Also by Rose Giallombardo

SOCIETY OF WOMEN: A STUDY OF A WOMEN'S PRISON

Juvenile Delinquency
A Book of Readings
second edition

Rose Giallombardo
The University of Chicago

John Wiley and Sons, Inc.
New York • *London* • *Sydney* • *Toronto*

Library of Congress Cataloging in Publication Data:

Giallombardo, Rose, ed.
  Juvenile delinquency

  Includes bibliographies.
  1. Juvenile delinquency—Addresses, essays,
lectures. I. Title.
HV9069.G445 1972   364.36'08   77-37645
ISBN 0-471-29727-5
ISBN 0-471-29728-3 (pbk.)

Printed in the United States of America

10 9 8 7 6 5 4 3 2

Preface

The second edition of this book retains the basic structure of the first edition, but the content of the sections has been substantially changed to include new areas of concern in the field of juvenile delinquency. Accordingly, some selections have been added and others have been deleted to update the book, consistent with the significant developments that have occurred in the field over the past six years.

This volume introduces the student of juvenile delinquency to some of the most important contemporary literature in the field. The nature of the selections makes the book easily adaptable to the framework of one-semester undergraduate and graduate courses in delinquency. It may be used along with supporting lectures and materials as the basic text, or to supplement the various basic textbooks in the field.

For some time there has been a need to bring together in one volume selections from the recent literature on juvenile delinquency which have been published in journals, books, and monographs. I contend that a knowledge of primary sources broadens the student's understanding of the subject matter. The intellectual excitement that is generated by reading the original expression of the scholars in the field cannot be duplicated by a study of the brief and skeletal summaries of source materials that are of necessity used in textbooks. Moreover, the limited resources of many college libraries and the ever-increasing class enrollments pose problems that the instructor finds difficult and often impossible to resolve. To help meet this difficulty, the articles in this volume have been reprinted in their entirety.

The literature dealing with delinquency is prodigious, and the task of selecting articles requires a willingness to compromise in making choices. The selections reprinted here are, for the most part, articles from the professional journals in social science or are lengthy selections from important books. They have been included because they deal with the sociological aspects of delinquency; and they either are important research contributions or provide valuable theoretical analyses and description. Nevertheless, even with the use of these restricting criteria in selecting materials it is not possible to include all the worthy sociological studies in a volume of this size. Also psychological, biological, and historical studies have been omitted because their inclusion would have meant the sacrifice of important sociological papers.

In order not to interfere with the work of the instructor, the brief introductory comments preceding each section do not impose a particular point of view on the student. They are intended solely to suggest connections and to bridge gaps between individual selections. The book has been planned and designed with the hope that it will engage the imagination and critical thinking of discerning students.

I gratefully thank the contributors and their publishers for generously permitting the selections to be reprinted. I also express my appreciation to Kathleen M. Carmody and to Deborah Herbert of Wiley who performed many of the editorial tasks that made the completion of this book possible.

Rose Giallombardo

Chicago, Illinois
February, 1972

Contents

section I

The Data of Delinquency: Problems of Definition and Measurement

The difficulties and confusion in determining the causes of delinquency originate in the extremely ambiguous use of the concept itself. Without a clear awareness of precisely what is meant by delinquency, no delineation of cause is possible. As the term is presently used, it may encompass almost any type of youthful behavior. The problem stems largely, Tappan maintains, from the contrasting views of those who deal with delinquents. Moreover, the problem of measurement is complicated by the distinction made between "adjudicated delinquents," those who have been processed through the courts, and "unofficial delinquents," those who are handled unofficially by the courts, police, and other agencies. Hence the statistics of juvenile delinquency are unreliable indexes of the amount of juvenile misconduct or of variations in it from one time period to another. Moreover, the problem of measurement is further complicated by the fact that middle-class delinquency is less often processed officially, which serves further to distort the exact dimensions of delinquency. Official records are unreliable as a basis for determining the extent or the nature of delinquent behavior.

In the first selection, the nature of delinquency, defining the conduct itself, and the legal status involved are cogently probed by Tappan. In order that the distinctions between delinquency, unofficial delinquency, and behavior problems may be understood, he contrasts the differing approaches of law and of casework to the youthful offender. In addition, he discusses the compromises that are present in the sociojudicial procedures of the children's court in relation to the general problem of definition and measurement. Throughout, Tappan stresses the importance of legal and social norms. The selection by Sellin and Wolfgang, "The Legal Basis of Juvenile Delinquency," explores further the broadness of the legal definition of delinquency and analyzes

1

the problem posed by the lack of uniformity from one state to another with respect to juvenile court jurisdictions.

The literature suggests that the increase in delinquency rates during the past three decades does not represent a genuine index of delinquent behavior but, instead, shows that the rates are linked to official policy. More specifically, the rates are related to the variable structures of family and community life, to a description of the volume of cases through selected children's courts, and to the variable nature of the court's function. In the selection by the President's Commission on Law Enforcement and Administration of Justice, the extent and volume of delinquency is considered.

As pointed out previously, the data on the amount and distribution of delinquency are neither complete nor known, and this causes much misunderstanding and controversy. Using three Western and Midwestern small cities, with populations of 10,000 to 30,000, Short and Nye studied high school students to ascertain the extent of admitted offenses.

The matter of undetected delinquency is also explored by Erickson and Empey. Employing official records and interviews with four subsamples, they analyse data on undetected and unacted upon violations by the courts in order to assess the nature of decision making by court authorities as this relates to the volume of delinquency. Their study also explores the implications of the self-reported violations by these groups for court statistics as a measure of youthful delinquent behavior in the community.

1

The Nature of Juvenile Delinquency

Paul Tappan

Annetta found some whisky at home and got drunk at the age of seven. Arnold stole some extract from a neighbor. His mother said, "Send him to the training school." Sarge whips his sisters. Cap stays out till midnight. J—— E—— and J—— B—— fight one another. Alvin stole his mother's stove and sold it. Melvin stole a pig from his father, who prevailed upon the juvenile court to commit him to the training school at the age of fifteen. An alcoholic parent complains that his daughter is "sassy." A boy strikes his alcoholic grandfather with a rock. Another is abusive to his mother and sister. Still another hacks up a package that his mother aims to send to another son. At the filling station that he was keeping during his father's absence Ritchey found a pint of whisky belonging to his father. Upon his father's return they got into a row. The father complained. Two months after a youth's father died, the boy wagered 40 cents against a bottle of wine in a game of dice. His mother said that she would send him to the training school next time. One mother complained that her boy was very troublesome and "just like his dad." Another parent heard that Jane left church one night and went to the school grounds with some boys. Gaylord is in when his mother is out and out when his mother is in. She works. Another mother had her fifteen-year-old son taken to jail from home because he was drunk. Jerry had a tantrum, during which he jerked the telephone off the wall. Speck's grandmother had him committed to the training school because he tried to leave town, and Mark's mother committed him after he stole a gallon of gasoline.[1]

What, then, is delinquency? Certainly there is no more central question in this study and probably none more difficult to answer. Yet it is important to see the nature of delinquency as clearly as possible and to understand the problems that have impeded efforts at definition. It is important, because on the interpretation of the term depend all those vital differences which set off the juvenile delinquent from the adult criminal at the one extreme and from the nonoffender at the other. In theory at least and, to a large degree, in fact, the delinquent child is dealt with differently from the criminal: in the conduct

[1] Austin L. Porterfield, *Youth in Trouble*, p. 17, 1946.

SOURCE. Paul Tappan, *Juvenile Delinquency*, New York: McGraw-Hill Book Company, 1949, pp. 3–13 and 15–30. Copyright 1949, McGraw-Hill Book Company. Reprinted with permission.

involved; the court and its methods employed; the treatment philosophy, purposes, and methods applied; and in the individual's status, reputation, and civil rights in the community after adjudication.

No less significant but far more difficult is the distinction between the delinquent and the individual who has no conflict with the law. Official delinquency usually implies involvement with the police, detention, court handling, damaging associations, semipunitive correctional treatment, and a role and stigma that are ineradicably injurious—notwithstanding all the idyllic euphemisms to the contrary that embellish the literature on "rehabilitative therapy." One must decide to whom these measures need to be applied and also who, in the name of justice, should be exempt from them. Incidentally, the student of the problem would like to know what phenomenon it is that he studies, its frequency, what is being done about it, and what should be done about it. It is a major thesis of the present work that, to a considerable extent, ineffective dealing with young deviants arises from the failure to determine and classify their problems and then to apply treatment that is appropriate to such careful classification.

The Legal View

The problem of definition flows in part from the contrasting views of those who deal with the delinquent. Broadly considered, two chief general types of approach may be observed: the judicial, or legal, view and the administrative, or case work, view. Conceptions of delinquency have been derived largely from these views, and they in turn tend to reflect the two main phases of juvenile court work: the adjudication of cases and their probation supervision. In the legal approach to misconduct, it is customary to describe offenses and penalties in specific terms in order to protect the citizen from arbitrary or unjust acts of police and judicial authority and, at the same time, to secure the community against those whose conduct has been shown in court to be dangerous. Lawyer and judge are inclined to stress as a precondition of treatment through criminal courts the following requirements: (1) that a specific charge be alleged against the defendant, (2) that it be defined in definite terms by law, (3) that the offense be proved rather conclusively, (4) that protection be given to the accused during trial against conviction by false, misleading, prejudicial, irrelevant, or immaterial evidence. The liberal political philosophy of Anglo-American democracy has evolved and refined these principles in reaction against the arbitrary, tyrannical excesses of political and administrative authoritarianism; they have become firmly embedded in the common law, constitutions, statutes, and institutional practices.

In relation to the young delinquent, as will be shown more fully below, this tradition of juristic liberalism has made for a partly "legalistic" handling of the offender, an attempt to distinguish as clearly as possible between delinquent and nondelinquent and to treat only the former with the sanctions of the state. The offender may be looked upon by the state as one functioning with greater or less freedom of will who has chosen to violate the law and who must be dealt with correctively to discourage him and others from further infractions. The full rigors of the criminal law are mitigated by reason of the offender's youth, but the judicial view would preserve in the hearings of children's courts a real test of the individual's status as a delinquent before applying to him the modern and individualized methods of treatment. The child is not a delinquent unless the court has found him so.

The Case Work Approach

In contrast with the procedural and normative formalism of the legal approach, case work brings to behavior problems a distinctly different set of methods and values. Its aims, generally, are therapeutic: to aid in the resolution of the individual's maladjustment by seeking out the social roots of his difficulties and attempting to mitigate the conflicts that have caused disturbance. Case work, then, essays to deal with a wide assortment of personal and group problems that represent failures in man's personal and social adjustments. Largely these are maladaptations in behavior: dependence, domestic conflict, desertion, drunkenness, unemployment, avoidance of responsibility, delinquency, the whole province of child-welfare work, and many others. Treating presumed causes and symptoms with methods devised to meet the particular needs of the individual situation is the essential function of case work.

The practitioner in applied sociology and case work ideally is nonmoralistic and nonpunitive in approach. His approach is nonmoralistic, because he either denies the freedom of the will or recognizes the profound significance of external forces in impelling conduct over which the individual has little or no control; he observes, moreover, that an understanding, sympathetic, nonmoralistic reaction encourages a more confident cooperation from the client, which facilitates treatment. His approach is nonpunitive, because the attribution of blame and the application of retributive measures are inconsistent with the recognition of causes of conduct extraneous to the individual "will" and, moreover, because experience shows the failure of retaliatory measures to produce the personal reconstruction which is sought. The social worker's approach is less formal than that of the legal mind, since categories and qualities of problem conduct are not so precisely established in the content of case work theory, nor are methods of treatment so definitively organized and equated, in general, to the problems of the case. In social work it is recognized that a given type of conduct may in different cases reflect quite different causes and that the treatment required to deal with the given behavior should depend on the factors that underlie the particular case rather than the behavior itself. It follows from this that there must be a far wider province of administrative discretion in the practice of case work than is employed by the judge in attempting to allocate responsibility for deviant behavior and to prescribe treatment suited to the subject. Moreover, interpretation and technique may differ considerably from one social agency to another or even, within an agency, from one case worker to another. To some extent the worker must operate empirically through trial and error to resolve the problems that confront him.

In contrast to the law's preoccupation with miscreants who have violated specific and official legal norms, then, social work is concerned with a multitude of problems of behavior that deviate from psychological, social, economic, and—sometimes—legal normality. Insofar as the case worker may deal with the law violator, he does so with the same nonmoralistic, nonpunitive assumptions that are applied to other deviants. The young antisocial child may be referred to any one of a variety of social agencies rather than to a court. In the agency his statutory infractions, if any, are not viewed separately from the remainder of his conduct but merely as incidents of the total problem to be dealt with for the purpose of improving adjustment. The focus of attention is upon the whole child. His illegalities are commonly interpreted as merely symptoms of the underlying maladjustments from which he suffers. In a proper case, where official authority appears to be needed, law-enforcement agencies may be called into operation, but much of the problem conduct that is handled by the case worker in the agency is identical with the illegal behavior that confronts the court. The agency, in the fulfillment of its purposes, makes no attempt at a specific definition of the type or degree of law violation or at a carefully controlled determination of the individual's innocence or guilt of the prohibited conduct. Rather, operating within the limitations of its means and purposes, the agency accepts as true the findings and interpretations of social investigation, and proceeds to over-all treatment of the case as inferred from the relatively loose methods (compared with the exacting requirements of legal evidence) of social inquiry. It should be noted, in addition, that the treatment techniques of the unofficial social agency lack the stigma of community disapproval that is inherent in the law's penalties. The very term "delinquent" is shunned because of its moralistic and legalistic implications. The child is called "unadjusted."

Judicial-Administrative Blending in the Children's Court

In the modern juvenile court there is a compromising of the legal and casework approaches: an effort at sociolegal handling of the child. Legal influences are inevitable and necessary in a court; they may be seen in the age limitations for delinquency, in the statutory specification of particular conduct deemed to be delinquent, in the preservation of some measure of procedural regularity and of due process rights, and in the very effort itself to provide children with special protec-

tion. Children were not only given a protected position, as early as the thirteenth century, at common law, before the ordinary courts, but also were considered in later chancery—along with other incompetents (females and imbeciles!)—to be wards of the state, shielded by the king's chancellor from injury or exploitation. The origin in chancery jurisdiction of many of the child's protections established an early informal and administration tradition in the legal handling of children's cases; thus, his contracts, property interests, and his rights and status might be ensured by administrative as well as strictly judicial measures. Much later, when juvenile courts were established, some followed this tradition as equity courts with wider powers and more informal methods than those of the common-law courts. However, equity, like the legal approach in general, has been characterized by rather definite rules of law governing conduct and regular procedures; its function has been chiefly the protection of those who lacked other adequate legal remedies.

In the nature of the juvenile court, case work practices are associated with probation treatment *after* the determination of delinquency. But in the emergence of specialized children's courts, the administrative approach was greatly extended beyond the limits that had been fixed in earlier law and equity. The developing ideology of social work was brought in to an increasing extent, particularly through the channels of a probation system that had already been set up in criminal courts before separate tribunals for juveniles were invented. After the birth of the juvenile court movement, the administrative approach received a great impetus from leaders in the field of juvenile probation who conceived the function of the court largely in terms of administrative social-work supervision, aimed at prevention and rehabilitation of problem cases.[2] Hence, important new influences developed to modify the traditional judicial process as it applied to the young offender. There is an expanded administrative emphasis today on the need to find the underlying social and psychological maladjustments of the child in the court, to see the total problem, and to resolve his difficulties by probation treatment. The specific delinquent act is considered to be relatively unimportant except as a symptom of the real problems. The model juvenile court statute of the National Probation Association neither defines the term "delinquent" nor applies it to court cases.[3]

The trend noted here has been fostered by the general terms in the provisions of children's court acts, which permit wide discretionary latitude in adjudication and treatment on the basis of vague standards of the conduct and the attitude of the child.[4] Thus a child whose behavior shows no specific and serious violation of the law may nevertheless be treated "preventively" if he is found to suffer from problems of social or psychological unadjustment. The growth of administrative process is seen in the effort of juvenile courts today to prevent misconduct through supervision by probation officers and to deal with children's problems in their early stages before more serious recalcitrance may develop. The large and growing amount of informal work performed by probation departments in cases that are not officially adjudicated is a part of this trend. This work reveals the effort of probation to function as an ordinary case work agency: "The juvenile court in its investigations and case work becomes an administrative social-work agency and must follow the example of the best private agencies in the fullest cooperation with others, taking advantage of the resources they offer in helping to work out the complicated and difficult problems often presented."[5] The significant point may be mentioned here, to be developed later, that in most jurisdictions neither

[2] Alice Scott Nutt, in "The Future of the Juvenile Court," *Nat. Prob. Assn. Yearb.*, 1939, p. 159, said: ". . . once certain services were begun as part of the court work they were continued as a matter of course and gathered strength through precedent, although the original reason for their initiation, namely, the absence in the community of other agencies performing these services, often no longer existed. The court frequently came to consider itself and to be considered a social agency rather than a socialized court, although strangely enough it often held itself apart from the social agencies of the community, and its probation officers spoke of themselves as a group separate and distinct from other social workers." (Reprinted by permission.)

[3] *A Standard Juvenile Court Act*, pp. 8–11, National Probation Association, New York, 1943.

[4] See Gilbert Cosulich, *Juvenile Court Laws of the United States*, pp. 34–47, National Probation Association, New York, 1939.

[5] It is not implied that professional case workers in private and public agencies share this view. To the contrary, see Alice Scott Nutt, *op. cit.*, pp. 163–164, where she says, "Because it is a court, the juvenile court has certain functions entirely apart from case work functions and a structure quite different from that of a nonjudicial agency. The court may use a socialized procedure, but because it is the offspring of the legal system this procedure is nevertheless a judicial one operating along legalistic lines. The handling of each official case in the juvenile court follows more or less a fixed routine. . . . The probation or case work is done under the direction of and within the framework of the law. . . . Several persons well known to this group have voiced their recognition of the limitations upon the development of the juvenile court as a case work agency and also their belief that instead of continuing to broaden its function it should concentrate on a definite and fairly limited field. They have argued that the court should limit its intake to children in whose cases a real issue arises; that the judicial and case work functions of the court should be separated; that the expansion of treatment services within the court administration should be opposed, and their development, specialization, and coordination in the educational and public welfare system should be encouraged."

probation staff nor judges are trained for a preventive case work function.

The administrative approach is revealed further by the quite successful resistance that comes frequently from probation officers, sometimes even from the judges themselves, to the legal requirements of proving an offense, excluding hearsay and prejudicial testimony, allowing counsel to the defendant, and permitting appeal. The argument runs that the court exists for the care, protection, and benefit of the child; it is therefore unnecessary to set up safeguards and frustrating limitations on the agency that would help him. There is a marked tendency among many leaders of the juvenile court movement today, in considering the child to be merely "unfortunate" or "unadjusted," to avoid reference to delinquency itself. They sometimes favor the burying of institutional statistics on the juvenile delinquent in some all-inclusive and innocuous category. This whole view appears to overlook the significant point that whatever he may be called, he is in fact treated as an offender through court control, and is himself often buried deeper in the correctional system than his statistics can be. A short quotation from each of two cases famous in the jurisprudence of the children's court will serve to illustrate this central problem of requiring proof of delinquency. How a particular jurisdiction resolves the issue determines to a great extent who may be considered a delinquent there.

The constitutional objections turn upon whether the act [the children's court act of Connecticut] is one for the punishment of crime and therefore subject . . . to the guaranties . . . in the Bill of Rights, or whether it is concerned with the care and protection which every state as *parens patriae* in some measure affords to all . . . who . . . are in some degree abnormal, and hence . . . *entirely of a civil nature* . . . if

such courts are not of a criminal nature, then they are not unconstitutional because of the nature of their procedure depriving persons brought before them of certain constitutional guaranties in favor of persons accused of crime. This principle has been recognized in many states where juvenile courts exist; in only one [Texas] has such an act been held entirely void, while in Missouri the validity of the act was based upon the statute in relation to constitutional provisions regarding courts.[6]

The proceeding here is under a widely different statute. . . . The concept of crime and punishment disappears. To the child, delinquent through the commission of an act criminal in nature, the state extends the same aid, care, and training which it had long given to the child who was merely incorrigible, neglected, abandoned, destitute, or physically handicapped. . . .

When it is said that even in cases of law-breaking delinquency, constitutional safeguards and the technical procedure of the criminal law may be disregarded, *there is no implication that a purely socialized trial of specific issue may properly or legally be had. The contrary is true. There must be a reasonably definite charge. The customary rules of evidence shown by long experience as essential to getting at the truth with reasonable certainty in civil trials must be adhered to.* The finding of fact must rest on the preponderance of evidence adduced under those rules. Hearsay, opinion, gossip, bias, prejudice, trends of hostile neighborhood feeling, the hopes and fears of social workers are all sources of error and have no more place in children's courts than in any other court.[7]

It should be noted in the above that, holding the children's court and its procedure to be noncriminal, these appellate decisions nevertheless affirm that juvenile cases come under the procedure of the civil law *and its due*

---

[6] *Cinque v. Boyd*, 121 Atl. 678 (June 1, 1923). (Italics not in the original.)

[7] *In the Matter of Arthur Lewis*, 260 N.Y. 171. (Italics not in the original.) See also Paul W. Tappan, *Juvenile Delinquency*, New York: McGraw-Hill Book Company, 1949, Appendix A, pp. 551–553.

process protections of fair trial of a real issue. Nevertheless, again and again in the literature on probation and juvenile courts and, moreover, in the practices of many of these courts, there is an assumption that, since they are "remedial instead of punitive," such safeguards as "appeals, rules of evidence, appearance of counsel, etc., [are] details of jurisprudence from which the juvenile court has been relieved."

This wedding of judicial and administrative process has not produced a wholly compatible marriage. Each strains to dominate the union—with results that are not always beneficial to the child who is subjected to its influence. The special danger is that in an "overlegalistic" court the experience of trial will be severe and traumatic. The child will less frequently be adjudicated a delinquent, but if he is, the treatment imposed may be based upon a moralistic and punitive ideology. In an "oversocialized" tribunal, on the other hand, there is danger that individuals will be exposed to court machinery and treatment who do not require state sanctions and who may, indeed, be injured by the crude tools to which courts are limited in their treatment efforts.

Modern probation tends to reflect the preventive views and administrative methods of professional case work, meritorious values within the framework of nonofficial case work agencies. But it should be remembered, ideal standards to the contrary, that the probation officer is generally not a case worker by professional training but rather an untrained, overworked, and undersupervised individual whose ability to carry out effective treatment is limited in addition by the coercive authority that the court setting implies. Also, he exercises far more power over the liberty of the child than does any professionally trained private case worker. The sociolegal compromise of the juvenile court fails when probation attempts to displace law and the courts by becoming an administrative social agency.[8] The compromise fails, too, when the judge attempts to operate a junior criminal court. Among the more than a thousand juvenile jurisdictions in the United States, both of those perversions of a liberalized justice are prevalent, but the former is becoming an especially common error. Later, consideration will be given to a better division of legal and social functions in the children's courts. Here concern has been only with the two conflicting spheres of ideology that have had so much to do with the determination of the official delinquent through the actual operation of the juvenile courts. The inclination of the court to assume a judicial attitude, on the one hand, or the administrative approach, on the other, determines to an important extent the probabilities of a child's being found delinquent and may influence as well the type of treatment he receives.

THE OFFICIAL DELINQUENT

The blending of conflicting concepts of delinquency is fully revealed in the definitions of juvenile delinquency that appear in children's court statutes. The disparity may be seen in the provisions for the courts possessing jurisdiction in these cases, in the age level of offenders covered by them, and in the types of conduct (substantive norms) established by law as delinquent.

Court Jurisdiction

The first juvenile court in the United States was one of equity jurisdiction, exemplifying the protective and noncriminal nature of the proceedings. Yet a majority of children's courts were originally set up as part of the criminal

[8] *Ibid.,* Chapter IX.

court system and, despite subsequent enactments, a large proportion of them still remains so. Thus juvenile cases are handled to a great extent today by some term of an ordinary court of original criminal jurisdiction or of general jurisdiction covering both criminal and civil cases; some are trial courts; others are courts of summary jurisdiction; a minority are distinct juvenile courts of separate jurisdiction; a few are probate or common pleas courts. Where special terms of court are established for children's cases, they are generally handled, nevertheless, by the nonspecialized judges, magistrates, and referees who try a variety of other cases. Usually the probation officers, too, are a part of the general system of probation that deals with adult criminal cases. In most juvenile courts there is a preservation of criminal court personnel, ideology, and, to a less marked extent, trial procedure and treatment methods. But the current trend is toward separate children's courts and separate probation departments to handle juveniles. There is a large and increasing admixture of informal, administrative, and case work methods filtering into these courts with considerable current dispute as to the role of legal and social methods in dealing with the child.

Age Levels of Delinquency

At common law the infant was held to be nonresponsible for crime up to the age of seven, lacking mental capacity to entertain the intent that is required for criminal behavior. From seven to fourteen the infant was presumed to be incapable of crime intellectually because of his immaturity, but this presumption might be rebutted by a showing that he had sufficient capacity to distinguish between right and wrong. From fourteen to twenty-one there was a rebuttable presumption

that the individual possessed criminal capacity and after twenty-one the presumption became conclusive insofar as age might affect capacity.[9] Distinctions in responsibility were based upon the notion of variations according to age among individuals deemed to possess free will in their power to distinguish right from wrong and thus to form the *mens rea* or culpable intent required in crime. This use of chronological maturity as a basis of discriminating between criminal and noncriminal has evolved into modern statutory law, with the underlying ideology preserved to a great extent.[10] A major change has been a pushing upward of the minimum age. Also, the presumption of juvenile nonresponsibility has been made absolute.

This use of chronological age as a criterion of delinquency may seem oddly arbitrary and out of place in an era of individualization. It is unfortunate, certainly, to hold a dull or emotionally unstable first offender criminally responsible if he is a young adult and to treat more leniently or with greater care an habitual, sophisticated, intelligent, and tough recalcitrant of fifteen (in some states sixteen, eighteen, or even twenty-one). From a psychiatric or case work point of view the individual's diagnosis and treatment should depend not on his years per se but on numerous more individuated

[9] See Blackstone, *Commentaries*, Book IV, Chap. II, quoted in Tappan, *op. cit.*, Chap. VIII, pp. 167–169.
[10] In *The Penal Law of the State of New York*, Sec. 817, appears the persisting survival of the common-law rule: "A child of the age of seven years and under the age of twelve years is presumed to be incapable of crime, but the presumption may be removed by proof that he had sufficient capacity to understand the act or neglect charged against him and to know its wrongfulness." This section is obsolete, except in regard to cases punishable by death or life imprisonment, but it survives in the statutes of this and other states.

factors, such as emotion, temperament, experiences, and physical condition. Despite the apparent excessive arbitrariness in the criterion of age, particularly in borderline cases where the child is just under or over the age set by statute, it should be recognized that the law must rely upon systems of rather definite classification to cover large numbers of cases. Arbitrariness is implicit in any system of classification; yet science as well as law is based upon classificatory devices. For the most part, legal categories have evolved as experience has shown their value for the purpose at hand.

Chronological age is a relevant criterion for distinguishing between antisocial groups, for it is a factor subject to easy verification and one which is highly correlated with specific items of maturity, balance, and physical condition with which the correctional system is properly concerned. Moreover, though it is impossible to individualize completely a system of justice, it is possible and usual today, within the framework of these age categories, to separate and subclassify treatment methods to meet particular groups of cases. The establishment of somewhat rough and variable age divisions, however lacking in nicety of discrimination the device may appear, does nevertheless promote a greater evenness of justice than would be possible under a legal system attempting to operate with a wide-open discretion for the judges and treatment experts. The requirements of justice are often enough disserved in the discretionary latitude now permitted where gross variations among authorities and their ideologies result in treating similar cases in radically dissimilar ways. A fair measure of just uniformity is ensured by classification norms such as age.

Under the statutes of a majority of states today, a child may be adjudicated delinquent if he is over the age of seven and under eighteen; thirty-two states confer either complete or partial jurisdiction over juvenile delinquency up to that age. Seven states extend jurisdiction to the age of twenty-one, but in each of these the criminal court has concurrent power to try serious cases, such as homicide, robbery, burglary, and rape. In eleven states, jurisdiction over the juvenile is terminated wholly or in part by the age of sixteen.

Delinquency as a Status

In addition to the shifting of the age factor, another significant change has developed in the establishment of delinquency as a status distinct from crime, dependent in part on age and in part on conduct. According to modern statutes a criminal charge against an infant must be dismissed on the ground of nonage: he is irresponsible by reason of immaturity. Nevertheless, such a person may be held as a juvenile delinquent and treated for his protection as a ward of the state. The status concept of delinquency has evolved from an appreciation of the danger that the young offender may easily become an adult criminal if no deterrent or rehabilitative influences play upon him. Hence, the contemporary effort to curb antisocial traits in their incipience. Adjudication to the status of delinquency does not establish a criminal record against the individual. Reports and records of the juvenile court may not be used against the child later in criminal trials. He loses no rights of citizenship, to hold public office, or to secure employment.

Nonetheless, these laws are generally a part of the criminal code; they are evolved from earlier criminal statutes governing incorrigible and wayward behavior. A considerable proportion of the child-defendants comes to the court (often, as indicated above, a part of the criminal court system) as serious offenders. It is natural that some of the contumely that devolves upon the adult criminal is attached to the young delinquent as well; the young offender is often considered and not infrequently treated as an intractable junior criminal. The curse of court adjudication and of institutional commitment or probation supervision is upon him. The stigma is just as real if not as horrendous as that of the convict.

Delinquency: Substantive Norms in the Law

Juvenile delinquency implies a special age range, a more or less distinct court jurisdiction, and a concept of status. These are all rather definite and specifically ascertainable. There is the further, most significant, and more difficult problem of the behavior denoted by that term. Here is real confusion in the purpose, philosophy, and content of the law—and a bewilderment to match in the practices of the courts.

A great part of the difficulty may be traced to the contrast drawn above between the legal and administrative approaches to the subject. The former characteristically specifies particular acts as offenses, operating under the theory that the blunt weapons of the law should be called into operation only after violations that appear clearly deleterious to social welfare. Exceptionally, as in the law of criminal attempt and of conspiracy, the effort is made to operate preventively by permitting prosecution where the conduct proscribed is not itself intrinsically harmful but, unless forestalled before the consummation of the intended acts, may seriously threaten harm to the group. Law of this sort has frequently been criticized for the ease with which evidence can be framed against innocent persons: usually the meaning of the statute is too imprecise and the probabilities of social harm too obscure. By and large, the formulation of statutory rules of conduct has tended to rest upon the standards that Professors Michael and Wechsler have stated. These standards have a special importance for delinquency legislation: "(1) What sorts of conduct is it both desirable and possible to deter; (2) what sorts indicate that persons who behave in those ways are dangerously likely to engage in socially undesirable behavior in the future; (3) will the attempt to prevent particular kinds of undesirable behavior by the criminal law do less good, as measured by the success of such efforts, than harm, as measured by their other and harmful results."[11] An evolving jurisprudence of delinquency has been less sure of its ground in this issue of conduct to be made taboo, perhaps, than has any other branch of the law.

Under the statutes of the various states, juvenile delinquency has come to include in part conduct that is specifically defined and clearly injurious. In considerable part, however, it is composed of vague and imprecise standards that look to preventive efforts and to the amelioration of social and psychological problems. Of the first type is the characteristic provision that a juvenile delinquent is any child "who violates any law of this state or of the United States or any municipal ordinance or who commits any act which if committed by an adult would be a crime. . . ."[12] This substantive provision is as definite as are the statutes defining adult criminal acts (though the courts are often in fact much less rigorous in their requirements of proof).

The omnibus provisions of these statutes, probably more vague as to

[11] Jerome Michael and Herbert Wechsler, *Criminal Law and Its Administration,* p. 11, 1940.
[12] *The Penal Law of the State of New York,* Sec. 486, Subsec. (a).

the class of individuals intended than any other part of the criminal code, are best illustrated by the common definition that the delinquent is one "who so deports himself as willfully to injure or endanger the morals or health of himself or others." Other recurring phrases of similar indefiniteness include the individual "who is incorrigible, ungovernable, or habitually disobedient and beyond the control of his parents, guardian, or other lawful authority" or "who, without just cause and without the consent of his parent, guardian, or other custodian, deserts his home or place of abode."[13] Obviously adjudication under such substantive provisions as these imposes upon the judge an onerous task of determining what conduct is reprehensible and dangerous, with very little assistance from the statute. This extends the administrative powers of the court to implement the statutory objectives, but the law may neglect to establish even general conduct norms to guide the tribunal's decision—which is customarily done for an ordinary administrative agency. The adjudicator may be an arbitrary despot in the application of his peculiar preferences. He may be enlightened, objective, and nonmoralistic, or ignorant and prejudiced. Under the elastic course-of-conduct clauses of these acts, the risk of adjudication as a delinquent depends considerably on the point of view of the judge and the probation officer who influences him.

In two jurisdictions, California and the District of Columbia, there is not even a statutory definition of delinquency. This follows the practice recommended under the standard juvenile court act of the National Probation Association which, in line with the case work theory of avoiding the very concept of delinquency itself, simply establishes the jurisdiction of the chil-

dren's court over those "(*b*) Whose occupation, behavior, environment, or associations are injurious to his welfare. (*c*) Who deserts his home or who is habitually disobedient or beyond the control of his parent or other custodian. (*d*) Who, being required by law to attend school, willfully violates rules thereof or absents himself therefrom. (*e*) Who violates any state law or municipal ordinance."[14] Query: How much difference does this approach make in the repute of the officially adjudicated child?

Legal Exceptions to the Delinquency Status

The statutory definitions of delinquency appear to reflect a dual purposing: there are clauses of a judicial slant to discourage specific acts of illegality and others bent toward administrative control over courses of conduct, which are designed to prevent the development of crime. This mixture of legal motives is not irreconcilable in logic, whatever difficulties it may involve in practice. Conceivably the court might, in turn, be reformative to the serious offender and preventive to the potential offender. But a more obvious confusion of purposes does appear in exceptions established to the jurisdiction of the children's courts in a number of states, e.g., the limitation that a child otherwise of delinquent age may be tried as a criminal where he is accused of committing a capital crime or certain other crimes.[15] The provision in various states for concurrent juris-

---

[13] *Ibid.*, Subsecs. (b) and (d).

[14] *A Standard Juvenile Court Act*, p. 10, 1943.
[15] California, Delaware, Louisiana, Vermont, and West Virginia except capital crimes. Colorado, Iowa, Massachusetts, Montana, New York, South Carolina, Tennessee, and United States courts except crimes punishable by death or life imprisonment. Florida, Maryland, North Carolina, Pennsylvania, and Rhode Island except certain other specific offenses.

diction of the criminal court and children's courts similarly displays an anomaly in the purposes of delinquency statutes. They first assert that the child is too immature to be responsible for crime or to suffer punishment therefor, and then except those crimes which are most retributively penalized in the law. These two cases from recent news releases reveal very well the anomalous contradictions of policy in dealing with the youngster:

JURY REFUSES TO INDICT

Youth, 13, in Fatal Shooting
Still to Face Children's Court

Thirteen-year-old Nicholas I—, of . . . , the Bronx, who last Friday shot and fatally wounded Rita P—, 8, . . . as she stood in front of 854 East 999 Street, will be arraigned today as a juvenile delinquent before Justice M— in Bronx Children's Court. Yesterday the Bronx Grand Jury refused to return an indictment against the youth after Chief Assistant District Attorney O— said he found no evidence of premeditation or intent to kill. Mr. O— said later that the Grand Jury could not return an indictment for manslaughter against a child under 16 years.[16]

BOY, 16, SENTENCED TO 25 YEARS TO LIFE

Nicholas T—, 16 years old, who had a record of juvenile delinquency for several years, was sentenced yesterday to serve twenty-five years to life for murder by Judge G— in Kings County Court. Only 15 at the time he was charged with the lead-pipe slaying . . . of Mrs. Pauline G—, 53, in her store . . . , the youth was found guilty May 7 of second-degree murder by an all-male blue-ribbon jury. Reviewing the boy's record of seven arrests since he was 8, Judge G— said he still had faith in the "fundamental goodness" of the youth of the country and absolved society from responsibility in the failure of the defendant to rehabilitate himself.

As the court concluded, the youth insisted that he was innocent of the crime. "What I did in the past, I admit, may have been bad," he said, "but of this charge I am not guilty. The jury was wrong."[17]

Observe the quaint spectacle of a child thirteen years old accused of murder. Such a child is ordinarily detained in jail without right to bail and goes before a police magistrate or justice of the peace for questioning in open court. There he may be bound over for action of the grand jury. In jail again, eventually he may be indicted by that body and held for trial before a jury "of his peers" whose duty it is to determine whether the child did commit a willful, deliberate, and premeditated homicide. (For any other offense it is conclusively presumed that he lacks the power of will and intent to commit crime.) But here it becomes the duty of the jury to decide whether this thirteen-year-old did "intend" to take the victim's life, whether he "planned" it—for even a moment—in advance. For the latter he may be punished by death or life imprisonment. For the former he may spend the entire productive period of his life in prison. Yet if, as in the case of Nicholas I——, the jury finds that the child acted without premeditation or intent, it can find him guilty of no crime at all. He may then be brought before the juvenile court as a delinquent to receive its relatively modest penalties or its therapy, as the case may be.

This is no mere relic of medieval justice or indeed even of nineteenth-century practice. It happens today as one may see all too often in the headlines of the daily papers. It is true that the child is no longer punished capitally for a long list of offenses. Nor, as in colonial days, for a short series (which included disobedience, smiting one's parents, and other "horrible"

---

[16] *The New York Times*, Sept. 6, 1946.

[17] *Ibid.*, May 28, 1946.

crimes).[18] But a child's age is not yet a bar to the death penalty or to a lifetime of retributive justice if he has deliberately taken the life of another.

BOY, 14, IS FREED IN GIRL'S DEATH[19]

TERM FOR BOY IN SHOOTING

Lad Who Fired "to See Someone Die" Gets 10 to 14 Years[20]

BOY, 15, GETS LIFE TERM

He Pleads Guilty to Slaying of Philadelphia Policeman[21]

BOY SLAYER GETS 30 YEARS

Codarre, 13, Is Sentenced for Attack on Girl of 10[22]

YOUTH, 15, ARRAIGNED IN MURDER OF BOY, 11[23]

BOY, 16, SEIZED AS SLAYER

Admits He Killed Youngster, 13, on Bronx Roof, Police Say[24]

4 CHILDREN SLAIN: BOY, 16, IS ACCUSED[25]

TEEN AGERS DESCRIBE KILLING POLICEMAN[26]

20 YEARS TO LIFE FOR ALBANY BOY, 15[27]

The Neglected or Dependent Child

Technically separate from juvenile delinquency, but included in the jurisdiction of the juvenile court, is the power to determine cases of neglected and dependent children. This protective function adds some further confusion to the effort to limit and define the delinquency concept, especially in that these children are often detained in and sometimes committed to the same institutions where delinquents are held. Frequently, too, their conduct problems overlap with those of delinquents to such an extent that any realistic behavioral discrimination is impossible. Whether a child be held delinquent, neglected, or dependent may depend chiefly on the petitioner and his motive rather than either the child's conduct or his more basic problems of unadjustment. Clearly many juvenile offenses are bred in parental neglect. This suggests the larger problem confronting children's courts as to the behavioral or situational elements that should be taken to constitute delinquency, an issue that will be considered in the next section.

There are provisions in some states establishing, in the courts that handle delinquents and neglected children, jurisdiction over other related problems, e.g., the dependent child, adoption, custody, the physically handicapped child, the mentally defective or disordered child, illegitimacy, or marriage of girls under sixteen.[28] In some states the children's court has jurisdiction to try as a misdemeanant the parent, guardian, or other custodian whose negligence in his duties has caused or contributed to the delinquency of the child.[29] The common

---

[18] For statute in Illinois, see Tappan, *op. cit.*, Appendix B, p. 554.
[19] *The New York Times*, May 8, 1946, and Aug. 7, 1946.
[20] *Ibid.*, May 28, 1947.
[21] *Ibid.*, Mar. 20, 1947.
[22] *Ibid.*, Dec. 7, 1943.
[23] *Ibid.*, Oct. 29, 1946.
[24] *Ibid.*, Oct. 24, 1946.
[25] *Ibid.*, May 28, 1947.
[26] *Ibid.*, May 29, 1947.
[27] *PM*, July 8, 1947.

[28] All but four states confer jurisdiction upon the children's court over neglect and dependency (Massachusetts, New York, New Mexico, and Texas). See Gilbert Cosulich, *op. cit.*, pp. 42–47, for a summary of the numerous states that provide for children's court control over the mentally defective or disordered child, issues of guardianship, adoption, custody, and legitimacy and for less common jurisdictional powers.
[29] Thirty-one states are listed by Cosulich as possessing jurisdiction to try adults charged with contributing to the delinquency, neglect, or dependency of a child; in the remainder some other court has this jurisdiction. See Cosulich, *op. cit.*, pp. 69–70.

informality of procedures employed in children's courts, particularly the allowance of hearsay testimony and hearings on imprecise issues, has been extended to threaten unjudicious criminal adjudication of adults under conditions that do not guard against injustice as do procedures of the ordinary criminal courts.

JUVENILE DELINQUENCY: ITS BEHAVIORAL CONTENT

In the discussion above of the substantive norms defining delinquency and the conflicting ideas of legal and case work personnel, the problem of attempting to delimit the behavioral content of delinquency has appeared in its general aspects. It was suggested that the judicial approach would require the statement and proof of fairly definite offenses. The administrative view, to the contrary, is that, since delinquents and their courts are not criminal in character, the latter being designed to aid children who are unadjusted, the courts should not seek to define and segregate delinquency but to discover and treat the maladjustments of children who appear before them. Out of these opposed ideologies have come varied statutory specifications. It is clear that these do not resolve the central issue of who should be brought before the court and adjudicated. Is the precocious and adventurous child who has run away from home once, or several times, a delinquent? Is the one who reacts rebelliously in a home pervaded by an atmosphere of incessant hostility a delinquent? Is a daughter in "bobby sox" who stays out later than her mother used to do, who seems "a little wild," and causes her fearful family much anxiety, a delinquent? Is the boy who expresses a desire, thoroughly normal in a healthy maturing preadolescent, to emancipate himself emotionally and

socially from his family and who behaves in a very independent fashion a delinquent? Is the youth who refuses to turn over his entire wage to his family? Is the girl who has become pregnant through ignorance, seduction, or curiosity? What are the effects on the child, his family, and the community when a fraction of the children who behave in these ways are adjudicated?

How, then, may one distinguish the problem child, the predelinquent, and the delinquent? Who among them belongs in court? A series of categories of deviation are set up below in order to consider the level at which a children's court should take control:

1.   Deviant situational factors, where the child is exposed to deleterious home and community influences:
   (a) Broken home
   (b) Variable, inadequate, or excessive discipline
   (c) Vice in the home
   (d) Economic insecurity
   (e) Unsupervised and unhealthy recreation
   (f) Slum neighborhood
   (g) Agencies of moral risk: cheap bars, theaters, poolrooms, etc.

2.   Behavior problems that represent some measure of personal unadjustment to the environment:
   (a) Thumb-sucking
   (b) Nail-biting
   (c) Temper tantrums
   (d) Enuresis
   (e) Masturbation

3.   Antisocial attitudes wherein the child reveals subjective reactions antagonistic to authority, but without serious overt aggressions:
   (a) Hostility
   (b) Isolation
   (c) Anxieties
   (d) Guilt feelings

4. "Waywardness" or "incorrigibility," the violation of relatively nonserious community conduct standards:

   (*a*) Idleness
   (*b*) Truancy
   (*c*) Running away from home
   (*d*) Fighting
   (*e*) Disobedience

5. Serious illegalities, the violation of criminal conduct norms:

   (*a*) Theft
   (*b*) Burglary
   (*c*) Robbery
   (*d*) Assault
   (*e*) Rape
   (*f*) Homicide

To most students of the problem it is clear that there is some child behavior which requires court attention due to the seriousness of its influence upon the community and the danger of continued criminalism. It is easy enough to justify a court's assuming control in the parent's stead under category 5 above in order to apply therapeutic, corrective, or deterrent treatment. It is also apparent, perhaps, that certain types of situational factors, attitudes, and deviant conduct may better be dealt with by nonjudicial social agencies, public or private, whenever possible. Many would agree that categories 1, 2, and 3, above, should be handled outside of court by noncourt personnel. This, however, leaves exceedingly difficult issues to resolve. If the community lacks appropriate agency facilities, such as case work organizations, mental-hygiene clinics, psychiatric resources, etc., should the court then take over in these cases to do as well as it can, with a view to preventing later more serious maladjustment? Or, though the community may provide these other facilities, if the child comes first to the court, should it attempt to deal with the problems discovered as an "administrative social agency" striving to provide the fullest possible service? However these questions may be answered, there is still the problem of what should be done with the "wayward" child, with that large range of behavior, attitude, and situation that lies between the extremes of criminalism on the one hand and mere slight deviation on the other. The cases under category 4 may be dealt with today either by court or social agency; they lie within the province of the courts by ancient legal tradition, and yet the majority of such cases are handled by the home or by any of a variety of social agencies. In this area there is much overlapping of effort, sometimes competition of agency resources, and frequently needs are met very inadequately or not at all because of the failure to work out a systematic philosophy and program for treatment.

The court may essay to deal with these situations "preventively" because of the alleged dangers of later delinquency or because it conceives its function broadly. A case work or group work agency may handle similar situations regularly, though with different tools, specific objectives, and consequences.

Neva Deardorff, assistant executive director of the Welfare Council, New York City, has pointed up this problem of defining delinquency in instances of so-called "incorrigible" behavior:

Not all disobedience, for instance, carries a connotation of moral turpitude. As everyone knows there are family situations from which any sensitive child would inevitably wish to run away, and some would have the courage to do so even though in the process they become "runaways." It would have to be decided whether rebels of this kind should go on the register of delinquents and, if so, under what diagnosis. Everyone who gives any thought to the matter knows that when a parent claims that a child is ungovernable it is well to see the kind of government that the parent

Table 1

COURT AND AGENCY DELINQUENCY:[*] CHILDREN REGISTERED FOR SPECIFIED REASONS
FOR REFERENCE BY ALL AGENCIES AND BY THE JUVENILE COURT[†]

(1) Reason for reference	(2) Children registered by all agencies for reason specified in (1)	(3) Children registered by the juvenile court for reason specified in (1)	(4) Per cent of all children registered for specified reason who were registered by the juvenile court for that reason
Traffic violations	591	585	99
Stealing	1,870	1,487	80
Assault, injury to person	187	148	79
Acts of carelessness or mischief	951	733	77
Being ungovernable	456	244	54
Sex offense	258	61	24
Truancy	3,488	177	5
Running away	819	16	2

[*] Edward E. Schwartz, Community Experiment in Delinquency Measurement, *Natl. Prob. Assn. Yearb.*, 1945, p. 173.

[†] Inasmuch as some children were referred to agencies for more than one reason, neither (2) nor (3) may be totaled without obtaining figures which include duplicate counts.

is imposing before jumping to the conclusion that the problem inheres in the child.[30]

Very convincing evidence of the difficulties inherent in the effort to define delinquency in terms of conduct appears in the results of two research studies on the incidence of court-adjudicated behavior and of similar behavior in other noncourt samples. The first of these studies came out of an effort, which was proposed by the U.S. Children's Bureau, to measure the total volume of delinquency in a single community, as recorded in court and by all the public agencies of the District of Columbia which have responsibility for dealing with delinquent children. The types of conduct that most frequently bring children into court are shown in

[30] Neva Deardorff, Central Registration of Delinquents, *Prob.*, vol. 13, p. 143, June, 1945. (Reprinted by permission.)

Table 1, together with data on the total number of children engaging in such behavior, the number brought before the juvenile court, and the proportion of all cases of the several types of conduct that appeared in court. It is apparent upon inspection that, save for the more serious types of law violation, juvenile court statistics include only a limited, and in some categories very small, proportion of cases of the kind with which criminal courts customarily deal. Moreover, these figures do not reveal the volume of similar cases handled by the private agencies of the community or by parents and others without resort to social agencies. Clearly whether or not one is officially delinquent depends not on his conduct alone but, to a great extent, on referral practices that obtain in the community (see Table 1).

The other study is even more suggestive of the anomaly implicit in juvenile court practices when conduct of the same order that may result in adjudication is regularly tolerated in vast numbers of other instances. Moreover, if a purpose of these courts is to prevent the development of serious misconduct, it is an error of function to manipulate many of these cases in court, since the result is so commonly recidivism and increasing recalcitrance. Professor Porterfield studied 2,049 cases of alleged delinquents in the Fort Worth area and broke down their conduct into fifty-five specific offenses ranging from "shooting spitwads at a wrestling match" to murder. He compared this sample with the admitted conduct of 337 students from three colleges of northern Texas. The summary table borrowed from his study reveals the frequency of these offenses in the histories of those who went to college rather than to court (see Table 2). It is of special interest to note in his detailed breakdown of the offenses and their frequency how often the college students had indulged in the "delinquent" or "predelinquent" peccadillos that send their less fortunate counterparts to court and frequently to the reformatory (see Table 3).

No clearer evidence is required to show the essentially sumptuary character of official definitions of delinquency as they operate from day to day in the court. It appears that the minor waywardness or incorrigibility of the college student's history is not only tolerated but proves to be of little detriment in his subsequent conformity to law and to the norms of society at large. What foundation is there to believe that the child of lower socioeconomic status with a similar conduct record will become seriously delinquent if he is not brought to court? It is known from disillusioning experience that many of them become progressively deviant *after* they have been exposed to court and training school. It is known, too, that similar cases dealt with simply by their parents or by nonstigmatic and unofficial social agencies do not become criminal. Does this not indicate that, in relation to "wayward" and other course-of-conduct provisions at any rate, control is better left whenever possible to noncourt facilities, the trenchant judicial authority being reserved for more serious cases that clearly require it? How frequently does society in effect manufacture, aggravate, and extend delinquency by preventive efforts on the predelinquent? Where is the administrative approach in the liberal and "socialized" but quasi-criminal court taking us?

Children's Court or Parents' Court?

A further and related problem affecting the behavioral content of delinquency remains to be stated: Whose

Table 2

PERCENTAGE OF STUDENTS REPORTING THE COMMISSION OF ONE OR MORE OF THE FIFTY-FIVE OFFENSES CHARGED AGAINST CHILDREN IN THE COURT AND AVERAGE NUMBER OF OFFENSES REPORTED BY EACH[*]

Offending group	Number in group	Percentage reporting one or more of the offenses	Average number of offenses reported
Precollege men	200	100.0	17.6
College men	100	100.0	11.2
Precollege women	137	100.0	4.7

[*] Porterfield, *Youth in Trouble,* p. 38.

Table 3

OFFENSES OF COLLEGE STUDENTS AND JUVENILE DELINQUENTS*

	Percentage of students						Percentage of juvenile court cases charged with the offense	
	Reporting the offense			Charged with the offense				
	Precollege		College men	Precollege		College men		
Offenses by types	Men	Women		Men	Women		Boys	Girls
Vagabondage:								
Suspicious character	0.0	0.0	0.0	0.0	0.0	0.0	9.0	4.9
Vagrancy	4.0	0.0	4.0	0.0	0.0	0.0	0.3	0.0
Begging	5.5	0.0	3.0	0.0	0.0	0.0	0.5	0.0
Peddling, no license	5.5	0.0	5.0	0.0	0.0	0.0	0.2	0.0
Runaway, wandering	14.5	4.3	2.0	0.0	0.0	0.0	42.0	31.5
Stranded transiency	14.5	0.0	12.0	0.0	0.0	0.0	†	†
Truancy	42.5	34.3	28.0	0.0	0.0	0.0	1.0	1.1
Loafing in a pool hall	48.0	0.0	46.0	0.0	0.0	0.0	0.3	0.0
Percentage charged in court: total				0.0	0.0	0.0	53.3	37.5
Liquor violations:								
Illegal manufacture	8.0	0.0	0.0	0.0	0.0	0.0	0.2	0.0
Illegal possession	35.5	2.9	47.0	0.0	0.0	0.0	0.1	0.0
Buying as a minor	38.0	2.2	53.0	0.0	0.0	0.0	0.1	0.0
Drunkenness	39.0	2.9	43.0	0.5	0.0	0.0	0.8	1.1
Percentage charged in court: total				0.5	0.0	0.0	1.2	1.1
Theft:								
Automobile theft	0.5	0.0	0.0	0.0	0.0	0.0	0.9	0.5‡
Bicycle theft	0.5	0.0	0.0	0.0	0.0	0.0	2.5	0.0
Theft of tools, money	5.5	0.0	1.0	0.0	0.0	0.0	3.8	0.0
Burglary·	7.5	0.0	4.0	0.0	0.0	0.0	7.0	0.0
Shoplifting	10.0	1.5	5.0	0.0	0.0	0.0	10.0	11.4
Miscellaneous, petty	23.0	8.8	11.0	0.0	0.0	0.0	2.7	4.1
Stealing melons, fruit	69.0	16.0	15.0	0.0	0.0	0.0	0.3	0.0
Percentage charged in court: total				0.0	0.0	0.0	27.2	16.0
Dishonesty (other than stealing):								
Forgery	2.5	5.1	1.0	0.0	0.0	0.0	0.2	1.6
False collection	8.0	2.2	10.0	0.0	0.0	0.0	0.2	0.0
Possessing stolen goods	20.0	3.6	14.0	0.0	0.0	0.0	1.4	0.0
Passing slugs, bad coins	24.0	0.0	14.0	0.0	0.0	0.0	0.1	0.0
Gambling	58.5	17.4	60.0	0.0	0.0	0.0	0.7	0.0
Percentage charged in court: total				0.0	0.0	0.0	2.6	1.6
Sex offenses:								
Attempt to rape	5.5	0.0	3.0	0.0	0.0	0.0	0.1	0.0
Indecent exposure	24.5	2.2	23.0	0.0	0.0	0.0	0.1	0.0
Extramarital coitus	58.5	0.7	59.0	0.0	0.0	0.0	0.5	11.4
Percentage charged in court: total				0.0	0.0	0.0	0.7	11.4

Table 3 (continued)

Offenses by types	Percentage of students						Percentage of juvenile court cases charged with the offense	
	Reporting the offense			Charged with the offense				
	Precollege		Col-lege men	Precollege		Col-lege men		
	Men	Women		Men	Women		Boys	Girls
Other cases:								
Carrying concealed weapons	14.0	0.0	0.0	0.0	0.0	0.0	0.2	0.0
Homicide, murder	0.5	0.0	0.0	0.0	0.0	0.0	0.2	0.5§
Homicide, negligent	0.5	0.0	0.0	0.5	0.0	0.0	0.1	0.0
Incorrigible	0.0	0.0	0.0	0.0	0.0	0.0	1.4	10.3
Neglected, abused, etc.	0.0	0.0	0.0	0.0	0.0	0.0	0.1	12.0
Miscellaneous appearance in court				2.0	0.0	4.0	0.0	2.1
Percentage charged in court: total				2.5	0.0	4.0	2.0	24.9

* Porterfield, *Youth in Trouble,* p. 41.
† See "Runaway."
‡ As accomplice.
§ Self-defense.

interests does the juvenile court propose to protect? Is it the child, the parent, or some other petitioner who persuades the court to action? In legal theory the court acts in a role of protector to serve its wards who have suffered from insufficiency in the aid and guidance of their natural parents. As stated in *Commonwealth v. Fisher,*[31]

. . . it is not for the punishment of offenders, but for the salvation of children, and points out the way by which the state undertakes to save, not particular children of a special class, but all children under a certain age, whose salvation may become the duty of the state in the absence of proper parental care or disregard of it by wayward children. No child under the age of sixteen years is excluded from its beneficent provisions. Its protecting arm is for all who have not attained that age and who may need its protection.

At the same time that statute and cases observe the objective to save the

[31] *Commonwealth v. Fisher,* 213 Pa. 48 (1905). See Tappan, *op. cit.,* Appendix A for a more complete quotation of this case.

child, the courts often appear in practice to shrink from any real subrogation to the parental role, tending simply to support parental authority by the added prestige and power of the state. It is anomalous when the parents have been, as they often are, an important contributing factor to the unadjustment of their offspring or have failed in efforts to guide and control them for the court to take jurisdiction and accede to the demands of those parents on adjudication and treatment. Courts and judges vary considerably in their inclination either to stand behind the parents or to blame and condemn them. The custom of the courts has been largely to assist parents in the latter's program of controlling the child, however, rather than to make an independent plan for his care based upon the total situation. Definitions of delinquency are based in part upon violation of parental standards and the courts are often deemed to be acting in the role of the parents. An equally unfortunate but contrasting practice that has become popular recently in some jurisdictions is to punish the parents for their children's delinquencies, usually treating the children too as offenders.[32] The provisions in many statutes for penalties against those responsible for or contributing to delinquency have permitted this opposite approach, popular in California, New York, and elsewhere.

This whole issue of parent-court relationship is important here in that the risk of a child's adjudication depends to so considerable an extent on whether the court conceives its primary function as protection of the child or support to the parent. In the former instance adjudication may often be avoided entirely whereas in the latter it is facilitated, whatever may be the consequent injury to the child. It appears that whether the child is a delinquent depends too much on whether the parent says he is, rather than on his actual conduct.

[32] A recent instance of this, which stirred considerable interest, was the case of a mother sentenced to a year in prison for contributing to the delinquency of her fourteen-year-old son. Upon appeal to the Appellate Division, the decision was reversed on the grounds of the improper hearsay testimony which the judge had allowed at the trial in children's court. The defendant was subsequently found to be insane and not, therefore, responsible for her own behavior, let alone that of her son. As Edwin Lukas, director of the Society for the Prevention of Crime, which appealed this case, pointed out, this mother was as much the victim of circumstances as was her son: "Mrs. R— was sent to this country like a piece of baggage at the age of 8 by parents who had too large a family to worry about her. She lived with childless relatives here. When she was 16, they tried to marry her off to a man twice her age. At 19 she married an older man and had two children by the time she was 20. Her husband abandoned her and she tried to find work to support her children, boarded out over the years. The woman deteriorated—she had no strength left. She tried to support her children, but she couldn't. Parents have contributed a great deal to the delinquency of their children. But just as children are seen as the products and victims of their environment, so are parents products and victims too." See *The New York Times*, Mar. 18, 1947.

What Conduct Results in Adjudication?

Of those children who are adjudicated in children's courts, the relative frequency of various offenses may be inferred from the petitions issued. In most jurisdictions theft, including automobile theft, burglary, and robbery, is the primary type of delinquency with mischievous behavior fairly close. Endangering the morals of oneself or others and running away from home follow with high rates and other assorted offenses trail behind with but a small proportion of each, such as truancy, property damage, unlawful entry, possession of a dangerous weapon, homicide, etc. Among girls the most common offenses are sex violations, incorrigibility, and running away. The accompanying table shows the ground of petition as reported to the U.S. Children's Bureau for 1945 (see Table 4).

Obviously, adjudications or petitions offer no accurate picture of the actual rates of delinquent conduct, or even of the order of their frequency. Truancy, running away, and unlawful entry, for example, occur much more frequently than court statistics indicate; their relative rates of adjudication vary greatly in different cities. The charges of incorrigibility and endangering the morals or health of a child, in the very nature of the allegations, are such that any estimate of their real frequency is futile: adjudication depends on the interpretation of the court.

DELINQUENCY DEFINED

It is suggested that the general terms of juvenile delinquency statutes permit courts to take hold under broad and imprecise circumstances of conduct, attitude, or social situation; that to a large and increasing extent these courts do in fact exercise this discretion to deal with cases deemed either presently delinquent or in danger of becoming so; that the same types of behavior and situation are handled by unofficial social agencies without stigma to the client; and that, in consequence of all this, "delinquency" has little specific behavioral content either in law or in fact, other than the provision that acts which would otherwise be crimes, in a juvenile are delinquency.

Hence, one emerges from a consideration of the elements entering into delinquency with an indefinite and unsatisfying conclusion. *The juvenile delinquent is a person who has been adjudicated as such by a court of proper jurisdiction* though he may be no dif-

ferent, up until the time of court contact and adjudication at any rate, from masses of children who are not delinquent. *Delinquency is any act, course of conduct, or situation which might be brought before a court and adjudicated* whether in fact it comes to be treated there or by some other resource or indeed remains untreated. It will be noted that under these definitions adjudicatable conduct may be defined as delinquent in the abstract, but it cannot be measured as delinquency until a court has found the facts of delinquency to exist.

Table 4

JUVENILE DELINQUENCY CASES, 1945: REASONS FOR REFERENCE TO COURT, IN BOYS' AND IN GIRLS' CASES DISPOSED OF BY 374 COURTS[*]

| | Juvenile-delinquency cases | | | | | |
| | Number | | | Per cent | | |
Reason for reference to court	Total	Boys	Girls	Total	Boys	Girls
Total cases	122,851	101,240	21,611			
Reason for reference reported	111,939	92,671	19,268	100	100	100
Stealing	40,879	38,610	2,269	37	42	12
Act of carelessness or mischief	19,241	17,779	1,462	17	19	8
Traffic violation	9,852	9,659	193	9	10	1
Truancy	8,681	6,164	2,517	8	7	13
Running away	9,307	5,652	3,655	8	6	19
Being ungovernable	9,840	5,542	4,298	9	6	22
Sex offense	5,990	2,579	3,411	5	3	18
Injury to person	3,224	2,828	396	3	3	2
Other reason	4,925	3,858	1,067	4	4	5
Reason for reference not reported	10,912	8,569	2,343			

[*] *Social Statistics,* p. 11, U.S. Children's Bureau, 1945.

2

The Legal Basis of Juvenile Delinquency

Thorsten Sellin and Marvin E. Wolfgang

A clear definition of fundamental concepts is a prime requisite for all research. Therefore, any study of delinquency must first establish the meaning of this term. This task has often been neglected by criminologists who have spent more time on examining the terms and concepts of the independent variables than of the dependent one—delinquency—which they have hoped to explain. As Mack has written: "It is impossible to undertake any such [etiological] research without having to decide first of all what you mean by delinquency. This is a condition which most textbooks and research papers acknowledge in their first paragraph and then go on to ignore."[1] The need for a definition of delinquency is equally stressed by Tappan, who states:

Certainly there is no more central question in this study and probably none more difficult to answer. Yet it is important to see the nature of delinquency as clearly as possible and to understand the problems that have impeded efforts at definition . . . , because on the interpretation of the term depend all those vital differences which set off the juvenile delinquent from the adult criminal at the one extreme and from the non-offender at the other.[2]

These quotations may appear strange in view of the fact that definitions of delinquency exist in laws that provide the basis for dealing with juvenile offenders. It is these definitions that have been used in the compilation of official statistics about delinquency and delinquents, on which so many studies have relied, or in classifying delinquents, when the researcher has had access to the original records of public agencies. Indeed, innumerable variables have been statistically correlated with the events covered by the legal terms "crime" and "delinquency" and provocative theories about these phenomena have been formulated, but even in the most sophisticated researches little or no account has been taken of the great diversity of conduct represented, not only by the inclusive designation of "delinquency" but even by such legal categories as "offenses against the per-

SOURCE. Thorsten Sellin and Marvin E. Wolfgang, *The Measurement of Delinquency*, New York: John Wiley and Sons, Inc., 1964, pp. 71–86. Reprinted with permission.

[1] J. A. Mack, "Juvenile delinquency research: A criticism," *Sociol. Rev.* N.S. 3:47–64 (July 1955), p. 56.

[2] Paul W. Tappan, *Juvenile Delinquency* (613 pp. New York: McGraw Hill, 1949), p. 3. Quoted by permission of publisher.

son," "offenses against property," criminal homicide, rape, robbery, burglary, larceny, and others. This, we think, is a cogent reason for the dissatisfaction with present definitions of juvenile delinquency and for the demand that something be done about it. But first, let us look at what the law calls delinquency.

This involves not only an examination of the specific statutes, which in creating juvenile courts also prescribed the scope of their jurisdiction in terms of the kinds of conduct and classes of juveniles affected, but also of the criminal law, since all juvenile court statutes in the United States provide that a child is a juvenile delinquent if he commits any act which would be a crime if done by an adult. Were delinquency limited to such conduct, our task would be simpler, but all jurisdicitions, except the federal, label a variety of other forms of conduct as delinquency. Sussmann has listed all of them in the order of their frequency and has shown, for each state, which ones are specified.[3] They number thirty-four, varying from truancy, incorrigibility, and running away from home to using tobacco in any form. No state has adopted all of them, but Indiana leads with seventeen; Maine, at the other extreme, names but one—"growing up in idleness and crime." Some of them could equally well come under the heading of dependency or neglect because the distinctions are often difficult to draw. As a matter of fact, some states classify as delinquency a condition which other states define as dependency or neglect.

The problem is not limited to the United States, as is seen from the following statement:

In many countries the meaning of juvenile delinquency is so broad that it embraces practically all manifestations of juvenile behavior. Under the influence of certain theories, juvenile delinquency is identified either with maladjustment or with forms of juvenile behavior which actually are more a reflection of poor living conditions or inadequate laws and regulations than a delinquent inclination. Thus, disobedience, stubbornness, lack of respect, being incorrigible, smoking without permission, collecting cigarette butts, hawking and the like are considered juvenile delinquency. Very often these "forms of delinquency" are hidden in statistical data under the vague term "other offenses." More often than would be desirable, these "offenders" are lumped together with real ones not only because services and institutions for them are not available but also because, according to some policies and practices, all of them are considered "maladjusted" and sent to the same institutions. The result is an artificial inflation of the juvenile delinquency problem and its "forms."[4]

Confusion results from these legal definitions of delinquency.

It is reasonable to believe [says Tappan] that all, or at least a vast majority of, normal children sometimes indulge in forms of behavior that might come within the purview of the juvenile court. Whether a given child will get into trouble depends largely on the interpretation that is attached to his conduct and the willingness or ability of the parent to deal with it. Considering the broad scope of legal provisions on insubordination, "questionable behavior," "injuring or endangering the morals or health of himself or others," truancy, running away, trespassing, and petty theft, it would be difficult to find any paragons of virtue who would be wholly ex-

---

[3] Frederick B. Sussmann, *Law of Juvenile Delinquency* (96 pp. New York: Oceana Publications, 1959), pp. 21–22.

[4] The Second United Nations Congress on The Prevention of Crime and the Treatment of Offenders (London, August 8–20, 1960). *New Forms of Juvenile Delinquency: Their Origin, Prevention and Treatment.* Report prepared by the Secretariat, A/Conf. 17/7.

onerated of delinquency, save through parental understanding and leniency.[5]

The lack of uniformity among jurisdictions makes comparative studies especially difficult. Although violations of criminal laws and ordinances are generally considered "delinquency" when committed by a juvenile, many states give exclusive jurisdiction to the criminal court if the violation is of a certain kind. This holds true for capital crimes in the federal code and in the laws of eleven states (Colorado, Georgia, Iowa, Maryland, Massachusetts, Minnesota, South Carolina, Tennessee, Delaware, Vermont, and West Virginia) and for crimes punishable by life imprisonment in the first eight of these mentioned; for murder in five states (Kansas, Louisiana, Montana, New Jersey, and Pennsylvania); for homicide (Texas); for manslaughter (Montana); for rape (Louisiana, Tennessee); for attempted rape (Louisiana); for crimes of violence (Illinois); for crimes punishable by more than ten years imprisonment (North Carolina); for infamous crimes (Maine); for traffic law (Indiana, New Jersey) or motor vehicle law offenses (Rhode Island); and for "any crime" (Florida).[6] Juveniles prosecuted for these offenses in the jurisdictions just mentioned fall outside of "delinquency" properly speaking. In studies of the illegal conduct of juveniles, they would, of course, have to be included, but if they have not been processed by juvenile courts they do not figure in the records of these courts which have so often been the chief source of data for delinquency studies.

Comparative analysis of such studies is complicated by still another problem, namely the lack of a standard definition of who is capable of engaging in "delinquency," both as to age and sex. Considering the fifty-two jurisdictions —constituted of fifty states, the District of Columbia, and the federal government—anyone under 21 years of age can commit a "delinquency" and therefore be adjudged a juvenile delinquent in 4 of the jurisdictions; under 19 in 2; under 18 in 28; under 17 in 10; and under 16 in 8. This is true for both sexes, but in one state that has a maximum limit of 19 for males, the limit is 21 for females; in two states these maxima are respectively 16 and 18, and in five states, 17 and 18. The effect of these diverse age limits on interstate research is easy to imagine, unless comparable age and sex groups have been used.

Except for the jurisdictions mentioned earlier, no state has given criminal courts exclusive jurisdiction over juveniles, but most have given them concurrent jurisdiction, which means that a juvenile in these states may, under certain circumstances, be adjudged a criminal rather than a delinquent. The scope of this power varies greatly among the jurisdictions, as may be seen from the tabulation on page 28, [Table 1] which takes only juvenile males into consideration.[7]

Although it can be seen that more than half of the jurisdictions (28) limit delinquency to illegal conduct by those under 18 years of age, there could be substantial errors made, for instance, in comparing the results of studies made in the eleven states, in which any juvenile may be prosecuted for crime, with those made in the two states (New Hampshire and Virginia) where criminal courts have no jurisdiction at all over those under 18.

In most states there is no lower age limit set for the adjudication of a child

[5] Paul W. Tappan, *op. cit.*, p. 32.
[6] Based on Sussman, *op. cit.*, pp. 65–77, as adapted from Paul W. Tappan, "Children and youth in the criminal court," *Ann. Amer. Acad. polit. and soc. Sci.* 261:128–136 (January 1949), pp. 129–130.

[7] Compiled from Sussman, *ibid.*

as delinquent; Mississippi and Texas place that limit at ten and New York at seven.[8]

Table 1

Where the original jurisdiction of the Juvenile Court extends to age	The Criminal Court has overlapping or concurrent jurisdiction over juveniles	
	above the age of	in ——— jurisdictions
21	11	1
	17	3
19	all ages	1
	14	1
18	all ages	11
	19–21	1
	11–21	1
	13	5
	15	8
	none	2
17	all ages	2
	9	1
	11	1
	15	1
	16	1
	none	4
16	all ages	2
	14	1
	none	5

Our brief discussion of how diversely "delinquency" and "delinquents" are defined in American statutes and how judicial administration may affect the assignment of an offense or an offender to the criminal or the delinquency area has been pursued to indicate one aspect of the difficulties involved in securing uniform and reliable data for the measurement of delinquency. Although these difficulties are especially great when data from different jurisdictions are involved, they are not absent in studies dealing with a single state or community. So long as the definition of delinquency in law in any jurisdiction includes so many ill-defined kinds of conduct and admits of the exercise of wide administrative discretion at all levels in handling juvenile offenders, the problem of standardization of data needed for measurement purposes will always face the student. Indeed, it has forced us, in the present research to develop a system of classifying delinquent acts which is in a sense independent of the labels attached to them by the law.

THE PENNSYLVANIA JUVENILE COURT ACT

The source documents used in our study are records of various kinds, compiled by the police of Philadelphia in connection with their routine enforcement of the law. So far as juveniles are concerned, such enforcement is circumscribed by what is considered to be delinquent conduct by the legislature of the Commonwealth of Pennsylvania and recorded in an act of June 2, 1933, Public Law 1433, with amendments of 1937, 1939, 1953. Section I, Subsection 2 and 4, contains the following definitions.

(2) The word "child," as used in this act, means a minor under the age of eighteen years.

(4) The words "delinquent child" include:

(a) A child who has violated any law of the Commonwealth or ordinance of any city, borough, or township;

(b) A child who, by reason of being wayward or habitually disobedient, is uncontrolled by his or her parent, guardian, custodian, or legal representative;

(c) A child who is habitually truant from school or home;

[8] Sol Rubin, "The legal character of juvenile delinquency," *Ann. Amer. Acad. polit. and soc. Sci.,* 261:1–8 (January 1949), p. 6.

(*d*) A child who habitually so deports himself or herself as to injure or endanger the morals or health of himself, herself, or others.

As can be seen, Section 1, Subsection 4a, defines delinquency as any act, which if committed by an adult would be a crime; and Subsections 4b, c, and d define delinquency in terms of an age status and constituting acts or conditions that could not be attributed to an adult.

THE STANDARD JUVENILE COURT ACT

The definition of delinquency, such as the one used in the Pennsylvania statute, is no longer supported by leading authorities. It is challenged, in particular, by the drafters of the Standard Juvenile Court Act. The first edition of this Act was published by the National Probation Association in 1925. It was revised and reissued in 1928, 1933, 1943, and 1959. Prepared by the Committee on Standard Juvenile Court Act of the National Probation and Parole Association, in cooperation with the National Council of Juvenile Court Judges and the United States Children's Bureau, the new act emphasizes the basic concept in *parens patriae*. Under the act, Article 1, Sections 2c and 2f, a "child" is defined as a person under 18 years of age and a "minor" as any person under 21 years of age. As in the 1943 and 1949 editions of the Act, the terms "delinquency" and "neglect" are avoided. Article 2, Section 8, Subsection 1 reads:

[Except as otherwise provided herein, the court shall have exclusive original jurisdiction in proceedings]
1. Concerning any child who is alleged to have violated any federal, state, or local law or municipal ordinance, regardless of where the violation occurred; or any minor alleged to have violated any federal, state,

or local law or municipal ordinance prior to having become 18 years of age. Such minor shall be dealt with under the provisions of this act relating to children. Jurisdiction may be taken by the court of the district where the minor is living or found, or where the offense is alleged to have occurred. When a minor 18 years of age or over already under the jurisdiction of the court is alleged to have violated any federal, state, or local law or municipal ordinance, the juvenile court shall have concurrent jurisdiction with the criminal court.[9]

This delimitation of the scope of juvenile delinquency has received recent support from two sources. The Second United Nations Congress on the Prevention of Crime and the Treatment of Offenders, London 1960, passed a resolution that stated: "The Congress considers that the scope of the problem of juvenile delinquency should not be unnecessarily inflated . . . it recommends that the meaning of the term juvenile delinquency should be restricted as far as possible to violations of the criminal law."[10]

The New York Joint Legislative Committee on Court Reorganization, in its draft of a Family Court Act, has taken a similar stand:

"Juvenile delinquent" is defined in the proposed legislation as "a person over seven and less than sixteen years of age who does any act which, if done by an adult would constitute a crime, and requires supervision, treatment or confinement." This definition, considerably narrower than the current definition, accords with the common understanding.[11]

[9] "Standard Juvenile Court Act," *National Probation and Parole Assoc. J.* 5:323–391 (October 1959), p. 344.
[10] See *Report Prepared by the Secretariat* (iv, 95 pp., New York: United Nations, 1961), p. 61.
[11] Joint Legislative Committee on Court Reorganization, II, "The Family Court Act," New York State, Daniel G. Albert, Chairman (Albany, N.Y., 1962), p. 6.

We believe that statistical collections and analyses in terms of the definitions of delinquency must adopt this delimitation if they are to provide a useful measurement or index of the volume, character or trend of delinquency.

Although the present research has had to depend on the definition of delinquency found in the Juvenile Court Act of Pennsylvania in selecting an appropriate sample of delinquent acts for analysis, we decided that it would be impossible to utilize the data on the "juvenile status" offenses in the construction of an index to delinquency. Such offenses are viewed by most writers only as predelinquent behavior or symptomatic of potential delinquent behavior. That is why it is often argued that they should not be labeled delinquency, and that is the chief reason behind the recommendations of the Standard Juvenile Court Act.

Truancy, for example, is a violation of a regulation requiring compulsory school attendance, but the explanation for truancy involves parental influence or lack of it or the failure of educational facilities and authorities to solve purely educational problems. To call the absence from classes delinquency places the truant in the same category with more serious violators of substantive legal codes. Shulman suggests: "Since chronic truancy often antedates serious delinquency by several years and may serve as a valuable warning signal of impending serious behavior disorder, we may raise the question of whether its formal handling as an aspect of juvenile delinquency is a proper one."[12]

The law presumes that children belong at home, and consequently a child who runs away from home is considered delinquent. But as in the case of in-

[12] Harry M. Shulman, *Juvenile Delinquency in American Society* (New York: Harper, 1961), p. 33.

corrigibility and ungovernable behavior, the problems of family neglect are the important issues to be considered by the juvenile court in handling these children rather than behavior that constitutes serious and injurious threats to other members of the community.

Excluding these and similar acts from use in the measurement of delinquency and concentrating only on violations by juveniles of the law and ordinances that, were they committed by adults, would be considered crimes, reduce but do not eliminate the problem of legal definitions and classifications. The substantive content of the definitions of these offenses in the criminal law therefore has to be considered since it is common practice in official statistics of delinquency, especially in police statistics, to classify delinquents and their conduct in categories designated by labels derived from the criminal law.

The Labels of the Criminal Law

Since police agencies are entrusted with the enforcement of the criminal law, it is both obvious and natural that, in the investigation of offenses, they think in terms of the specific definitions of crime contained in the law. When a complaint is made and they investigate the incident, or when they observe an offense being committed, its objective characteristics lead them to call it burglary, robbery, larceny, etc. And when they prepare reports on the incidents on some standard forms, these labels are recorded and furnish the basis for later periodic tabulations of the number of different offenses the police have dealt with whether or not an offender is taken into custody. The result is that when juveniles are apprehended by the police, their offenses are not labeled "delinquency" but are given appropriate criminal designations or, in the case of juvenile status offenses, a specific designation supplied by the juvenile court law, such as truancy, runaway, incorrigibility, etc.

No police department, to our knowledge, publishes any statistics of juvenile *offenses*. Since most offenses are committed by unknown persons, those committed by juveniles can be segregated only when an apprehension is made. Even then, however, the practice is to publish only statistics of juvenile *delinquents* without reference to the number of offenses of different legal categories that have been "cleared" by their apprehension. In any event, such statistics are commonly relied on today as indicators of the movement and character of juvenile delinquency. Therefore, it becomes necessary to ask if (*a*) the criminal law labels best characterize delinquency and (*b*) if customary practices of statistical classification of juvenile offenses present the best picture of such delinquency.

Answers to these questions are complicated by the fact that the problems they involve are not independent of one another. The criminal law of a state may contain a very large number of distinctive crime designations, several hundreds of them, but when police departments record offenses with a view to their later inclusion in statistics, they are accustomed to use relatively few such designations and give the same label to a variety of offenses that resemble one another in some way. This practice has become more and more common and has been greatly stimulated by the formulation of the Uniform Classification of Offenses in the early 1930's. This classification is used in national statistics of offenses known to the police and of persons charged with offenses and published in *Unifrom Crime Reports* issued by the FBI and based on reports now submitted by most civil police agencies in the United States. The classification, as slightly revised in 1958, contains 26 offense categories. Police agencies periodically submit reports to the FBI on standard forms containing these categories; and to facilitate the preparation of these reports the police now tend to label offenses not according to the more specific designations in the criminal law but by the code numbers and titles used in the Uniform Classification.

UNIFORM CLASSIFICATION OF OFFENSES

Part 1

1. Criminal homicide
   a. Murder and non-negligent manslaughter
   b. Manslaughter by negligence
2. Forcible rape
3. Robbery
4. Aggravated assault
5. Burglary—breaking or entering
6. Larceny-theft (except auto theft)
   a. $50 and over in value
   b. Under $50 in value
7. Auto theft

Part 2

8. Other assaults
9. Forgery and counterfeiting
10. Embezzlement and fraud
11. Stolen property: Buying, receiving, possessing
12. Weapons: Carrying, possessing, etc.
13. Prostitution and commercialized vice
14. Sex offenses (except forcible rape, prostitution, and commercialized vice)
15. Offenses against the family and children
16. Narcotic drug laws
17. Liquor laws (except drunkenness)
18. Drunkenness
19. Disorderly conduct
20. Vagrancy
21. Gambling
22. Driving while intoxicated
23. Violation of road and driving laws
24. Parking violations
25. Other violations of traffic and motor vehicle laws
26. All other offenses

Each of the titles in the above classification is derived from the criminal law but of necessity each covers a considerable variety of illegal conduct. When juvenile delinquency which violates the criminal law is subsumed under them, the result is a highly simplified and considerably distorted picture of that delinquency. A few illustrations will suffice. They will be limited largely to some of the titles of offenses which in *Uniform Crime Reports* are considered as "index crimes," that is, susceptible of use as a measurement of criminality. These are murder and non-negligent manslaughter, forcible rape, robbery, aggravated assault, burglary-breaking and entering, larceny or theft of property valued at 50 dollars or more, and auto theft (motor vehicle theft). It should be recalled that so far as juveniles are concerned, these titles are applicable only in descriptions of *offenses* attributable to juveniles or to *apprehended juveniles* charged with their commission.

Robbery

This title implies to most people that there is only one kind of robbery, that it is terrible and that it connotes taking something of value from a person, usually with violence. Yet, evidence points to significant differences in the quality of these acts.[13] As Beattie points out,

. . . there is no knowledge of the variation that has occurred in different types of robbery. Such increases or decreases as have been observed may be due to variations in armed robbery or in strong-arm robbery, which in some instances amounts to no more than drunk rolls. Reports are often received today that children have been engaged in highjacking coins from

each other. These incidents have been reported as robberies.[14]

The victim-offender relationship is also important, by sex, age, and other variables. There is certainly a vast difference between a 16-year-old boy's forcing a gas station attendant at the point of a gun to give up money from the cash register and an eight-year-old boy's twisting the arm of another eight-year-old boy in the school corridor in order to take his lunch money. Both acts are classified legally and statistically as robbery. This same kind of situation was referred to in the 1956 Annual Report of the Crime Prevention Association of Philadelphia:

And again, what is "highway robbery"? In the thinking of the American people, this indeed is a serious offense. Yet we know of a case last year in which a 14-year-old approached another boy of similar age and demanded 15 cents; the boy accosted stated he had only a quarter. The "highway robber" took the quarter, had it changed and returned to the other boy 10 cents. *This offense is listed as highway robbery.* Another instance involved two boys who extorted 20 cents daily for a week from another boy as he went to and from school. This youthful highjacking was reported by the victim's parents to the police; charge against the two offenders— highway robbery. Now we must admit that such extortion and highjacking is nasty behavior but to call this highway robbery and still keep a straight face is naive.[15]

Burglary

Burglary is another example of the need for subclassifications, for while it

---

[13] These differences in adult robberies have recently been examined in some detail by F. H. McClintock and Evelyn Gibson, *Robbery in London* (xix, 147 pp. London: Macmillan, 1961).

[14] *Crime in California 1958*, p. 18. See also Nochem S. Winnet, *Twenty-Five Years of Crime Prevention* (Philadelphia: Philadelphia Crime Association) *Annual Report 1956*, p. 1: "Hundreds of robberies were reported. An analysis showed many of them involved petty sums, one as low as ten cents, a tribute exacted by one school child from another."

[15] *Ibid.*, p. 11.

is an offense that has shown a steady increase over the past years, we are never sure what kind of burglary has been increasing. The California Report has raised this same question: "Is the increase in safe burglary, large-scale residential and commercial burglary, or in just smallscale pilferings that are technically burglary? A large part of the latter could be the result of juvenile behavior. Under present classification methods, this question cannot be answered."[16] There are wide variations in the state statutes that define burglary. Although breaking into a locked car is defined as burglary in California and is reported thus in many instances, it is an offense that is often reported by many law enforcement agencies as petty theft and classified as larceny.

Some of these problems were raised in papers presented in 1960 before the Social Statistics Section of the American Statistical Association. It was pointed out, for example, that broad crime groupings are used to tally major offenses which differ according to some element in definition. The following cases were given as illustrations:

(A) Two juveniles while on school vacation break into a neighbor's barn, steal some nails, a hammer, and a saw in order to build a treehouse nearby; (B) a prowler sneaks into an unoccupied bedroom and rummages for money or jewlery while the occupants are having dinner downstairs; (C) a team of thugs, armed and with heavy burglar tools force entrance into an office and attack a safe. Each of these cases is classified ordinarily as a "burglary" according to police statistical practices.[17]

Both from the viewpoint of police protective services and of threats of danger to life or property, these acts are clearly distinguishable, but the differential variables are hidden in formal statistical tabulations that use legal categories. Such factors as the presence or absence of violence to obtain entry, the legal or illegal presence of the offender at the scene of the crime, the amount of property loss or damage, etc., are totally neglected.

Assaults

The legal definitions of aggravated assaults, sexual assaults, rape and similar offenses against the person each cover a variety of forms of conduct. The 1958 California report again suggests:

. . . because of the relationship of the parties or the conditions under which the assaults occurred, many altercations, largely domestic quarrels, characterized in reports as aggravated assault, do not seem to fall in the general area of felonious assault. There is need to sub-classify this type of offense in order to arrive at a true picture of assault.[18]

A New Jersey analysis of juvenile court cases a decade ago alluded to the same problem: "Personal injury, while having a higher percentage of dismissals as malicious mischief, does not carry comparable value under analysis. A majority of personal injury complaints were not assault cases per se—proper classification would be street fighting."[19] Moreover, the differences between a simple assault and battery and aggravated assault and battery are such that not only police variations but statutory provisions as well lend confusion rather than clarity to the classification problems. The legal nomenclature often distorts the true character of an attack on the person because of the difficulties of determining "grievous bodily harm" or

[16] *Crime in California 1958*, p. 18.
[17] Edward V. Comber, "Discussion," *Proc. Social Statistics Section 1960.* (viii, 211 pp., Washington, D.C.: American Statistical Association, n.d., mimeo.); pp. 36–37.

[18] *Crime in California 1958*, p. 18.
[19] *Children in New Jersey Courts 1953*, p. 24.

extent of the injury and because suspects are often willing to confess to a simple assault or the police and courts are willing to accept a plea of guilty to a simple assault in order to obtain a conviction even when the more serious aggravated assault occurred.[20]

Rape

The categories of rape—even forcible rape—assault with attempt to ravish, sexual license, and sexual offenses generally fail to provide qualitative information on the broad range of activities and on the dimensions of seriousness or injury that may be involved in these acts. Forcible rape can range from violent and unprovoked attacks on women by strangers to a common pickup in a barroom that ends in greater sexual intimacy than the woman intended. The lines between forcible rape, statutory rape, fornication, and contributing to the delinquency of a minor are never clear from statistical tabulations that merely use these legal terms. Without examination of the detailed descriptions in police reports, the compilation of data in tabular form usually fail to represent important distinctions in the facts. As the United Nations Congress in 1960 reported on an attempt to collect international data on sex offenses: " 'Sexual license' was too vague. The replies do not always make clear what kind of offenses are referred to: Full sexual relations or sexual games between children? Relations between lovers, sexual promiscuity, dissolute behavior, prostitution?"[21]

Certainly there are vast differences in the types of offenses that are listed as "assault with intent to ravish." The conduct of a 16-year-old boy, who attacks a 30-year-old woman, drags her into a dark alley to assault her sexually but is thwarted by screams and the appearance of a police officer, is surely different from a 9-year-old boy's exploratory sexual curiosity with a neighbor girl aged 8. When she innocently tells her mother about the afternoon's adventure, and when the mother imagines horrendous things, calls the police, and has the boy arrested, this case like the previous one is listed as "assault with intent to ravish." Once again, Beattie has remarked:

Much has been said in recent years of the apparent growth of viciousness in certain types of crime. There is no basis upon which to determine whether or not there has been such a growth. There have been many cases that have received a great deal of publicity, but without careful classification, it cannot be known whether the impression of increase is backed by fact.[22]

We believe that these illustrations suffice to show that the use of the broad titles of offenses derived from the Uniform Classification of Offenses for a description of delinquency chargeable to juveniles would be an unsatisfactory procedure that cannot provide sensitive measures of delinquency.

A second problem arises out of certain arbitrary practices of classifying and ordering offenses in official statistics of delinquency. These practices are directly attributable to the manner in which the Uniform Classification is applied in accordance with the instructions governing its use. There are, of course, many ways of presenting offense statistics. The offenses involved could be listed alphabetically, or grouped in broad classes—for instance, offenses against the person, offenses against property, etc.—with appropriate sub-

---

[20] See Donald J. Newman, "Pleading guilty for considerations: A study of bargain justice," *J. Crim. Law, Criminol., and Police Sci.*, 46:780–790, March–April, 1956.

[21] United Nations Congress, London, August 8–20, 1960, A/Conf. 17/6, p. 64.

[22] *Crime in California 1958*, p. 19.

classes, or grouped according to the Uniform Classification, to mention but a few patterns. For reasons already stated the last mentioned method is the most common one in American police statistics.

There are two built-in features of the use of this classification which reduce its value. First, an implicit hypothesis underlies it, namely that its 26 classes are arranged in decreasing order of seriousness. The hypothesis is not completely invalid. Certainly most offenses in Part 1 of the classification are more injurious than most of those in Part 2, but arson, kidnapping, abortion, blackmail and extortion, and malicious mischief now falling into the last class of "all other offenses," and simple assault and battery (item 8) and embezzlement and fraud (item 10) may in fact involve more personal injury or loss of property, for instance, than many of the offenses listed among the "index crimes" under rape, aggravated assault, burglary and larceny. Therefore, the present grouping of the offenses by the broad legal labels employed does not provide the best typology of offenses based on an hypothesis of degree of seriousness, not to mention the fact that it does not provide for differential weighting of the classes, nor of the great number of variants among the offenses included in any single class. One theft of fifty dollars is given as much weight as one homicide, and one such theft as much weight as one of $5000.[23]

Second, the manner in which the classification is used conceals a great deal of delinquency known to the police because it offers no possibility of counting all the *components* of a de-

linquent event. The problem does not arise in the case of uncomplicated events. A mere breaking and entering can be classified as burglary, but suppose that in committing this offense a juvenile also steals property of great value, and on being surprised, assaults and wounds the owner with a dangerous weapon. The instructions for classifying this total event require that only the offense highest in the order of the Uniform Classification be counted—in this instance, the aggravated assault and battery. This conceals both the burglary and the theft. If a juvenile holds up the occupants of an automobile, kills the driver, rapes his female companion, and steals her pocket book, jewelry, and the car, this complex event must be counted as one non-negligent criminal homicide (item 1) and the rape and the thefts will be concealed. All kinds of other complex events could be cited to show that the manner in which offenses are commonly tabulated for statistical presentation results in an incomplete picture even of the delinquency known to the police.

The conclusion seems inescapable that when an offense is given, in official police statistics, a broad legal label which does not allow for adequate discriminatory separation and weighting of the variants covered by it, and when all but the hypothetically most serious component of a delinquency event are concealed by the procedure followed in scoring offenses, the resulting statistics are not adequate for the measurement of delinquency.

The Philadelphia Police Department faithfully applies the Uniform Classification of Offenses and the instructions for its use, except that it regards item 12 of the classification as applying only to guns. In addition, it has extracted several distinct classes from "other offenses," thereby reducing the size of that residue. These classes are: arson,

---

[23] For a more detailed discussion of these and related problems, see Marvin E. Wolfgang, "Uniform crime reports: A critical appraisal," *University of Pennsylvania Law Rev.* 111:708–738 (April 1963).

corner lounging, malicious mischief, trespassing, incorrigible, runaway, and weapons other than guns. Furthermore, it has defined a total of 267 subclasses in order to secure statistics useful for internal administrative purposes.

Important as are the qualitative differences among the types of conduct now indiscriminately grouped statistically with the aid of a legal nomenclature, criminologists have taken little or no cognizance of them in researches dependent on such sources of data. Unlike scholars in most other fields of scientific research, they have, in such instances, relied upon terms, concepts, and definitions of units of investigation that they themselves did not establish. In the present research we have tried to solve this problem by an operational definition and classification of delinquent acts which cuts across legal categories.

3

Facts About Delinquency

America's best hope for reducing crime is to reduce juvenile delinquency and youth crime. In 1965 a majority of all arrests for major crimes against property were of people under 21, as were a substantial minority of arrests for major crimes against the person. The recidivism rates for young offenders are higher than those for any other age group. A substantial change in any of these figures would make a substantial change in the total crime figures for the Nation.

One of the difficulties of discussing the misconduct, criminal or not, of young people is that "juvenile" and "youth" are not precise definitions of categories of people. People are legally juveniles in most States until they pass their 18th birthdays, but in some States they stop being juveniles after they turn 16 or remain juveniles until they turn 21. The problems and behavior patterns of juveniles and youths often are similar.

To prevent and control delinquency, we must first know something about the nature of delinquency and the dimensions of the problem. We need to know how serious delinquency is. How much

SOURCE. The President's Commission on Law Enforcement and Administration of Justice, "Facts About Delinquency" from *The Challenge of Crime in a Free Society,* Washington, D.C.: U.S. Government Printing Office, 1967, pp. 55–57. Reprinted with permission.

of it is there? How many of our youth are involved? What sorts of illegal acts do they commit? What have the trends in delinquency been in the past, and what can we expect in the future? We also need knowledge about the people who become delinquent—information such as where most delinquents live and under what economic conditions.

But we are severely limited in what we can learn today. The only juvenile statistics regularly gathered over the years on a national scale are the FBI's Uniform Crime Reports, based on arrest statistics, and the juvenile court statistics of the Children's Bureau of the U.S. Department of Health, Education, and Welfare, based on referrals of juveniles from a variety of agencies to a sample of juvenile courts. These reports can tell us nothing about the vast number of unsolved offenses, or about the many cases in which delinquents are dealt with informally instead of being arrested or referred to court. Supplementing this official picture of delinquency are self-report studies, which rely on asking selected individuals about their delinquent acts. While efforts are made to insure the validity of the results by such means as guaranteeing anonymity, and verifying results with official records and unofficial checks, such studies have been conducted only on a local and sporadic basis, and they vary greatly in quality.

Clearly, there is urgent need for more and better information. Nonetheless, enough is available to give some of the rough outlines of juvenile delinquency in the United States.

SERIOUSNESS OF THE DELINQUENCY PROBLEM

Volume

Enormous numbers of young people appear to be involved in delinquent acts. Indeed, self-report studies reveal that perhaps 90 percent of all young people have committed at least one act for which they could have been brought to juvenile court. Many of these offenses are relatively trivial—fighting, truancy, running away from home. Statutes often define juvenile delinquency so broadly as to make virtually all youngsters delinquent.

Even though most of these offenders are never arrested or referred to juvenile court, alarming numbers of young people are. Rough estimates by the Children's Bureau, supported by independent studies, indicate that one

in every nine youths—one in every six male youths—will be referred to juvenile court in connection with a delinquent act (excluding traffic offenses) before his 18th birthday.

Youth is apparently responsible for a substantial and disproportionate part of the national crime problem. Arrest statistics can give us only a rough picture —probably somewhat exaggerated since it is likely that juveniles are more easily apprehended than adults. In addition, it may be that juveniles act in groups more often than adults when committing crimes, thus producing numbers of juvenile arrests out of proportion with numbers of crimes committed. But even with these qualifications, the figures are striking. FBI figures reveal that of all persons arrested in 1965 (not counting traffic offenders) about 30 percent were under 21 years of age, and about 20 percent were under 18 years of age. Arrest rates are highest for persons aged 15 through 17, next highest for those aged 18 through 20, dropping off quite directly with increases in age, as table 1 below indicates.

Table 1

ARREST RATES FOR DIFFERENT AGE GROUPS—1965 [RATES PER 100,000 POPULATION]

Age Groups	Arrest Rates for all Offenses (Excluding Traffic)	Arrest Rates for Willful Homicide, Forcible Rape, Robbery, Aggravated Assault	Arrest Rates for Larceny, Burglary, Motor Vehicle Theft
11 to 14	3,064.4	71.0	1,292.3
15 to 17	8,050.0	222.8	2,467.0
18 to 20	7,539.6	299.8	1,452.0
21 to 24	6,547.2	296.6	833.7
25 to 29	5,366.9	233.6	506.7
30 to 34	5,085.8	177.5	354.4
35 to 39	4,987.4	132.5	260.4
40 to 44	4,675.3	94.0	185.4
45 to 49	4,102.0	65.3	131.9
50 and over	1,987.4	24.2	55.2
Overall rate	3,349.9	99.9	461.5

Source. FBI, Uniform Crime Reports Section, unpublished data. Estimates for total U.S. population.

The picture looks even worse if attention is directed to certain relatively serious property crimes—burglary, larceny, and motor vehicle theft. The 11- to 17-year-old age group, representing 13.2 percent of the population, was responsible for half of the arrests for these offenses in 1965 (table 2). Table 1 shows that the arrest rates for these offenses are much higher for the 15- to 17-year-olds than for any other age group in the population. But not all of the acts included within these categories are equally serious. Larceny includes thefts of less than $50, and most motor vehicle thefts are for the purpose of securing temporary transportation and do not involve permanent loss of the vehicle. Moreover, although juveniles account for more than their share of arrests for many serious crimes, these arrests are a small part of all juvenile arrests. Juveniles are most frequently arrested or referred to court for petty larceny, fighting, disorderly conduct, liquor-related offenses, and conduct not in violation of the criminal law such as curfew violation, truancy, incorrigibility, or running away from home.

It is an older age group—beyond the jurisdiction of almost all juvenile courts —that has the highest arrest rate for crimes of violence. The 18- to 24-year-old group, which represents only 10.2 percent of the population, accounts for 26.4 percent of the arrests for willful homicide, 44.6 percent of the arrests for rape, 39.5 percent of the arrests for robbery, and 26.5 percent of the arrests for aggravated assult (table 2).

Table 2

PERCENT OF ARRESTS ACCOUNTED FOR BY DIFFERENT AGE GROUPS—1965
(PERCENT OF TOTAL)

	Persons 11–17	Persons 18–24	Persons 25 and over
Population	13.2	10.2	53.5
Willful homicide	8.4	26.4	65.1
Forcible rape	19.8	44.6	35.6
Robbery	28.0	39.5	31.4
Aggravated assault	14.2	26.5	58.7
Burglary	47.7	29.0	19.7
Larceny, (includes larceny under $50)	49.2	21.9	24.3
Motor vehicle theft	61.4	26.4	11.9
Willful homicide, rape, robbery, aggravated assault	18.3	31.7	49.3
Larceny, burglary, motor vehicle theft	50.5	24.7	21.2

Source. FBI, Uniform Crime Reports Section, unpublished data. Estimates for total U.S. population.

Trends

In recent years the number of delinquency arrests has increased sharply in the United States, as it has in several Western European countries studied by the Commission. Between 1960 and 1965, arrests of persons under 18 years of age jumped 52 percent for willful homicide, rape, robbery, aggravated assault, larceny, burglary and motor vehicle theft. During the same period, arrests of person 18 and over for these offenses rose only 20 percent. This is explained in large part by the disproportionate increase in the population under

18 and, in particular, the crime-prone part of that population—the 11- to 17-year-old age group.

Official figures may give a somewhat misleading picture of crime trends. Over the years there has been a tendency toward more formal records and actions, particularly in the treatment of juveniles. In addition, police efficiency may well have increased. But, considering other factors together with the official statistics, the Commission is of the opinion that juvenile delinquency has increased significantly in recent years.

The juvenile population has been rising, and at a faster rate than the adult population. And an increasing proportion of our society is living in the cities where delinquency rates have always been highest. These trends and the increase in the total volume of crime that they appear to foretell are testimony enough that programs for the prevention and control of delinquency deserve our full attention.

WHO THE DELINQUENTS ARE

Almost all youths commit acts for which they could be arrested and taken to court. But it is a much smaller group that ends up being defined officially as delinquent.

Official delinquents are predominantly male. In 1965 boys under 18 were arrested five times as often as girls. Four times as many boys as girls were referred to juvenile court.

Boys and girls commit quite different kinds of offenses. Children's Bureau statistics based on large-city court reports reveal that more than half of the girls referred to juvenile court in 1965 were referred for conduct that would not be criminal if committed by adults; only one-fifth of the boys were referred for such conduct. Boys were referred to court primarily for larceny, burglary, and motor vehicle theft, in order of frequency; girls for running away, ungov-

ernable behavior, larceny, and sex offenses.

Delinquents are concentrated disproportionately in the cities, and particularly in the larger cities. Arrest rates are next highest in the suburbs, and lowest in rural areas.

Delinquency rates are high among children from broken homes. They are similarly high among children who have numerous siblings.

Delinquents tend to do badly in school. Their grades are below average. Large numbers have dropped one or more classes behind their classmates or dropped out of school entirely.

Delinquents tend to come from backgrounds of social and economic deprivation. Their families tend to have lower than average incomes and social status. But perhaps more important than the individual family's situation is the area in which a youth lives. One study has shown that a lower class youth has little chance of being classified as delinquent if he lives in an upper class neighborhood. Numerous studies have revealed the relationship between certain deprived areas—particularly the slums of large cities—and delinquency.

It is inescapable that juvenile delinquency is directly related to conditions bred by poverty. If the Fulton County census tracts were divided into five groups on the basis of the economic and educational status of their residents, we would find that 57% of Fulton County's juvenile delinquents during 1964 were residents of the lowest group which consists of the principal poverty areas of the City of Atlanta. Only 24% of the residents of the county lived within these tracts. Report of the Atlanta Commission on Crime and Juvenile Delinquency, *Opportunity for Urban Excellence* (1966), p. 24.

Thus Negroes, who live in disproportionate numbers in slum neighborhoods, account for a disproportionate number of arrests. Numerous studies indicate that what matters is where in the city one is growing up, not religion or nationality or race. The studies by Shaw and McKay, discussed under "Crime and the Inner City," in chapter 2, followed a number of different national groups—Germans, Irish, Poles, Italians—as they moved from the grim center of the city out to better neighborhoods. They found that for all groups the delinquency rates were highest in the center and lowest on the outskirts of the city.

There is no reason to expect a different story for Negroes. Indeed, McKay found Negro delinquency rates decreasing from the center of the city outward, just as they did for earlier migrant groups. And when delinquency rates of whites and Negroes are compared in areas of similar economic status, the differences between them are markedly reduced. But for Negroes, movement out of the inner city and absorption into America's middle class have been much slower and more difficult than for any other ethnic or racial group. Their attempts to move spatially, socially, economically have met much stiffer resistance. Rigid barriers of residential segregation have prevented them from moving to better neighborhoods as their desire and capacity to do so have developed, leading to great population density and to stifling overcrowding of housing, schools, recreation areas. Restricted access to jobs and limited upward mobility in those jobs that are available have slowed economic advance.

It is likely that the official picture exaggerates the role played by social and economic conditions, since slum offenders are more likely than suburban offenders to be arrested and referred to juvenile court. In fact, recent self-report studies reveal suburban and middle-class delinquency to be a more significant problem than was once assumed. But there is still no reason to doubt that delinquency, and especially the most serious delinquency, is committed disproportionately by slum and lower-class youth.

A balanced judgment would seem to be that, while there is indeed unreported delinquency and slower resort to official police and court sanctions in middle-class areas than in the central sectors of our cities, there is also an absolute difference in the amount and types of crimes committed in each area. In short, the vast differences represented in official statistics cannot be explained by differential police or court action toward children of varying backgrounds. There are, in fact, real differences leading to more frequent assaults, thefts, and breaking and entering offenses in lower socioeconomic areas of our urban centers. Wheeler and Cottrell, Juvenile Delinquency—Its Prevention and Control (Russell Sage Foundation 1966), pp. 12–13.

4

Extent of Unrecorded Delinquency, Tentative Conclusions

James F. Short, Jr. and F. Ivan Nye

The frequency and nature of delinquent behavior committed by adolescents never arrested or committed to institutions has been regarded by criminologists as an important but unknown dimension of delinquent behavior. The informed layman also is aware that only a portion of delinquent behavior is followed by arrest and conviction; further, that conviction and committal to a "training school" is much more likely to follow delinquent behavior if the adolescent is from the "wrong side of the tracks." The picture of delinquent behavior obtained from official records only, and particularly the punitive action of the courts, is known to be incomplete and seriously biased.

That concern with unrecorded delinquency is high is indicated by the great interest shown in the pioneer studies of Robinson,[1] Schwartz,[2] Por-

terfield,[3] and the Cambridge-Somerville Youth Study,[4] in texts and in recent papers by the writers.[5] Cohen has called for an extension of such studies,[6] and a number of other investigators are pursuing research projects dealing with unrecorded delinquency.[7]

* From two larger studies of adolescent delinquency and adjustment supported in part by grants from the Social Science Research Council and the College Committee on Research of the State College of Washington.

[1] Sophia Robison, *Can Delinquency Be Measured?* (New York: Columbia University Press, 1936).

[2] Edward E. Schwartz, "A Community Experiment in the Measurement of Juvenile Delinquency," reprinted from *Nat. Prob. Assoc. Yearbook,* 1945 (Washington: U.S.G.P.O., 1947).

[3] Austin L. Porterfield, *Youth in Trouble* (Fort Worth: Leo Potishman Foundation, 1946), Chapter 2.

[4] Fred J. Murphy, Mary M. Shirley, and Helen L. Witmer, "The Incidence of Hidden Delinquency," *Am. Jour. of Orthopsychiatry,* 16 (October, 1946), 686–696.

[5] Albert K. Cohen, *Delinquent Boys: The Culture of the Gang* (Glencoe, Illinois: The Free Press, 1955), 37–41; for the authors' statement as to the importance of such data, see James F. Short, Jr. and F. Ivan Nye, "Reported Behavior as a Criterion of Deviant Behavior," *Soc. Problems* (Winter, 1957–1958).

[6] Albert K. Cohen, *Sociological Research in Juvenile Delinquency,* paper read before American Orthopsychiatric Association, March, 1956.

[7] The authors are aware of studies under way in Chicago, Kansas City, Indiana,

SOURCE. James F. Short, Jr. and F. Ivan Nye, "Extent of Unrecorded Delinquency, Tentative Conclusions," from *Journal of Criminal Law, Criminology and Police Science,* Volume 49, November–December 1958, pp. 296–302. Copyright © 1958, The Williams and Wilkins Company, Baltimore, Maryland.

Table 1

REPORTED DELINQUENT BEHAVIOR AMONG BOYS IN THREE SAMPLES

Type of offense	Percent admitting commission of offense			Percent admitting commission of offense more than once or twice		
	M.W.	West	Tr.S.	M.W.	West	Tr.S.
Driven a car without a driver's license or permit	81.1	75.3	91.1	61.2	49.0	73.4
Skipped school	54.4	53.0	95.3	24.4	23.8	85.9
Had fist fight with one person	86.7	80.7	95.3	32.6	31.9	75.0
"Run away" from home	12.9	13.0	68.1	2.8	2.4	37.7
School probation or expulsion	15.3	11.3	67.8	2.1	2.9	31.3
Defied parents' authority	22.2	33.1	52.4	1.4	6.3	23.6
Driven too fast or recklessly	49.7	46.0	76.3	22.7	19.1	51.6
Taken little things (worth less than $2) that did not belong to you	62.7	60.6	91.8	18.5	12.9	65.1
Taken things of medium value ($2–$50)	17.1	15.8	91.0	3.8	3.8	61.4
Taken things of large value ($50)	3.5	5.0	90.8	1.1	2.1	47.7
Used force (strong-arm methods) to get money from another person	6.3	—	67.7	2.4	—	35.5
Taken part in "gang fights"	24.3	22.5	67.4	6.7	5.2	47.4
Taken a car for a ride without the owner's knowledge	11.2	14.8	75.2	4.5	4.0	53.4
Bought or drank beer, wine, or liquor (include drinking at home)	67.7	57.2	89.7	35.8	29.5	79.4
Bought or drank beer, wine, or liquor (outside your home)	43.0	—	87.0	21.1	—	75.0
Drank beer, wine, or liquor in your own home	57.0	—	62.8	24.1	—	31.9
Deliberate property damage	60.7	44.8	84.3	17.5	8.2	49.7
Used or sold narcotic drugs	1.4	2.2	23.1	0.7	1.6	12.6
Had sex relations with another person of the same sex (not masturbation)	12.0	8.8	10.9	3.9	2.9	3.1
Had sex relations with a person of the opposite sex	38.8	40.4	87.5	20.3	19.9	73.4
Gone hunting or fishing without a license (or violated other game laws)	74.0	62.7	66.7	39.6	23.5	44.8
Taken things you didn't want	15.7	22.5	56.8	1.4	3.1	26.8
"Beat up" on kids who hadn't done anything to you	15.7	13.9	48.7	3.1	2.8	26.2
Hurt someone to see them squirm	22.7	15.8	33.4	2.8	3.2	17.5

The methodology of the investigations which form the basis for this paper have been described elsewhere and will not be repeated here.[8] The present paper deals with (1) types and frequency of delinquent behavior as indicated by 23 specific delinquent acts ranging from driving without a license to grand larceny and drug use, and by the use of delinquency scales derived from these items; (2) comparison of

Tennessee, Columbus, Ohio, New York City, and in the State of Washington.

[8] F. Ivan Nye and James F. Short, Jr., "Scaling Delinquent Behavior," *Amer. Sociol. Rev.*, 22 (June, 1957); F. Ivan Nye, *Family Relationships and Delinquent Behavior* (New York: John Wiley and Sons, 1958) Chapter 1; James F. Short, Jr., *The Study of Juvenile Delinquency by*

Reported Behavior—An Experiment in Method and Preliminary Findings, paper read at the annual meetings of the American Sociological Society, Washington, D. C., 1955 (dittoed).

delinquent behavior in western and mid-western high school students; and (3) comparison of unrecorded delinquency with official records of delinquency.

The data were gathered by anonymous questionnaire in the classroom under the supervision of the writers. A 75 percent sample was taken from the three western high schools (cities of 10,000 to 30,000 population) and a 100 percent sample in three smaller mid-western communities. Approximately 99 percent of the questionnaires were usable.[9] In addition to being considered generally suitable for present research purposes, these particular communities possessed the positive advantage that active and informed lay people were ready to sponsor the project and interpret it to the community.

The measures of delinquent behavior used in this paper are based upon a list of behavior items commonly referred to in the laws relating to delinquent and criminal behavior. Delinquency has been defined in descriptive terms rather than in terms of legalistic categories. For example, we refer to stealing things of a certain value, rather than to descriptions of property offenses, e.g., robbery, burglary, larceny, etc.

HIGH SCHOOL POPULATIONS

Because they seem likely to be more representative of the general population than are college or training school populations, we have concentrated our research on high school populations. Table 1 presents the percentage of boys in our two high school samples, western and mid-western, and in the western

[9] Questionnaires were administered by one or both writers, assisted by other staff members or graduate students of the Department of Sociology of the State College of Washington. For further methodological details, see references cited in footnote 8.

training school group, who report committing each of 21 delinquency items, and the percentage who admit committing these offenses more than once or twice. Table 2 presents these data for the high school and training school girls.

From these tables it is apparent that the types of delinquent behavior studied are extensive and variable in the populations studies. We have compared students in the western and mid-western samples in order to secure an estimate of the stability of responses in two non-institutionalized populations. Populations in these two regional samples differ in such respects as city size and population mobility. The mid-western sample is comprised of three small communities: a suburb of a large city, a rural town, and a consolidated rural school district. The western sample comprises three small contiguous cities. The population of the mid-western communities has been fairly stable since 1940, in contrast to the rapid population growth experienced by the western cities. These samples are alike in important respects, however. Ethnic composition is similar, both populations being overwhelmingly native caucasian, and age and sex are controlled. Perhaps of greater importance, both populations are non-institutionalized.

Few statistically significant differences between our two non-institutionalized groups are found in Tables 1 and 2.[10] This may be taken as an indication

[10] Samples from both finite and hypothetical universes are treated. The western state samples represent 25 per cent regular-interval samples of the high school population. Mid-western and training school samples represent 100 per cent samples of the individuals in those selected grades in the mid-western high schools and 100 per cent samples of the training schools.

Nine of 21 possible comparisons of the percentage of western and mid-western boys who admit committing these offenses are significant at least at the .05 level. Eight of these 9 offenses are committed

Table 2

REPORTED DELINQUENT BEHAVIOR AMONG GIRLS IN THREE SAMPLES

Type of offense	Percent admitting commission of offense			Percent admitting commission of offense more than once or twice		
	M.W.	West	Tr.S.	M.W.	West	Tr.S.
Driven a car without a driver's license or permit	60.1	58.2	68.3	33.6	29.9	54.4
Skipped school	40.3	41.0	94.0	10.1	12.2	66.3
Had fist fight with one person	32.7	28.2	72.3	7.4	5.7	44.6
"Run away" from home	9.8	11.3	85.5	1.0	1.0	51.8
School probation or expulsion	2.7	3.7	63.4	0.3	0.2	29.3
Defied parents' authority	33.0	30.6	68.3	3.7	5.0	39.0
Driven too fast or recklessly	20.9	16.3	47.5	5.7	5.4	35.0
Taken little things (worth less than $2) that did not belong to you	36.0	30.0	77.8	5.7	3.5	48.1
Taken things of medium value ($2–$50)	3.4	3.9	58.0	1.0	0.6	29.6
Taken things of large value ($50)	2.0	1.3	30.4	1.7	0.9	10.1
Used force (strong-arm methods) to get money from another person	1.3	—	36.7	0.3	—	21.5
Taken part in "gang fights"	9.7	6.5	59.0	1.7	1.1	27.7
Taken a car for a ride without the owner's knowledge	5.4	4.5	36.6	1.0	0.6	20.7
Bought or drank beer, wine, or liquor (include drinking at home)	62.7	44.5	90.2	23.1	17.6	80.5
Bought or drank beer, wine, or liquor (outside your home)	28.7	—	83.9	10.8	—	75.3
Drank beer, wine, or liquor in your own home	54.2	—	71.1	16.4	—	42.2
Deliberate property damage	21.7	13.6	65.4	5.7	1.6	32.1
Used or sold narcotic drugs	1.3	0.5	36.9	0.3	0.3	23.8
Had sex relations with another person of the same sex (not masturbation)	5.4	3.6	25.0	1.7	0.5	12.5
Had sex relations with a person of the opposite sex	12.5	14.1	95.1	4.1	4.8	81.5
Gone hunting or fishing without a license (or violated other game laws)	20.6	20.3	27.5	5.7	3.9	21.3
Taken things you didn't want	6.4	3.6	43.0	0.7	0.6	13.9
"Beat up" on kids who hadn't done anything to you	5.7	3.1	37.8	1.0	0.9	18.3
Hurt someone to see them squirm	10.4	9.3	35.4	1.0	1.1	20.7

by a higher percentage of mid-western boys. When percentage of boys admitting commission of these offenses more than once or twice is compared, only 6 significant differences (at .05 level) are found, 5 of these being higher for the mid-western boys. When mid-western and western girls are compared as to commission of these offenses, 5 significant differences are found, all being committed by a higher percentage of mid-western girls. Only 1 significant difference between these groups of non-institutionalized girls is found when percentages admitting commission of the 21 offenses more than once or twice is compared.

of stability and reliability of the responses obtained from the two samples. Comparison of 16 and 17 year old high school boys on a seven-item delinquency scale, based upon these same data, indicates agreement between the two groups of boys in 90.7 percent of the scale responses.[11] We note that such

[11] These data are described and graphically presented in F. Ivan Nye and James F. Short, Jr., "Scaling Delinquent Behavior," op. cit.

differences as are found in Tables 1 and 2 indicate that delinquent behavior is somewhat more widespread in the smaller, older, more structured midwestern sample than in the larger, newer, growing western communities.

The most common offenses reported "more than once or twice" by high school boys and girls in Tables 1 and 2 are traffic offenses, truancy, and drinking. Boys also report considerable fighting, stealing (of small things), heterosexual relations, and game violations.

Comparisons of western institutionalized and non-institutionalized boys and girls on the delinquency items in Tables 1 and 2 indicate that significantly higher proportions of the "official" delinquents commit virtually all of the offenses, and commit them more often, than do the high school students.[12] Exceptions to this pattern are found only in the case of homosexual relations among the boys, driving a car without a license among girls, and game violations among both boys and girls. In spite of the statistical significance of these comparisons, however, it is apparent that there is a good deal of "overlapping" between institutionalized and non-institutionalized boys and girls in the frequency of commission of our delinquency items.

In order to specify more precisely the amount of such overlapping, indexes of delinquent behavior in the form of Guttman-type scales have been constructed. Scales for 16 and 17 year old boys, consisting of seven and eleven delinquency items, have been described elsewhere.[13] These scales proved to

be nearly equal in their ability to differentiate between institutionalized and non-institutionalized boys. On the seven-item scale, a cutting point is found which maximizes the difference in delinquency involvement between the two groups of boys at 71 percent (see Table 3). At this cutting point, 86 percent of the non-institutionalized boys had been accounted for, as compared with only 14 percent of the training school boys. This difference on the eleven-item scale was maximized at 67 percent.[14] The amount of overlapping between institutionalized and non-institutionalized boys is here specified more closely than has been done in previous research. We have cited only the maximum differences between the two groups. Thus, if we were to study "delinquent" and "non-delinquent" boys by comparing our institutionalized and

things (worth less than $2) that did not belong to you, buying or drinking beer, wine, or liquor (include drinking at home), skipping school without a legitimate excuse, purposely damaging or destroying public or private property, sex relations with a person of the opposite sex, and defying parents' authority to their faces. Offenses added for the eleven-item scale were: taking things of medium value, taking things of large value, running away from home, and narcotics violations. These data were rescored following the Israel "Gamma" technique in order to remove "idiosyncratic" elements, prior to scaling. For the procedure, and an exposition of its rationale, see M. W. Riley, J. W. Riley, and Jackson Toby, *Scale Analysis* (New Brunswick: Rutgers University Press, 1954), Chapter 18.

[14] It is interesting to compare these findings with results of the delinquency scale of the California Psychological Inventory, as obtained by Gough. Comparing a broad cross section of delinquents (as indicated by their being institutionalized or. classed as "high school disciplinary problems") and non-delinquents on this scale, he found a cutting point above which 70 percent of his male delinquents fell, as compared to 20 percent of his male non-delinquents. See Harrison Gough, *Systematic Validation of a Test for Delinquency*, paper delivered at the annual meeting of the American Psychological Association, 1954 (mimeographed).

[12] This conclusion is based upon statistical comparison of figures presented in Tables 1 and 2, for our institutionalized and non-institutionalized western state boys and girls.

[13] F. Ivan Nye and James F. Short, Jr., *op. cit.* The seven-item scale included the following delinquency items: driving a car without a license or permit, taking little

Table 3

DELINQUENT BEHAVIOR SCORES OF HIGH SCHOOL AND TRAINING SCHOOL BOYS AGED
16 AND 17°

Scale type	Delinquent behavior score	High school		Training school	
		Frequency	Cumulative percent	Frequency	Cumulative percent
1	00	0	0	0	0
2	01	128	22	0	0
3	02	40	29	0	0
4	03	60	40	0	0
5	04	105	58	3	2
6	05	28	63	2	4
7	06	26	68	3	6
8	07	25	72	2	8
9	08	80	86	7	14
10	09	31	92	24	32
11	10	27	96	8	39
12	11	6	97	11	48
13	12	6	98	15	60
14	13	5	99	16	72
15	14	3	100	34	100
		570		125	

° No scores were obtained for one training school and eight high school boys.

non-institutionalized groups, on the basis of the seven-item scale we would in fact be studying a group of delinquent boys, 14 percent of whom are less delinquent than are 14 percent of the "non-delinquent" boys. Comparisons can, of course, be obtained at any point along the scale.

A nine-item scale for the 16 and 17 year old western high school and training school girls differentiates somewhat more clearly between the two groups.[15] On this scale a maximum difference of 80 percent is found at scale type 09 (see Table 4). At this point on the scale 90.4 percent of the high school girls and only 10.4 percent of the training school girls are accounted for. That is, only about 10 percent of the high school girls are more delinquent than is indicated by scale type 08, while nearly 90 percent of the training school

girls fall into this more delinquent category.

SEX DIFFERENCES

Comparison of boys and girls within the high school sample indicates a higher proportion of boys committing nearly all offenses. With few exceptions such differences are statistically significant (at .01 level). This finding is similar to that revealed by official data, though the 5 to 1 ratio of boys to girls reported by the Children's Bureau[16] is not found in many cases, suggesting a bias in under-reporting female delinquency on the part of official data. Offenses for which significant differences between the sexes are not found are generally those offenses for which girls are most often apprehended, e.g. running away from home, defying

15 The girls' scale consisted of the offenses included in the eleven-item boys' scale, with the exception of taking things of large value and narcotics violations.

16 U. S. Department of Health, Education and Welfare, Social Security Administration, Children's Bureau, *Juvenile Court Statistics,* 1955, Children's Bureau Statistical Series, *Number 37.*

Table 4

DELINQUENT BEHAVIOR SCORES OF HIGH SCHOOL AND TRAINING SCHOOL GIRLS AGED 16 AND 17°

Scale type	Delinquent behavior score	High school		Training school	
		Frequency	Cumulative percent	Frequency	Cumulative percent
1	00	135	26	1	2
2	01	72	40	0	2
3	02	21	44	1	4
4	03	74	59	1	6
5	04	61	71	0	6
6	05	52	81	0	6
7	06	15	84	1	8
8	07	11	86	1	10
9	08	22	90	0	10
10	09	10	92	1	12
11	10	23	97	6	25
12	11	9	99	4	33
13	12	2	99	7	48
14	13	5	100	25	100
		512		48	

° No scores were obtained for two training school and one high school girls.

parents' authority (incorrigibility), and drinking. The fact that significantly higher proportions of boys in both samples report engaging in heterosexual relations and the fact that girls are most often referred to court for such activities presumably reflects society's greater concern for the unsupervised activities of girls.

Fewer statistically significant differences are found between training school boys and girls than was the case in our samples of high school students. Significantly greater percentages of the boys report committing 11 of the 24 offenses studied, and 13 of these offenses "more than once or twice." For nine of these offenses the recorded differences are not significant. Four of the offenses are reported by larger percentages of training school girls. These include running away from home, defying parents' authority, narcotics violations, and homosexual relations. A higher percentage of girls also report heterosexual relations, though this difference is not statistically significant. With the exception of nar-

cotics violations, these are offenses for which girls are most often apprehended. The offenses reported by the highest percentage of training school boys, with the exception of fighting, which is a part of "growing up," are also those for which boys are most often apprehended, viz., stealing and traffic offenses.

ARREST RATES

Arrest rates for the high school and training school samples described above are not available. Data from the first phase of our research program, comparing college and training school students, indicate that non-institutionalized (college) students experience arrest in a far smaller proportion of offenses which they report committing than do training school students.[17] This is es-

[17] James F. Short, Jr., "A Report on the Incidence of Criminal Behavior, Arrests, and Convictions in Selected Groups," *Proc. of the Pacific Sociol. Soc.*, 1954, published as Vol. 22, No. 2 of *Research Studies of the State College of Washington* (June 1954), 110–118, see Table 3, p. 117.

pecially true of girls, for college girls report arrests only for traffic offenses. These arrest data bear a close relationship to officially available data. For both training school boys and girls arrest rates are highest for offenses against the person exclusive of sex offenses. Arrest rates for property offenses are more than twice as high among boys as among girls in the training school populations, while the reverse is true of sex offenses among these groups. Arrests among college men are reported in only a small percentage of property offenses (.3 percent as compared to 13.7 percent for training school boys), behavior problem offenses (2.3 percent compared to 15.1 percent for training school boys), and "casual" offenses (1.9 percent compared to 5.2 percent).

SOCIO-ECONOMIC DISTRIBUTION

Finally, the socio-economic characteristics associated with delinquent behavior among our high school and training school populations have been studied.[18] For this purpose analysis of delinquent behavior by individual behavior items and by scale type was made, holding constant sex categories and two age groups in the western and midwestern states. Similar analysis was made for adolescents 16 and older in the "training schools" of the western state. Few significant differences were found between socio-economic strata. Such differences as were found indicated greater delinquent involvement within the highest socio-economic category as often as in the lowest.

CONCLUSIONS

While recognizing the limitations of our definition of delinquent behavior,

[18] F. Ivan Nye, James F. Short, Jr., and V. J. Olson, "Socio-Economic Status and Delinquent Behavior," *Amer. Jour. of Sociol.,* 63 (January, 1958).

in terms of the behavior categories studied, and the limitations of the samples employed, it appears that the following tentative conclusions regarding the extent of juvenile delinquency in the non-institutionalized population are warranted:

1. Delinquent conduct in the non-institutionalized population is extensive and variable.

2. Delinquent conduct as we have measured it is similar in extent and nature among non-institutionalized high school students in widely separated sections of the country.

3. Delinquent conduct *reported* by institutionalized and non-institutionalized students is similar to delinquency and crime as treated officially in the following respects:

(*a*) Non-institutionalized boys admit committing virtually all delinquencies more frequently than do non-institutionalized girls, "once or twice" and "more than once or twice"; fewer differences exist, and these differences are smaller, between institutionalized boys and girls.

(*b*) The offenses for which boys are most often arrested are generally those which they most often admit committing, e.g., property offenses, traffic violations, truancy, destruction of property, drinking; a few offenses are reported by large proportions of boys which are not often recorded in official statistics, e.g., game violations and fist fights.

(*c*) The offenses for which girls are most often arrested are, with the exception of sex offenses among high school girls, generally the offenses which girls most often admit committing, e.g., sex offenses, incorrigibility, running away. A few offenses are reported by high proportions of girls which do not find their way into official statistics.

(*d*) Significantly greater proportions of training school boys and girls admit committing virtually all delinquencies, and admit committing them more frequently, than do high school boys and girls.

(*e*) When training school students are compared with high school students on a composite scale of delinquency activities, there is considerable overlapping between groups of both boys and girls, but training school students as a group rank significantly higher, in terms of seriousness of involvement in delinquent behavior, than do high school students.

(*f*) Differences on the delinquency scales, and in the commission of individual delinquencies, are greater between high school and training school girls than between high school and training school boys.

(*g*) Variation in the proportion of reported delinquencies which result in arrest are similar to variations in the "cleared by arrest" figures collected by the Federal Bureau of Investigation.

4. Delinquent conduct reported by non-institutionalized students differs from official data in the following ways:

(*a*) Arrests—comparison of college and training school students indicates that training school students are arrested in higher proportions of all classes of delinquencies which they admit committing than college students.

(*b*) Socio-economic status—delinquency within the non-institutionalized populations studied is distributed more evenly throughout the socio-economic structure of society than are official cases, which are found disproportionately in the lower socio-economic strata.

Further research of this nature may be expected to provide additional clues as to the extent and nature of delinquent behavior in various segments of the population. By such means the structural correlates of delinquency, together with other important etiological considerations, may be better understood. Reported delinquent behavior as a method warrants and requires further investigation.[19] The present status of research by reported behavior is regarded as still in a pioneer stage. It provides an alternative to the use of institutionalized populations and court records, with new opportunities for research in delinquent behavior and comprehension of it.

[19] For a discussion of advantages, as well as methodological problems of this approach, see James F. Short, Jr., and F. Ivan Nye, "Reported Behavior as a Criterion of Deviant Behavior," *op. cit.*

5

Court Records, Undetected Delinquency and Decision-Making

*Maynard L. Erickson and Lamar T. Empey**

There is almost universal dissatisfaction with the accuracy of official records on delinquency.[1] Yet, at present, there are

* Mr. Erickson is Research Director of the Provo Experiment in Delinquency Rehabilitation, Brigham Young University. Mr. Empey is Director of the Provo Experiment.

Grateful acknowledgement is expressed by the authors to Monroe J. Paxman for his cooperation and support and to the Ford Foundation for the grant under which this research was conducted. Appreciation is also extended to Stanton Wheeler, Peter Garabedian, and James Short for their helpful criticisms.

SOURCE. Maynard L. Erickson and La-Mar T. Empey, "Court Records, Undetected Delinquency and Decision-Making" from *Journal of Criminal Law, Criminology and Police Science,* Volume 54, No. 4, December 1963, pp. 456–469. Reprinted with permission.

[1] Discussions and criticisms are legion. A sample might include: Cressey, *The State of Criminal Statistics,* 3 NAT'L PROBATION & PAROLE ASS'N J. 230 (1957); McQueen, *A Comparative Prospective on Juvenile Delinquency,* in A SYMPOSIUM ON DELINQUENCY: PATTERNS, CAUSES AND CURES 1–21 (1960); Sellin, *The Basis of a Crime Index,* 22 J. CRIM. L. & C. 335 (1931); Sutherland, PRINCIPLES OF CRIMINOLOGY 29–30 (1947); Taft, CRIMINOLOGY 61–65 (1956); and VanVechten, *Differential Criminal Case Mortality in Selected Jurisdictions,* 7 AM. SOC. REV. 833 (1942).

On the other hand, Perlman and

few realistic alternatives. Official records must be used, not only to provide statistical information on delinquent trends, but to act as an information base on the qualitative characteristics (i.e., delinquent types) of offenders. It is this base upon which many important practical and theoretical decisions are presently dependent. A host of provocative problems relative to each of these uses merits serious attention. Two are discussed below.

The first has to do with the currently increasing emphasis on preventing delinquency.[2] If prevention is to be suc-

Schwartz, noting a high degree of agreement in trends between police and court records on juveniles, feel the two are subject to common determining factors. See Perlman, *The Meaning of Juvenile Delinquency Statistics,* 13 Fed. Prob. 63 (Sept. 1949). See also Perlman, *Reporting Juvenile Delinquency,* 3 NAT'L PROBATION & PAROLE ASS'N J. 242 (1957); and Schwartz, *Statistics of Juvenile Delinquency in the United States,* 261 ANNALS 9 (1949).

[2] A good example is President Kennedy's creation of the President's Committee on Juvenile Delinquency and Youth Crime; see Executive Order 10940, and THE FEDERAL DELINQUENCY PROGRAM OBJECTIVE AND OPERATION UNDER THE PRESIDENT'S COMMITTEE ON JUVENILE DELINQUENCY AND YOUTH CRIME, AND THE JUVENILE DELINQUENCY AND YOUTH OFFENSES CONTROL ACT OF 1961 (1962).

53

cessful, it must forestall delinquent behavior before it becomes a matter of official record. But how much is known about the whole body of delinquent acts which do not become a matter of official concern? How accurately do official statistics reveal the *actual* extent and types of offenses committed? Answers to these questions are needed before revisions in control strategies can proceed rationally toward desired goals.

At present most control decisions are without the benefit of answers to important questions. Most people are left in a quandary as to whether official records understate or overstate the problem. For example, as a result of finding a vast number of undetected violations in their study, Murphy, Shirley and Witmer concluded that "even a moderate increase in the amount of attention paid to [them] by law-enforcement authorities could create a semblance of a 'delinquency wave' without there being the slightest change in adolescent behavior."[3]

Therefore, perhaps even more basic than deciding what should be done, we need more information in deciding whether, to what extent, or along what dimensions anything needs to be done. A greater knowledge of the nature of *undetected offenses* among the adolescent population might be important in determining prevention (and treatment) strategies.

A second problem has to do with the research on delinquency. Few authorities would dispute the value of using legal norms, in contrast to diffuse moral or extralegal concepts, to define a delinquent act. But the extension of this use to practical purposes often results

in the development of extreme, either-or dichotomies: delinquent or nondelinquent, institutionalized or noninstitutionalized.

It is an obvious oversimplification to believe in the validity of such dichotomies. Delinquent behavior is not an attribute—something which one either is or is not, such as male or female, plant or animal. It is "a more or less thing,"[4] possibly distributed along one or more continua.

Even so, many sophisticated efforts to develop specific criminal or delinquent typologies based on this premise must still depend on the either-or nature of official records as the major criterion for selecting samples for study. Once this is done, analyses tend to proceed in one of two directions: (1) either to rely further upon official records for specific information on such things as offense patterns; or (2) to reject as unimportant the official offense pattern in favor of psychological, cultural, or interactional factors.[5] This latter action is usually taken on the premise that the delinquent act is merely a symptom of some more basic cause and that to understand or perhaps remove the cause is what is important. But, in either case, the paradox remains: the court record serves as the basic criterion for sample selection.[6]

---

[3] Murphy, Shirley & Witmer, *The Incidence of Hidden Delinquency*, 16 AM. J. ORTHOPSYCHIATRY 696 (1946). See also, Porterfield, YOUTH IN TROUBLE (1946); and a summary of studies in COHEN, DELINQUENT BOYS: THE CULTURE OF THE GANG 36–44 (1955).

[4] Short, *The Sociocultural Context of Delinquency*, 6 CRIME & DELINQUENCY 365, 366 (1960).

[5] For excellent summaries and bibliographies on typological developments in criminology, see: Gibbons & Garrity, *Some Suggestions for the Development of Etiological and Treatment Theory in Criminology*, 38 SOCIAL FORCES 51 (1960); Grant, *Inquiries Concerning Kinds of Treatment for Kinds of Delinquents*, CALIFORNIA BOARD OF CORRECTIONS MONOGRAPH NO. 2, at 5 (1961).

[6] For example, such diverse typologies as those produced by Clyde Sullivan, Douglas and Marguerite Grant, in *The Development of Interpersonal Maturity, Applications to Delinquency*, 20 PSYCHIATRY 373 (1957), and Gresham Sykes, in THE SOCI-

Any strong bias in it will likely color what is found. Thus, it may be that refined analyses based upon official samples are based also upon a rather questionable foundation.

So long as samples are selected on this basis, there is a possibility that important information is being excluded. What of the possibility, for example, that there are patterns of delinquent activity which are etiologically distinct?[7] What of the possibility that the search for different configurations of variables has been inadequate because of the incompleteness of official records on delinquent activity? Even further, what of the possibility that official records do not even reveal the pattern of offenses which most commonly characterizes an offender?

The fact that many studies have found age and sex to be more highly correlated with delinquency than a host of other supposedly more important etiological variables,[8] suggests the need to explore these questions. The addition of information on the actual, not official, amount and type of delinquency in which an individual has been involved might be an aid in filling many of the gaps which exist. One important gap would have to do with the extent to which, and under what circumstances, the delinquent offense pattern should be treated as an *independent* rather than as a dependent variable. What might be revealed if it were viewed as a variable which helps to explain rather

than one which is always explained by other factors?

THE PRESENT RESEARCH

This research is a modest attempt to provide some information on the questions just raised:

1. What is revealed about the total volume of delinquency when undetected offenses are enumerated? What offenses are most common?

2. To what degree do violations go undetected? To what extent do they go unacted upon in the courts?[9]

3. Do non-official delinquents—young people that have never been convicted—commit delinquencies equal in number and seriousness to those committed by officially designated offenders?[10]

4. How useful are traditional dichotomies—delinquent or nondelinquent, institutionalized or noninstitutionalized —in distinguishing groups of offenders one from another?

5. How valid are court records as an index of the total volume and types of offenses in which individuals are most commonly involved?

In seeking answers to such questions as these, this research sought: (1) to examine reported lawbreaking across an adolescent continuum extending from those who had never been officially declared delinqent, through those who had appeared in court once, to those who were "persistent" offenders; and (2) to question adolescent respondents across the whole spectrum of legal norms for which they might have been taken

---

ETY OF CAPTIVES (1958), must still rely upon official definition for their basic samples of offenders.

[7] This question has been raised in Gibbons & Garrity, *supra* note 5, at 51; Short, *supra* note 4, at 366.

[8] Short, "The Study of Juvenile Delinquency by Reported Behavior—An Experiment in Method and Preliminary Findings" at 12 (unpublished paper read at the annual meeting of the American Sociological Association, 1955).

[9] For studies dealing with the problem of undetected delinquency, see: Murphy, Shirley & Witmer, *supra* note 3; Wallerstein & Wyle, *Our Law-Abiding-Lawbreakers*, 25 Fed. Prob. 110 (April 1947); Wilson, *How To Measure the Extent of Juvenile Delinquency*, 41 J. CRIM. L. & C. 435 (1950).

[10] Porterfield's work, *op. cit. supra* note 3, throws some light on this question; however, the evidence is not conclusive.

to court. In all, they were asked about 22 violations.[11]

The Sample

The sample included only males, ages 15–17 years. It was made up of four subsamples:

1. A subsample of 50 randomly selected high school boys who had never been to court.

2. A subsample of 30 randomly selected boys who had been to court once.[12]

3. A subsample of 50 randomly selected, repeat offenders who were on probation. The respondents in this sample were assigned to a special community treatment program. If the program had not existed, 32 percent of these offenders would have been incarcerated, and 68 percent on regular probation.[13]

4. A subsample of 50 randomly se-

---

[11] Unfortunately, no data on sex violations can be presented. Two things stood in the way. The first was a general policy of high school administrators against questions on sex. The second had to do with possible negative reactions by parents against questions because of the brutal sex slaying of an 11-year-old girl and several attacks on women which occurred at the very time we began our study. For these reasons we did not attempt to gather these data for fear they might endanger the whole study.

[12] Since this study was part of a larger study comparing persistent delinquents—incarcerated and unincarcerated—with non-delinquent high school students, data were not collected initially from one-time offenders. Consequently, they had to be collected especially for this group. However, time and budgetary considerations required that the sample of one-time offenders be limited to 30.

[13] They are assignees to the Provo Experiment in Delinquency Rehabilitation. All assignees are, by design, persistent offenders. Assignment is made on a random basis and includes both offenders who might otherwise be left on regular probation and offenders who might otherwise be incarcerated in the State Industrial School. See Empey & Rabow, The Provo Experiment in Delinquency Rehabilitation, 26 AM. SOC. REV. 693 (1961).

lected, incarcerated offenders. Subsamples 1, 2, and 3 were drawn from the same community population. Subsample 4 was drawn from a statewide population of incarcerated offenders.

It was necessary to keep the number of respondents relatively small because each respondent was questioned at length about the whole spectrum of legal norms for which he might have been taken to court—22 different violations in all. As will be seen, this questioning resulted in the accumulation of a large mass of data which turned out to be expensive and difficult to handle.

Data Collection

All respondents were contacted in person by the authors. The study was explained to them and they were asked to participate. There were no refusals. Data were gathered by means of a detailed interview which was conducted as follows:

First, each of the 22 offenses were described in detail. For example, under the section regarding breaking and entering, it is not enough to ask a boy, "Have you ever broken into a place illegally?" He wants to know what constitutes "a place": a car, a barn in the country, an unlocked garage? All of these had to be defined.

Second, after the act was defined, the respondent was asked if he had ever committed the offense. In judging his response, attention was paid to nonverbal cues—blushes, long pauses, nervousness—as well as to verbal cues. These cues served as guides to further questions, probes and reassurances.

Third, if the respondent admitted having committed the offense, he was asked how many times he had done so. Again, considerable time and effort were spent in obtaining an estimate, the idea being that greater accuracy could be obtained by this means than by fitting answers to a predetermined code or having him respond to such general categories as "'none," "a few times," or "a great many times." In the case of habitual offenders, however, it was necessary on some offenses to have them estimate a range—15–20 times, 200–250 times—rather than a specific number.

Finally, the respondent was asked if he had ever been *caught, arrested,* or *to court* for each type of offense. If so, he was asked how many times this had occurred.

Methodological Problems

Besides the methodological problems inherent in any reported data, there are others peculiar to the nature of this type of study.[14] Perhaps the most important has to do with the method of obtaining data. An extended pilot study[15] and pretests, using both interviews and questionnaires, suggested that interviews could provide more complete and reliable data. Two main considerations led to this conclusion.

The first had to do with the lack of literacy skills among persistent delinquents. Two 15-year-olds in this study could neither read nor write; others had great trouble with simple instructions and questions. In our opinion, therefore, an interview was the only alternative for the delinquent subsamples.

Second, in addition to the need for comparable data, our pilot studies indicated that high school samples had trouble understanding specific questions and supplying the data wanted. There-

fore, the value of using an interview for this group, as for delinquents, seemed to outweigh the virtues of an anonymous questionnaire.

We did not find the confrontation of an interview to be generally harmful. By using only three skilled interviewers, it became possible to anticipate recurring difficulties and to deal more effectively with them. These interviewers encountered two types of problems.

The first was the resistance on the part of high school students to revealing offenses. Patience, skepticism regarding replies, probes, and reassurances seemed to encourage candor. The second was a memory problem. Habitual offenders were not so reluctant to admit offenses, but they had often committed them so frequently that they could make an easy estimate neither as to number nor the age at which they began. Probes and extended discussions helped considerably here in settling upon a reasonable estimate.

One possible problem regarding the validity of these data has to do with the perceptions of respondents regarding the "'social desirability" of answering questions according to social expectation. What is each respondent's reference group? How does he perceive the interview? Are his responses biased by special perceptions of each?

For example, if, among delinquents, it is desirable to exhibit extensive delinquent behavior, then, at least up to a certain point, the less delinquent an individual is, the more likely he may be to inflate his own actual violations. The converse might also be true for the conventional boy. Actually, as will be seen later, our findings tended to question the premise that social expectation influences boys' answers (or at least they failed to establish its validity). Nondelinqents reported so much delinquent behavior that it became difficult to assess the extent to which official de-

[14] See Short, *supra* note 8; and Short & Nye, *Reported Behavior as a Criterion of Deviant Behavior*, 5 SOCIAL PROBLEMS 210 (Winter 1957–1958).

[15] Erickson, "An Experiment To Determine the Plausibility of Developing an Empirical Means of Differentiating Between Delinquents and Nondelinquents Without Consideration to Involvement in Legal Process," (unpublished Masters Thesis, Brigham Young University, 1960).

linquents, by contrast, might have inflated their own illegal behavior.

By way of determining validity, the names of all respondents were run through court records. None of those who had been to court failed to say so in the interview, nor did anyone fail to describe the offense(s) for which he was charged.

Few responses were so distorted as to be questionable. For example, no one maintained complete detachment from lawbreaking; no one admitted having committed all offenses. These findings tended to parallel the experience of Short and Nye in this regard.[16]

FINDINGS

1. *What is revealed about the total volume of delinquency when undetected offenses are enumerated? What offenses are most common?*

The number of violations which respondents admitted having committed was tremendous. So great was the volume that it posed some difficulty for display and analysis. A comprehensive table, Table I, was prepared for use throughout the paper. The reader's patience is requested in referring to it.

The first two colums of Table I deal with the total volume of reported delinquency. These columns rank types of offenses in terms of the total frequency with which they were reported by all four samples. The frequencies reported for one-time offenders (N = 30) has been inflated by two-fifths in order to make them comparable to the other subsamples (N = 50). This inflation is also reflected in the *totals column* of Table I for the entire sample.[17] (Many

[16] Short & Nye, *supra* note 14, at 211.
[17] It is impossible to assess any increase in error which might have resulted from this inflation. If there is bias in the sample of 30, it will have been magnified. See Hansen, Hurwitz & Madow, SAMPLE SURVEY METHOD AND THEORY (1953). Insofar as sample size, *per se*, is concerned,

other refinements and differences among subsamples in this comprehensive table will be discussed later.)

Three types of offenses were most common: theft (24,199)—especially of articles worth less than $2 (15,175)—, traffic (23,946), and the purchase and drinking of alcohol (21,698).

Grouped somewhat below these three were open defiance of authority—parents and others—(14,639); violations of property, including breaking and entering (12,278); retreatist activities such as running away (9,953); offenses against person (9,026); and finally such offenses as gambling (6,571). In the case of smoking, the total number of respondents who smoke habitually, rather than the estimated number of times all have smoked, was obtained. Of the 200, 86 reported smoking habitually.

2. *To what degree do violations go undetected? To what extent do they go unacted upon in the courts?*

The reader is again referred to Table I where, along with the volume of delinquent violations, the percentage of each of those violations which went (1) *undetected* and (2) *unacted upon* in court is presented.

With regard to detection, respondents were asked after each reported violation to tell whether they had been *caught by anyone*: parents, police, or others. With regard to court action, they were asked to report *any* appearance, *formal or informal*, before *any* officer of the court: judge, referee, or probation officer. (It was this question which served as an outside check on reliability. As noted above, respondents were generally very accurate.)

error would not have been significantly decreased had this sample of 30 been increased to 50. Both (N = 30) and (N = 50) are very small proportions of the total population of one-time offenders.

More than nine times out of ten—almost ten times out of ten—most offenses go *undetected* and *unacted upon*. This is especially true with respect to so-called minor violations: traffic offenses, theft of articles worth less than $50, buying and drinking liquor, destroying property, skipping school, and so on.

As might be expected, the picture changes with respect to more serious violations—theft of articles worth more than $50, auto theft, breaking and entering, forgery, and so on. Fewer of these offenses went undetected and unacted upon. Yet, even in these cases, eight out of ten reported that their violations went undetected and nine out of ten did not result in court action.

3. *Do nonofficial delinquents—young people who have never been convicted —commit delinquencies equal in number and seriousness to those committed by officially designated offenders?*

The answer to this question illustrates the extreme importance of distinguishing between the *frequency* with which a given norm or set of norms is violated by two different samples and the proportion of respondents in each sample who report having violated them. The distinction helps to avoid the pitfall of concluding that, because large *proportions* of two different samples—i.e., students and institutionalized delinquents—have committed various offenses, the samples are equally delinquent in terms of total volume. Because of early studies, this impression regarding the total volume of delinquency in different samples has become almost traditional, even though it was not embraced by the authors of these studies.[18] The fact is that the *frequency*, as well as the types of offenses, with which individuals violated certain statutes turns out to be vitally important.

18 See PORTERFIELD, *op. cit. supra* note 3.

By way of example, consider Table II. It presents the *proportions* of respondents in the four different samples who reported committing various offenses. On some offenses—theft of articles worth less than $2, traffic violations, and destroying property—there is little to choose among the four samples. Most young people in each sample reported having committed them.

The proportions of all 180 boys who reported committing various offenses were as follows: petty theft (93%), gambling (85%), driving without a license (84%), skipping school (83%), destroying property (80%), other traffic offenses (77%), drinking (74%), fighting (70%), defying others (64%), and thefts of from $2 to $50 (59%).

However, it would be premature and superficial to conclude that, because large *proportions* of the entire sample have committed these offenses, the subsamples are equally delinquent. On only two offenses—gambling and traffic—did the proportions of nondelinquents exceed those of the delinquent subsamples. (However, the proportions for the nondelinquents and one-time offenders were very much the same.)

Furthermore, a re-examination of Table I reveals that the *frequency* with which official offenders violate the law is in excess of the *frequency* with which non-official offenders violate it. (Again, however, non-official and one-time offenders differ very little. More will be said on them later.) The chief distinctions were between non- and one-time offenders, on the one hand, and the two subsamples of persistent offenders on the other.

If non- and one-time offenders are combined—because of their similarity —the cumulative violations of persistent offenders exceed their violations by thousands: thefts, excluding forgery (20,836 vs. 2,851); violations of property (10,828 vs. 1,450); violations of

Table I

EXTENT OF VIOLATIONS AND PER CENT UNDETECTED AND UNACTED UPON

| | | Entire Adolescent Sample [a] | | | Subsamples | | | | | | | | | | | | | |
| | | | | | Nondelinquents [b] | | | One-Time Offenders [c] | | | Delinquents Community [d] | | | Delinquents Incarcerated [e] | | |
Offense	Rank	Total Offenses	% Unde-tected	% Unacted Upon	Total Offenses	% Unde-tected	% Unacted Upon	Total Offenses	% Unde-tected	% Unacted Upon	Total Offenses	% Unde-tected	% Unacted Upon	Total Offenses	% Unde-tected	% Unacted Upon
Traffic Offenses	1															
Driving without license		11,796	98.9	99.7	1,845	99.6	100.0	512	98.7	98.7	2,386	98.0	99.1	7,053	99.1	99.9
Traffic viol. (not lic.)		12,150	98.2	99.3	2,040	98.3	99.9	2,142	98.4	98.7	3,068	96.8	98.4	4,900	99.0	98.8
Total		23,946	98.6	99.5	3,885	98.9	100.0	2,654	98.4	98.6	5,454	97.3	98.7	11,953	99.0	99.8
Theft	2															
Articles less than $2		15,175	97.1	99.8	966	91.7	100.0	1,738	96.5	99.6	7,886	98.6	99.8	4,585	95.6	99.8
Articles worth $2 to $50		7,396	97.1	99.1	60	83.3	100.0	80	93.8	95.8	4,671	98.5	99.2	2,585	94.8	99.1
Articles more than $50		294	71.0	92.8	1	100.0	100.0	2	100.0	100.0	90	66.7	91.1	201	72.6	93.5
Auto theft		822	88.9	95.5	4	100.0	100.0	0	0.0	0.0	169	84.6	93.5	649	90.0	96.0
Forgery		512	93.4	97.5	0	0.0	0.0	0	0.0	0.0	60	70.0	90.0	452	96.5	98.5
Total		24,199	96.3	99.3	1,031	91.3	100.0	1,820	96.3	99.4	12,876	98.0	99.4	8,472	94.5	99.0
Alcohol and Narcotics	3															
Buying beer or liquor		8,890	99.6	99.9	18	100.0	100.0	57	94.1	100.0	1,453	99.6	100.0	7,362	99.6	99.9
Drinking beer or liquor		12,808	98.8	99.8	219	100.0	100.0	270	100.0	100.0	4,173	99.0	99.7	8,146	98.6	99.8
Selling narcotics		1	100.0	100.0	0	0.0	0.0	0	0.0	0.0	0	0.0	0.0	1	100.0	100.0
Using narcotics		74	100.0	100.0	0	0.0	0.0	0	0.0	0.0	3	100.0	100.0	71	100.0	100.0
Total		21,773	99.1	99.9	237	100.0	100.0	327	99.0	100.0	5,629	99.1	99.8	15,580	99.1	99.9
Open Defiance of Authority	4															
Defying parents		8,142	99.7	99.9	138	100.0*	100.0	128	100.0*	100.0	4,804	99.7*	99.9	3,072	99.8*	99.9
Defying others		6,497	99.4	99.7	124	100.0*	100.0	170	100.0*	100.0	1,478	99.3*	99.3	4,725	99.5*	99.9
Total		14,639	99.5	99.9	262	100.0*	100.0	298	100.0*	100.0	6,282	99.6*	99.8	7,797	99.6*	99.9

Table I (Cont.)

EXTENT OF VIOLATIONS AND PER CENT UNDETECTED AND UNACTED UPON

	N	%	%	N	%	%	N	%	%	N	%	%	N	%	%
5 Property Violations															
Breaking and entering	1,622	85.6	94.4	67	94.0	100.0	102	98.4	100.0	527	84.4	93.5	926	84.9	94.2
Destroying property	10,645	98.5	99.7	477	97.1	100.0	800	98.5	99.7	4,927	98.7	99.6	4,441	98.7	99.4
Setting fires (arson)	11	40.0	90.0	2	0.0	0.0	2	0.0	100.0	0	0.0	0.0	7	100.0	100.0
Total	12,278	96.8	99.0	546	96.7	100.0	904	96.5	99.6	5,454	97.3	99.0	5,374	96.4	98.5
6 Retreatist Activities															
Running away from home	578	86.8	94.7	19	100.0	100.0	19	100.0	100.0	103	75.0	87.4	437	89.0	96.1
Skipping school	9,375	93.9	99.8	377	94.7	100.0	698	93.1	100.0	3,478	93.2	99.8	4,822	94.4	99.8
Total	9,953	93.5	99.5	396	94.9	100.0	717	93.2	100.0	3,581	92.6	99.5	5,259	94.0	99.5
7 Offenses Against Person															
Armed robbery	46	80.4	91.3	0	0.0	0.0	0	0.0	0.0	22	68.2	90.9	24	91.7	91.7
Fighting, assault	8,980	99.7	99.9	354	100.0*	100.0	103	100.0*	100.0	2,207	99.9*	99.8	6,316	99.6*	99.9
Total	9,026	99.6	99.9	354	100.0*	100.0	103	100.0*	100.0	2,229	99.6*	99.7	6,340	99.5*	99.9
8 Others															
Gambling	6,571	99.9	99.8	1,185	100.0	100.0	2,400	100.0	100.0	1,186	99.3	99.5	2,800	99.9	100.0
Smoking (habitually)	86	87.1	91.8	1	—*	100.0	3	50.0	100.0	39	—*	94.9	43	—*	88.4

a Number of Respondents = 180, except on Arson (N = 136) and Gambling (N = 171).

b N = 50.

c Actual N = 30. However, figures in this column have been inflated as though N = 50. This was done to make frequencies comparable with other subsamples.

d N = 50, except on Arson (N = 15) and Gambling (N = 41).

e N = 50, except on Arson (N = 41).

* Because of their nature, these offenses almost never remain undetected by someone in authority. Thus, these figures refer to per cent *un-arrested*, rather than *undetected*.

person (8,569 vs. 457); and violations involving the purchase and drinking of alcohol (21,134 vs. 564).

In addition, as shown in Table II, far smaller proportions of non- and one-time offenders committed offenses of a "serious" nature than did persistent offenders: theft of articles worth more than $50 (2% vs. 50%), auto theft (2% vs. 52%), forgery (0% vs. 25%), and armed robbery (0% vs. 9%).

The significance of these data, then,

Table II

PROPORTION OF RESPONDENTS COMMITTING OFFENSES

Offense		Per Cent Rank of Total[a]	Subsamples			
			Non-Delinquents[b]	One-Time Offenders[c]	Delinquents Community[d]	Delinquents Incarcerated[e]
Theft	1					
Less than $2		93	92	98	96	86
Worth $2 to $50		59	22	36	78	90
More than $50		26	2	2	46	54
Auto theft		29	2	2	54	60
Forgery		13	0	0	16	34
Others	2					
Gambling		85	90	100	56	72
Smoking (habitually)		42	2	4	76	86
Traffic Offenses	3					
Driving without license		84	72	78	94	92
Traffic viol. (not lic.)		77	84	84	72	66
Retreatist Activities	4					
Running away from home		38	22	24	46	60
Skipping school		83	66	68	96	100
Property Violations	5					
Breaking and entering		59	32	46	74	84
Destroying property		80	66	84	86	84
Setting fires (arson)		6	2	2	0	8
Alcohol and Narcotics	6					
Buying beer or liquor		29	4	8	46	58
Drinking beer or liquor		74	52	66	84	94
Selling narcotics		0.5	0	0	0	2
Using narcotics		4	0	0	2	12
Offenses against Person	7					
Armed robbery		5	0	0	4	14
Fighting, assault		70	52	60	82	86
Open Defiance of Authority	8					
Defying parents		53	40	44	64	64
Defying others		64	52	54	72	78

[a] Number of respondents = 200, except on arson (N = 156) and gambling (N = 191).

[b] N = 50.

[c] N = 30.

[d] N = 50, except on arson (N = 16) and gambling (N = 41).

[e] N = 50, except on arson (N = 41).

seems to be that one should guard against the use of *proportions* of total populations as a measure of delinquent involvement without also taking into account the *frequency* with which these proportions commit violations. Although in two cases proportionately fewer of the delinquent samples had committed certain violations, those who had committed them did so with much greater *frequency* than official nondelinquent samples.

4. *How useful are traditional dichotomies—delinquent or nondelinquent, institutionalized or noninstitutionalized —in distinguishing groups of offenders one from another?*

A series of tests was run, beginning on the nondelinquent end of the continuum, to discover where, if any, there were discriminating dichotomies on the volume of delinquent offenses, either between delinquent and nondelinquent subsamples or between institutionalized and noninstitutionalized offenders.

Chi Square was used as a test of significance. This test examines the possibility that any difference between groups could have occurred by chance. If differences are so great as to suggest that factors other than chance are responsible, it then suggests the confidence one might have in making that assumption.

To lend further refinement, a measure of association (T) was used to indicate the degree of relationship, when any difference was significant,[19] between official status and total volume of delinquency. For example, if Chi Square indicated that a delinquent and nondelinquent sample differed significantly on a given offense, the measure of association (T) suggests the power of that offense to distinguish between these two samples.

[19] Hagood & Price, STATISTICS FOR SOCIOLOGISTS 370–71 (1952).

An effort was made to increase the validity of all comparisons by diminishing the impact of the large number of offenses commited by a few individuals. Thus, instead of making a gross comparison between two samples on the total number of times an offense was committed, respondents in each sample were ordered according to the number of times they reported committing an offense (i.e., 1–3 times, 4–6 times, etc.). Comparisons were then made between the number of respondents from each sample found in each category.

The wisdom of doing this can be illustrated by examining Table I. Persistent delinquents in the community reported having committed more petty theft than institutionalized offenders, while the reverse is true for auto theft. But these differences were largely due to the excessive activities of a few individuals. By taking them into account, the tests could more accurately reflect real, overall differences. If we had not accounted for them, excessively large differences between samples might have been suggested when, in fact, they did not exist.

OFFICIAL NONDELINQUENTS VERSUS OFFICIAL ONE-TIME OFFENDERS. The first comparison was between the subsamples of 50 high school boys who had *no* court record and the 30 one-time offenders.[20] In this particular comparison, only one significant difference past the .05 level of confidence was found; the offense was *destruction of property*. Official offenders were more likely to have been involved.

[20] This and other comparisons have the serious weakness of dealing with only a limited number of boys. But, at the same time, two things must be recalled: (1) that such comparisons involve an enumeration of violations which, in most cases, was very large; and (2) that it was necessary to limit the number of respondents because of the time and money involved in gathering and analyzing data on such a large number of violations.

Comparisons on such offenses as stealing articles worth more than $50, auto theft, armed robbery, forgery, etc., were meaningless because they were seldom, if ever, reported by either group. This in itself tells us much about the similarity of these two groups.

This dichotomy, then—official nondelinquent vs. one-time offenders—did not prove to be discriminating.

OFFICIAL ONE-TIME VERSUS PERSISTENT OFFENDERS. The second comparison was between one-time offenders and the subsample of 50 boys who were non-incarcerated persistent offenders. Differences between these two on most offenses were marked.

Persistent offenders were significantly—that is, 99 times out of 100—more inclined than one-time offenders, as a group, to have stolen expensive and inexpensive items, skipped school, defied parents, bought and drunk liquor, smoked regularly, stolen autos, fought, and driven without a license. There was also a significant difference past the .05 level with regard to forgery.

They did not differ significantly from one-time offenders on such things as running away from home, breaking and entering, destroying property, or committing most types of traffic violations. They could not be compared on such offenses as armed robbery, arson, or selling and using narcotics because of the small number of violations by both groups, but especially by one-time offenders.

This dichotomy, then—one-time versus persistent offenders in the community—was generally discriminating.

INSTITUTIONALIZED VERSUS NONINSTITUTIONALIZED OFFENDERS. The final comparisons had to do with the institutionalized versus noninstitutionalized dichotomy. First, the sample of institutionalized offenders (Subsample 4) was compared with those noninstitutionalized offenders who had been to court once (Subsample 2). As might be expected, differences were significant on virtually all offenses. The samples seemed to represent two different populations because of the much heavier involvement of the institutionalized offenders (Subsample 4) in delinquency.

Second, institutionalized offenders (Subsample 4) were compared with the subsample of persistent offenders who had not been institutionalized (Subsample 3). The two did not differ significantly.

Persistent institutionalized offenders as a group reported having committed more traffic offenses, forgeries, auto thefts, offenses involving alcohol, and fights than persistent noninstitutionalized offenders. The latter, meanwhile, reported considerably more petty thefts, thefts of items worth up to $50, defying parents, and destruction of property. But these differences were due largely to a few extreme individuals. Consequently, as explained earlier, when tests of significance took this fact into account, the modal behavior of boys in the two samples tended to be very much the same.

Consequently, the only significant difference between these two subsamples was on habitual smoking; more boys in the reformatory smoked regularly. Otherwise, the two samples might be taken as representative of the same population insofar as the modal volume and nature of their offenses were concerned.

The significance of this finding is diluted somewhat by the fact that only two-thirds of the noninstitutionalized group (Subsample 3) would have been on probation (and free in the community) had they not been attending a special rehabilitative program. Nevertheless, the findings strongly support the idea that a dichotomy which distinguishes, without qualification, between *institutionalized* and *noninstitu-*

tionalized offenders may not be valid. *Persistency* rather than institutionalization seems to be the more important variable in distinguishing groups. In this study, for example, the clearest distinction among official offenders was between *one-time* offenders, on one hand, and persistent offenders—whether institutionalized or noninstitutionalized—on the other.

This finding suggests that where persistent offenders are involved, the decision to incarcerate one group and to leave the other in the community might be highly subjective. Factors other than the extent and seriousness of these offenses seem to determine whether they are incarcerated or not.

Because of the significance of this finding, both samples of persistent offenders were combined and compared with the two subsamples on the nondelinquent end of the continuum (Subsamples 1 and 2, the official nondelinquents and one-time offenders) which likewise had been found not to differ. By combining samples in this way, comparisons could be made more reliable because of larger numbers with which to work. The results are displayed in Table III.

Differences were strong and striking. On virtually all offenses, the chances were less than one in a thousand that they could have occurred by chance (see Table III). Furthermore, all relationships were positive as indicated by the measures of association (T). This means that persistent offenders report having committed more of virtually every offense. Those offenses which best distinguished them from official non- or one-time offenders were smoking regularly (T = .78), skipping school (T = .50), theft of articles worth $2 to $50 (T = .46), theft of articles worth more than $50 (T = .45), auto theft (T = .45), and drinking alcohol (T = .42).

This finding re-emphasizes the idea that the old dichotomies may be misleading. Persistency is the most distinguishing variable.

To what extent this finding may be generalized is hard to say. Many of the most significant differences—smoking regularly, all kinds of theft, drinking, fighting, and skipping school—are associated with behavior often thought to be more characteristic of the lower than the middle class. Other offense patterns may have been characteristic of their setting in a Mormon subculture. However, such offenses as auto theft, forgery, breaking and entering, or stealing items worth more than $50 were also highly discriminating between these two samples and are likely to draw strong official reaction anywhere.

The implication of these findings for both practice and research seems to be that the unqualified use of traditional dichotomies—i.e., delinquent versus non-delinquent or institutionalized versus noninstitutionalized—may be unreliable. A further examination of undetected offenses on other populations, to test the validity of these dichotomies, might be an important prerequisite to their future use as an important source of data.

5. How valid are court records as an index of the total volume and types of offenses which are committed?

COURT RECORDS AS AN INDEX OF VOLUME. Evidence presented earlier indicated that the great majority of all delinquent offenses remain undetected and unacted upon. It might be concluded, therefore, that official records do not accurately reflect the total volume of delinquency. However, this might not be true.

It may be that official records are useful in reflecting volume by (1) distinguishing between those who have been heavily delinquent from those who

Table III

COMPARISON OF OFFICIAL NON- AND ONE-TIME
OFFENDERS WITH PERSISTENT OFFENDERS

Offense	Probability that Differences Could be Due to Chance	Degree of Association Between Volume and Official Classification
Theft		
Articles less than $2	.001	.28
Articles worth $2 to $50	.001	.46
Articles more than $50	.001	.45
Auto theft	.001	.45
Forgery	.001	.31
Property Violations		
Breaking and entering	.001	.34
Destroying property	.001	.24
Setting fires (arson)	a	
Offenses Against Person		
Armed robbery	a	
Fighting, assault	.001	.41
Open Defiance of Authority		
Defying parents	.001	.27
Defying others	.001	.34
Retreatist Activities		
Running away from home	.001	.32
Skipping school	.001	.50
Traffic Offenses		
Driving without license	.001	.36
Traffic viol. (not lic.)	.05	.17
Alcohol and Narcotics		
Buying beer or liquor	.001	.40
Drinking beer or liquor	.001	.42
Selling narcotics	a	
Using narcotics	a	
Others		
Gambling	.001	.29
Smoking (habitually)	.001	.78

a Offense not committed enough times to test differences.

have not; and/or (2) reflecting a tiny but consistently accurate portion of all offenses.

One method of treating these possibilities is to calculate the correlation between the actual number of court appearances for a given population and the number of violations it reports having committed. This calculation was made.

A coefficient of correlation was calculated for all 180 respondents. To do this and still maintain specificity, court appearances were broken into 9 categories—never been to court, been to court one time, two times, three times . . . nine or more times. The total number of reported violations was broken into 11 categories—never, 1–50, 51–100, 101–150 . . . 501 or more. The degree of association between these two variables was then calculated.

A correlation of .51 was obtained. This coefficient is statistically significant, indicating the existence of a relationship between appearing in court and the total number of violations one has committed; that is, the greater the number of reported violations, the greater likelihood that an individual will have appeared in court.

On one hand, this coefficient leaves much to be desired in terms of accurate predictability. A coefficient of .51 means that 26 percent of the variation in the number of court appearances among the 180 respondents could be associated with variations in the number of delinquent offenses they reported having committed.

When only 26 percent of the violation rates, using specific categories, is explained in terms of court appearances, the ability of these appearances to supply a good index of the actual number of violations may be highly questionable.

To further illustrate this point we found a correlation of .56 between dropping out of school and the number of reported violations. This suggested that whether or not individuals had dropped out of school was as accurate or possibly more accurate a predictor of reported violations than court records. (For those respondents incarcerated in the Utah State Industrial School, this meant dropping out of school prior to incarceration, not because of incarceration.)

One would not expect official delinquency rates to be an exact match of the volume of delinquency. Seriousness is also very important. Society demands that stronger measures be taken for serious violations.

In order to examine its significance, correlation coefficients were run between court appearance and a series of single violations, extending all the way from misdemeanors to felonies. The results are displayed in Table IV.

As might be expected, reported felonies correlated more highly with court appearances than did reported misde-

Table IV

CORRELATION COEFFICIENT BETWEEN COURT APPEARANCES
AND REPORTED NUMBER OF VIOLATIONS

Offense	Correlation	Percentage of Variation Explained
Misdemeanors		
A. Taken singly		
Skipping school	.17	.03
Theft (less than $2)	.19	.04
Theft $2 to $50)	.20	.04
Traffic violations (all types)	.18	.03
B. Combined	.15	.02
Felonies [a]		
A. Taken singly		
Theft (more than $50)	.25	.06
Auto theft	.43	.18
Breaking and entering	.40	.15
Forgery	.05	.003
B. Combined	.29	.08

[a] Armed robbery, arson and the selling and use of narcotics were not included because the number reporting such violations was small.

meanors. However, taken singly, the correlation between any one of the felonies (theft of articles worth more than $50, auto theft, breaking and entering, and forgery)[21] was not so high as that between the total *volume* of violations and court appearance.

Furthermore, even though the total number of reported violations for the felonies, when they were combined and then correlated with court appearance, produced a higher coefficient (.29) than did the combined misdemeanors (.15), this correlation (.29) was considerably lower than the correlation (.51) between the total volume of offenses and court appearance.

This finding raises questions regarding the traditional assumption that the court record is a better index of serious violations than it is of the total number of offenses an individual has committed. One might speculate, however, that the finding is due to the inaccuracy of reported data. But if one were to discard these reported data as inaccurate, he would have to ignore the fact that, except for seriousness, these findings met other assumptions rather consistently regarding distinctions between persistent and nonpersistent offenders, as to both frequency and seriousness. And they also seemed capable of making more precise distinctions in the direction of theoretical expectations among various dichotomies than court records.

Thus, these findings also raise important questions regarding the accuracy of official records as an index of volume and seriousness. But it is difficult either to assess the amount of combined error inherent in these court and reported data or to generalize from them to other police and court jurisdictions.

21 Armed robbery, arson, and the selling and use of narcotics were not included in this analysis because the number reporting such violations was small.

COURT RECORDS AND TYPES OF OFFENSES. One of the major problems raised in the introduction had reference to the adequacy of official records for the purpose of conducting typological research. There are at least two different levels of complication.

The first has to do with the validity of the official dichotomies—delinquent or nondelinquent, institutionalized or noninstitutionalized—which are used as the major criteria for distinguishing groups and setting up research samples. The foregoing analysis has already suggested some possible difficulties. It suggests that important qualifications may be needed.

The second level of complication comes in specific attempts to establish delinquent typologies based not only upon basic dichotomies but upon the offense patterns which are revealed by court records. To be accurate, these records would have to reflect reliably an individual's major offense pattern, with respect to both number and seriousness. Some test of their ability to do so was made.

The first part of the analysis was concerned with volume. It sought to determine how well the court record reflected, without special regard to seriousness, the offense which each respondent reported having committed *most often*. The court record proved to be a fair index for offenders who had been to court only once. Sixteen of 30, half of them, had appeared in court for the types of offenses they reported having committed most often.

But this was not the case for the more persistent offenders. The more delinquent they tended to be, the less predictive the court record was of their most commonly reported violations. For example, only 26 of the 100 official, persistent delinquents had appeared in court more often for their major areas of offense than for other offenses. Nineteen of the 100 had *never* appeared in court for their reported major areas of offense. Thus, if these reported data are valid, the court record for this latter group would not give any clues as to the types of offenses they reported having committed most frequently.

In between these two extremes were 55 other boys, all of whom had been to court for their major patterns of offense, but they had also been there equally as often for other offenses. Consequently, even for them court records would fail to provide a clear picture of the most commonly reported offense patterns.

With regard to seriousness, the foregoing analysis has already suggested that court records may be a relatively poor index of the total number of *serious* violations. But what of individual offenders rather than their total offenses? How well does the court record eventually select boys who report having committed *serious* violations?

Answers to such questions are important. Although an offender may have a long record of petty violations, his commission of a serious offense, such as breaking and entering, will more likely type him as a burglar than a petty thief.

In order to examine this dimension, a crude "seriousness" classification was established. Five judges and five chief probation officers from Utah's six juvenile districts[22] were asked to rank 25 offenses according to seriousness. The first ten of these offenses were then selected to serve as the *serious* criterion. They were:

1. Rape[23]   3. Arson
2. Selling narcotics 4. Using narcotics

5. Armed robbery 9. Homo-
6. Breaking and   sexuality[23]
   entering   10. Theft of
7. Forgery   items worth
8. Auto theft   more than $50

Two specific questions were examined: (1) How accurate is the court record in reflecting the most *serious* offense each respondent has committed (in terms of the hierarchy of eight serious violations)? (2) How accurate is the court record in reflecting each offender's most frequently committed *serious* violation?

For a relatively large group, the court record could supply no information regarding these questions. This group was comprised primarily of the official nondelinquents and one-time offenders. Twenty-three of the 50 nondelinquents (46%) and 14 of the 30 one-time offenders (47%) had committed one or more of the serious violations, but none had ever been to court for any of them. (The close similarity between the nondelinquents and one-time offenders in this study is again illustrated.)

By contrast, a much higher proportion of the two most delinquent samples had not only committed serious offenses —i.e., 88 of 100—but had also been to court for committing them—i.e., 77 of the 88 (or 88%).

Upon reading such information one might conclude that official records are likely biased against persistent offenders. It should be recalled from Table I, however, that respondents in the two most delinquent samples reported having committed many more serious offenses than the less delinquent subsamples. Court records, therefore, may simply reflect the greater probability of being caught because of excessive violations.

[22] Utah has one of the two State Juvenile Court Systems in the United States. Connecticut has the other. Judges are appointed for six-year terms; they must be members of the bar. Chief probation officers are selected on the basis of a state merit system examination, and training and experience in correctional work.

[23] It will be recalled that data on rape and homosexuality are not presented in this paper. Therefore, the seriousness classification includes the eight remaining offenses.

For this group of 77 persistent offenders who had been to court, the court record was accurate for 65 percent of them in reflecting the most serious offense they had committed. It said nothing of the remaining 35 percent. If, therefore, the premise is accepted that an offender would likely be typed on the basis of his most serious known offense, the court record would be accurate approximately two-thirds of the time for his select group. This is encouraging in some ways because it is persistent offenders with whom officials and researchers have been most concerned.

On the other hand, the large proportion of juveniles whose serious offenses remained undetected might easily have been typed in the same way had they been apprehended. Yet, without official action, many of them apparently make a reasonable, conventional adjustment.

A second qualification has to do with the ability of the court record to reflect not only an individual's most *serious* violation, but the type(s) of *serious* violation(s) he commits most frequently. Another premise might be that an individual should be typed on the basis of frequency of seriousness rather than extremity of seriousness. For example, it may be preferable to type an individual as an auto thief for having been to court three times for auto theft than to type him as an armed robber for having been to court once for armed robbery.

The court records were somewhat less accurate in this regard. About half (39) of the 77 persistent offenders who had appeared in court for serious violations had appeared there more often for the types of *serious* violations they reported committing most often than for any other *serious* violation. However, the picture for this group of 39 was muddied somewhat because 52 percent of them had appeared in court just as

often, or more often, for other offenses not considered serious.

For the other half of the 77 offenders who had not been to court more often for their most common serious violation, 20 (26%) had *never* been to court for their most common *serious* offense. And 18 (23%) had been to court just as often for other *serious* offenses. In these cases, the court record would not be an accurate means for typing an individual according to *serious* offense.

CONCLUSION

In conclusion, official records seemed more accurate in reflecting an individual's single most *serious* violation that the pattern of offenses, either *serious* or *nonserious*, which he most commonly commits.

On the surface, these findings may seem more encouraging from the treatment and control, than the research, standpoints. That is, court records, when compared with reported behavior, did distinguish persistent offenders (with whom officials are most concerned) from one-time offenders or nondelinquents, in terms of both number and seriousness of violation. Furthermore, they seemed quite efficient in indicating the most *serious* violations which persistent offenders had committed.

However, a great deal of refined information regarding types of offenders is needed if treatment and control strategies are to be effective. And, even though such information may be most needed for the persistent offender, it cannot be supplied, even for him, until more is known about two things: (1) about any differences or similarities between him and those juveniles who, if they were apprehended, might be typed the same way; and (2) about the offense patterns of him and others who, though they are apprehended, often remain largely unincorporated into the official record. Varying degrees of such information are needed no matter what theoretical orientation one takes towards developing typologies for treatment and control purposes.

Obviously, the findings which led to these conclusions must be qualified because of the data from which they were derived and the methodological problems inherent in obtaining them. Yet, even if they are only partially correct, they indicate one possible reason why we have encountered so much difficulty in pinpointing important etiological and treatment variables.

If different patterns of delinquency have important significance for the administration of justice, for prevention and treatment strategies, and for research purposes, data which could be used to supplement official records seem needed. At least it would seem important to explore the possibility that re-

ported data on undetected offenses might be helpful in understanding delinquency.

The methods for obtaining such data need not be greatly different from those which are used in a variety of other areas, clinical and scientific. Possible legal and constitutional questions would have to be explored. Yet, we are not without precedent in the clinical field where the communication of important information is privileged.

Furthermore, reported data might also open avenues to more detailed examination of the circumstances surrounding the commission of delinquent acts: Who is present? How are the acts carried out? What social and psychological variables seem to be operating? And then attempts might be made to relate such questions to court, control, and research strategies.

section II

Development of Delinquent Behavior

Many theories have been advanced to account for the development of delinquent behavior, and explanations for delinquent behavior have varied with time and place. Sociology has expanded the analysis of delinquency and crime well beyond the narrow individual-centered theories that once prevailed. Attempts by sociologists to relate delinquency to the social structure have helped us to understand delinquent and criminal acts as though they were integral elements of social life rather than aberrations.

The student will appreciate how knowledge of the legal definition of delinquency is important in understanding the statutory norms which stipulate that certain forms of behavior are consigned delinquent status. This status is part of the long process that leads to delinquent careers. In outlining the development of the delinquent career, Tannenbaum shows how being processed by various agencies, being labeled as a delinquent, and being stigmatized ascribe to the individual a social role, change his public image and self-conception, and generate a set of appropriate responses. These responses often involve exclusion from avenues of legitimate opportunity and hence may function to make attractive illegitimate events.

Sutherland's "Theory of Differential Association" is essentially a culture transmission view. He hypothesizes that criminal behavior is learned in a pattern of communication. Persons acquire patterns of criminal behavior by the same learning process with which they acquire patterns of lawful behavior. The delinquent career, then, is integrally related to an excess of definitions favorable to violation of law over definitions unfavorable to violation of law. According to Sutherland, when a person becomes criminal, he does so because of isolation from anticriminal patterns.

According to the anomie theory of Merton, deviant behavior, at least in part, involves "selective adherence to accepted social norms and occurs in areas of specific structural strains in a social system."

Merton suggests that anomie develops because of a breakdown in the relationship between goals that place great stress on success and to which all groups in our society are indoctrinated, without equivalent emphasis on institutional or legitimate channels of access to these goals. In the areas where the discrepancy between goals and means is greatest, a condition of anomie prevails, and individuals resort to illegitimate means to achieve the goals.

A modification of Merton's theory appears in Cohen's theory of delinquent subcultures. This concept is also rooted in the discrepancy between culture goals and institutionalized means. However, according to Cohen's formulation, the delinquent subculture is a reaction formation to socially induced stresses that our social-class system inflicts on working-class boys. He attempts to explain the formation of what he describes as the "non-utilitarian, malicious, and negativistic" behavior of working-class gang boys. Critiques of Cohen's position have been made on several grounds. Kitsuse and Dietrich contend that the postulation of a sharp break between the value systems of the middle and working classes is dubious, and that support for the theory is inadequate. Sykes and Matza question whether a gang boy actually rejects middle-class values, and they suggest that he rationalizes his deviant behavior by five techniques of neutralization or rationalization. Another response to Cohen's thesis is the portrayal of lower-class gang delinquency by Miller, who suggests that lower-class boys are virtually unaffected by middle-class traditions. He contends that much of lower-class delinquency may be viewed as a reflection of certain "focal concerns" that are characteristic of the urban lower-class way of life.

Cloward and Ohlin distinguish varieties of delinquent subcultures and try to account for them in terms of socially structured anomie based on interclass conflict and the availability of legitimate and illegitimate opportunity structures differentially organized on an ethnic and neighborhood basis. This theory has had a great impact on our approach to delinquency and its prevention in several action programs throughout the country.

In the article that follows, Reckless attempts to explain why all children living in a delinquency area do not engage in deviant behavior. Reckless' containment theory may be viewed as an attempt to integrate certain individual and social theories of delinquency causation. Tangri and Schwartz, however, take issue with the conclusions drawn in several studies that utilize Reckless' treatment of self as being basically atheoretical, and they suggest that severe restrictions are placed on the predictive value of the self-concept variable.

Hirschi and Selvin review statements of noncausality in delinquency research and draw conclusions regarding the possibility for change in the social structure.

The article by Reiss and Rhodes, "An Empirical Test of Differential Association Theory," presents findings that cannot be interpreted as clearly supporting the differential association hypothesis. These writers emphasize the difficulty in operationalizing the hypothesis in a manner that will make a valid test of the relationship of association with delinquent others through time.

The relationship between social class and illegal behavior, which has been so forcefully set forth in earlier papers, is challenged by Clark and Wenninger. They suggest that illegal acts within small communities or "status areas" of a large metropolitan center are related to community-wide norms to which juveniles adhere regardless of their social class origins. Finally, the basic issues of social status and delinquency are explored in the study by LaMar Empey and Maynard Erickson. Although they report different kinds of delinquency between status levels, they find that the lower-class and middle-class groups do not differ significantly from each other.

There is wide belief that the chief source of delinquent behavior lies in family disorganization. The practice followed by a few judges, of punishing the parents of delinquents, is a reflection of this belief, although the family influences that may be related to delinquent behavior are seldom specified, apart from vague references to, for example, "lack of proper supervision." Although it is extremely difficult to indicate exactly what influence the family has on delinquency, a number of studies suggest that the broken home and socialization to delinquent norms within the family are related to it. The selection by Monahan stresses the deleterious influence of a broken home on the child's development, whether through death, desertion, long separation, or divorce, and the consequences for delinquent behavior.

This section concludes with LaMar Empey's article, "Delinquency Theory and Recent Research," in which his examination of current research raises important questions concerning current theory on delinquency.

6.

Point of View

Frank Tannenbaum

The criminal is a social human being; he is adjusted; he is not necessarily any of the things that have been imputed to him. Instead of being unadjusted he may ‚be quite adjusted to his group, and instead of being "unsocial" he may show all of the characteristics we identify as social in members of other groups. The New York Crime Commission says, "He is adjusted to his own social group and violently objects to any social therapy that would make him maladjusted to it."[1]

Crime is a maladjustment that arises out of the conflict between a group and the community at large. The issue involved is not whether an individual is maladjusted to society, but the fact that his adjustment to a special group makes him maladjusted to the large society because the group he fits into is at war with society.

The difficulty with the older theory [of deviant behavior] is that it assumed that crime was largely an individual matter and could be dealt with when the individual was dealt with. Instead, most delinquencies are committed in groups; most criminals live in, operate

with, and are supported by groups. We must face the question of how that group grew up into a conflict group and of how the individual became adjusted to that group rather than to some other group in society. The study of the individual in terms of his special physical or psychical idiosyncrasies would have as much bearing on the question why he became a member of a criminal group as it would on the question why he joined the Ku Klux Klan, was a member of a lynching bee, joined the I. W. W., became a member of the Communist or Socialist party, joined the Seventh Day Adventists or the Catholic Church, took to vegetarianism, or became a loyal Republican. The point is that a person's peculiar physical or psychic characteristics may have little bearing on the group with which he is in adjustment.

The question is not how a criminal is distinguished in his nature from a non-criminal, but how he happened to be drawn into a criminal group and why that criminal group developed that peculiar position of conflict with the rest of society. The important facts, therefore, are to be sought in his behavior history.

Criminal behavior originates as part

[1] State of New York. Report of the Crime Commission, 1930. Legislative Document (1930) No. 98, p. 243.

SOURCE. Frank Tannenbaum, "Point of View," *Crime and the Community,* Boston: Ginn and Company, 1938, pp. 8–22. Copyright 1938, Columbia University Press.

of the random movement of children in a world of adults, a world with attitudes and organized institutions that stamp and define the activities of the little children. The career of the criminal is a selective process of growth within that environment, and the adult criminal is the product and summation of a series of continued activities and experience. The adult criminal is usually the delinquent child grown up.

The delinquent child is all too frequently "the truant of yesterday."[2] The truant is the school child who found extra-curricular activities more appealing and less burdensome than curricular ones. The step from the child who is a behavior problem in school to the truant is a natural one; so, too, is the step from truancy to delinquency, and that from delinquency to crime. In the growth of his career is to be found the important agency of the gang. But "the majority of gangs develop from the spontaneous play-group."[3]

The play group becomes a gang through coming into conflict with some element in the environment. A single illustration will indicate the process.

The beginning of the gang came when the group developed an enmity toward two Greeks who owned a fruit store on the opposite corner. The boys began to steal fruit on a small scale. Finally they attempted to carry off a large quantity of oranges and bananas which were displayed on the sidewalks, but the Greeks gave chase. This was the signal for a general attack, and the fruit was used as ammunition. The gang had a good start from this episode.[4]

But even after the gang has been formed, in its early stages its activities are not necessarily delinquent, and de-

linquent and non-delinquent activities may have the same meaning for the children. "We would gather wood together, go swimming, or rob the Jews on Twelfth Street."[5] The conflict may arise from play.

We did all kinds of dirty tricks for fun. We'd see a sign "Please keep the street clean," but we'd tear it down and say, "We don't feel like keeping it clean." One day we put a can of glue in the engine of a man's car. We would always tear things down. That would make us laugh and feel good, to have so many jokes.[6]

Or the jokes may be other ways of annoying people. "Their greatest fun consists in playing tag on porches and having people chase them."[7] Or it may be more serious annoyance: "such as throwing stones at windows of homes and ridiculing persons in the street who are known as 'odd characters.' "[8] Even a murder may arise out of the ordinary by-play of two gangs of young boys in rivalry.

Dey picked on us for two years, but even den we wouldn't a shot if "Stinky" —the big guy and the leader of the El-stons—hadn't jumped out of his dugout in a coal pile Saturday and waved a long bayonet wid a red flag on one end of it and an American flag upside down on de udder and dared us to come over de tracks.[9]

Once the gang has been developed, it becomes a serious competitor with other institutions as a controlling factor in the boy's life. The importance of the gang lies in its being the only social world of the boy's own age and, in a sense, of his own creation. All other agencies belong to elders; the gang belongs to the boy. Whether he is a

---

[2] State of New York. Report of the Crime Commission, 1927. Legislative Document (1927) No. 94, p. 285.
[3] Frederic M. Thrasher, *The Gang*, p. 29. Chicago, 1927.
[4] Thrasher, *op. cit.*, p. 29.

[5] *Ibid.*, p. 36.
[6] *Ibid.*, pp. 94–95.
[7] New York Crime Commission, 1927 Report, p. 371.
[8] *Ibid.*, p. 370.
[9] Thrasher, *op. cit.*, p. 180.

leader or just one of the pack, whether his assigned rank has been won by force or ingenuity or represents a lack of superior force or ingenuity, once that rank is established the child accepts it and abides by the rules for changing it.

Children are peculiarly sensitive to suggestion.

It is known that young people and people in general have little resistance to suggestion, that fashions of thought and fashions of dress spread rapidly through conversation and imitation, and that any form of behavior may be normalized through conversation and participation of numbers.[10]

In the boy's gang, conversation, gossip, approval, participation, and repetition will make any kind of behavior whatsoever normal.

The gang is important because the reaction of others is the source of the greater part of the individual's conduct. Conduct is learned in the sense that it is a response to a situation made by other people. The smile, the frown, approval and disapproval, praise and condemnation, companionship, affection, dislike, instruments, opportunities, denial of opportunities, are all elements at hand for the individual and are the source of his behavior. It is not essential that the whole world approve; it is essential that the limited world to which the individual is attached approve. What other people think is the more important because what they think will express itself in what they do and in what they say; and in what they do or say, in the way they look, in the sound of their voices, in the physical posture that they assume, the individual finds the stimuli that call out those particular attitudes that will bring the needed and desired approval from his immediate face-to-face companionship.

[10] William I. Thomas and Dorothy S. Thomas, *The Child in America*, p. 164. New York, 1928.

It is here that we must look for the origin of criminal behavior. It is here, largely, that the roots of conduct difficulties are to be found. What one learns to do, one does if it is approved by the world in which one lives. That world is the very limited world which approves of the conduct one has learned to seek approval for. The group, once it becomes conscious of itself as an entity, tends to feed and fortify itself in terms of its own values. The contrast with the rest of the world merely strengthens the group, and war merely enhances its resistance.

THE GROUP AND THE COMMUNITY

Once the differentiation of the gang has taken place, it becomes a competitor for the child's allegiance, and wins in a certain number of cases.

The growing child in a modern large city is exposed to a variety of conflicting stimuli, interests, and patterns. Not only are there differences between the family, the school, the church, and the street gang, but the family itself may be representative of a series of differences between parents and children, between father and mother, between older and younger children. The pattern is uneven, the demands are contradictory. What is approved in one place is derided and condemned in another.

Behavior is a matter of choice as to whose approval you want. And whose approval you want may be determined by such invisible and subtle influences as whom you like, who has given you pleasure, who has commended you. Conflicting demands for the growing child's loyalty are the source of much of the difficulty.

The fact that the gang wins in many instances does not reflect upon the children. It reflects upon the other agencies that are competing for the child's adherence. Of a dozen children who have come into conflict with the other groups in the community and have given their loyalty to the gang instead, the victory of the gang may have had a different cause in each case.

The family by its internal weakness may have been a contributory factor. The father or mother or an older brother may have been delinquent, or there may have been sharp conflict of opinions and attitudes in the family, or constant bickering and incompatibility between the parents. The father may have been dead and the mother forced away from home so that the children were left unsupervised, or an ignorant and poverty-stricken mother may have encouraged the child to bring in food or money whether earned or stolen, or the father may have been a drunkard and given to seriously mistreating the child and breaking down the loyalty and unity which are essential to the slow maturation of systematic habit formation. In these and innumerable other examples that might be cited of family inadequacy we have a source for the acceptance by the child of his playmates and gang affiliates *as a substitute for the home.* Gang membership under these circumstances may be a perfectly natural reaction and a seeking for fun, contentment, and status. That the fun may take on delinquent forms is another matter and depends on the opportunities for such uses of leisure within the environment as make delinquency an alternative, or by-product, of gang activity.

If the family itself is a unit and well co-ordinated, it still may contribute to delinquency by forcing upon the child an incompatible pattern. The dislike of the pattern, again, may arise from many different reasons, none of which are in themselves evidence of moral turpitude or psychical deficiency on the part of the child.

The objections to going to school

may arise from lack of good hearing, from poor eyesight, from undernourishment, from being left-handed, from dislike for the teacher because of favoritism, from being taken away from playmates because the family moves, from lack of interest in intellectual pursuits, from being either too big or too small for the grade, from undue competition with other children within the family, from a desire for excitement which the school does not provide, from having poor clothes and being ashamed to go to school, from a too rapid maturing, from a too slow development, from losing a grade because of illness, or from any number of other causes. That is, even in a "good" family, where moral standards are rigid, habits regular, ambitions high, there may still be adequate cause for the child to fall out of the pattern of the family interest because there are insufficient insight and sympathy for his needs, with the consequent conversion of the difficulty into conflict.

Truancy may in some degree have its roots in physical defect.

Thus, only 2.9 per cent of normal school children were suffering from malnutrition, whereas 26.2 per cent of truants were undernourished. Seven and three-tenths per cent of normal school children had defective vision, whereas 20.1 per cent of truants were so handicapped. Forty-nine and four-tenths per cent of normal children had defective teeth, whereas 91.2 per cent of truants had bad teeth.[11]

The physical defect may not be a direct cause of truancy, but it may contribute to that disgust with the school which may be directly responsible for truancy. "These are children in whom a definite attitude of dislike or even of disgust toward school has been built up."[12]

[11] New York Crime Commission, 1927 Report, p. 287.
[12] *Ibid.*, p. 285.

If the deviation could be compensated by having its need met, then the conflict might never arise and the competition of the gang would not be serious. But ordinarily it is not met.

Under our system of compulsory education we force into schools many, many children who would otherwise have been kept, or at least allowed to stay, at home —the "delicate" child, the excessively shy child, the child with some obvious defect, the child who does not care especially for books or activities that appeal only to the intellect. Now we make all of these children attend school, but we have not yet adapted our educational system to their needs.[13]

The difficulties of the child who is forced out of step in the school system, either through poor health or through lack of aptitude for scholastic endeavor, are met by the school authorities in terms of conflict, discipline, and tradition.

This group has been regarded by school teachers and administrators as more or less of an enigma, because these children stand out so decidedly from their playmates as being free from the domination of school discipline. Threats, punishment, hearings at the Bureau of Attendance, pleas of parents, frequently even commitments to the truant school do not seem to be successful in breaking up this attitude of unyielding resistance to compulsory schooling. It is because the truant is usually such an enigma to the average school administrator that he arouses so much ire. The response of the school administrator to the problem of truancy takes very little cognizance of the specific factors which have entered into the individual case of truancy. His response is in terms of an established tradition.[14]

Another source of failure of the other

agencies within the community to fulfill the demands made upon them for winning the loyalty and cooperation of the child who ultimately becomes delinquent may have no direct relation to the family or to the school, but be the result of the environment. The family may live in such crowded quarters as to force the child into the street to such an extent that street life takes the place of family life. The family may be living in a neighborhood where houses of prostitution are located; where gangsters gather; where there is a great deal of perversion of one sort or another; where street pilfering is a local custom; where there is hostility to the police; where there is race friction and warfare; where the children, without the knowledge of their parents, may find means of employment in illicit ways such as acting as procurers for prostitutes or as messengers and go-betweens for criminals; where they can observe the possession of guns, the taking of dope; where they can hear all sorts of tales and observe practices or be invited to participate in practices, or become conscious of habits, attitudes, morals, which are entirely in conflict with the teaching, habits, and points of view of the family in which they live. And because the family under these conditions may be an inadequate instrument for the purpose of supervising and co-ordinating all the child's activities, the family may lose the battle for the imposition of its own standards just because there was a lack of time, energy, space, for the doing of the things that needed to be done or for the provision of the room that the children required for the development of their normal play life.

The activities which are taken as a substitute for those provided by the community may be innocent enough in themselves. The New York Crime Commission found that the activities of truants, as a rule, were not delinquent

[13] White-Williams Foundation: Five Years' Review for the Period Ending December 31, 1921, p. 8.
[14] New York Crime Commission, 1927 Report, p. 285.

activities: the children flew pigeons, went fishing, rode in the subway and the "L," went to the movies, went to a park, shot craps, collected junk, went to work, peddled fruit, went auto riding with older boys, hitched on the backs of wagons, delivered wet wash, and stole lead pipe for sale. These activities, we see, were for the children an adequate substitute for the school which they did not particularly enjoy; instead of doing required things which were not particularly attractive to them—they almost all liked mechanical shop work but were generally indifferent to purely intellectual endeavor—these children turned to the endless opportunities for adventure in the city streets. Here they are free of physical restraint, can avoid any authority they do not wish to acknowledge, may use their wits and legs and voices for objectives they themselves set.

But these and other activities carried on during truancy or in spare time are carried on in a group. The gang tends to dominate the children's activities as soon as conflict arises. And conflict arises frequently over issues much less conspicuous than stealing. In the congested neighborhoods where most of the young delinquent gangs arise, the elements of conflict between the old and the young are natural and difficult to avoid. The old want peace, security, quiet, routine, protection of property. The young want just the opposite: chiefly room, noise, running about, unorganized mischief, fighting, shouting, yelling.

The crowded homes provide no place for the children, and therefore force them into the streets for play. Not only the homes are congested, but the streets are, too. In densely populated sections children engaged in even the mildest activities seem in the way. The absence of open spaces on the one hand and the conflict of interests on the other provide many occasions for opposition, dispute, and difference.

Gang KK. This group of 12 boys, ranging in age from 12 to 15 years, were all American-born. They were fond of athletics and had made a habit of playing hand-ball against the rear wall of a moving picture theatre. Their yells disturbed the patrons of the theatre, and the management frequently ordered them away from the premises. They left, but returned. Finally, in anger, the movie proprietor called a patrol wagon and had them loaded into it. They were arraigned in the Children's Court, but discharged. None of these boys had previous court records. They consisted partly of boys who lived in the immediate neighborhood, and partly of former residents, who still kept up their intimacy with the group.[15]

Here is an illustration of the difficulty in its simplest form. It is no crime to play handball against a wall. Nor is it a crime to yell and shout while the playing proceeds. In fact, the shouting, yelling, rough-housing, are an integral part of the game. It would be no game at all if this loud verbalization could not go on. The patrons are watching a picture and the noise disturbs them. The owner wants to keep his customers. A natural conflict has arisen, and no compromise is possible: the children cannot promise not to play or shout, the patrons cannot help being annoyed. The alternative is a different place to play. But a different place may not exist; there may be only one available wall and ground in the neighborhood. The children are arrested. A definition of evil has been created, a court record has been set up. The beginning of a career may have been marked. A differentiation has now been created which would never have arisen if the interests of the children were as highly considered as those of

[15] State of New York. Report of the Crime Commission, 1928, p. 620. Legislative Document (1928) No. 23.

the patrons of the theater or of the owner. The children needed space and a wall; these should have been provided in some form that would not involve the children with the court, the police, the patrol wagon, with which they had had no previous contact.

The process of gang formation may be stimulated also by the natural efforts of parents to maintain their own social standards in a continual process of classification, of separation of the "good" and the "bad," the right and the wrong. Parents carry their attitudes over to their children by talk, gossip, approval, condemnation, punishment, and reward. A system of values, judgments, differentiations, and classifications makes itself felt very early in the children's lives, and may have any number of grounds: religious, racial, economic, social, professional, and occupational. The more differentiation in the community, the greater the heterogeneity of the population, the less internal unity and sympathy, the greater the ease with which gangs are formed. In a sense, therefore, the gangs derive from the natural conflict that exists within the community itself.

Gangs are not merely spatial relationships—blocks, neighborhoods—but they are social relationships. The Irish gangs, the Jewish gangs, the Italian gangs, the Polish gangs, the gangs of English-speaking and non-English-speaking members of the community, are all evidence of the range of conflict within which the individual finds an outlet, recognition, and companionship.

A MATTER OF DEFINITION

In the conflict between the young delinquent and the community there develop two opposing definitions of the situation. In the beginning the definition of the situation by the young delinquent may be in the form of play, adventure, excitement, interest, mischief, fun. Breaking windows, annoying people, running around porches, climbing over roofs, stealing from pushcarts, playing truant—all are items of play, adventure, excitement. To the community, however, these activities may and often do take on the form of a nuisance, evil, delinquency, with the demand for control, admonition, chastisement, punishment, police court, truant school. This conflict over the situation is one that arises out of a divergence of values. As the problem develops, the situation gradually becomes redefined. The attitude of the community hardens definitely into a demand for suppression. There is a gradual shift from the definition of the specific acts as evil to a definition of the individual as evil, so that all his acts come to be looked upon with suspicion. In the process of identification his companions, hang-outs, play, speech, income, all his conduct, the personality itself, become subject to scrutiny and question. From the community's point of view, the individual who used to do bad and mischievous things has now become a bad and unredeemable human being. From the individual's point of view there has taken place a similar change. He has gone slowly from a sense of grievance and injustice, of being unduly mistreated and punished, to a recognition that the definition of him as a human being is different from that of other boys in his neighborhood, his school, street, community. This recognition on his part becomes a process of self-identification and integration with the group which shares his activities. It becomes, in part, a process of rationalization; in part, a simple response to a specialized type of stimulus. The young delinquent becomes bad because he is defined as bad and because he is not believed if he is good. There is a persistent demand for consistency in character. The community cannot deal with people whom it cannot define. Reputation is this sort of public definition. Once it is established, then unconsciously all agencies combine to maintain this definition even when they apparently and consciously attempt to deny their own implicit judgment.

Early in his career, then, the incipient professional criminal develops an attitude of antagonism to the regulated orderly life that he is required to lead. This attitude is hardened and crystallized by opposition. The conflict becomes a clash of wills. And experience too often has proved that threats, punishments, beatings, commitments to institutions, abuse and defamation of one sort or another, are of no avail. Punishment breaks down against the child's stubbornness. What has happened is that the child has been defined as an "incorrigible" both by his contacts and by himself, and an attempt at a direct breaking down of will generally fails.

The child meets the situation in the only way he can, by defiance and escape—physical escape if possible, or emotional escape by derision, anger, contempt, hatred, disgust, tantrums, destructiveness, and physical violence. The response of the child is just as intelligent and intelligible as that of the schools, of the authorities. They have taken a simple problem, the lack of fitness of an institution to a particular child's needs, and have made a moral issue out of it with values outside the child's ken. It takes on the form of war between two wills, and the longer the war lasts, the more certainly does the child become incorrigible. The child will not yield because he cannot yield —his nature requires other channels for pleasant growth; the school system or society will not yield because it does not see the issues involved as between the incompatibility of an institution and a child's needs, sometimes physical needs, and will instead attempt to twist the child's nature to the institution with that consequent distortion of the child which makes an unsocial career inevitable. The verbalization of the conflict in terms of evil, delinquency, incorrigibility, badness, arrest, force, punishment, stupidity, lack of intelligence, truancy, criminality, gives the innocent divergence of the child from the straight road a meaning that it did not have in the beginning and makes its continuance in these same terms by so much the more inevitable.

The only important fact, when the issue arises of the boy's inability to acquire the specific habits which organized institutions attempt to impose upon him, is that this conflict becomes the occasion for him to acquire another series of habits, interests, and attitudes as a substitute. These habits become as effective in motivating and guiding conduct as would have been those which the orderly routine social institutions attempted to impose had they been acquired.

This conflict gives the gang its hold, because the gang provides escape, security, pleasure, and peace. The gang also gives room for the motor activity which plays a large role in a child's life. The attempt to break up the gang by force merely strengthens it. The arrest of the children has consequences undreamed of, for several reasons.

First, only some of the children are caught though all may be equally guilty. There is a great deal more delinquency practiced and committed by the young groups than comes to the attention of the police. The boy arrested, therefore, is singled out in specialized treatment. This boy, no more guilty than the other members of his group, discovers a world of which he knew little. His arrest suddenly precipitates a series of institutions, attitudes, and experiences which the other children do not share. For this boy there suddenly appear the police, the patrol wagon, the police station, the other delinquents and criminals found in the police lock-ups, the court with all its agencies such as bailiffs, clerks, bondsmen, lawyers, probation officers. There are bars, cells, handcuffs, criminals. He is questioned, examined, tested, investigated. His history is gone into, his family is brought into court. Witnesses make their appearance. The boy, no different from the rest of his gang, suddenly becomes the center of a major drama in which all sorts of unexpected characters play important roles. And what is it all about? About the accustomed things his gang has done and has been doing for a long time. In this entirely new world he is made conscious of himself as a different human being than he was before his arrest. He becomes classified as a thief, perhaps, and the entire world about him has suddenly become a different place for him and will remain different for the rest of his life.

THE DRAMATIZATION OF EVIL

The first dramatization of the "evil" which separates the child out of his group for specialized treatment plays a greater role in making the criminal than perhaps any other experience. It cannot be too often emphasized that for the child the whole situation has become different. He now lives in a different world. He has been tagged. A new and hitherto non-existent environment has been precipitated out for him.

The process of making the criminal, therefore, is a process of tagging, defining, identifying, segregating, describing, emphasizing, making conscious and self-conscious; it becomes a way of stimulating, suggesting, emphasizing, and evoking the very traits that are complained of. If the theory of relation of response to stimulus has any meaning, the entire process of dealing with

the young delinquent is mischievous insofar as it identifies him to himself or to the environment as a delinquent person.

The person becomes the thing he is described as being. Nor does it seem to matter whether the valuation is made by those who would punish or by those who would reform. In either case the emphasis is upon the conduct that is disapproved of. The parents or the policeman, the older brother or the court, the probation officer or the juvenile institution, insofar as they rest upon the thing complained of, rest upon a false ground. Their very enthusiasm defeats their aim. The harder they work to reform the evil, the greater the evil grows under their hands. The persistent suggestion, with whatever good intentions, works mischief, because it leads to bringing out the bad behavior that it would suppress. The way out is through a refusal to dramatize the evil. The less said about it the better. The more said about something else, still better.

The hard-drinker who keeps thinking of not drinking is doing what he can to initiate the acts which lead to drinking. He is starting with the stimulus to his habit. To succeed he must find some positive interest or line of action which will inhibit the drinking series and which by instituting another course of action will bring him to his desired end.[16]

The dramatization of the evil therefore tends to precipitate the conflict situation which was first created through some innocent maladjustment. The child's isolation forces him into companionship with other children similarly defined, and the gang becomes his means of escape, his security. The life of the gang gives it special mores, and the attack by the community upon

---

[16] John Dewey, *Human Nature and Conduct*, p. 35. New York, 1922.

these mores merely overemphasizes the conflict already in existence, and makes it the source of a new series of experiences that lead directly to a criminal career.

In dealing with the delinquent, the criminal, therefore, the important thing to remember is that we are dealing with a human being who is responding normally to the demands, stimuli, approval, expectancy, of the group with whom he is associated. We are dealing not with an individual but with a group.

In a study of 6,000 instances of stealing, with reference to the number of boys involved, it was found that in 90.4 per cent of the cases two or more boys were known to have been involved in the act and were consequently brought to court. Only 9.6 per cent of all the cases were acts of single individuals. Since this study was based upon the number of boys brought to court, and since in many cases not all of the boys involved were caught and brought to court, it is certain that the percentage of group stealing is therefore even greater than 90.4 per cent. It cannot be doubted that delinquency, particularly stealing, almost invariably involves two or more persons.[17]

That group may be a small gang, a gang of children just growing up, a gang of young "toughs" of nineteen or twenty, or a gang of older criminals of thirty. If we are not dealing with a gang we may be dealing with a family. And if we are not dealing with either of these especially we may be dealing with a community. In practice all these factors—the family, the gang, and the community—may be important in the development and the maintenance of that attitude towards the world which makes a criminal career a normal, accepted and approved way of life.

Direct attack upon the individual in these circumstances is a dubious under-

taking. By the time the individual has become a criminal his habits have been so shaped that we have a fairly integrated character whose whole career is in tune with the peculiar bit of the environment for which he has developed the behavior and habits that cause him to be apprehended. In theory isolation from that group ought to provide occasion for change in the individual's habit structure. It might, if the individual were transplanted to a group whose values and activities had the approval of the wider community, and in which the newcomer might hope to gain full acceptance eventually. But until now isolation has meant the grouping in close confinement of persons whose strongest common bond has been their socially disapproved delinquent conduct. Thus the attack cannot be made without reference to group life.

The attack must be on the whole group; for only by changing its attitudes and ideals, interests and habits, can the stimuli which it exerts upon the individual be changed. Punishment as retribution has failed to reform, that is, to change character. If the individual can be made aware of a different set of values for which he may receive approval, then we may be on the road to a change in his character. But such a change of values involves a change in stimuli, which means that the criminal's social world must be changed before he can be changed.

THE SCAPEGOAT IS A SNARE AND A DELUSION

The point of view here developed rejects all assumptions that would impute crime to the individual in the sense that a personal shortcoming of the offender is the cause of the unsocial behavior. The assumption that crime is caused by any sort of inferiority, physiological or psychological, is here completely and unequivocally repudiated.

---

[17] Clifford R. Shaw and Earl D. Myers, "The Juvenile Delinquent," The Illinois Crime Survey, pp. 662-663. Chicago, 1929.

This of course does not mean that morphological or psychological techniques do not have value in dealing with the individual. It merely means that they have no greater value in the study of criminology than they would have in the study of any profession. If a poor IQ is a bad beginning for a career in medicine, it is also a poor beginning for a career in crime. If the psychiatrist can testify that a psychopath will make an irritable doctor, he can prove the same for the criminal. But he can prove no more. The criminal differs from the rest of his fellows only in the sense that he has learned to respond to the stimuli of a very small and specialized group; but that group must exist or the criminal could not exist. In that he is like the mass of men, living a certain kind of life with the kind of companions that make that life possible.

This explanation of criminal behavior is meant to apply to those who more or less consistently pursue the criminal career. It does not necessarily presume to describe the accidental criminal or the man who commits a crime of pas-sion. Here perhaps the theories that would seek the cause of crime in the individual may have greater application than in attempting to deal with those who follow a life of crime. But even in the accidental criminal there is a strong presumption that the accident is the outcome of a habit situation. Any habit tends to have a background of social conditioning.

A man with the habit of giving way to anger may show his habit by a murderous attack upon some one who has offended. His act is nonetheless due to habit because it occurs only once in his life. The essence of habit is an acquired predisposition to *ways* or modes of response, not to particular acts except as, under special conditions, these express a way of behaving. Habit means special sensitiveness or accessibility to certain classes of stimuli, standing predilections and aversions, rather than bare recurrence of specific acts. It means will.[18]

In other words, perhaps the accidental criminal also is to be explained in terms such as we used in discussing the professional criminal.

[18] Dewey, *op. cit.*, p. 42.

7.

Theory of Differential Association

Edwin H. Sutherland

The following paragraphs state a genetic theory of criminal behavior on the assumption that a criminal act occurs when a situation appropriate for it, as defined by the person, is present. The theory should be regarded as tentative, and it should be tested by the factual information and theories which are applicable.

GENETIC EXPLANATION OF CRIMINAL BEHAVIOR

The following statement refers to the process by which a particular person comes to engage in criminal behavior.

1. *Criminal behavior is learned.* Negatively, this means that criminal behavior is not inherited, as such; also, the person who is not already trained in crime does not invent criminal behavior, just as a person does not make mechanical inventions unless he has had training in mechanics.

2. *Criminal behavior is learned in interaction with other persons in a process of communication.* This communication is verbal in many respects but includes also "the communication of gestures."

3. *The principal part of the learning of criminal behavior occurs within intimate personal groups.* Negatively, this means that the impersonal agencies of communication, such as movies and newspapers, play a relatively unimportant part in the genesis of criminal behavior.

4. *When criminal behavior is learned, the learning includes (a) techniques of committing the crime, which are sometimes very complicated, sometimes very simple; (b) the specific direction of motives, drives, rationalizations, and attitudes.*

5. *The specific direction of motives and drives is learned from definitions of the legal codes as favorable or unfavorable.* In some societies an individual is surrounded by persons who invariably define the legal codes as rules to be observed, while in others he is surrounded by persons whose definitions are favorable to the violation of the legal codes. In our American society these definitions are almost always mixed, with the consequence that we have culture conflict in relation to the legal codes.

6. *A person becomes delinquent because of an excess of definitions favorable to violation of law over definitions*

SOURCE. Edwin H. Sutherland, *Principles of Criminology,* seventh edition, revised by Donald R. Cressey, Philadelphia: J. B. Lippincott Company, 1955, pp. 80–83. Reprinted with the permission of J. B. Lippincott Company.

unfavorable to violation of law. This is the principle of differential association. It refers to both criminal and anti-criminal associations and has to do with counteracting forces. When persons become criminal, they do so because of contacts with criminal patterns and also because of isolation from anti-criminal patterns. Any person inevitably assimilates the surrounding culture unless other patterns are in conflict; a Southerner does not pronounce "r" because other Southerners do not pronounce "r." Negatively, this proposition of differential association means that associations which are neutral so far as crime is concerned have little or no effect on the genesis of criminal behavior. Much of the experience of a person is neutral in this sense, e.g., learning to brush one's teeth. This behavior has no negative or positive effect on criminal behavior except as it may be related to associations which are concerned with the legal codes. This neutral behavior is important especially as an occupier of the time of a child so that he is not in contact with criminal behavior during the time he is so engaged in the neutral behavior.

7. *Differential associations may vary in frequency, duration, priority, and intensity.* This means that associations with criminal behavior and also associations with anti-criminal behavior vary in those respects. "Frequency" and "duration" as modalities of associations are obvious and need no explanation. "Priority" is assumed to be important in the sense that lawful behavior developed in early childhood may persist throughout life, and also that delinquent behavior developed in early childhood may persist throughout life. This tendency, however, has not been adequately demonstrated, and priority seems to be important principally through its selective influence. "Intensity" is not precisely defined but it has

to do with such things as the prestige of the source of a criminal or anti-criminal pattern and with emotional reactions related to the associations. In a precise description of the criminal behavior of a person these modalities would be stated in quantitative form and a mathematical ratio be reached. A formula in this sense has not been developed, and the development of such a formula would be extremely difficult.

8. *The process of learning criminal behavior by association with criminal and anti-criminal patterns involves all of the mechanisms that are involved in any other learning.* Negatively, this means that the learning of criminal behavior is not restricted to the process of imitation. A person who is seduced, for instance, learns criminal behavior by association, but this process would not ordinarily be described as imitation.

9. *While criminal behavior is an expression of general needs and values, it is not explained by those general needs and values since non-criminal behavior is an expression of the same needs and values.* Thieves generally steal in order to secure money, but likewise honest laborers work in order to secure money. The attempts by many scholars to explain criminal behavior by general drives and values, such as the happiness principle, striving for social status, the money motive, or frustration, have been and must continue to be futile since they explain lawful behavior as completely as they explain criminal behavior. They are similar to respiration, which is necessary for any behavior but which does not differentiate criminal from non-criminal behavior.

It is not necessary, at this level of explanation, to explain why a person has the associations which he has; this certainly involves a complex of many things. In an area where the delinquency rate is high, a boy who is sociable, gregarious, active, and athletic is very likely to come in contact with the other boys in the neighborhood, learn delinquent behavior from them, and become a gangster; in the same neighborhood the psychopathic boy who is isolated, introverted, and inert may remain at home, not become acquainted with the other boys in the neighborhood, and not become delinquent. In another situation, the sociable, athletic, aggressive boy may become a member of a scout troop and not become involved in delinquent behavior. The person's associations are determined in a general context of social organization. A child is ordinarily reared in a family; the place of residence of the family is determined largely by family income; and the delinquency rate is in many respects related to the rental value of the houses. Many other aspects of social organization affect the kinds of associations a person has.

The preceding explanation of criminal behavior purports to explain the criminal and non-criminal behavior of individual persons. As indicated earlier, it is possible to state sociological theories of criminal behavior which explain the criminality of a community, nation, or other group. The problem, when thus stated, is to account for variations in crime rates and involves a comparison of the crime rates of various groups or the crime rates of a particular group at different times. The explanation of a crime rate must be consistent with the explanation of the criminal behavior of the person, since the crime rate is a summary statement of the number of persons in the group who commit crimes and the frequency with which they commit crimes. One of the best explanations of crime rates from this point of view is that a high crime rate is due to social disorganization. The term "social disorganization" is not entirely satisfactory, and it seems preferable to substitute for it the term "differential social organization." The postulate on which this theory is based, regardless of the name, is that crime is rooted in the social organization and is an expression of that social organization. A group may be organized for criminal behavior or organized against criminal behavior. Most communities are organized both for criminal and anti-criminal behavior, and in that sense the crime rate is an expression of the differential group organization. Differential group organization as an explanation of variations in crime rates is consistent with the differential association theory of the processes by which persons become criminals.

8.

Social Structure and Anomie

Robert K. Merton

There persists a notable tendency in sociological theory to attribute the malfunctioning of social structure primarily to those of man's imperious biological drives which are not adequately restrained by social control. In this view, the social order is solely a device for "impulse management" and the "social processing" of tensions. These impulses which break through social control, be it noted, are held to be biologically derived. Nonconformity is assumed to be rooted in original nature.[1] Conformity is by implication the result of an utilitarian calculus or unreasoned conditioning. This point of view, whatever its other deficiencies, clearly begs one question. It provides no basis for determining the nonbiological conditions which induce deviations from prescribed patterns of conduct. In this paper, it will be suggested that certain phases of social structure generate the circumstances in which infringement of social codes constitutes a "normal" response.[2]

The conceptual scheme to be outlined is designed to provide a coherent, systematic approach to the study of socio-cultural sources of deviate behavior. Our primary aim lies in discovering how some social structures *exert a definite pressure* upon certain persons in the society to engage in nonconformist rather than conformist conduct. The many ramifications of the scheme cannot all be discussed; the problems mentioned outnumber those explicitly treated.

Among the elements of social and cultural structure, two are important for our purposes. These are analytically separable although they merge imperceptibly in concrete situations. The first consists of culturally defined goals, purposes, and interests. It comprises a frame of aspirational reference. These goals are more or less integrated and

oriented, if not approved, response. This statement does not deny the relevance of biological and personality differences which may be significantly involved in the *incidence* of deviate conduct. Our focus of interest is the social and cultural matrix; hence we abstract from other factors. It is in this sense, I take it, that James S. Plant speaks of the "normal reaction of normal people to abnormal conditions." See his *Personality and the Cultural Pattern*, 248, New York, 1937.

[1] E.g., Ernest Jones, *Social Aspects of Psychoanalysis*, 28, London, 1924. If the Freudian notion is a variety of the "original sin" dogma, then the interpretation advanced in this paper may be called the doctrine of "socially derived sin."

[2] "Normal" in the sense of a culturally

SOURCE. Robert K. Merton, "Social Structure and Anomie," from *American Sociological Review*, Volume 3, October 1938, pp. 672-682. Reprinted with the permission of the American Sociological Association and the author.

involve varying degrees of prestige and sentiment. They constitute a basic, but not the exclusive, component of what Linton aptly has called "designs for group living." Some of these cultural aspirations are related to the original drives of man, but they are not determined by them. The second phase of the social structure defines, regulates, and controls the acceptable modes of achieving these goals. Every social group invariably couples its scale of desired ends with moral or institutional regulation of permissible and required procedures for attaining these ends. These regulatory norms and moral imperatives do not necessarily coincide with technical or efficiency norms. Many procedures which form the standpoint of *particular individuals* would be most efficient in securing desired values, e.g., illicit oil-stock schemes, theft, fraud, are ruled out of the institutional area of permitted conduct. The choice of expedients is limited by the institutional norms.

To say that these two elements, culture goals and institutional norms, operate jointly is not to say that the ranges of alternative behaviors and aims bear some constant relation to one another. The emphasis upon certain goals may vary independently of the degree of emphasis upon institutional means. There may develop a disproportionate, at times, a virtually exclusive, stress upon the value of specific goals, involving relatively slight concern with the institutionally appropriate modes of attaining these goals. The limiting case in this direction is reached when the range of alternative procedures is limited only by technical rather than institutional considerations. Any and all devices which promise attainment of the all important goal would be permitted in this hypothetical polar case.[3]

[3] Contemporary American culture has been said to tend in this direction. See

This constitutes one type of cultural malintegration. A second polar type is found in groups where activities originally conceived as instrumental are transmuted into ends in themselves. The original purposes are forgotten, and ritualistic adherence to institutionally prescribed conduct becomes virtually obsessive.[4] Stability is largely ensured while change is flouted. The range of alternative behaviors is severely limited. There develops a tradition-bound, sacred society characterized by neophobia. The occupational psychosis of the bureaucrat may be cited as a case in point. Finally, there are the intermediate types of groups where a balance between culture goals and institutional means is maintained. These are the significantly integrated and relatively stable, though changing, groups.

André Siegfried, *America Comes of Age,* 26–37. New York, 1927. The alleged extreme(?) emphasis on the goals of monetary success and material prosperity leads to dominant concern with technological and social instruments designed to produce the desired result, inasmuch as institutional controls become of secondary importance. In such a situation, innovation flourishes as the *range of means* employed is broadened. In a sense, then, there occurs the paradoxical emergence of "materialists" from an "idealistic" orientation. Cf. Durkheim's analysis of the cultural conditions which predispose toward crime and innovation, both of which are aimed toward efficiency, not moral norms. Durkheim was one of the first to see that "contrairement aux idées courantes le criminel n'apparait plus comme un être radicalement insociable, comme une sorte d'élément parasitaire, de corps étranger et inassimilable, introduit au sein de la société; c'est un agent régulier de la vie sociale." See *Les Règles de la Méthode Sociologique,* 86–89, Paris, 1927.

[4] Such ritualism may be associated with a mythology which rationalizes these actions so that they appear to retain their status as means, but the dominant pressure is in the direction of strict ritualistic conformity, irrespective of such rationalizations. In this sense, ritual has proceeded farthest when such rationalizations are not even called forth.

An effective equilibrium between the two phases of the social structure is maintained as long as satisfactions accrue to individuals who conform to both constraints, viz., satisfactions from the achievement of the goals and satisfactions emerging directly from the institutionally canalized modes of striving to attain these ends. Success, in such equilibrated cases, is twofold. Success is reckoned in terms of the product and in terms of the process, in terms of the outcome and in terms of activities. Continuing satisfactions must derive from sheer *participation* in a competitive order as well as from eclipsing one's competitors if the order itself is to be sustained. The occasional sacrifices involved in institutionalized conduct must be compensated by socialized rewards. The distribution of statuses and roles through competition must be so organized that positive incentives for conformity to roles and adherence to status obligations are provided *for every position* within the distributive order. Aberrant conduct, therefore, may be viewed as a symptom of dissociation between culturally defined aspirations and socially structured means.

Of the types of groups which result from the independent variation of the two phases of the social structure, we shall be primarily concerned with the first, namely, that involving a disproportionate accent on goals. This statement must be recast in a proper perspective. In no group is there an absence of regulatory codes governing conduct, yet groups do vary in the degree to which these folkways, mores, and institutional controls are effectively integrated with the more diffuse goals which are part of the culture matrix. Emotional convictions may cluster about the complex of socially acclaimed ends, meanwhile shifting their support from the culturally defined implementation of these ends. As we shall see, certain aspects of the social structure may generate countermores and antisocial behavior precisely because of differential emphases on goals and regulations. In the extreme case, the latter may be so vitiated by the goal-emphasis that the range of behavior is limited only by considerations of technical expediency. The sole significant question then becomes, which available means is most efficient in netting the socially approved value?[5] The technically most feasible procedure, whether legitimate or not, is preferred to the institutionally prescribed conduct. As this process continues, the integration of the society becomes tenuous and anomie ensues.

Thus, in competitive athletics, when the aim of victory is shorn of its institutional trappings and success in contests becomes construed as "winning the game" rather than "winning through circumscribed modes of activity," a premium is implicitly set upon the use of illegitimate but technically efficient means. The star of the opposing football team is surreptitiously slugged; the wrestler furtively incapacitates his opponent through ingenious but illicit techniques; university alumni covertly subsidize "students" whose talents are largely confined to the athletic field. The emphasis on the goal has so attenuated the satisfactions deriving from sheer participation in the competitive activity that these satisfactions are vir-

[5] In this connection, one may see the relevance of Elton Mayo's paraphrase of the title of Tawney's well-known book. "Actually the problem *is not that of the sickness of an acquisitive society; it is that of the acquisitiveness of a sick society.*" *Human Problems of an Industrial Civilization*, 153, New York, 1933. Mayo deals with the process through which wealth comes to be a symbol of social achievement. He sees this as arising from a state of anomie. We are considering the unintegrated monetary-success goal as an element in producing anomie. A complete analysis would involve both phases of this system of interdependent variables.

tually confined to a successful outcome. Through the same process, tension generated by the desire to win in a poker game is relieved by successfully dealing oneself four aces, or, when the cult of success has become completely dominant, by sagaciously shuffling the cards in a game of solitaire. The faint twinge of uneasiness in the last instance and the surreptitious nature of public delicts indicate clearly that the institutional rules of the game *are known* to those who evade them, but that the emotional supports of these rules are largely vitiated by cultural exaggeration of the success-goal.[6] They are microcosmic images of the social macrocosm.

Of course, this process is not restricted to the realm of sport. The process whereby exaltation of the end generates a *literal demoralization,* i.e., a deinstitutionalization, of the means is one which characterizes many[7] groups in which the two phases of the social structure are not highly integrated. The extreme emphasis upon the accumulation of wealth as a symbol of success[8] in our own society militates against the completely effective control of institutionally regulated modes of acquiring a fortune.[9] Fraud, corruption, vice, crime, in short, the entire catalogue of proscribed behavior, becomes increasingly common when the emphasis on the *culturally induced* success-goal becomes divorced from a coordinated institutional emphasis. This observation is of crucial theoretical importance in examining the doctrine that antisocial behavior most frequently derives from biological drives breaking through the restraints imposed by society. The difference is one between a strictly utilitarian interpretation which conceives man's ends as random and an analysis which finds these ends deriving from the basic values of the culture.[10]

Our analysis can scarcely stop at this juncture. We must turn to other aspects of the social structure if we are to deal with the social genesis of the varying rates and types of deviate behavior characteristic of different societies. Thus far, we have sketched three ideal types of social orders constituted by distinctive patterns of relations between culture ends and means. Turning from

---

[6] It is unlikely that interiorized norms are completely eliminated. Whatever residuum persists will induce personality tensions and conflict. The process involves a certain degree of ambivalence. A manifest rejection of the institutional norms is coupled with some latent retention of their emotional correlates. "Guilt feelings," "sense of sin," "pangs of conscience" are obvious manifestations of this unrelieved tension; symbolic adherence to the nominally repudiated values or rationalizations constitute a more subtle variety of tensional release.

[7] "Many," and not all, unintegrated groups, for the reason already mentioned. In groups where the primary emphasis shifts to institutional means, i.e., when the range of alternatives is very limited, the outcome is a type of ritualism rather than anomie.

[8] Money has several peculiarities which render it particularly apt to become a symbol of prestige divorced from institutional controls. As Simmel emphasized, money is highly abstract and impersonal.

However acquired, through fraud or institutionally, it can be used to purchase the same goods and services. The anonymity of metropolitan culture, in conjunction with this peculiarity of money, permits wealth, the sources of which may be unknown to the community in which the plutocrat lives, to serve as a symbol of status.

[9] The emphasis upon wealth as a success-symbol is possibly reflected in the use of the term "fortune" to refer to a stock of accumulated wealth. This meaning becomes common in the late sixteenth century (Spenser and Shakespeare). A similar usage of the Latin *fortuna* comes into prominence during the first century B.C. Both these periods were marked by the rise to prestige and power of the "bourgeoisie."

[10] See Kingsley Davis, "Mental Hygiene and the Class Structure," *Psychiatry,* 1928, 1: esp. 62–63; Talcott Parsons, *The Structure of Social Action,* 59–60, New York, 1937.

these types of *culture patterning,* we find five logically possible, alternative modes of adjustment or adaptation *by individuals* within the culture-bearing society or group.[11] These are schematically presented in the following table, where (+) signifies "acceptance," (−) signifies "elimination," and (±) signifies "rejection and substitution of new goals and standards."

	Culture goals	Institutionalized means
I. Conformity	+	+
II. Innovation	+	−
III. Ritualism	−	+
IV. Retreatism	−	−
V. Rebellion[12]	±	±

Our discussion of the relation between these alternative responses and other phases of the social structure must be prefaced by the observation that persons may shift from one alternative to another as they engage in different social activities. These categories refer to role adjustments in specific situations, not to personality *in toto.* To treat the development of this process in various spheres of conduct would introduce a complexity unmanageable within the confines of this paper. For this reason, we shall be concerned primarily with economic activity in the broad sense, "the production, exchange, distribution, and consumption of goods

and services" in our competitive society, wherein wealth has taken on a highly symbolic cast. Our task is to search out some of the factors which exert pressure upon individuals to engage in certain of these logically possible alternative responses. This choice, as we shall see, is far from random.

In every society, Adaptation I (conformity to both culture goals and means) is the most common and widely diffused. Were this not so, the stability and continuity of the society could not be maintained. The mesh of expectancies which constitutes every social order is sustained by the modal behavior of its members falling within the first category. Conventional role behavior oriented toward the basic values of the group is the rule rather than the exception. It is this fact alone which permits us to speak of a human aggregate as comprising a group or society.

Conversely, Adaptation IV (rejection of goals and means) is the least common. Persons who "adjust" (or maladjust) in this fashion are, strictly speaking, *in* the society but not *of* it. Sociologically, these constitute the true "aliens." Not sharing the common frame of orientation, they can be included within the societal population merely in a fictional sense. In this category are *some* of the activities of psychotics, psychoneurotics, chronic autists, pariahs, outcasts, vagrants, vagabonds, tramps, chronic drunkards, and drug addicts.[13] These have relinquished, in certain spheres of activity, the culturally

---

[11] This is a level intermediate between the two planes distinguished by Edward Sapir; namely, culture patterns and personal habit systems. See his "Contribution of Psychiatry to an Understanding of Behavior in Society," *Amer. J. Sociol.,* 1937, 42:862-870.

[12] This fifth alternative is on a plane clearly different from that of the others. It represents a *transitional* response which seeks to *institutionalize* new procedures oriented toward revamped cultural goals shared by the members of the society. It thus involves efforts to *change* the existing structure rather than to perform accommodative actions *within* this structure, and introduces additional problems with which we are not at the moment concerned.

[13] Obviously, this is an elliptical statement. These individuals may maintain some orientation to the values of their particular differentiated groupings within the larger society or, in part, of the conventional society itself. Insofar as they do so, their conduct cannot be classified in the "passive rejection" category (IV). Nels Anderson's description of the behavior and attitudes of the bum, for example, can readily be recast in terms of our analytical scheme. See *The Hobo,* 93-98, *et passim,* Chicago, 1923.

defined goals, involving complete aim-inhibition in the polar case, and their adjustments are not in accord with institutional norms. This is not to say that in some cases the source of their behavioral adjustments is not in part the very social structure which they have in effect repudiated nor that their very existence within a social area does not constitute a problem for the socialized population.

This mode of "adjustment" occurs, as far as structural sources are concerned, when both the culture goals and institutionalized procedures have been assimilated thoroughly by the individual and imbued with affect and high positive value, but where those institutionalized procedures which promise a measure of successful attainment of the goals are not available to the individual. In such instances, there results a two-fold mental conflict insofar as the moral obligation for adopting institutional means conflicts with the pressure to resort to illegitimate means (which may attain the goal) and inasmuch as the individual is shut off from means which are both legitimate *and* effective. The competitive order is maintained, but the frustrated and handicapped individual who cannot cope with this order drops out. Defeatism, quietism, and resignation are manifested in escape mechanisms which ultimately lead the individual to "escape" from the requirements of the society. It is an expedient which arises from continued failure to attain the goal by legitimate measures and from an inability to adopt the illegitimate route because of internalized prohibitions and institutionalized compulsives, *during which process the supreme value of the success-goal has as yet not been renounced.* The conflict is resolved by eliminating *both* precipitating elements, the goals and means. The escape is complete, the conflict is eliminated, and the individual is associalized.

Be it noted that where frustration derives from the inaccessibility of effective institutional means for attaining economic or any other type of highly valued "success," that Adaptations II, III, and V (innovation, ritualism, and rebellion) are also possible. The result will be determined by the particular personality, and thus, the *particular* cultural background, involved. Inadequate socialization will result in the innovation response whereby the conflict and frustration are eliminated by relinquishing the institutional means and retaining the success-aspiration; an extreme assimilation of institutional demands will lead to ritualism wherein the goal is dropped as beyond one's reach but conformity to the mores persists; and rebellion occurs when emancipation from the reigning standards, due to frustration or to marginalist perspectives, leads to the attempt to introduce a "new social order."

Our major concern is with the illegitimacy adjustment. This involves the use of conventionally proscribed but frequently effective means of attaining at least the simulacrum of culturally defined success,—wealth, power, and the like. As we have seen, this adjustment occurs when the individual has assimilated the cultural emphasis on success without equally internalizing the morally prescribed norms governing means for its attainment. The question arises, Which phases of our social structure predispose toward this mode of adjustment? We may examine a concrete instance, effectively analyzed by Lohman,[14] which provides a clue to the answer. Lohman has shown that specialized areas of vice in the near north side of Chicago constitute a "normal" response to a situation where the cultural emphasis upon pecuniary success has

[14] Joseph D. Lohman, "The Participant Observer in Community Studies," *Amer. Sociol. Rev.*, 1937, 2:890–898.

been absorbed, but where there is little access to conventional and legitimate means for attaining such success. The conventional occupational opportunities of persons in this area are almost completely limited to manual labor. Given our cultural stigmatization of manual labor, and its correlate, the prestige of white collar work, it is clear that the result is a strain toward innovational practices. The limitation of opportunity to unskilled labor and the resultant low income cannot compete *in terms of conventional standards of achievement* with the high income from organized vice.

For our purposes, this situation involves two important features. First, such antisocial behavior is in a sense "called forth" by certain conventional values of the culture *and* by the class structure involving differential access to the approved opportunities for legitimate, prestige-bearing pursuit of the culture goals. The lack of high integration between the means-and-end elements of the cultural pattern and the particular class structure combine to favor a heightened frequency of antisocial conduct in such groups. The second consideration is of equal significance. Recourse to the first of the alternative responses, legitimate effort, is limited by the fact that actual advance toward desired success-symbols through conventional channels is, despite our persisting open-class ideology,[15] rela-

tively rare and difficult for those handicapped by little formal education and few economic resources. The dominant pressure of group standards of success is, therefore, on the gradual attenuation of legitimate, but by and large ineffective, strivings and the increasing use of illegitimate, but more or less effective, expedients of vice and crime. The cultural demands made on persons in this situation are incompatible. On the one hand, they are asked to orient their conduct toward the prospect of accumulating wealth and on the other, they are largely denied effective opportunities to do so institutionally. The consequences of such structural inconsistency are psychopathological personality, and/or antisocial conduct, and/or revolutionary activities. The equilibrium between culturally designated means and ends becomes highly unstable with the progressive emphasis on attaining the prestige-laden ends by any means whatsoever. Within this context, Capone represents the triumph of amoral intelligence over morally prescribed "failure," when the channels of vertical mobility are closed or narrowed[16] *in a*

---

[15] The shifting historical role of this ideology is a profitable subject for exploration. The "office-boy-to-president" stereotype was once in approximate accord with the facts. Such vertical mobility was probably more common then than now, when the class structure is more rigid. (See the following note.) The ideology largely persists, however, possibly because it still performs a useful function for maintaining the *status quo*. For insofar as it is accepted by the "masses," it constitutes a useful sop for those who might rebel against the entire structure, were this consoling hope removed. This ideology now serves to lessen the probability of Adaptation V. In short, the role of this notion

has changed from that of an approximately valid empirical theorem to that of an ideology, in Mannheim's sense.

[16] There is a growing body of evidence, though none of it is clearly conclusive, to the effect that our class structure is becoming rigidified and that vertical mobility is declining. Taussig and Joslyn found that American business leaders are being *increasingly* recruited from the upper ranks of our society. The Lynds have also found a "diminished chance to get ahead" for the working classes in Middletown. Manifestly, these objective changes are not alone significant; the individual's subjective evaluation of the situation is a major determinant of the response. The extent to which this change in opportunity for social mobility has been recognized by the least advantaged classes is still conjectural, although the Lynds present some suggestive materials. The writer suggests that a case in point is the increasing frequency of cartoons which observe in a tragi-comic vein that "my old man says everybody can't be President. He says if ya can get three days a week steady on W.P.A. work ya ain't

society which places a high premium on economic affluence and social ascent for all its members.[17]

This last qualification is of primary importance. It suggests that other phases of the social structure besides the extreme emphasis on pecuniary success must be considered if we are to understand the social sources of antisocial behavior. A high frequency of deviate behavior is not generated simply by "lack of opportunity" or by this exaggerated pecuniary emphasis. A comparatively rigidified class structure, a feudalistic or caste order, may limit such opportunities far beyond the point which obtains in our society today. It is only when a system of cultural values extols, virtually above all else, certain *common* symbols of success *for the population at large* while its social structure rigorously restricts or completely eliminates access to approved modes of acquiring these symbols *for a considerable part of the same population* that antisocial behavior ensues on a considerable scale. In other words, our egalitarian ideology denies by implication the existence of noncompeting groups and individuals in the pursuit of pecuniary success. The same body of success-symbols is held to be desirable for all.

doin' so bad either." See F. W. Taussig and C. S. Joslyn, *American Business Leaders*, New York, 1932; R. S. and H. M. Lynd, *Middletown in Transition*, 67 ff., chap. 12, New York, 1937.

[17] The role of the Negro in this respect is of considerable theoretical interest. Certain elements of the Negro population have assimilated the dominant caste's values of pecuniary success and social advancement, but they also recognize that social ascent is at present restricted to their own caste almost exclusively. The pressures upon the Negro which would otherwise derive from the structural inconsistencies we have noticed are hence not identical with those upon lower class whites. See Kingsley Davis, *op. cit.*, 63; John Dollard, *Caste and Class in a Southern Town*, 66 ff., New Haven, 1936; Donald Young, *American Minority Peoples*, 581, New York, 1932.

These goals are held to *transcend class lines*, not to be bounded by them, yet the actual social organization is such that there exist class differentials in the accessibility of these *common* success-symbols. Frustration and thwarted aspiration lead to the search for avenues of escape from a culturally induced intolerable situation; or unrelieved ambition may eventuate in illicit attempts to acquire the dominant values.[18] The American stress on pecuniary success and ambitiousness for all thus invites exaggerated anxieties, hostilities, neuroses, and antisocial behavior.

This theoretical analysis may go far toward explaining the varying correlations between crime and poverty.[19] Poverty is not an isolated variable. It is one in a complex of interdependent social and cultural variables. When viewed in such a context, it represents quite different states of affairs. Poverty as such, and consequent limitation of opportunity, are not sufficient to induce a conspicuously high rate of criminal

[18] The psychical coordinates of these processes have been partly established by the experimental evidence concerning *Anspruchsniveau* and levels of performance. See Kurt Lewin, *Vorsatz, Wille und Bedurfnis*, Berlin, 1926; N. F. Hoppe, "Erfolg und Misserfolg," *Psychol. Forschung*, 1930, 14:1–63; Jerome D. Frank, "Individual Differences in Certain Aspects of the Level of Aspiration," *Amer. J. Psychol.*, 1935, 47:119–128.

[19] Standard criminology texts summarize the data in this field. Our scheme of analysis may serve to resolve some of the theoretical contradictions which P. A. Sorokin indicates. For example, "not everywhere nor always do the poor show a greater proportion of crime . . . many poorer countries have had less crime than the richer countries . . . . The [economic] improvement in the second half of the nineteenth century, and the beginning of the twentieth, has not been followed by a decrease of crime." See his *Contemporary Sociological Theories*, 560–561, New York, 1928. The crucial point is, however, that poverty has varying social significance in different social structures, as we shall see. Hence, one would not expect a linear correlation between crime and poverty.

behavior. Even the often mentioned "poverty in the midst of plenty" will not necessarily lead to this result. Only insofar as poverty and associated disadvantages in competition for the culture values approved for *all* members of the society are linked with the assimilation of a cultural emphasis on monetary accumulation as a symbol of success is antisocial conduct a "normal" outcome. Thus, poverty is less highly correlated with crime in southeastern Europe than in the United States. The possibilities of vertical mobility in these European areas would seem to be fewer than in this country, so that neither poverty *per se* nor its association with limited opportunity is sufficient to account for the varying correlations. It is only when the full configuration is considered, poverty, limited opportunity, and a commonly shared system of success symbols, that we can explain the higher association between poverty and crime in our society than in others where rigidified class structure is coupled with *differential class symbols of achievement*.

In societies such as our own, then, the pressure of prestige-bearing success tends to eliminate the effective social constraint over means employed to this end. "The-end-justifies-the-means" doctrine becomes a guiding tenet for action when the cultural structure unduly exalts the end and the social organization unduly limits possible recourse to approved means. Otherwise put, this notion and associated behavior reflect a lack of cultural coordination. In international relations, the effects of this lack of integration are notoriously apparent. An emphasis upon national power is not readily coordinated with an inept organization of legitimate, i.e., internationally defined and accepted, means for attaining this goal. The result is a tendency toward the abrogation of international law, treaties become scraps of paper, "undeclared warfare" serves as a technical evasion, the bombing of civilian populations is rationalized,[20] just as the same societal situation induces the same sway of illegitimacy among individuals.

The social order we have described necessarily produces this "strain toward dissolution." The pressure of such an order is upon outdoing one's competitors. The choice of means within the ambit of institutional control will persist as long as the sentiments supporting a competitive system, i.e., deriving from the possibility of outranking competitors and hence enjoying the favorable response of others, are distributed throughout the entire system of activities and are not confined merely to the final result. A stable social structure demands a balanced distribution of affect among its various segments. When there occurs a shift of emphasis from the satisfactions deriving from competition itself to almost exclusive concern with successful competition, the resultant stress leads to the breakdown of the regulatory structure.[21] With the resulting attenuation of the institutional imperatives, there occurs an approximation of the situation erroneously held by utilitarians to be typical of society generally wherein calculations of advantage and fear of punishment are the sole regulating agencies. In such situations, as Hobbes observed, force and fraud come to constitute the sole virtues in view of their relative efficiency in attaining goals—which were for him, of course, not culturally derived.

It should be apparent that the fore-

[20] See M. W. Royse, *Aerial Bombardment and the International Regulation of War*, New York, 1928.

[21] Since our primary concern is with the socio-cultural aspects of this problem, the psychological correlates have been only implicitly considered. See Karen Horney, *The Neurotic Personality of Our Time*, New York, 1937, for a psychological discussion of this process.

going discussion is not pitched on a moralistic plane. Whatever the sentiments of the writer or reader concerning the ethical desirability of coordinating the means-and-goals phases of the social structure, one must agree that lack of such coordination leads to anomie. Insofar as one of the most general functions of social organization is to provide a basis for calculability and regularity of behavior, it is increasingly limited in effectiveness as these elements of the structure become dissociated. At the extreme, predictability virtually disappears and what may be properly termed cultural chaos or anomie intervenes.

This statement, being brief, is also incomplete. It has not included an exhaustive treatment of the various structural elements which predispose toward one rather than another of the alternative responses open to individuals; it has neglected, but not denied the relevance of, the factors determining the specific incidence of these responses; it has not enumerated the various concrete responses which are constituted by combinations of specific values of the analytical variables; it has omitted, or included only by implication, any consideration of the social functions performed by illicit responses; it has not tested the full explanatory power of the analytical scheme by examining a large number of group variations in the frequency of deviate and conformist behavior; it has not adequately dealt with rebellious conduct which seeks to refashion the social framework radically; it has not examined the relevance of cultural conflict for an analysis of culture-goal and institutional-means malintegration. It is suggested that these and related problems may be profitably analyzed by this scheme.

9.

The Delinquency Subculture

Albert K. Cohen

In the following pages we present a portrait of the delinquent subculture. In presenting a thumbnail description of any widely distributed subculture it is impossible to do full justice to the facts, for no brief account can deal with all the varieties and nuances which actually exist. The subcultures of the medical profession, the professional gambler or the jitterbug have many local versions, as does the delinquent subculture. Nonetheless, it is possible, for each of these subcultures, to draw a picture which represents certain themes or traits which run through all the variants. This "ideal-typical" or "full-blown" picture will be fully realized in some of the variants and only approximated, in various degrees, in others. This much, however, may be said for our description of the delinquent subculture. It is a real picture, drawn from life. It is the picture most familiar to students of juvenile delinquency, especially those who, like the group worker, encounter the delinquent gang in its natural habitat, the streets and alleys of our cities. It is the picture that stands out most prominently in the literature of juvenile delinquency. Compare it to a generalized picture of a pear, in which the distinctively pear-like features are accentuated. Many pears will look very like our picture; others will only approximate it. However, if our picture is truly drawn, it will give us a good idea of the shape which distinguishes pears in general from other fruits. This is the kind of validity which we claim for our portrait of the delinquent subculture.

THE CONTENT OF THE DELINQUENT SUBCULTURE

The common expression, "juvenile crime," has unfortunate and misleading connotations. It suggests that we have two kinds of criminals, young and old, but only one kind of crime. It suggests that crime has its meanings and its motives which are much the same for young and old; that the young differ from the old as the apprentice and the master differ at the same trade; that we distinguish the young from the old only because the young are less "set in their ways," less "confirmed" in the same criminal habits, more amenable to treatment and more deserving, because of their tender age, of special consideration.

The problem of the relationship be-

SOURCE. Albert K. Cohen, *Delinquent Boys: The Culture of the Gang*, Glencoe, Illinois: The Free Press, 1958, pp. 23–36, 121–137, 183–184, 185–186, 192, and 193. Copyright © 1955, The Free Press, a Corporation. Reprinted with the permission of The Macmillan Company.

tween juvenile delinquency and adult crime has many facets. To what extent are the offenses of children and adults distributed among the same legal categories, "burglary," "larceny," "vehicle-taking," and so forth? To what extent, even when the offenses are legally identical, do these acts have the same meaning for children and adults? To what extent are the careers of adult criminals continuations of careers of juvenile delinquency? We cannot solve these problems here, but we want to emphasize the danger of making facile and unproven assumptions. If we assume that "crime is crime," that child and adult criminals are practitioners of the same trade, and if our assumptions are false, then the road to error is wide and clear. Easily and unconsciously, we may impute a whole host of notions concerning the nature of crime and its causes, derived from our knowledge and fancies about adult crime, to a large realm of behavior to which these notions are irrelevant. It is better to make no such assumptions; it is better to look at juvenile delinquency with a fresh eye and try to explain what we see.

What we see when we look at the delinquent subculture (and we must not even assume that this describes *all juvenile* crime) is that it is *non-utilitarian, malicious* and *negativistic.*

We usually assume that when people steal things, they steal because they want them. They may want them because they can eat them, wear them or otherwise use them; or because they can sell them; or even—if we are given to a psychoanalytic turn of mind—because on some deep symbolic level they substitute or stand for something unconsciously desired but forbidden. All of these explanations have this in common, that they assume that the stealing is a means to an end, namely, the possession of some object of value, and that it is, in this sense, rational and

"utilitarian." However, the fact cannot be blinked—and this fact is of crucial importance in defining our problem—that much gang stealing has no such motivation at all. Even where the value of the object stolen is itself a motivating consideration, the stolen sweets are often sweeter than those acquired by more legitimate and prosaic means. In homelier language, stealing "for the hell of it" and apart from considerations of gain and profit is a valued activity to which attaches glory, prowess and profound satisfaction. There is no accounting in rational and utilitarian terms for the effort expended and the danger run in stealing things which are often discarded, destroyed or casually given away. A group of boys enters a store where each takes a hat, a ball or a light bulb. They then move on to another store where these things are covertly exchanged for like articles. Then they move on to other stores to continue the game indefinitely. They steal a basket of peaches, desultorily munch on a few of them and leave the rest to spoil. They steal clothes they cannot wear and toys they will not use. Unquestionably, most delinquents are from the more "needy" and "underprivileged" classes, and unquestionably many things are stolen because they are intrinsically valued. However, a humane and compassionate regard for their economic disabilities should not blind us to the fact that stealing is not merely an alternative means to the acquisition of objects otherwise difficult of attainment.[1]

[1] See H. M. Tiebout and M. E. Kirkpatrick, "Psychiatric Factors in Stealing," *American Journal of Orthopsychiatry,* 2 (April, 1932), 114–123, which discusses, in an exceptionally lucid manner, the distinction between motivating factors which center around the acquisition of the object and those which center around the commission of the act itself.

The non-utilitarian nature of juvenile delinquency has been noted by many stu-

Can we then account for this stealing by simply describing it as another form of recreation, play or sport? Surely it is that, but why is this form of play so attractive to some and so unappealing to others? Mountain climbing, chess, pinball, number pools and bingo are also different kinds of recreation. Each of us, child or adult, can choose from a host of alternative means for satisfying our common "need" for recreation. But every choice expresses a preference, and every preference reflects something about the chooser or his circumstances that endows the object of his choice with some special quality or virtue. The choice is not self-explanatory nor is it arbitrary or random. Each form of recreation is distributed in a characteristic way among the age, sex and social class sectors of our population. The ex-

planation of these distributions and of the way they change is often puzzling, sometimes fascinating and rarely platitudinous.

By the same logic, it is an imperfect answer to our problem to say: "Stealing is but another way of satisfying the universal desire for status." Nothing is more obvious from numberless case histories of subcultural delinquents that they steal to achieve recognition and to avoid isolation or opprobrium. This is an important insight and part of the foundation on which we shall build. But the question still haunts us: "Why is stealing a claim to status in one group and a degrading blot in another?"

If stealing itself is not motivated by rational, utilitarian considerations, still less are the manifold other activities which constitute the delinquent's repertoire. Throughout there is a kind of *malice* apparent, an enjoyment in the discomfiture of others, a delight in the defiance of taboos itself. Thrasher quotes one gang delinquent:

> We did all kinds of dirty tricks for fun. We'd see a sign, "Please keep the streets clean," but we'd tear it down and say: "We don't feel like keeping it clean." One day we put a can of glue in the engine of a man's car. We would always tear things down. That would make us laugh and feel good, to have so many jokes.°

The gang exhibits this gratuitous hostility toward non-gang peers as well as adults. Apart from its more dramatic manifestations in the form of gang wars, there is keen delight in terrorizing "good" children, in driving them from playgrounds and gyms for which the gang itself may have little use, and in general in making themselves obnoxious to the virtuous. The same spirit is evident in playing hookey and in misbehavior in school. The teacher and her

dents. ". . . while older offenders may have definitely crystallized beliefs about profitable returns from anti-social conduct, it is very clear that in childhood and in earlier youth delinquency is certainly not entered into as a paying proposition in any ordinary sense." William Healy and Augusta F. Bronner, *New Light on Delinquency and Its Treatment* (New Haven, Conn.: Yale University Press, 1936), p. 22. "The juvenile property offender's thefts, at least at the start are usually 'for fun' and not for gain." Paul Tappan, *Juvenile Delinquency* (New York: McGraw-Hill Book Company, 1949), p. 143. "Stealing, the leading predatory activity of the adolescent gang, is as much a result of the sport motive as of a desire for revenue." Frederic M. Thrasher. *The Gang* (Chicago: University of Chicago Press, 1936), p. 143. "In its early stages, delinquency is clearly a form of play." Henry D. McKay, "The Neighborhood and Child Conduct," *Annals of the American Academy of Political and Social Science*, 261 (January, 1949), 37. See also Barbara Bellow et al., "Prejudice in Seaside," *Human Relations*, 1 (1947), 15–16 and Sophia M. Robison et al., "An Unsolved Problem in Group Relations," *Journal of Educational Psychology*, 20 (November, 1946), 154–162. The last cited paper is an excellent description of the non-utilitarian, malicious and negativistic quality of the delinquent subculture and is the clearest statement in the literature that a satisfactory theory of delinquency must make sense of these facts.

° Frederic M. Thrasher, *The Gang* (Chicago: University of Chicago Press, 1936), pp. 94–95.

rules are not merely something onerous to be evaded. They are to be *flouted*. There is an element of active spite and malice, contempt and ridicule, challenge and defiance, exquisitely symbolized, in an incident, described to the writer by Mr. Henry D. McKay, of defecating on the teacher's desk.[2]

All this suggests also the intention of our term "negativistic." The delinquent subculture is not only a set of rules, a design for living which is different from or indifferent to or even in conflict with the norms of the "respectable" adult society. It would appear at least plausible that it is defined by its "negative polarity" to those norms. That is, the delinquent subculture takes its norms from the larger culture but turns them upside down. The delinquent's conduct is right, by the standards of his subculture, precisely *because* it is wrong by the norms of the larger culture.[3]

[2] To justify the characterization of the delinquent subculture as "malicious" by multiplying citations from authorities would be empty pedantry. The malice is evident in any detailed description of juvenile gang life. We commend in particular, however, the cited works of Thrasher, Shaw and McKay and Robison et al. One aspect of this "gratuitous hostility" deserves special mention, however, for the benefit of those who see in the provision of facilities for "wholesome recreation" some magical therapeutic virtue. "On entering a playground or a gym the first activity of gang members is to disrupt and interrupt whatever activities are going on. Nongang members flee, and when the coast is clear the gang plays desultorily on the apparatus or carries on horseplay." Sophia Robison et al., *op. cit.*, p. 159. See, to the same effect, the excellent little book by Kenneth H. Rogers, *Street Gangs in Toronto* (Toronto: The Ryerson Press, 1945), pp. 18–19.

[3] Clifford R. Shaw and Henry D. McKay, in their *Social Factors in Juvenile Delinquency*, Vol. 2 of National Commission on Law Observance and Enforcement, *Report on the Causes of Crime* (Washington: U. S. Government Printing Office, 1931), p. 241, come very close to making this point quite explicitly: "In fact the standards of these groups may represent a complete reversal of the standards and norms of conventional society. Types of

"Malicious" and "negativistic" are foreign to the delinquent's vocabulary, but he will often assure us, sometimes ruefully, sometimes with a touch of glee or even pride, that he is "just plain mean."

In describing what might be called the "spirit" of the delinquent culture, we have suggested also its *versatility*. Of the "antisocial" activities of the delinquent gangs, stealing, of course, looms largest. Stealing itself can be, and for the gang usually is, a diversified occupation. It may steal milk bottles, candy, fruit, pencils, sports equipment and cars; it may steal from drunks, homes, stores, schools and filling stations. No gang runs the whole gamut but neither is it likely to "specialize" as do many adult criminal gangs and "solitary" delinquents. More to our point, however, is the fact that stealing tends to go hand-in-hand with "other property offenses," "malicious mischief," "vandalism," "trespass" and "truancy." This quality of versatility and the fusion of versatility and malice are manifest in the following quotation:

We would get some milk bottles in front of the grocery store and break them in somebody's hallway. Then we would break windows or get some garbage cans and throw them down someone's front stairs. After doing all this dirty work and running through alleys and yards, we'd go over to a grocery store. There, some of the boys would hide in a hallway while I would get a basket of grapes. When the man came after me, why the boys would jump out of their places and each grab a basket of grapes.[*]

Dozens of young offenders, after relating to the writer this delinquent episode and that, have summarized: "I guess

conduct which result in personal degradation and dishonor in a conventional group, serve to enhance and elevate the personal prestige and status of a member of the delinquent group."
[*] Clifford R. Shaw and Henry D. McKay, *Social Factors in Juvenile Delinquency, op. cit.*, p. 18.

we was just ornery." A generalized, diversified, protean "orneriness," not this or that specialized delinquent pursuit, seems best to describe the vocation of the delinquent gang.[4]

Another characteristic of the subculture of the delinquent gang is *short-run hedonism*. There is little interest in long-run goals, in planning activities and budgeting time, or in activities involving knowledge and skills to be acquired only through practice, deliberation and study. The members of the gang typically congregate, with no specific activity in mind, at some street corner, candy store or other regular rendezvous. They "hang around," "rough-housing," "chewing the fat" and "waiting for something to turn up." They may respond impulsively to somebody's suggestion to play ball, go swimming, engage in some sort of mischief or do something else that offers excitement. They do not take kindly to organized and supervised recreation, which subjects them to a regime of schedules and impersonal rules. They are impatient, impetuous and out for "fun," with little heed to the remoter gains and costs. It is to be noted that this short-run hedonism is not inherently delinquent, and indeed it would be a serious error to think of the delinquent gang as dedicated solely to the cultivation of juvenile crime. Even in the most seriously delinquent gang only a small fraction of the "fun" is specifically and intrinsically delinquent. Furthermore, short-run hedonism is not characteristic of delinquent groups alone. On the contrary, it is common throughout the social class from which delinquents characteristically come. However, in the delinquent gang it reaches its finest flower. It is the fabric, as it were, of

which delinquency is the most brilliant and spectacular thread.[5]

Another characteristic not peculiar to the delinquent gang but a conspicuous ingredient of its culture is an emphasis on *group autonomy,* or intolerance of restraint except from the informal pressures within the group itself. Relations with gang members tend to be intensely solidary and imperious. Relations with other groups tend to be indifferent, hostile or rebellious. Gang members are unusually resistant to the efforts of home, school and other agencies to regulate, not only their delinquent activities, but any activities carried on within the group, and to efforts to compete with the gang for the time and other resources of its members. It may be argued that the resistance of gang members to the authority of the home may not be a result of their membership in gangs but that membership in gangs, on the contrary, is a result of ineffective family supervision, the breakdown of parental authority and the hostility of the child toward the parents; in short, that the delinquent gang recruits members who have already achieved autonomy. Certainly a previous breakdown in family controls facilitates recruitment into delinquent

---

[4] *Federal Probation,* 18 (March, 1954), 3–16 contains an extremely valuable symposium on vandalism, which highlights all of the characteristics we have imputed to the delinquent subculture. . . .

[5] See the splendid report on "Working with a Street Gang" in Sylvan S. Furman (ed.), *Reaching the Unreached* (New York: New York City Youth Board, 1952), pp. 112–121. On this quality of short-run hedonism we quote, p. 13:

One boy once told me, "Now, for example, you take an average day. What happens? We come down to the restaurant and we sit in the restaurant, and sit and sit. All right, say, er . . . after a couple of hours in the restaurant, maybe we'll go to a poolroom, shoot a little pool, that's if somebody's got the money. O. K., a little pool, come back. By this time the restaurant is closed. We go in the candy store, sit around the candy store for a while, and that's it, that's all we do, man."

See also Barbara Bellow et al., *op. cit.,* pp. 4–15, and Ruth Topping, "Treatment of the Pseudo-Social Boy," *American Journal of Orthopsychiatry,* Vol. 13 (April, 1943), pp. 353–360.

gangs. But we are not speaking of the autonomy, the emancipation of *individuals*. It is not the individual delinquent but the gang that is autonomous. For many of our subcultural delinquents the claims of the home are very real and very compelling. The point is that the gang is a separate, distinct and often irresistible focus of attraction, loyalty and solidarity. The claims of the home versus the claims of the gang may present a real dilemma, and in such cases the breakdown of family controls is as much a casualty as a cause of gang membership.[6]

SOME ATTEMPTS AT EXPLANATION

The literature on juvenile delinquency has seldom come to grips with the problem of accounting for the content and spirit of the delinquent subculture. To say that this content is "traditional" in certain areas and is "handed down" from generation to generation is but to state the problem rather than to offer a solution. Neither does the "social disorganization" theory[7] come to grips with the facts. This theory holds that the delinquent culture flourishes in the "interstitial areas" of our great cities. These are formerly "good" residential areas which have been invaded by industry and commerce, are no longer residentially attractive, and are inhabited by a heterogeneous, economically depressed and highly mobile population with no permanent stake in the community. These people lack the solidarity, the community spirit, the motivation and the residential stability necessary for organization, on a neighborhood basis,

for the effective control of delinquency. To this argument we may make two answers. First, recent research has revealed that many, if not most, such "interstitial" and "slum" areas are by no means lacking in social organization. To the observer who has lived in them, many such areas are anything but the picture of chaos and heterogeneity which we find drawn in the older literature. We find, on the contrary, a vast and ramifying network of informal associations among like-minded people, not a horde of anonymous families and individuals, strangers to one another, rudely jostling one another in the struggle for existence. The social organization of the slum may lack the spirit and the objectives of organization in the "better" neighborhoods, but the slum is not necessarily a jungle. In the "delinquency area" as elsewhere, there is an awareness of community, an involvement of the individual in the lives and doings of the neighborhood, a concern about his reputation among his neighbors. The organization which exists may indeed not be adequate for the effective control of delinquency and for the solution of other social problems, but the qualities and defects of organization are not to be confused with the absence of organization.[8] However, granting the absence of community pressures and concerted action for the repression of delinquency, we are confronted by a second deficiency in this argument. It is wholly negative. It accounts for the presence of delinquency by the absence of effective constraints. If one is disposed to be delinquent, the absence of constraint will facilitate the expression of these impulses. It will not, however, account for the presence of these impulses. The social disorganization argument leaves

---

[6] The solidarity of the gang and the dependence of its members upon one another are especially well described in Barbara Bellow et al., *op. cit.*, p. 16 and Sophia Robison et al., *op. cit.*, p. 158.

[7] See Clifford R. Shaw and Henry D. McKay, *Social Factors in Juvenile Delinquency, op. cit.*, p. 111.

[8] See William Foote Whyte, "Social Organization in the Slums," *American Sociological Review*, 8 (February, 1943), 34–39.

open the question of the origin of the impulse, of the peculiar content and spirit of the delinquent subculture.

Another theory which has enjoyed some vogue is the "culture conflict" theory.[9] According to this view, these areas of high mobility and motley composition are lacking in cultural unity. The diverse ethnic and racial stocks have diverse and incongruent standards and codes, and these standards and codes are in turn inconsistent with those of the schools and other official representatives of the larger society. In this welter of conflicting cultures, the young person is confused and bedeviled. The adult world presents him with no clear-cut and authoritative models. Subject to a multitude of conflicting patterns, he respects none and assimilates none. He develops no respect for the legal order because it represents a culture which finds no support in his social world. He becomes delinquent.

From the recognition that there exists a certain measure of cultural diversity, it is a large step to the conclusion that the boy is confronted by such a hodgepodge of definitions that he can form no clear conception of what is "right" and "wrong." It is true that some ethnic groups look more tolerantly on certain kinds of delinquency than others do; that some even encourage certain minor forms of delinquency such as picking up coal off railroad tracks; that respect for the courts and the police are less well established among some groups and that other cultural differences exist. Nonetheless, it is questionable that there is any ethnic or racial group which positively encourages or even condones stealing, vandalism, habitual truancy and the general negativism which characterizes the delinquent subculture. The existence of culture conflict must not be

allowed to obscure the important measure of consensus which exists on the essential "wrongness" of these activities, except under special circumstances which are considered mitigating by this or that ethnic subculture. Furthermore, if we should grant that conflicting definitions leave important sectors of conduct morally undefined for the boy in the delinquency area, we must still explain why he fills the gap in the particular way he does. Like the social disorganization theory, the culture conflict theory is at best incomplete. The delinquent subculture is not a fund of blind, amoral, "natural" impulses which inevitably well up in the absence of a code of socially acquired inhibitions. It is itself a positive code with a definite if unconventional moral flavor, and it demands a positive explanation in its own right.

Another view which currently commands a good deal of respect we may call the "illicit means" theory.[10] According to this view our American culture, with its strongly democratic and equalitarian emphasis, indoctrinates all social classes impartially with a desire for high social status and a sense of ignominy attaching to low social status. The symbols of high status are to an extraordinary degree the possession and the conspicuous display of economic goods. There is therefore an unusually intense desire for economic goods diffused throughout our population to a degree unprecedented in other societies. However, the means and the opportunities for the legitimate achieve-

---

[9] See Clifford R. Shaw and Henry D. McKay, *Social Factors in Juvenile Delinquency, op. cit.*, p. 115.

[10] See Clifford R. Shaw and Henry D. McKay, *Juvenile Delinquency and Urban Areas: A Study of Rates of Delinquents in Relation to Differential Characteristics of Local Communities in American Cities* (Chicago: University of Chicago Press, 1942), pp. 180–181. Henry D. McKay, *op. cit.*, p. 35, and Robert K. Merton, "Social Structure and Anomie," *American Sociological Review*, 3 (October, 1938) 672–682.

ment of these goals are distributed most unequally among the various segments of the population. Among those segments which have the least access to the legitimate channels of "upward mobility" there develop strong feelings of deprivation and frustration and strong incentives to find other means to the achievement of status and its symbols. Unable to attain their goals by lawful means, these disadvantaged segments of the population are under strong pressure to resort to crime, the only means available to them.

This argument is sociologically sophisticated and highly plausible as an explanation for adult professional crime and for the property delinquency of some older and semi-professional juvenile thieves. Unfortunately, it fails to account for the non-utilitarian quality of the subculture which we have described. Were the participant in the delinquent subculture merely employing illicit means to the end of acquiring economic goods, he would show more respect for the goods he has thus acquired. Furthermore, the destructiveness, the versatility, the zest and the wholesale negativism which characterizes the delinquent subculture are beyond the purview of this theory. None of the theories we have considered comes to grips with the data: the distinctive content of the delinquent subculture. . . .

WHAT THE DELINQUENT SUBCULTURE HAS TO OFFER

The delinquent subculture, we suggest, is a way of dealing with the problems of adjustment we have described. These problems are chiefly status problems: certain children are denied status in the respectable society because they cannot meet the criteria of the respectable status system. The delinquent subculture deals with these problems by providing criteria of status which these children *can* meet.

This statement is highly elliptical and is based upon a number of assumptions whose truth is by no means self-evident. It is not, for example, self-evident that people whose status positions are low must necessarily feel deprived, injured or ego-involved in that low status. Whether they will or not depends upon several considerations.

Our ego-involvement in a given comparison with others depends upon our "status universe." "Whom do we measure ourselves against?" is the crucial question. In some other societies virtue may consist in willing acceptance of the role of peasant, low-born commoner or member of an inferior caste and in conformity to the expectations of that role. If others are richer, more nobly born or more able than oneself, it is by the will of an inscrutable Providence and not to be imputed to one's own moral defect. The sting of status inferiority is thereby removed or mitigated; one measures himself only against those of like social position. We have suggested, however, that an important feature of American "democracy," perhaps of the Western European tradition in general, is the tendency to measure oneself against "all comers." This means that, for children as for adults, one's sense of personal worth is at stake in status comparisons with all other persons, at least of one's own age and sex, whatever their family background or material circumstances. It means that, in the lower levels of our status hierarchies, whether adult or juvenile, there is a chronic fund of motivation, conscious or repressed, to elevate one's status position, either by striving to climb within the established status system or by redefining the criteria of status so that one's present attributes become status-giving assets. It has been suggested, for example, that such typically working-class forms of Protestantism as the Holiness sects owe their appeal to the fact that they reverse the respectable status system; it is the humble, the simple and the dispossessed who sit at the right hand of God, whereas worldly goods, power and knowledge are as nothing in His eyes. In like manner, we offer the view that the delinquent subculture is one solution to a kindred problem on the juvenile level.

Another consideration affecting the degree of privation experienced in a given status position is the "status source." A person's status, after all, is how he stands in somebody's eyes. Status, then, is not a fixed property of the person but varies with the point of view of whoever is doing the judging. I may be revered by some and despised by others. A crucial question then becomes: "Whose respect or admiration do I value?" That *you* think well or ill of me may or may not *matter* to me.

It may be argued that the working-class boy does not *care* what middle-class people think of him, that he is ego-involved only in the opinions of his family, his friends, his working-class neighbors. A definitive answer to this argument can come only from research designed to get at the facts. This research, in our opinion, is yet to be done. There is, however, reason to believe that most children are sensitive *to some degree* about the attitudes of *any persons* with whom they are thrown into more than the most superficial kind of contact. The contempt or indifference of others, particularly of those like schoolmates and teachers, with whom we are constrained to associate for long hours every day, is difficult, we suggest, to shrug off. It poses a problem with which a person may conceivably attempt to cope in a variety of ways. He

may make an active effort to change himself in conformity with the expectations of others; he may attempt to justify or explain away his inferiority in terms which will exculpate him; he may tell himself that he really doesn't care what these people think; he may react with anger and aggression. But the least probable response is simple, uncomplicated, honest indifference. If we grant the probable truth of the claim that most American working-class children are most sensitive to status sources on their own level, it does not follow that they take lightly rejection, disparagement and censure from other status sources.

Even on their "own" social level, the situation is far from simple. The "working-class," we have repeatedly emphasized, is not culturally homogeneous. Not only is there much diversity in the cultural standards applied by one's own working-class neighbors and kin, so that it is difficult to find a "working-class" milieu in which "middle-class" standards are not important. In addition, the "working-class" culture we have described is, after all, an ideal type; most working-class *people* are culturally ambivalent. Due to lack of capacity, of the requisite "character structure" or of "luck," they may be working class in terms of job and income; they may have accepted this status with resignation and rationalized it to their satisfaction; and by example, by class-linked techniques of child training and by failure to support the middle-class agencies of socialization they may have produced children deficient in the attributes that make for status in middle-class terms. Nevertheless, all their lives, through all the major media of mass indoctrination—the schools, the movies, the radio, the newspapers and the magazines—the middle-class powers-that-be that manipulate these media have been trying to "sell" them on middle-class values and the middle-class standard of living. Then there is the "propaganda of the deed," the fact that they have seen with their own eyes working-class contemporaries "get ahead" and "make the grade" in a middle-class world. In consequence of all this, we suspect that few working-class parents unequivocally repudiate as intrinsically worthless middle-class objectives. There is good reason to believe that the modesty of working-class aspirations is partly a matter of trimming one's sails to the available opportunities and resources and partly a matter of unwillingness to accept the discipline which upward striving entails.

However complete and successful a person's accommodation to an humble status, the vitality of middle-class goals, of the "American dream," is nonetheless likely to manifest itself in his aspirations for his children. His expectations may not be grandiose, but he will want his children to be "better off" than he. Whatever his own work history and social reputation may be, he will want his children to be "steady" and "respectable." He may exert few positive pressures to "succeed," and the experiences he provides his children may even incapacitate them for success; he may be puzzled at the way they "turn out." But whatever the measure of his own responsibility in accounting for the product, he is not likely to judge that product by unadulterated "corner-boy" standards. Even "corner-boy" parents, although they may value in their children such corner-boy virtues as generosity to friends, personal loyalty and physical prowess, are likely also to be gratified by recognition by middle-class representatives and by the kinds of achievement for which the college-boy way of life is a prerequisite. Even in

the working-class milieu from which he acquired his incapacity for middle-class achievement, the working-class corner-boy may find himself at a status disadvantage as against his more upwardly mobile peers.

Lastly, of course, is that most ubiquitous and inescapable of status sources, oneself. Technically, we do not call the person's attitudes towards himself "status" but rather "self-esteem," or, when the quality of the self-attitude is specifically moral, "conscience" or "superego." The important question for us is this: To what extent, if at all, do boys who are typically "working-class" and "corner-boy" in their overt behavior evaluate themselves by "middle-class," "college-boy" standards? For our overt behavior, however closely it conforms to one set of norms, need not argue against the existence or effectiveness of alternative and conflicting norms. The failure of our own behavior to conform to our own expectations is an elementary and commonplace fact which gives rise to the tremendously important consequences of guilt, self-recrimination, anxiety and self-hatred. The reasons for the failure of self-expectations and overt conduct to agree are complex. One reason is that we often internalize more than one set of norms, each of which would dictate a different course of action in a given life-situation; since we can only *do* one thing at a time, however, we are forced to choose between them or somehow to compromise. In either case, we fall short of the full realization of our own expectations and must somehow cope with the residual discrepancy between those expectations and our overt behavior.

We have suggested that corner-boy children (like their working-class parents) internalize middle-class standards to a sufficient degree to create a fundamental ambivalence towards their own corner-boy behavior. Again, we are on somewhat speculative ground where fundamental research remains to be done. The coexistence within the same personality of a corner-boy and a college-boy morality may appear more plausible, however, if we recognize that they are not simple antitheses of one another and that parents and others may in all sincerity attempt to indoctrinate both. For example, the goals upon which the college-boy places such great value, such as intellectual and occupational achievement, and the college-boy virtues of ambitiousness and pride in self-sufficiency are not as such disparaged by the corner-boy culture. The meritoriousness of standing by one's friends and the desire to have a good time here and now do not by definition preclude the desire to help oneself and to provide for the future. It is no doubt the rule, rather than the exception, that most children, college-boy and corner-boy alike, would like to enjoy the best of both worlds. *In practice,* however, the substance that is consumed in the pursuit of one set of values is not available for the pursuit of the other. The sharpness of the dilemma and the degree of the residual discontent depend upon a number of things, notably, the intensity with which both sets of norms have been internalized, the extent to which the life-situations which one encounters compel a choice between them, and the abundance and appropriateness of the skills and resources at one's disposal. The child of superior intelligence, for example, may find it easier than his less gifted peers to meet the demands of the college-boy standards without failing his obligations to his corner-boy associates.

It is a plausible assumption, then, that the working-class boy whose status is low in middle-class terms *cares* about that status, that this status confronts him with a genuine problem of adjustment. To this problem of adjustment there are a variety of conceivable responses, of which participation in the creation and the maintenance of the delinquent subculture is one. Each mode of response entails costs and yields gratifications of its own. The circumstances which tip the balance in favor of the one or the other are obscure. One mode of response is to desert the corner-boy for the college-boy way of life. To the reader of Whyte's *Street Corner Society* the costs are manifest. It is hard, at best, to be a college-boy and to run with the corner-boys. It entails great effort and sacrifice to the degree that one has been indoctrinated in what we have described as the working-class socialization process; its rewards are frequently long-deferred; and for many working-class boys it makes demands which they are, in consequence of their inferior linguistic, academic and "social" skills, not likely ever to meet. Nevertheless, a certain proportion of working-class boys accept the challenge of the middle-class status system and play the status game by the middle-class rules.

Another response, perhaps the most common, is what we may call the "stable corner-boy response." It represents an acceptance of the corner-boy way of life and an effort to make the best of a situation. If our reasoning is correct, it does not resolve the dilemmas we have described as inherent in the corner-boy position in a largely middle-class world, although these dilemmas may be mitigated by an effort to disengage oneself from dependence upon middle-class status-sources and by withdrawing, as far as possible, into a sheltering community of like-minded working-class children. Unlike the delinquent response, it avoids the radical rupture of good relations with even working-class adults and does not represent as irretrievable a renunciation of upward mobility. It does not incur the active hostility of middle-class persons and therefore leaves the way open to the pursuit of some values, such as jobs, which these people control. It represents a preference for the familiar, with its known satisfactions and its known imperfections, over the risks and uncertainties as well as the moral costs of the college-boy response, on the one hand, and the delinquent response on the other.

What does the delinquent response have to offer? Let us be clear, first, about what this response is and how it differs from the stable corner-boy response. The hallmark of the delinquent subculture is the explicit and wholesale repudiation of middle-class standards and the adoption of their very antithesis. *The corner-boy culture is not specifically delinquent.* Where it leads to behavior which may be defined as delinquent, e.g., truancy, it does so not because nonconformity to middle-class norms *defines* conformity to corner-boy norms but because conformity to middle-class norms *interferes with* conformity to corner-boy norms. The corner-boy plays truant because he does not like school, because he wishes to escape from a dull and unrewarding and perhaps humiliating situation. But truancy is not defined as intrinsically valuable and status-giving. The member of the delinquent subculture plays truant because "good" middle-class (and working-class) children do not play truant. Corner-boy resistance to being herded and marshalled by middle-class figures is not the same as the delinquent's flouting and jeering of those middle-class figures and active ridicule of those who submit. The corner-boy's ethic of reciprocity, his quasi-communal attitude toward the property of in-group members, is shared by the delinquent.

But this ethic of reciprocity does not sanction the deliberate and "malicious" violation of the property rights of persons outside the in-group. We have observed that the differences between the corner-boy and the college-boy or middle-class culture are profound but that in many ways they are profound differences in emphasis. We have remarked that the corner-boy culture does not so much repudiate the value of many middle-class achievements as it emphasizes certain other values which make such achievements improbable. In short, the corner-boy culture temporizes with middle-class morality; the full-fledged delinquent subculture does not.

It is precisely here, we suggest, in the refusal to temporize, that the appeal of the delinquent subculture lies. Let us recall that it is characteristically American, not specifically working-class or middle-class, to measure oneself against the widest possible status universe, to seek status against "all comers," to be "as good as" or "better than" anybody—anybody, that is, within one's own age and sex category. As long as the working-class corner-boy clings to a version, however attenuated and adulterated, of the middle-class culture, he must recognize his inferiority to working-class and middle-class college-boys. The delinquent subculture, on the other hand, permits no ambiguity of the status of the delinquent relative to that of anybody else. In terms of the norms of the delinquent subculture, defined by its negative polarity to the respectable status system, the delinquent's very nonconformity to middle-class standards sets him above the most exemplary college boy.

Another important function of the delinquent subculture is the legitimation of aggression. We surmise that a certain amount of hostility is generated among working-class children against middle-class persons, with their airs of superiority, disdain or condescension and against middle-class norms, which are, in a sense, the cause of their status-frustration. To infer inclinations to aggression from the existence of frustration is hazardous; we know that aggression is not an inevitable and not the only consequence of frustration. So here too we must feel our way with caution. Ideally, we should like to see systematic research, probably employing "depth interview" and "projective" techniques, to get at the relationship between status position and aggressive dispositions toward the rules which determine status and toward persons variously distributed in the status hierarchy. Nevertheless, despite our imperfect knowledge of these things, we would be blind if we failed to recognize that bitterness, hostility and jealousy and all sorts of retributive fantasies are among the most common and typically human responses to public humiliation. However, for the child who temporizes with middle-class morality, overt aggression and even the conscious recognition of his own hostile impulses are inhibited, for he acknowledges the *legitimacy* of the rules in terms of which he is stigmatized. For the child who breaks clean with middle-class morality, on the other hand, there are no moral inhibitions on the free expression of aggression against the sources of his frustration. Moreover, the connection we suggest between status-frustration and the aggressiveness of the delinquent subculture seems to us more plausible than many frustration-aggression hypotheses because it involves no assumptions about obscure and dubious "displacement" of aggression against "substitute" targets. The target in this case is the manifest cause of the status problem.

It seems to us that the mechanism of "reaction-formation" should also play a part here. We have made much of the corner-boy's basic ambivalence, his uneasy acknowledgement, while he lives by the standards of his corner-boy culture, of the legitimacy of college-boy standards. May we assume that when the delinquent seeks to obtain unequivocal status by repudiating, once and for all, the norms of the college-boy culture, these norms really undergo total extinction? Or do they, perhaps, linger on, underground, as it were, repressed, unacknowledged but an ever-present threat to the adjustment which has been achieved at no small cost? There is much evidence from clinical psychology that moral norms, once effectively internalized, are not lightly thrust aside or extinguished. If a new moral order is evolved which offers a more satisfactory solution to one's life problems, the old order usually continues to press for recognition, but if this recognition is granted, the applecart is upset. The symptom of this obscurely felt, ever-present threat is clinically known as "anxiety," and the literature of psychiatry is rich with devices for combatting this anxiety, this threat to a hard-won victory. One such device is reaction-formation. Its hallmark is an "exaggerated," "disproportionate," "abnormal" intensity of response, "inappropriate" to the stimulus which seems to elicit it. The unintelligibility of the response, the "over-reaction," becomes intelligible when we see that it has the function of reassuring the actor against an *inner* threat to his defenses as well as the function of meeting an external situation on its own terms. Thus we have the mother who "compulsively" showers "inordinate" affection upon a child to reassure herself against her latent hostility and we have the male adolescent whose awkward and immoderate masculinity reflects a basic insecurity about his own sex-role. In like manner, we would expect the delinquent boy who, after all, has been socialized in a soci-

ety dominated by a middle-class morality and who can never quite escape the
blandishments of middle-class society,
to seek to maintain his safeguards
against seduction. Reaction-formation,
in his case, should take the form of an
"irrational," "malicious," "unaccountable" hostility to the enemy within the
gates as well as without: the norms of
the respectable middle-class society.[11]

[11] No single strand of our argument concerning the motivation of the delinquent
subculture is entirely original. All have
been at least adumbrated and some quite
trenchantly formulated by others.
   The idea that aggressive behavior, including crime and delinquency, are often
reactions to difficulties in achieving status
in legitimate status systems has been remarked by many, although the systematic
linkage between the particular status problems we have described and social class
position has not been well developed in
the literature. Caroline B. Zachry, for example, in *Emotion and Conduct in Adolescence* (New York: D. Appleton-Century
Company, 1940), pp. 187, 200–209, 245–
246, has a thoughtful discussion of the
ego-damage resulting from inability to
compete effectively in school and of the
function of aggressive behavior in maintaining self-esteem. Arthur L. Wood, in Social Disorganization and Crime," *Encyclopedia of Criminology* (New York: Philosophical Library, 1949), pp. 466–471,
states that the highest crime rates tend
to occur in those minority culture groups
"which have become acculturated to the
majority-group patterns of behavior, but
due to hostility toward them they have
failed to succeed in competition for social
status." Robert B. Zajonc, in "Aggressive
Attitudes of the 'Stranger' as a Function
of Conformity Pressures," *Human Relations*, 5 (1952), 205–216, has experimentally tested the general hypothesis, although
not in connection with delinquency or
crime, that a "need to conform" with a
pattern of behavior coupled with inability
to conform successfully generates hostile
attitudes towards that pattern.
   The general notion of negativism as an
ego-salving type of reaction-formation,
which plays such an important part in
the theory we have outlined, is common in
the psychoanalytical literature. It has been
brilliantly developed with specific reference to criminality in a paper by George
Devereux, "Social Negativism and Criminal Psychopathology," *Journal of Criminal
Psychopathology*, 1 (April, 1940), 322–338
and applied to other behavior problems in

If our reasoning is correct, it should
throw some light upon the peculiar
quality of "property delinquency" in
the delinquent subculture. We have already seen how the rewardingness of a
college-boy and middle-class way of
life depends, to a great extent, upon
general respect for property rights. In
an urban society, in particular, the possession and display of property are the
most ready and public badges of reputable social-class status and are, for that
reason, extraordinarily ego-involved.
That property actually is a reward for
middle-class morality is in part only a
plausible fiction, but in general there
is certainly a relationship between the
practice of that morality and the possession of property. The middle-classes
have, then, a strong interest in scrupu-
lous regard for property rights, not only
because property is "intrinsically" valuable but because the full enjoyment of
their status requires that that status be
readily recognizable and therefore that
property adhere to those who earn it.
The cavalier misappropriation or destruction of property, therefore, is not
only a diversion or diminution of
wealth; it is an attack on the middle-
class where their egos are most vulnerable. Group stealing, institutionalized
in the delinquent subculture, is not just
a way of *getting* something. It is a
means that is the antithesis of sober
and diligent "labour in a calling." It
expresses contempt for a way of life by
making its opposite a criterion of status.
Money and other valuables are not, as
such, despised by the delinquent. For
the delinquent and the non-delinquent
alike, money is a most glamorous and
efficient means to a variety of ends and
one cannot have too much of it. But, in
the delinquent subculture, the stolen

George Devereux and Malcolm E. Moos,
"The Social Structure of Prisons, and the
Organic Tensions," *Journal of Criminal
Psychopathology*, 4 (October, 1942), 306–
324.

dollar has an odor of sanctity that does not attach to the dollar saved or the dollar earned.

This delinquent system of values and way of life does its job of problem-solving most effectively when it is adopted as a group solution. The efficacy of a given change in values as a solution and therefore the motivation to such a change depends heavily upon the availability of "reference groups" within which the "deviant values" are already institutionalized, or whose members would stand to profit from such a system of deviant values if each were assured of the support and concurrence of the others. So it is with delinquency. We do not suggest that joining in the creation or perpetuation of a delinquent subculture is the only road to delinquency. We do believe, however, that for most delinquents delinquency would not be available as a response were it not socially legitimized and given a kind of respectability, albeit by a restricted community of fellow-adventurers. In this respect, the adoption of delinquency is like the adoption of the practice of appearing at the office in open-collar and shirt sleeves. Is it much more comfortable, is it more sensible than the full regalia? Is it neat? Is it dignified? The arguments in the affirmative will appear much more forceful if the practice is already established in one's milieu or if one senses that others are prepared to go along if someone makes the first tentative gestures. Indeed, to many of those who sweat and chafe in ties and jackets, the possibility of an alternative may not even occur until they discover that it has been adopted by their colleagues.

This way of looking at delinquency suggests an answer to a certain paradox. Countless mothers have protested that their "Johnny" was a good boy until he fell in with a certain bunch. But the mothers of Johnny's companions hold the same view with respect to their own offspring. It is conceivable and even probable that some of these mothers are naive, that one or more of these youngsters are "rotten apples" who infected the others. We suggest, however, that all of the mothers may be right, that there is a certain chemistry in the group situation itself which engenders that which was not there before, that group interaction is a sort of catalyst which releases potentialities not otherwise visible. This is especially true when we are dealing with a problem of status-frustration. Status, by definition, is a grant of respect from others. A new system of norms, which measures status by criteria which one can meet, is of no value unless others are prepared to apply those criteria, and others are not likely to do so unless one is prepared to reciprocate.[12]

We have referred to a lingering ambivalence in the delinquent's own value system, an ambivalence which threatens the adjustment he has achieved and which is met through the mechanism of reaction-formation. The delin-

[12] The distinguished criminologist, Sutherland, apparently had this in mind when he wrote: "It is not necessary that there be bad boys inducing good boys to commit offenses. It is generally a mutual stimulation, as a result of which each of the boys commits delinquencies which he would not commit alone." Edwin H. Sutherland, *Principles of Criminology* (Philadelphia: J. B. Lippincott Company, 1947), p. 145. Having made the point, however, Sutherland failed to develop its implications, and in his general theory of criminal behavior the function of the group or the gang is not collectively to *contrive* delinquency but merely to *transmit* the delinquent tradition and to provide protection to the members of the group. Fritz Redl, on the other hand, in "The Psychology of Gang Formation and the Treatment of Juvenile Delinquents," *The Psychoanalytic Study of the Child*, Vol. 1 (New York: International Universities Press, 1945), pp. 367–377, has developed at considerable length the ways in which the group makes possible for its members behavior which would otherwise not be available to them.

quent may have to contend with another ambivalence, in the area of his status sources. The delinquent subculture offers him status *as against* other children of whatever social level, but it offers him this status *in the eyes of* his fellow delinquents only. To the extent that there remains a desire for recognition from groups whose respect has been forfeited by commitment to a new subculture, his satisfaction in his solution is imperfect and adulterated. He can perfect his solution only by rejecting as status sources those who reject him. This too may require a certain measure of reaction-formation, going beyond indifference to active hostility and contempt for all those who do not share his subculture. He becomes all the more dependent upon his delinquent gang. Outside that gang his status position is now weaker than ever. The gang itself tends toward a kind of sectarian solidarity, because the benefits of membership can only be realized in active face-to-face relationships with group members.

This interpretation of the delinquent subculture has important implications for the "sociology of social problems." People are prone to assume that those things which we define as evil and those which we define as good have their origins in separate and distinct features of our society. Evil flows from poisoned wells; good flows from pure and crystal fountains. The same source cannot feed both. Our view is different. It holds that those values which are at the core of "the American way of life," which help to motivate the behavior which we most esteem as "typically American," are among the major determinants of that which we stigmatize as "pathological." More specifically, it holds that the problems of adjustment to which the delinquent subculture is a response are determined, in part, by those very values which respectable society holds most sacred. The same value system, impinging upon children differently equipped to meet it, is instrumental in generating both delinquency and respectability.

10.

Delinquent Boys: A Critique

John I. Kitsuse and David C. Dietrick

One of the most provocative theoretical formulations concerning juvenile delinquency is that contained in Albert K. Cohen's *Delinquent Boys: The Culture of the Gang.*[1] The reviews of Cohen's monograph are enthusiastic in their praise,[2] and one textbook has already incorporated the theory of the delinquent subculture as the major framework for the discussion of juvenile delinquency.[3] Sykes and Matza, Wilensky and Lebeaux, Merton, and Kobrin and Finestone[4] have questioned various

propositions and implications of Cohen's thesis, but their discussions are limited to rather specific issues. In view of the impressive reception which has greeted Cohen's work, his theory of the delinquent subculture deserves a more detailed and systematic examination.

The primary concern of Cohen's inquiry is stated clearly and repeatedly throughout the study: the theoretical task is to explain the content and distribution of the delinquent subculture. Cohen offers his theory to fill a gap in the cultural transmission theories of delinquency which assert that individuals become delinquent because they learn the values, attitudes, and techniques of the delinquent group. The theory of the delinquent subculture attempts to account for the content of what the delinquent learns. Thus, Cohen does *not* purport to present a theory of delinquency.

° This paper has benefited from the criticism and suggestions from many sources. We wish especially to acknowledge the helpful comments of Aaron V. Cicourel, Scott Greer, and Donald R. Cressey.

[1] Glencoe, Ill.: Free Press, 1955.

[2] See reviews by Frank E. Hartung, *American Sociological Review*, 20 (December, 1955), pp. 751–752; Donnell M. Poppenfort, *American Journal of Sociology*, 62 (July, 1956), pp. 125–126; Hermann Mannheim, *British Journal of Sociology*, 7 (June, 1956), pp. 147–152; Max Benedict, *The British Journal of Delinquency*, 7 (October, 1956), pp. 323–324; Gilbert Shapiro, *Dissent*, 3 (Winter, 1956), pp. 89–92.

[3] Jessie Bernard, *Social Problems at Midcentury*, New York: Dryden, 1957, Chapter 18.

[4] See, respectively, Gresham M. Sykes and David Matza, "Techniques of Neutralization," *American Sociological Review*, 22 (December, 1957), pp. 664–670; Harold Wilensky and Charles Lebeaux, *Industrial*

Society and Social Welfare, New York: Russell Sage Foundation, 1958, Chapter 9; Robert K. Merton, *Social Theory and Social Structure*, Glencoe, Ill.: Free Press, 1957, pp. 177–179; and Solomon Kobrin and Harold Finestone, "A Proposed Framework for the Analysis of Juvenile Delinquency," presented at the meeting of the American Sociological Society, August, 1958.

SOURCE. John I. Kitsuse and David C. Dietrick, "Delinquent Boys: A Critique," from *American Sociological Review*, Volume 24, April 1959, pp. 208–215. Reprinted with the permission of the American Sociological Association and the authors.

Although Cohen is explicit about the limited and specific nature of the problem he is addressing, his theory has been interpreted and discussed as a theory of juvenile delinquency.[5] Indeed, the psychological terms in which Cohen couches his discussion and the logic of his thesis invite such an interpretation. In this paper, therefore, Cohen's thesis is critically examined both as a theory of the delinquent subculture and as a theory of delinquency. We contend that (1) Cohen does not present adequate support, either in theory or in fact, for his explanation of the delinquent subculture, (2) the methodological basis of the theory renders it inherently untestable, (3) the theory is ambiguous concerning the relation between the *emergence* of the subculture and its *maintenance*, and (4) the theory should include an explanation of the persistence of the subculture if it is to meet an adequate test. In the following section, we remain close to Cohen's statements and analyze them for their internal consistency.

THE THEORY OF THE DELINQUENT SUBCULTURE

Cohen addresses himself to the task of constructing a theory which will explain two sets of "known facts": first, the content of what he calls the "delinquent subculture," which is characterized by maliciousness, non-utilitarianism, and negativism; and, second, the concentration of that subculture among the male, working-class segment of the population.[6]

[5] See, e.g., Bernard, *op. cit.*; Marshall B. Clinard, *Sociology of Deviant Behavior*, New York: Rinehart, 1957, pp. 182–183.

[6] Cohen, *op. cit.*, pp. 36–44. It should be noted that Cohen's assertion that the *delinquent subculture* is concentrated in the working-class is based on an inference from data, not specifically classified with respect to their subcultural character, which suggest the concentration of *delinquency* in that social stratum.

The propositions in Cohen's theory may be stated briefly as follows:

1. The working-class boy faces a characteristic problem of adjustment which is qualitatively different from that of the middle-class boy.
2. The working-class boy's problem is one of "status-frustration," the basis of which is systematically generated by his early exposure to the working-class pattern of socialization.
3. The working-class boy's socialization handicaps him for achievement in the middle-class status system.
4. Nevertheless, he is thrust into this competitive system where achievement is judged by middle-class standards of behavior and performance.
5. Ill-prepared and poorly motivated, the working-class boy is frustrated in his status aspirations by the agents of middle-class society.
6. The delinquent subculture represents a "solution" to the working-class boy's problem, for it enables him to "break clean" with the middle-class morality and legitimizes hostility and aggression "without moral inhibitions on the free expression of aggression against the sources of his frustration."[7]
7. Thus, the delinquent subculture is characterized by non-utilitarian, malicious, and negativistic values as "an attack on the middle-class where their egos are most vulnerable. . . . It expresses contempt for a way of life by making its opposite a criterion of status."[8]

The Working-Class Boy's Problem

What are the logic and the evidence presented in support of Cohen's theory? He begins by noting the class differentials in the socialization experience of the child which handicap the working-class boy in his competition for status in

[7] *Ibid.*, p. 132.
[8] *Ibid.*, p. 134.

the middle-class system. For example: the working-class boy's social and cultural environment does not systematically support the middle-class ethic of ambition to get ahead; he is not socialized in techniques of discipline and hard work; his behavior is oriented to immediate satisfactions rather than to future goals. Thus, the working-class boy is not socialized to middle-class norms. "To this extent he is less likely to identify with these norms, to 'make them his own,' and to be able to conform to them easily and 'naturally.' "[9]

What then is the basis for the working-class boy's fundamental ambivalence toward the middle-class system that seeks and finds a solution in the delinquent subculture? His ambivalence, according to Cohen, is due to the fact that, in American society, children are compared with "all comers" by a single standard of performance which embodies the norms of the middle class. Neither the working-class boy nor his parents can ignore or deny the dominance of middle-class norms, for they comprise the code of "the distinguished people who symbolize and represent the local and national communities with which the children identify."[10] Confronted by the obvious dominance and prestige of middle-class values, the working-class boy is drawn to the "American Dream."

We note a persistent ambiguity in Cohen's statements. The working-class boy faces a problem of adjustment "to the degree to which he values the good opinion of middle-class persons or because he has to some degree internalized middle-class standards himself. . . ."[11] On the other hand, Cohen acknowledges, "it may be argued that the working-class boy does not *care* what middle-class people think of

him."[12] He suggests, and rightly so, that this is an empirical question. Nevertheless, Cohen proceeds to develop his thesis with the assertion that "there is, however, reason to believe that most children are sensitive *to some degree* about the attitudes of *any persons* with whom they are thrown into more than the most superficial kind of contact."[13]

Cohen's reasons for rejecting the argument that the working-class boy may not care what middle-class people think (which is crucial for his theory) are not convincing. Indeed, his statements about the working-class boy's socialization lend strong support to the contrary view.[14] If there are in fact class differences in socialization, surely they may be expected to insulate the working-class boy from the responses of middle-class people. Furthermore, it would appear that the working-class boy's problem is a minor one if it depends on "the degree to which he values middle-class persons" or if it rests upon the argument that he is "sensitive *to some degree*" about the attitudes of others. On the strength of his statements, the rejected proposition seems equally plaus-

---

[9] *Ibid.*, p. 97.
[10] *Ibid.*, p. 87.
[11] *Ibid.*, p. 119.

[12] *Ibid.*, p. 123, Cohen's emphasis.
[13] *Ibid.*, p. 123, Cohen's emphases.
[14] Thus Cohen states, "In general, the working-class person appears to be more dependent upon and 'at home' in primary groups [presumably among his own social class] and to avoid secondary, segmental relationships more than the middle-class person" (*ibid.*, p. 97). Again, "The working-class child is more often thrown upon his own or the company of an autonomous group of peers" (p. 100). He suggests further that "At the same time, it seems likely, although this aspect of differential socialization has not been so well explored, that the working-class child is more dependent emotionally and for the satisfaction of many practical needs upon his relationships to his peer groups. . . . Satisfactory emotional relationships with his peers are likely to be more important, their claims to be more imperious, and the rewards they offer to compete more effectively with parental [and we might add, teacher] expectations" (p. 101).

ible, namely, that the working-class boy is *not* oriented to status in the middle-class system. As Cohen himself suggests, "satisfactory emotional relationships with his peers are likely to be more important" for the working-class boy than for his middle-class counterpart.

The Reaction-Formation Concept

Cohen's explanation of the distinctive content of the delinquent subculture and "what it has to offer" to the working-class boy is anchored in the concept of "reaction-formation." His use of this psychological concept deserves careful examination, for reaction-formation provides the key to his explication of the non-utilitarian, malicious, and negativistic character of the delinquent subculture.

A reaction-formation is a psychological mechanism which "attempts to deny or to repress some impulses, or to defend the person against some instinctual danger. . . . the original opposite attitudes still exist in the unconscious."[15] In the context of Cohen's argument, the "impulse" is the working-class boy's desire for middle-class status which, if expressed, would only be frustrated. Therefore, the reaction-formation is instituted against it.

Is the ambivalence described by Cohen sufficient warrant for the introduction of this psychological concept? Cohen states that the reaction-formation in the case of the working-class boy who responds to the delinquent subculture "should take the form of an 'irrational,' 'malicious,' and 'unaccountable' hostility to the enemy within the gates as well as without: the norms of the respectable middle-class society." He suggests: "the unintelligibility of the response, the 'overreaction,' becomes

intelligible when we see that it has the function of reassuring the actor against an *inner* threat to his defenses as well as the function of meeting an external situation on its own terms. . . . we would expect the delinquent boy, who, after all, has been socialized in a society dominated by a middle-class morality and who can never quite escape the blandishments of middle-class society, to seek to maintain his safeguards against seduction."[16]

Clearly, Cohen's use of reaction-formation assumes that the delinquent boy is *strongly and fundamentally ambivalent* about status in the middle-class system, and that he "cares" so intensely about improving his status within the system that he is faced with a genuine problem of adjustment. Cohen's theory stands on this assumption which is, by his own admission, on "somewhat speculative ground where fundamental research remains to be done."[17]

Cohen's description of the social and cultural conditions of the working-class boy is a tenuous base from which to posit the internalization of middle-class values. A more reasonable and obvious question is: How under such conditions are such values significantly communicated to the working-class boy at all? According to Cohen, in his daily encounters with the middle-class system, the working-class boy suffers humiliation, shame, embarrassment, rejection, derision, and the like as a consequence of his family background. Similarly, in the settlement houses, recreation centers, and other welfare agencies, the working-class boy is exposed to the "critical or at best condescending surveillance of people who are 'foreigners' to his community and who appraise him in terms of values *which he does not share*. . . . To win favor of the peo-

---

[15] Otto Fenichel, *Psychoanalytic Theory of Neurosis*, New York: Norton, 1945, p. 151.

[16] Cohen, *op. cit.*, p. 133, Cohen's emphasis.

[17] *Ibid.*, p. 127.

ple in charge he must change his habits, his values, his ambitions, his speech and his associates. Even were these things possible, the game might not be worth the candle. So, having sampled what they have to offer, he turns to the street or to his 'clubhouse' in a cellar where 'facilities' are meager but human relations more satisfying."[18] In this description of the working-class boy's perceptions of the middle-class system, the implication is clear that it is not that the working-class boy's status aspirations are frustrated (that is, he is motivated but is unable to achieve prestigeful status in the middle-class system), but rather that he does not want to strive for status in the system, and that he resents the intrusion of "foreigners" who seek to impose upon him an irrelevant way of life.

Cohen's image of the working-class boy, who admittedly is extremely dependent upon his gang, standing alone to face humiliation at the hands of middle-class agents is difficult to comprehend. To add to this picture of the pre-teen and teen-ager an intense desire to gain status in the middle-class system, which when frustrated provides sufficient basis for a reaction-formation response, is to overdraw him beyond recognition. Even in "Elmtown," to which Cohen refers, it is difficult to conceive of the working-class boy exposed to the middle-class environment unprotected by the support of his peer group. When we realize that Cohen's formulation applies, presumably, more directly to schools in urban areas which are predominantly working-class in composition, confusion is compounded.

Again, *why* does Cohen insist upon the working-class boy's ambivalence toward the middle-class system? His discussion of alternative subcultural responses among working-class boys to the problem of status-frustration may

provide a clue. He specifies three modes of response: that of the college boy, of the "stable corner-boy," and of the delinquent boy. The college boy deserts the corner-boy way of life and accepts the "challenge of the middle-class status system," conforming to its rules.[19] The stable corner-boy culture "does not so much repudiate the value of middle-class achievements as it emphasizes certain other values which make such achievements improbable. . . . the corner-boy culture temporizes the middle-class morality."[20] It is the delinquent response, legitimized by the subculture, that represents the reaction-formation of a whole-hearted repudiation of middle-class morality.

It would appear that, of the three categories of respondents, the working-class boys who find a solution in the delinquent subculture are those who are faced with the most serious problems of status-frustration and ambivalence. The logic of the reaction-formation thesis leads us to conclude that, of the three modes of adjustment, the delinquent boys' is an expression of the *most serious* problems of status-frustration and ambivalence. We must assume that the intensity of the hostility and aggression against the middle-class system is a measure of status-frustration and ambivalence.

Theoretically, the college boy is equally ambivalent about the middle-class system, yet Cohen does not invoke the concept of reaction-formation to account for *his* (the college boy's) rejection of (or reaction against) working-class values. If the price of the working-class boy's accommodation to the middle-class system is that he must "change his habits, his values, his ambitions, his speech and his associates," would not the college-boy response entail more than an acceptance of the

[18] *Ibid.*, p. 117, emphasis added.

[19] *Ibid.*, p. 128.
[20] *Ibid.*, p. 130.

challenge to compete within the system on its own terms?[21]

The Description of the Delinquent Subculture

Cohen's emphasis upon the "positive" aspect of the college-boy response contrasts with his stress upon the "negative" aspect of the delinquent response, which leads him, we suggest, to describe the delinquent subculture as an irrational, malicious attack on the middle-class system. This raises the more fundamental question about his *description* of the subculture, "the facts to be explained."

"Non-utilitarian," "malicious," and "negativistic" are, we suggest, interpretive categories of description which are not independent of Cohen's explanation of the delinquent subculture. For example, the imputation of intent, implicit in his description of malice, is open to serious doubt.[22] We do not deny that subculture delinquency is marked by such distinctive characteristics as the systematic extortion of money from younger, defenseless children. What is at issue here is the interpretation of this kind of delinquent behavior, an interpretation directed systematically at the middle-class as a consequence of the frustration of ambivalent status aspirations.

It is important that we keep apace the facts. Cohen's description of the delinquent subculture does not fit the behavior of contemporary delinquent gangs.[23] They are not engaged in replacing one stolen hat with another from store to store, or delighting in the terrorizing of "good" children by driving them from playgrounds and gyms. The delinquents whose activities are organized by a delinquent subculture are attending to more serious enterprises. There is no absence of rational, calculated, utilitarian behavior among delinquent gangs, as they exist today. To describe the activities of such gangs as non-utilitarian, malicious, and negativistic gives the misleading view that they somehow represent a child's angry outbursts against the injustices of a world he never made.

It is also important to guard against the tendency to apply different standards for interpreting the behavior of class-differentiated groups. There is ample evidence in the daily press that middle-class adolescents are engaged in the kinds of activities that Cohen cites to support his description of the working-class delinquent subculture. To be sure, such reports appear less frequently under banner headlines than do the exploits of working-class delinquents; and middle-class delinquency does not prompt, as does working-class delinquency, editorial clamor for a radical and thorough revision of programs of control. For example, acts of vandalism committed by college boys on the facilities rented for fraternity dances and other occasions occur with

---

[21] *Ibid.,* p. 127.

[22] Martha M. Eliot, Chief of the Children's Bureau, has observed, "We are too inclined to make vandalism a catch-all phrase which imputes to the vandal hostile antagonisms toward society, then to compound the catch-all by saying that vandals, by and large, are teen-agers. But if teen-agers are vandals, why are they any more so than children of any age?" What is Vandalism"? *Federal Probation,* 18 (March, 1954), p. 3.

[23] See, e.g., Sam Glane, "Juvenile Gangs in East Side Los Angeles," *Focus,* 29 (September, 1950), pp. 136–141; Dale Kramer and Madeline Karr, *Teen-Age Gangs,* New York: Henry Holt, 1953; Stacy V. Jones, "The Cougars—Life with a Brooklyn Gang," *Harper's Magazine,* 209 (November, 1954), pp. 35–43; Paul C. Crawford, Daniel I. Malamud, and James R. Dumpson, *Working with Teen-Age Gangs,* New York: New York Welfare Council, 1950; Harrison E. Salisbury, "The Shook-Up Generation," *New York Times,* March 24–30, 1958; Dan Wakefield, "The

annual regularity.[24] In view of the great probability that such instances of middle-class gang delinquency are substantially under-reported, it would be an arbitrary preconception to dismiss them as no more than scattered and rare occurrences.

THE TEST OF COHEN'S THEORY

In the preceding discussion we argue that, first, Cohen does not present adequate support for his formulation of "the working-class boy's problem," second, his description of the working-class boy's ambivalence toward the middle-class system does not warrant the use of the reaction-formation concept, and third, his description of the delinquent subculture, the "facts" to which his theory is addressed, is open to question. While these criticisms are presented as logical ambiguities and inconsistencies in Cohen's statements, it may be maintained nevertheless that empirical research demonstrates the validity of his major thesis. In turning to this question, we suspend the criticisms formulated above, and examine the methodology of Cohen's theory.

Gang That Went Good," *Harper's Magazine*, 216 (June, 1958), pp. 36–43.

[24] One Southern California college fraternity has depleted a long list of rental facilities where their patronage is no longer solicited. The last dance held by this fraternity was the scene of a minor riot which required a force of thirty regular and reserve police officers to control. Acts of vandalism included ripping fixtures from the walls, entering the ballroom dripping with water from the swimming pool, tearing radio antennae from police cars, etc. Lest this example be dismissed as institutionalized saturnalia, other instances may be cited which the community was less willing to view as mere pranks. In Los Angeles, a group of high school seniors of undisputedly middle-class families committed an "unprovoked" act of setting fire to a school building. In another case, several middle-class adolescents in Glendale, California were convicted for stomping on the hoods and roofs of automobiles in that city. And so on.

The Historical Method and Empirical Research

What, then, are the research directives of the theory of the delinquent subculture? When this problem is analyzed, Cohen's methodology presents numerous difficulties, for his theory is an historical construction addressed to the explanation of the *emergence* of an existing subculture and its *present* concentration among the working-class male population. Furthermore, the basic propositions of this explanation utilize concepts which require data about the psychological characteristics of past populations.

Cohen's use of the present indicative in the development of his theory is misleading, for the interpretation of the rise of the delinquent subculture requires historical data. It is not that the working-class boy *is* ambivalent about middle-class values; the theory requires only that at some unspecified time when the delinquent subculture emerged, the working-class boy *was* ambivalent about middle-class values.

Subculture Maintenance and Motivation

There is no objection per se to a plausible explanation that cannot be tested if the explanation is viewed as an heuristic device for the generating of hypotheses. If then a direct test of Cohen's theory through the measurement of deduced empirical regularities is not possible as a practical matter, is it feasible to approach the problem from a functional point of view? The question may be phrased: What are the necessary conditions for the maintenance of the delinquent subculture? On this question, Cohen's statements are quite explicit. Commenting on the fact that his theory is not concerned with the processes by which one boy becomes delinquent while another does not, Cohen writes:

We have tried to show that a subculture owes its existence to the fact that it provides a solution to certain problems of adjustment shared among a community of individuals. However, it does not follow that for every individual who participates these problems provide the sole or sufficient source of motivation. Indeed, there may be some participants to whose motivation these problems contribute very little. . . . Our delinquent subculture . . . is not a disembodied set of beliefs and practices but is "carried" and supported by groups with distinctive personnel. A position in this organization or affiliation with this or that particular member may offer other satisfactions which help to account for the participation of certain members but do not help to explain the content of the culture in which they participate.[25]

An implication of this statement is that the maintenance of the delinquent subculture is not wholly dependent upon the motivational structure which explains its emergence. Not *every* individual who participates in the delinquent subculture need be so motivated and, for some, such motivation may be peripheral if not irrelevant. Clearly an investigation of the motivations which lead individuals to participate in the delinquent subculture does not constitute even an indirect test of the theory. For the statement may be read to mean that once the subculture is established, it can be maintained by the behavior of individuals who bring a diverse range of motivations to the gangs which embody the delinquent subculture. Thus, functionally, the delinquent subculture requires another explanation.

The Double Dilemma: Theory and Method

The theoretical significance of Cohen's explanation of the emergence of

25 Cohen, *op. cit.,* p. 148.

the delinquent subculture, however, lies precisely in its relevance for an explanation of the maintenance of that subculture. Were this not so, the theory could be dismissed as merely plausible and untestable or as incapable of generating hypotheses about regularities other than the pre-existing "facts" which it explains. We suggest that the statement quoted above presents a methodological dilemma by divorcing the dynamics of the etiology of the delinquent subculture from the dynamics of its maintenance. Cohen is correct of course in asserting that, theoretically, the former does not necessarily require the same motivational dynamics as the latter. However, the ambiguity of his statement lies in his implicit concession that *some* of the participants in the subculture must have the characteristic motivational structure posited in the theory.

The research dilemma posed by Cohen's theory is two-fold. Methodologically, the historical method relies upon data concerning the psychological dynamics of a population which are difficult if not impossible to obtain. Theoretically, the motivational dynamics posited as necessary for the *emergence* of the delinquent subculture is considered either (*a*) independent of the motivational dynamics necessary for the *maintenance* of the subculture, or (*b*) dependent upon it in some unspecified relationship.

In view of these difficulties, it may be fruitful to turn the problem around and ask: What are the consequences of participation in the delinquent subculture for the motivational structure of the participants? This question places the theory of the delinquent subculture in its proper relation to the value-transmission theories of delinquency and directs us to examine the heuristic value of Cohen's theory. Viewing his theory from this perspective, the following propositions about the maintenance of the delinquent subculture may be stated:

1. The individual learns the values of the delinquent subculture through his participation in gangs which embody that subculture.

2. The motivations of individuals for participating in such gangs are varied.

3. The malicious, non-utilitarian, and negativistic behavior which is learned through participation in the subculture is met by formal negative sanctions, rejection, and limitation of access to prestigeful status within the middle-class system.

4. Thus, participation in the delinquent subculture creates similar problems for all its participants.

5. The participants' response to the barriers raised to exclude them from status in the middle-class system (that is, the "problem") is a hostile rejection of the standards of "respectable" society and an emphasis upon status within the delinquent gang.

6. The hostile rejection response reinforces the malicious, non-utilitarian, and negativistic norms of the subculture.

The formulation suggested here relates Cohen's explanation of the emergence of the delinquent subculture with an explanation of its maintenance. It hypothesizes that the delinquent subculture persists because, once established, it creates for those who participate in it the very problems which were the bases for its emergence. It is possible to derive the further hypothesis that the motivational structure of the participants of the subculture displays characteristics similar to those described by Cohen.

CONCLUSIONS

In this paper, we have critically examined Cohen's monograph for its implications for theory and method. The problems raised in the first part of our critique cannot be resolved by logical argumentation. Indeed, we have suggested that insofar as they are consequences of the historical method, research to test the validity of Cohen's statements, as a practical matter, is impossible. If, however, the theory of the delinquent subculture is read for its heuristic value, its significance for theory and research is not limited to the field of juvenile delinquency, but extends to the more general problem of the dynamics of subcultural maintenance.

11.

Techniques of Neutralization: A Theory of Delinquency

Gresham M. Sykes and David Matza

In attempting to uncover the roots of juvenile delinquency, the social scientist has long since ceased to search for devils in the mind or stigma of the body. It is now largely agreed that delinquent behavior, like most social behavior, is learned and that it is learned in the process of social interaction.

The classic statement of this position is found in Sutherland's theory of differential association, which asserts that criminal or delinquent behavior involves the learning of (a) techniques of committing crimes and (b) motives, drives, rationalizations, and attitudes favorable to the violation of law.[1] Unfortunately, the specific content of what is learned —as opposed to the process by which it is learned—has received relatively little attention in either theory or research. Perhaps the single strongest school of thought on the nature of this content has centered on the idea of a delinquent sub-culture. The basic characteristic of the delinquent sub-culture,

it is argued, is a system of values that represents an inversion of the values held by respectable, law-abiding society. The world of the delinquent is the world of the law-abiding turned upside down, and its norms constitute a countervailing force directed against the conforming social order. Cohen[2] sees the process of developing a delinquent sub-culture as a matter of building, maintaining, and reinforcing a code for behavior which exists by opposition, which stands in point by point contradiction to dominant values, particularly those of the middle class. Cohen's portrayal of delinquency is executed with a good deal of sophistication, and he carefully avoids overly simple explanations such as those based on the principle of "follow the leader" or easy generalizations about "emotional disturbances." Furthermore, he does not accept the delinquent sub-culture as something given, but instead systematically examines the function of delinquent values as a viable solution to the lower-

[1] E. H. Sutherland, *Principles of Criminology*, revised by D. R. Cressey, Philadelphia: Lippincott, 1955, pp. 77–80.

[2] Albert K. Cohen, *Delinquent Boys*, Glencoe, Ill.: The Free Press, 1955.

SOURCE. Gresham M. Sykes and David Matza, "Techniques of Neutralization: A Theory of Delinquency," from *The American Journal of Sociology*, Volume 22, December 1957, pp. 664–670. Copyright © 1957, University of Chicago Press. Reprinted with the permission of the University of Chicago Press.

class, male child's problems in the area of social status. Yet in spite of its virtues, this image of juvenile delinquency as a form of behavior based on competing or countervailing values and norms appears to suffer from a number of serious defects. It is the nature of these defects and a possible alternative or modified explanation for a large portion of juvenile delinquency with which this paper is concerned.

The difficulties in viewing delinquent behavior as springing from a set of deviant values and norms—as arising, that is to say, from a situation in which the delinquent defines his delinquency as "right"—are both empirical and theoretical. In the first place, if there existed in fact a delinquent sub-culture such that the delinquent viewed his illegal behavior as morally correct, we could reasonably suppose that he would exhibit no feelings of guilt or shame at detection or confinement. Instead, the major reaction would tend in the direction of indignation or a sense of martyrdom.[3] It is true that some delinquents do react in the latter fashion, although the sense of martyrdom often seems to be based on the fact that others "get away with it," and indignation appears to be directed against the chance events or lack of skill that led to apprehension. More important, however, is the fact that there is a good deal of evidence suggesting that many delinquents *do* experience a sense of guilt or shame, and its outward expression is not to be dismissed as a purely manipulative gesture to appease those in authority. Much of this evidence is,

to be sure, of a clinical nature or in the form of impressionistic judgments of those who must deal first hand with the youthful offender. Assigning a weight to such evidence calls for caution, but it cannot be ignored if we are to avoid the gross stereotype of the juvenile delinquent as a hardened gangster in miniature.

In the second place, observers have noted that the juvenile delinquent frequently accords admiration and respect to law-abiding persons. The "really honest" person is often revered, and if the delinquent is sometimes overly keen to detect hypocrisy in those who conform, unquestioned probity is likely to win his approval. A fierce attachment to a humble, pious mother or a forgiving, upright priest (the former, according to many observers, is often encountered in both juvenile delinquents and adult criminals) might be dismissed as rank sentimentality, but at least it is clear that the delinquent does not necessarily regard those who abide by the legal rules as immoral. In a similar vein, it can be noted that the juvenile delinquent may exhibit great resentment if illegal behavior is imputed to "significant others" in his immediate social environment or to heroes in the world of sport and entertainment. In other words, if the delinquent does hold to a set of values and norms that stand in complete opposition to those of respectable society, his norm-holding is of a peculiar sort. While supposedly thoroughly committed to the deviant system of the delinquent sub-culture, he would appear to recognize the moral validity of the dominant normative system in many instances.[4]

[3] This form of reaction among the adherents of a deviant sub-culture who fully believe in the "rightfulness" of their behavior and who are captured and punished by the agencies of the dominant social order can be illustrated, perhaps, by groups such as Jehovah's Witnesses, early Christian sects, nationalist movements in colonial areas, and conscientious objectors during World Wars I and II.

[4] As Weber has pointed out, a thief may recognize the legitimacy of legal rules without accepting their moral validity. Cf. Max Weber, *The Theory of Social and Economic Organization* (translated by A. M. Henderson and Talcott Parsons), New York: Oxford University Press, 1947, p.

In the third place, there is much evidence that juvenile delinquents often draw a sharp line between those who can be victimized and those who cannot. Certain social groups are not to be viewed as "fair game" in the performance of supposedly approved delinquent acts while others warrant a variety of attacks. In general, the potentiality for victimization would seem to be a function of the social distance between the juvenile delinquent and others, and thus we find implicit maxims in the world of the delinquent such as "don't steal from friends" or "don't commit vandalism against a church of your own faith."[5] This is all rather obvious, but the implications have not received sufficient attention. The fact that supposedly valued behavior tends to be directed against disvalued social groups hints that the "wrongfulness" of such delinquent behavior is more widely recognized by delinquents than the literature has indicated. When the pool of victims is limited by considerations of kinship, friendship, ethnic group, social class, age, sex, etc., we have reason to suspect that the virtue of delinquency is far from unquestioned.

In the fourth place, it is doubtful if many juvenile delinquents are totally immune from the demands for conformity made by the dominant social order. There is a strong likelihood that the family of the delinquent will agree with respectable society that delinquency is wrong, even though the family may be engaged in a variety of illegal activities. That is, the parental posture conductive to delinquency is

125. We are arguing here, however, that the juvenile delinquent frequently recognizes *both* the legitimacy of the dominant social order and its moral "rightness."

[5] Thrasher's account of the "Itschkies"—a juvenile gang composed of Jewish boys—and the immunity from "rolling" enjoyed by Jewish drunkards is a good illustration. Cf. F. Thrasher, *The Gang,* Chicago: The University of Chicago Press, 1947, p. 315.

not apt to be a positive prodding. Whatever may be the influence of parental example, what might be called the "Fagin" pattern of socialization into delinquency is probably rare. Furthermore, as Redl has indicated, the idea that certain neighborhoods are completely delinquent, offering the child a model for delinquent behavior without reservations, is simply not supported by the data.[6]

The fact that a child is punished by parents, school officials, and agencies of the legal system for his delinquency may, as a number of observers have cynically noted, suggest to the child that he should be more careful not to get caught. There is an equal or greater probability, however, that the child will internalize the demands for conformity. This is not to say that demands for conformity cannot be counteracted. In fact, as we shall see shortly, an understanding of how internal and external demands for conformity are neutralized may be crucial for understanding delinquent behavior. But it is to say that a complete denial of the validity of demands for conformity and the substitution of a new normative system is improbable, in light of the child's or adolescent's dependency on adults and encirclement by adults inherent in his status in the social structure. No matter how deeply enmeshed in patterns of delinquency he may be and no matter how much this involvement may outweigh his associations with the law-abiding, he cannot escape the condemnation of his deviance. Somehow the demands for conformity must be met and answered; they cannot be ignored as part of an alien system of values and norms.

In short, the theoretical viewpoint

[6] Cf. Solomon Kobrin, "The Conflict of Values in Delinquency Areas," *American Sociological Review,* 16 (October, 1951), pp. 653–661.

that sees juvenile delinquency as a form of behavior based on the values and norms of a deviant sub-culture in precisely the same way as law-abiding behavior is based on the values and norms of the larger society is open to serious doubt. The fact that the world of the delinquent is embedded in the larger world of those who conform cannot be overlooked, nor can the delinquent be equated with an adult thoroughly socialized into an alternative way of life. Instead, the juvenile delinquent would appear to be at least partially committed to the dominant social order in that he frequently exhibits guilt or shame when he violates its proscriptions, accords approval to certain conforming figures, and distinguishes between appropriate and inappropriate targets for his deviance. It is to an explanation for the apparently paradoxical fact of his delinquency that we now turn.

As Morris Cohen once said, one of the most fascinating problems about human behavior is why men violate the laws in which they believe. This is the problem that confronts us when we attempt to explain why delinquency occurs despite a greater or lesser commitment to the usages of conformity. A basic clue is offered by the fact that social rules or norms calling for valued behavior seldom if ever take the form of categorical imperatives. Rather, values or norms appear as *qualified* guides for action, limited in their applicability in terms of time, place, persons, and social circumstances. The moral injunction against killing, for example, does not apply to the enemy during combat in time of war, although a captured enemy comes once again under the prohibition. Similarly, the taking and distributing of scarce goods in a time of acute social need is felt by many to be right, although under other circumstances private property is held inviolable. The normative system of a society, then, is marked by what Williams has termed *flexibility;* it does not consist of a body of rules held to be binding under all conditions.[7]

This flexibility is, in fact, an integral part of the criminal law in that measures for "defenses to crimes" are provided in pleas such as nonage, necessity, insanity, drunkenness, compulsion, self-defense, and so on. The individual can avoid moral culpability for his criminal action—and thus avoid the negative sanctions of society—if he can prove that criminal intent was lacking. *It is our argument that much delinquency is based on what is essentially an unrecognized extension of defenses to crimes, in the form of justifications for deviance that are seen as valid by the delinquent but not by the legal system or society at large.*

These justifications are commonly described as rationalizations. They are viewed as following deviant behavior and as protecting the individual from self-blame and the blame of others after the act. But there is also reason to believe that they precede deviant behavior and make deviant behavior possible. It is this possibility that Sutherland mentioned only in passing and that other writers have failed to exploit from the viewpoint of sociological theory. Disapproval flowing from internalized norms and conforming others in the social environment is neutralized, turned back, or deflected in advance. Social controls that serve to check or inhibit deviant motivational patterns are rendered inoperative, and the individual is freed to engage in delinquency without serious damage to his self-image. In this sense, the delinquent both has his cake and eats it too, for he remains committed to the dominant normative system and yet so

[7] Cf. Robin Williams, Jr., *American Society,* New York: Knopf, 1951, p. 28.

qualifies its imperatives that violations are "acceptable" if not "right." Thus the delinquent represents not a radical opposition to law-abiding society but something more like an apologetic failure, often more sinned against than sinning in his own eyes. We call these justifications of deviant behavior techniques of neutralization; and we believe these techniques make up a crucial component of Sutherland's "definitions favorable to the violation of law." It is by learning these techniques that the juvenile becomes delinquent, rather than by learning moral imperatives, values, or attitudes standing in direct contradiction to those of the dominant society. In analyzing these techniques, we have found it convenient to divide them into five major types.

The Denial of Responsibility

Insofar as the delinquent can define himself as lacking responsibility for his deviant actions, the disapproval of self or others is sharply reduced in effectiveness as a restraining influence. As Justice Holmes has said, even a dog distinguishes between being stumbled over and being kicked, and modern society is no less careful to draw a line between injuries that are unintentional, i.e., where responsibility is lacking, and those that are intentional. As a technique of neutralization, however, the denial of responsibility extends much further than the claim that deviant acts are an "accident" or some similar negation of personal accountability. It may also be asserted that delinquent acts are due to forces outside of the individual and beyond his control such as unloving parents, bad companions, or a slum neighborhood. In effect, the delinquent approaches a "billiard ball" conception of himself in which he sees himself as helplessly propelled into new situations. From a psychodynamic viewpoint, this orientation toward one's own

actions may represent a profound alienation from self, but it is important to stress the fact that interpretations of responsibility are cultural constructs and not merely idiosyncratic beliefs. The similarity between this mode of justifying illegal behavior assumed by the delinquent and the implications of a "sociological" frame of reference or a "humane" jurisprudence is readily apparent.[8] It is not the validity of this orientation that concerns us here, but its function of deflecting blame attached to violations of social norms and its relative independence of a particular personality structure.[9] By learning to view himself as more acted upon than acting, the delinquent prepares the way for deviance from the dominant normative system without the necessity of a frontal assault on the norms themselves.

The Denial of Injury

A second major technique of neutralization centers on the injury or harm involved in the delinquent act. The criminal law has long made a distinction between crimes which are *mala in se* and *mala prohibita*—that is between acts that are wrong in themselves and acts that are illegal but not immoral— and the delinquent can make the same kind of distinction in evaluating the wrongfulness of his behavior. For the delinquent, however, wrongfulness may turn on the question of whether or not anyone has clearly been hurt by his deviance, and this matter is open to a variety of interpretations. Vandalism, for example, may be defined by the

[8] A number of observers have wryly noted that many delinquents seem to show a surprising awareness of sociological and psychological explanations for their behavior and are quick to point out the causal role of their poor environment.

[9] It is possible, of course, that certain personality structures can accept some techniques of neutralization more readily than others, but this question remains largely unexplored.

delinquent simply as "mischief"—after all, it may be claimed, the persons whose property has been destroyed can well afford it. Similarly, auto theft may be viewed as "borrowing," and gang fighting may be seen as a private quarrel, an agreed upon duel between two willing parties, and thus of no concern to the community at large. We are not suggesting that this technique of neutralization, labeled the denial of injury, involves an explicit dialectic. Rather, we are arguing that the delinquent frequently, and in a hazy fashion, feels that his behavior does not really cause any great harm despite the fact that it runs counter to law. Just as the link between the individual and his acts may be broken by the denial of responsibility, so may the link between acts and their consequences be broken by the denial of injury. Since society sometimes agrees with the delinquent, e.g., in matters such as truancy, "pranks," and so on, it merely reaffirms the idea that the delinquent's neutralization of social controls by means of qualifying the norms is an extension of common practice rather than a gesture of complete opposition.

The Denial of the Victim

Even if the delinquent accepts the responsibility for his deviant actions and is willing to admit that his deviant actions involve an injury or hurt, the moral indignation of self and others may be neutralized by an insistence that the injury is not wrong in light of the circumstances. The injury, it may be claimed, is not really an injury; rather, it is a form of rightful retaliation or punishment. By a subtle alchemy the delinquent moves himself into the position of an avenger and the victim is transformed into a wrong-doer. Assaults on homosexuals or suspected homosexuals, attacks on members of minority groups who are said to have

gotten "out of place," vandalism as revenge on an unfair teacher or school official, thefts from a "crooked" store owner—all may be hurts inflicted on a transgressor, in the eyes of the delinquent. As Orwell has pointed out, the type of criminal admired by the general public has probably changed over the course of years and Raffles no longer serves as a hero;[10] but Robin Hood, and his latter day derivatives such as the tough detective seeking justice outside the law, still capture the popular imagination, and the delinquent may view his acts as part of a similar role.

To deny the existence of the victim, then, by transforming him into a person deserving injury is an extreme form of a phenomenon we have mentioned before, namely, the delinquent's recognition of appropriate and inappropriate targets for his delinquent acts. In addition, however, the existence of the victim may be denied for the delinquent, in a somewhat different sense, by the circumstances of the delinquent act itself. Insofar as the victim is physically absent, unknown, or a vague abstraction (as is often the case in delinquent acts committed against property), the awareness of the victim's existence is weakened. Internalized norms and anticipations of the reactions of others must somehow be activated if they are to serve as guides for behavior; and it is possible that a diminished awareness of the victim plays an important part in determining whether or not this process is set in motion.

The Condemnation of the Condemners

A fourth technique of neutralization would appear to involve a condemnation of the condemners or, as McCorkle and Korn have phrased it, a rejection of the rejectors.[11] The delinquent shifts

[10] George Orwell, *Dickens, Dali, and Others*, New York: Reynal, 1946.
[11] Lloyd W. McCorkle and Richard

UNIVERSITY
BOOK STORES
49

- 4 NOV 74

$008.25 —— 2

6562 $008.25 TOTL

the focus of attention from his own deviant acts to the motives and behavior of those who disapprove of his violations. His condemners, he may claim, are hypocrites, deviants in disguise, or impelled by personal spite. This orientation toward the conforming world may be of particular importance when it hardens into a bitter cynicism directed against those assigned the task of enforcing or expressing the norms of the dominant society. Police, it may be said, are corrupt, stupid, and brutal. Teachers always show favoritism and parents always "take it out" on their children. By a slight extension, the rewards of conformity—such as material success—become a matter of pull or luck, thus decreasing still further the stature of those who stand on the side of the law-abiding. The validity of this jaundiced viewpoint is not so important as its function in turning back or deflecting the negative sanctions attached to violations of the norms. The delinquent, in effect, has changed the subject of the conversation in the dialogue between his own deviant impulses and the reactions of others; and by attacking others, the wrongfulness of his own behavior is more easily repressed or lost to view.

The Appeal to Higher Loyalties

Fifth, and last, internal and external social controls may be neutralized by sacrificing the demands of the larger society for the demands of the smaller social groups to which the delinquent belongs, such as the sibling pair, the gang, or the friendship clique. It is important to note that the delinquent does not necessarily repudiate the imperatives of the dominant normative system, despite his failure to follow them.

Rather, the delinquent may see himself as caught up in a dilemma that must be resolved, unfortunately, at the cost of violating the law. One aspect of this situation has been studied by Stouffer and Toby in their research on the conflict between particularistic and universalistic demands, between the claims of friendship and general social obligations, and their results suggest that "it is possible to classify people according to a predisposition to select one or the other horn of a dilemma in role conflict."[12] For our purposes, however, the most important point is that deviation from certain norms may occur not because the norms are rejected but because others norms, held to be more pressing or involving a higher loyalty, are accorded precedence. Indeed, it is the fact that both sets of norms are believed in that gives meaning to our concepts of dilemma and role conflict.

The conflict between the claims of friendship and the claims of law, or a similar dilemma, has of course long been recognized by the social scientist (and the novelist) as a common human problem. If the juvenile delinquent frequently resolves his dilemma by insisting that he must "always help a buddy" or "never squeal on a friend," even when it throws him into serious difficulties with the dominant social order, his choice remains familiar to the supposedly law-abiding. The delinquent is unusual, perhaps, in the extent to which he is able to see the fact that he acts in behalf of the smaller social groups to which he belongs as a justification for violations of society's norms, but it is a matter of degree rather than of kind.

"I didn't mean it." "I didn't really

Korn, "Resocialization Within Walls," *The Annals of the American Academy of Political and Social Science*, 293 (May, 1954), pp. 88–98.

12 See Samuel A. Stouffer and Jackson Toby, "Role Conflict and Personality," in *Toward a General Theory of Action*, edited by Talcott Parsons and Edward A. Shils, Cambridge, Mass.: Harvard University Press, 1951, p. 494.

hurt anybody." "They had it coming to them." "Everybody's picking on me." "I didn't do it for myself." These slogans or their variants, we hypothesize, prepare the juvenile for delinquent acts. These "definitions of the situation" represent tangential or glancing blows at the dominant normative system rather than the creation of an opposing ideology; and they are extensions of patterns of thought prevalent in society rather than something created *de novo*.

Techniques of neutralization may not be powerful enough to fully shield the individual from the force of his own internalized values and the reactions of conforming others, for as we have pointed out, juvenile delinquents often appear to suffer from feelings of guilt and shame when called into account for their deviant behavior. And some delinquents may be so isolated from the world of conformity that techniques of neutralization need not be called into play. Nonetheless, we would argue that techniques of neutralization are critical in lessening the effectiveness of social controls and that they lie behind a large share of delinquent behavior. Empirical research in this area is scattered and fragmentary at the present time, but the work of Redl,[13] Cressey,[14] and others has supplied a body of significant data that has done much to clarify the theoretical issues and enlarge the fund of supporting evidence. Two

[13] See Fritz Redl and David Wineman, *Children Who Hate,* Glencoe, Ill.: The Free Press, 1956.

[14] See D. R. Cressey, *Other People's Money,* Glencoe, Ill.: The Free Press, 1953.

lines of investigation seem to be critical at this stage. First, there is need for more knowledge concerning the differential distribution of techniques of neutralization, as operative patterns of thought, by age, sex, social class, ethnic group, etc. On a priori grounds it might be assumed that these justifications for deviance will be more readily seized by segments of society for whom a discrepancy between common social ideals and social practice is most apparent. It is also possible, however, that the habit of "bending" the dominant normative system—if not "breaking" it—cuts across our cruder social categories and is to be traced primarily to patterns of social interaction within the familial circle. Second, there is need for a greater understanding of the internal structure of techniques of neutralization, as a system of beliefs and attitudes, and its relationship to various types of delinquent behavior. Certain techniques of neutralization would appear to be better adapted to particular deviant acts than to others, as we have suggested, for example, in the case of offenses against property and the denial of the victim. But the issue remains far from clear and stands in need of more information.

In any case, techniques of neutralization appear to offer a promising line of research in enlarging and systematizing the theoretical grasp of juvenile delinquency. As more information is uncovered concerning techniques of neutralization, their origins, and their consequences, both juvenile delinquency in particular and deviation from normative systems in general may be illuminated.

12.

Lower Class Culture as a Generating Milieu
of Gang Delinquency

Walter B. Miller

The etiology of delinquency has long been a controversial issue and is particularly so at present. As new frames of reference for explaining human behavior have been added to traditional theories, some authors have adopted the practice of citing the major postulates of each school of thought as they pertain to delinquency, and of going on to state that causality must be conceived in terms of the dynamic interaction of a complex combination of variables on many levels. The major sets of etiological factors currently adduced to explain delinquency are, in simplified terms, the physiological (delinquency results from organic pathology), the psychodynamic (delinquency is a "behavioral disorder" resulting primarily from emotional disturbance generated by a defective mother-child relationship), and the environmental (delinquency is the product of disruptive forces, "disorganization," in the actor's physical or social environment).

This paper selects one particular kind of "delinquency"[1]—law-violating acts

committed by members of adolescent street corner groups in lower class communities—and attempts to show that the dominant component of motivation underlying these acts consists in a directed attempt by the actor to adhere to forms of behavior, and to achieve standards of value, as they are defined within that community. It takes as a premise that the motivation of behavior in this situation can be approached most productively by attempting to understand the nature of cultural forces impinging on the acting individual as they are perceived *by the actor himself* —although by no means only that segment of these forces of which the actor is consciously aware—rather than as they are perceived and evaluated from the reference position of another cul-

[1] The complex issues involved in deriving a definition of "delinquency" cannot be discussed here. The term "delinquent" is used in this paper to characterize behavior or acts committed by individuals within specified age limits which if known to official authorities could result in legal action. The concept of a "delinquent" individual has little or no utility in the approach used here; rather, specified types of *acts* which may be committed rarely or frequently by few or many individuals are characterized as "delinquent."

SOURCE. Walter B. Miller, "Lower Class Culture as a Generating Milieu of Gang Delinquency," from *The Journal of Social Issues*, Volume 14, No. 3, 1958, pp. 5–19. Reprinted with the permission of *The Journal of Social Issues*.

tural system. In the case of "gang" delinquency, the cultural system which exerts the most direct influence on behavior is that of the lower class community itself—a long-established, distinctively patterned tradition with an integrity of its own—rather than a so-called "delinquent subculture" which has arisen through conflict with middle class culture and is oriented to the deliberate violation of middle class norms.

The bulk of the substantive data on which the following material is based was collected in connection with a service-research project in the control of gang delinquency. During the service aspect of the project, which lasted for three years, seven trained social workers maintained contact with twenty-one corner group units in a "slum" district of a large eastern city for periods of time ranging from ten to thirty months. Groups were Negro and white, male and female, and in early, middle, and late adolescence. Over eight thousand pages of direct observational data on behavior patterns of group members and other community residents were collected; almost daily contact was maintained for a total time period of about thirteen worker years. Data include workers' contact reports, participant observation reports by the writer —a cultural anthropologist—and direct tape recordings of group activities and discussions.[2]

[2] A three-year research project is being financed under National Institutes of Health Grant M-1414 and administered through the Boston University School of Social Work. The primary research effort has subjected all collected material to a uniform data-coding process. All information bearing on some seventy areas of behavior (behavior in reference to school, police, theft, assault, sex, collective athletics, etc.) is extracted from the records, recorded on coded data cards, and filed under relevant categories. Analysis of these data aims to ascertain the actual nature of customary behavior in these areas and

FOCAL CONCERNS OF LOWER CLASS CULTURE

There is a substantial segment of present-day American society whose way of life, values, and characteristic patterns of behavior are the product of a distinctive cultural system which may be termed "lower class." Evidence indicates that this cultural system is becoming increasingly distinctive, and that the size of the group which shares this tradition is increasing.[3] The lower class way of life, in common with that of all distinctive cultural groups, is characterized by a set of focal concerns—areas or issues which command widespread and persistent attention and a high degree of emotional involvement. The specific concerns cited here, while by no means confined to the American lower classes, constitute a distinctive *patterning* of concerns which differs significantly, both in rank order and weighting, from that of American middle class culture. Chart 1 presents a highly schematic and simplified listing of six of the major concerns of lower class culture. Each is conceived as a "dimension" within which a fairly wide and varied range of alternative behav-

the extent to which the social work effort was able to effect behavioral changes.

[3] Between 40 and 60 per cent of all Americans are directly influenced by lower class culture, with about 15 per cent, or twenty-five million, comprising the "hard core" lower class group—defined primarily by its use of the "female-based" household as the basic form of child-rearing unit and of the "serial monogamy" mating pattern as the primary form of marriage. The term "lower class culture" as used here refers most specifically to the way of life of the "hard core" group; systematic research in this area would probably reveal at least four to six major subtypes of lower class culture, for some of which the "concerns" presented here would be differently weighted, especially for those subtypes in which "law-abiding" behavior has a high overt valuation. It is impossible within the compass of this short paper to make the finer intracultural distinctions which a more accurate presentation would require.

Chart 1

FOCAL CONCERNS OF LOWER CLASS CULTURE

Area	Perceived alternatives (state, quality, condition)	
1. Trouble:	law-abiding behavior	law-violating behavior
2. Toughness:	physical prowess, skill; "masculinity"; fearlessness, bravery, daring	weakness, ineptitude; effeminacy; timidity, cowardice, caution
3. Smartness:	ability to outsmart, dupe, "con"; gaining money by "wits"; shrewdness, adroitness in repartee	gullibility, "con-ability"; gaining money by hard work; slowness, dull-wittedness, verbal maladroitness
4. Excitement:	thrill; risk, danger; change, activity	boredom; "deadness," safeness; sameness, passivity
5. Fate:	favored by fortune, being "lucky"	ill-omened, being "unlucky"
6. Autonomy:	freedom from external constraint; freedom from superordinate authority; independence	presence of external constraint; presence of strong authority; dependency, being "cared for"

ior patterns may be followed by different individuals under different situations. They are listed roughly in order of the degree of *explicit* attention accorded each and, in this sense, represent a weighted ranking of concerns. The "perceived alternatives" represent polar positions which define certain parameters within each dimension. As will be explained in more detail, it is necessary in relating the influence of these "concerns" to the motivation of delinquent behavior to specify *which* of its aspects is oriented to, whether orientation is *overt* or *covert, positive* (conforming to or seeking the aspect) or *negative* (rejecting or seeking to avoid the aspect).

The concept "focal concern" is used here in preference to the concept "value" for several interrelated reasons: (1) It is more readily derivable from direct field observation. (2) It is descriptively neutral—permitting independent consideration of positive and negative valences as varying under dif-

ferent conditions, whereas "value" carries a built-in positive valence. (3) It makes possible more refined analysis of subcultural differences, since it reflects actual behavior, whereas "value" tends to wash out intracultural differences since it is colored by notions of the "official" ideal.

Trouble

Concern over "trouble" is a dominant feature of lower class culture. The concept has various shades of meaning; "trouble" in one of its aspects represents a situation or a kind of behavior which results in unwelcome or complicating involvement with official authorities or agencies of middle class society. "Getting into trouble" and "staying out of trouble" represent major issues for male and female, adults and children. For men, "trouble" frequently involves fighting or sexual adventures while drinking; for women, sexual involvement with disadvantageous consequences. Expressed desire to avoid behavior which violates moral or legal norms is often based less on an explicit commitment to "official" moral or legal standards than on a desire to avoid "getting into trouble," e.g., the complicating consequences of the action.

The dominant concern over "trouble" involves a distinction of critical importance for the lower class community —that between "law-abiding" and "non-law-abiding" behavior. There is a high degree of sensitivity as to where each person stands in relation to these two classes of activity. Whereas in the middle class community a major dimension for evaluating a person's status is "achievement" and its external symbols, in the lower class personal status is very frequently gauged along the law-abiding–non-law-abiding dimension. A mother will evaluate the suitability of her daughter's boyfriend less on the basis of his achievement potential than on the basis of his innate "trouble" potential. This sensitive awareness of the opposition of "trouble-producing" and "non-trouble-producing" behavior represents both a major basis for deriving status distinctions and an internalized conflict potential for the individual.

As in the case of other focal concerns, which of two perceived alternatives—"law-abiding" or "non-law-abiding"—is valued varies according to the individual and the circumstances; in many instances there is an overt commitment to the "law-abiding" alternative, but a covert commitment to the "non-law-abiding." In certain situations, "getting into trouble" is overtly recognized as prestige-conferring; for example, membership in certain adult and adolescent primary groupings ("gangs") is contingent on having demonstrated an explicit commitment to the law-violating alternative. It is most important to note that the choice between "law-abiding" and "non-law-abiding" behavior is still a choice within lower class culture; the distinction between the policeman and the criminal, the outlaw and the sheriff, involves primarily this one dimension; in other respects they have a high community of interests. Not infrequently brothers raised in an identical cultural milieu will become police and criminals respectively.

For a substantial segment of the lower class population "getting into trouble" is not in itself overtly defined as prestige-conferring, but is implicitly recognized as a means to other valued ends, e.g., the covertly valued desire to be "cared for" and subject to external constraint, or the overtly valued state of excitement or risk. Very frequently "getting into trouble" is multi-functional and achieves several sets of valued ends.

Toughness

The concept of "toughness" in lower class culture represents a compound combination of qualities or states. Among its most important components are physical prowess, evidenced both by demonstrated possession of strength and endurance and by athletic skill; "masculinity," symbolized by a distinctive complex of acts and avoidances (bodily tatooing, absence of sentimentality, non-concern with "art," "literature," conceptualization of women as conquest objects, etc.); and bravery in the face of physical threat. The model for the "tough guy"—hard, fearless, undemonstrative, skilled in physical combat—is represented by the movie gangster of the thirties, the "private eye," and the movie cowboy.

The genesis of the intense concern over "toughness" in lower class culture is probably related to the fact that a significant proportion of lower class males are reared in a predominantly female household and lack a consistently present male figure with whom to identify and from whom to learn essential components of a "male" role. Since women serve as a primary object of identification during pre-adolescent years, the almost obsessive lower class concern with "masculinity" probably resembles a type of compulsive reaction-formation. A concern over homosexuality runs like a persistent thread through lower class culture. This is manifested by the institutionalized practice of baiting "queers," often accompanied by violent physical attacks, an expressed contempt for "softness" or frills, and the use of the local term for "homosexual" as a generalized pejorative epithet (e.g., higher class individuals or upwardly mobile peers are frequently characterized as "fags" or "queers"). The distinction between "overt" and "covert" orientation to aspects of an area of concern is especially important in regard to "toughness." A positive overt evaluation of behavior defined as "effeminate" would be out of the question for a lower class male; however, built into lower class culture is a range of devices which permit men to adopt behaviors and concerns which in other cultural milieux fall within the province of women, and at the same time to be defined as "tough" and manly. For example, lower class men can be professional short-order cooks in a diner and still be regarded as "tough." The highly intimate circumstances of the street corner gang involve the recurrent expression of strongly affectionate feelings towards other men. Such expressions, however, are disguised as their opposite, taking the form of ostensibly aggressive verbal and physical interaction (kidding, "ranking," roughhousing, etc.).

Smartness

"Smartness," as conceptualized in lower class culture, involves the capac-
ity to outsmart, outfox, outwit, dupe, "take," "con" another or others and the concomitant capacity to avoid being outwitted, "taken," or duped oneself. In its essence, smartness involves the capacity to achieve a valued entity— material goods, personal status— through a maximum use of mental agility and a minimum use of physical effort. This capacity has an extremely long tradition in lower class culture and is highly valued. Lower class culture can be characterized as "non-intellectual" only if intellectualism is defined specifically in terms of control over a particular body of formally learned knowledge involving "culture" (art, literature, "good" music, etc.), a generalized perspective on the past and present conditions of our own and other societies, and other areas of knowledge imparted by formal educational institutions. This particular type of mental attainment is, in general, overtly disvalued and frequently associated with effeminacy; "smartness" in the lower class sense, however, is highly valued.

The lower class child learns and practices the use of this skill in the street corner situation. Individuals continually practice duping and outwitting one another through recurrent card games and other forms of gambling, mutual exchanges of insults, and "testing" for mutual "con-ability." Those who demonstrate competence in this skill are accorded considerable prestige. Leadership roles in the corner group are frequently allocated according to demonstrated capacity in the two areas of "smartness" and "toughness"; the ideal leader combines both, but the "smart" leader is often accorded more prestige than the "tough" one—reflecting a general lower class respect for "brains" in the "smartness" sense.[4]

[4] The "brains-brawn" set of capacities are often paired in lower class folk lore or accounts of lower class life, e.g., "Brer

The model of the "smart" person is represented in popular media by the card shark, the professional gambler, the "con" artist, the promoter. A conceptual distinction is made between two kinds of people: "suckers," easy marks, "lushes," dupes, who work for their money and are legitimate targets of exploitation; and sharp operators, the "brainy" ones, who live by their wits and "getting" from the suckers by mental adroitness.

Involved in the syndrome of capacities related to "smartness" is a dominant emphasis in lower class culture on ingenious aggressive repartee. This skill, learned and practiced in the context of the corner group, ranges in form from the widely prevalent semi-ritualized teasing, kidding, razzing, "ranking," so characteristic of male peer group interaction, to the highly ritualized type of mutual insult interchange known as "the dirty dozens," "the dozens," "playing house," and other terms. This highly patterned cultural form is practiced on its most advanced level in adult male Negro society, but less polished variants are found throughout lower class culture—practiced, for example, by white children, male and female, as young as four or five. In essence, "doin' the dozens" involves two antagonists who vie with each other in the exchange of increasingly inflammatory insults, with incestuous and perverted sexual relations with the mother a dominant theme. In this form of insult interchange, as well as on other less ritualized occasions for joking, semi-serious, and serious mutual invective, a very high premium is placed on ingenuity, hair-trigger responsiveness, inventiveness, and the acute exercise of mental faculties.

Fox" and "Brer Bear" in the Uncle Remus stories, or George and Lennie in "Of Mice and Men."

Excitement

For many lower class individuals the rhythm of life fluctuates between periods of relatively routine or repetitive activity and sought situations of great emotional stimulation. Many of the most characteristic features of lower class life are related to the search for excitement or "thrill." Involved here are the highly prevalent use of alcohol by both sexes and the widespread use of gambling of all kinds—playing the numbers, betting on horse races, dice, cards. The quest for excitement finds what is perhaps its most vivid expression in the highly patterned practice of the recurrent "night on the town." This practice, designated by various terms in different areas ("honky-tonkin' "; "goin' out on the town"; "bar hoppin' "), involves a patterned set of activities in which alcohol, music, and sexual adventuring are major components. A group or individual sets out to "make the rounds" of various bars or night clubs. Drinking continues progressively throughout the evening. Men seek to "pick up" women, and women play the risky game of entertaining sexual advances. Fights between men involving women, gambling, and claims of physical prowess, in various combinations, are frequent consequences of a night of making the rounds. The explosive potential of this type of adventuring with sex and aggression, frequently leading to "trouble," is semi-explicitly sought by the individual. Since there is always a good likelihood that being out on the town will eventuate in fights, etc., the practice involves elements of sought risk and desired danger.

Counterbalancing the "flirting with danger" aspect of the "excitement" concern is the prevalence in lower class culture of other well-established patterns of activity which involve long periods of relative inaction or passivity. The term "hanging out" in lower class culture refers to extended periods of standing around, often with peer mates, doing what is defined as "nothing," "shooting the breeze," etc. A definite periodicity exists in the pattern of activity relating to the two aspects of the "excitement" dimension. For many lower class individuals the venture into the high risk world of alcohol, sex, and fighting occurs regularly once a week, with interim periods devoted to accommodating to possible consequences of these periods, along with recurrent resolves not to become so involved again.

Fate

Related to the quest for excitement is the concern with fate, fortune, or luck. Here also a distinction is made between two states—being "lucky" or "in luck" and being unlucky or jinxed. Many lower class individuals feel that their lives are subject to a set of forces over which they have relatively little control. These are not directly equated with the supernatural forces of formally organized religion, but relate more to a concept of "destiny," or man as a pawn of magical powers. Not infrequently this often implicit world view is associated with a conception of the ultimate futility of directed effort towards a goal: if the cards are right, or the dice good to you, or if your lucky number comes up, things will go your way; if luck is against you, it's not worth trying. The concept of performing semi-magical rituals so that one's "luck will change" is prevalent; one hopes as a result to move from the state of being "unlucky" to that of being "lucky." The element of fantasy plays an important part in this area. Related to and complementing the notion that "only suckers work" (Smartness) is the idea that once things start going your way, relatively independent of your own effort, all good

things will come to you. Achieving great material rewards (big cars, big houses, a roll of cash to flash in a fancy night club), valued in lower class as well as in other parts of American culture, is a recurrent theme in lower class fantasy and folk lore; the cocaine dreams of Willie the Weeper or Minnie the Moocher present the components of this fantasy in vivid detail.

The prevalence in the lower class community of many forms of gambling, mentioned in connection with the "excitement" dimension, is also relevant here. Through cards and pool which involve skill, and thus both "toughness" and "smartness"; or through race horse betting, involving "smartness"; or through playing the numbers, involving predominantly "luck," one may make a big killing with a minimum of directed and persistent effort within conventional occupational channels. Gambling in its many forms illustrates the fact that many of the persistent features of lower class culture are multifunctional—serving a range of desired ends at the same time. Describing some of the incentives behind gambling has involved mention of all of the focal concerns cited so far—Toughness, Smartness, and Excitement, in addition to Fate.

Autonomy

The extent and nature of control over the behavior of the individual—an important concern in most cultures—has a special significance and is distinctively patterned in lower class culture. The discrepancy between what is overtly valued and what is covertly sought is particularly striking in this area. On the overt level there is a strong and frequently expressed resentment of the idea of external controls, restrictions on behavior, and unjust or coercive authority. "No one's gonna push *me* around," or "I'm gonna tell him he can take the job and shove it. . . ." are commonly expressed sentiments. Similar explicit attitudes are maintained to systems of behavior-restricting rules, insofar as these are perceived as representing the injunctions and bearing the sanctions of superordinate authority. In addition, in lower class culture a close conceptual connection is made between "authority" and "nurturance." To be restrictively or firmly controlled is to be cared for. Thus the overtly negative evaluation of superordinate authority frequently extends as well to nurturance, care, or protection. The desire for personal independence is often expressed in such terms as "I don't need *nobody* to take care of me. I can take care of myself!" Actual patterns of behavior, however, reveal a marked discrepancy between expressed sentiment and what is covertly valued. Many lower class people appear to seek out highly restrictive social environments wherein stringent external controls are maintained over their behavior. Such institutions as the armed forces, the mental hospital, the disciplinary school, the prison or correctional institution, provide environments which incorporate a strict and detailed set of rules, defining and limiting behavior and enforced by an authority system which controls and applies coercive sanctions for deviance from these rules. While under the jurisdiction of such systems, the lower class person generally expresses to his peers continual resentment of the coercive, unjust, and arbitrary exercise of authority. Having been released, or having escaped from these milieux, however, he will often act in such a way as to insure recommitment, or choose recommitment voluntarily after a temporary period of "freedom."

Lower class patients in mental hospitals will exercise considerable ingenuity to insure continued commitment while voicing the desire to get out; delinquent boys will frequently "run" from a correctional institution to activate efforts to return them; to be caught and returned means that one is cared for. Since "being controlled" is equated with "being cared for," attempts are frequently made to "test" the severity or strictness of superordinate authority to see if it remains firm. If intended or executed rebellion produces swift and firm punitive sanctions, the individual is reassured, at the same time that he is complaining bitterly at the injustice of being caught and punished. Some environmental milieux, having been tested in this fashion for the "firmness" of their coercive sanctions, are rejected, ostensibly for being too strict, actually for not being strict enough. This is frequently so in the case of "problematic" behavior by lower class youngsters in the public schools, which generally cannot command the coercive controls implicitly sought by the individual.

A similar discrepancy between what is overtly and covertly desired is found in the area of dependence-independence. The pose of tough rebellious independence often assumed by the lower class person frequently conceals powerful dependency cravings. These are manifested primarily by obliquely expressed resentment when "care" is not forthcoming rather than by expressed satisfaction when it is. The concern over autonomy-dependency is related both to "trouble" and "fate." Insofar as the lower class individual feels that his behavior is controlled by forces which often propel him into "trouble" in the face of an explicit determination to avoid it, there is an implied appeal to "save me from myself." A solution appears to lie in arranging things so that his behavior will be coercively restricted by an externally imposed set of controls strong enough to forcibly restrain his inexplicable inclination to get into trouble. The periodicity observed in connection with the "excitement" dimension is also relevant here; after involvement in trouble-producing behavior (assault, sexual adventure, a "drunk"), the individual will actively seek a locus of imposed control (his wife, prison, a restrictive job); after a given period of subjection to this control, resentment against it mounts, leading to a "break away" and a search for involvement in further "trouble."

FOCAL CONCERNS OF THE LOWER CLASS ADOLESCENT STREET CORNER GROUP

The one-sex peer group is a highly prevalent and significant structural form in the lower class community. There is a strong probability that the prevalence and stability of this type of unit is directly related to the prevalence of a stabilized type of lower class child-rearing unit—the "female-based" household. This is a nuclear kin unit in which a male parent is either absent from the household, present only sporadically, or, when present, only minimally or inconsistently involved in the support and rearing of children. This unit usually consists of one or more females of child-bearing age and their offspring. The females are frequently related to one another by blood or marriage ties, and the unit often includes two or more generations of women, e.g., the mother and/or aunt of the principal child-bearing female.

The nature of social groupings in the lower class community may be clarified if we make the assumption that it is the *one-sex peer unit* rather than the two-parent family unit which represents the most significant relational unit for both sexes in lower class communities. Lower class society may be pictured as comprising a set of age-graded one-sex groups which constitute the major psychic focus and reference group for

those over twelve or thirteen. Men and women of mating age leave these groups periodically to form temporary marital alliances, but these lack stability, and after varying periods of "trying out" the two-sex family arrangement, they gravitate back to the more "comfortable" one-sex grouping, whose members exert strong pressure on the individual *not* to disrupt the group by adopting a two-sex household pattern of life.[5] Membership in a stable and solidary peer unit is vital to the lower class individual precisely to the extent to which a range of essential functions —psychological, educational, and others—are not provided by the "family" unit.

The adolescent street corner group represents the adolescent variant of this lower class structural form. What has been called the "delinquent gang" is one subtype of this form, defined on the basis of frequency of participation in law-violating activity; this subtype should not be considered a legitimate unit of study per se, but rather as one particular variant of the adolescent street corner group. The "hanging" peer group is a unit of particular importance for the adolescent male. In many cases it is the most stable and solidary primary group he has ever belonged to; for boys reared in female-based households the corner group provides the first real opportunity to learn essential aspects of the male role in the context of peers facing similar problems of sex-role identification.

The form and functions of the adolescent corner group operate as a selective mechanism in recruiting members.

[5] Further data on the female-based household unit (estimated as comprising about 15 per cent of all American "families") and the role of one-sex groupings in lower class culture are contained in Walter B. Miller, Implications of Urban Lower Class Culture for Social Work. *Social Service Review*, 1959, 33, No. 3.

The activity patterns of the group require a high level of intragroup solidarity; individual members must possess a good capacity for subordinating individual desires to general group interests as well as the capacity for intimate and persisting interaction. Thus highly "disturbed" individuals, or those who cannot tolerate consistently imposed sanctions on "deviant" behavior cannot remain accepted members; the group itself will extrude those whose behavior exceeds limits defined as "normal." This selective process produces a type of group whose members possess to an unusually high degree both the *capacity* and *motivation* to conform to perceived cultural norms, so that the nature of the system of norms and values oriented to is a particularly influential component of motivation.

Focal concerns of the male adolescent corner group are those of the general cultural milieu in which it functions. As would be expected, the relative weighting and importance of these concerns pattern somewhat differently for adolescents than for adults. The nature of this patterning centers around two additional "concerns" of particular importance to this group—concern with "belonging," and with "status." These may be conceptualized as being on a higher level of abstraction than concerns previously cited, since "status" and "belonging" are achieved *via* cited concern areas of Toughness, etc.

Belonging

Since the corner group fulfills essential functions for the individual, being a member in good standing of the group is of vital importance for its members. A continuing concern over who is "in" and who is not involves the citation and detailed discussion of highly refined criteria for "in-group" membership. The phrase "he hangs with us" means "he is accepted as a member in good standing by current consensus"; conversely, "he don't hang with us" means he is not so accepted. One achieves "belonging" primarily by demonstrating knowledge of and determination to adhere to the system of standards and valued qualities defined by the group. One maintains membership by acting in conformity with valued aspects of Toughness, Smartness, Autonomy, etc. In those instances where conforming to norms of this reference group at the same time violates norms of other reference groups (e.g., middle class adults, institutional "officials"), immediate reference group norms are much more compelling since violation risks invoking the group's most powerful sanction: exclusion.

Status

In common with most adolescents in American society, the lower class corner group manifests a dominant concern with "status." What differentiates this type of group from others, however, is the particular set of criteria and weighting thereof by which "status" is defined. In general, status is achieved and maintained by demonstrated possession of the valued qualities of lower class culture—Toughness, Smartness, expressed resistance to authority, daring, etc. It is important to stress once more that the individual orients to these concerns *as they are defined within lower class society;* e.g., the status-conferring potential of "smartness" in the sense of scholastic achievement generally ranges from negligible to negative.

The concern with "status" is manifested in a variety of ways. Intragroup status is a continued concern and is derived and tested constantly by means of a set of status-ranking activities; the intragroup "pecking order" is constantly at issue. One gains status within the group by demonstrated superiority in

Toughness (physical prowess, bravery, skill in athletics and games such as pool and cards), Smartness (skill in repartee, capacity to "dupe" fellow group members), and the like. The term "ranking," used to refer to the pattern of intra-group aggressive repartee, indicates awareness of the fact that this is one device for establishing the intragroup status hierarchy.

The concern over status in the adolescent corner group involves in particular the component of "adultness," the intense desire to be seen as "grown up," and a corresponding aversion to "kid stuff." "Adult" status is defined less in terms of the assumption of "adult" responsibility than in terms of certain external symbols of adult status—a car, ready cash, and, in particular, a perceived "freedom" to drink, smoke, and gamble as one wishes and to come and go without external restrictions. The desire to be seen as "adult" is often a more significant component of much involvement in illegal drinking, gambling, and automobile driving than the explicit enjoyment of these acts as such.

The intensity of the corner group member's desire to be seen as "adult" is sufficiently great that he feels called upon to demonstrate qualities associated with adultness (Toughness, Smartness, Autonomy) to a much greater degree than a lower class adult. This means that he will seek out and utilize those avenues to these qualities which he perceives as available with greater intensity than an adult and less regard for their "legitimacy." In this sense the adolescent variant of lower class culture represents a maximization or an intensified manifestation of many of its most characteristic features.

Concern over status is also manifested in reference to other street corner groups. The term "rep" used in this regard is especially significant and has broad connotations. In its most fre-

quent and explicit connotation, "rep" refers to the "toughness" of the corner group as a whole relative to that of other groups; a "pecking order" also exists among the several corner groups in a given interactional area, and there is a common perception that the safety or security of the group and all its members depends on maintaining a solid "rep" for toughness vis-a-vis other groups. This motive is most frequently advanced as a reason for involvement in gang fights: "We *can't* chicken out on this fight; our rep would be shot!"; this implies that the group would be relegated to the bottom of the status ladder and become a helpless and recurrent target of external attack.

On the other hand, there is implicit in the concept of "rep" the recognition that "rep" has or may have a dual basis —corresponding to the two aspects of the "trouble" dimension. It is recognized that group as well as individual status can be based on both "law-abiding" and "law-violating" behavior. The situational resolution of the persisting conflict between the "law-abiding" and "law-violating" bases of status comprises a vital set of dynamics in determining whether a "delinquent" mode of behavior will be adopted by a group, under what circumstances, and how persistently. The determinants of this choice are evidently highly complex and fluid, and rest on a range of factors including the presence and perceptual immediacy of different community reference-group loci (e.g., professional criminals, police, clergy, teachers, settlement house workers), the personality structures and "needs" of group members, the presence in the community of social work, recreation, or educational programs which can facilitate utilization of the "law-abiding" basis of status, and so on.

What remains constant is the critical importance of "status" both for the members of the group as individuals and for the group as a whole insofar as members perceive their individual destinies as linked to the destiny of the group, and the fact that action geared to attain status is much more acutely oriented to the fact of status itself than to the legality or illegality, morality or immorality of the means used to achieve it.

LOWER CLASS CULTURE AND THE MOTIVATION OF DELINQUENT BEHAVIOR

The customary set of activities of the adolescent street corner group includes activities which are in violation of laws and ordinances of the legal code. Most of these center around assault and theft of various types (the gang fight; auto theft; assault on an individual; petty pilfering and shoplifting; "mugging"; pocketbook theft). Members of street corner gangs are well aware of the law-violating nature of these acts; they are not psychopaths, or physically or mentally "defective"; in fact, since the corner group supports and enforces a rigorous set of standards which demand a high degree of fitness and personal competence, it tends to recruit from the most "able" members of the community.

Why, then, is the commission of crimes a customary feature of gang activity? The most general answer is that the commission of crimes by members of adolescent street corner groups is motivated primarily by the attempt to achieve ends, states, or conditions which are valued and to avoid those that are disvalued within their most meaningful cultural milieu, through those culturally available avenues which appear as the most feasible means of attaining those ends.

The operation of these influences is well illustrated by the gang fight—a prevalent and characteristic type of corner group delinquency. This type of activity comprises a highly stylized and culturally patterned set of sequences. Although details vary under different circumstances, the following events are generally included. A member or several members of group A "trespass" on the claimed territory of group B. While there they commit an act or acts which group B defines as a violation of their rightful privileges, an affront to their honor, or a challenge to their "rep." Frequently this act involves advances to a girl associated with group B; it may occur at a dance or party; sometimes the mere act of "trespass" is seen as deliberate provocation. Members of group B then assault members of group A, if they are caught while still in B's territory. Assaulted members of group A return to their "home" territory and recount to members of their group details of the incident, stressing the insufficient nature of the provocation ("I just *looked* at her! Hardly even said anything!"), and the unfair circumstances of the assault ("About *twenty* guys jumped just the *two* of us!"). The highly colored account is acutely inflammatory; group A, perceiving its honor violated and its "rep" threatened, feels obligated to retaliate in force. Sessions of detailed planning now occur; allies are recruited if the size of group A and its potential allies appears to necessitate larger numbers; strategy is plotted, and messengers dispatched. Since the prospect of a gang fight is frightening to even the "toughest" group members, a constant rehearsal of the provocative incident or incidents and declamations of the essentially evil nature of the opponents accompany the planning process to bolster possibly weakening motivation to fight. The excursion into "enemy" territory sometimes results in a full scale fight; more often group B cannot be found, or the police appear and stop the fight, "tipped off" by an anonymous informant. When this occurs, group members express disgust and disappointment; secretly there is much relief; their honor has been avenged without incurring injury; often the anonymous tipster is a member of one of the involved groups.

The basic elements of this type of delinquency are sufficiently stabilized and recurrent as to constitute an essentially ritualized pattern, resembling both in structure and expressed motives for action classic forms such as the European "duel," the American Indian tribal war, and the Celtic clan feud. Although the arousing and "acting out" of individual aggressive emotions are inevitably involved in the gang fight, neither its form nor motivational dynamics can be adequately handled within a predominantly personality-focused frame of reference.

It would be possible to develop in considerable detail the processes by which the commission of a range of illegal acts is either explicitly supported by, implicitly demanded by, or not materially inhibited by factors relating to the focal concerns of lower class culture. In place of such a development, the following three statements condense in general terms the operation of these processes:

1. Following cultural practices which comprise essential elements of the total life pattern of lower class culture automatically violates certain legal norms.

2. In instances where alternate avenues to similar objectives are available, the non-law-abiding avenue frequently provides a relatively greater and more immediate return for a relatively smaller investment of energy.

3. The "demanded" response to certain situations recurrently engendered within lower class culture involves the commission of illegal acts.

The primary thesis of this paper is that the dominant component of the motivation of "delinquent" behavior engaged in by members of lower class corner groups involves a positive effort to achieve states, conditions, or qualities valued within the actor's most significant cultural milieu. If "conformity to immediate reference group values" is the major component of motivation of "delinquent" behavior by gang members, why is such behavior frequently referred to as negativistic, malicious, or rebellious? Albert Cohen, for example, in *Delinquent Boys* (Glencoe, Ill.: Free Press, 1955) describes behavior which violates school rules as comprising elements of "active spite and malice, contempt and ridicule, challenge and defiance." He ascribes to the gang "keen delight in terrorizing 'good' children, and in general making themselves obnoxious to the virtuous." A recent national conference on social work with "hard-to-reach" groups characterized lower class corner groups as "youth groups in conflict with the culture of their (sic) communities." Such characterizations are obviously the result of taking the middle class community and its institutions as an implicit point of reference.

A large body of systematically interrelated attitudes, practices, behaviors, and values characteristic of lower class culture are designed to support and maintain the basic features of the lower class way of life. In areas where these differ from features of middle class culture, action oriented to the achievement and maintenance of the lower class system may violate norms of middle class culture and be perceived as deliberately non-conforming or malicious by an observer strongly cathected to middle class norms. This does not mean, however, that violation of the middle class norm is the dominant component of motivation; it is a by-product of action primarily oriented to the lower class system. The standards of lower class culture cannot be seen merely as a reverse function of middle class culture—as middle class standards "turned upside down"; lower class culture is a distinctive tradition many centuries old with an integrity of its own.

From the viewpoint of the acting individual, functioning within a field of well-structured cultural forces, the relative impact of "conforming" and "rejective" elements in the motivation of gang delinquency is weighted preponderantly on the conforming side. Rejective or rebellious elements are inevitably involved, but their influence during the actual commission of delinquent acts is relatively small compared to the influence of pressures to achieve what is valued by the actor's most immediate reference groups. Expressed awareness by the actor of the element of rebellion often represents only that aspect of motivation of which he is explicitly conscious; the deepest and most compelling components of motivation—adherence to highly meaningful group standards of Toughness, Smartness, Excitement, etc.—are often unconsciously patterned. No cultural pattern as well established as the practice of illegal acts by members of lower class corner groups could persist if buttressed primarily by negative, hostile, or rejective motives; its principal motivational support, as in the case of any persisting cultural tradition, derives from a positive effort to achieve what is valued within that tradition, and to conform to its explicit and implicit norms.

13.

Illegitimate Means, Differential Opportunity and Delinquent Subcultures

Richard Cloward and Lloyd E. Ohlin

THE AVAILABILITY OF
ILLEGITIMATE MEANS

Social norms are two-sided. A prescription implies the existence of a prohibition, and vice versa. To advocate honesty is to demarcate and condemn a set of actions which are dishonest. In other words, norms that define legitimate practices also implicitly define illegitimate practices. One purpose of norms, in fact, is to delineate the boundary between legitimate and illegitimate practices. In setting this boundary, in segregating and classifying various types of behavior, they make us aware not only of behavior that is regarded as right and proper but also of behavior that is said to be wrong and improper. Thus the criminal who engages in theft or fraud does not invent a new way of life; the possibility of employing alternative means is acknowledged, tacitly at least, by the norms of the culture.

This tendency for proscribed alternatives to be implicit in every prescription, and vice versa, although widely recognized, is nevertheless a reef upon which many a theory of delinquency has foundered. Much of the criminological literature assumes, for example, that one may explain a criminal act simply by accounting for the individual's readiness to employ illegal alternatives of which his culture, through its norms, has already made him generally aware. Such explanations are quite unsatisfactory, however, for they ignore a host of questions regarding the *relative availability* of illegal alternatives to various potential criminals. The aspiration to be a physician is hardly enough to explain the fact of becoming a physician; there is much that transpires between the aspiration and the achievement. This is no less true of the person who wants to be a successful criminal. Having decided that he "can't make it legitimately," he cannot simply choose among an array of illegitimate means, all equally available to him. It is assumed in the theory of anomie that access to conventional means is differentially distributed, that some individuals, because of their social class, enjoy

SOURCE. Richard Cloward and Lloyd E. Ohlin, "Illegitimate Means, Differential Opportunity and Delinquent Subcultures," from *Delinquency and Opportunity*, Glencoe, Illinois: The Free Press, 1961, pp. 145–159. Copyright © 1960, The Free Press, a Corporation. Reprinted with the permission of The Macmillan Company.

certain advantages that are denied to those elsewhere in the class structure. For example, there are variations in the degree to which members of various classes are fully exposed to and thus acquire the values, knowledge, and skills that facilitate upward mobility. It should not be startling, therefore, to suggest that there are socially structured variations in the availability of illegitimate means as well. In connection with delinquent subcultures, we shall be concerned principally with differentials in access to illegitimate means within the lower class.

Many sociologists have alluded to differentials in access to illegitimate means without explicitly incorporating this variable into a theory of deviant behavior. This is particularly true of scholars in the "Chicago tradition" of criminology. Two closely related theoretical perspectives emerged from this school. The theory of "cultural transmission," advanced by Clifford R. Shaw and Henry D. McKay, focuses on the development in some urban neighborhoods of a criminal tradition that persists from one generation to another despite constant changes in population.[1] In the theory of "differential association," Edwin H. Sutherland described the processes by which criminal values are taken over by the individual.[2] He asserted that criminal behavior is learned, and that it is learned in interaction with others who have already

incorporated criminal values. Thus the first theory stresses the value systems of different areas; the second, the systems of social relationships that facilitate or impede the acquisition of these values.

Scholars in the Chicago tradition, who emphasized the processes involved in learning to be criminal, were actually pointing to differentials in the availability of illegal means—although they did not explicitly recognize this variable in their analysis. This can perhaps best be seen by examining Sutherland's classic work, *The Professional Thief*. "An inclination to steal," according to Sutherland, "is not a sufficient explanation of the genesis of the professional thief."[3] The "self-made" thief, lacking knowledge of the ways of securing immunity from prosecution and similar techniques of defense, "would quickly land in prison . . . a person can be a professional thief only if he is recognized and received as such by other professional thieves." But recognition is not freely accorded: "Selection and tutelage are the two necessary elements in the process of acquiring recognition as a professional thief. . . . A person cannot acquire recognition as a professional thief until he has had tutelage in professional theft, *and tutelage is given only to a few persons selected from the total population.*" For one thing, "the person must be appreciated by the professional thieves. He must be appraised as having an adequate equipment of wits, front, talking-ability, honesty, reliability, nerve and determination." Furthermore, the aspirant is judged by high standards of performance, for only "a very small percentage of those who start on this process ever reach the stage of professional thief. . . ." Thus motivation and pressures toward deviance do not fully account for deviant

---

[1] See esp. C. R. Shaw, *The Jack-Roller* (Chicago: University of Chicago Press, 1930); Shaw, *The Natural History of a Delinquent Career* (Chicago: University of Chicago Press, 1931); Shaw et al., *Delinquency Areas* (Chicago: University of Chicago Press, 1940); and Shaw and H. D. McKay, *Juvenile Delinquency and Urban Areas* (Chicago: University of Chicago Press, 1942).

[2] E. H. Sutherland, ed., *The Professional Thief* (Chicago: University of Chicago Press, 1937); and Sutherland, *Principles of Criminology*, 4th Ed. (Philadelphia: Lippincott, 1947).

[3] All quotations in this paragraph are from *The Professional Thief, op. cit.*, pp. 211–213. Emphasis added.

behavior any more than motivation and pressures toward conformity account for conforming behavior. The individual must have access to a learning environment and, once having been trained, must be allowed to perform his role. Roles, whether conforming or deviant in content, are not necessarily freely available; access to them depends upon a variety of factors, such as one's socioeconomic position, age, sex, ethnic affiliation, personality characteristics, and the like. The potential thief, like the potential physician, finds that access to his goal is governed by many criteria other than merit and motivation.

What we are asserting is that access to illegitimate roles is not freely available to all, as is commonly assumed. Only those neighborhoods in which crime flourishes as a stable, indigenous institution are fertile criminal learning environments for the young. Because these environments afford integration of different age-levels of offender, selected young people are exposed to "differential association" through which tutelage is provided and criminal values and skills are acquired. To be prepared for the role may not, however, ensure that the individual will ever discharge it. One important limitation is that more youngsters are recruited into these patterns of differential associations than the adult criminal structure can possibly absorb. Since there is a surplus of contenders for these elite positions, criteria and mechanisms of selection must be evolved. Hence a certain proportion of those who aspire may not be permitted to engage in the behavior for which they have prepared themselves.

Thus we conclude that access to illegitimate roles, no less than access to legitimate roles, is limited by both social and psychological factors. We shall here be concerned primarily with socially structured differentials in illegit-imate opportunities. Such differentials, we contend, have much to do with the type of delinquent subculture that develops.

LEARNING AND PERFORMANCE STRUCTURES

Our use of the term "opportunities," legitimate or illegitimate, implies access to both learning and performance structures. That is, the individual must have access to appropriate environments for the acquisition of the values and skills associated with the performance of a particular role, and he must be supported in the performance of the role once he has learned it.

Tannenbaum, several decades ago, vividly expressed the point that criminal role performance, no less than conventional role performance, presupposes a patterned set of relationships through which the requisite values and skills are transmitted by established practitioners to aspiring youth:

It takes a long time to make a good criminal, many years of specialized training and much preparation. But training is something that is given to people. People learn in a community where the materials and the knowledge are to be had. A craft needs an atmosphere saturated with purpose and promise. The community provides the attitudes, the point of view, the philosophy of life, the example, the motive, the contacts, the friendships, the incentives. No child brings those into the world. He finds them here and available for use and elaboration. The community gives the criminal his materials and habits, just as it gives the doctor, the lawyer, the teacher, and the candlestick-maker theirs.[4]

Sutherland systematized this general point of view, asserting that opportunity consists, at least in part, of learning structures. Thus "criminal behavior is

[4] Frank Tannenbaum, "The Professional Criminal," *The Century*, Vol. 110 (May-Oct. 1925), p. 577.

learned" and, furthermore, it is learned "in interaction with other persons in a process of communication." However, he conceded that the differential-association theory does not constitute a full explanation of criminal behavior. In a paper circulated in 1944, he noted that "criminal behavior is partially a function of opportunities to commit [i.e., to perform] specific classes of crime, such as embezzlement, bank burglary, or illicit heterosexual intercourse." Therefore, "while opportunity may be partially a function of association with criminal patterns and of the specialized techniques thus acquired, it is not determined entirely in that manner, and consequently differential association is not the sufficient cause of criminal behavior."[5]

To Sutherland, then, illegitimate opportunity included conditions favorable to the performance of a criminal role as well as conditions favorable to the learning of such a role (differential associations). These conditions, we suggest, depend upon certain features of the social structure of the community in which delinquency arises.

DIFFERENTIAL OPPORTUNITY: A HYPOTHESIS

We believe that each individual occupies a position in both legitimate and illegitimate opportunity structures. This is a new way of defining the situation. The theory of anomie views the individual primarily in terms of the legitimate opportunity structure. It poses questions regarding differentials in access to legitimate routes to success-goals; at the same time it assumes either that illegitimate avenues to success-goals are freely available or that differentials in their availability are of little signifi-

cance. This tendency may be seen in the following statement by Merton:

Several researches have shown that specialized areas of vice and crime constitute a "normal" response to a situation where the cultural emphasis upon pecuniary success has been absorbed, but where there is little access to conventional and legitimate means for becoming successful. The occupational opportunities of people in these areas are largely confined to manual labor and the lesser white-collar jobs. Given the American stigmatization of manual labor *which has been found to hold rather uniformly for all social classes,* and the absence of realistic opportunities for advancement beyond this level, the result is a marked tendency toward deviant behavior. The status of unskilled labor and the consequent low income cannot readily compete *in terms of established standards of worth* with the promises of power and high income from organized vice, rackets and crime. . . . [Such a situation] leads toward the gradual attenuation of legitimate, but by and large ineffectual, strivings and the increasing use of illegitimate, but more or less effective, expedients.[6]

The cultural-transmission and differential-association tradition, on the other hand, assumes that access to illegitimate means is variable, but it does not recognize the significance of comparable differentials in access to legitimate means. Sutherland's "ninth proposition" in the theory of differential association states:

Though criminal behavior is an expression of general needs and values, it is not explained by those general needs and values since non-criminal behavior is an expression of the same needs and values. Thieves generally steal in order to secure money, but likewise honest laborers work in order to secure money. The attempts by many scholars to explain criminal behavior by general drives and values, such as the happiness principle, striving for so-

[5] See A. K. Cohen, Alfred Lindesmith, and Karl Schuessler, eds., *The Sutherland Papers* (Bloomington, Ind.: Indiana University Press, 1956), pp. 31–35.

[6] R. K. Merton, *Social Theory and Social Structure,* Rev. and Enl. Ed. (Glencoe, Ill.: Free Press, 1957), pp. 145–146.

cial status, the money motive, or frustration, have been and must continue to be futile since they explain lawful behavior as completely as they explain criminal behavior.[7]

In this statement, Sutherland appears to assume that people have equal and free access to legitimate means regardless of their social position. At the very least, he does not treat access to legitimate means as variable. It is, of course, perfectly true that "striving for social status," "the money motive," and other socially approved drives do not fully account for either deviant or conforming behavior. But if goal-oriented behavior occurs under conditions in which there are socially structured obstacles to the satisfaction of these drives by legitimate means, the resulting pressures, we contend, might lead to deviance.

The concept of differential opportunity structures permits us to unite the theory of anomie, which recognizes the concept of differentials in access to legitimate means, and the "Chicago tradition," in which the concept of differentials in access to illegitimate means is implicit. We can now look at the individual, not simply in relation to one or the other system of means, but in relation to both legitimate and illegitimate systems. This approach permits us to ask, for example, how the relative availability of illegitimate opportunities affects the resolution of adjustment problems leading to deviant behavior. We believe that the way in which these problems are resolved may depend upon the kind of support for one or another type of illegitimate activity that is given at different points in the social structure. If, in a given social location, illegal or criminal means are not readily available, then we should not expect a

criminal subculture to develop among adolescents. By the same logic, we should expect the manipulation of violence to become a primary avenue to higher status only in areas where the means of violence are not denied to the young. To give a third example, drug addiction and participation in subcultures organized around the consumption of drugs presuppose that persons can secure access to drugs and knowledge about how to use them. In some parts of the social structure, this would be very difficult; in others, very easy. In short, there are marked differences from one part of the social structure to another in the types of illegitimate adaptation that are available to persons in search of solutions to problems of adjustment arising from the restricted availability of legitimate means.[8] In this sense, then, we can think of individuals as being located in two opportunity structures—one legitimate, the other illegitimate. Given limited access to success-goals by legitimate means, the nature of the delinquent response that may result will vary according to the availability of various illegitimate means.[9]

[7] *Principles of Criminology, op. cit.,* pp. 7–8.

[8] For an example of restrictions on access to illegitimate roles, note the impact of racial definitions in the following case: "I was greeted by two prisoners who were to be my cell buddies. Ernest was a first offender, charged with being a 'hold-up' man. Bill, the other buddy, was an old offender, going through the machinery of becoming a habitual criminal, in and out of jail. . . . The first thing they asked me was, 'What are you in for?' I said, 'Jack-rolling.' The hardened one (Bill) looked at me with a superior air and said, 'A hoodlum, eh? An ordinary sneak thief. Not willing to leave jack-rolling to the niggers, eh? That's all they're good for. Kid, jack-rolling's not a white man's job.' I could see that he was disgusted with me, and I was too scared to say anything" (Shaw, *The Jack-Roller, op. cit.,* p. 101).

[9] For a discussion of the way in which the availability of illegitimate means influences the adaptations of inmates to prison life, see R. A. Cloward, "Social Con-

ILLEGITIMATE OPPORTUNITIES AND THE SOCIAL STRUCTURE OF THE SLUM

When we say that the form of delinquency that is adopted is conditioned by the presence or absence of appropriate illegitimate means, we are actually referring to crucial differences in the social organization of various slum areas, for our hypothesis implies that the local milieu affects the delinquent's choice of a solution to his problems of adjustment. One of the principal ways in which slum areas vary is in the extent to which they provide the young with alternative (albeit illegitimate) routes to higher status. Many of the works in the cultural-transmission and differential-association tradition are focused directly on the relationship between deviant behavior and lower-class social structure. By reconceptualizing aspects of that tradition, we hope to make our central hypothesis more explicit.

Integration of Different Age-Levels of Offender

In their ecological studies of the urban environment, Shaw and McKay found that delinquency tended to be confined to limited areas and to persist in these areas despite demographic changes. Hence they spoke of "criminal traditions" and of the "cultural transmission" of criminal values.[10] As a result of their observations of slum life, they concluded that particular importance must be assigned to the relationships between immature and sophisticated offenders—which we call the integration of different age-levels of offender. They suggested that many

youngsters are recruited into criminal activities as a direct result of intimate associations with older and more experienced offenders:

Stealing in the neighborhood was a common practice among the children and approved of by the parents. Whenever the boys got together they talked about robbing and made more plans for stealing. I hardly knew any boys who did not go robbing. The little fellows went in for petty stealing, breaking into freight cars, and stealing junk. The older guys did big jobs like stick-ups, burglary, and stealing autos. The little fellows admired the "big shots" and longed for the day when they could get into the big racket. Fellows who had "done time" were the big shots and looked up to and gave the little fellows tips on how to get by and pull off big jobs.[11]

Thus the "big shots"—conspicuous successes in the criminal world—become role-models for youth, much more important as such than successful figures in the conventional world, who are usually socially and geographically remote from the slum area. Through intimate and stable associations with these older criminals, the young acquire the values and skills required for participation in the criminal culture. Further, structural connections between delinquents, semimature criminals, and the adult criminal world, where they exist, provide opportunities for upward mobility; where such integrative arrangements do not exist, the young are cut off from this alternative pathway to higher status.

Integration of Conventional and Deviant Values

Shaw and McKay were describing deviant learning structures—that is, alternative routes by which people seek access to the goals that society holds to be worthwhile. Their point was that

---

trol in the Prison," *Theoretical Studies of the Social Organization of the Prison*, Bulletin No. 15 (New York: Social Science Research Council, March 1960), pp. 20–48.

[10] See esp. *Delinquency Areas, op. cit.*, Chap. 16.

[11] Shaw, *The Jack-Roller, op. cit.*, p. 54.

access to criminal roles and advancement in the criminal hierarchy depend upon stable associations with older criminals from whom the necessary values and skills may be learned. Yet Shaw and McKay failed to give explicit recognition to the concept of illegitimate means and the socially structured conditions of access to them—probably because they tended to view slum areas as "disorganized." Although they consistently referred to illegitimate *activities* as "organized," they nevertheless tended to label high-rate delinquency *areas* "disorganized" because the values transmitted were criminal rather than conventional. Hence they sometimes made statements which we now perceive to be internally inconsistent, such as the following:

This community situation was not only disorganized and thus ineffective as a unit of control, but it was characterized by a high rate of juvenile delinquency and adult crime, not to mention the widespread political corruption which had long existed in the area. Various forms of stealing and many organized delinquent and criminal gangs were prevalent in the area. These groups exercised a powerful influence and tended to create a community spirit which not only tolerated but actually fostered delinquent and criminal practices.[12]

Sutherland was among the first to perceive that the concept of social disorganization tends to obscure the stable patterns of interaction which exist among carriers of criminal values: "the organization of the delinquent group, which is often very complex, is social disorganization only from an ethical or some other particularistic point of view."[13] Like Shaw and McKay, he had observed that criminal activities in lower-class areas were organized in terms of a criminal value system, but he also observed that *this alternative value system was supported by a patterned system of social relations.* That is, he recognized the fact that crime, far from being a random, unorganized activity, is often an intricate and stable system of arrangements and relationships. He therefore rejected the "social disorganization" perspective: "At the suggestion of Albert K. Cohen, this concept has been changed to differential group organization, with organization for criminal activities on one side and organization against criminal activities on the other."[14]

William F. Whyte, in his classic study of an urban slum, carried the empirical description of the structure and organization of illegal means a step further. Like Sutherland, Whyte rejected the position of Shaw and McKay that the slum is *dis*organized simply because it is organized according to principles different from those in the conventional world:

It is customary for the sociologist to study the slum district in terms of "social disorganization" and to neglect to see that an area such as Cornerville has a complex and well-established organization of its own. . . . I found that in every group there was a hierarchical structure of social relations binding the individuals to one another and that the groups were also related hierarchically to one another. Where the group was formally organized into a political club, this was immediately apparent, but for informal groups it was no less true.[15]

But Whyte's view of the slum differed somewhat from Sutherland's in that Whyte's emphasis was not on "differential group organization"—the idea that the slum is composed of two discrete

[12] Shaw, *The Natural History of a Delinquent Career, op. cit.*, p. 229.

[13] Cohen, Lindesmith, and Schuessler, eds., *The Sutherland Papers, op. cit.*, p. 21.

[14] *Ibid.*

[15] W. F. Whyte, *Street Corner Society,* Enl. Ed. (Chicago: University of Chicago Press, 1955), p. viii.

systems, conventional and deviant. He stressed, rather, the way in which the occupants of various roles in these two systems become integrated in a single, stable structure which organizes and patterns the life of the community. Thus Whyte showed that individuals who participate in stable illicit enterprises do not constitute a separate or isolated segment of the community but are closely integrated with the occupants of conventional roles. He noted, for example, that "the rackets and political organizations extend from the bottom to the top of Cornerville society, mesh with one another, and integrate a large part of the life of the district. They provide a general framework for the understanding of the actions of both 'little guys' and 'big shots.' "[16]

In a recent article, Kobrin has clarified our understanding of slum areas by suggesting that they differ in the *degree* to which deviant and conventional value systems are integrated with each other. This difference, we argue, affects the relative accessibility of illegal means. Pointing the way to the development of a "typology of delinquent areas based on variations in the relationship between these two systems," Kobrin describes the "polar types" on such a continuum. The integrated area, he asserts, is characterized not only by structural integration between carriers of the two value systems but also by reciprocal participation by carriers of each in the value system of the other. Thus, he notes:

Leaders of [illegal] enterprises frequently maintain membership in such conventional institutions of their local communities as churches, fraternal and mutual benefit societies and political parties. . . . Within this framework the influence of each of the two value systems is reciprocal, the leaders of illegal enterprise participat-

ing in the primary orientation of the conventional elements in the population, and the latter, through their participation in a local power structure sustained in large part by illicit activity, participating perforce in the alternate, criminal value system.[17]

The second polar type consists of areas in which the relationships between carriers of deviant and conventional values break down because of disorganizing forces such as "drastic change in the class, ethnic, or racial characteristics of [the] population." Kobrin suggests that in such slums "the bearers of the conventional culture and its value system are without the customary institutional machinery and therefore in effect partially demobilized with reference to the diffusion of their value system." At the same time, areas of this type are "characterized principally by the absence of systematic and organized adult activity in violation of the law, despite the fact that many adults in these areas commit violations." Thus both value systems remain implicit, but the fact that neither is "systematic and organized" precludes the possibility of effective integration.

How does the accessibility of illegal means vary with the relative integration of conventional and criminal values in a given area? Although Kobrin does not take up this problem explicitly, he does note that the integrated area apparently constitutes a "training ground" for the acquisition of criminal values and skills. Of his first polar type he says:

The stable position of illicit enterprise in the adult society of the community is reflected in the character of delinquent conduct on the part of children. While delinquency in all high-rate areas is intrinsically disorderly in that it is unrelated

[16] *Ibid.*, p. xii.

[17] Solomon Kobrin, "The Conflict of Values in Delinquency Areas," *American Sociological Review*, Vol. 16 (Oct. 1951), pp. 657–658.

to official programs for the education of the young, in the [integrated community] boys may more or less realistically recognize the potentialities for personal progress in local society through access to delinquency. In a general way, therefore, delinquent activity in these areas constitutes a training ground for the acquisition of skill in the use of violence, concealment of offense, evasion of detection and arrest, and the purchase of immunity from punishment. Those who come to excel in these respects are frequently noted and valued by adult leaders in the rackets who are confronted, as are the leaders of all income-producing enterprises, with problems of the recruitment of competent personnel.[18]

Kobrin makes no mention of the extent to which learning structures and opportunities for criminal careers are available in the unintegrated area. Yet the fact that neither conventional nor criminal values are articulated in this type of area as he describes it suggests that the appropriate learning structures —principally integration of different age-levels of offenders—are not available. Furthermore, Kobrin's description of adult violative activity in such areas as "unorganized" suggests that illegal opportunities are severely limited. Even if youngsters were able to secure adequate preparation for criminal roles, the social structure of such neighborhoods would appear to provide few opportunities for stable criminal careers. Kobrin's analysis—as well as that of Whyte and others before him—sup-

[18] *Ibid.*

ports our conclusion that *illegal opportunity structures tend to emerge only when there are stable patterns of accommodation between the adult carriers of conventional and of deviant values.* Where these two value systems are implicit, or where the carriers are in open conflict, opportunities for stable criminal-role performance are limited. Where stable accommodative relationships exist between the adult carriers of criminal and conventional values, institutionalized criminal careers are available. The alienated adolescent need not rely on the vagaries of private entrepreneurship in crime, with the attendant dangers of detection and prosecution, imprisonment, fluctuations in income, and the like. Instead, he may aspire to rise in the organized criminal structure and to occupy a permanent position in some flourishing racket. Secure in such a position, he will be relatively immune from prosecution and imprisonment, can expect a more or less stable income, and can look forward to acceptance by the local community—criminal and conventional.

Some urban neighborhoods, in short, provide relief from pressures arising from limitations on access to success-goals by legitimate means. Because alternative routes to higher status are made available to those who are ambitious, diligent, and meritorious, the frustrations of youth in these neighborhoods are drained off. Where such pathways do not exist, frustrations become all the greater.

14.

A New Theory of Delinquency and Crime

Walter C. Reckless

Containment theory is an explanation of conforming behavior as well as deviancy.[1] It has two reinforcing aspects: an inner control system and an outer control system. Are there elements within the self and within the person's immediate world that enable him to hold the line against deviancy or to hew to the line of social expectations? The assumption is that strong inner and reinforcing outer containment constitutes an insulation against normative deviancy (not constitutional or psychological deviancy), that is, violation of the sociolegal conduct norms.

A MIDDLE RANGE THEORY

Containment theory does not explain the entire spectrum of delinquency and crime. It does not explain crime or delinquency which emerges from strong inner pushes, such as compulsions, anxieties, phobias, hallucinations, personality disorders (including inadequate, unstable, antisocial personalities, etc.), from organic impairments such as brain damage and epilepsy, or from neurotic

[1] For the complete statement on containment theory, see Walter C. Reckless, *The Crime Problem*, 3rd Ed. New York: Appleton-Century-Crofts, 1961, pp. 335–359.

mechanisms (exhibitionists, peepers, fire setters, compulsive shop lifters). All told these cases are minimal. And containment theory does not explain criminal or delinquent activity which is a part of "normal" and "expected" roles and activities in families and communities, such as the criminal tribes of India, Gypsy vocations and trades (very similar to the former), begging families, and certain phases of delinquency subculture and organized crime. Between these two extremes in the spectrum of crime and delinquency is a very large middle range of norm violation, perhaps as big as two thirds to three quarters of officially reported cases as well as the unreported cases of delinquency and crime. Containment theory seeks to explain this large middle range of offenders. According to its place on the spectrum of delinquency and crime, one might say that it occupies the middle position.

A QUICK REVIEW OF CRIMINOLOGICAL THEORIES

Before proceeding further, it might be a good idea to see in what directions theory in criminology is pointing at present. Since the early nineteenth century we have had a long succession

SOURCE. Walter C. Reckless, "A New Theory of Delinquency and Crime, from *Federal Probation*, Volume 25, December 1961, pp. 42–46. Reprinted with the permission of *Federal Probation*.

of theories, most of which have not stood the test of time. It is possible to assemble these theories into three main camps of schools: (1) biological and constitutional theory—often called the school of criminal biology—in which the mainsprings of deviancy are sought in the inherited physical and mental makeup of man; (2) psychogenic theory, in which the formation of antisocial character is traced to faulty relationships within the family in the first few years of life; and (3) sociological theory, in which the pressures and pulls of the social milieu produce delinquent and criminal behavior.

Mention should be made of some of the specific theories. The dominating theory in Europe today is still the all-inclusive one which falls into the school of criminal biology. It points to the inheritance of weaknesses or pronenesses toward crime and delinquency (plus pressure from a bad environment).[2] Many variants of this theory have shown up in recent years: The attempt to prove inheritance of proneness through the method of studying criminal twins (Lange);[3] the attempt to identify body-mind types (Kretschmer);[4] the general acceptance throughout Europe in the past 25 years of several criminally oriented types of psychopaths, based on inherited proneness (according to Kurt Schneider);[5] the attempt to identify and explain habitual (serious) offenders as contrasted with occasional offenders or offenders of opportunity, according to early onset which in turn points to

inheritance of proneness (Irwin Frey);[6] the specification of the mesomorphic somatotype (muscular) as the type of constitution which is most usually related to delinquency (first according to William Sheldon[7] and later to the Gluecks).[8]

The psychogenic school probably claims August Aichhorn as its fountainhead. According to Aichhorn,[9] faulty development in the first few years of life makes it impossible for the child to control his impulses. The child lingers on as a sort of aggrandizing infant, living in the pleasure principle and failing to develop the reality principle in life. Friedlander[10] indicates that this faulty development in the first few years of life adds up to an antisocial character structure, incapable of handling reality properly. Redl,[11] who is also a disciple of Aichhorn, calls attention to the failure of the child to develop a management system over his impulsivity; that is, fails to develop a good ego and super ego.

The sociologists, ever since Ferri[12] (Italy, c. 1885), have been calling attention to bad environmental conditions. This was echoed by Bonger,[13] who placed the blame for dispropor-

[6] Irwin Frey, *Die Frühkriminelle Rückfallsverbrecher.* Basel, 1951, pp. 95–98, 103, 253.
[7] William H. Sheldon, *Varieties of Delinquent Youth.* New York: Harper and Brothers, 1949, p. 727.
[8] Sheldon and Eleanor Glueck, *Physique and Delinquency.* New York: Harper and Brothers, 1956, p. 219.
[9] August Aichhorn, *Wayward Youth.* New York, 1936.
[10] Kate Friedlander, *The Psycho-Analytic Approach to Delinquency.* New York: International Universities Press, 1947.
[11] Fritz Redl and David Wineman, *Children Who Hate.* Glencoe, Illinois: The Free Press, 1951.
[12] Enrico Ferri, *Criminal Sociology.* New York: Appleton and Co., 1896.
[13] W. G. Bonger, *Criminality and Economic Conditions,* translated by H. P. Horton. Boston: Little, Brown and Co., 1916.

[2] Franz Exner, *Kriminologie.* Berlin, 1949, pp. 115–120.
[3] Johannes Lange, *Crime and Destiny,* translated by Charlotte Haldane. New York: C. Boni, 1930.
[4] E. Kretschmer, *Physique and Character,* translated by W. I. H. Sprott. New York: Harcourt, Brace and Co., 1925.
[5] Kurt Schneider, *Psychopathische Persönlichkeiten,* 6th Ed. Berlin, 1943.

tional crime and delinquency among the proletariat on the pressures of the capitalistic system. However, the American sociologists in the twenties pointed to conditions of social or community disorganization, rather than factors related to poverty. They became engrossed with identifying the location and characteristics of high delinquency areas of the city, specifying family disruption and conflict instead of broken home, and calling attention to the modal importance of companionship in delinquency.

It was not until around 1940 that a basic American sociological theory of delinquency and criminal behavior was propounded. This was done by Sutherland and it was called differential association.[14] According to this theory, delinquent or criminal behavior is learned as is most other kinds of behavior— learned in association with others, according to the frequency, intensity, priority, and duration of contacts. Sutherland's theory really is not basically different from the one announced by Tarde[15] 50 years earlier, which regarded criminal behavior as a product of limitation of circulating patterns. Glaser[16] fairly recently proposed differential identification as a substitute for differential association. One takes over the models of behavior from those (reference) groups with which one identifies. But this does not have to be a face-to-face or person-to-person identification. (One can identify with the Beatniks without having actual physical contact with them.)

Still more recently Albert Cohen,[17]

picking up the lead from Whyte's *Street-Corner Society,* contended that working class boys who turned their backs on middle class virtues and values found the solution for their status problems in the delinquency subculture of the gang. And most recent of all is the theory propounded by Cloward and Ohlin[18] that urban slum boys gravitate to delinquency subculture when they discover they do not have access to legitimate avenues of success.

COMMENT ON THE THEORIES

Working backward in commenting on these theories, one might say that Cloward's theory only applies to those forms of delinquency which are part and parcel of the role structure of delinquency subculture. Jackson Toby[19] makes the estimate that this might only be 10 percent of the whole spectrum of delinquency. Assuming that Cloward's focus is very restricted, his theory does not account for the boys who do not gravitate toward the fighting gang, the criminal gang, and the retreatist groups (drugs). It does not specify that the ones who do gravitate to the three types of subculture have internalized an awareness of inaccessibility to legitimate success goals. It does not indicate that there are degrees of participation in gangs and that delinquency involvement of some members might be nil.

Cohen's theory has somewhat more merit. Somewhere and somehow in the growing-up process, slum boys turn their backs on middle class values and look to street-corner groups to come to their aid. But Cohen is not able to specify the boys who do or do not

[14] Edwin H. Sutherland, *Principles of Criminology,* 4th Ed. Philadelphia: J. B. Lippincott Co., 1947, pp. 6–7.
[15] Gabriel Tarde, *Penal Philosophy,* translated by R. Howell. Boston: Little, Brown and Co., 1912.
[16] Daniel Glaser, "Criminality Theories and Behavioral Images," *American Journal of Sociology,* Vol. 61, 1956, p. 440.
[17] Albert K. Cohen, *Delinquent Boys:*

The Culture of the Gang. Glencoe, Illinois: The Free Press, 1955, pp. 128–133.
[18] R. A. Cloward and Lloyd Ohlin, *Delinquency and Opportunity.* Glencoe, Illinois: The Free Press, 1960.
[19] Private circulated comment on the Cloward and Ohlin book, 1961.

turn their backs on middle class virtues and opportunities and gravitate to the street corner. He does not indicate whether only some of the boys on the street corner get involved in delinquent acts, as Shaw and Thrasher did a generation ago. So we have two interesting sociological formulations here, but not much realistic applicability.

Sutherland's differential association theory was meant to be a general theory, applying to the entire spectrum of delinquency and crime, from low to high in the class structure and across the board in personality. The trouble with Sutherland's theory (as well as Tarde's and Glaser's) is that it does not explain who *does* and who *does not* take up with carriers of delinquent patterns or who internalizes and who does not internalize delinquent models of behavior.

Coming now to the contributors to theory in the psychogenic school (Aichhorn, Redl, et al.), one should observe that at the most they only occupy a small end of the total spectrum of delinquency and crime. It is granted that there are some individuals whose ego and superego development is too weak or poor to control impulses and to handle ordinary expectancies. But it is not at all clear just which children succumb to or are recipients of faulty socialization in the first few years of life. And it is not clear just which of the children, teen-agers, late adolescents, and adults who are supposed to have little control over their impulse system run afoul the laws and regulations of society and those who do not.

One certainly finds it difficult to specify just exactly what the proneness is that is supposed to be the mainspring of serious, habitual, and early-starting offenders (criminal biology). It seems to be a sort of weakness in character. The evidence for the inheritance of proneness is very skimpy and most un-

impressive, a sort of unreliable family-tree assessment by clinicians.

William Sheldon was able to specify the different kinds of somatotypes much more definitely than Kretschmer was able to specify his body-mind types. A group of 200 problem youth in a Boston hostel, according to Sheldon, tended to have mesomorphic (athletic) body types along with several related forms of mental deviancy. The Gluecks discovered that among 500 delinquent and 500 nondelinquent boys the delinquents showed up very much more mesomorphic than the nondelinquents. The mesomorphs were found by the Gluecks to have a higher delinquency potential than other body types. Associated with mesomorphy were strength, social assertiveness, uninhibited motor responses, less submissiveness to authority. While mesomorphy does not explain all of delinquent behavior in the Gluecks' sample, it is certainly associated with a large segment of it and seems to reinforce many of the mental, emotional, and family traits connected with delinquency. Future studies will have to confirm the mesomorphic potential in delinquency.

GLUECKS: 4 TO 1 CAUSAL LAW

Out of their research on 500 delinquent and 500 nondelinquent boys, the Gluecks[20] proposed a five point causal law. According to this formulation, delinquents are distinguishable from nondelinquents (1) physically, in being essentially mesomorphic; (2) temperamentally, in being restless, impulsive, aggressive, destructive; (3) emotionally, in being hostile, defiant, resentful, assertive, nonsubmissive; (4) psychologically, in being direct, concrete learners; (5) socioculturally, in being

[20] Sheldon and Eleanor Glueck, *Unraveling Juvenile Delinquency*. New York: The Commonwealth Fund, 1950, pp. 281–282.

reared by unfit parents. This might be looked upon as a 4 to 1 law: four parts individual and one part situational. Items 2, 3, and 5 were chosen from among more than 100 overlapping traits, which distinguished delinquents from nondelinquents. The use of more sophisticated statistical methods would have enabled the Gluecks to find the two or three components within this maze of overlapping items which basically differentiate the delinquents from the nondelinquents. Nevertheless, the 4 to 1 causal law still stands as one of the few formulations which is worth attempting to confirm, qualify, or disprove by more rigorous research methods in the future. The law covers most of the spectrum of juvenile delinquency as we know it in the United States, certainly insofar as the full spectrum is represented by 500 boys from Boston who had been committed by juvenile courts to state schools in Massachusetts for delinquency.

INGREDIENTS OF INNER AND OUTER CONTAINMENT

In contrast to the buck-shot approach of the Gluecks, that is, shooting out in all directions to explore and discover, containment theory seeks to ferret out more specifically the inner and outer controls over normative behavior. It is attempting to get closer on the target of delinquency and crime by getting at the components which regulate conduct.

Inner containment consists mainly of self components, such as self-control, good self-concept, ego strength, well-developed superego, high frustration tolerance, high resistance to diversions, high sense of responsibility, goal orientation, ability to find substitute satisfactions, tension-reducing rationalizations, and so on. These are the inner regulators.

Outer containment represents the structural buffer in the person's immediate social world which is able to hold him within bounds. It consists of such items as a presentation of a consistent moral front to the person, institutional reinforcement of his norms, goals, and expectations, the existence of a reasonable set of social expectations, effective supervision and discipline (social controls), provision for reasonable scope of activity (including limits and responsibilities) as well as for alternatives and safety-valves, opportunity for acceptance, identity, and belongingness. Such structural ingredients help the family and other supportive groups contain the individual.

Research will have to ferret out the one or two elements in inner and outer containment which are the basic regulators of normative behavior. Undoubtedly in the lists cited above there are items which, if present, determine the existence of other items and cause most of the regulation of conduct. Likewise, research must indicate the way in which the inner and outer regulatory systems operate conjointly. How much self-strength must be present in a fluid world with very little external buffer? How much weakness in self-components is an effective external buffer able to manage?

SUPPORTING RESEARCH

The research and observations so far which give support to containment theory are the following:

1. According to Albert J. Reiss,[21] as a result of a study of Chicago delinquents who failed and succeeded on probation, the relative weakness of personal and social controls accounts for most cases of delinquency. Reiss found,

[21] Albert J. Reiss, Jr., "Delinquency as the Failure of Personal and Social Controls," *American Sociological Review,* Vol. 16, 1951, pp. 196–206.

however, that the personal controls had more predictive efficiency than the social controls as far as recidivism was concerned.

2. Nye[22] presented evidence to the effect that trends toward delinquent behavior are related to four control factors: (a) direct control which comes from discipline, restrictions, punishments; (b) internalized control which is the inner control of conscience; (c) indirect control which is exerted by not wanting to hurt or go against the wishes of parents or other individuals with whom the person identifies; and (d) the availability of alternative means to goals. Nye contends that his social control theory should not be applied to compulsive behavior or the behavior influenced by delinquency subcultures. He feels that the more indirect control is effective, the less need for direct control; the more internalized control is effective, the less need for any other type of control.

3. Reckless and Dinitz[23] found that a favorable concept of self insulated 12-year-old boys in the slum against delinquency, including perceptions about self, companions, home, and school. A poor concept of self, including perceptions that one is likely to get into trouble, his friends are in trouble, his

[22] F. Ivan Nye, *Family Relationships and Delinquent Behavior*. New York: John Wiley and Sons, Inc., 1958, pp. 3–4.
[23] Walter C. Reckless, Simon Dinitz, and Ellen Murray, "Self Concept as an Insulator against Delinquency," *American Sociological Review*, Vol. 21, 1956, p. 745; "The Self Component in Potential Delinquency and Potential Non-Delinquency," *ibid.*, Vol. 22, 1957, p. 569; Dimon Dinitz, Barbara Ann Kay, and Walter C. Reckless, "Group Gradients in Delinquency Potential and Achievement Score of Sixth Graders," *American Journal of Orthopsychiatry*, Vol. 28, 1958, pp. 598–605: Frank Scarpitti et al., "The 'Good' Boy in a High Delinquency Area: Four Years Later," *American Sociological Review*, Vol. 25, 1960, pp. 555–558.

family and home are unsatisfactory, that he will not finish school, and so on, was associated with delinquency vulnerability in 12-year-old slum boys. Four years later, followup contact revealed that the good self-concept group had pretty much held the line and the favorable direction, while the poor self-concept group had gravitated in unfavorable directions, 35 percent being involved with the law three times on an average. Reckless and Dinitz look upon a good or poor self-concept as an internalization of favorable or unfavorable socialization.

4. As a result of his observations on hyperaggressive, hostile children, Redl[24] identifies 22 functions of the ego in managing life situations. He conceives of the ego as the manager in the behavior control system, while the super ego is looked upon as the system which gives the signals to the ego. Redl, as is true of Aichhorn disciples, recognizes, particularly at the extremes, ego shortage and ego strength as well as a sick conscience and a healthy one.

Containment theory points to the regulation of normative behavior through resistance to deviancy as well as through direction toward legitimate social expectations. It may very well be that most of the regulation is in terms of a defense or buffer against deflection. At any rate, it appears as if inner and outer containment occupies a central or core position in between the pressures and pulls of the external environment and the inner drives or pushes. Environmental pressures may be looked upon as a condition associated with poverty or deprivation, conflict and discord, external restraint, minority group status, limited access to success

[24] Fritz Redl and David Wineman, *Children Who Hate*. Glencoe, Illinois: The Free Press, 1951, pp. 74–140.

in an opportunity structure. The pulls of the environment represent the distractions, attractions, temptations, patterns of deviancy, advertising, propaganda, carriers of delinquent and criminal patterns (including pushers), delinquency subculture, and so forth. The ordinary pushes are the drives, motives, frustrations, restlessness, disappointments, rebellion, hostility, feelings of inferiority, and so forth. One notices at once that Bonger as well as Cloward fall into pressure theory, while Tarde, Sutherland, and Glaser fall into pull theory.

In a vertical order, the pressures and pulls of the environment are at the top or the side of containing structure, while the pushes are below the inner containment. If the individual has a weak outer containment, the pressures and pulls will then have to be handled by the inner control system. If the outer buffer of the individual is relatively strong and effective, the individual's inner defense does not have to play such a critical role. Likewise, if the person's inner controls are not equal to the ordinary pushes, an effective outer defense may help hold him within bounds. If the inner defenses are of good working order, the outer structure does not have to come to the rescue of the person. Mention has already been made of the fact that there are some extraordinary pushes, such as compulsions, which cannot be contained. The inner and outer control system is usually not equal to the task of containing the abnormal pushes. They are uncontainable by ordinary controls.

SEVEN TESTS OF VALIDITY

1. Containment theory is proposed as the theory of best fit for the large middle range of cases of delinquency and crime. It fits the middle range cases better than any other theory.

2. It explains crimes against the person as well as the crimes against property, that is the mine run of murder, assault, and rape, as well as theft, robbery, and burglary.

3. It represents a formulation which psychiatrists, psychologists, and sociologists, as well as practitioners, can use equally well. All of these experts look for dimensions of inner and outer strength and can specify these strengths in their terms. Differential association and/or pressure of the environment leave most psychiatrists and psychologists cold, and an emphasis on push theory leaves the sociologists for the most part cold. But all of the experts can rally around inner and outer weaknesses and strengths.

4. Inner and outer containment can be discovered in individual case studies. Weaknesses and strengths are observable. Containment theory is one of the few theories in which the microcosm (the individual case history) mirrors the ingredients of the macrocosm (the general formulation).

5. Containment theory is a valid operational theory for treatment of offenders: for restructuring the milieu of a person or beefing up his self. The most knowledgeable probation workers, parole workers, and institutional staff are already focusing to some extent on helping the juvenile or adult offender build up ego strength, develop new goals, internalize new models of behavior. They are also working on social ties, anchors, supportive relationships, limits, and alternative opportunities in helping to refashion a new containing world for the person.

6. Containment theory is also an effective operational theory for prevention. Children with poor containment can be spotted early. Programs to help insulate vulnerable children against delinquency must operate on internaliza-

tion of stronger self components and the strengthening of containing structure around the child.

7. Internal and external containment can be assessed and approximated. Its strengths and weaknesses can be specified for research. There is good promise that such assessments can be measured in a standard way.

Finally, it is probable that the theory which will best supplement containment theory in the future will be "damage theory," according to which a light to dark spectrum of damage produces maladjustment and deviancy. The problem here is to find measures to isolate the less serious and less obvious damage cases and to estimate how far into the middle range of delinquency and crime the lighter impairments go.

15.

Delinquency Research and the Self-Concept Variable

Sandra S. Tangri and Michael Schwartz

A wide variety of variables have been related to delinquency rates. These include demographic variables,[1] social structural variables,[2] variables having to do with perception of the social structures,[3] and occasionally personality variables.[4] In a recent paper by Himelhoch,[5] the point is made, without much elaboration, that personality variables may indeed be necessary for an adequate prediction scheme in delinquency research. He makes a plea in his paper for multi-level analyses which ought to include at one time variables of structure, perception of structure, and personality.

A case can be made for engaging in such research on a number of counts. In the first place, while structural variables seem to be the primary focus in delinquency research carried on by sociologists, the results of their studies can by no means be taken as heartening. For example, in a recent paper by Westie and Turk, in which they examine the question of the relationship of social class to delinquency, they point out that it is quite possible to support findings which indicate more delinquency in the lower class then the middle class, more delinquency in the middle class than the lower class, or no differences by class, on the basis of both current research and theory.[6] Similarly, those studies which relate demographic variables to delinquency rates do not by any means achieve the same results.

While some students of delinquency have been able to find that delinquents and non-delinquents have differing per-

SOURCE. Sandra S. Tangri and Michael Schwartz, "Delinquency Research and the Self-Concept Variable" from *Journal of Criminal Law, Criminology and Police Science*, Volume 58, June 1967, pp. 182–190. Reprinted with permission.
[1] See especially Chilton, "Continuity in Delinquency Area Research: A Comparison of Studies for Baltimore, Detroit, and Indianapolis, 29 AM. SOC. REV., 71–83 (1964).
[2] For example, see Cloward & Ohlin, *Delinquency and Opportunity* (1960).
[3] See Short, Jr., Rivera & Tennyson, *Perceived Opportunities, Gang Membership and Delinquency*, 30 AM. SOC. REV., 56–67 (1965).
[4] Reckless, Dinitz & Murray, *Self-Concept and an Insulator Against Delinquency*, 21 AM. SOC. REV. 744–746 (1956).
[5] Himelhoch, *Delinquency and Opportunity: an End and a Beginning of Theory*, Gouldner & Miller, Eds., *Applied Sociology*, 189–206 (1965).

[6] Westie & Turk, "A Strategy for Research on Social Class and Delinquency," 56 *J. Crim. L., C. & P. S.* 454–462 (1965).

ceptions of the structure which they confront, in no case has it been determined that those perceptions precede delinquency or non-delinquency or are a consequence of delinquency or non-delinquency. That very criticism can be made of studies which claim to discriminate between delinquents and non-delinquents on the basis of personality measures, although studies of personality variables and delinquency are most uncommon in the sociological literature.

Apparently the major point, which is not made with the strength necessary in Himelhoch's paper, is that delinquency research has reached a stage where study designs ought to include variables at all of the levels we have mentioned, and that designs aimed at discriminating between groups are, at this stage, less important than are designs aimed at determining the amount of variance which can be accounted for in delinquency and non-delinquency by variables at a number of levels of analysis. In other words, we are now due for designs in delinquency research which are analysis of variance designs.

If the ambiguity and contractions in our univariate forms of analysis are ever to be understood, then it seems that the analysis of variance design is one which ought to be employed. It does have the virtue of giving the researcher an indication of the ways in which the interactions of variables from different levels of analysis combine to account for delinquency, and it seems that there is every indication that an understanding of the interaction effects of these variables may prove to be vastly more fruitful than a continued pursuit of univariate studies.

As Himelhoch has argued, however, sociologists concerned with delinquency research seem either to ignore variables at the level of personality, or to take them as given. Variables of personality

seem to be in the domain of the psychologists and therefore out of the realm of the sociologist's competence or research concern. Perhaps that is a great error. There is available in our discipline a tradition of thought in the realm of personality and socialization which is not only respectable but also growing in measurement sophistication and applicability in empirical research. That is, of course, the tradition of symbolic interactionism.

Some sociologists have, in the past, investigated personality or self variables, keeping constant the social structural variables. Most important and impressive among these studies are the ones conducted by Professor Reckless and his associates, in which self-concept is viewed as a variable which seems effective in insulating boys against delinquency or in making them more vulnerable. Because this research has been so widely quoted and reprinted, and because it is practically the only research by sociologists in the area of delinquency which claims to handle variables of personality and self, it is wise, we believe, to undertake a thoroughgoing analysis of those researches, their designs, and the findings in order to determine what sociologists have been able to learn about delinquency and personality, as well as to determine what remains to be done in that area.

The behavior of the non-delinquent in a high delinquency area has occasioned a good deal of interest because of its possible implications for policies of social control. None of the studies by the Reckless group, however, draw such implications although they all claim to have discovered a crucial variable which differentiates delinquents and non-delinquents, and delinquents who have and have not been in contact with legal authorities as offenders. They do suggest that "self theory seems . . . to be the best operational basis for designing effective prevention and treatment measures."[7]

This proposal is elaborated no further. As they state, the crucial variable is self-concept or "self-evaluation":

> It is proposed that a socially appropriate or inappropriate concept of self and other is the basic component that steers the youthful person away from or toward delinquency and that those appropriate or inappropriate concepts represent differential response to various environments and confrontations of delinquent patterns.[8]

In this discussion we shall review the methodology and detailed results of several studies, and attempt to evaluate the extent to which these impose certain restrictions on the broad interpretation quoted above.

THE ORIGINAL STUDY: SELF CONCEPT AS AN INSULATOR AGAINST DELINQUENCY[9]

This was the first of the series of articles on the problem and deals exclusively with the boys whom we shall refer to as "good boys".

For this study, all thirty sixth-grade teachers in schools located in the highest white deliquency areas of Columbus, Ohio, were asked to nominate those white boys who would not, in their opinion, ever experience police or juvenile court contact; and the teachers were asked to give their reasons. Half of those eligible were nominated (i.e., 192). Of those, 51 students (27.3%) could not be located because of summer vacation. Of the remaining 141 boys, sixteen (11.3%) already had rec-

ords and were eliminated from the sample. This left 125 "good boys"—and their mothers—who were interviewed. Each boy was administered the delinquency proness (DE) and social responsibility (RE) scales of Gough's California Personality Inventory (CPI); a questionnaire on his occupational preference (the data from which do not appear among the results); and each was asked questions about his concept of himself, his family, and his interpersonal relations.

The results obtained for the "good boys" were: (1) Low scores on the DE scale and high scores on the RE scale; (2) "self-evaluations" which were law-abiding and obedient; and (3) very favorable perceptions of family interaction, and lack of resentment of close family (mother) supervision; (4) these families were maritally, residentially, and economically stable. The authors concluded: "Insulation against delinquency is an ongoing process reflecting internalization of non-delinquent values and conformity to the expectations of significant others".

Critique

1. The first and obvious problem is that, without knowing parallel results on a control group of so-called "bad boys", we cannot conclude that these results actually differentiate the two populations. Since this comparison is subsequently made at the time of a later study, we shall postpone further discussion of this issue.

2. Insofar as the term "insulation" implies present and/or future predictiveness as to actual delinquent behavior, the following difficulties arise:

(a) It is perhaps a truism to point out that court records do not contain evidence of all law-violating behavior, and particularly in the case of minors.

---

[7] Reckless, Dinitz & Kay, "The Self Component in Potential Delinquency and Non-Delinquency," **22** *Am. Soc. Rev.,* 570 (1957).

[8] *Ibid,* p. 569.

[9] Reckless, Dinitz & Murray, *op cit supra* note 4.

Therefore, it is probably safe to guess that the previous offenders constituting 11.3% of the "good boys" is an underestimate. It is about half the proportion of previous offenders later found among the "bad boys".

(b) Since these boys were only 12 years old at this time, it would be more reasonable to look for a correlation between present "self-concept" and future "delinquency". Most of these boys (99 out of 125) were relocated in school four years later (at age 16), and four of them had been in "contact" with the police or juvenile court or both, one time each during the intervening years. Even this interval might be questioned as to whether it provides an adequate time span in which to validate actual "insulation". Together with the 16 "good boys" who were eliminated for this reason from the original sample, this makes 20 boys, or 14.4% of the 141 nominated "good boys" who were originally located.

(c) What is required is a comparison of the proportion of "contacts" among those scoring like "good boys" and those scoring like "bad boys" on the DE and RE scales from both actual groups of "good boys" and "bad boys" as nominated by the teachers. The analysis is not made anywhere, and is precluded by the exclusion of the 16 "contact" cases from the study of "good boys".

3. There is some clarification needed as to the use of teacher's nominations in this design. We have already seen that there is not a perfect correlation between the teacher's evaluations of the boys and their actual (non-) delinquency, as operationally defined in this study.

(a) If the authors wanted to investigate that relationship, they would not have eliminated 11.3% of the "good boys" who had already experienced "contact" with juvenile court or police.

Such an investigation would have shed an interesting sidelight on why, in spite of being capable of making a good impression, these boys also had police or court records. What if they had turned out to have relatively positive self-concepts instead of relatively negative ones —contrary to the author's later assumption? We would be in a much better position to evaluate the author's conclusion if they had elected to gather these data. On the other hand, it must be pointed out that the authors were presumably not interested in investigating this relationship. From their point of view, it could be argued that there is no need for a perfect correlation. The assumption is only that you have a little better chance of getting a pure non-delinquent sample if you have two criteria; that the delinquent who can slip by one of them is less likely to slip by both.

(b) Nevertheless, the margin of uncertainty about the meaning of the teachers' nominations is magnified by the fact that only one-half of the eligible students were nominated. Who are the remaining boys? We wonder how many of those not nominated as "good boys" and with no "contact" experience would have been found to have poor self-concepts? And how many of these would have had "contact" with the police or juvenile court? Conversely, we wonder how many of those not nominated but with no "contact" would have been found to have poor self-concepts. The magnitudes involved are certainly great enough to reverse or eliminate the reported relationships.

The fact remains, however, that if we are really interested in determining the effect of the self-concept upon delinquency vulnerability, then we ought not look for delinquent and non-delinquent groups, but rather for groups with clearly good and clearly bad self-concepts. How those would be distributed between later delinquent and non-delinquent groups would better determine the effect of self-concept as independent variable, upon delinquency as the dependent one. Clearly, a major issue in much of this research has to do with the delineation of the experimental variables. If self-concept is an "insulator against delinquency", this implies that self-concept is an independent variable. But the research causes confusion because self-concept is treated as the dependent variable.

(c) There is some reason to feel uneasy also about the fairly high percentage (27.3%) of "good boys" who could not be located (i.e., 51 out of 192). This is particularly so when we compare the similar percentage for the "bad boys" nominated in the later study: 6.5% (or 7 out of 108). Thus, the original population of "good boys" (192) has been reduced by 34.9% (51 + 16 = 67), whereas no comparable shrinkage occurred in the "bad boy" population.

4. Our most serious concern, however, is with the instruments used to evaluate self-concept.

(a) In terms of the most elementary Meadian psychology, the relationship between frame of reference and self-evaluation, i.e., the correlation between teachers' nominations and the boys' responses to CPI items is not surprising. The CPI items obviously are drawn from a middle-class frame of reference, as are the teachers' impressions. They do not sample from an alternative frame of reference, in which positive instead of negative values might be placed on the same response. But we do not know whether a revised scoring procedure in itself could be sensibly interpreted. Therefore, we would prefer to substitute a less culture-bound measure such as the semantic differential, in which the individual is free to operate in terms

of any (unspecified) frame of reference. (We will have more to say about this problem presently, in some general comments.)

(b) Viewed in this light, one might hypothesize that because of this frame of reference, boys who are nominated as "good" will continue to test positive on the CPI, until they are caught in a delinquent act, at which time—and not until—the middle-class frame of reference would operate to devalue their behavior, and supposedly that part of their self-concept. Unfortunately, no such separate analysis was made.

THE "GOOD BOYS" FOUR YEARS LATER[10]

Some of the questions raised in the previous section about the interpretation of the "insulation" of the "good boys" in these studies may now be answered. Of the original 125 on whom data had been collected, only 103 boys (82.4%) were relocated, now age 16, but only 90 of them were still in school. The others were not retested. These boys' homeroom teachers were again requested to nominate the boys as (a) ones who would not experience difficulty with the law, (b) ones who would get into trouble, or (c) ones about whom the teacher was unsure, and why. Each of the boys was again checked through police and juvenile court files "for official or unofficial violation behavior in the intervening years," and their school records were checked. Their mothers or mother-surrogates were again interviewed.

The results were as follows: Ninety-five of the boys were again nominated by their teachers as unlikely to get into trouble with the law. The reasons in-

[10] Scarpitti, Murray, Dinitz & Reckless, "The 'Good' Boy in a High Delinquency Area: Four Years Later, **25** *Am. Soc. Rev.* 555–558 (1960).

dicated "quietness," "good family," and "good student." Four of these boys had become known to the police or juvenile court, or both—one time each during the intervening years. Ninety-six boys were enrolled in the academic program, although they showed a more or less normal distribution scholastically and in attendance (in which respect there had been no significant change over time). Ninety-eight expected to finish high school. Ninety-one remained aloof from boys in trouble with the law. The families of these boys, who were found in the original study to be typical of the families in the school areas in terms of father's occupation, were not nearly as residentially mobile as anticipated. (A separate analysis comparing the respondents who remained in the high delinquency areas with those who had achieved upward mobility revealed no significant difference on any of the indices included.) The boys' responses on the tests "and, apparently, in behavior as well," were consistent with their earlier performances.

On an additional measure, the Short-Nye seven-items scale of admitted delinquent behavior, "The good boys appear almost angelic." The authors question, however, the reliability of this result because they were unable to replicate the Short-Nye scale in any of their own more recent studies and because of the lack of anonymity of the boys, ". . . and their younger age." The boys' reports on their families were again favorable, somewhat more so than previously.

Critique

1. Now it is somewhat more clear that self-concept is the independent variable and that delinquency is the dependent one. At least it is clear if one keeps the first paper in mind. Of greatest interest is the finding that most of

the "good boys" located again are still in school ($99/103 = 96.1\%$), and all but three are in the academic program. We wonder if this might not imply that the factor differentiating good from bad boys is ability to perform adequately in school. Glueck's findings on comparative intelligence between the normal and reformatory population would tend to support this interpretation: "It will be seen that the reformatory population contains a considerable excess of dull, borderline, and feebleminded groups."[11]

2. There are, however, several reasons why this interpretation may be unwarranted:

(a) The later studies do not give information on how many of the "bad boys" similarly remained in school (and in an academic program).

(b) Even if we found the proportion to be radically different, it would be quite reasonable to argue that this was because of their delinquency, lack of motivation, rejection by their teachers, or any one of a number of other factors than intelligence *per se*. However, it might have been helpful for narrowing the possible interpretations to have such a measure, providing it too wasn't class-biased.

(c) Of the boys still in school, half were still in the compulsory attendance age bracket.

3. In the relocation of the "good boys", 22 of the original sample were lost. Although this is three times as many as were lost from the "bad boy" sample, because of the fact that the original nominees from the population were almost 50% more for the "good boys" than for the "bad boys", it means in effect that the retested samples were approximately in the same proportions

[11] Glueck, S. & E., *Five Hundred Criminal Careers,* 156 (1939).

to the original populations for both groups: $99/141 = 70.2\%$ of the "good boys" and $70/101 = 69.3\%$ of the "bad boys."

4. We are also faced again with the questionable interpretation of the teachers' nominations. Why were they again asked to nominate each boy as a likely or unlikely candidate for trouble?

(a) In this case they were not choosing the boys out of the total class; if they had, perhaps fewer would have been nominated as "good boys".

(b) We do not know whether the four "good boys" still in school but not renominated were nominated as likely to get into trouble, or whether in their case the teacher was "unsure" (an additional category not previously used).

(c) It is interesting to point out that the four boys who had police or court contact in the intervening years are not these four (who were *not* renominated), but are among those the teachers again nominated as unlikely to get into trouble.

(d) It is not clear whether these are the only boys out of those relocated who had been "in trouble," or whether they are the only ones out of those still in school. If the latter is the case, and it appears to be, then there remains some question about the "insulation" of the four boys *not* in school.

(e) We are left with 95 "good boys" (67.4%) out of the original 141 nominated and tested about whom we can weigh with some (but not absolute) confidence that they have not been delinquent. Because of the unfortunate reporting of data, we cannot determine the comparable figure for the "bad boys." We know there were 20 offenders among the original "good boys" at the end of the study, but we don't know how many there were among the "bad boys" (because some of the earlier and later offenders may be the same boys).

THE SELF COMPONENT IN POTENTIAL DELINQUENCY AND NON-DELINQUENCY,[12] A SELF-GRADIENT AMONG POTENTIAL DELINQUENTS[13]

The sample of potential delinquents were nominated a year after the "good boys" study by 37 sixth-grade teachers in the same 20 schools in a white high delinquency area in Columbus, Ohio. Approximately one-fourth (108) of those eligible were nominated as "headed for police and juvenile court contact." Apparently population growth in the area had increased the white sixth-grade population by about 13% (from ca. 384 to ca. 432) and the number of sixth-grade teachers by 23% (from 30 to 37). (There may have been a greater increase in the area's Negro population than in its white population.) Only seven of these boys could not be located; the remaining 101, and their mothers, were interviewed. A check of the police and juvenile court files revealed that 24 of these twelve-year-old boys (23%) were already on record for previous offenses which ranged from charges of incorrigibility to theft.

The results, when compared with the first study, were as follows:

The "bad boy" scores . . . were significantly higher on the DE and lower on the RE scales than those made by the 'good boys' of the first study. Indeed, this mean delinquency vulnerability score was higher than that achieved by any of the non-delinquents and non-disciplinary sample subjects treated in other studies. Similarly, the mean social responsibility score was lower than those recorded in other studies for all but prisoners, delinquents, and school disciplinary cases. These scores seem to validate the judgments of the

[12] Reckless, Dinitz & Kay, *op cit supra* note 7.

[13] Dinitz, Reckless & Kay, "A Self-Gradient Among Potential Delinquents," **49** *J. Crim. L., C. & P. S.* 230–233 (1958).

teachers in selecting these boys as ones who would get into future difficulties with the law.

Not only do these scales appear to differentiate between the potentially delinquent and non-delinquent, but even more importantly they were found to descriminate within the sample of nominated delinquents between those boys who had and those who had not experienced previous court contact. . . . These differences between the contact and non-contact groups on both sides were statistically significant.[14]

Critique

(We shall not repeat the points already discussed as parts of the preceding sections.)

1. Adding to the confusion of possible interpretations already mentioned is the fact that the samples were not "designed" in a parallel manner. It will be recalled that in order to isolate "a truly non-delinquent group" for the first study, the investigators discarded sixteen cases (11.3%) of the "good boys" who could be located. This procedure would lead one to think that the interest was in fact correlating certain psychological patterns with behavioral patterns. However, we find that in the second study no such "purity" is attempted, and the 77 boys (76.8% of the 101 "bad boys" located) who did not have records for previous offenses were retained in the sample. Had the parallel operation been carried out, the "truly delinquent" group would have been considerably smaller, thus altering the statistical results of the measure. However, it should be pointed out that this type of attrition would have led to more, rather than less, significant results. The problem, therefore, is not the validity of the statistics, but rather the *interpretation* in comparing two non-parallel groups.

2. The second most critical point to

14 *Ibid*, p. 231.

make is that there is further contamination of variables due to the fact that the teachers' knowledge of the boys' involvement with the law "undoubtedly influenced" their nominations. Therefore, we have neither an independent "nomination variable" nor independent behavior variable. (We shall subsequently discuss the possible contamination of the third and critical variable, the test and interview responses.)

3. Although it is not possible to infer *a priori* whether any bias in sampling occurred because of the increase in number of teachers participating (37 as against 30 in the first study), it should be noted that there were large teacher differences in the number of "bad boys" nominated. In some classrooms 60% of the eligible boys were nominated, whereas nine teachers nominated no one. (There was an average of 11.7 white boys per class, out of whom an average of 2.9 were nominated as headed for trouble.) These differences may reflect school policy to segregate potential disrupters, but we do not know.

We should point out that the statement that "these scores seem to validate the judgment of the teachers in selecting these boys as ones who would get into future difficulties with the law" implies some "validation" of the teachers' nominations against the nominees' later (future) actual behavior. This interpretation clearly may be unwarranted insofar as the only relationship being described is that teachers' nominations succeeded in creating two groups (at two different times) whose average scores on the DE and RE scales were significantly different. Moreover, we do not know how many of the same teachers were involved in both tests.

5. With respect to the comparisons of the "contact cases" and "non-contact cases," the conclusion that "it is apparent that the contact cases in many re-

spects seem to be confirmed in their delinquent self-concepts to a greater extent than are the others" is justified in light of the results. What is not warranted, however, is the investigators' projected *evaluation* of his self-concept as a negative one to the boys being studied. A delinquent self-concept is not necessarily a negative concept.

DELINQUENCY VULNERABILITY[15]

The follow-up study four years later of the "bad boys" succeeded in relocating 70 boys, now 16 years old. We know nothing of how many were in school or in an academic program, and there is no report of second set of teachers' nominations. Twenty-seven (38.6%) of these seventy boys "had had serious and frequent contact with the court during the four-year interlude. These 27 boys averaged slightly more than three contacts with the court, involving separate complaints for delinquency." However, we do not know how many (if any) of these 27 are the same boys (24 of them) who had already had records at the time of the first testing, or whether they are different boys from the original population. As was mentioned earlier, both the "good" and "bad" follow-up samples are approximately the same proportion of the originally located, but untested, nominee groups. The "good" group lost 11.3% of its boys before testing began because of their delinquency records, whereas none of the located "bad boys" was dropped. The "bad" group, on the other hand, diminished proportionately more in size between the first and second testing, which may be considered more serious because it was an *uncontrolled* shrinkage of the *tested* population. The result is that the "good"

15 Dinitz, Scarpitti, & Reckless, "Delinquency Vulnerability: A Cross-Group and Longitudinal Analysis," **27** *Am. Soc. Rev.* 515–517 (1962).

follow-ups constitute 82.4% of their originally tested group and the "bad" follow-up constitute only 69.3% of theirs. Results of the second follow-up indicated that the "bad boys" mean score on the DE scale had not changed (it was 23.6 and at second testing was 23.4), and was still significantly "worse" than the "good boys" (whose mean score was 14.2, and at the second testing 13.6). The authors also note that "whereas the individual scores of the 70 'bad' boys on the DE scale at age 16 correlated with their scores at 12 years of age to the extent of r = .78," the "coefficient of correlation (r) of the DE scores for the boys in the 'good' cohort at 16 and at 12 years of age was only .15." They do not attempt to give any explanation for this difference in the groups' longitudinal stability. Certainly this is a most important finding and requires further understanding.

GENERAL COMMENTS

There are criticisms which pertain to the series of studies as a whole, and which are so important as to restrict severely the authors' interpretations given, even if all the foregoing is deemed irrelevant or incorrect. Of major concern to us are the measures which were used to define operationally the boys' self-concepts. In the first place, it is not made quite clear in the original studies whether the conclusions with regard to self-concept are based on the Gough (DE and RE) CPI Scales, or whether the conclusion is based on the boys' answers to questions about their expectations of getting into trouble, or whether it was based on attitude items such as whether "any real trouble persons have with the law can be 'fixed' if they know the right people," whether it had to do with their descriptions of their home life or the degree to which they and their mothers (or mother-surrogates) seemed to agree.

It would be helpful in deciding which items are appropriate to a self-concept measure to differentiate between questions of *fact* and questions of *evaluation.* It is our opinion that only the latter is relevant to self-concept. Therefore, insofar as the boy states facts as he perceives them about his present behavior, the age and delinquency of his companions, "activity level" (whatever that is), whether he relies more on his friends or his parents for advice, etc., he tells us nothing about whether he thinks these are good or bad things, i.e., how these reflect on him personally and in his own judgment. Even in his judgment about the likelihood of his getting into trouble in the future, we do not know whether (1) this is self-criticism, (2) a badge of bravado, or (3) whether the prediction is accurate.

If we look at the operational definitions which are more ambiguously stated in the later studies, we see that they consist primarily of these kinds of statements:

On a nine-item quasi-scale or inventory, which measures the boys' favorable or unfavorable *projections of self in reference to getting into trouble with the law,* the cohort of 103 sixteen-year-old insulated slum boys showed an average score of 15.8. In this instance, the inventory was scored from 10 for the most favorable answers to 19 for the most unfavorable answers on all nine items. The 70 vulnerable 16-year-old slum boys scored an average of 18.9 on this quasi-scale.[16]

Could not these results be regarded as a statistically reasonable prediction by the boys of future events based on their respective past histories? Could it not be possible that the "bad boys" take some pride in their "record" and consider it a necessary adjunct to their self-image to be "tough" and "in trouble"?

Later in the same article quoted

[16] *Ibid,* p. 516. (Emphasis added.)

above, the following operational definition is given:

Regarding favorable or unfavorable concepts of self as measured by responses to questions such as "up to now, do you think things have gone your way?" or "do you feel that grown ups are usually against you?" or "do you expect to get an even break from people in the future?" there was no major change in the percentage distribution of the responses of the two cohorts at age 12 and at age 16. The good cohort had a very high percentage of favorable responses and the bad cohort a low percentage favorable responses. On all three questions listed above, the percentage of favorable responses for the 103 good boys at age 16 was 90. For the 70 bad boys at 16 the percentage of favorable responses on the first of the above listed questions was 50; on the second, 29; on the third, 30.[17]

It is reasonable again to ask whether the "bad boys" responses are not simply realistic reflections of the fact that these same boys ". . . who had already been in trouble with the law defined themselves significantly more often than the others as likely candidates for getting into further difficulties with the police and the courts."[18]

Does it not reflect the fact that their mothers think so too; and that their teachers think so? Is not just another way of saying that their "family affectional relationships" are not satisfactory? But, does it also necessarily mean that these boys have no recourse but to accept these negative evaluations of *these* others *as their own evaluations of themselves?* We would argue that this is not the case, but that these boys look elsewhere for positive self-reflection, and that they may find it in their friends, which is the meaning of their seeking advice from friends more than from

[17] *Ibid,* p. 517.
[18] Dinitz, Reckless & Kay, *op cit supra* note 7, at p. 232.

parents. A major problem appears to be that the authors may have selected sets of others for the boys, i.e., mother and teacher, both of whom are not significant "others" from the boys' own points of view.[19]

In summary, we would say that these studies have demonstrated:

1. That there is a certain amount of agreement between teachers and parents on the likelihood of certain boys getting into trouble; it has not demonstrated that this consensus agrees with either present or future actual experience.

2. That boys are aware of the judgments their elders make of them; it has not demonstrated the boys' acceptances of these evaluations of them as their own.

3. That this is true for the so-called "good boys" as well the "bad boys"; and we still do not know whether the former think well of themselves and the latter do not.

The primary problem that is raised by Reckless' treatment of self is this: from any collection of questionnaire or interview responses, what kinds of conclusions can we draw about the self? It is not enough to say that these responses represent the subject's self. Since almost anything one can say may have some bearing on the self, we must have rules for extracting that aspect or implication of the statement relevant to self; otherwise we have no basis for distinguishing self from non-self, for everything is self. And that is the trouble with these studies. If everything is self, then self becomes another word for everything and its value is destroyed! A general hodgepodge of items from the CPI, questions asked of mother, son and

teacher all thrown into the pot of self seems to destroy the meaning of self for research usage.

Vastly improved measurement in all of sociology is necessary. But adequate self-concept measurement is a dire necessity. We do not wish, however, to belabor the point. This research represents an important contribution to delinquency theory as well as to general social psychology. The papers have been reprinted in numbers of books of readings. It has been our experience that teachers, school administrators, public officials concerned with youth problems and others are very much aware of the Reckless *et al.* studies and in some cases try to operate in terms of these findings. But it would seem that there are some problems with this work which require adequate investigation. Nevertheless, Professor Reckless has opened an important door.

Our second comment in general has to do with the interpretation of the correspondence between the two studies. It will be remembered that the two cohorts were examined a year apart and taken from the same schools. They were not done contemporaneously This may have had the advantage of avoiding invidious comparisons between the two groups of boys. However, in order to have confidence in the lack of bias on the part of the *investigators who administered the tests and interviewed the parents,* we would have to know whether or not they knew which cohort they were interviewing. In light of the fact that the data on the students in the good cohort were published soon after the data on the bad cohort were collected, (which means, in effect, that the results were known sometime earlier), and considering the fact that all these studies have been done by substantially the same group of investigators, we are inclined to believe that the investigators' own interviewers knew which cohort

---

[19] Schwartz & Tangri, "A Note on Self-Concept As An Insulator Against Delinquency," **30** *Am. Soc. Rev.* 922–926 (1965).

was which *while they were collecting data.*

Finally, we would point out that a theoretical link is missing from this research. Why should poor self-concept leave the individual vulnerable to delinquency? It might be argued, for example, that a poor self-concept ought to produce behavior more in conformity with the demands of significant others like mother or teacher. Or does poor self-concept lead to rejecting the rejectors and subsequent attributions of significance to those others who prove rewarding to the self (say, delinquent peers)?

Is it enough to indicate that more nominated "bad boys" than "good boys" become delinquent, even though the number of "bad boys" who become delinquent is less than 50% of the total nominated. In short, we are not yet convinced that "self-concept" is a major contributor to the variance in delinquent behavior. No small part of our skepticism arises from the atheoretical orientation of the Reckless work.

Even if all the foregoing criticism of this research were to be determined to be incorrect, the fact of the matter is that until this same form of research is undertaken in a somewhat more sophisticated way and a design is formed which includes not only self variables but also structural and cognitive (such as perception of structure) variables, and until the interaction effects from all of these levels as well as the main effects of each are understood, then it will continue to be impossible to develop predictive accuracy with reference to juvenile delinquency.

16.

False Criteria of Causalily in Delinquency Research*

Travis Hirschi and Hanan C. Selvin

Smoking per se is not a cause of lung cancer. Evidence for this statement comes from the thousands of people who smoke and yet live normal, healthy lives. Lung cancer is simply unknown to the vast majority of smokers, even among those who smoke two or more packs a day. Whether smoking is a cause of lung cancer, then, depends upon the reaction of the lung tissues to the smoke inhaled. The important thing is not whether a person smokes, but how his lungs react to the smoke inhaled. These facts point to the danger of imputing causal significance to superficial variables. In essence, it is not smoking as such, but the carcinogenic ele-ments in tobacco smoke that are the real causes of lung cancer.[1]

The task of determining whether such variables as broken homes, gang membership, or anomie are "causes" of delinquency benefits from a comparison with the more familiar problem of deciding whether cigarette smoking "causes" cancer. In both fields many statistical studies have shown strong relations between these presumed causes and the observed effects, but the critics of these studies often attack them as "merely statistical." This phrase has two meanings. To some critics it stands for the belief that only with ex-perimental manipulation of the inde-pendent variables is a satisfactory causal inference possible. To others it is a brief way of saying that observing a statistical association between two phenomena is only the first step in plausibly inferring casuality. Since no one proposes trying to give people cancer or to make them delinquent, the fruitful way toward bet-ter causal analyses in these two fields is

* This is publication A-56 of the Survey Research Center, University of California, Berkeley. We are grateful to the Ford Foundation for financial support of the larger study from which this paper is drawn. An early account of this study, which does not include the present paper, is *The Methodological Adequacy of De-linquency Research*, Berkeley: Survey Re-search Center, 1962. Ian Currie, John Lofland, Alan B. Wilson, and Herbert L. Costner made useful criticisms of previous versions of this paper.

SOURCE. Travis Hirschi and Hanan C. Selvin, "False Criteria of Causality in De-linquency Research," from *Social Prob-lems,* Volume 13, No. 3, Winter 1966, pp. 254–268. Reprinted with permission.

[1] This is a manufactured "quotation"; its source will become obvious shortly.

to concentrate on improving the statistical approach.

In setting this task for ourselves we can begin with one area of agreement: all statistical analyses of causal relations in delinquency rest on observed associations between the independent and dependent variables. Beyond this there is less agreement. Following Hyman's reasoning,[2] we believe that these two additional criteria are the minimum requirements for an adequate causal analysis: (1) the independent variable is causally prior to the dependent variable (we shall refer to this as the criterion of "causal order"), and (2) the original association does not disappear when the influences of other variables causally prior to both of the original variables are removed ("lack of spuriousness").[3]

The investigator who tries to meet these criteria does not have an easy time of it.[4] Our examination of statistical research on the causes of delinquency shows, however, that many investigators do not try to meet these criteria but instead invent one or another new criterion of causality—or, more often, of noncausality, perhaps because noncausality is easier to demonstrate. To establish causality one must forge a chain of three links (association, causal order, and lack of spuriousness), and the possibility that an antecedent variable not yet considered may account for the observed relation makes the third link inherently weak.

To establish noncausality, one has only to break any one of these links.[5]

Despite the greater ease with which noncausality may be demonstrated, many assertions of noncausality in the delinquency literature turn out to be invalid. Some are invalid because the authors misuse statistical tools or misinterpret their findings. But many more are invalid because the authors invoke one or another false criterion of noncausality. Perhaps because assertions of noncausality are so easy to demonstrate, these invalid assertions have received a great deal of attention.

A clear assertion that certain variables long considered causes of delinquency are not really causes comes from a 1960 *Report to The Congress:*

Many factors frequently cited as causes of delinquency are really only concomitants. They are not causes in the sense that if they were removed delinquency would decline. Among these factors are:
Broken homes.
Poverty.
Lack of recreational facilities.
Poor physical health.
Race.
Working mothers.[6]

---

[2] Herbert H. Hyman, *Survey Design and Analysis.* Glencoe, Illinois: The Free Press, 1955, chs. 5–7.

[3] Hyman appears to advocate another criterion as well: that a chain of intervening variables must link the independent and dependent variables of the original relation. We regard this as psychologically or theoretically desirable but not as part of the minimum methodological requirements for demonstrating causality in nonexperimental research.

[4] Hirschi and Selvin, *op. cit.*

[5] Popper calls this the asymmetry of verifiability and falsifiability. Karl R. Popper, *The Logic of Scientific Discovery,* New York: Basic Books, 1959, esp. pp. 27–48. For a fresh view of the verification-falsification controversy, see Thomas S. Kuhn, *The Structure of Scientific Revolutions,* Chicago: University of Chicago Press, 1962. Kuhn discusses Popper's views on pp. 145–146. Actually, it is harder to establish non-causality than our statement suggests, because of the possibility of "spurious independence." This problem is discussed in Hirschi and Selvin, *op. cit.,* pp. 38–45, as "elaboration of a zero relation."

[6] U.S. Department of Health, Education, and Welfare, *Report to The Congress on Juvenile Delinquency,* United States Government Printing Office, 1960, p. 21. The conclusion that "poor housing" is not a cause of delinquency is based on Mildred Hartsough, *The Relation Between Housing and Delinquency,* Federal Emergency Administration of Public Works, Housing

According to this report, all of these variables are statistically associated with delinquency, i.e., they are all "concomitants." To prove that they are not causes of delinquency it is necessary either to show that their relations with delinquency are spurious or that they are effects of delinquency rather than causes. Since all of these presumptive causes appear to precede delinquency, the only legitimate way to prove noncausality is to find an antecedent variable that accounts for the observed relations. None of the studies cited in the *Report* does this.[7] Instead, the assertion that broken homes, poverty, lack of recreational facilities, race, and working mothers are not causes of delinquency appears to be based on one or more of the following false "criteria":[8]

1. Insofar as a relation between two variables is not *perfect*, the relation is not causal.
   a. Insofar as a factor is not a *necessary condition* for delinquency, it is not a cause of delinquency.
   b. Insofar as a factor is not a *sufficient condition* for delinquency, it is not a cause of delinquency.
2. Insofar as a factor is not *"characteristic"* of delinquents, it is not a cause of delinquency.
3. If a relation between an independent variable and delinquency is found for a *single value of a situational or contextual factor*, then the situational or contextual factor cannot be a cause of delinquency.[9]
4. If a relation is observed between an independent variable and delinquency and if a psychological variable is suggested as *intervening* between these two variables, then the original relation is not causal.
5. *Measurable* variables are not causes.
6. If a relation between an independent variable and delinquency is *conditional* upon the value of other variables, the independent variable is not a cause of delinquency.

In our opinion, all of these criteria of noncausality are illegitimate. If they were systematically applied to any field of research, no relation would survive the test. Some of them, however, have

---

Division, 1936. The conclusion that "poor physical health" is not a cause is based on Edward Piper's "unpublished Children's Bureau manuscript summarizing the findings of numerous investigators on this subject." Since we have not examined these two works, the following conclusions do not apply to them.

[7] The works cited are: broken homes, Negly K. Teeters and John Otto Reinemann, *The Challenge of Delinquency,* New York: Prentice-Hall, 1950, pp. 149–154; poverty, Bernard Lander, *Toward an Understanding of Juvenile Delinquency,* New York: Columbia University Press, 1954; recreational facilities, Ethel Shanas and Catherine E. Dunning, *Recreation and Delinquency,* Chicago: Chicago Recreation Commission, 1942; race, Lander, *op. cit.*; working mothers, Eleanor E. Maccoby, "Children and Working Mothers," *Children,* 5 (May-June, 1958), pp. 83–89.

[8] It is not clear in every case that the researcher himself reached the conclusion of noncausality or, if he did, that this conclusion was based on the false criteria discussed below. Maccoby's article, for example, contains a "conjectural explanation" of the relation between mother's employment and delinquency (i.e., without presenting any statistical evidence she suggests that the original relation came about through some antecedent variable), but it appears that the conclusion of noncausality in the *Report* is based on other statements in her work.

[9] All of the foregoing criteria are related to the "perfect relation" criterion in that they all require variation in delinquency that is unexplained by the "noncausal" variable. A more general statement of criterion 3 would be: "if variable X is related to delinquency when there is no variation in variable T, then variable T is not a cause of delinquency." In order for this criterion to be applicable, there must be some residual variation in delinquency after T has had its effect.

Although both forms of this criterion fairly represent the reasoning involved in some claims of non-causality, and although both are false, the less explicit version in the text is superficially more plausible. This inverse relation between explicitness and plausibility is one reason for the kind of methodological explication presented here.

a superficial plausibility, both as stated or implied in the original works and as reformulated here. It will therefore be useful to consider in some detail just why these criteria are illegitimate and to see how they appear in delinquency research.

FALSE CRITERION 1. *Insofar as a relation between two variables is not perfect, the relation is not causal.*

Despite the preponderance of Negro delinquency, one must beware of imputing any causal significance to race per se. There is no *necessary* concomitance between the presence of Negroes and delinquency. In Census Tracts 9-1 and 20-2, with populations of 124 and 75 Negro juveniles, there were no recorded cases of delinquency during the study period. The rates of Negro delinquency also vary as widely as do the white rates indicating large differences in behavior patterns that are not a function or effect of race per se. It is also of interest to note that in at least 10% of the districts with substantial Negro juvenile populations, the Negro delinquency rate is lower than the corresponding white rate.[10]

There are three facts here: (1) not all Negroes are delinquents; (2) the rates of Negro delinquency vary from place to place; (3) in some circumstances, Negroes are less likely than whites to be delinquent. These facts lead Lander to conclude that race has no causal significance in delinquency.

In each case the reasoning is the same: each fact is another way of saying that the statistical relation between race and delinquency is not perfect, and this apparently is enough to disqualify race as a cause. To see why

[10] Bernard Lander, *Towards an Understanding of Juvenile Delinquency*, New York: Columbia University Press, 1954, p. 32. Italics in original. An alternative interpretation of the assumptions implicit in this quotation is presented in the discussion of criterion 6, below.

this reasoning is invalid one has only to ask for the conditions under which race *could be* a cause of delinquency if this criterion were accepted. Suppose that the contrary of the first fact above were true, that *all* Negroes are delinquent. It would then follow necessarily that Negro delinquency rates would not vary from place to place (fact 2) and that the white rate would never be greater than the Negro rate (fact 3). Thus in order for race to have "any" causal significance, all Negroes must be delinquents (or all whites non-delinquents). In short, race must be perfectly related to delinquency.[11]

Now if an independent variable and a dependent variable are perfectly associated,[12] no other independent variable

[11] Strictly speaking, in this quotation Lander does not demand that race be perfectly related to delinquency, but only that all Negroes be delinquents (the sufficient condition of criterion 1-b). Precedent for the "perfect relation" criterion of causality appears in a generally excellent critique of crime and delinquency research by Jerome Michael and Mortimer J. Adler published in 1933: "There is still another way of saying that none of the statistical findings derived from the quantitative data yields answers to etiological questions. The findings themselves show that every factor which can be seen to be in some way associated with criminality is also associated with non-criminality, and also that criminality is found in the absence of every factor with which it is also seen to be associated. In other words, what has been found is merely additional evidence of what we either knew or could have suspected, namely, that there is a plurality of related factors in this field." *Crime, Law and Social Science*, New York: Harcourt Brace, p. 53.

[12] "Perfect association" here means that all of the cases fall into the main diagonal of the table, that (in the 2 × 2 table) the independent variable is both a necessary and a sufficient cause of the dependent variable. Less stringent definitions of perfect association are considered in the following paragraphs. Since Lander deals with ecological correlations, he could reject race as a cause of delinquency even if it were perfectly related to delinquency at the census tract level, since the ecological and the individual correlations are not identical.

is needed: that is, perfect association implies single causation, and less-than-perfect association implies multiple causation. Rejecting as causes of delinquency those variables whose association with delinquency is less than perfect thus implies rejecting the principle of multiple causation. Although there is nothing sacred about this principle, at least at the level of empirical research it is more viable than the principle of single causation. All studies show that more than one independent variable is needed to account for delinquency. In this field, as in others, perfect relations are virtually unknown. The researcher who finds a less-than-perfect relation between variable X and delinquency should not conclude that X is not a cause of delinquency, but merely that it is not the *only* cause.[13]

For example, suppose that tables like the following have been found for variables A, B, C, and D as well as for X:

Delinquency by X, where X is neither a necessary nor a sufficient condition for delinquency, but may be one of several causes.

	X	Not X
Delinquent	40	20
Nondelinquent	60	80

The researcher using the perfect relation criterion would have to conclude that none of the causes of delinquency has yet been discovered. Indeed, this criterion would force him to conclude that there are *no causes* of delinquency except *the* cause. The far-from-perfect relation between variable X and delinquency in the table above leads him to reject variable X as a cause of delinquency. Since variables A, B, C, and D

[13] We are assuming that the causal order and lack of spuriousness criteria are satisfied.

are also far from perfectly related to delinquency, he must likewise reject them. Since it is unlikely that *the* cause of delinquency will ever be discovered by quantitative research, the researcher who accepts the perfect relation criterion should come to believe that such research is useless: all it can show is that there are *no* causes of delinquency.

FALSE CRITERION 1a. *Insofar as a factor is not a necessary condition for delinquency, it is not a cause of delinquency.*

The "not necessary" (and of course the "not sufficient") argument against causation is a variant of the "perfect relation" criterion. A factor is a necessary condition for delinquency if it must be present for delinquency to occur—e.g., knowledge of the operation of an automobile is a necessary condition for auto theft (although all individuals charged with auto theft need not know how to drive a car). In the following table the independent variable X is a necessary (but not sufficient[14]) condition for delinquency.

Delinquency by X, where X is a necessary but not sufficient condition for delinquency.

	X	Not X
Delinquent	67	0
Nondelinquent	33	100

The strongest statement we can find in the work cited by the Children's

[14] To say that X is a necessary condition for delinquency means that all delinquents are X (i.e., that the cell in the upper right of this table is zero); to say that X is a sufficient condition for delinquency implies that all X's are delinquent (i.e., that the cell in the lower left is zero); to say that X is a necessary and sufficient condition for delinquency means that all X's and no other persons are delinquent (i.e., that both cells in the minor diagonal of this table are zero).

Bureau in support of the contention that the broken home is not a cause of delinquency is the following:

We can leave this phase of the subject by stating that the phenomenon of the physically broken home is a cause of delinquent behavior is, in itself, not so important as was once believed. In essence, it is not that the home is broken, but rather that the home is inadequate, that really matters.[15]

This statement suggests that the broken home is not a necessary condition for delinquency (delinquents may come from intact but "inadequate" homes). The variable with which the broken home is compared, inadequacy, has all the attributes of a necessary condition for delinquency: a home that is "adequate" with respect to the prevention of delinquency will obviously produce no delinquent children. If, as appears to be the case, the relation between inadequacy and delinquency is a matter of definition, the comparison of this relation with the relation between the broken home and delinquency is simply an application of the illegitimate "necessary conditions" criterion. Compared to a necessary condition, the broken home is "not so important." Compared to some (or some *other*) *measure* of inadequacy, however, the broken home may be very important. For that matter, once "inadequacy" is empirically defined, the broken home may turn out to be one of its important causes. Thus the fact that the broken home is not a necessary condition for delinquency does not justify the statement that the broken home is "not [a cause of delinquency] in the sense that if [it] were removed delinquency would decline."[16]

[15] Teeters and Reinemann, *op. cit.*, p. 154.
[16] *Report to The Congress*, p. 21. Two additional illegitimate criteria of causality listed above are implicit in the quotation

FALSE CRITERION 1b. *Insofar as a factor is not a sufficient condition for delinquency, it is not a cause of delinquency.*

A factor is a sufficient condition for delinquency if its presence is invariably followed by delinquency. Examples of sufficient conditions are hard to find in empirical research.[17] The nearest one comes to such conditions in delinquency research is in the use of predictive devices in which several factors taken together are virtually sufficient for delinquency.[18] (The fact that several variables are required even to approach sufficiency is of course one of the strongest arguments in favor of multiple causation.) Since sufficient conditions are rare, this unrealistic standard can be used against almost any imputation of causality.

First, however, let us make our position clear on the question. Poverty per se is not a cause of delinquency or criminal behavior; this statement is evidenced by the

from Teeters and Reinemann. "Inadequacy of the home" could be treated as an intervening variable which interprets the relation between the broken home and delinquency (criterion 4) or as a theoretical variable of which the broken home is an indicator (criterion 5). These criteria are discussed below.
[17] In his *Theory of Collective Behavior* (New York: The Free Press of Glencoe, 1963) Neil J. Smelser suggests sets of necessary conditions for riots, panics, and other forms of collective behavior; in this theory the entire set of necessary conditions for any one form of behavior is a sufficient condition for that form to occur.
[18] In the Gluecks' prediction table, those with scores of 400 or more have a 98.1% chance of delinquency. However, as Reiss has pointed out, the Gluecks *start* with a sample that is 50% delinquent. Had they started with a sample in which only 10% were delinquent, it would obviously have been more difficult to approach sufficiency. Sheldon Glueck and Eleanor Glueck, *Unraveling Juvenile Delinquency*, Cambridge: Harvard University Press, 1950, pp. 260–262; Albert J. Reiss, Jr., "Unraveling Juvenile Delinquency. II. An Appraisal of the Research Methods," *American Journal of Sociology*, 57:2, 1951, pp. 115–120.

courage, fortitude, honesty, and moral stamina of thousands of parents who would rather starve than steal and who inculcate this attitude in their children. Even in the blighted neighborhoods of poverty and wretched housing conditions, crime and delinquency are simply nonexistent among most residents.[19]

Many mothers, and some fathers, who have lost their mates through separation, divorce, or death, are doing a splendid job of rearing their children.[20]

Our point of view is that the structure of the family *itself* does not cause delinquency. For example, the fact that a home is broken does not cause delinquency, but it is more difficult for a single parent to provide material needs, direct controls, and other important elements of family life.[21]

The error here lies in equating "not sufficient" with "not *a* cause." Even if every delinquent child were from an impoverished (or broken) home—that is, even if this factor were a necessary condition for delinquency—it would still be possible to show that poverty is not a sufficient condition for delinquency.

In order for the researcher to conclude that poverty is a cause of delinquency, it is not necessary that all or most of those who are poor become delinquents.[22] If it were, causal variables would be virtually impossible to find. From the standpoint of social action, this criterion can be particularly unfortunate. Suppose that poverty were a necessary but not sufficient condition for delinquency, as in the table on

page 258. Advocates of the "not sufficient" criterion would be forced to conclude that, if poverty were removed, delinquency would not decline. As the table clearly shows, however, removal of poverty under these hypothetical conditions would *eliminate* delinquency!

To take another example, Wootton reports Carr-Saunders as finding that 28% of his delinquents and 16% of his controls came from broken homes and that this difference held in both London and the provinces. She quotes Carr-Saunders' "cautious" conclusion:

We can only point out that the broken home may have some influence on delinquency, though since we get control cases coming from broken homes, we cannot assert that there is a direct link between this factor and delinquency.[23]

Carr-Saunders' caution apparently stems from the "non sufficient" criterion, for unless the broken home is a sufficient condition for delinquency, there must be control cases (nondelinquents) from broken homes.

In each of these examples the attack on causality rests on the numbers in a single table. Since all of these tables show a non-zero relation, it seems to us that these researchers have misinterpreted the platitude "correlation is not causation." To us, this plautitude means that one must go beyond the observed fact of association in order to demonstrate causality. To those who employ one or another variant of the perfect relation criterion, it appears to mean that there is something suspect in any numerical demonstration of association. Instead of being the first evidence for causality, an observed association becomes evidence against causality.

---

[19] Teeters and Reinemann, *op. cit.*, p. 127.
[20] *Ibid.*, p. 154.
[21] F. Ivan Nye, *Family Relationships and Delinquent Behavior*, New York: John Wiley, 1958, p. 34. Italics in original.
[22] We are of course assuming throughout this discussion that the variables in question meet what we consider to be legitimate criteria of causality.

[23] Barbara Wootton, *Social Science and Social Pathology*, New York: Macmillan, 1959, p. 118.

FALSE CRITERION 2. *Insofar as a factor is not "characteristic" of delinquents, it is not a cause of delinquency.*

Many correlation studies in delinquency may conquer all these hurdles and still fail to satisfy the vigorous demands of scientific causation. Frequently a group of delinquents is found to differ in a statistically significant way from a nondelinquent control group with which it is compared. Nevertheless, the differentiating trait may not be at all characteristic of the delinquent group. Suppose, for example, that a researcher compares 100 delinquent girls with 100 nondelinquent girls with respect to broken homes. He finds, let us say, that 10% of the nondelinquents come from broken homes, whereas this is true of 30% of the delinquent girls. Although the difference between the two groups is significant, the researcher has not demonstrated that the broken home is characteristic of delinquents. The fact is that 70% of them come from unbroken homes. Again, ecological studies showing a high correlation between residence in interstitial areas and delinquency, as compared with lower rates of delinquency in other areas, overlook the fact that even in the most marked interstitial area nine tenths of the children do not become delinquent.[24]

This argument is superficially plausible. If a factor is not characteristic, then it is apparently not important. But does "characteristic" mean "important"? No. Importance refers to the variation accounted for, to the size of the association, while "being characteristic" refers to only one of the conditional distributions (rows or columns) in the table (in the table on page 258, X is characteristic of delinquents because more than half of the delinquents are X). This is not enough to infer association, any more than the statement that 95% of the Negroes in some sample are illiterate can be taken to say anything

[24] Milton L. Barron, *The Juvenile in Delinquent Society*, New York: Knopf, 1954, pp. 86–87.

about the association between race and illiteracy in that sample without a corresponding statement about the whites. In the following table, although Negroes are predominantly ("characteristically") illiterate, race has no effect on literacy, for the whites are equally likely to be illiterate.

	Race	
	Negro	White
Literate	5	5
Illiterate	95	95

More generally, even if a trait characterizes a large proportion of delinquents and also characterizes a large proportion of nondelinquents, it may be less important as a cause of delinquency than a trait that characterizes a much smaller proportion of delinquents. The strength of the relation is what matters—that is, the *difference* between delinquents and nondelinquents in the proportion having the trait (in other words, the difference between the conditional distributions of the dependent variable). In the quotation from Barron at the beginning of this section, would it make any difference for the imputation of causality if the proportions coming from broken homes had been 40% for the nondelinquents and 60% for the delinquents, instead of 10 and 30%? Although broken homes would now be "characteristic" of delinquents, the percentage difference is the same as before. And the percentage difference would still be the same if the figures were 60 and 80%, but now broken homes would be characteristic of *both* nondelinquents and delinquents!

The "characteristic" criterion is thus statistically irrelevant to the task of assessing causality. It also appears to be inconsistent with the principle of multiple causation, to which Barron else-where subscribes.[25] If delinquency is really traceable to a plurality of causes," then some of these causes may well "characterize" a minority of delinquents. Furthermore, this "inconsistency" is empirical as well as logical: in survey data taken from ordinary populations it is rare to find that any group defined by more than three traits includes a majority of the cases.[26]

FALSE CRITERION 3. *If a relation between an independent variable and delinquency is found for a single value of a situational or contextual factor, that situational or contextual factor cannot be a cause of delinquency.*

No investigation can establish the causal importance of variables that do not vary. This obvious fact should be even more obvious when the design of the study restricts it to single values of certain variables. Thus, the researcher who restricts his sample to white Mormon boys cannot use his data to determine the importance of race, religious affiliation, or sex as causes of delinquency. Nevertheless, students of

delinquency who discover either from research or logical analysis that an independent variable is related to delinquency in certain situations or contexts often conclude that these situational or contextual variables are not important causes of delinquency. Since personality or perceptual variables are related to delinquency in most kinds of social situations, social variables have suffered most from the application of this criterion:

Let the reader assume that a boy is returning home from school and sees an unexpected group of people at his doorstep, including a policeman, several neighbors, and some strangers. He may suppose that they have gathered to welcome him and congratulate him as the winner of a nation-wide contest he entered several months ago. On the other hand, his supposition may be that they have discovered that he was one of several boys who broke some windows in the neighborhood on Halloween. If his interpretation is that they are a welcoming group he will respond one way; but if he feels that they have come to "get" him, his response is likely to be quite different. In either case he may be entirely wrong in his interpretation. *The important point, however, is that the external situation is relatively unimportant.* Rather, what the boy himself thinks of them [it] and how he interprets them [it] is the crucial factor in his response.[27]

There are at least three independent "variables" in this illustration: (1) the external situation—the group at the doorstep; (2) the boy's past behavior —entering a contest, breaking windows, etc.; (3) the boy's interpretation of the group's purpose. As Barron notes, variable (3) is obviously important in determining the boy's response. It does not follow from this, however, that variables (1) and (2) are unimportant. As a matter of fact, it is easy to see how vari-

---

[25] *Ibid.*, pp. 81–83.

[26] There are two reasons for this: the less-than-perfect association between individual traits and the fact that few traits are simple dichotomies. Of course, it is always possible to take the logical complement of a set of traits describing a minority and thus arrive at a set of traits that does "characterize" a group, but such artificial combinations have too much internal heterogeneity to be meaningful. What, for example, can one say of the delinquents who share the following set of traits; not Catholic, not middle class, not of average intelligence?

The problem of "characteristic" traits arises only when the dependent variable is inherently categorical (Democratic; member of a gang, an athletic club, or neither) or is treated as one (performs none, a few, or many delinquent acts). In other words, this criterion arises only in tabular analysis, not where some summary measure is used to describe the association between variables.

[27] Barron, *op. cit.*, pp. 87–88. Italics added.

able (2), the boy's past behavior, could influence his interpretation of the group's purpose and thus affect his response. If he had not broken any windows in the neighborhood, for example, it is less likely that he would think that the group had come to "get" him, and it is therefore less likely that his response would be one of fear. Since Barron does not examine the relation between this situational variable and the response, he cannot make a legitimate statement about its causal importance.

Within the context of this illustration it is impossible to relate variable (1), the group at the doorstep, to the response. The reason for this is simple: this "variable" does not vary—it is fixed, given, constant. In order to assess the influence of a group at the doorstep (the external situation) on the response, it would be necessary to compare the effects of groups varying in size or composition. Suppose that there was no group at the doorstep. Presumably, if this were the case, the boy would feel neither fear nor joy. Barron restricts his examination of the relation between interpretation and response to a single situation, and on this basis concludes that what appears to be a necessary condition for the response is *relatively unimportant!*

In our opinion, it is sometimes better to say nothing about the effects of a variable whose range is restricted than to attempt to reach some idea of its importance with inadequate data. The first paragraph of the following statement suggests that its authors are completely aware of this problem. Nevertheless, the concluding paragraphs are misleading:

We recognized that the Cambridge-Somerville area represented a fairly restricted socio-economic region. Although the bitter wave of the depression had passed, it had left in its wake large num-

bers of unemployed. Ten years after its onset, Cambridge and Somerville still showed the effects of the depression. Even the best neighborhoods in this study were lower middle class. Consequently, our results represent only a section of the class structure.

In our sample, however [*therefore*], there is not a *highly* significant relation between "delinquency areas," or subcultures, and crime. If we had predicted that every child who lived in the poorer Cambridge-Somerville areas would have committed a crime, we would have been more often wrong than right. Thus, current sociological theory, by itself, cannot explain why the majority of children, even those from the "worst" areas, never became delinquent.

Social factors, in our sample, were not strongly related to criminality. The fact that a child's neighborhood did not, by itself, exert an independently important influence may [*should not*] surprise social scientists. Undeniably, a slum neighborhood can mold a child's personality—but apparently only if other factors in his background make him susceptible to the subculture that surrounds him.[28]

FALSE CRITERION 4. *If a relation is observed between an independent variable and delinquency and if a psychological variable is suggested as intervening between these two variables, then the original relation is not causal.*

[28] William McCord and Joan McCord, *Origins of Crime*, New York: Columbia University Press, 1959, pp. 71 and 167.

In a study restricted to "known *offenders*" in which the dependent variable is the *seriousness* of the *first offense* Richard S. Sterne concludes: "Delinquency cannot be fruitfully controlled through broad programs to prevent divorce or other breaks in family life. The prevention of these would certainly decrease unhappiness, but it would not help to relieve the problem of delinquency." Since the range of the dependent variable, delinquency, is seriously reduced in a study restricted to *offenders*, such conclusions can not follow from the data. *Delinquent Conduct and Broken Homes*, New Haven: College and University Press, 1964, p. 96.

There appear to be two elements in this causal reasoning. One is the procedure of *conjectural interpretation.*[29] The other is the confusion between *explanation,* in which an antecedent variable "explains away" an observed relation, and *interpretation,* in which an intervening variable links more tightly the two variables of the original relation. In short, the vanishing of the partial relations is assumed, not demonstrated, and this assumed statistical configuration is misconstrued.

This criterion is often encountered in a subtle form suggestive of social psychological theory:

The appropriate inference from the available data, on the basis of our present understanding of the nature of cause, is that whether poverty, broken homes, or working mothers are factors which cause delinquency depends upon the meaning the situation has for the child.[30]

It now appears that neither of these factors [the broken home and parental discipline] is so important in itself as is the child's reaction to them.[31]

A factor, whether personal or situational, does not become a cause unless and until it first becomes a motive.[32]

The appropriate inference about whether some factor is a cause of delin-

quency depends on the relation between that factor and delinquency (and possibly on other factors causally prior to both of these). All that can be determined about meanings, motives, or reactions that *follow from* the factor and *precede* delinquency can only strengthen the conclusion that the factor is a cause of delinquency, not weaken it.

A different example may make our argument clearer. *Given* the bombing of Pearl Harbor, the crucial factor in America's response to this situation was its interpretation of the meaning of this event. Is one to conclude, therefore, that the bombing of Pearl Harbor was relatively unimportant as a cause of America's entry into World War II? Intervening variables of this type are no less important than variables further removed from the dependent variable, but to limit analysis to them, to deny the importance of objective conditions, is to distort reality as much as do those who ignore intervening subjective states.[33]

This kind of mistaken causal inference can occur long after the original analysis of the data. A case in point is the inference in the *Report to The Congress*[34] that irregular employment of the mother does not cause delinquency. This inference appears to come from misreading Maccoby's reanalysis of the Glueck's results.

Maccoby begins by noting that "the association between irregular employment and delinquency suggests at the outset that it may not be the mother's absence from home per se which creates adjustment problems for the children. Rather, the cause may be found in the conditions of the mother's em-

---

[29] Like conjectural explanation, this is an argument, unsupported by statistical data, that the relation between two variables would vanish if the effects of a third variable were removed; here, however, the third variable "intervenes" causally between the original independent and dependent variables.

[30] Sophia Robison, *Juvenile Delinquency,* New York: Holt, Rinehart and Winston, 1961, p. 116.

[31] Paul W. Tappan, *Juvenile Delinquency,* New York: McGraw-Hill, 1949, p. 135.

[32] Sheldon and Eleanor Glueck, *Family Environment and Delinquency,* Boston: Houghton-Mifflin, 1962, p. 153. This statement is attributed to Bernard Glueck. No specific reference is provided.

[33] "Write your own life history, showing the factors *really* operative in you coming to college, contrasted with the external social and cultural factors of your situation." Barron, *op. cit.,* p. 89.

[34] *Op. cit.,* p. 21.

ployment or the family characteristics leading a mother to undertake outside employment."[35] She then lists several characteristics of the sporadically working mothers that might account for the greater likelihood of their children becoming delinquent. For example, many had a history of delinquency themselves. In our opinion, such conjectural "explanations" are legitimate guides to further study but, as Maccoby says, they leave the causal problem unsettled:

It is a moot question, therefore, whether it is the mother's sporadic employment as such which conduced to delinquency in the sons; equally tenable is the interpretation that the emotionally disturbed and antisocial characteristics of the parents produced both a sporadic work pattern on the part of the mother and delinquent tendencies in the son.[36]

Maccoby's final step, and the one of greatest interest here, is to examine simultaneously the effects of mother's employment and mother's supervision on delinquency. From this examination she concludes:

It can be seen that, whether the mother is working or not, the quality of the supervision her child receives is paramount. If the mother remains at home but does not keep track of where her child is and what he is doing, he is far more likely to become a delinquent (within this highly selected sample), than if he is closely watched. Furthermore, if a mother who works does arrange adequate care for the

child in her absence, he is no more likely to be delinquent . . . than the adequately supervised child of a mother who does not work. But there is one more lesson to be learned from the data: among the working mothers, a majority did not in fact arrange adequate supervision for their childen in their absence.[37]

It is clear, then, that regardless of the mother's employment status, supervision is related to delinquency. According to criterion 3, employment status is therefore not a cause of delinquency. It is also clear that when supervision is held relatively constant, the relation between employment status and delinquency disappears. According to criterion 4, employment status is therefore *not* a cause of delinquency. This appears to be the reasoning by which the authors of the *Report to The Congress* reject mother's employment as a cause of delinquency. But criterion 3 ignores the association between employment status and delinquency and is thus irrelevant. And criterion 4 treats what is probably best seen as an intervening variable as an antecedent variable and is thus a misconstruction of a legitimate criterion. Actually, the evidence that allows the user of criterion 4 to reach a conclusion of noncausality is, at least psychologically, evidence of *causality*. The disappearance of the relation between mother's employment and delinquency when supervision is held relatively constant makes the "How?" of the original relation clear: working mothers are less likely to provide adequate supervision for their children, and inadequately supervised children are more likely to become delinquent.

FALSE CRITERION 5. *Measurable variables are not causes.*

In tract 11–1, and to a lesser extent in tract 11–2, the actual rate [of delinquency]

[35] Eleanor E. Maccoby, "Effects upon Children of Their Mothers' Outside Employment," in Norman W. Bell and Ezra F. Vogel (eds.), *A Modern Introduction to The Family,* Glencoe, Illinois: The Free Press, 1960, p. 523. In fairness to the Children's Bureau report, it should be mentioned that Maccoby's argument against the causality of the relation between mother's employment and delinquency has a stronger tone in the article cited there (see footnote 7) than in the version we have used as a source of quotations.

[36] *Ibid.*

[37] *Ibid.,* p. 524.

is lower than the predicted rate. We suggest that these deviations [of the actual delinquency rate from the rate predicted from home ownership] point up the danger of imputing a causal significance to an index, per se, despite its statistical significance in a prediction formula. It is fallacious to impute causal significance to home ownership as such. In the present study, the author hypothesizes that the extent of home-ownership is probably highly correlated with, and hence constitutes a measure of community anomie.[38]

As a preventive, "keeping youth busy," whether through compulsory education, drafting for service in the armed forces, providing fun through recreation, or early employment, can, at best, only temporarily postpone behavior that is symptomatic of more deep-seated or culturally oriented factors. . . . Merely "keeping idle hands occupied" touches only surface symptoms and overlooks underlying factors known to generate norm-violating behavior patterns.[39]

The criterion of causation that, in effect, denies causal status to measurable variables occurs frequently in delinquency research. In the passages above, home ownership, compulsory education, military service, recreation, and early employment are all called into question as causes of delinquency. In their stead one finds as causes anomie and "deep-seated or culturally oriented factors." The appeal to abstract as opposed to more directly measurable variables appears to be especially persuasive. Broad general concepts embrace such a variety of directly measurable variables that their causal efficacy becomes almost self evident. The broken home, for example, is no match for the "inadequate" home:

[T]he physically broken home as a cause of delinquent behavior is, in itself, not so

important as was once believed. In essence, it is not that the home is broken, but rather that the home is inadequate, that really matters.[40]

The persuasiveness of these arguments against the causal efficacy of measurable variables has two additional sources: (1) their logical form resembles that of the legitimate criterion "lack of spuriousness"; (2) they are based on the seemingly obvious fact that "operational indices" (measures) do not *cause* the variations in other operational indices. Both of the following arguments can thus be brought against the assertion that, for example, home ownership causes delinquency.

Anomie causes delinquency. Home ownership is a measure of anomie. Anomie is thus the "source of variation" in both home ownership and delinquency. If the effects of anomie were removed, the observed relation between home ownership and delinquency would disappear. This observed relation is thus causally spurious.

Home ownership is used as an indicator of anomie, just as responses to questionnaire items are used as indicators of such things, as "authoritarianism," "achievement motivation," and "religiosity." No one will argue that the responses to items on a questionnaire *cause* race hatred, long years of self-denial, or attendance at religious services. For the same reason, it is erroneous to think that home ownership "causes" delinquency.

Both of these arguments beg the question. As mentioned earlier, conjectural explanations, altogether legitimate guides to further study, leave the causal problem unsettled. The proposed "antecedent variable" may or *may not* actually account for the observed relation.

---

38 Lander, *op. cit.*, p. 71.
39 William C. Kvaraceus and Walter B. Miller, *Delinquent Behavior: Culture and the Individual,* National Education Association, 1959, p. 39.

40 Teeters and Reinemann, *op. cit.,* p. 154.

Our argument assumes that the proposed antecedent variable is directly measurable. In the cases cited here it is not. If the antecedent variable logic is accepted as appropriate in these cases, all relations between measurable variables and delinquency may be said to be causally spurious. If anomie can "explain away" the relation between *one* of its indicators and delinquency, it can explain away the relations between *all* of its indicators and delinquency.[41] No matter how closely a given indicator measures anomie, the indicator is not anomie, and thus not a cause of delinquency. The difficulty with these conjectural explanations is thus not that they may be false, but that they are *non-falsifiable*.[42]

The second argument against the causality of measurable variables overlooks the following point: it is one thing to use a measurable variable as an indicator of another, not directly measurable, variable; it is something else again to assume that the measurable variable is *only* an indicator. Not owning one's home may indeed be a useful indicator of anomie; it may, at the same time, be a potent cause of delinquency in its own right.

The user of the "measurable variables are not causes" criterion treats measurable variables as epiphenomena. He strips these variables of all their causal efficacy (and of all their meaning) by treating them merely as indexes, and by using such words as *per se, as such,* and *in itself*.[43] In so doing, he begs rather than answers the important question: Are these measurable variables causes of delinquency?

FALSE CRITERION 6. *If the relation between an independent variable and delinquency is conditional upon the value of other variables, the independent variable is not a cause of delinquency.*

The rates of Negro delinquency also vary as widely as do the white rates indicating large differences in behavior patterns that are not a function or effect of race per se. It is also of interest to note that in at least 10 percent of the districts with substantial Negro juvenile populations, the Negro delinquency rate is lower than the corresponding white rate.[44]

The appropriate inference from the available data, on the basis of our present understanding of the nature of cause, is that whether poverty, broken homes, or working mothers are factors which cause delinquency depends upon the meaning the situation has for the child.[45]

Both of these quotations make the same point: the association between an independent variable and delinquency depends on the value of a third variable. The original two-variable relation thus becomes a three-variable conditional relation. In the first quotation, the relation between race and delinquency is shown to depend on some (unspecified) property of census tracts. In the second quota-

---

[41] As would be expected, Lander succeeds in disposing of all the variables in his study as causes of delinquency—even those he says at some points are *"fundamentally* related to delinquency."

[42] While Lander throws out his measurable independent variables in favor of anomie, Kvaraceus and Miller throw out their measurable dependent variable in favor of "something else." "Series of norm-violating behaviors, which run counter to legal codes and which are engaged in by youngsters [delinquency], are [is] only symptomatic of something else in the personal make-up of the individual, in his home and family, or in his cultural milieu." *Op. cit.,* p. 34. The result is the same, as the quotations suggest.

[43] The appearance of these terms in the literature on delinquency almost invariably signals a logical difficulty.

[44] Lander, *op. cit.,* p. 32. This statement is quoted more fully above (see footnote 10).

[45] See footnote 30.

tion, each of three variables is said to "interact" with "the meaning of the situation" to cause delinquency.

One consequence of showing that certain variables are only conditionally related to delinquency is to invalidate what Albert K. Cohen has aptly named "the assumption of intrinsic pathogenic qualities"—the assumption that the causal efficacy of a variable is, or can be, independent of the value of other causal variables.[46] Invalidating this assumption, which Cohen shows to be widespread in the literature on delinquency, is a step in the right direction. As many of the quotations in this paper suggest, however, the discovery that a variable has no *intrinsic* pathogenic qualities has often led to the conclusion that it has no pathogenic qualities at all. The consequences of accepting this conclusion can be shown for delinquency research and theory.

Cloward and Ohlin's theory that delinquency is the product of lack of access to legitimate means *and* the availability of illegitimate means assumes, as Palmore and Hammond have shown,[47] that each of these states is a necessary condition for the other—i.e., that lack of access to legitimate and access to illegitimate means "interact" to produce delinquency. Now, if "conditional relations" are non-causal, neither lack of access to legitimate nor the availability of illegitimate means is a cause of delinquency, and one could manipulate either without affecting the delinquency rate.

Similarly absurd conclusions could be drawn from the results of empirical research in delinquency, since all relations

between independent variables and delinquency are at least conceivably conditional (the paucity of empirical generalizations produced by delinquency research as a whole shows that most of these relations have already actually been found to be conditional).[48]

Although conditional relations may be conceptually or statistically complicated and therefore psychologically unsatisfying, their discovery does not justify the conclusion that the variables involved are not causes of delinquency. In fact, the researcher who would grant causal status only to unconditional relations will end by granting it to none.

Any one of the criteria of causality discussed in this paper makes it possible to question the causality of most of the relations that have been or could be revealed by quantitative research. Some of these criteria stew from perfectionistic interpretations of legitimate criteria, others from misapplication of these legitimate criteria. Still others, especially the argument that a cause must be "characteristic" of delinquents, appear to result from practical considerations. (It would indeed be valuable to the practitioner if he could point to some easily identifiable trait as the "hallmark" of the delinquent.) Finally, one of these criteria is based on a mistaken notion of the relation between abstract concepts and measurable variables—a notion that only the former can be the causes of anything.

The implications of these standards of causality for practical efforts to reduce delinquency are devastating. Since nothing that can be pointed to in the

---

[46] "Multiple Factor Approaches," in Marvin E. Wolfgang *et al.* (eds.), *The Sociology of Crime and Delinquency,* New York: John Wiley, 1962, pp. 78–79.

[47] Erdman B. Palmore and Phillip E. Hammond, "Interacting Factors in Juvenile Delinquency," *American Sociological Review,* 29 (December, 1964), pp. 848–854.

[48] After reviewing the findings of twenty-one studies as they bear on the relations between twelve commonly used independent variables and delinquency, Barbara Wootton concludes: "All in all, therefore, this collection of studies, although chosen for its comparative methodological merit, produces only the most meager, and dubiously supported generalizations." *Op. cit.,* p. 134.

practical world is a cause of delinquency (e.g., poverty, broken homes, lack of recreational facilities, working mothers), the practitioner is left with the task of combatting a nebulous "anomie" or an unmeasured "inadequacy of the home"; or else he must change the adolescent's interpretation of the "meaning" of events without at the same time changing the events themselves or the context in which they occur.

Mills has suggested that accepting the principle of multiple causation implies denying the possibility of radical change in the social structure.[49] Our analysis suggests that rejecting the principle of multiple causation implies denying the possibility of *any* change in the social structure—since, in this view, nothing causes anything.

[49] C. Wright Mills, "The Professional Ideology of Social Pathologists," *American Journal of Sociology*, 44 (September, 1942), pp. 165–180, esp. pp. 171–172.

17.

An Empirical Test of Differential Association Theory*

Albert J. Reiss, Jr., and A. Lewis Rhodes

A basic postulate in sociological writing about delinquents is that delinquent behavior is essentially group behavior. Sociologists have shown that groups enter into delinquent activity in a number of ways. Breckinridge and Abbott were among the first to point out that not only are most delinquent offenses committed in groups but that most lone offenders are influenced by companions.[1] Somewhat later, Shaw and Meyer[2] and Shaw and McKay[3] estimated the

* We wish to thank Otis Dudley and Beverly Duncan, Lloyd E. Ohlin and Guy E. Swanson for critical comments and suggestions.

SOURCE. Albert J. Reiss, Jr., and A. Lewis Rhodes, "An Empirical Test of Differential Association Theory" from *Journal of Research in Crime and Delinquency*, Volume 1, No. 1, January 1964, pp. 5–18. Reprinted with permission.

[1] Sophonisba P. Breckinridge and Edith Abbot, *The Delinquent Child and the Home*, New York: The Russell Sage Foundation, 1917, pp. 34–35.
[2] Clifford R. Shaw and Earl D. Meyer, "The Juvenile Delinquent," in *The Illinois Crime Survey*, Illinois Association for Criminal Justice, 1929, p. 662.
[3] Clifford R. Shaw and Henry D. McKay, "Social Factors in Juvenile Delinquency: A Study of the Community, the Family, and the Gang in relation to Delinquent Behavior," National Commission on Law Observance and Enforcement, *Report on*

extent to which juvenile delinquency is group activity, showing that less than 20 percent are lone offenders in juvenile court samples. Shaw and McKay also showed that the modal size of offending groups is two and three participants, and that not all group delinquency is committed by well organized gangs.[4] More recently Enyon and Reckless demonstrated that companionship is usually present at the onset of admitted delinquency as well as in officially recorded delinquency.[5] These studies for the United States and similar ones in other countries clearly establish that most delinquent behavior is committed as group activity.

Following Sutherland, many sociologists reason that delinquent behavior is genetically a function of learning delinquency through association with delinquents within intimate personal groups.[6] That this hypothesis is not

the Causes of Crime, Washington, D.C.: USGPO, 1931, Volume II, No. 13, Chapter VI, esp. pp. 194–199.
[4] *Ibid.*, p. 195.
[5] Thomas G. Enyon and Walter C. Reckless, "Companionship at Delinquency Onset," *The British Journal of Criminology*, 2 (October, 1961), 167–68.
[6] Albert Cohen, Alfred Lindesmith and

demonstrated is troublesome to some sociologists[7] and a basis for criticism by others.[8] Criticism of the hypothesis rests on a logical argument that empirical evidence of association in delinquent acts merely demonstrates concomitance of behavior, whereas a temporal sequence of the effects of association must be demonstrated.[9]

It is one thing to demonstrate that most delinquents associate with other delinquents, participate with them in delinquent activity or are members of a group where others are delinquent and that conforming boys and girls generally associate with other conformers, or belong to groups where behavior is essentially conforming to societal norms. It is quite another to demonstrate that delinquent behavior occurs after induction into a delinquent group, or that delinquency occurs as group activity after a group is formed. Apart from the methodological issues raised by a causal demonstration of group effects on individual behavior and the nature of criteria for an adequate test of differential association theory, there are problems of conceptualizing group effects and operationalizing concepts in differential association theory.

TESTING THE THEORY

Sutherland never explicitly formulated his hypothesis of differential association in operational terms and Short questions whether it lends itself to operationalization without reformulation.[10] Short, however, devised a test of differential association theory to show that the frequency, duration, priority and intensity of association with delinquent and anti-delinquent culture and behavior varies among delinquent and non-delinquent groups. He defined intensity of association as a subject's perception of the delinquency of his best friends and concludes that, among his operational measures of differential association, this measure of intensity is most consistently and strongly related to the delinquency of youth.[11] Short's test rests on a *subject's definition* of best friends as delinquent. The main purpose of this paper is to make a test similar to Short's on the effect of intensity of association, using, however, data on the *actual delinquency* known and reported by a boy and his best friends. We propose to examine whether the probability of an individual engaging in several different kinds of delinquent acts is associated with his close friends also having engaged in these acts. It should be apparent that a failure to demonstrate that one's close friends have delinquent behavior patterns similar to one's own in no way contradicts or supports the hypothesis that most delinquent behavior occurs as group activity. Rather, it would simply put in doubt the judgment that boys who engage in a kind of delinquent activity are generally also in *intimate* association with one another.

Sutherland's differential association hypothesis holds that variation in fre-

Karl Schuessler, *The Sutherland Papers*, Bloomington: Indiana University Press, 1956, pp. 8–11.

[7] Donald R. Cressey, "Epidemiology and Individual Conduct: A Case from Criminology," *Pacific Sociological Review*, 3 (Fall, 1960), and James F. Short, Jr., "Differential Association as a Hypothesis: Problems of Empirical Testing," *Social Problems*, 8 (Summer, 1960), pp. 14–25.

[8] The most pointed criticism has been made by the Gluecks. Sheldon and Eleanor Glueck, *Unraveling Juvenile Delinquency*, Cambridge: Harvard University Press, 1950, pp. 146–149 and 163–164. See also Marshall Clinard, "Criminological Research," in Robert K. Merton, Leonard Broom and Leonard S. Cottrell, Jr. (eds.), *Sociology Today: Problems and Prospects*. New York: Basic Books, Inc., 1959, Chapter 23.

[9] Sheldon Glueck, "Theory and Fact in Criminology," *British Journal of Delinquency*, 7 (July, 1956), 92–109.

[10] James F. Short, Jr., *op. cit.*, p. 17.
[11] James F. Short, Jr., *op. cit.*, p. 18.

quency, duration, priority and intensity of association with delinquent behavior patterns accounts for delinquent behavior. The homophily hypothesis holds that one is likely to select as best friends those whose values and behavior are similar to one's own[12] while coalition theory argues that all other things being equal, constraints on members who deviate from the expectations of the group lead to their behaving in conformity with these standards.[13] Though not explicitly stated in any theory, both group selection and group constraint hypotheses lead to the same conclusion: one's close friends should have a delinquency history similar to one's own.

It is apparent, however, that there is considerable variation over time in the cliques to which an adolescent belongs, in whom he will select as his best friends, and in the kinds of delinquent activity in which he will engage. Shaw pointed out, for example, that Sidney in the course of his delinquent career from 7 to 17 years of age was officially known to have been involved in delinquency with 11 different companions, representing three distinct groups whose activities and traditions were delinquent in character, and that he was never implicated in any offense with more than three delinquents.[14] Recognizing that current best friends are not necessarily companions from past delinquent association, it seems consistent with differential association theory to argue that, if

current best friends comprise a salient primary group, and if past behavior serves as a basis for mutual communication and action within it (which it need not), then boys currently in intense association with one another should show similar patterns of delinquency. Assuming that specific techniques for committing delinquent acts are communicated in primary association, it follows that all, or none, of the boys in close friendship triads should report committing a given kind of offense. Within a triadic friendship group, there should be no dyads committing a given type of offense, since group constraint should produce homogeneity in behavior. It should be clear that whether or not boys in close friendship groups show similarity in delinquent behavior because they select one another on this basis, or as a result of association, failure to show that delinquency histories of boys in close friendship groups are the same casts doubt at least upon the *specificity* of any learned delinquent behavior in intense association with others. Since Sutherland did not restrict his hypothesis to lower class delinquents, behavioral homophily should hold regardless of social class.[15]

To show that one's close friends are also delinquent is not to show that they have an effect on all of one's delinquent activity. Shaw and McKay early showed that stealing is more likely to be a group offense than are offenses against the home and school.[16] Enyon and Reckless have gone further to show that companionship characterizes first participation in some kinds of offenses more than in others. Companions were present in 100 per cent of boys' first involvement in gang fights but only 56 per cent of the cases of first running away from

[12] Paul F. Lazarsfeld and Robert K. Merton, "Friendship as Social Process: A Substantive and Methodological Analysis," in Morroe Berger, et. al., *Freedom and Control in Modern Society*, New York: D. Van Nostrand Co., Inc., esp. footnote 19.

[13] John W. Thibaut and Harold H. Kelley, *The Social Psychology of Groups*, New York: John W. Wiley, Inc., 1959, pp. 208 and 210, and L. Festinger and J. Thibaut, "Interpersonal Communication in Small Groups," *Journal of Abnormal and Social Psychology*, XLVI (1951), 92–100.

[14] Clifford R. Shaw and Henry D. McKay, *op. cit.*, p. 221.

[15] *The Sutherland Papers, op. cit.*, p. 19. pp. 32–33 and pp. 58–59.

[16] Clifford R. Shaw and Henry D. McKay, *op. cit.*, pp. 195–196.

home.[17] While our study cannot demonstrate the precise effect of friendship on delinquency patterns, it investigates the extent to which there is covariation in a boy's delinquent behavior and that of his friends for different kinds of delinquent behavior.

Sociological theories on delinquent subcultures that are consistent with Sutherland's differential association hypothesis postulate that members of delinquent subcultures become highly dependent upon one another, particularly for status gratification. As Short points out, it follows that members of such groups, having a more intense association with one another, should show greater similarity in their patterns of delinquency than do members of other delinquent groups.[18] Cohen's general theory of delinquent subcultures holds that subcultural delinquent groups should be homogeneous in behavior for a variety of delinquent offenses against property and persons. It is implicit in his theory that middle class boys will show less similarity and versatility in their delinquency.[19] Miller holds that delinquency is endemic in lower class culture. It would be consistent with his theory to argue that delinquent behavior of lower class boys is independent of the commission of the act by other members of the group.[20]

THE INVESTIGATION

The investigation was designed to gather information on the actual delinquent behavior of boys in close friendship cliques. A sample of 378 boys was drawn from a base population of all white males between the ages of 12 and 16 who were registered in one of 45 public, private or parochial junior or senior high schools in Davidson County, Tennessee during the 1957 school year. Strata were designed so as to select disproportionately lower- and middle-class delinquent boys.[21]

Each clique is a triad composed of a boy selected in the stratified probability sample of 378 boys and his two closest friends. Given a large population from which the sample of boys was drawn, only a few sample cases chose the same "closest" friend. Effects of overlapping friendship choice or of pyramiding therefore are negligible. Information was gathered for 299 triads and 79 dyads. The dyads are pairs where a boy selected only one "best friend." Data are presented in this paper only for the 299 triads. Each step was replicated for the 79 dyads and the results are similar where the number of dyads makes comparison possible.

The index person in each triad was classified into one of seven conforming or delinquent types.[22] The career-*oriented delinquent* is the most delinquent person in the classification schema. He is oriented toward the adult criminal world and maintains contact with adult criminals. The largest group of delinquents are *peer-oriented* and directed in their goals and behavior. The lone

[17] Thomas G. Enyon and Walter C. Reckless, *op. cit.*, Table 3, p. 170.
[18] James F. Short, Jr., *op. cit.*, p. 17.
[19] Albert K. Cohen, *Delinquent Boys: The Culture of the Gang*, Glencoe: The Free Press, 1955, pp. 157–169.
[20] Walter Miller, "The Impact of a 'Total Community' Delinquency Control Project," *Social Problems*, 10 (Fall, 1962), 169–191.

[21] This is a more efficient sample design inasmuch as delinquency is a relatively low incidence phenomenon in the general population. The methodological problems encountered in dealing with a low incidence phenomenon in a population have been discussed in Daniel Glaser, "Differential Association and Criminological Prediction," *Social Problems*, 8 (Summer, 1960), p. 7; Albert J. Reiss, Jr., "Unraveling Juvenile Delinquency II: An Appraisal of the Research Methods," *American Journal of Sociology*, 57 (September, 1951), 118–119.
[22] Albert J. Reiss, Jr. and A. Lewis Rhodes, "The Distribution of Juvenile Delinquency in the Social Class Structure," *American Sociological Review*, 26 (October, 1961), Chart I.

delinquent is our *nonconforming isolate*. There are four types of conforming boys. The *conforming nonachiever* is comparable to William Whyte's "corner boy" and the *conforming achiever* to his "college boy," if social class attributes are disregarded.[23] The *hyperconformer* disregards conventional for strict conformity while the *conforming isolate* is outside the clique system. Peer-oriented delinquents, conforming nonachievers, and achievers are divided into white-collar and blue-collar status based on father's occupation.[24]

The dependent variable, self-reported delinquent behavior, was measured by asking each boy how often he had done any of the following things, whether alone or with others, and by inquiring about the conditions related to it: taken little things worth less than $2? $2 to $50? more than $50? purposely damaged or destroyed property? taken a car without the owner's permission or knowledge? beat up somebody bad enough to be arrested?[25] Self-reports include virtually all cases of officially recorded delinquency. Only delinquent acts committed after age 10 are data for this paper.

Self-reported delinquent acts were tabulated for each of the six categories of delinquent act for the 299 triads arranged in the 10 types of conforming-delinquent, SES groups.[26] This tabulation provided information on kind of

delinquent behavior reported by none, one, two or all members of the triad in each of the 10 conforming-delinquent groups. A model was then constructed to give the expected delinquent behavior composition of the triad, using actual rate of delinquency for the sample of boys for estimation purposes. The model is based on the expansion of the binomial.[27] Our use of the binomial ignores variability in response patterns by friendship choice, e.g. + (original) − (first best friend) + (second best friend) and ++− or −++ are all treated as two boys expected (or actual) to commit the act. This disregard of response order seems warranted for we cannot determine whether the original subject models his behavior on that of his two closest friends, or whether he chooses friends who have similar behavior, or whether they copy his behavior.

The observed distribution of boys in triads reporting they committed an act of delinquency is then compared with the expected distribution. The chi square test of goodness of fit is used to test the significance of the departure of the observed measure from the hypothetical one of the binomial.[28] Occasionally, the conventional test of the significance of difference between two proportions is used to test whether there is any significant difference in the number of observed and expected triads where all members of the triad reported committing the act.

Very briefly, this paper attempts to shed light on three closely related ques-

[23] William F. Whyte, *Street Corner Society*, Chicago: University of Chicago Press, 1937.

[24] Albert J. Reiss, Jr. and A. Lewis Rhodes, *op. cit.*, pp. 721–722.

[25] Readers will note the similarity of these questions with the Nye-Short delinquency scale items: Ivan F. Nye and James F. Short, Jr., "Scaling Delinquent Behavior," *American Sociological Review*, 22 (June, 1957), 326–331.

[26] The authors express their appreciation to NAL, State University of Iowa for use of the IBM 650. A special program for rapid tabulation of response patterns in triads was developed for this study.

[27] $f(x) = \dfrac{3!}{x!(3-x)!} \, p^x(q)^{3-x}$

where x is the number of boys expected to commit the act (0, 1, 2 or 3); p is the proportion of the subgroup reporting commission of the act; q is the proportion of the subgroup not reporting commission of the act.

[28] No test was made if the expected frequency in any cell was less than two or less than five in two cells of a 2×3 table.

tions that are germane to propositions about the group nature of delinquency and the empirical testing of differential association theory: (1) Does the probability of an individual committing kinds of delinquent acts depend upon his close friends committing these acts? (2) Is there variation in dependence upon friends committing delinquent acts among different kinds of delinquent behavior? (3) Is the probability of committing a delinquent act less dependent upon one's friends committing the act in some kinds of conforming or delinquent groups than in others?

FINDINGS

Boys generally choose boys as close friends whose law-abiding or delinquent behavior is similar to their own. Table 1 answers our first question in comparing reported delinquent behavior of boys in triads with that expected from the proportion of boys in the sample who reported committing specific kinds of delinquency. For each kind of delinquent behavior, *the probability of an individual committing a specific delinquent act depends upon the commission of the act by other members of the friendship triad.* More of the triads in Table 1 than expected from the binomial are made up of boys, all or none of whom engaged in the same kind of delinquent act. The more serious the offense, the greater the difference between observed and expected proportions of triads where *all* of the boys committed the same kind of delinquent offense. Confidence in the finding that the probability for a boy committing a delinquent act is not independent of the behavior of his close friends is increased with the observation that fewer of the triads than expected have only one boy reporting he engaged in the delinquent activity. Table 2 restates the conclusion in a way that aids the interpretation. For each kind of act, significantly more

of the original sociometric subjects who reported the offense, than of those who did not, have friends who also committed the act.

Nonetheless, Tables 1 and 2 make apparent considerable variation in delinquent behavior homophily of close friendship triads. Of the triads in Table 1 where at least one boy reported committing auto theft or assault, three-fifths have only one boy reporting he committed the act. By way of contrast, but one-fourth of the triads where at least one boy committed an act of vandalism and one in five for petty larceny are made up of boys where only one reported committing the act. Original sociometric subjects in Table 2 are more likely to choose boys as friends who also committed acts of vandalism or theft under two dollars than they are to have chosen boys as friends who also committed acts of auto larceny or assault, when they report having done these things. We must conclude in answer to our second question that although, in the aggregate, commission of a kind of delinquent act is not independent of the commission of the act by other members of a close friendship triad, the correlation varies with kind of delinquent behavior and is far from perfect for any kind.

We know from previous studies that roughly four-fifths of all boys arrested for delinquency had associates in the offense for which they were arrested, and that at least that high a proportion of delinquent boys have as close friends boys who have committed some kind of delinquent act. We must conclude then, that close friendship choices are more closely correlated with delinquency *per se* than with specialization or engagement in all specific kinds of delinquency.

Attention has been called to the ambiguity in formulation of Sutherland's differential association theory rendering difficult both operationalization of the

Table 1

OBSERVED (f), EXPECTED (f_e)[1] AND SUM OF EXPECTED (f^Σ)[2] FOR CONFORMING-DELINQUENT SUBGROUPS. NUMBER OF WHITE MALE TRIADS CLASSIFIED BY NUMBER OF MALES IN EACH TRIAD WHO REPORTED DELINQUENT BEHAVIOR ONE OR MORE TIMES FOR SIX KINDS OF DELINQUENT BEHAVIOR

Kind of Delinquent Behavior	Percent Reporting Behavior	Number in Triad Reporting Delinquent Behavior				Number of Triads	P (χ^2)a
		0	1	2	3		
Auto theft	12						
f_e		204	83	11*	1*	299	<.001
f		229	42	17	11	299	
f^Σ		227	43	19	10	299	
Theft over $50	12						
f_e		204	84	11*	1*	299	<.001
f		236	31	18	14	299	
f^Σ		232	37	19	11	299	
Theft: $2–$50	18						
f_e		111	130	51	7	299	<.001
f		161	65	36	37	299	
f^Σ		150	78	44	27		
Assault	28						
f_e		168	107	23*	2*	299	<.001
f		200	61	18	20	299	
f^Σ		189	74	26	10	299	
Vandalismb	—b						
f_e		44	116	103	31	294	<.001
f		75	84	78	57	294	
f^Σ		60	103	86	45	294	
Theft under $2b	—b						
f_e		27	98	120	49	294	<.001
f		52	80	77	85	294	
f^Σ		42	88	97	67	294	

[1] Expected frequencies are calculated for the binomial using the proportion of boys in the sample who reported committing each kind of delinquency.

[2] Expected frequencies were calculated for the binomial for each of 10 conforming-delinquent subgroups. The sum of these expected values is reported here.

a χ^2 computed for actual (f) with expected (f_e) values only.

b Offense committed two or more times.

* Cell frequencies combined for computation of χ^2.

theory and deductions from it. An altogether literal deduction from Sutherland's theory, though he never made it, is that either all or none of the boys in a close friendship triad should report committing the same kind of offense. It is immediately apparent from inspec-tion of Tables 1 and 2 that there is a substantial number of triads where only one or two members of the triad committed the same kind of delinquent act, thereby calling into question any postulate about the homogeneity of law-violative behavior in triads through

Table 2

PERCENT OF TRIADS WITH NUMBER OF
FRIENDS COMMITTING DELINQUENT ACT
BY ORIGINAL SUBJECTS DELINQUENT BE-
HAVIOR, FOR SIX KINDS OF DELINQUENT
BEHAVIOR

Original Subject's Delinquent Act	Number of Friends Committing Same Kind of Act				
	0	1	2	Total	$P(\chi^2)$
Auto theft					
Yes	45	28	27	40	.001
No	88	9	3	259	
Theft over $50					
Yes	29	29	42	34	.001
No	89	8	3	265	
Theft: $2–$50					
Yes	24	32	44	84	.001
No	75	21	4	215	
Assault					
Yes	35	27	38	52	.001
No	81	17	2	247	
Vandalism					
Yes	16	41	43	134	.001
No	47	39	14	160	
Theft under $2					
Yes	9	37	54	158	.001
No	38	48	14	136	

differential association. Let us assume, however, as does a variant of coalition theory, that when two members of a triad engage in a given kind of behavior, the third member is under strong pressure to do likewise.[29] We would expect, then, that there should be relatively few, if any, close friendship triads with only two members engaging in delinquent behavior. Expressing the triads where *all* members commit the same kind of delinquent act as a per cent of all triads where two or three members commit the act, the following distribution results; auto theft (65 percent); theft over $50 (64 percent); theft $2-$50 (80 percent); assault (83 percent); vandalism (71 percent); theft under $2 (82 percent). The distribu-

[29] See footnote 13.

tion supports the contention that there is pressure toward uniformity of behavior in these triads. In two-thirds or more of the triads, for each kind of delinquent offense, all members report they committed the act, i.e., if more than one did it, it was probably three. There remained, nonetheless, a substantial minority of triads in which only two members committed the same kind of delinquency. The more serious offenses are least likely to show triadic uniformity.

Thus far two main ways of accounting for the observed distribution of delinquent associates in close friendship triads have been introduced. We first examined whether the sample of triads was a sample drawn from a binomial based on the rate of a specified kind of delinquency, and we concluded that the departure of the observed distribution from the binomial exceeded that ordinarily encountered in random sampling. The probability of an individual committing a specific kind of delinquent act depends upon the commission of the act by other members of the friendship triad. We then examined whether the sample of triads conformed to predictions from Sutherland's differential association theory or coalition theory. Inasmuch as there was a substantial number of triads with only one or two members reporting they engaged in a specific kind of delinquent behavior, we are led to question the postulate that differential association is a necessary and sufficient condition explaining delinquency. Table 3 summarizes these comparisons and is a convenient way of raising the further question whether the observed distribution of triads departs more from the random distribution than the expected one based on the differential association hypothesis. Although no test of statistical significance is employed, it seems clear that the observed distribution is closer to the binomial than to the expected distribution based on the differential association hypothesis.

Table 3

COMPARISON OF REPORTED BEHAVIOR IN 299 DELINQUENT TRIADS (f) WITH RANDOM EXPECTATION (f_e) AND NUMBER EXPECTED UNDER DIFFERENTIAL ASSOCIATION EFFECT ON BEHAVIOR OF ORIGINAL MEMBER OF SOCIOMETRIC TRIAD $(f_d)^2$ FOR SIX KINDS OF DELINQUENT BEHAVIOR

Type of Delinquency and Number in Triad Committing Act	$f_e{}^1$	f	$f_d{}^2$
Auto theft			
3	*	11	40
2 or 1	95	59	0
0	204	229	259
Theft over $50			
3	*	14	34
2 or 1	95	49	0
0	204	236	265
Theft: $2–$50			
3	7	37	84
2 or 1	181	101	0
0	112	161	215
Assault			
3	2	20	52
2 or 1	129	79	0
0	168	200	247
Vandalism			
3	121	138	220
2 or 1	172	151	0
0	5	10	79
Theft under $2			
3	49	85	158
2 or 1	218	157	0
0	27	52	136

[1] The proportion of boys in the sample who reported each kind of delinquency is used to set up the binomial of triads.

[2] The expected values for differential association are the marginal frequencies of original subjects committing and not committing a specific kind of delinquent act.

* Less than one case.

The reciprocation of sociometric choices, the delinquency orientation and behavior of boys chosen as close friends, and the content and seriousness of a boy's delinquent offenses were the main criteria in classifying a boy into a particularly conforming or delinquent type in our study. The *type* and *content* of the delinquent offenses of his close friends were not used as criteria in classifying a boy into a particular group. Although classification of a boy and his friends into a conforming or delinquent subtype then is not independent of classification by type of delinquent behavior, there still can be considerable variation in the delinquent behavior among the members of a triad within any kind of delinquent group. Given the possibility of variation in type and content of delinquent offense within a triad, we compared the triads in each subtype of conforming or delinquent group to see whether boys in each subtype chose as close friends boys who committed acts of delinquency similar to their own. Table 4 compares the reported behavior of boys in each subtype of conforming or delinquent triad with the behavior expected from the proportion of boys in each type who reported committing each kind of act. Such comparisons should permit us to learn whether membership in a specific kind of conforming or delinquent group has any effect upon one's delinquent behavior independent of the rate of delinquency within that type of group.

Inspection of Table 4 shows that there is little significant variation between observed and expected values for any of the conforming-delinquent groups. The answer to our third question then is that selection of close friends who commit a specific kind of act within a given type of conforming-delinquent group is largely a function of the rate of that kind of delinquency within each group. The more boys there are committing any kind of offense in a type of group, the more likely one is to have groups in which all members

Table 4

OBSERVED (f) AND EXPECTED (f_e)[1] NUMBER OF WHITE MALE TRIADS CLASSIFIED BY NUMBER OF MALES IN EACH TRIAD WHO REPORTED DELINQUENT BEHAVIOR FOR EACH OF SIX KINDS OF DELINQUENCY IN EACH TYPE OF CONFORMING-DELINQUENT SUBGROUP

Type of Conforming or Delinquent Group		Theft under $2 more than once				Vandalism more than once				Theft: $2–$50 once or more				Assault once or more				Theft over $50 once or more				Auto theft once or more			
		0	1	2	3	0	1	2	3	0	1	2	3	0	1	2	3	0	1	2	3	0	1	2	3
Career oriented: B.C.	f_e	*	3	12	17†	*	4	13	15	*	2	11	19	1	7	14	10†	1	6	14	11	1	8	14	9
	f	1	4	7	20	3	2	9	18	*	3	10	19	2	9	7	14	2	6	11	13	4	5	12	11
Peer oriented: B.C.	f_e	1	7	19	16	2	12	19	10	7	19	16	4	22	19	5	2	27	16	3	*	29	14	2	*
	f	1	10	13	19	4	8	22	9	9	18	12	7	24	15	5	2	28	15	2	1	28	17	1	0
Peer oriented: W.C.	f_e	0	0	0	9	*	0	2	6	*	2	4	3	3	4	2	*	3	4	2	*	5	3	1	*
	f	0	0	0	9	0	0	3	6	1	1	3	4	3	4	2	0	4	1	4	*	5	3	1	0
Conf. nonachv: B.C.	f_e	10	29	27	8	16	32	21	5	42	27	6	*	55	18	2	*	69	6	*	*	69	6	*	*
	f	15	23	24	12	19	29	18	8	45	22	5	3	59	12	2	2	70	4	1	0	68	6	1	0
Conf. nonachv: W.C.	f_e	1	4	12	12	1	8	13	7	9	13	6	1	18	9	2	*	27	2	*	*	18	9	2	*
	f	1	4	11	13	2	9	9	9	12	9	4	4	21	5	1	2	27	2	0	0	19	8	2	0
Nonconf. isolate	f_e	1	2	3	1	1	1	2	1	6	1	0	0	4	2	1	0	7	0	0	0	7	0	0	0
	f	4	4	1	2	2	2	2	1	6	1	0	0	5	1	1	0	7	0	0	0	7	0	0	0
Conf. achiever: B.C.	f_e	8	10	4	*	10	9	3	*	19	3	*	*	17	5	0	0	22	0	0	0	22	0	0	0
	f	8	9	4	1	11	8	2	1	20	1	1	0	17	5	0	0	22	0	0	0	22	0	0	0
Conf. achiever: W.C.	f_e	10	21	16	4†	17	23	10	1	40	10	1	0	45	6	0	0	49	2	0	0	48	3	*	0
	f	14	17	12	8	22	16	8	5	41	9	1	0	45	6	0	0	49	2	0	0	48	3	0	0
Conf. isolate	f_e	6	8	3	0	8	8	3	0	17	1	1	0	15	3	0	0	17	1	1	0	18	0	0	0
	f	7	6	3	1	6	6	6	5	17	1	0	0	15	3	0	0	17	1	0	0	18	0	0	0
Hyperconformer	f_e	5	4	1	0	7	3	0	0	10	0	0	0	9	1	0	0	10	0	0	0	10	0	0	0
	f	5	3	2	0	6	4	0	0	10	0	0	0	9	1	0	0	10	0	0	0	10	0	0	0

* Expected frequency is less than one case.
† Null hypothesis rejected for this comparison: $P(\chi^2) < .05$.
[1] Proportion of boys in each conforming-delinquent subgroup who reported each kind of delinquency is used to set up binomial of triads for each subgroup.

commit that kind of offense. Put in another way, our classification of boys into conforming and delinquent types of groups accounts in large part for the tendency for boys to choose as close friends boys who commit delinquent acts similar to their own. This can be seen by turning again to Table 1 where we observe that the sum of the expected values for the conforming-delinquent subgroups is remarkably like that observed for all triads, particularly for the serious offenses of auto theft and theft over $50. These two types of offenses are more clearly concentrated in the career- and peer-oriented delinquent types, of course. The similarity between the sum of the expected values for subgroups and the actual behavior reported within triads is less marked for the less serious offenses, offenses which occur quite frequently in most conforming and delinquent groups.

These observations (a summary of which is aided by comparing the f and f Σ values in Table 1) suggest that a model of random selection accounts for subcultural or career-oriented delinquents associating most frequently with boys who commit delinquent acts similar to their own, given our classification of them into that type of delinquent group. This finding, of course, should not obscure the fact that the classification system does discriminate among types of conforming and delinquent boys. Career-oriented delinquents are easily distinguished from all other types by the fact that for every kind of offense, at least two-thirds of the triads are made up of boys who committed the same kind of offense. There are significantly more career-oriented triads in which all members engaged in every kind of offense than in any other type of delinquent group except that peer-oriented white-collar delinquents have significantly more triads in which all

members committed theft under two dollars.

We have shown that for each kind of delinquent behavior reported in this study, the probability of an individual committing a specific act of delinquency is dependent upon the commission of the act by other members of the triad. Except for Sutherland's original formulation of differential association theory, most contemporary sociological theories emphasize a qualitative difference between middle and lower class delinquency. In Table 5 we ask whether the finding that a boy's delinquent behavior depends upon his close friends engaging in it is independent of the social class status of the boys. It clearly is not for all types of offenses. Among blue-collar boys, the probability of a boy engaging in any specific kind of delinquency depends upon his close friends engaging in it but among white-collar boys this is true only for theft involving amounts of less than $50 or for vandalism. Apparently when middle class delinquent boys engage in serious delinquent behavior it is relatively independent of their close friendship choices.

Our interviews with subjects were structured so as to avoid mention by name of close friends in delinquency. To do so would violate peer norms about "squealers" and at times jeopardize rapport. Many respondents nevertheless volunteered names of their co-participants for delinquent acts in which they had associates and these were usually persons mentioned as "closest friends." Each respondent was explicitly asked for each reported delinquent offense whether he was (always, usually, sometimes or never) alone (or with one or more persons) when committing it. Table 6 presents this information only for those triads in which all members reported committing a specific kind of delinquent act. The objective is to in-

Table 5

OBSERVED (f) AND EXPECTED (f_e)[1] NUMBER OF WHITE MALE TRIADS CLASSIFIED BY NUMBER OF MALES IN EACH TRIAD WHO REPORTED DELINQUENT BEHAVIOR FOR SIX KINDS OF DELINQUENT BEHAVIOR, CONTROLLING ON SOCIAL CLASS OF ORIGINAL SUBJECT IN EACH TRIAD

Kind of Delinquent Behavior	Number in Triad Reporting Delinquent Behavior by Social Class									
	White Collar Triads					Blue Collar Triads				
	0	1	2	3	$P(\chi^2)$	0	1	2	3	$P(\chi^2)$
Done One or More Times										
Auto theft										
f_e	72	16	1	*		100	61	13	1	
f	72	14	3	0	p>.90	122	28	14	11	p<.001
Theft over $50										
f_e	76	12	1	*		96	64	14	1	
f	80	5	4	0	p>.20	122	25	14	14	p<.001
Assault										
f_e	65	22	2	*		80	72	21	2	
f	69	15	3	2	p>.30	102	41	14	18	p<.001
Theft: $2-$50										
f_e	42	36	10	1		46	77	44	8	
f	54	19	8	8	p<.001	74	44	28	29	p<.001
Done More than Once										
Vandalism										
f_e	13	36	31	9		22	64	64	21	
f	24	25	20	20	p<.001	37	47	51	36	p<.001
Theft under $2										
f_e	6	27	38	18		13	52	73	33	
f	15	21	23	30	p<.001	25	46	48	52	p<.001

* Expected frequency is less than one case.

[1] The proportion of boys in each social class subgroup who reported committing each kind of delinquency is used to set up the binominal of triads for each social class subgroup.

vestigate whether unanimous reporting of engaging in a kind of delinquent behavior in a triad means they engaged in the behavior as group activity. Evidently this is not always the case. It is apparent that, for close friendship groups where all members committed the same kind of act, participants are most likely to report vandalism as group activity and least likely to report theft under $2 as group activity. This finding is consistent with that of Enyon and Reckless on the percentage of cases in which companions were present at first occurrence of admitted delinquency, it being higher for acts of vandalism (91 percent) than for taking things under $2 (69 percent).[30]

[30] Thomas G. Enyon and Walter C. Reckless, op. cit., Table 4.

Table 6

PERCENT OF TRIADS WHERE ALL BOYS ADMIT DELINQUENT ACTS IN WHICH ALL BOYS ALSO INDICATE COMMISSION OF ACT WITH SOME-ONE ELSE, BY KIND OF ACT AND TYPE OF TRIAD

Type of Conforming or Delinquent Triad	Kind of Delinquent Act											
	Theft < $2 once or more		Vandalism once or more		Theft: $2–$50 once or more		Assault once or more		Theft > $50 once or more		Auto Theft once or more	
	Percent	Number	Percent	Number	Percent	Number	Percent	Number	Percent	Number	Percent	Number
Career oriented: B.C.	45	22	86	21	74	19	79	14	100	13	82	11
Peer oriented: B.C.	45	29	74	19	43	7	50	2	0	1	0	0
Peer oriented: W.C.	22	9	100	7	75	4		0		0	0	0
Conf. nonachv: B.C.	32	25	80	20	67	3	0	2		0	0	0
Conf. nonachv: W.C.	42	19	92	13	100	4	50	2		0	0	0
Nonconf. isolate	20	5	100	3		0		0		0	0	0
Conf. achiever: B.C.	0	6	80	5		0		0		0	0	0
Conf. achiever: W.C.	5	19	80	10		0		0		0	0	0
Conf. isolate	25	4	100	2		0		0		0	0	0
Hyperconformer		0		0		0		0		0	0	0

If attention is directed to variation in group involvement in delinquency among our conforming-delinquent types of triads, there is substantial evidence that only career-oriented delinquents report group involvement for all types of offense other than theft under $2. The career-oriented delinquent is apparently most likely to commit his offenses with accomplices.

SUMMARY AND CONCLUSIONS

The main question for this paper was whether boys in close friendship groups have the same specific patterns of delinquent behavior. The reported delinquent behavior of boys in close friendship triads was compared with that expected for six kinds of delinquent· behavior. Two different ways of accounting for the observed distribution were examined.

The first compares the observed delinquent behavior of boys in triads with a binomial based on the rate for each kind of delinquency in the population. We concluded that the probability for an individual committing a specific kind of delinquent act depends upon the commission of the act by other members of the triad. This dependence upon close friends engaging in delinquent activity is not independent of the social class status of boys for all kinds of offenses, however. Among blue-collar boys, the probability of a boy engaging in any of the six kinds of delinquency depends upon his close friends engaging in it but among white-collar boys this is true only for the less serious offenses.

The second comparison asks whether the behavior of boys in triads departs from predictions from Sutherland's differential association theory or coalition theory that there be uniform conformity in conforming groups and uniformity of specific kinds of delinquent behavior in

delinquent groups. We concluded there is considerable departure from this explanatory model even when only those groups are considered where at least two boys engaged in the same kind of delinquency. The observed distribution of delinquency in close friendship triads departs somewhat less from the random than the differential association model, at least for the more serious offenses.

There is in fact considerable variation in the delinquent behavior homophily of friendship triads. The degree to which commission of a kind of delinquent act depends upon its commission by other members of the triad varies considerably by type of delinquency. Vandalism and petty larceny, the more common offenses, are commonly committed by two or three members of the triad while a majority of the triads where at least one member committed auto theft or assault are made up of only one member committing the offense. Behavioral homophily in triads does not mean that boys always or usually commit these offenses together, since there is evidence that theft under $2 is least likely to involve group activity. Two things seem evident from these findings, that delinquent behavior homophily in close friendship triads does not necessarily involve association in the commission of offenses and that some offenses are more clearly group activity than others.

Our classification of boys into conforming and delinquent subgroups accounts in large part for the selection of close friends who commit delinquent acts similar to one's own. While career-oriented delinquent boys generally have the highest proportion of triads where boys commit the same kind of delinquent act, they also have the highest overall rate of delinquency for each kind of act. The main problem is to account for the higher rate of delinquency among these boys. Certainly the effect of one's close friends on delinquency does not appear to be a sufficient reason to account for this higher rate since a substantial minority of career-oriented delinquent boys are in close friendship triads where at least one other boy does not commit the same kind of offense and the convergence of boys who commit the same kind of delinquent act in close friendship triads is not greater than that one would expect from the rate of delinquency among these boys.

This study cannot be construed as a test of the genetic formulation of the differential association hypothesis. To the extent that the findings of this study are valid and our logical inferences correctly drawn, however, they may be disappointing to proponents of differential association theory. The association of boys with the *same kind* of delinquent behavior in close friendship triads while somewhat greater than chance is well below what one would expect from the learning hypothesis in differential association theory and the results are not independent of social class. Close friendship choices are more closely correlated with delinquency *per se* than with participation in specific patterns of delinquency presumably learned from others.

The results also cannot be interpreted as clearly supporting one of the major theories of delinquent behavior over that of another, though some postulates in these theories seem supported over others. The main sociological theories of subcultural delinquency such as those of Cohen and Walter Miller postulating differences between lower and middle class gang behavior find some support in this study. Delinquency among middle class boys, particularly for the more serious delinquent offenses, is independent of friendship choices while among lower class boys the probability of committing any kind of delinquent activity

is related to the delinquent activity of one's close friends. The fact that selection of close friends who commit specific kinds of delinquency within each type of conforming-delinquent group is largely a function of the rate of delinquency within each group lends support to Walter Miller's contention that delinquency is endemic in lower class culture. Nonetheless, if Miller is correct, convergence of delinquent patterns of behavior in friendship groups should not exceed chance since he argues that the pressures toward deviance come from outside the immediate peer group. The fact that the probability of a lower class boy's committing any specific kind of delinquency is dependent upon the commission of the act by other members of the group therefore is at odds with Miller's formulation. The model of differential association seems even a less powerful one in accounting for our observed patterns of behavior in close friendship triads than does Miller's formulation, however.

The fact that a substantial proportion of career-oriented delinquent boys do show a marked similarity in delinquent activity, particularly for the more serious offenses, is consistent with Cohen's formulation emphasizing the versatility of delinquency among subcultural delinquents. That some of these groups may be specialized in specific kinds of delinquent activity was not investigated.

This study perhaps only serves to emphasize the difficulty in testing inferences from differential association theory. It perhaps is unnecessary to repeat what is already well stated, that we need to operationalize the hypothesis in such a way as to test the relationship of association with delinquent others through time. Of considerable importance, however, in future research would be an investigation of the "deviant" cases which do not conform to expectations of the differential association model. How can one account for the fact that all members of delinquent groups do not conform to the same patterns of delinquency? Why are some members of close friendship groups delinquent and not others? What are the patterns of recruitment to peer groups and how stable is peer group structure?

18.

Socio-Economic Class and Area as Correlates
of Illegal Behavior among Juveniles

John P. Clark and Eugene P. Wenninger

Until recently almost all efforts to discover characteristics that differentiate juveniles who violate legal norms from those who do not have compared institutional and non-institutional populations. Though many researchers still employ a "delinquent" or "criminal" sample from institutions,[1] there is a growing awareness that the process through which boys and girls are selected to populate our "correctional" institutions may cause such comparison studies to distort seriously the true picture of illegal behavior in our society. Therefore, conclusions based upon such studies are subject to considerable criticism[2] if generalized beyond the type of population of the particular institution at the time of the study. Although the study of adjudicated offenders is important, less encumbered studies of the violation of legal norms hold more promise for those interested in the more general concept of deviant behavior.

Though it, too, has methodological limitations, the anonymous-questionnaire procedure has been utilized to obtain results reflecting the rates and patterns of illegal behavior among juveniles from different social classes, ages, sexes, and ethnic groups in the general population.[3] The results of

* The total project of which this paper is a part was sponsored by the Ford Foundation and the University of Illinois Graduate Research Board. Professor Daniel Glaser was very helpful throughout the project and in the preparation of this paper.

[1] An outstanding example of this type of research design is Sheldon and Eleanor Glueck, *Unraveling Juvenile Delinquency,* New York: The Commonwealth Fund, 1950.

[2] See Marshall B. Clinard, *Sociology of Deviant Behavior,* New York: Rinehart, 1958, p. 124, for his assessment of the validity of the study by Sheldon and Eleanor Glueck, *Unraveling Juvenile Delinquency.*

[3] Most outstanding are those by Austin L. Porterfield, *Youth in Trouble,* Fort Worth, Texas: Leo Potishman Foundation, 1946; F. Ivan Nye and James F. Short, "Scaling Delinquent Behavior," *American Sociological Review,* 22 (June, 1957), pp. 326–331; and Robert A. Dentler and Lawrence J. Monroe, "Early Adolescent Theft," *American Sociological Review,* 26 (October, 1961), 733–743; Fred J. Murphy, Mary M. Shirley, and Helen L. Witmer, "The Incidence of Hidden Delinquency," *American Journal of Orthopsychiatry,* 16 (October, 1946), pp. 686–696.

SOURCE. John P. Clark and Eugene P. Wenninger, "Socio-economic Class and Area as Correlates of Illegal Behavior among Juveniles," from *American Sociological Review,* Volume 27, December 1962, pp. 826–834. Reprinted with the permission of the American Sociological Association and the authors.

these studies have offered sufficient evidence to indicate that the patterns of illegal behavior among juveniles may be dramatically different from what was heretofore thought to be the case.

Some of the most provocative findings have been those that challenge the almost universally accepted conclusion that the lower socio-economic classes have higher rates of illegal behavior than do the middle or upper classes. For example, neither the Nye-Short study[4] nor that of Dentler and Monroe[5] revealed any significant difference in the incidence of certain illegal or "deviant" behaviors among occupational-status levels—a finding quite at odds with most current explanations of delinquent behavior.

Although most of the more comprehensive studies in the social class tradition have been specifically concerned with a more-or-less well-defined portion of the lower class (i.e., "delinquent gangs,"[6] or "culture of the gang," or "delinquent subculture"[7]), some authors have tended to generalize their findings and theoretical formulations rather specifically to the total lower class population of juveniles.[8] These

latter authors certainly do not profess that *all* lower class children are equally involved in illegal behavior, but by implication they suggest that the incidence of illegal conduct (whether brought to the attention of law enforcement agencies or not) is more pervasive in this class than others because of some unique but fundamental characteristics of the lower social strata. For example, Miller has compiled a list of "focal concerns" toward which the lower class supposedly is oriented and because of which those in this class violate more legal norms with greater frequency than other classes.[9] Other authors point out that the lower classes are disadvantaged in their striving for legitimate goals and that they resort to deviant means to attain them.[10] Again, the result of this behavior is higher rates of illegal behavior among the lower socio-economic classes.

Therefore, there *appears* to be a direct conflict between the theoretical formulations of Miller, Cohen, Merton, Cloward and Ohlin, and those findings reported by Nye and Short and Dentler and Monroe. This apparent discrepancy in the literature can be resolved, however, if one hypothesizes that the rates of illegal conduct among the social classes vary with the type of community[11] in which they are found. Were this so, it would be possible for studies which have included certain types of communities to reveal differential illegal

---

[4] James F. Short, "Differential Association and Delinquency," *Social Problems,* 4 (January, 1957), pp. 233-239; F. Ivan Nye, *Family Relationships and Delinquent Behavior,* New York: John Wiley, 1958; James E. Short and F. Ivan Nye, "Reported Behavior as a Criterion of Deviant Behavior," *Social Problems,* 5 (Winter, 1957–1958), pp. 207–213; F. Ivan Nye, James F. Short, and Virgil J. Olson, "Socio-Economic Status and Delinquent Behavior," *American Journal of Sociology,* 63 (January, 1958), pp. 381–389.

[5] Dentler and Monroe, *op. cit.*

[6] Richard A. Cloward and Lloyd E. Ohlin, *Delinquency and Opportunity: A Theory of Delinquent Gangs,* New York: The Free Press of Glencoe, 1961.

[7] Albert K. Cohen, *Delinquent Boys: The Culture of the Gang,* Glencoe, Ill.: Free Press, 1955.

[8] Walter B. Miller, "Lower Class Culture as a Generating Milieu of Gang Delinquency," *Journal of Social Issues,* 14 (No. 3, 1958), pp. 5–19.

[9] *Ibid.*

[10] Cohen, *op. cit.*, Cloward and Ohlin, *op. cit.*, and Robert K. Merton, *Social Theory and Social Structure,* Glencoe, Ill.: Free Press, 1957, pp. 146-149.

[11] In this report "type of community" is used to refer in a general way to a geographic and social unit having certain distinctive demographic qualities, such as occupational structure, race, social class, and size. Designations such as "rural farm," or "Negro lower class urban," or "middle class suburbia," have long been utilized to describe such persistent physical-social characteristics.

behavior rates among social classes while studies which have involved other types of communities might fail to detect social class differences.

Whereas the findings and formulations of Merton, Cohen, Cloward and Ohlin, and Miller are oriented, in a sense, toward the "full range" of social situations, those of Nye-Short and Dentler-Monroe are very specifically limited to the types of populations used in their respective studies. It is important to note that the communities in which these latter studies were conducted ranged only from rural to small city in size. As Nye points out, "They are thus urban but not metropolitan."[12] Yet, most studies of "delinquent gangs" and "delinquent subcultures" have been conducted in metropolitan centers where these phenomena are most apparent. Perhaps it is only here that there is a sufficient concentration of those in the extreme socio-economic classes to afford an adequate test of the "social class hypothesis."

In addition to the matter of social class concentration and size, there is obviously more than one "kind" of lower class and each does not have rates or types of illegal behavior identical to those of the others. For example, most rural farm areas, in which occupations, incomes, and educational levels are indicative of lower class status, as measured by most social class indexes, consistently have been found to have low rates of misconduct—in fact lower than most urban middle class communities.

Therefore, to suggest the elimination of social class as a significant correlate to the quantity and quality of illegal behavior before it has been thoroughly examined in a variety of community situations seems somewhat premature. Reiss and Rhodes concluded as a re-

sult of study of class and juvenile court rates by school district that "it is clear that there is no simple relationship between ascribed social status and delinquency."[13] In order to isolate the factor of social class, to eliminate possible effects of class bias in the rate at which juvenile misbehavior is referred to court, as well as to vary the social and physical environs in which it is located, we chose in this study to compare rates of admitted illegal behavior among diverse communities within the northern half of Illinois. Our hypotheses were:

1. Significant differences in the incidence of illegal behavior exist among communities differing in predominant social class composition within a given metropolitan area.

2. Significant differences in the incidence of illegal behavior exist among similar social class strata located in different types of community.

3. Differences in the incidence of illegal behavior among different social class populations within a given community are not significant.

THE STUDY

The data used to test the above hypotheses were gathered in 1961 as part of a larger exploratory study of illegal behavior (particularly theft) among juveniles and its relationship to socio-economic class, type of community, age, race, and various attitudinal variables, such as attitude toward law, feelings of alienation, concept of self, and feelings of being able to achieve desired goals. Subsequent reports will deal with other aspects of the exploratory study.

---

[12] Nye, Short, and Olson, *op. cit.*, p. 383.

[13] Albert J. Reiss and Albert L. Rhodes, "The Distribution of Juvenile Delinquency in the Social Class Structure," *American Sociological Review*, 26 (October, 1961), pp. 720–732.

A total of 1154 public school students from the sixth through the twelfth grades in the school systems of four different types of communities were respondents to a self-administered, anonymous questionnaire given in groups of from 20 to 40 persons by the senior author. Considerable precaution was taken to insure reliability and validity of the responses. For example, assurances were given that the study was not being monitored by the school administration; questions were pretested to eliminate ambiguity; and the administration of the questionnaire was made as threat-free as possible.

The four communities represented in the study were chosen for the unique social class structure represented by each. The Duncan "Socio-Economic Index for All Occupations"[14] was used to determine the occupational profile of each community by assigning index scores to the occupation of the respondents' fathers. The results are summarized in Table 1.

The overwhelming majority of the

[14] Albert J. Reiss, Jr., Otis Dudley Duncan, Paul K. Hatt, and Cecil C. North, *Occupations and Social Status*, New York: The Free Press of Glencoe, 1961, especially pp. 109–161 prepared by Otis D. Duncan.

respondents comprising the *rural farm* population live on farms, farming being by far the most common occupation of their fathers. Many of the fathers who were not listed as farmers are, in fact, "part-time" farmers. Therefore, though the Duncan Index would classify most of the residents in the lower class, most of these public school children live on farms in a prosperous section of the Midwest. The sixth, seventh, and eighth graders were drawn from schools located in very small villages. Grades 9–12 were drawn from the high school which was located in open-farm land.

The *lower urban* sample is primarily composed of children of those with occupations of near-equal ranking but certainly far different in nature from those of the rural farm community. The lower urban sample was drawn from a school system located in a very crowded and largely Negro area of Chicago. The fathers (or male head of the family) of these youngsters are laborers in construction, waiters, janitors, clean-up men, etc. Even among those who place relatively high on the Duncan Scale are many who, in spite of their occupational title, reside, work, and socialize almost exclusively in the lower class community.

Table 1

DUNCAN SOCIO-ECONOMIC-INDEX SCORES BASED ON OCCUPATION OF FATHER

	Type of community			
Score	Rural farm %	Lower urban %	Industrial city %	Upper urban %
(1) 0–23	75.9	40.4	36.4	5.7
(2) 24–47	9.9	15.5	19.3	4.8
(3) 48–71	4.7	12.5	22.9	43.9
(4) 72–96	1.5	4.2	10.0	34.6
(5) Unclassifiable°	8.0	27.4	11.4	11.0
Total	100 (N—274)	100 (N—265)	100 (N—280)	100 (N—335)

° This category included those respondents from homes with no father and those respondents who did not furnish adequate information for reliable classification. The 27.4 per cent figure in the lower urban community reflects a higher proportion of "fatherless" homes rather than greater numbers of responses which were incomplete or vague in other ways.

As Table 1 demonstrates, the occupational structure of the *industrial city* is somewhat more diffuse than the other communities, though consisting primarily of lower class occupations. This city of about 35,000 is largely autonomous, although a small portion of the population commutes daily to Chicago. However, about two-thirds of these students have fathers who work as blue-collar laborers in local industries and services. The median years of formal education of all males age 25 or over is 10.3.[15] The median annual family income is $7,255.[16] The population of this small city contains substantial numbers of Polish and Italian Americans and about 15 per cent Negroes.

Those in the *upper urban* sample live in a very wealthy suburb of Chicago. Nearly three-fourths of the fathers in these families are high-level executives or professionals. The median level of education for all males age 25 or over is 16 plus.[17] The median annual family income is slightly over $20,000 —80 per cent of the families make $10,000 or more annually.[18]

With two exceptions, representative sampling of the public school children was followed within each of these communities: (1) those who could not read at a fourth grade level were removed in all cases, which resulted in the loss of less than one-half per cent of the total sample, and (2) the sixth-grade sample in the industrial city community was drawn from a predominantly Negro, working class area and was, therefore, non-representative of the total community for that grade-level only. All the students from grades 6 through 12 were used in the rural farm community "sample."

[15] *U.S. Census of Population: 1960*, Final Report PC (1)–15C, p. 15–296.
[16] *Ibid.*, p. 15–335.
[17] *Ibid.*, p. 15–305.
[18] *Ibid.*, p. 15–344.

MEASURE OF ILLEGAL BEHAVIOR

An inventory of 36 offenses was initially assembled from delinquency scales, legal statutes, and the FBI Uniform Crime Reports. In addition to this, a detailed list of theft items, ranging from candy to automobiles, was constructed. The latter list was later combined into two composite items (minor theft and major theft) and added to the first list, enlarging the number of items in this inventory to 38 items as shown in Table 2. No questions on sex offenses were included in this study, a restriction found necessary in order to gain entrance into one of the school systems.

All respondents were asked to indicate if they had committed each of these offenses (including the detailed list of theft items) *within the past year,* thus furnishing data amenable to age-level analysis.[19] If the respondents admitted commission of an offense, they so indicated by disclosing the number of times (either 1, 2, 3, or 4 or more) they had done so. The first four columns of Table 2 reveal the percentage of students who admitted having indulged in each specific behavior one or more times *during the past year.*

Specific offense items were arranged in an array from those admitted by the highest percentage of respondents to those admitted by the lowest percentage of respondents. Obviously the "nuisance" offenses appear near the top while the most serious and the more situationally specific fall nearer the end of the listing.[20] Several offenses are

[19] Rates of illegal behavior were found to increase until age 14–15 and then to decrease.
[20] Ordinarily, not receiving 100 per cent admission to the first few offenses listed would have raised doubt as to the validity of those questionnaires on which these extremely common offenses were not admitted. In the Nye-Short study such questionnaires were discarded. However, since the

Table 2

PERCENTAGE OF RESPONDENTS ADMITTING INDIVIDUAL OFFENSES AND SIGNIFICANCE OF DIFFERENCES BETWEEN SELECTED COMMUNITY COMPARISONS

Offense	Community (1) Industrial city N = 280	(2) Lower urban N = 265	(3) Upper urban N = 335	(4) Rural farm N = 274	Significance of differences* (1–2)	(2–3)	(3–4)
1. Did things my parents told me not to do.	90	87	85	82	X	X	X
2. Minor theft (compilation of such items as the stealing of fruit, pencils, lipstick, candy, cigarettes, comic books, money less than $1, etc.).	79	78	80	73	X	X	X
3. Told a lie to my family, principal, or friends.	80	74	77	74	X	X	X
4. Used swearwords or dirty words out loud in school, church, or on the street so other people could hear me.	63	58	54	51	X	X	X
5. Showed or gave someone a dirty picture, a dirty story, or something like that.	53	39	58	54	1	3	X
6. Was out at night just fooling around after I was supposed to be home.	49	50	51	35	X	X	3
7. Hung around other people who I knew had broken the law lots of times or who were known as "bad" people.	49	47	27	40	X	2	4
8. Threw rocks, cans, sticks, or other things at passing car, bicycle, or person.	41	37	33	36	X	X	X
9. Slipped into a theater or other place without paying.	35	40	39	22	X	X	3

* Code: X = no significant difference.
1, 2, 3, or 4 = significant differences at .05 level or higher. The numbers indicate which of the communities in the comparison is higher in incidence of the offense.
n = too few offender cases to determine significant level.

Table 2—Continued

10. Major theft (compilation of such items as the stealing of auto parts, autos, money over $1, bicycles, radios and parts, clothing, wallets, liquor, guns, etc.).	37	40	29	20	X	2	3
11. Went into another person's house, a shed, or other building without their permission.	31	16	31	42	1	3	4
12. Gambled for money or something else with people other than my family.	30	22	35	26	X	3	3
13. Got some money or something from others by saying that I would pay them back even though I was pretty sure I wouldn't.	35	48	26	14	2	2	3
14. Told someone I was going to beat-up on them unless they did what I wanted them to do.	33	28	24	32	X	X	4
15. Drank beer, wine, or liquor without my parents' permission.	38	37	26	12	X	2	3
16. Have been kicked out of class or school for acting up.	27	28	31	22	X	X	3
17. Threw nails, or glass, or cans in the street.	31	29	21	17	X	X	X
18. Used a slug or other things like this in candy, coke, or coin machines.	24	35	18	12	2	2	3
19. Skipped school without permission.	24	36	18	11	2	2	3
20. Helped make a lot of noise outside a church, or school, or any other place in order to bother the people inside.	17	37	18	15	X	2	X
21. Threw rocks, or sticks or any other thing in order to break a window, or street light, or thing like that.	24	26	22	16	X	X	3
22. Said I was going to tell something on someone unless they gave me money, candy, or something else I wanted.	23	28	17	19	X	2	X
23. Kept or used something that I knew had been stolen by someone else.	29	36	15	16	X	2	X

Table 2—Continued

Offense	Community				Significance of differences*		
	(1) Industrial city N = 280	(2) Lower urban N = 265	(3) Upper urban N = 335	(4) Rural farm N = 274	(1-2)	(2-3)	(3-4)
24. Tampered or fooled with another person's car, tractor, or bicycle while they weren't around.	26	13	19	24	1	3	X
25. Started a fist fight.	26	22	15	18	X	2	X
26. Messed up a restroom by writing on the wall, or leaving the water running to run onto the floor, or upsetting the waste can.	18	33	14	17	X	2	X
27. Hung around a pool hall, bar, or tavern.	21	18	10	23	X	2	4
28. Hung around the railroad tracks and trains.	16	13	23	16	X	3	3
29. Broke down or helped to break down a fence, gate, or door on another person's place.	15	14	8	8	X	2	X
30. Took part in a "gang fight."	12	18	7	7	X	2	X
31. Ran away from home.	12	12	8	7	X	X	X
32. Asked for money, candy, a cigarette or other things from strangers.	12	12	6	7	X	2	X
33. Carried a razor, switch-blade, or gun to be used against other people.	8	16	3	4	2	2	X
34. "Beat up" on kids who hadn't done anything to me.	8	5	5	6	X	X	X
35. Broke or helped break up the furniture in a school, church, or other public building.	8	4	2	8	X	X	4
36. Attacked someone with the idea of killing them.	3	6	1	3	2	1	n
37. Smoked a reefer or used some sort of dope (narcotics).	3	4	1	3	X	n	n
38. Started a fire or helped set a fire in a building without the permission of the owner.	3	2	1	3	X	n	n

apparently committed very infrequently by school children from the sixth to twelfth grades regardless of their social environs.

FINDINGS

In order to determine whether significant differences exist in the incidence of illegal behavior among the various types of communities, a two-step procedure was followed. First, each of the four communities was assigned a rank for each offense on the basis of the percentage of respondents admitting commission of that offense. These ranks were totaled across all offenses for each community. The resultant numerical total provided a very crude over-all measure of the relative degree to which the sample population from each community had been involved in illegal behavior during the past year. The results were (from most to least illegal behavior): industrial city, lower urban, upper urban, and rural farm. However, there was little over-all difference in the sum of ranks between upper urban and rural farm and even less difference between the industrial city and lower urban areas.

In the second step the communities were arranged in the order given above and then the significance of the difference between adjacent pairs was determined by applying the Wilcoxon matched-pairs signed-ranks test. Only those comparisons which involve either industrial city or lower urban versus upper urban or rural farm result in any significant differences.[21] This finding is

compatible with the above crude ranking procedure.

On the basis of these findings the first hypothesis is supported, while the second hypothesis received only partial support. Lower urban juveniles reported significantly more illegal behavior than did the juveniles of the upper urban community, and the two lower class communities of industrial city and lower urban appear to be quite similar in their high rates, but another lower class area composed largely of farmers has a much lower rate, similar to that of the upper urban area.

Much more contrast among the rates of juvenile misconduct in the four different communities than is indicated by the above results becomes apparent when one focuses on individual offenses. As the last column in Table 2 reveals, and as could be predicted from the above, there are few significant differences in the rates on each offense between the industrial city and lower urban communities. The few differences that do occur hardly fall into a pattern except that the lower urban youth seem to be oriented more toward violence (carrying weapons and attacking persons) than those in the industrial city.

However, 16 of a possible 35 relationships are significantly different in the upper urban-rural farm comparison, a fact that could not have been predicted from the above results. Apparently, variation in one direction on certain offenses tends to be neutralized by variation in the opposite direction on other offenses when the Wilcoxon test is used. There are greater actual differ-

---

respondents were asked in this study to admit their offenses during the past year only, it was thought that less than 100 per cent admission would be highly possible when one considers the entire age range. Undoubtedly some of the respondents who did not admit these minor offenses were falsifying their questionnaires.

[21] Significance of differences were calculated between pairs of communities across *all* 38 offenses by using the Wil-

coxon matched-pairs signed-ranks test (described in Sidney Siegel, *Non-Parametric Statistics*, New York: McGraw-Hill Book Company, Inc., 1956, pp. 75–83). The results of this procedure were:

1–2—P .35	1–3—P .00006
2–3—P .0034	1–4—P .0006
3–4—P .90	2–4—P .016

ences in the nature of illegal behavior between these two communities than is noticeable when considered in more summary terms. (It might be pointed out here, parenthetically, that this type of finding lends support to the suggestion by Dentler and Monroe that the comparison of criterion groups on the basis of "omnibus scales" may have serious shortcomings.)[22]

Rural farm youngsters are more prone than those in the upper urban area to commit such offenses as trespassing, threatening to "beat up" on persons, hanging around taverns, and being with "bad" associates—all relatively unsophisticated acts. Although some of the offenses committed more often by those who live in the upper urban community are also unsophisticated (throwing rocks at street lights, getting kicked out of school classes, and hanging around trains), others probably require some skill to perform successfully and probably depend on supportive peer-group relationships. For example, these data reveal that upper urban juveniles are more likely than their rural farm counterparts to be out at night after they are supposed to be at home, drink beer and liquors without parents' permission, engage in major theft, gamble, skip school, and slip into theaters without paying. In addition to their likely dependence upon peer-groups, perhaps these offenses are more easily kept from the attention of parents in the urban setting than in open-farm areas.

The greatest differences between rates of illegal conduct occur between the lower urban and upper urban communities, where 21 of a possible 35 comparisons reach statistical significance, the lower urban rates being higher in all except five of these. Although the upper urban youngsters are more likely to pass "dirty pictures,"

gamble, trespass, hang around trains, and tamper with other people's cars, their cousins in the lower class area are more likely to steal major items, drink, skip school, destroy property, fight, and carry weapons. The latter offenses are those normally thought to be "real delinquent acts" while the upper urban offenses (with the exception of vehicle tampering) are not generally considered to be such.

To summarize briefly, when the rates of juvenile misconduct are compared on individual offenses among communities, it appears that as one moves from rural farm to upper urban to industrial city and lower urban, the incidence of most offenses becomes greater, especially in the more serious offenses and in those offenses usually associated with social structures with considerable tolerance for illegal behavior.

While most emphasis is placed here on the differences, one obvious finding, evident in Table 2, is that in most of the nuisance offenses (minor theft, lying to parents, disobeying parents, swearing in public, throwing objects to break things or into the streets) there are no differences among the various communities. Differences appear to lie in the more serious offenses and those requiring a higher degree of sophistication and social organization.

The Reiss-Rhodes findings tend to refute theories of delinquent behavior which imply a high delinquency proneness of the lower class regardless of the "status area" in which it is found.[23] In view of this report, and since Nye-Short and Dentler-Monroe were unable to detect inter-class differences, inter-class comparisons were made within the four community types of this study.

---

[22] Dentler and Monroe, op. cit., p. 734.

[23] Reiss and Rhodes, op. cit., p. 729. The concept of "status areas" is used here as it was used by Reiss and Rhodes to designate residential areas of a definite social class composition.

Following the technique employed by Nye and Short, only those students age 15 and younger were used in these comparisons in order to neutralize the possible effects of differential school dropout rates by social classes in the older categories.

With the exception of the industrial city, no significant inter-class differences in illegal behavior rates were found within community types when either the Wilcoxon test was used for all offenses or when individual offense comparisons were made.[24] This finding supports hypothesis 3. It could account for the inability of Nye-Short and Dentler-Monroe to find differences among the socio-economic classes from several relatively similar communities in which their studies were conducted. It is also somewhat compatible with the Reiss and Rhodes findings. However, we did not find indications of higher rates of illegal conduct in the predominant socio-economic class within most areas, as the Reiss and Rhodes data suggested.[25] This may have been a function of the unique manner in which the socio-economic categories had to be combined for comparison purposes in this study. These findings, however, are logical in that boys and girls of the minority social classes within a

[24] Because of small numbers in social classes within certain communities, categories were collapsed or ignored for comparison purposes as shown below. Refer to Table 1 for designation of categories. The Wilcoxon matched-pairs signed-ranks test was used.

Rural farm	
category 1 versus 2, 3, 4	insignificant
Lower urban	
category 1 versus 2, 3, 4	insignificant
category 1 versus 5	insignificant
categories 2, 3, 4 versus 5	insignificant
Industrial city	
category 1 versus 2	significant
category 2 versus 3, 4	significant
category 1 versus 3, 4	insignificant
Upper urban	
category 3 versus 4	insignificant

[25] Reiss and Rhodes, *op. cit.*, p. 729.

"status area" would likely strive to adhere to the norms of the predominant social class as closely as possible whether these norms were legal or illegal.

Within the industrial city the second socio-economic category (index scores 24–47) was slightly significantly lower than either extreme category when the Wilcoxon test was used. Since the largest percentage of the sample of the industrial city falls in the lowest socio-economic category (0–23) and since this category evidences one of the highest rates of misconduct, the finding for this community is somewhat similar to the Reiss-Rhodes findings.

CONCLUSIONS

The findings of this study tend to resolve some of the apparent conflicts in the literature that have arisen from previous research concerning the relationship between the nature of illegal behavior and socio-economic class. However, some of the results contradict earlier reports.

Our findings are similar to those of Nye-Short and Dentler-Monroe in that we failed to detect any significant differences in illegal behavior rates among the social classes of rural and small urban areas. However, in keeping with the class-oriented theories, we did find significant differences, both in quantity and quality of illegal acts, among communities or "status areas," each consisting of one predominant socio-economic class. The lower class areas have higher illegal behavior rates, particularly in the more serious types of offenses. Differences among the socio-economic classes within these "status areas" were generally insignificant (which does not agree with the findings of Reiss and Rhodes), although when social class categories were compared across communities, significant differences were found. All this suggests some extremely interesting relationships.

1. The pattern of illegal behavior within small communities or within "status areas" of a large metropolitan center is determined by the predominant class of that area. Social class differentiation within these areas is apparently not related to the incidence of illegal behavior. This suggests that there are community-wide norms which are related to illegal behavior and to which juveniles adhere regardless of their social class origins. The answer to the obvious question of how large an urban area must be before socio-economic class becomes a significant variable in the incidence of illegal behavior is not provided by this study. It is quite likely that in addition to size, other considerations such as the ratio of social class representation, ethnic composition, and the prestige of the predominant social class relative to other "status areas" would influence the misconduct rates. The population of 20,-000 of the particular upper urban community used in this study is apparently not of sufficient size or composition to provide for behavior autonomy among the social classes in the illegal behavior sense. There is some evidence, however, that an industrial city of roughly 40,000 such as the one included here is on the brink of social class differentiation in misconduct rates.

2. Though the juveniles in all communities admitted indulgence in several nuisance offenses at almost equal rates, serious offenses are much more likely to have been committed by lower class urban youngsters. Perhaps the failure of some researchers to find differences among the social classes in their misconduct rates can be attributed to the relatively less serious offenses included in their questionnaires or scales. It would seem to follow that any "sub-culture" characterized by the more serious delinquencies, would be found only in large, urban, lower class areas. However, the data of this study, at best, can only suggest this relationship.

3. Lastly, these data suggest that the present explanations that rely heavily on socio-economic class as an all-determining factor in the etiology of illegal behavior should be further specified to include data such as this study provides. For example, Cohen's thesis that a delinquent subculture emerges when lower class boys discover that they must satisfy their need for status by means other than those advocated in the middle class public schools should be amended to indicate that this phenomenon apparently occurs only in large metropolitan centers where the socio-economic classes are found in large, relatively homogeneous areas. In the same manner, Miller's theory of the relationship between the focal concerns of the lower class culture and delinquency may require closer scrutiny. If the relationship between focal concerns to illegal behavior that Miller has suggested exists, then those in the lower social class (as determined by father's occupation) who live in communities or "status areas" that are predominantly of some other social class, are apparently not participants in the "lower class culture;" or, because of their small numbers, they are being successfully culturally intimidated by the predominant class. Likewise, those who are thought to occupy middle class positions apparently take on lower class illegal behavior patterns when residing in areas that are predominantly lower class. This suggests either the great power of prevailing norms within a "status area" or a limitation of social class, as it is presently measured, as a significant variable in the determination of illegal behavior.

RESEARCH QUESTIONS

At least three general questions that demand further research emerge from this study:

1. What dimension (in size and other demographic characteristics) must an urban area attain before socio-economic class becomes a significant variable in the determination of illegal behavior patterns?

2. What are the specific differences between lower class populations and social structures located in rural or relatively small urban areas and those located in large, concentrated areas in metropolitan centers that would account for their differential illegal behavior rates, especially in the more serious offenses?

3. The findings of this study suggest that the criteria presently used to determine social class levels may not be the most conducive to the understanding of variation in the behavior of those who fall within these classes, at least for those within the juvenile ages. A substitute concept is that of "status area" as operationalized by Reiss and Rhodes. For example, the differentiating characteristics of a large, Negro, lower class, urban "status area" could be established and would seem to have greater predictive and descriptive power than would the social class category as determined by present methods. Admittedly, this suggestion raises again the whole messy affair of "cultural area typologies" but area patterns of behaviors obviously exist and must be handled in some manner. Research effort toward systematically combining the traditional socio-economic class concept with that of cultural area might prove extremely fruitful by providing us with important language and concepts not presently available.

19.

Hidden Delinquency and Social Status*

LaMar T. Empey and Maynard L. Erickson

Available data regarding the relationship of social status to delinquency are limited and contradictory. On one hand, almost all official statistics report the incidence of delinquency to be concentrated most heavily among lower-status juveniles.[1] The evidence has been suf-

* This work was financed in part by grants from the Ford Foundation and The Office of Juvenile Delinquency and Youth Development, U.S. Department of Health, Education and Welfare. Grateful acknowledgment is expressed to both.

SOURCE. LaMar T. Empey and Maynard L. Erickson, "Hidden Delinquency and Social Status" from Social Forces, Volume 44, No. 4 June 1966, pp. 546–554. Reprinted with permission.

[1] For examples see: Ernest W. Burgess, "The Economic Factor in Juvenile Delinquency," Journal of Criminal Law, Criminology and Police Science, 43 (May-June 1952), pp. 29–42; Cletus Dirksen, Economic Factors in Delinquency (Milwaukee: Bruce Publishing Co., 1948); Joseph W. Eaton and Kenneth Polk, Measuring Delinquency: A Study of Probation Department Referrals (Pittsburgh: University of Pittsburgh Press, 1961), p. 4; Bernard Lander, Juvenile Delinquency (New York: Columbia University Press, 1954); Clifford R. Shaw and Henry D. McKay, Juvenile Delinquency in Urban Areas (Chicago: University of Chicago Press, 1942); Wm. W. Wattenberg and J. J. Balistrieri, "Gang Membership and Juvenile Delinquency," American Sociological Review, 15 (December 1950), pp. 744–752 and Albert K. Cohen's analysis of several studies in Delinquent Boys: The Culture of the Gang (Glencoe, Illinois: The Free Press, 1955), pp. 37–44.

ficiently persuasive as to lead to a large body of theory designed to explain it: Merton,[2] Cohen,[3] Cloward and Ohlin,[4] Miller,[5] and others.

Yet, there have always been those who argue that the supporting evidence is nothing more than a statistical artifact. Warner and Lunt,[6] Porterfield,[7] Barron[8] and Kvaraceus[9] have all con-

[2] Robert K. Merton, Social Theory and Social Structure (Glencoe, Illinois: The Free Press, 1957), chaps. 4–5.

[3] Cohen, op. cit.

[4] Richard A. Cloward and Lloyd E. Ohlin, Delinquency and Opportunity: A Theory of Delinquent Gangs (Glencoe, Illinois: The Free Press, 1960).

[5] Walter B. Miller, "Lower Class Culture as a Generating Milieu of Gang Delinquency," The Journal of Social Issues, 14 (1958), pp. 5–19.

[6] Lloyd Warner and Paul S. Lunt, The Social Life of a Modern Community (New Haven: Yale University Press, 1941), p. 427.

[7] "Delinquency and Its Outcome in Court and College," American Journal of Sociology, 49 (1943), pp. 199–204; "The Complainant in the Juvenile Court," Sociology and Social Research, 28 (January-February 1944), pp. 171–181; and Youth in Trouble (Ft. Worth, Texas: The Leo Potishman Foundation, 1946).

[8] Milton A. Barron, The Juvenile in Delinquent Society (New York: Alfred A. Knopf, 1956), p. 32.

[9] William C. Kvaraceus, What Research Says to the Teacher: Juvenile Delinquency (Washington, D.C.: National Education Association, August, 1958), pp. 331–332.

cluded that the reason some juveniles are officially charged while others are not is a function of social status. But is their conclusion based on fact or what Cohen calls "egalitarian proclivities and sentimental humanitarianism?"[10]

The answer is not easy to find. On one hand, the empirical findings of Nye, Short and Olsen support Porterfield's pioneer studies which suggested that there is no direct association between delinquency and social status.[11] On the other hand, Gold reported a statistically reliable relationship between white, low-status boys and delinquency.[12] Meanwhile, a recent conference involving investigators who had been concerned with studying hidden delinquency ended up in some disagreement over the matter,[13] some contending there were differences among status levels, others questioning it.

The same kinds of disagreement exist with respect to the *kinds* of delinquent acts which young people from different status levels commit. Ohlin maintains, for example, that middle-status delinquency is "petty" in comparison with low-status delinquency. The latter is more deeply ingrained and possesses a much greater potential for the development of a criminal career.[14] Myerhoff and Myerhoff agree. In their observa-

tions of deviant, middle-class youth, they conclude that the violations of these groups were more often capricious and manipulative than violent.[15]

Karacki and Toby, on the other hand, found fighting gangs that did not come from economically deprived homes. These gangs placed emphasis upon many of the characteristics traditionally associated with lower-class delinquent groups: physical aggression, loyalty to delinquent peers and a search for immediate gratification.[16] Shanley located a similar group of middle- and upper-class boys in the suburbs of Los Angeles. This small minority had patterns of police contact which were every bit as extensive and serious as samples of adjudicated delinquents from lower-class neighborhoods.[17] Herskovitz *el al.*, found likewise. They noted that, among incarcerated offenders, there were comparatively few differences in the nature of offenses committed by middle- and upper- as contrasted to low-status juveniles.[18]

THIS STUDY

This study is concerned with a rather comprehensive analysis of the subject. It utilizes *self-reported* data on delinquency as a means for examining both the *amounts* and *kinds* of delinquent

[10] Cohen, *op. cit.*, p. 42.

[11] F. Ivan Nye, James Short, and V. J. Olsen, "Socio-Economic Status and Delinquent Behavior," *American Journal of Sociology*, 63 (January 1958), pp. 318–389.

[12] Martin Gold, "Socio-Economic Distributions of Juvenile Delinquency," University of Michigan, Institute for Social Research paper presented at the annual meeting of the American Psychological Asociation, Los Angeles, September, 1964.

[13] Robert H. Hardt and George E. Bodine, *Development of Self-Report Instruments in Delinquency Research*, A Conference Report (Syracuse, New York: Syracuse University, Youth Development Center 1965), pp. 12–13.

[14] Lloyd E. Ohlin, *The Development of Opportunities for Youth* (Syracuse, New York: Syracuse University, Youth Development Center, 1960), pp. 8–9.

[15] Howard L. Myerhoff and Barbara G. Myerhoff, "Field Observations of Middle-Class Groups," *Social Forces*, 42 (March 1964), pp. 328–336.

[16] Larry Karacki and Jackson Toby, "The Uncommitted Adolescent: Candidates for Gang Socialization," *Sociological Inquiry*, 32 (Spring 1962), pp. 203–215.

[17] Fred J. Shanley, "Middle-class Delinquency as a Social Problem," paper presented at the annual meeting of the Pacific Sociological Association, Salt Lake City, April, 1965, p. 2.

[18] Herbert H. Herskovitz, Murray Leven, and George Spivak, "Anti-Social Behavior of Adolescents from Higher Socio-Economic Groups," *Journal of Nervous and Mental Diseases*, 125 (November 1959), pp. 1–9.

acts which juveniles from different status levels have committed.

The sample was drawn in Utah and included only white males, ages 15-17 years. Negro and Mexican boys were excluded for two reasons: (1) because they constitute a very small minority in Utah; and (2) because their exclusion permitted ethnic status to be eliminated as a contributing influence. The overall sample was made up of four subsamples:

1. *Fifty randomly selected high school boys who had never been to court;*
2. *Thirty randomly selected boys who had been to court once* (responses for this group have been inflated as though $N = 50$ in order to make them equal with other subsamples);[19]
3. *Fifty randomly selected offenders who were on probation* (these respondents were all repeaters and all had been assigned to the Provo Experiment in Delinquency Rehabilitation, a special community treatment program.[20] If the program had not existed, 32 percent of these offenders would have been incarcerated, and 68 percent on regular probation); and
4. *Fifty randomly selected, incarcerated offenders.*

Subsamples 1, 2, and 3 were drawn from a county population of 110,000 people. Subsample 4 was drawn from a statewide population of incarcerated offenders.

[19] It is impossible to assess any increase in error which might have resulted from this inflation. If there is bias in the sample of 30, it will have been magnified. If not, the change in sample size is not especially significant since both ($N = 30$ and $N = 50$) are very small proportions of the total population of one-time offenders.
[20] LaMar T. Empey and Jerome Rabow, "The Provo Experiment in Delinquency Rehabilitation," *American Sociological Review*, 26 (October 1961), pp. 679–696.

Data Collection

All respondents were contacted in person by the authors. Data were gathered by means of a detailed interview which was conducted as follows:[21] (1) each of 22 different offenses was defined in detail; (2) the respondent was asked if he had ever committed the offense; (3) how many times he had done so; (4) if he had ever been caught, arrested, or brought to court for the offense; and (5) if so, how many times he had been detected, arrested, or brought to court.

The names of all respondents were checked through court records as a means of testing response validity. The findings confirmed those of both Short and Nye[22] and Gold[23] that the majority of respondents seemed to be telling the truth about their offenses. However, the problem of determining both validity and reliability is a great one and any conclusions must consider that fact.[24]

Measurement of Social Status

The occupational status of the father or guardian was used as the criterion for defining the status level for each respondent. It was measured by means of an occupational prestige scale which was formed by combining the Hatt-North[25] and Smith[26] scales.[27]

[21] For greater detail on data collection and methodological problems, see Maynard L. Erickson and LaMar T. Empey, "Court Records, Undetected Delinquency and Decision-making," *The Journal of Criminal Law, Criminology and Police Science*, 54 (December 1963), pp. 456–469.
[22] James F. Short and Ivan Nye, "Reported Behavior as a Criterion of Deviant Behavior," *Social Problems*, 5 (Winter 1957-1958), pp. 207–213.
[23] Gold, *op. cit.*, pp. 8–10.
[24] For an analysis of the subject see Hardt and Bodine, *op. cit.*
[25] Paul K. Hatt and C. C. North, "Jobs and Occupations: A Popular Evaluation," in *Class, Status and Power* (ed.), R. Bendix and S. M. Lipset (Glencoe, Illinois: The Free Press, 1953), pp. 411–126.
[26] Mapheus Smith, "An Empirical Scale

This scale ranks occupations from *0* to *100* in terms of prestige. However, for purposes of this analysis it was collapsed into three main categories based upon the occupations located in the lower, middle and upper thirds of the scale.

Twenty-nine percent of the respondents were located in the *lower* category which was made up primarily of unskilled or semiskilled occupations. Fifty-five percent were located in the *middle* category. It included skilled occupations, owners of small businesses and a variety of white-collar jobs. Finally, 16 percent were located in the *upper* category which included most professions, a variety of business positions, scientists, and artists.

No attempt is made to assess the accuracy of equating these three status categories with the "lower," "middle" and "upper" classes. That complex problem cannot be solved here. Instead the scale is simply one way of ordering respondents empirically through the use of occupation as perhaps the most important, single measure of status.[28]

FINDINGS

Overall, the 180 respondents reported a tremendous number of violations, running into the thousands on all but a few serious offenses such as arson, selling and using narcotics, forgery and armed robbery. Furthermore, the large number

of violations reported by them was not restricted to a minority. Virtually all respondents reported having committed not one but a variety of different offenses. More than nine times out of ten, they said, these offenses went undetected and unacted upon.[29]

So striking were their reports that one was reminded of the 20-year-old statement of Murphy, Shirley and Witmer who, in noting similar figures, concluded that "even a moderate increase in the amount of attention paid to [them] by law enforcement authorities could create a semblance of a 'delinquency wave' without there being the slightest change in adolescent behavior."[30] One wonders to what extent the current "delinquency wave" is a function of this very phenomenon and, whether, if attention were focused elsewhere, it might also result in a "crime wave" among white-collar and other segments of adult society.

STATUS AND DELINQUENCY

This sample is of limited utility in comparing the delinquency of different status levels, both because it is small and because it relies heavily on data from *official* delinquents. However, there are factors which compensate for these problems and suggest that some confidence can be placed in the findings: (1) because tests of significance were used in such a way as to provide a conservative and stringent test of differences, and (2) because the findings were so consistent throughout, both in (officially) delinquent and non-delinquent subsamples, that there is undoubtedly

of Prestige of Occupations," *American Sociological Review,* 8 (April 1943), pp. 185–192.

[27] For greater detail on this combination, see LaMar T. Empey, "Social Class and Occupational Aspiration: A Comparison of Absolute and Relative Measurement," *American Sociological Review,* 21 (December, 1956), pp. 705–706.

[28] W. Lloyd Warner, M. Meeker and K. Eells, *Social Class in America* (Chicago: Social Science Research Associates, 1949), pp. 167–168; and Leona Tyler, *The Psychology of Human Differences* (New York: Appleton-Century-Crofts, 1947), pp. 145–146.

[29] For a great deal of detail on both the numbers of violations and the proportions of respondents involved, see Erickson and Empey, *op. cit.*

[30] Fred J. Murphy, M. M. Shirley, and Helen L. Witmer, "The Incidence of Hidden Delinquency," *American Journal of Orthopsychiatry,* 16 (October 1946), pp. 686–696.

some reliability in the directions noted here.

Despite the finding that these adolescents reported having committed a great number of violations, the data provided little support for the notion that there are status differences. Most respondents on one status level were no more nor no less delinquent than most respondents on another. If, and when, status differences did occur, they occurred because of the excessive violations of a small minority, not because of the general activities of one whole group versus another.

This conclusion was reached on the basis of two kinds of statistical analyses. The first utilized *chi square* in such a way as to provide a stringent examination of possible differences. Instead of lumping all respondents from each status level together and making gross comparisons between total groups, respondents were ordered according to the number of times they reported having committed each offense (i.e., 0, 1-3 times, 4-6 times, etc.). The *chi square* test was then run comparing the number of respondents from each subsample who were found in each of these categories. This test had the effect of eliminating gross differences because it ruled out the possible impact of a large number of offenses which might have been committed by only a few individuals and presented, instead, a more accurate picture of all respondents. It permitted a much better comparison of all individuals in one group with all individuals in another because it controlled for excesses on the extremes.

This comparison revealed very few differences among low- and middle-status respondents. The delinquency patterns for boys on these two status levels were not only similar but each of them also tended to be somewhat more delinquent than upper-status respondents on exactly the same offenses. For ex-

ample, low- and middle-status boys were significantly more inclined ($P<.05$ or greater) than upper-status boys to have stolen items worth $2.00-$50.00, stolen autos, skipped school, smoked regularly and drank more. But even so, the most important consideration is that, out of 22 items, only these few differences were statistically significant among the three status levels.

Second, a correlation analysis was used as a means of analyzing the data in another way. Instead of relating status position to each of the 22 offenses, attempts were made to construct scales which would combine several offenses into unidimensional patterns to see if these patterns were related in some way to status. Three Guttman scales were developed:

1. A *general theft* scale made up of dichotomous items and including theft of articles or money valued at less than $2.00, theft of articles or money valued from $2.00-$50.00 and theft of articles worth more than $50.00. The coefficient of reproducibility for the scale is .91.

2. A *serious theft* scale made up of dichotomous items and including theft of articles or money worth more than $50.00, auto theft, and theft involving breaking and entering. The coefficient of reproducibility for this scale was .93.

3. A *common delinquency* scale made up of dichotomous items and including illegal drinking, petty theft, open defiance of people in authority, skipping school and fighting. The coefficient of reproducibility was .91.[31]

When the single scores from each of these scales were correlated with status position, a slight, positive correlation was found between low-status and a

[31] For details on these scales see Maynard L. Erickson and LaMar T. Empey, "Class, Peers and Delinquency," *Sociology and Social Research*, 49 (April 1965), pp. 268–282.

greater amount of delinquency: .20 for *general theft*, .17 for *serious theft*, and .17 for *common delinquency*. But, when analysis of variance was used to trace down the source of the variation, it was found to exist, not between low-status respondents and the other two, but between upper-status respondents and the other two. On all three delinquency scales, low- and middle-status respondents did not differ significantly from each other while both differed from upper-status respondents. Thus, the slight correlation that was discovered was due more to the lower amount of delinquency on the extreme upper end of the status ladder than to a high concentration solely on the lower end.

The important thing to remember, therefore, is that the predictive efficiency of status position for this sample is extremely poor, explaining only four percent of the variance on *general theft* and only three percent on both *serious theft* and *common delinquency*. This finding stands out because it is so different from that which came to light when, instead of social status, respondents were compared in terms of their official designation as delinquent or nondelinquent.

Delinquency and Official Position

It will be recalled that the overall sample included respondents in four subsamples who, in *official* terms, were non-delinquent, one-time offenders, serious offenders on probation and incarcerated offenders. A comparison of these groups, using *chi square*, revealed that, while *non and one-time* offenders did not differ significantly from each other, both of them differed significantly on virtually every offense from *serious offenders* who were on probation or were incarcerated. The likelihood was less than one in a thousand that the differences between them could have occurred by chance. Boys whose official

position placed them on probation or in an institution, reported having been far more delinquent. On many offenses their reported violations exceeded those of non- and one-time offenders by thousands.

Thus, while these findings tended to support the Porterfield thesis that differences do not exist between adolescents from different status levels, they did not support his thesis that nondelinquents have committed as many offenses as official delinquents who are on probation or incarcerated. It would be a mistake, therefore, to assume, as he did, that official standing is a function entirely of social status. However, since these findings are based on self-reported data, it could be argued that differences are due to non-official offenders who wish to hide their delinquency and serious offenders who wish to advertise it. But this hardly seems to be the case.

It is not as though non- and one-time offenders did not reveal incriminating evidence. They did. It was just by comparison with officially serious offenders that they seemed to be less delinquent. Meanwhile, it could be argued that offenders who are already in the toils of the law would have much to lose by revealing incriminating evidence. Yet, they did.

It seems, therefore, that actual involvement in more delinquency seems to have been a major reason why some boys were labeled as serious offenders and others were not. What the process was that led to their excessive delinquency, the data do not reveal; that is, whether they were excessively delinquent *prior* to becoming labeled as delinquent or whether the label was self-fulfilling in some way. It would be extremely important, therefore, for subsequent studies to pursue this issue, to determine whether official attention seems to precede excessive delinquency, or whether excessive delinquency precedes official attention.

Kinds of Delinquency

Despite the failure to locate strong differences according to amount of delinquency, there were hints that there were some differences among status levels with respect to *kinds* of delinquency, especially among the minority of respondents who have been the most delinquent. These hints were confirmed when a different series of statistical tests were run.

In order to concentrate upon offense patterns, as contrasted to individuals, a study was made of the cases in which the proportion of violations committed by each status group, on each offense, may have exceeded the proportions of respondents contributed by that level to the total sample. For example, the middle-status group, with 55 percent of the respondents, committed 90 percent of the forgeries. Obviously, middle-status respondents, *as a group*, had been significantly more involved in forgeries than the other two. A *chi square* test on the significance of differences among proportions confirmed the conclusion.[32] Thus, despite the fact that most individuals in that group had not committed any more or less forgeries than *most* individuals in the others, those few who did commit such offenses tended almost always to be from the middle-status.

In the simplest sense, therefore, more detail was sought through comparing groups, rather than individuals within groups, saying nothing about whether the violations of each group were contributed by a large number or only a few individuals within it. The findings were these:

[32] For an example of the test used, see Helen M. Walker and Joseph Lev, *Statistical Inference* (New York, Henry Holt & Co., 1953), pp. 94–95.

UPPER-STATUS DELINQUENCY. The upper-status group consisted *16 percent* of the total sample but contributed only nine percent of the total violations. Compared to the other two, in terms of both volume and seriousness, it was considerably less delinquent.

Among respondents who were on probation or incarcerated, upper-status boys contributed only six percent of all offenses even though they comprised nine percent of the two subsamples. Thus, even though these boys were in serious trouble—i.e., on probation or incarcerated—they had contributed, as a group, significantly fewer than their share of violations. They exceeded the other two status groups on only one offense: defying parents $(P < .001)$. Apparently parent-child tensions for the upper-status group constitute an important source of difficulty. Defying parents was more strongly associated with being labeled a serious offender among upper-status than low- or middle-status boys.

MIDDLE-STATUS DELINQUENCY. The middle-status group consistuted 55 *percent* of the total sample and contributed 59 percent of the total violations. The significant thing about its delinquency, however, is the type and extent of certain violations, not its overall violation rate.

Looking at the total sample, this group was inclined to exceed others in five major areas: (1) general traffic (63 percent of the violations); (2) theft in general, including forgery (90%); (3) defying people other than parents (83%); (4) property violations of all types including breaking and entering (67%), destroying property (70%) and arson (84%); and (5) armed robbery (87%). These items and the extent to which observed differences are real, when the middle is compared separately with each of the other two status groups, are displayed in Table 1.

Many of the violations in Table 1 are

Table 1

COMPARISON OF MIDDLE-STATUS DELINQUENCY WITH OTHERS

Offense	Middle (55% of Sample) % of Violations	Lower (29% of Sample) % of Violations	Signif. Level	Upper (16% of Sample) % of Violations	Signif. Level
Traffic					
General traffic	63	22	.001	15	.05
Theft					
Articles less than $2.00	61	29	.001	10	.001
Articles, $2.00 to $50.00	69	26	.001	5	.001
Articles more than $50.00	59	33	N.S.	8	.05
Forgery	90	9	.001	1	.001
Defiance					
Defying people other than parents	83	16	.001	1	.001
Property Violations					
Breaking and entering	67	24	.001	8	.001
Destroying property	70	22	.001	8	.001
Arson	85	10	.05	5	.05
Retreatist					
Running away	85	12	.001	3	.001
Offenses Against Person					
Armed robbery	88	12	.10	0	—

notable for their seriousness: felony thefts, forgery, breaking and entering, arson and armed robbery. The fact that the middle-status group was high on these items is important. As shown in Table 2, they reported having committed over *two-thirds* of the *serious* violations in both the non- and one-time offender, and the probation and incarcerated, groups. The primary mitigating factor was that most of the serious offenses were apparently committed by those boys who had already been officially designated as persistent offenders. All non- and one-time offenders reported only 173 serious violations, most of which were for breaking and entering, as contrasted to 1,628 for respondents in the persistent category. Even so, it is notable that the proportionate rate of serious violations for the middle-

Table 2

PERCENT OF SERIOUS OFFENSES COMMITTED BY DIFFERENT STATUS GROUPS

Status	Non- and One-Time Offenders N	%	Probation and Incarcerated Offenders N	%
Lower	8	5	521	32
Middle	124	72	1055	65
Upper	41	23	52	3
Total	173	100	1628	100

status group remains significantly high throughout. Thus, even though there may be a large number of differences among the various delinquent and nondelinquent subsamples in the study, this particular one remained consistent throughout.

Overall, then, the middle-status group was more inclined to activities of a destructive and serious quality. However, the fact that this tendency did not show up quite so strongly in the previous analysis, when tests were designed to maximize individual, rather than group differences, implies the existence of a group among middle-status respondents which, when it becomes delinquent, is excessively delinquent. This implication was further confirmed by the finding that among respondents who were on probation or incarcerated, the middle-status group had committed significantly ($P < .005$ or greater) more violations than the upper-status group on all but four items (theft of more than $50.00, defying parents, arson and smoking habitually) and more than the low-status group on all but six items (buying alcohol, using narcotics, defying parents, skipping school, fighting and smoking habitually). Consequently, this group, rather than middle-status respondents across the board, seems to have contributed to the disproportionate number of serious and destructive offenses reported by the middle-status group.

LOW-STATUS DELINQUENCY. The pattern of offenses for low-status respondents is displayed in Table 3. With 29 percent of the total sample, they reported 32 percent of the total violations and were disproportionately high on the following offenses: driving without a license (44 percent of total violations), stealing articles worth more than $50.00 (33%), auto theft (38%), buying alcohol (58%), drinking alcohol (33%), using narcotics (64%), defying parents (39%), skipping school (46%), and fighting and assault (52%).

They differed significantly from the other two status groups on all these offenses except for stealing articles worth more than $50.00 where the differences

between them and middle-status respondents was not great enough. They also tended to smoke regularly more often than the other two but differences were not significant.

This pattern for low-status respondents might have been more predictable than for the middle-status group. For example, it is common to assume that skipping school, using narcotics, or fighting is more characteristic of low- than middle- or upper-status juveniles.

Even the findings with respect to traffic violations seem consistent with previous preconceptions; namely, that, while low-status juveniles may be less inclined than the other two groups to violate traffic laws in general, probably because they do not have means to drive as much, they are *more* inclined to steal autos and drive without a license. One could speculate that, with lower literacy skills and less legitimate access to a car, they would be more likely to commit these offenses.

However, when the low-status respondents in the *non- and one-time* offender category were compared with those in the *probation and incarcerated* category, some interesting things came to light. Low-status respondents in the first category constituted only 17 percent of the sample but reported 24 percent of the offenses. The pattern of offenses just described was the one most pronounced.

But in the *probation and incarcerated* category, some marked changes occurred. Low-status boys constituted a much heavier proportion of the total number of respondents (41%) but contributed a much smaller proportion of the total violations (34%). The differences between them and upper-status respondents tended to persist but compared to middle-status respondents, their contribution to the total number of violations declined heavily. They remained significantly higher than middle-

Table 3

COMPARISON OF LOW-STATUS DELINQUENCY WITH OTHERS

Offense	Lower (29% of Sample) % of Violations	Middle (55% of Sample) % of Violations	Signif. Level	Upper (16% of Sample) % of Violations	Signif. Level
Traffic					
Driving without a license	44	51	.001	4	.001
Theft					
Articles more than $50.00	33	59	N.S.	8	.01
Auto theft	38	60	.05	2	.001
Alcohol and narcotics					
Buying alcohol	58	37	.001	5	.001
Drinking alcohol	33	59	.05	8	.001
Using narcotics	64	36	.005	0	—a
Defiance					
Defying parents	41	39	.001	19	.005
Retreatist					
Skipping school	46	47	.001	7	.001
Offenses against person					
Fighting and assault	52	45	.001	2	.001
Others					
Smoking regularly	39	52	N.S.	9	N.S.

a No reported violations.

status respondents only on the offenses of buying alcohol, using narcotics, fighting and defying parents. Otherwise, as mentioned earlier, middle-status boys who eventually became probation violators, or were incarcerated, were the ones who seemed to have been extremely delinquent.

IMPLICATIONS

One can only speculate as to the reasons for these findings. The need for qualification is always present. The size of the sample is one limitation; it inhibits generalization. But it also points to the problems of gathering valid data on a subject such as this. In this particular study, sample size had to be limited because of the time consumed in locating, obtaining cooperation from, and interviewing respondents. And, as it turned out, the sheer quantity of violations that were recorded became a difficult matter for description and display.

A second problem was the geographic location of the study. Perhaps the influences responsible for the findings were inherent in the relatively small Utah cities from which the respondents came. The same study, conducted in a large, urban center may have resulted in an entirely different picture. But, again, it may be an oversimplification to assume that conditions of poverty, ethnicity and class in metropolitan centers would result in distinctions among status levels of the kind which did not appear here.

One important factor to be remembered is that the prevailing subculture in which these data were gathered was Mormon. It is generally believed that this subculture retains a traditional belief system emphasizing obedience to parents, hard work, and observance of the law even more than our large cities. Yet, if familial and community controls are ineffective in this setting, then one might expect even less control in large metropolitan centers. It could be hypothesized, therefore, that the amount of delinquency for all status levels would be greater there. We cannot know until more data such as these are gathered on *actual* rather than *official* delinquency.

The data on both the amount and kinds of hidden delinquency committed by these respondents imply that official records provide information only on the tip, not on the entire iceberg, of delinquency. If this is the case, they suggest why so much difficulty has been encountered in pinpointing important variables. Adequate information has not been available.

The lack of information has been qualitative as well as quantitative. For example, even though in this study we met daily for a period of months with many of the respondents from the probations and incarcerated subsamples, we formed incorrect impressions about them. It was our impression that virtually all of these officially serious respondents had low-status roots. They wore clothes, used language, and had hairdos which were alike and which, generally, are associated with low-status. Yet, it was not until we gathered objective data on their backgrounds that we discovered that we were wrong. The regular "uniform" was being worn by middle- as well as low-status boys. Only upper-status boys were exceptional. We concluded, therefore, that the uniform was a symbol of a life-style, as much the result of membership in a delinquent subsystem as of membership in a low social stratum. The implication is that, if different patterns of delinquency have important significance for the administration of justice, for prevention and treatment strategies and for research purposes, then far more data are needed on hidden delinquency. They are needed to determine the shape of the total iceberg.

20.

Family Status and the Delinquent Child: A Reappraisal And Some New Findings

Thomas P. Monahan

When a child loses a parent through death, desertion, divorce, or long separation, some form of deprivation is bound to result.[1] Where, as is generally the case, the male parent is missing, the child is placed under an obvious economic handicap. Absence of either parent may also cause a certain affectional loss for the child. In addition, the complementary control, example, and guidance given by both parents is wanting and complete socialization of the child is rendered more difficult.

At the death of a parent no cultural opposition is imposed upon the situation. Rather, social and economic assistance, both public and private, is readily forthcoming. Furthermore, the acquisition of a stepparent through remarriage of the remaining parent may even reestablish something of a family norm for the bereaved child.

But, in cases of desertion and divorce (and illegitimacy) we have an entirely different set of circumstances. Here we frequently find the child exposed to a highly emotionalized atmosphere of discontent and discord. The child most often remains with the mother only, financial support may be withheld by the father, or the parents may fight over the child's custody. In case of desertion no new father may legally become part of the child's home. And the subtle challenge of public disapproval of the family situation and the psychological impact of a seeming rejection by one's parents may becloud the child's outlook.

Divorce in many cases is indeed simply a formal recognition or acknowledgment of an already socially broken home, and it is generally appreciated that the home in constant discord might cause the child more harm than if the

* The assistance of Mr. Frank S. Drown, Statistician for the Philadelphia Municipal Court, in the preparation of this paper is gratefully acknowledged.

[1] As James H. S. Bossard and Eleanor S. Boll say in *Family Situations* (Philadelphia: University of Pennsylvania Press, 1943), p. 163, "But however specific the situation of the Incomplete Family, in the great average of broken homes the child loses more than he gains." For a treatment of deprivation from the psychiatric and mental health point of view, see John Bowlby, *Maternal Care and Mental Health* (Geneva: World Health Organisation, 1952) and G. E. Gardner, "Separation of the Parents and the Emotional Life of the Child," *Mental Hygiene,* 40 (January 1956), 53–64.

SOURCE. Thomas P. Monahan, "Family Status and the Delinquent Child: A Reappraisal and Some New Findings," from *Social Forces,* Volume 35, March 1957, pp. 251–258. Reprinted with the permission of the University of North Carolina Press.

parental relationship were severed. Such reasoning has merit, but, interestingly enough, this argument has been used to justify divorce rather than to plead for the rehabilitation or prevention of unhappy families. Such a viewpoint, it should also be noted, contradicts another social philosophy which holds that even a bad home is better than no home at all for the child.

There are many varieties of broken homes and many correspondingly different kinds of family relationships involved. Even the social disparateness in family structure which results from long-term hospitalization, military service, or employment of the breadwinner away from home may bring about some serious consequences for the members of a family. On the other hand, the conventional family structure may cloak a host of baneful influences or situations harmful to a child's wholesome development. To say it in another way, all broken homes are not bad ones, and all conventional types are not good ones.

This article is not concerned with a delineation of all possible types of homes and their effect on children, but rather it is restricted to a consideration of the more evident types of broken homes as they relate to children who are apprehended for committing delinquent acts.

DELINQUENCY STUDIES OF BROKEN HOMES

With the establishment of juvenile courts in the United States around 1900 and the compilation of social statistics on youth who were brought before these courts, observers were struck by the high proportion—40 to 50 percent —of all delinquent children who came from broken homes. Since it was far beyond normal expectancy that such a proportion of all youth was similarly disadvantaged, early writers saw broken homes to be an important, if not the greatest single proximate (causal), factor in understanding juvenile delinquency.[2]

There was no denial that the broken home was only one of a number of factors to take into account and that the age of the child and the quality of the home life, as well as the mere fact of a break, were important. A number of studies have shown, however, that abnormal or defective family relationships are much more prevalent among families of delinquent children than among families of comparable children who do not become delinquent.[3] This aspect of the matter is a subject unto itself.

Not counting the statistical tabula-

[2] G. B. Mangold, *Problems of Child Welfare* (New York: Macmillan Co., 1930), p. 406; Mabel Rhoades, "A Case Study of Delinquent Boys in the Juvenile Court of Chicago," *American Journal of Sociology*, 13 (July 1907), 3–25; S. P. Breckenridge and E. Abbott, *The Delinquent Child and the Home* (New York: Russell Sage Foundation, 1912); C. A. Ellwood, "The Instability of the Family as a Cause of Child Dependency and Delinquency," *Survey*, 24 (September 1910), pp. 886–889; Municipal Court of Philadelphia, *Annual Report* (1918), pp. 98–99.

[3] See, for instance, John Slawson, "Marital Relations of Parents and Juvenile Delinquency," *Journal of Delinquency*, 8 (September–November 1923), 280–283, and *The Delinquent Boy* (Boston: Gorham Press, 1926); Cyril Burt, *The Young Delinquent* (New York: D. Appleton and Co., 1925); Mabel Elliott, *Correctional Education and the Delinquent Girl* (Harrisburg, Pennsylvania State Department of Welfare, 1929); K. D. Lumpkin, "Factors in the Commitment of Correctional School Girls in Wisconsin," *American Journal of Sociology*, 37 (September 1931), 222–230; T. E. Sullenger, "Juvenile Delinquency, A Product of the Home," *Journal of Criminal Law and Criminology*, 24 (March–April 1934), pp. 1088–1092; W. Healy and A. Bronner, *New Light on Delinquency and Its Treatment* (New Haven, Connecticut: Yale University Press, 1936), pp. 29–30; A. M. Carr-Saunders, H. Mannheim, and E. Rhodes, *Young Offenders* (New York: Macmillan Co., 1944), p. 70; and Connecticut Public Welfare Council, *Needs of Neglected and Delinquent Children* (Hartford, Connecticut, 1946).

tions of many juvenile courts over the years, dozens of studies have been made which deal with the broken home and juvenile delinquency or crime. Some of the early studies attempted to estimate the proportion of broken homes in the population at large from existing census data, to use for a comparison with their special groups of delinquent or institutionalized children.[4] A common conclusion was that delinquent children had about twice the proportion of broken homes as did children in the general population. A few comparisons were made of boys in the same school or city area, revealing a greater prevalence of broken homes among the delinquent group; one such comparison of several groups of children in 1918 suggested that more orphans were found in the delinquent group.[5]

The first major attempt at a controlled comparison was made by Slawson in 1923, using delinquent boys in four state institutions and boys in three New York City public schools, from which he concluded that there were over twice as many broken homes in his delinquent group.[6] Concurrently, in England, Cyril Burt analyzed a group of misbehaving ("delinquent") children and public school children of the same age and social class. Although his classification of "defective family relationships" included other factors besides the broken home, he, too, found the problem children to be doubly disfavored.[7] And, in 1929, Mabel Elliott compared the family structure of her group of Sleighton Farm girls—mostly sex offenders—with that of a group of Philadelphia working-class, continuation school girls, revealing the respective proportions of broken homes to be 52 and 22 percent.[8]

Even greater refinement was introduced into the question by Shaw and McKay when they compared boys against whom official delinquency petitions were filed in the juvenile court of Chicago in 1929 with other boys drawn from the public school population of the same city areas.[9] They found that a rather high proportion (29 percent) of the school boys 10 to 17 years of age came from broken homes. After the school population data were carefully adjusted statistically for age and ethnic composition to make them comparable with the delinquent group, the propor-

[4] E. H. Schideler, "Family Disintegration and the Delinquent Boy in the United States," *Journal of Criminal Law and Criminology*, 8 (January 1918), 709–732; E. Bushong, "Family Estrangement and Juvenile Delinquency," *Social Forces*, 5 (September 1926), pp. 79–83; W. Roach, "Record of Juvenile Delinquency in Benton County, Oregon, 1907–1929," *Journal of Juvenile Research*, 14 (January 1930), 34–40; M. G. Caldwell, "Home Conditions of Institutional Delinquent Boys in Wisconsin," *Social Forces*, 8 (March 1930), pp. 390–397; S. B. Crosby, "A Study of Alameda County Delinquent Boys, with Special Emphasis upon the Group Coming from Broken Homes," *Journal of Juvenile Research*, 13 (July 1929), 220–230. For a recent study see New Jersey Department of Institutions and Agencies, Trenton, New Jersey, *The Welfare Reporter*, 5 (January 1951), 17.

[5] F. G. Bonser, *School Work and Spare Time*, Cleveland Recreation Survey (Philadelphia: William Fell, 1918), pp. 36–40; E. H. Johnson, "The Relation of Conduct Difficulties of a Group of Public School Boys to Their Mental Status and Home Environment," *Journal of Delinquency*, 6 (November 1921), p. 563; E. H. Sutherland, *Criminology* (Philadelphia: J. B. Lippincott Co., 1924), and study by Roy D. Young cited therein, p. 143.

[6] Slawson, "Marital Relations of Parents and Juvenile Delinquency," *loc. cit.*, p. 280.

[7] Burt, *op. cit.*, pp. 51, 90 ff.

[8] Elliott, *op. cit.*, p. 28.

[9] C. R. Shaw and H. D. McKay, *Report on the Causes of Crime, Vol. II, Social Factors in Juvenile Delinquency* (Washington, D. C.: National Commission on Law Observance and Enforcement, Government Printing Office, 1931), pp. 261–284, and Shaw and McKay, "Are Broken Homes a Causative Factor in Delinquency?" *Social Forces*, 10 (May 1932), pp. 514–524, and discussion pp. 525–533.

tion of broken homes rose to 36.1 per-cent for the school group, as compared to 42.5 percent for the delinquent boys. This result, as Shaw and McKay inter-preted it, "suggests that the broken home, as such, is not an important fac-tor in the case of delinquent boys in the Cook County juvenile court," while other writers further interpreted the findings as showing that broken homes generally are "relatively insignificant in relation to delinquency."[10] Even accept-ing the above figures for Chicago, mathematical exception has been taken to such interpretations.[11]

DISAGREEMENT AMONG AUTHORITIES

Thus there arose a sharp divergence of opinion among sociologists as to the importance of the broken home as a factor in delinquency. Standard refer-ences in criminology refer to this lack of agreement and "welter of conflicting opinion," but they offer no clarification of the question.[12] Indeed one senses somewhat of a partisan approach in the differing selection of references and the interpretations of extant information.

Rather significantly, Hodgkiss' study of Chicago girls, done at about the same time and in the same manner as the Shaw-McKay inquiry, disclosed that 67 percent of the delinquent girls and 45 percent of the controls came

from broken homes.[13] These figures were less readily dismissed. Again the high percentage of broken homes among the control group is remarkable. Probably because of difficulties sur-rounding the collection of such data from school children, the studies have not been repeated in Chicago.

OTHER STUDIES

Six other investigations published after the Shaw-McKay report deserve special mention. First, Cavan, in her study of school children in 1930, placed in opposition information on several classes of children in the same locality. The proportion of broken homes in-creased consistently from the control group of boys (21 percent) to the pre-delinquent boys (35 percent), to the institutionalized boys (49 percent), to the institutionalized girls (71 per-cent).[14] Second, in a study of Spokane, Washington, public school boys, 14 to 17 years of age, and delinquent boys in 1937, Weeks and Smith made a careful comparison only to find that broken homes among the delinquents (41 per-cent) were far more numerous than among the control group of boys (27 percent), even when refined according to a number of social categories.[15] Third, in the mid-1930's, Merrill matched 300 run-of-the-mill cases re-ferred to the court of a rural California county with other children selected ac-cording to age, sex, and neighborhood (school). In this case 51 percent of the delinquents were found to come from broken homes versus 27 percent for the

[10] Shaw and McKay, *Report on the Causes of Crime*, loc. cit., p. 392; and Sutherland, *Principles of Criminology* (Philadelphia: J. B. Lippincott Co., 1947), p. 159.

[11] J. B. Maller in Shaw and McKay, "Are Broken Homes a Causative Factor in Delinquency?" loc. cit., pp. 531–533.

[12] Teeters in N. Teeters and J. O. Reine-mann, *The Challenge of Delinquency* (New York: Prentice-Hall, 1950), p. 153. Compare Sutherland, *Criminology* 1924 ed. versus 1947 ed.; and H. M. Shulman's summarization, "The Family and Juvenile Delinquency," *Annals of the American Academy of Political and Social Science*, 261 (January 1949), pp. 21–31.

[13] M. Hodgkiss, "The Influence of Broken Homes and Working Mothers," *Smith College Studies in Social Work*, 3 (March 1933), pp. 259–274.

[14] R. S. Cavan, *The Adolescent in the Family* (New York: D. Appleton-Century Co., 1934), pp. 220–221.

[15] H. A. Weeks and M. G. Smith, "Juve-nile Delinquency and Broken Homes in Spokane, Washington," *Social Forces*, 18 (October 1939), pp. 48–55.

control group.[16] Fourth, Wittman and Huffman's study of teen-aged youth in Elgin, Illinois, disclosed that a very high disproportion of the institutionalized delinquents came from broken homes as compared to high school students in the same area.[17] Fifth, the Gluecks carefully paired 500 boys from the general school population with 500 delinquent (correctional school) boys in the Boston area. They found that only 50 percent of the delinquent boys had been living with their own parents, whereas the control group of boys were living with both parents in 71 percent of the cases.[18] Sixth, a study of pre-war delinquents was made in England by Carr-Saunders and others, using an individual-matching technique (boys under 16 years), with the following results: delinquents had a much higher proportion of broken homes than the controls (28 percent versus 16 percent), and there was a greater amount of separation and divorce in the delinquent group of broken homes.[19]

A PARTIAL SUMMATION

Thus, in comparisons of delinquents with control samples, and in statistical adjustments of delinquency data for age, ethnic, and neighborhood biases, the children with intact families have shown a clear and persistent advantage over those from broken homes. This is especially true for the females. In addition to this, the home of the delinquent child appears to be much more "defective," "immoral," or "inadequate" than are homes in general. In broken homes one seems to find a conjunction of deprivations and positive influences toward criminal behavior.

From an over-all viewpoint it is well to remember that a large proportion of children from broken homes do not become delinquent, but this hardly refutes the inescapable fact that more children from broken homes, as compared to those from unbroken homes, become delinquent. Even among families having delinquents, siblings are more often delinquent in the broken family group.[20]

For the social analyst, the broken home may be regarded either as a symptom or as a consequence of a larger process, but for the child it becomes a social fact with which he has to abide. In a very real sense the abnormal structure of his family may impede his own normal adjustment and in some cases may bring him into conflict with the requirements of the larger society, more so than if he were surrounded by a conventional family milieu. That so many children surpass this handicap is an exemplification of their own resilience and a demonstration of the presence of other forces acting towards the child's socialization in the community, rather than a proof of the unimportance of normal family life in the development of norms of conduct or the unimportance of the handicaps experienced by the child in the broken home.

[16] M. Merrill, *Problems of Child Delinquency* (New York: Houghton Mifflin Co., 1947), pp. 66, 311.

[17] M. P. Wittman and A. V. Huffman, "A Comparative Study of Developmental, Adjustment, and Personality Characteristics of Psychotic, Psychoneurotic, Delinquent, and Normally Adjusted Teen Aged Youths," *Journal of Genetic Psychology,* 66 (June 1945), 167–182.

[18] S. Glueck and E. Glueck, *Unraveling Juvenile Delinquency* (Cambridge, Massachusetts: Harvard University Press, 1950), p. 88. However, if one includes prolonged absence of a parent because of delinquency, illness, and the like, 34 percent of the control group of children experienced a broken home prior to their inclusion in the study, versus 60 percent of the delinquent children (p. 122).

[19] Carr-Saunders et al., *op. cit.,* pp. 60. 149.

[20] N. D. Hirsch, *Dynamic Causes of Juvenile Crime* (Cambridge, Massachusetts: Sci-Art Publishers, 1937), pp. 66, 79.

In former years when divorce was less common and desertion less apparent perhaps, broken homes were probably thought to be largely a result of the death of a parent. The material and other losses to such children may not have been readily perceived. How such a simple event as death could wreak enduring havoc with the child's development was difficult to discern. Hence, disbelief in the importance of orphanhood as to delinquency causation, coupled with the very unsatisfactory nature of the early studies, no doubt led some sociologists to take exception to the prevailing beliefs and to question the whole relationship.

A convergence of information from the other disciplines as to the deleterious effects of divorce and desertion or family separations upon the child, as well as a psychological appreciation of the different nature of these types of family disruption, brought a more unanimous acknowledgment of the importance of the *socially* broken home. In some quarters the recent "wave" of delinquency has been interpreted to be a result of the growth of divorce and separation. However, information on the particular family relationships of children in the community and those who become delinquent are generally lacking. We know that over the past 50 years there has been a lessening of orphanhood through improvement in life expectancy, and an upward rise in family dissolutions through desertion and divorce, until now there seems to have been a reversal in the relative importance of the two factors of death and social discord in the breaking up of a child's family. Oddly enough, in spite of the change in the nature of broken homes, the high over-all proportion of delinquent children from broken homes apparently has not changed significantly.

A SIX-YEAR STUDY OF PHILADELPHIA RECORDS

In order to throw some additional light upon the subject of broken homes, some special tabulations were made of all delinquency charges—44,448 cases, of which 24,811 were first offenders—disposed of in the Philadelphia Municipal Court in the period 1949–1954.

METHODOLOGICAL PROBLEMS

Accuracy of Data

In cases which are adjusted before going to court or which receive no investigation, children are quite often the only source of some of the information recorded. The precision of the data suffers thereby, especially if one is interested in the details of family relationships. Erratic or unreasonable fluctuations in the statistics sometimes disclose the unreliability of information derived from court records, as Breckenridge and Abbott, for instance, suggest may have been the case for some early Chicago data.[21] A high degree of reliability may obtain in some jurisdictions, but one must always use particular sets of data with reservations.

Types of Data

The proportion and types of broken homes among juvenile offenders are known to vary greatly according to racial or ethnic group, sex and age, and certain offenses. As one proceeds from first offenders to the recidivists, from those dismissed to those adjudged delinquent, and from the probationary types to those who require institutionalization, it may be expected that one will find an increasing proportion of broken homes. Unfortunately, very little attention has been given to the correspon-

[21] Breckenridge and Abbott, *op. cit.*, p. 92.

dence between the degree of broken homes and the type of data being studied. A number of early studies, for instance, were concerned exclusively with special types of offenders, recidivists and institutionalized children.[22] Since chronic offenders represent a special class, and other cases may be institutionalized *because* they come from broken homes, there is a basic weakness in using such selective kinds of information to demonstrate a relationship between broken homes and unlawful behavior of juveniles.

Lack of Population Statistics

Perhaps the greatest stumbling block in all attempts to analyze and interpret statistics on delinquency has been the lack of population data which would show the family situation of children as a whole. For nearly 50 years this deficiency in census compilations has been bemoaned by many students of the subject, and a wide variety of crude estimates have been made. If such information were tabulated from census cards and classified according to governmental units for age, color, and neighborhood area (census tracts), we could begin to assess this problem with more certainty. Among different elements of the population the proportion and types of broken homes vary so greatly that one must be cautious in using particular kinds of data for comparative purposes. It should be recognized that the percentages of broken homes in some control groups (Shaw-McKay, Hodgkiss, and Glueck) do not purport to represent the condition prevailing among the population as a whole. In general, no more than 20 percent of all children of juvenile court age have broken homes, with the pro-

portion among the nonwhites being about twice that for the whites.[23]

FAMILY STATUS OF DELINQUENTS BY SEX AND COLOR

As shown in Table 1, the proportion of broken homes among Negroes is considerably greater than among the whites, and girls in each group are more often from broken homes than are boys in each class. The range of broken homes extends from about one-third of all cases of white boys to three-fourths of the cases of Negro girls, with white girls and Negro boys showing less than 50 percent with intact families.

The families of first offenders show a lesser degree of fragmentation, whereas those who offended in a prior year (Class I recidivists) are from families particularly marked by a greater degree of orphanhood, illegitimacy, and social disruption. Including children who are recidivists increases the proportion of broken homes in the whole.

The parents of Negro delinquents are less often legally separated and more often unmarried or living apart than are the parents of white children. Girls, of course, with a higher proportion of broken homes also show a higher degree of orphanhood; but, except for a moderate excess of orphanhood of Negro boys as compared to white boys, the impact of death is not an outstanding element of difference between the two classes. Initial disorganization and informal social disorganization of family status are most characteristic of Negro delinquent children.

RECIDIVISM BY FAMILY STATUS

Recidivism betokens not merely the frequency or probability of repetition of infractions of the law, but also the like-

---

[22] References available on request.

[23] References on population estimates available on request.

Table 1

PERCENTAGE DISTRIBUTION OF JUVENILE DELINQUENTS IN PHILADELPHIA BY TYPE OF FAMILY STATUS, ALL CASES, FIRST OFFENDERS, AND CLASS I RECIDIVISTS, 1949–1954*

| | Boys | | | | | | Girls | | | | | |
| | White | | | Negro | | | White | | | Negro | | |
	All cases	First offenders	Recid-ivists	All cases	First offenders	Recid-ivists	All cases	First offenders	Recid-ivists	All cases	First offenders	Recid-ivists
With whom child was living												
Number of cases	17,772	11,236	4,108	18,317	8,706	5,708	2,919	1,984	504	4,378	2,736	933
Total	100.0	100.0	100.0	100.0	100.0	100.0	100.0	100.0	100.0	100.0	100.0	100.0
With both own parents	67.5	72.4	58.6	41.7	47.2	37.8	43.6	48.4	31.4	24.6	27.3	19.8
Father only	3.1	2.6	4.4	4.0	3.8	4.2	5.1	4.6	6.3	4.4	5.2	2.8
Mother only	17.9	15.5	22.0	39.4	35.2	42.1	27.0	26.1	30.8	45.4	46.7	42.2
Mother and stepfather	4.9	4.2	5.9	2.8	2.8	2.8	7.1	7.0	7.1	2.7	2.7	2.7
Father and stepmother	1.6	1.3	1.7	1.4	1.4	1.4	3.3	3.1	2.4	1.8	2.0	1.3
Adoptive parents	0.1	0.1	0.2	†	†	†	0.2	0.3	—	0.2	0.1	0.5
Other family home	4.9	3.9	7.2	10.7	9.6	11.7	13.7	10.5	22.0	20.9	16.0	30.7
(Excluded: in institution)	(2.5)	(0.4)	(5.9)	(1.4)	(0.1)	(2.3)	(5.6)	(0.9)	(12.5)	(2.0)	(0.1)	(4.7)
Marital status of parents												
Number of cases	18,138	11,244	4,323	18,456	8,643	5,813	3,076	1,996	571	4,443	2,717	968
Total	100.0	100.0	100.0	100.0	100.0	100.0	100.0	100.0	100.0	100.0	100.0	100.0
Own parents living together	67.8	73.1	58.7	42.1	47.8	38.1	44.6	49.7	33.6	25.7	27.9	22.5
Parents unmarried	2.3	1.6	3.6	13.0	10.7	14.2	5.8	4.1	10.2	22.0	20.3	25.5
Mother dead	3.6	2.9	4.6	5.2	4.8	5.6	7.1	6.3	8.6	7.9	7.5	8.4
Father dead	8.3	7.7	9.5	10.4	9.8	11.0	12.2	11.0	12.6	10.4	10.4	10.8
Both parents dead	0.6	0.5	0.6	1.7	1.7	1.8	1.7	1.6	1.9	2.5	2.1	3.6
Father deserted mother	1.0	0.7	1.4	2.7	2.3	2.9	2.2	1.7	4.2	3.7	3.6	3.6
Mother deserted father	0.3	0.2	0.5	0.3	0.2	0.3	0.8	0.8	1.1	0.4	0.3	0.3
Both parents deserted	0.1	0.1	0.1	0.2	0.2	0.2	0.2	0.1	0.3	†	†	—
Parents living apart	9.6	7.9	12.9	22.2	20.1	24.0	15.0	14.0	18.4	24.8	25.4	22.5
Parents divorced	6.4	5.3	8.1	2.2	2.4	1.9	10.4	10.7	9.1	2.6	2.5	2.8

* Each time a child is dealt with on a new delinquency charge is called a case. Class I recidivists does not include second offenses in the calendar year for recidivist children. Cases not reporting as to family status or parental status are excluded from the percentage distribution.

† Less than 0.05 percent.

lihood of the development of a pattern of such behavior, or even a career of criminality in adulthood. It is a reasonable conjecture that if a broken home predisposes a child to commit a delinquent act, then it follows, to state it simply, that lacking the necessary parental guidance and control in the first place, this tendency toward misconduct will continue throughout the period of childhood and there will be a greater recurrence of offenses among children in broken homes. Some studies have, in fact, revealed a greater degree of recidivism among children in broken homes.[24] One cannot ignore this evidence by assuming that there is a selective apprehension of youth on the basis of their home conditions rather than a direct operation of the law.

The deleterious effect of broken homes upon children as regards the repetition of their delinquencies is portrayed in Table 2. In all sex and color groups children who are living with both parents are much less likely to appear again on charges of delinquency. Since family status is a changing thing for the child, the pattern cannot be delineated with perfect clarity, because a child living with both own parents in 1949 may have committed an offense after his home was broken in 1950 or later, thus blurring the picture. However, calendar year figures disclose essentially the same pattern and serve to show that further refinements would minimize the contrasts only moderately.

As between the types of marital status, further meaningful differences appear. The exceedingly high proportion of recidivism among institutional children is no doubt related to their

unusual background of deprivation and their likelihood of offending by running away. For white boys the percentage of all cases in the recidivist class increases from 32 where both parents are married and living together, to 38 where the father is dead and the boy is with his mother, to 42 where both parents are dead and the child is with a surrogate family, to 46 percent where the parents are living apart and the child is with the mother, to 49 where the parents are divorced, to 55 where the boy is living with his unmarried mother. In general the same pattern holds for both sex and color groups, except that the recidivism contrast among the types of broken homes for Negroes is not as well defined or as great. This could betoken a greater ambiguity or inaccuracy of Negro data, or a lesser significance to the Negro child as to the specific manner by which his home is broken.[25]

Interestingly enough, although girls more often come from broken homes, to an observable degree they are less likely to engage in repeated offenses, whatever the type of broken home. Explanation for this may lie in the fundamentally different nature of offenses of boys and girls.

Where the child, especially the girl, remains with the mother there appears to be less likelihood of recidivism. The death of the mother, as compared to the death of the father, also leads to somewhat greater recidivism; while the loss of both parents is particularly severe on the Negro girls. For the most part, a child living in another family home and not with one of his parents is more likely to commit repeated offenses.

DIFFERENTIAL TREATMENT BY FAMILY STATUS

In Philadelphia, except for the handling of complaints which are rather

[24] M. E. Kirkpatrick, "Some Significant Factors in Juvenile Recidivism," *American Journal of Orthopsychiatry*, 7 (July 1937), p. 356; Carr-Saunders et al., *op. cit.*, pp. 39, 99; Slawson, *The Delinquent Boy*, pp. 373–374.

[25] Cavan, *The Adolescent in the Family*, pp. 60, 63, 90.

Table 2

JUVENILE DELINQUENCY CASES IN PHILADELPHIA: REPEATED OFFENSES AS A PERCENTAGE OF TOTAL OFFENSES, OR RECIDIVISM BY FAMILY STATUS 1949–1954

	Boys									Girls								
			Deceased									Deceased						
	Total	Own parents living together	Mother	Father	Both	Desertion	Parents living apart	Divorced	Not married	Total	Own parents living together	Mother	Father	Both	Desertion	Parents living apart	Divorced	Not married
Total																		
White	38	33	49	43	(46)	55	50	49	58	35	28	42	41	(38)	(47)	40	33	54
Negro	53	47	57	56	55	59	58	49	61	39	34	42	39	50	41	37	41	43
With both own parents																		
White	32	32							54	24	24							
Negro	46	46								31	31							
With father only																		
White	48		45	38		56	54	(38)	(63)	38		(32)				(23)		
Negro	56		53	55		61	59			26		(25)						
With mother only																		
White	45						46	51	55	34			34		35	30	(28)	50
Negro	58						57	45	62	36			33			34		38
With mother and stepfather																		
White	46			46				45		33			(39)				30	
Negro	52			54				48		37			(36)					
With father and stepmother																		
White	49		49					50		(36)		(40)						
Negro	53		53							(33)		(30)						

Table 2—Continued

	Girls									Boys								
	Total	Own parents living together	Deceased Mother	Deceased Father	Deceased Both	Desertion	Parents living apart	Divorced	Not married	Total	Own parents living together	Deceased Mother	Deceased Father	Deceased Both	Desertion	Parents living apart	Divorced	Not married
In other family home																		
White	50	38	49	(56)	(42)		52	(53)	(66)	48	(45)	(48)	(63)			(56)		
Negro	57	54	60	59	54	(54)	59		46	52	(56)	51		47		48		55
In institution																		
White	91	96					(90)			89	(93)							
Negro	98	(100)					(98)			98								

Note. Cells with less than 50 cases not calculated; cells with 50–99 cases shown in parentheses. Excluding children in institutions, the total-total and total-own parents living together percentages of recidivism become: whites—37, 32, 32, 25, and Negroes—53, 46, 38, 32, for boys and girls respectively.

trifling, law officers routinely deliver all children who are apprehended in the commission of delinquent acts into the hands of juvenile court authorities. They do not adjudicate or dispose of cases in the police station. Hence, in Philadelphia, as compared to other areas of the country, a much higher proportion of allegedly delinquent children receive treatment by the court, and the information on these cases approaches a completeness and representativeness as regards all children apprehended in the commission of delinquent acts. There does not seem to be any great tendency for policewomen, who arrest nearly 30 percent of the girls, to turn girls over to their parents rather than to charge them with delinquency. Indeed, girls show the same excessively high proportion of broken homes no matter what the type of offense may be.

The same proportion of broken homes appears in both the minor and major offense groups, as shown in Table 3. However, children who are living with both parents are much more likely to be dismissed by the intake interviewing staff, whereas the children from broken homes are more often held for court. The parentless child (one or both natural parents absent from home) is more often adjudged delinquent or in need of care, and a rather high proportion of them are committed to institutions for delinquents.

From these figures on first offenders it should be evident that the use of court arraignment and institutional statistics can give a rather distorted picture regarding the family status of delinquent children in general.[26]

[26] Cf., P. M. Smith, "Broken Homes and Juvenile Delinquency," *Sociology and Social Research*, 39 (May–June 1955), pp. 307–311; and New Jersey, *op. cit.*, p. 18, fn. 4.

Table 3

PERCENTAGE DISTRIBUTION OF JUVENILE DELINQUENTS IN PHILADELPHIA FROM BROKEN HOMES AMONG APPREHENDED FIRST OFFENDERS FOR TOTAL AND MAJOR OFFENSES, MANNER OF REFERRAL AND DISPOSITION, 1949–1954°

	Boys		Girls	
Treatment stage	White	Negro	White	Negro
Total first offenders	27.7	53.0	52.0	73.2
Major offense group†	27.4	54.2	48.0	72.3
Source of referral				
Policeman	27.9	53.1	50.0	71.3
Policewoman	—	—	54.7	75.6
Railroad police	21.7	42.4	—	—
Initial action				
Adjusted by staff	21.6	45.0	43.9	59.6
Held for court	35.0	60.9	55.3	76.8
Disposition, all cases				
Dismissed	23.1	47.1	46.1	66.1
Adjudged "delinquent"	38.7	64.5	57.4	77.5
Placed on probation	35.2	63.1	52.3	74.9
Committed to institution for delinquents	49.8	68.3	59.9	83.8

° With both own parents, married and living together. In 19 out of 20 of these cases the illegitimate child (see Table 1) does not live with both his natural parents. The smallest figure represented by a percentage is 130 (Negro girls committed to an institution for delinquents).

† Major offenses include injury to person, carrying deadly weapons, arson, vandalism, robbery, burglary, theft, drug and liquor violations, and sex offenses.

POPULATION COMPARISONS

Some 14 percent of all Philadelphia children *under 16 years* of age were *not* in husband-wife families in 1934–1936 (11 percent of the white and 31 percent of the Negro children).[27] At that time, in about 30 percent of all cases of delinquent boys and 50 percent of all cases of delinquent girls under 16 years of age, the children were living with one parent only, and no stepparent, or in a substitute family. Delinquency cases for the same age group in 1940 showed the following proportions of such incomplete families: white boys 27 percent, Negro boys 55 percent, white girls 43 percent, and Negro girls 70 percent.

The 1950 Census for Philadelphia revealed that 7 percent of the white children and 33 percent of the nonwhite children *under 18 years* of age were *not* in census-classified husband-wife families. In 1940 the corresponding figures were 13 percent for the whites and 33 percent for the nonwhites.[28] Any adjustment for the age factor does not seem warranted because the proportion of broken homes among delinquent first offenders, 1949–1954, is practically the same for children of all ages.

With *incomplete* families among *first offenders* (1949–1954) under 18 years of age amounting to 22 percent for the white boys and 49 percent for the Negro boys, it should certainly be appar-

ent that in their respective groups broken homes predispose these boys to acts of delinquency. Among the females the proportions from incomplete families are so high (42 percent for white girls and 68 percent for Negro girls) that there can hardly be any doubt as to the importance of parental deprivation to them.

CONCLUSION

One large minority in the population consistently shows twice the average rate of socially broken homes and twice the average rate of delinquency. Other groups with strong family cohesiveness show below average rates of delinquency. Such apparent associations cannot be dismissed as happenstance.

On the whole very little disagreement has been expressed over the probable harmful influence of the socially broken home on the child. This does not gainsay, however, the deprivation consequent to the loss of a parent through death. Indeed, the same high proportions of delinquents were found to come from broken homes more than a generation ago when orphanhood loomed larger as the reason for family disruption. Of even more importance to the child than the nature of the break is the fact of a break in his home.

All in all, the stability and continuity of family life stands out as a most important factor in the development of the child. It would seem, therefore, that the place of the home in the genesis of normal or delinquent patterns of behavior should receive greater practical recognition. The relationship is so strong that, if ways could be found to do it, a strengthening and preserving of family life, among the groups which need it most, could probably accomplish more in the amelioration and prevention of delinquency and other problems than any other single program yet devised.

[27] United States Social Security Board, *Statistics of Family Composition in Selected Areas of the United States,* 1934–1936, Vol. 6, Philadelphia, Bureau Memorandum No. 45 (February 1942), pp. 3, 196–197; and Municipal Court of Philadelphia, *Annual Reports.*
[28] United States Bureau of the Census, *Population—Families, Types of Families, 1940* (Washington, D.C.: Government Printing Office, 1943), pp. 24, 90; and *General Characteristics of Families, 1950* Special Report P-E, No. 2A (Washington, D. C.: Government Printing Office, 1955), pp. 174, 180.

21.

Delinquency Theory and Recent Research*

LaMar T. Empey

Attempts to explain delinquency traditionally have been concerned with two fundamental sets of data: (1) evidence from official sources that delinquency is concentrated most heavily among lower-class juveniles[1] and (2) evidence that the delinquent act is typically a group phenomenon, not a solitary enterprise.[2] The result has been a

number of influential theories which, despite many differences, have a common theme,[3] viz., that delinquency is primarily the product of provincial lower-class gangs whose members share a common subculture. The factors which set delinquents apart from nondelinquents are thought to be their face-to-face interactions within gangs,

* Appreciation is expressed to William Fawcett Hill, Malcolm W. Klein, Solomon Kobrin, Sanford Labovitz, Steven G. Lubeck, George Newland, and James F. Short, Jr. for their review of and comments on this article.

SOURCE. LaMar T. Empey, "Delinquency Theory and Recent Research," from *Journal of Research in Crime and Delinquency*, Volume 4, No. 1, January 1967, pp. 28–42. Reprinted with permission.

[1] For examples see Ernest W. Burgess, "The Economic Factor in Juvenile Delinquency," *Journal of Criminal Law, Criminology and Police Science*, May-June 1952, pp. 29–42; Joseph W. Eaton and Kenneth Polk, *Measuring Delinquency: A Study of Probation Department Referrals* (Pittsburgh: University of Pittsburgh Press, 1961), p. 4; Clifford R. Shaw and Henry D. McKay, *Juvenile Delinquency in Urban Areas* (Chicago: University of Chicago Press, 1942); and Albert K. Cohen's analysis of several studies in *Delinquent Boys: The Culture of the Gang* (Glencoe: Free Press, 1955), pp. 37–44.

[2] For examples see William Healy and Augusta F. Bronner, *New Light on Delinquency and Its Treatment* (New Haven: Yale University Press, 1936), p. 52; Sheldon and Eleanor Glueck, *Delinquents in*

the Making (New York: Harper, 1952), p. 89; Clifford R. Shaw and Henry D. McKay, "Social Factors in Juvenile Delinquency," *Report on the Causes of Crime* (Washington: National Commission on Law Observance and Enforcement, 1931), pp. 195–96; Joseph D. Lohman, *Juvenile Delinquency* (Cook County: Office of the Sheriff, 1957), p. 8; Norman Fenton, *The Delinquent Boy and the Correctional School* (Claremont: Claremont Colleges Guidance Center, 1935), as quoted by Karl G. Garrison, *Psychology of Adolescence* (New York: Prentice-Hall, 1956), p. 350; and Peter Scott, "Gangs and Delinquent Groups in London," *British Journal of Delinquency*, July 1956, pp. 4–26.

[3] Cohen, *op. cit. supra* note 1; Richard A. Cloward and Lloyd E. Ohlin, *Delinquency and Opportunity: A Theory of Delinquent Gangs* (Glencoe: Free Press, 1960); Walter B. Miller, "Lower-Class Culture as a Generating Milieu of Gang Delinquency," *Journal of Social Issues*, Summer 1958, pp. 5–19. See also Frederic M. Thrasher, *The Gang: A Study of 1,313 Gangs in Chicago*, abridged and with a new introduction by James F. Short, Jr. (Chicago: University of Chicago Press, 1963); and Lewis Yablonsky, *The Violent Gang* (New York: Macmillan, 1962).

253

the deviant norms and beliefs which the gangs engender, and the group rewards and publicity which the gangs provide.

Comparatively little attention has been paid to middle-class delinquency, principally because middle-class delinquency has not been considered serious, either in frequency or in form.[4] However, a growing number of empirical studies question both the basic facts which the theories must encompass and the theoretical constructs themselves. This paper reviews some of the questions that have been raised.

SOCIAL CLASS AND DELINQUENCY

The accuracy of official statistics regarding the relationship of social class to delinquency has long been a bone of contention. Many people have argued that official records are biased.[5] The reason, they say, that lower-class juveniles are overrepresented in delinquency statistics is simply that official agencies are more inclined to record the offenses of lower-class offenders. But can this conclusion be substantiated by fact or is it, as Cohen asks, the product of "egalitarian proclivities and sentimental humanitarianism"?[6]

Universality of Inverse Relation between Class and Delinquency

The first issue that reflects on Cohen's question has to do with the universality of the supposed inverse relation between social class and delinquency. On one hand, the Short and Strodtbeck studies of delinquent gangs in Chicago tended to support official findings. Lower-class gang boys *were* the most delinquent. They were followed, in turn, by lower-class non-gang boys and then by middle-class boys. These differences held up for both Negro and white respondents, although Negro gang members were not so different from their Negro middle-class peers as were white gang boys from white middle-class peers.[7]

On the other hand, most studies of undetected delinquency in smaller cities and towns have not found significant differences among adolescents from different classes,[8] and those which have, have reported differences which are not nearly so strong as those indicated by official data.[9] For example, Gold, in a

[4] For some discussions of the subject see Ralph W. England, Jr., "A Theory of Middle-Class Delinquency," *Journal of Criminal Law, Criminology and Police Science*, April 1960, pp. 535–40; Herbert A. Bloch and Arthur Niederhoffer, *The Gang: A Study of Adolescent Behavior* (New York: Philosophical Library, 1958); Cohen, *op. cit. supra* note 1, pp. 88–91; William C. Kvaraceus and Walter B. Miller, *Delinquent Behavior, Culture and the Individual* (Washington: National Education Association, 1959), pp. 77–84.

[5] Austin L. Porterfield, *Youth in Trouble* (Fort Worth: Leo Potishman Foundation, 1946), *passim;* Milton A. Barron, *The Juvenile in Delinquent Society* (New York: Alfred A. Knopf, 1956), p. 32; Lloyd Warner and Paul S. Lunt, *The Social Life of a Modern Community* (New Haven: Yale University Press, 1941), p. 427; and William C. Kvaraceus, *What Research Says to the Teacher: Juvenile Delinquency* (Washington: National Education Association, 1958), pp. 331–32.

[6] Cohen, *op. cit. supra* note 1, p. 42.

[7] James F. Short, Jr. and Fred L. Strodtbeck, *Group Process and Delinquency* (Chicago: University of Chicago Press, 1965), pp. 164–71.

[8] F. Ivan Nye, James F. Short, Jr., and V. J. Olsen, "Socio-Economic Status and Delinquent Behavior," *American Journal of Sociology*, January 1958, pp. 318–29; John P. Clark and Eugene P. Wenninger, "Socio-Economic Class and Area as Correlates of Illegal Behavior Among Juveniles," *American Sociological Review*, December 1962, pp. 826–34; Robert Dentler and Lawrence J. Monroe, "Early Adolescent Theft," *American Sociological Review*, October 1961, pp. 733–43; and Porterfield, *op. cit. supra* note 5. An exception is Albert J. Reiss, Jr. and Albert L. Rhodes, "The Distribution of Juvenile Delinquency in the Social Class Structure," *American Sociological Review*, October 1961, pp. 730–32.

[9] LaMar T. Empey and Maynard L. Erickson, "Hidden Delinquency and Social Status," *Social Forces*, June 1966, pp. 546–54; and Martin Gold, "Undetected Delinquent Behavior," *Journal of Research in Crime and Delinquency*, January 1966, pp. 27–46.

Michigan study, found a statistically significant, inverse relation between class and delinquency, but the strength of the relationship was extremely slight, a coefficient of −.12.[10] The degree of variance which could be explained by this relationship would be small indeed.

Empey and Erickson report similar findings from Utah.[11] The degrees of association between social class and three different delinquency scales were: for *general* theft, −.20; for *serious* theft, −.17; and for *common* delinquency, −.17. They discovered further that the inverse relationship was due more to a small amount of delinquency among upper-class respondents than it was to an excessive amount of delinquency among lower-class respondents. The lower- and middle-class groups did not differ significantly from each other while the degree of difference between each of them and the upper-class group was considerable.

Actual Violations versus Apprehension

Empirical studies have indicated that the amount of undetected delinquency is great.[12] The degree of apprehension is extremely low, somewhere between 3 and 5 per cent of all self-reported offenses. Yet, when apprehension does occur, officials are more likely to record and process lower-class youngsters.[13]

The picture is further confused by the fact that the police and other officials are charged by juvenile court law to respond to poor home and family conditions, neglect, truancy, and other factors which may come to light when some "predatory" act is detected. Their interest is often solicitous rather than punitive, but since these factors are more often associated with lower-class than middle-class juveniles, the former are more inclined to be processed legally. These two conditions distort the idea of the epidemiological character of delinquency and probably lend credence to the notion of an inverse relation between class and delinquency.

Seriousness

There are many who feel that the offenses of lower-class youngsters are more likely to be serious. Ohlin, for example, maintains that middle-class delinquency is "petty" in comparison with lower-class delinquency.[14] The inclination to violate the law, he believes, is more deeply ingrained in the lower-class youngster who therefore possesses a greater potential for the development of a criminal career. The evidence pertinent to this question is limited but that which is available is not entirely supportive of Ohlin's position.

The Myerhoffs, in their observations of middle-class "gangs" in Los Angeles, reported that the violations of these "gangs" were often more "mischievous"

---

[10] Gold, *op. cit. supra* note 9, pp. 40–43.

[11] Empey and Erickson, *op. cit. supra* note 9. pp. 549–50. See also Maynard L. Erickson and LaMar T. Empey, "Class Position, Peers and Delinquency," *Sociology and Social Research*, April 1965, pp. 271–72.

[12] Maynard L. Erickson and LaMar T. Empey, "Court Records, Undetected Delinquency and Decision-Making," *Journal of Criminal Law, Criminology and Police Science*, December 1963, pp. 456–69; Fred J. Murphy, M. Shirley, and Helen L. Witmer, "The Incidence of Hidden Delinquency," *American Journal of Orthopsychiatry*, October 1946, pp. 686–96; Gold, *op. cit. supra* note 9; and Porterfield, *op. cit. supra* note 5.

[13] Gold found that the police were more likely to record lower-class offenders; see Gold, *op. cit. supra* note 9, p. 38. Empey and Erickson found that low-class adolescents were overrepresented in a training school in proportion to the offenses they reported having committed; see Empey and Erickson, *op. cit. supra* note 9.

[14] Lloyd E. Ohlin, *The Development of Opportunities for Youth* (New York: Youth Development Center, Syracuse University, 1960), pp. 8–9; and Cloward and Ohlin, *op. cit. supra* note 3, p. 12.

than violent.[15] However, violence is not the only dimension of seriousness. Included in these "mischievous" acts was the frequent and regular theft of articles that were by no means small nor inexpensive: radios, phonographs, car accessories, television sets, all usually taken from employers or personal acquaintances.

Such findings were corroborated by Empey and Erickson in a more systematic enumeration of offenses in a *nonmetropolitan* center.[16] They found that, while the more serious forms of delinquency were less common among all class groups, such violations as grand theft, forgery, breaking and entering, destroying property, and even arson, when they did occur, were more often committed by middle- than lower-class juveniles. This rather surprising finding held true whether the self-reported data came from boys with no official record or boys who were incarcerated in a training school.[17] Middle-class groups in both populations were the ones who rated disproportionately high on these kinds of offenses.

Even with respect to violence, Karacki and Toby found fighting gangs that did not come from economically deprived homes.[18] These gangs placed emphasis on many of the characteristics traditionally associated with lower-class delinquent groups: physical aggression, loyalty to peers, and immediate gratification. Shanley located a similar group of middle- and upper-class boys in the suburbs of Los Angeles who had patterns of police contact which were as extensive and serious as samples of adjudicated delinquents from lower-class neighborhoods.[19] Finally, other analyses suggest that particular patterns of delinquency may be associated as much with differences in place of residence—rural, urban, or type of neighborhood—as with social class position.[20]

In summary, these findings suggest that the inverse relationship between social class and delinquency may be less potent than has been traditionally assumed and that we should search for other determinants;[21] social class by itself may be a poor clue. The behavior of some middle-class groups suggests that we might discover as many differences *within* classes regarding delinquency as we now discover between them. In other words, instead of using a two- or three-celled table to compare lower-, middle-, and upper-class groups across the board, we should use four- or six-celled tables to compare the delinquent acts of various groups within, as

[15] Howard L. and Barbara G. Myerhoff, "Field Observations of Middle-Class Gangs," *Social Forces*, March 1964, pp. 328–36. See also Andrew Greely and James Casey, "An Upper-Middle-Class Deviant Gang," *American Catholic Sociological Review*, Spring 1963, pp. 33–41.

[16] Empey and Erickson, *op. cit. supra* note 9, pp. 551–54.

[17] Albert H. Herskovitz, Murray Levene, and George Spivak, "Anti-Social Behavior of Adolescents from Higher Socio-Economic Groups," *Journal of Nervous and Mental Diseases*, November 1959, pp. 1–9. They found no sharply different patterns between middle- and low-class incarcerated offenders and little variation in the seriousness of their offenses.

[18] Larry Karacki and Jackson Toby, "The Uncommitted Adolescent: Candidates for Gang Socialization," *Sociological Inquiry*, Spring 1962, pp. 203–15.

[19] Fred J. Shanley, "Middle-Class Delinquency as a Social Problem," paper presented at the Annual Meetings of the Pacific Sociological Association, Salt Lake City, April 1965, p. 2. A recent article in *Life* magazine was also devoted to the extensive drug use and other delinquent patterns of middle-class groups on Sunset Strip in Hollywood. The Strip is also the locale of the heaviest concentration of "gay" (homosexual) hangouts in the city; see *Life*, August 26, 1966, pp. 75–83.

[20] Irving Spergel, *Racketville, Slumtown, Haulburg: An Exploratory Study of Delinquent Subcultures* (Chicago: University of Chicago Press, 1964); and Clark and Wenninger, *op. cit. supra* note 8.

[21] Identification with particular sets of peers is one that has appeared. See Erickson and Empey, *op. cit. supra* note 11, pp. 272–81.

well as between, classes.[22] More precise distinctions of this type might provide better clues to the nature delinquency than do gross comparisons between classes.

DIMENSIONS OF GROUP DELINQUENCY

What about the second set of facts which theory must fit—the proposition that delinquency is typically a group phenomenon? The available evidence has a paradoxical quality which illustrates both the complexity of the subject and the meagerness of our information.

There are few findings which question seriously the basic proposition that delinquency is typically a group phenomenon. Most studies, including some which use self-reported data, place the incidence of group delinquency somewhere between 60 and 90 per cent of the total.[23] It may be that with more systematic data this range will be extended, since some offenses—defying parents or running away—are by nature less likely to be group-related than others. However, the group aspects of delinquency seem to be well established with a modal figure of about 75 per cent.

What is not well established is a consensus regarding the nature of delinquent groups—their cohesiveness, their structural qualities, their subcultural characteristics. The most commonly used term to refer to delinquent groups has been the word "gang." The term has

been so overworked and is so imprecise that its use in scientific discourse may well be questioned. An examination of evidence relative to the cohesiveness and structural qualities of delinquent groups illustrates the elusiveness of the "gang" and other group concepts.

Group Cohesiveness

Conflicting themes run through the literature regarding cohesiveness. The first theme, exemplified most clearly by Thrasher and the Chicago school, emphasizes the idea that delinquent groups are characterized by *internal* cohesion—*esprit de corps,* solidarity, cooperative action, shared tradition, and a strong group awareness.[24] Despite the qualifications which Thrasher placed on this theme—and he did qualify it— there is no denying that a traditional perspective has developed emphasizing the romantic quality of delinquent gangs, the free and easy life, the joint commitments of members to one another. The key to this theme is its emphasis upon the culture-generating qualities and attractiveness of the peer group.

The second theme, as Bordua notes, is irrationalistic and deterministic in its emphasis. "Gang boys are driven," he notes, "not attracted. Their lives are characterized by desperation rather than fun."[25] Such theories as those of Cohen,[26] Cloward and Ohlin,[27] and Miller[28] emphasize the idea that lower-

---

[22] Miller, for example, noted differences in theft behavior among three different groups, all *within* the lower class. See Walter B. Miller, "Theft Behavior in City Gangs," *Juvenile Gangs in Context: Theory, Research and Action,* Malcolm W. Klein and Barbara G. Myerhoff, eds. (New York: Prentice-Hall, 1967).

[23] See note 2 of this paper for relevant studies. Unpublished data in our possession on self-reported delinquency, both from Utah and California, confirm this figure.

[24] Thrasher, *op. cit. supra* note 3, pp. 40–46. See also Short's discussion of this theme in his introduction to the abridged edition, *passim.*

[25] David J. Bordua, "Some Comments on Theories of Group Delinquency," *Sociological Inquiry,* Spring 1962, pp. 245–46; see also David J. Bordua, "A Critique of Sociological Interpretations of Gang Delinquency," *Annals of the American Academy of Political and Social Science,* November 1961, pp. 120–36.

[26] Cohen, *op. cit.* supra note 1.

[27] Cloward and Ohlin, *op. cit. supra* note 3.

[28] Miller, *op. cit. supra* note 3.

class children are downgraded in both the child and the adult status hierarchies of our middle-class institutions. They are ill-prepared by family background and cultural heritage to achieve successfully and, as a consequence, their lives are characterized by frustration, negativistic retaliation, alienation, and radical separation from conventional successes and satisfactions. This theme is much less romantic in its emphasis than the first and implies, not internal attraction, but external pressure as the source of gang cohesion.

It is the role of the individual youngster in the social structure, not his role in the street group, that is of primary significance. He is alienated before he enters the group, not because of it. The group is simply the instrument that translates his individual discontent into a collective solution.[29] By implication, the group can do little to remedy his sensitivity to the middle-class measuring rod, to provide him with the material and social satisfactions to which he aspires.

The fundamental question, then, asks what the forces are that hold delinquent groups together. Are they the group rules and loyalties which emerge from gratifying relationships within the group, as the first theme suggests, or are they due to the position of gang boys in the class structure as suggested by the second theme?

First of all, we are confronted with the apparent fact that, if the delinquent group were not rewarding to the individual, it would cease to exist. In this vein, Short and Strodtbeck have observed that when it comes to assuming adult roles—occupation and marriage —". . . . the lure of the gang may spell disaster."[30] Even when challenging jobs

are obtained for them, when the pay is good or when gang members are married and have children, the lure of the street is not easily forgotten and any inclination to return to it is supported by the gang. The implication, of course, is one of *internal* cohesiveness and attraction: gang membership has much to offer. However, as might be expected, there are other interpretations.

In this issue of the *Journal of Research in Crime and Delinquency*, Klein and Crawford argue that *internal* sources of lower-class gang cohesion are weak.[31] Group goals which might be unifying are minimal, membership stability is low, loyalty is questionable, and even the names of gangs—Gladiators, Vice Lords, Egyptian Kings—are unifying only when external threat is present. When the threat is diminished, cohesion is diminished. It is their feeling that were it not for the external pressures of police and other officials, the threats of rival groups, or the lack of acceptance by parents and employers, many delinquent gangs would have nothing to unify them. By themselves, such gangs do not develop the kinds of group goals and instrumentally oriented activities which are indicative of much organization.

Group Cohesion and Delinquent Acts

The commission of delinquent acts seems to illustrate this lack of organization. One of the most striking things about them is not their planned and patterned characteristics but their episodic and highly situational character.[32] One would think that if delinquent

[29] Bordua, *op. cit. supra* note 25, pp. 252–57.
[30] Short and Strodtbeck, *op. cit. supra* note 7, pp. 221–34.

[31] Malcolm W. Klein and Lois Y. Crawford, "Groups, Gangs and Cohesiveness," *Journal of Research in Crime and Delinquency,* January 1967, pp. 63.
[32] Many works allude to this phenomenon. For examples see Thrasher, *op. cit. supra* note 3; Short and Strodtbeck, *op. cit. supra* note 7; and Yablonsky, *op. cit. supra* note 3.

groups were highly cohesive or highly structured this would not be the case. Yet, most delinquent acts are more spontaneous than planned and, even though they involve groups, they rarely involve all members of a gang acting together.

Even complex crimes reveal considerable spontaneity and what Matza calls "shared misunderstanding."[33] Thrasher describes three college students who began to phantasize about robbing a post-office.[34] Subsequent interviews with them revealed that none of them wanted to be involved in the actual robbery but the more they talked the deeper they became involved, each hoping, actually believing, that the others would call a halt to this crazy phantasy but each reluctant, on his own, to "chicken out." The result was that, in a state of almost total individual disbelief, they robbed the post-office and found themselves in legal custody.

Careful observation of delinquents reveals countless repetitions of this phenomenon—the wandering kinds of interaction that lead to delinquent acts and the mixed rather than solidary motivations that accompany them. Even in regard to fighting, as Miller points out, "A major objective of gang members is to put themselves in the posture of fighting without actually having to fight."[35]

Group Cohesion and Member Interaction

Observations of delinquent gangs led Short and Strodtbeck, like Klein and Crawford, to depreciate nostalgic references to "that old gang of mine" and to deny the image of the delinquent gang as a carefree and solidary group.

They report that such an interpretation may derive more from the projections of middle-class observers than from the realities that dominate street life.[36] They document this interpretation with a considerable amount of data.

They found that, compared with others, gang boys were characterized by a long list of "social disabilities": unsuccessful school adjustment, limited social and technical skills, a low capacity for self-assertion, lower intelligence scores, and also a tendency to hold other gang members in low esteem.[37] Interaction within the gang seemed to be characterized by an omnipresent tone of aggression as a result of these disabilities and the insecurities they engendered.

This account is complemented by Matza's use of the term "sounding," which refers to the incessant plumbing and testing through insult by delinquent boys of one another's status and commitment to delinquency.[38] Miller speaks of the "focal concerns" of lower-class gang culture as toughness, smartness, and excitement.[39] Whatever the terms, it appears that delinquent boys are under constant pressure to protect status and assert masculinity.

While this pressure to project a particular image may not be qualitatively different from many of the highly stylized kinds of interaction found in a host of other status-conscious groups, the point is that such interaction is not characteristic, at least hypothetically, of *primary* groups. Primary groups, ideally, are supposed to provide warmth and support. With the constant "sounding" that goes on in delinquent groups it is questionable whether lower-class gangs

---

[33] David Matza, *Delinquency and Drift* (New York: Wiley, 1964), pp. 35–59.

[34] Thrasher, *op. cit. supra* note 3, pp. 300–03.

[35] Walter B. Miller, "Violent Crimes in City Gangs," *Annals of the American Academy of Political and Social Science,* March 1965, p. 110.

[36] Short and Strodtbeck, *op. cit. supra* note 7, p. 231.

[37] *Ibid.,* ch. 10 and 12.

[38] Matza, *op. cit. supra* note 33, pp. 53–55.

[39] Miller, *op. cit. supra* note 3, p. 519.

are conducive to close friendships.[40]

The picture that is painted suggests that gang members, like inmates in a prison, are held together, not by feelings of loyalty and solidarity, but by forces much less attractive. It is not that structure is lacking but that it is defensive and highly stylized, not supportive. Group members stay together simply because they feel they have more to lose than to gain by any breach in their solidarity. While they may appear to the outsider to be dogmatic, rigid, and unyielding in their loyalty to each other, the sources of this loyalty are not internal but external. Remove the pressure and you remove the cohesion.

Seeming to comment on this very point, Short and Strodtbeck report that they "find the capacity of lower-class gangs to elaborate and enforce norms of reciprocity is very much below what might be required to sustain the group if alternative forms of gratification were available."[41] Similarly, Matza argues that the majority of delinquents are not strongly committed either to delinquent groups or to a criminal career but are "drifters" who are held together by a kind of pluralistic ignorance.[42] When in the company of others, the boy is inclined to attribute to them a greater commitment to delinquent relationships and values than he has himself.

These points of view indicate the need for more direct investigation of delinquent group cohesiveness *per se* and for the study of middle-class as well as lower-class groups. Our lack of information is so great that we do not have even an adequate baseline from

which to begin; that is, we know very little about the cohesiveness and inherent gratifications of adolescent groups in general. Therefore, until we can establish a baseline, it will be difficult either to generalize about delinquent groups or to compare them with other groups. Furthermore, the possible lack of cohesiveness in delinquent groups raises questions regarding the nature of delinquent subculture. If delinquent groups are not cohesive and internally gratifying, can it be expected that delinquents, especially those in the lower class, have either the personal motivation or the organizational skills to promote and maintain a deviant subculture which is in total opposition to prevailing values?

DELINQUENT SUBCULTURE

Such theorists as Cloward and Ohlin have defined the subcultural concept in narrow terms.[43] They see a delinquent subculture as unique and as autonomous. Organization around a specific delinquent activity, they say, distinguishes a delinquent subculture from other subcultures. Such behaviors as truancy, drunkenness, property destruction, or theft are legally delinquent activities but these they would not include as characteristic of a delinquent subculture unless they were the focal activities around which the dominant beliefs and roles of a group were organized.

The narrowness and rigor of their postulates regarding criminal, retreatist, and conflict-oriented subcultures characterize the logical structure of their theory but do these postulates accurately characterize delinquent groups and subculture? Are they this focused? Are they this unique and autonomous?

When Short and his associates set about trying to study these kinds of subcultures, they had extreme difficulty

[40] Short and Strodtbeck, *op. cit. supra* note 7, p. 233. See also Lewis Yablonsky, "The Delinquent Gang as a Near-Group," *Social Problems*, Fall 1959, pp. 108–17.

[41] Short and Strodtbeck, *op. cit. supra* note 7, p. 280.

[42] Matza, *op. cit. supra* note 33, pp. 27–30, 56.

[43] Cloward and Ohlin, *op. cit. supra* note 3, p. 7.

in locating them.[44] They found a number of gangs in which marijuana smoking was rather common and in which there was experimentation with heroin and pills, but it took more than a year of extensive inquiries among police and local adults to locate a clearly drug-oriented group. They never did find a full-blown criminal group. Consequently, they concluded that their failure casts doubt on the generality of the Cloward-Ohlin postulates.[45]

Short, *et al.*, had no difficulty in locating a number of gangs who were well-known for their conflict, toughness, and fighting but one still must question what it means to say that the "focal" concern of gangs is conflict. The bulk of even the most delinquent boys' time is spent in nondelinquent activity and their delinquent acts make up a long list of different offenses.[46] How precise can we be, then, in referring to the characteristics of a "conflict" subculture or gang?

In observing "typical," "tough" city gangs over a two-year period, Miller found that assault was *not* the most dominant form of activity.[47] In fact, two-thirds of the male gang members who were observed were not known to have engaged in *any* assaultive crimes over the two-year period and 88 per cent did not appear in court on such a charge. Similarly, Klein and his colleagues in Los Angeles have found that less than 10 per cent of the recorded offenses for gang members are assaultive.[48] Instead, the *frequency* with which adolescents commit a long list of different offenses seems to better char-

acterize their commitments to delinquency than their persistent adherence to a particular offense pattern.[49] There seems to be limited empirical support for the idea of autonomous and highly focused delinquent subcultures and somewhat more support for the notion of a ubiquitous, "parent" subculture of delinquency in which there is a "garden-variety" of delinquent acts.[50]

A ubiquitous, but amorphous, subculture would be more consistent with the notion of weak internal bonds in delinquent groups and highly situational delinquent acts than with the idea of internally cohesive groups who participate in planned and highly patterned delinquent activities. Furthermore, if delinquent subculture is not highly focused and autonomous, question is raised regarding its relation to the larger culture.

Subculture: Contraculture or Infraculture?

Most contemporay theory has suggested that lower-class delinquent subculture is *contra*culture[51] in which status is gained by demonstrated opposition to prevailing middle-class standards.[52] Theories of middle-class delinquency suggest that the delinquent group is a collective response to adolescent efforts to establish sexual identity and to deal with frustrations attendant on the transition from childhood to adulthood.[53] But does this mean that a middle-class de-

---

[44] Short and Strodtbeck, *op. cit. supra* note 7, pp. 10–13.

[45] *Ibid.*, p. 13.

[46] Short, Introduction in Thrasher, *op. cit.*, *supra* note 3, pp. xlvii–xlviii.

[47] Miller, *op. cit. supra* note 35, pp. 105, 111.

[48] Malcolm W. Klein, Youth Studies Center, University of Southern California, Personal Communication, September 1966.

[49] Erickson and Empey, *op. cit. supra* note 12, pp. 465–69; and Gold, *op. cit. supra* note 9, pp. 27–46.

[50] Albert K. Cohen and James F. Short, Jr., "Research in Delinquent Subcultures," *Journal of Social Issues,* Summer 1958, pp. 20–36.

[51] J. Milton Yinger, "Contraculture and Subculture," *American Sociological Review,* October 1960, pp. 625–35.

[52] Cohen, *op. cit. supra* note 1; Cloward and Ohlin, *op. cit. supra* note 3; and Miller, *op. cit. supra* note 3.

[53] England, *op. cit. supra* note 4; Bloch and Niederhoffer, *op. cit. supra* note 4.

linquent group is, like a lower-class gang, the instrument that translates individual discontent into a delinquent *contra*culture?

Matza takes issue with the notion of *contra*culture on any class level and emphasizes a subtle but important distinction. He argues that "there is a subculture of delinquency but it is not a delinquent subculture."[54] American culture, he believes, is not a simple puritanism exemplified by the middle-class. Instead, it is a complex and pluralistic culture in which, among other cultural traditions, there is a "subterranean" tradition—an *infra*culture of delinquency.[55]

This *infra*culture does not represent ignorance of the law nor even general negation of it; instead, it is a complex relationship to law in a *symbiotic* rather than an oppositional way. It is not a separate set of beliefs which distinguish delinquents from other youth, or youth from adults; it is the part of the overall culture which consists of the personal, more deviant, and less-publicized version of officially endorsed values. The two sets of traditions—conventional and deviant—are held simultaneously by almost everyone in the social system and, while certain groups may be influenced more by one than the other, both determine behavior to a considerable degree.

Daniel Bell's analysis of crime as an American way of life is probably a good illustration of Matza's point.[56] Bell notes that Americans are characterized by an "extremism" in morality, yet they also have an "extraordinary" talent for compromise in politics and a "brawling" economic and social history. These contradictory features form the basis for an intimate and symbolic relationship between crime and politics, crime and economic growth, and crime and social change, not an oppositional relationship. The tradition of wanting to "get ahead" is no less an ethic than wanting to observe the law.

Crime has been a major means by which a variety of people have achieved the American success ideal and obtained respectability, if not for themselves, for their children. The basic question, therefore, is whether this deviant tradition contributes more than we realize to the behavior of younger as well as older people. Rather than delinquent subculture being uniquely the property of young people, it may have roots in the broader culture.

Empirical investigation of the matter would seem to involve two questions: (1) the extent to which adolescents legitimate official, conventional patterns and (2) the extent to which they simultaneously participate in, or espouse in some way, deviant patterns. With reference to the first question both Korbin[57] and Gordon *et al.*[58] suggest that adolescents from all strata are inclined to legitimate official patterns. The gang members they studied did not seem to be alienated from the goals of the larger society and ". . . even the gang ethic, is not one of 'reaction formation' *against* widely shared conceptions of the 'good' life." Gang, low-class

---

[54] Matza, *op. cit. supra* note 33, p. 33; and David Matza and Gresham M. Sykes, "Juvenile Delinquency and Subterranean Values," *American Sociological Review,* October 1961, pp. 712–19.

[55] The idea of *infra*culture was suggested by J. A. Pitt-Rivers, *The People of the Sierra* (Chicago: University of Chicago Press, 1961), who referred to "infrastructure" rather than "infraculture."

[56] Daniel Bell, *The End of Ideology* (Glencoe: Free Press, 1959), pp. 115–36.

[57] Solomon Kobrin "The Conflict of Values in Delinquency Areas," *American Sociological Review,* October 1951, pp. 653–61.

[58] Robert A. Gordon, James F. Short, Jr., Desmond F. Cartwright, and Fred L. Strodtbeck, "Values and Gang Delinquency," *American Journal of Sociology,* September 1963, pp. 109–28, as reproduced in Short and Strodtbeck, *op. cit. supra* note 7, ch. 3.

and middle-class boys, Negro and white ". . . *evaluated images representing salient features of the middle-class styles of life equally high.*"[59] This finding confirmed that of Gold in Michigan with a much different population[60] and led to the conclusion that ". . . if the finding is valid, three separate theoretical formulations [Cohen, Miller, and Cloward-Ohlin] fail to make sufficient allowance for the meaningfulness of middle-class values to members of gangs."[61] In fact, given the strength of the findings, one wonders whether we are correct in referring to official values as "middle-class" values or whether we should be using some more inclusive term.

The second question, regarding the simultaneous possession of deviant patterns, presents a more confused picture. A curious omission in our conjectures and research has been our failure to examine the extent to which deviant values are widely transmitted to young people. Several elaborate theories hypothesize that all children, including those in the lower class, are conditioned by official, "middle-class" stimuli. They watch television, listen to the radio, go to the movies, read the ads, and attend middle-class dominated schools; as a consequence, they acquire common desires for status, recognition, and achievement. Despite these conjectures, we have not had similar conjectures regarding the possible transmission of deviant patterns.

Kvaraceus and Miller have suggested that middle-class delinquency represents an upward diffusion of lower-class attitudes and practices;[62] but are lower-class patterns all that are diffused? To what extent are children on all class levels conditioned not just by lower-class values but by mass stimuli which emphasize violence, toughness, protest, kicks, and expedience? These are certainly important aspects of our "brawling" American history, a part of our cultural tradition. If we pay too little heed to them then we may be inclined to overemphasize the narrowness and autonomy of delinquent subculture, especially as the sole possession of the lower class. It is seductively easy to overemphasize the uniqueness of problem people and thereby to obscure their similarities to non-problem people. For example, studies of self-reported delinquency reveal that the extent of hidden law violation is widespread,[63] so widespread, indeed, that Murphy, Shirley, and Witmer were led to remark that "even a moderate increase in the amount of attention paid to it by law enforcement authorities could create the semblance of a 'delinquency wave' without there being the slightest change in adolescent behavior."[64] This finding, coupled with the questionable strength of the theory of an inverse relationship between social class and delinquency, suggests that, unless we are to assume that deviant traditions actually predominate, they must occupy a symbiotic tie of some kind with conformist traditions.

Conventional Values and Deviance

In order to investigate the matter further, several factors should be considered. One important factor is the nature of adult-youth relationships. What perspectives, for example, are transmitted from adults to youth? Is the youthful search for "kicks" or the irresponsible acquisition of wealth and

[59] Short and Strodtbeck, *op. cit. supra* note 7, pp. 271, 59. Italics theirs.
[60] Martin Gold, *Status Forces in Delinquent Boys* (Ann Arbor: University of Michigan, Institute for Social Research, 1963).
[61] Short and Strodtbeck, *op. cit. supra* note 7, p. 74.
[62] Kvaraceus and Miller, *op. cit. supra* note 4, pp. 77–79.

[63] Erickson and Empey, *op. cit. supra* note 12; and Gold, *op. cit. supra* note 9.
[64] Murphy, Shirley, and Witmer, *op. cit. supra* note 12.

leisure profoundly different from adult desires for the same things or, rather, a projection of them? A double standard for judging adult and youthful behavior is certainly not uncommon and could be far more influential than a double standard distinguishing between the sexes. Personal access to various adult role models, as contrasted to a vague and abstract relationship with them, would likely affect the selection of deviant or conformist behavior. The absence of a strong personal relationship would make the juvenile more dependent upon the images projected by such secondary sources as the movies or television.

A second important factor has to do with the relative valences of delinquent and conformist values for different populations of adolescents. How do they balance? Short and Strodtbeck found that, while conventional prescriptions were generally accepted, subterranean, deviant values were accepted differentially. While gang boys were as willing as lower- and middle-class nongang boys to legitimate official prescriptions, they were not as inclined to support official proscriptions.[65] This particular research failed to explore other important aspects of the issue.

Besides obtaining some indication of the general valences of both deviant and conventional values, we need to explore their valences in various specific contexts. We know, for example, that if changes in group context or social situation occur, both behavior and the espousal of particular values are likely to change also. The citizen who is in favor of racial equality in a general way is often one of the first to sell his home when integration occurs in his neighborhood. Specific considerations alter his behavior. Similarly, the delinquent boy, when placed in the context of having to exercise leadership over his peers

in a conventional setting, will often act remarkably like a conventional adult. His actions are suprisingly stereotyped, a response not to norms in general but to norms as they apply in a specific context.

In studying the relative valences of conventional and deviant proscriptions we also need to compare not only lower-class gang boys with others, as Short and Strodtbeck did, but excessively delinquent boys from other classes with their peers as well. We need a better indication of the extent to which deviant values are diffused either throughout the entire class structure or through subgroups on all class levels.

Finally, we need more careful study of the way official and societal responses to juvenile behavior contribute to definitions of delinquency and delinquent subcultures, either by overemphasizing their uniqueness or by contributing to their development. Becker argues that the process by which some juveniles but not others are labeled may be as crucial in defining the problem as the behavior of the juveniles themselves.[66] For example, as mentioned earlier, there are those who think that the coalescence and persistence of delinquent gangs may be due as much to external pressure from official and other sources as to the internal gratifications and supposedly unique standards of those groups.

The contribution which could be made by a study of official systems— the police, the courts, the correctional agencies—would be clarification of the total *gestalt* to which officials respond: how legal statutes, official policies, and perceptual cues affect the administration of juvenile justice.[67] It seems ap-

---

[65] Short and Strodtbeck, *op. cit. supra* note 7, pp. 59–76.

[66] Howard S. Becker, *Outsiders: Studies in the Sociology of Deviance* (Glencoe: Free Press, 1963), ch. 1.

[67] See Irving Piliavin and Scott Brian, "Police Encounters with Juveniles," *American Journal of Sociology*, September 1964, pp. 206–15; Joseph D. Lohman, James T.

parent that official and societal reactions to juveniles are due not entirely to criminalistic behavior but also (1) to acts which, if committed by adults, would not warrant legal action and (2) to a number of "social disabilities" that are popularly associated with deviance: unkempt appearance, inappropriate responses due to lack of interpersonal skills, and educational deficiencies.[68]

These are characteristics which traditionally have been more closely associated with lower- than middle-class juveniles and are characterized in legal terms by truancy, dependency, or incorrigibility. It would be important to learn the extent to which these identifying characteristics, as contrasted to demonstrably delinquent *values*, contribute to the definition of some groups, but not others, as seriously delinquent. Since only a small fraction of their time and attention is devoted to law violation, even among the most seriously delinquent, the meanings which these juveniles assign to themselves are usually far less sinister than the meanings which officials assign to them.

CONCLUSION

It seems apparent that, in order to complete the picture of the total phenomenon, we need a series of related studies which would, first, identify a representative population of adolescents, their class positions, their value-beliefs and commitments, various mea-

sures of delinquent acts (self-reported and official), their symptoms of disability, and their group affiliations; and, second, follow these adolescents through the institutional paths—educational, economic, or correctional—along which they are routed by officials. Which juveniles are processed legally and on what criteria? In what ways are they the same or different from nonprocessed juveniles in terms of values, class position, group affiliations, actual delinquent acts, and so on.

Given such research we might then be in a better position to know not only what the consequences are for those who are apprehended and processed by legal and correctional institutions but also what the consequences are for those who are *not* processed. This would most certainly apply to middle-class as well as lower-class juveniles. Hopefully, we might gain better insight into the total mosaic composed of delinquent values, actual behavior, and official reaction. Are delinquent values widely shared and is delinquent behavior common? Does legal or semilegal processing contribute to the solidification of delinquent groups? Is there differential treatment of juveniles based not on actual behavioral or value differences but on other identifying characteristics? Information of this type would help to indicate whether delinquent subculture is *contra*culture or *infra*culture.

We are only recently becoming aware of the extent of the symbiotic and mutually supporting characteristics of official and client roles in a long list of social systems; for example, policeman-offender, captor-captive, teacher-pupil, therapist-patient, caseworker-client. These are inextricably tied together by a host of traditional expectations and definitions. Change one and you are likely to change the other. We need to know more clearly the extent to which

---

Carey, Joel Goldfarb, and Michael J. Rowe, *The Handling of Juveniles From Offense to Disposition* (Berkeley: University of California, 1965); and Nathan Goldman, *The Differential Selection of Juvenile Offenders for Court Appearance* (National Research and Information Center, National Council on Crime and Delinquency, 1963).

[68] For conflicting evidence, see A. W. McEachern and Riva Bouzer, "Factors Related to Disposition in Juvenile Police Contacts," *Juvenile Gang in Context*, Klein and Myerhoff, eds., *op. cit. supra* note 22.

these definitions and the systems of which they are a part make delinquency and delinquents appear to be what they are, as well as the standards, beliefs, and behavior which may be unique to delinquents. Interactive relations be- tween and among juveniles and official agencies may be as important as the behavior exhibited by juveniles in de- limiting delinquency for purposes of both etiological inquiry and social con- trol.

section III

The Emperical Structure
of Delinquent Groups

There is considerable evidence that most juvenile delinquency is a
group phenomenon. Because delinquency occurs in groups, the struc-
tur of the gang is an important area for study by sociologists. Lack
of empirical data, however, has led us to assume that the delinquent
gang is virtually a closed social system, and that its influence on the
gang member is pervasive. The selections in this section provide some
of the recent analyses of the empirical structure of delinquent groups.

In the first article, Yablonsky suggests an interesting conceptualization of the gang as a "near-group." He describes gangs as informal,
short-lived, secondary groups without a clear-cut, stable delinquent
structure. According to his observations, their diffuse and malleable
structure makes it possible for them to meet the varied and individual
needs of their members.

Important issues concerning the structure and values of delinquent
groups are also raised by observations of middle-class gangs. With the
exception of the leadership role, the groups described by the Myerhoffs manifest all the characteristics identified by Yablonsky as those
of a near-group.

The investigation by Carl Werthman and Irving Piliavin of the
interaction between policemen and gang members in a metropolitan
area in the West indicates that the nature of the relationship between
gang members and policemen has its roots in an ecological conflict
over legitimate claims to certain social settings. An analysis is given of
the way policemen and gang boys perceive and construct their social
worlds in a response to this situation. In the next selection Werthman
continues the discussion of the function of social definitions, and
traces the consequences of the gang boy's *autonomy* both in the home
and in the school setting.

In the Miller article, data are presented on the behavior of twenty-
one corner gangs which describes the amount and types of violence

that distinguished these city gangs. The theme of violence also concerns Thomas Gannon. Gannon's intensive study of the characteristics of a New York "defensive" gang examines the function of group status symbols and status threats in gang conflicts.

22.

The Delinquent Gang as a Near-Group

Lewis Yablonsky

This paper is based on four years of research and direct work with some 30 delinquent gangs in New York City. During this period I directed a crime prevention program on the upper West Side of Manhattan for Morningside Heights, Inc., a community social agency sponsored by 14 major institutions including Columbia University, Barnard, Teacher's College, Union Theological Seminary, and Riverside Church.

Approaches used in data gathering included field study methods, participant observation, role-playing, group interaction analysis, and sociometry. The data were obtained through close daily interaction with gang boys over the four-year period during which I was the director of the project.

Although data were obtained on 30 gangs, the study focused on two, the Balkans and the Egyptian Kings. It was the latter which committed the brutal killing of a polio victim, Michael Farmer, in an upper west side park of

* This is a revised version of a paper delivered at The Eastern Sociological Meetings in New York City, April 11, 1959. The theory of near-groups and gang data presented in this paper is part of a forthcoming volume on gangs by the author.

New York City. The trial lasted over three months and received nation-wide attention. These two groups were intensively interviewed and contributed heavily to the formulation of a theory of near-groups. In addition to the analysis of the gang's structure, a number of delinquent gang war events produced vital case material.

There is a paucity of available theory based on empirical evidence about the structure of delinquent gangs. Two landmarks in the field are Thrasher's *The Gang* and Whyte's *Street Corner Society*. Some recent publications and controversy focus on the emergence of gangs and their function for gang members. Professor Cohen deals with gangs as sub-cultures organized by working-class boys as a reaction to middle-class values (1). In a recent publication Block and Nederhoffer discuss gangs as organizations designed to satisfy the adolescent's striving for the attainment of adult status (2).

Although partial group structuring has been extensively discussed in sociological literature on "groups," "crowds," and "mobs," my gang research revealed that these collectivity constructs did not seem to adequately describe and properly abstract the un-

SOURCE. Lewis Yablonsky, "The Delinquent Gang as a Near-Group," from *Social Problems,* Volume 7, No. 2, Fall 1959, pp. 108–117. Reprinted with the permission of the Society for the Study of Social Problems and the author.

derlying structural characteristics of the delinquent gang. Consequently, I have attempted here to construct a formulation which would draw together various described social dimensions of the gang under one conceptual scheme. I call this formulation Near-Group Theory.

NEAR-GROUP THEORY

One way of viewing human collectivities is on a continuum of organization characteristics. At one extreme, we have a highly organized, cohesive, functioning collection of individuals as members of a sociological group. At the other extreme, we have a mob of individuals characterized by anonymity, disturbed leadership, motivated by emotion, and in some cases representing a destructive collectivity within the inclusive social system. When these structures are observed in extreme, their form is apparent to the observer. However, in viewing these social structures on a continuum, those formations which tend to be neither quite a cohesive integrated group nor a disturbed malfunctioning mob or crowd are often distorted by observers in one or the other direction.

A central thesis of this paper is that mid-way on the group-mob continuum are collectivities which are neither groups nor mobs. These are structures prevalent enough in a social system to command attention in their own right as constructs for sociological analysis. Near-groups are characterized by some of the following factors: (1) diffuse role definition, (2) limited cohesion, (3) impermanence, (4) minimal consensus of norms, (5) shifting membership, (6) disturbed leadership, and (7) limited definition of membership expectations. These factors characterize the near-group's "normal" structure.

True groups may manifest near-group structure under stress, in transition, or when temporarily disorganized; however, at these times they are moving toward or away from their normative, permanent structure. The near-group manifests its homeostasis in accord with the factors indicated. It never fully becomes a *group* or a *mob*.

THE GANG AS A NEAR-GROUP PATTERN

Some recent sociological theory and discourse on gangs suffers from distortions of gang structure to fit a group rather than a near-group conception. Most gang theorizing begins with an automatic assumption that gangs are defined sociological groups. Many of these misconceived theories about gangs in sociological treatises are derived from the popular and traditional image of gangs held by the general public as reported in the press, rather than as based upon empirical scientific investigation. The following case material reveals the disparities between popular reports of gang war behavior and their organization as revealed by more systematic study.

The official report of a gang fight, which made headlines in New York papers as the biggest in the city's history, detailed a gang war between six gangs over a territorial dispute.* The police, social workers, the press, and the public accepted a defined version of groups meeting in battle over territory. Research into this gang war incident, utilizing a near-group concept of gangs, indicates another picture of the situation.

N. Y. DAILY NEWS

NIP 200—PUNK FIGHT NEAR COLUMBIA CAMPUS
by Grover Ryder and Jack Smee

A flying squad of 25 cops, alerted by a civilian's tip, broke up the makings of one

* New York Newspaper Headlines—June 11, 1955.

of the biggest gang rumbles in the city's turbulent teen history last night at the edge of Columbia University campus on Morningside Heights.

N. Y. HERALD TRIBUNE

POLICE SEIZE 38, AVERT GANG BATTLE—RIVERSIDE PARK RULE WAS GOAL

Police broke up what they said might have been "a very serious" battle between two juvenile factions last night as they intercepted thirty-eight youths.

N. Y. TIMES

GANG WAR OVER PARK BROKEN BY POLICE

The West Side police broke up an impending gang fight near Columbia University last night as 200 teen-agers were massing for battle over exclusive rights to the use of Riverside Park.

N. Y. JOURNAL-AMERICAN

6-GANG BATTLE FOR PARK AVERTED NEAR GRANT'S TOMB COPS PATROL TROUBLE SPOT

Police reinforcements today patrolled Morningside Heights to prevent a teen-aged gang war for "control" of Riverside Park.

WORLD-TELEGRAM AND SUN

HOODLUM WAR AVERTED AS COPS ACT FAST
38 to 200 Seized near Columbia
by Richard Graf

Fast police action averted what threatened to be one of the biggest street gang fights in the city's history as some 200 hoodlums massed last night on the upper West Side to battle over "exclusive rights" to Riverside Park.

Depth interviews with 40 gang boys, most of whom had been arrested at the scene of the gang fight, revealed a variety of reasons for attendance at the battle. There were also varied perceptions of the event and the gangs involved reported simply in the press

as "gangs battling over territory." Some of the following recurring themes were revealed in the gang boys' responses.

Estimates of number of gang boys present varied from 80 to 5,000.

Gang boys interviewed explained their presence at the "battle" as follows:

I didn't have anything to do that night and wanted to see what was going to happen.

Those guys called me a Spic and I was going to get even. [He made this comment even though the "rival" gangs were mostly Puerto Ricans.]

They always picked on us. [The "they" is usually a vague reference.]

I always like a fight; it keeps up my rep.

My father threw me out of the house; I wanted to get somebody and heard about the fight.

The youth who was responsible for "calling on" the gang war—the reputed Balkan Gang leader—presented this version of the event:

That night I was out walkin' my dog about 7:30. Then I saw all these guys coming from different directions. I couldn't figure out what was happening. Then I saw some of the guys I know and I remembered we had called it on for that night.

I never really figured the Politicians [a supposed "brother Gang" he had called] would show.

Another boy added another dimension to "gang war organization":

How did we get our name? Well, when we were in the police station, the cops kept askin' us who we were. Jay was studying history in school—so he said how about The Balkans. Let's call ourselves Balkans. So we told the cops—we're the Balkans—and that was it.

Extensive data revealed this was not a case of two organized groups meeting in battle. The press, public, police, social workers, and others projected group conceptions onto a near-group activity. Most of the youths at the scene of the gang war were, in fact, participating in a kind of mob action. Most had no real concept of belonging to any gang or group; however, they were interested in a situation which might be exciting and possibly a channel for expressing some of their aggressions and hostilities. Although it was not necessarily a defined war, the possibilities of a stabbing or even a killing were high —with a few hundred disturbed and fearful youths milling around in the undefined situation. The gang war was not a social situation of two structured teen-aged armies meeting on a battlefield to act out a defined situation; it was a case of two near-groups in action.

Another boy's participation in this gang war further reveals its structure. The evening of the fight he had nothing to do, heard about this event, and decided that he would wander up to see what was going to happen. On his way to the scene of the rumored gang fight he thought it might be a good idea to invite a few friends "just to be on the safe side." This swelled the final number of youths arriving at the scene of the gang fight, since other boys did the same. He denied (and I had no reason to disbelieve him) belonging to either of the gangs, and the same applied to his friends. He was arrested at the scene of "battle" for disorderly conduct and weapon-carrying.

I asked him why he had carried a knife and a zip gun on his person when he went to the gang fight if he did not belong to either of the reputed gangs and intended to be merely a "peaceful observer." His response: "Man, I'm not going to a rumble without packin'." The boy took along weapons for self-defense in the event he was attacked. The possibilities of his being attacked in an hysterical situation involving hundreds of youths who had no clear idea of what they were doing at the scene of a gang fight was, of course, great. Therefore, he was correct (within his social framework) in taking along a weapon for self-protection.

These characteristic responses to the situation when multiplied by the numbers of others present characterizes the problem. What may be a confused situation involving many aggressive youths (belonging to near-groups) is often defined as a case of two highly mechanized and organized gang groups battling each other with definition to their activities.

In another "gang war case" which made headlines, a psychotic youth acted out his syndrome by stabbing another youth. When arrested and questioned about committing the offense, the youth stated that he was a member of a gang carrying out retaliation against another gang which was out to get him. He attributed his assault to gang affiliation.

The psychotic youth used the malleable near-group, the gang, *as his psychotic* syndrome. Napoleon, God, Christ, and other psychotic syndromes, so popular over the years, may have been replaced on city streets by gang membership. Not only is it a convenient syndrome, but some disturbed youths find their behavior as rational, accepted, and even aggrandized by many representatives of society. Officials such as police officers and social workers, in their interpretation of the incident, often amplify this individual behavior by a youth into a group gang war condition because it is a seemingly more logical explanation of a senseless act.

In the case of the Balkans, the societal response of viewing them as a group rather than a near-group solidified their structure. After the incident, as one leader stated it, "lots more kids wanted to join."

Another gang war event further reveals the near-group structure of the gang. On the night of July 30, 1957, a polio victim named Michael Farmer was beaten and stabbed to death by a gang varyingly known as the Egyptian Kings and the Dragons. The boys who participated in this homicide came from the upper West Side of Manhattan. I had contact with many of these boys prior to the event and was known to others through the community program I directed. Because of this prior relationship the boys cooperated and responded openly when I interviewed them in the institutions where they were being held in custody.*

Responses to my interviews indicated the near-group nature of the gang. Some of the pertinent responses which reveal this characteristic of the Egyptian King gang structure are somewhat demonstrated by the following comments made by five of the participants in the killing. (These are representative comments selected from over ten hours of recorded interviews.)

I was walking uptown with a couple of friends and we ran into Magician [one of the Egyptian King gang leaders] and them there. They asked us if we wanted to go to a fight, and we said yes. When he asked me if I wanted to go to a fight, I couldn't say no. I mean, I could say no, but for old time's sake, I said yes.

Everyone was pushin' and I pulled out my knife. I saw this face—I never seen it before, so I stabbed it.

He was laying on the ground lookin' up at us. Everyone was kicking, punching, stabbing. I kicked him on the jaw

or someplace; then I kicked him in the stomach. That was the least I could do was kick 'im.

They have guys watching you and if you don't stab or hit somebody, they get you later. I hit him over the head with a bat. [Gang youths are unable to articulate specific individuals of the vague "they" who watch over them.]

I don't know how many guys are in the gang. They tell me maybe a hundred or a thousand. I don't know them all. [Each boy interviewed had a different image of the gang.]

These comments and others revealed the gang youths' somewhat different perceptions and rationale of gang war activity. There is a limited consensus of participants as to the nature of gang war situations because the gang structure—the collectivity which defines gang war behavior—is amorphous, diffuse, and malleable.

Despite the fact of gang phenomena taking a diffuse form, theoreticians, social workers, the police, the press, and the public autistically distort gangs and gang behavior toward a gestalt of clarity. The rigid frame of perceiving gangs as groups should shift to the fact of gangs as near-groups. This basic redefinition is necessary if progress is to be made in sociological diagnosis as a foundation for delinquent gang prevention and correction.

THE DETACHED GANG WORKER

The detached-worker approach to dealing with gangs on the action level is increasingly employed in large cities and urban areas throughout the country. Simply stated, a professional, usually a social worker, contacts a gang in their milieu on the street corner and attempts to redirect their delinquent patterns into constructive behavior.

Because of the absence of an ade-

---

* The research and interviewing at this time was combined with my role as consultant to the Columbia Broadcasting System. I assisted in the production of a gang war documentary narrated by Edward R. Murrow, entitled "Who Killed Michael Farmer?" The documentary tells the story of the killing through the actual voices of the boys who committed the act.

quate perceptual framework, such as the near-group concept, detached gang workers deal with gang collectivities as if they were organized like other groups and social organizations. The following principle stated in a New York City Youth Board manual on the detached gang worker approach reveals this point of view:

Participation in a street gang or club, like participation in any natural group, is a part of the growing-up process of adolescence. Such primary group associations possess potentialities for positive growth and development. Through such a group, the individual can gain security and develop positive ways of living with other individuals. Within the structure of his group the individual can develop such characteristics as loyalty, leadership, and community responsibility (3, p. 107).

This basic misconception not only produces inaccurate reports and theories about gang structure but causes ineffectual work with gangs on the action level. This problem of projecting group structure onto gangs may be further illuminated by a cursory examination of detached gang-worker projects.

Approaching the gang as a group, when it is not, tends to project onto it a structure which formerly did not exist. The gang worker's usual set of notions about gangs as groups includes some of the following distortions: (1) the gang has a measurable number of members, (2) membership is defined, (3) the role of members is specified, (4) there is a consensus of understood gang norms among gang members, and (5) gang leadership is clear and entails a flow of authority and direction of action.

These expectations often result in a group-fulfilling prophecy. A group may form as a consequence of the gang worker's view. In one case a gang worker approached two reputed gang leaders and told them he would have a bus to take their gang on a trip to the country. This gang had limited organization; however, by travel-time there were 32 gang members ready to go on the trip. The near-group became more organized as a result of the gang worker's misconception.

This gang from a near-group point of view was in reality comprised of a few disturbed youths with rich delusional systems who had need to view themselves as leaders controlling hordes of other gang boys in their fantasy. Other youths reinforce this ill-defined collectivity for a variety of personal reasons and needs. The gang, in fact, had a shifting membership, no clarity as to what membership entailed, and individualized member images of gang size and function.

The detached worker, as an agent of the formal social system, may thus move in on a gang and give a formerly amorphous collectivity structure and purpose through the projection of group structure onto a near-group.

NEAR-GROUP STRUCTURE

Research into the structure of 30 groups revealed three characteristic levels of membership organization. In the center of the gang, on the first level, are the most psychologically disturbed members—the leaders. It is these youths who require and need the gang most of all. This core of disturbed youths provides the gang's most cohesive force. In a gang of some 30 boys there may be five or six who are central or core members because they desperately need the gang in order to deal with their personal problems of inadequacy. These are youths always working to keep the gang together and in action, always drafting, plotting, and talking gang warfare. They are the center of the near-group activity.

At a second level of near-group organization in the gang, we have youths who claim affiliation to the gang but only participate in it according to their emotional needs at given times. For example, one of the Egyptian Kings reported that if his father had not given him a "bad time" and kicked him out of the house the night of the homicide, he would not have gone to the corner and become involved in the Michael Farmer killing. This second-level gang member's participation in the gang killing was a function of his disturbance on that particular evening. This temporal gang need is a usual occurrence.

At a third level of gang participation, we have peripheral members who will join in with gang activity on occasion, although they seldom identify themselves as members of the gang at times. This type of gang member is illustrated by the youth who went along with the Egyptian Kings on the night of the Farmer killing, as he put it, "for old time's sake." He just happened to be around on that particular evening and went along due to a situational condition. He never really "belonged" to the gang nor was he defined by himself or others as a gang member.

The size of gangs is determined in great measure by the emotional needs of its members at any given point. It is not a measure of actual and live membership. Many of the members exist only on the thought level. In the gang, if the boys feel particularly hemmed in (for paranoid reasons), they will expand the number of their near-group. On the other hand, at other times when they feel secure, the gang's size is reduced to include only those youths known on a face-to-face basis. The research revealed that, unlike an actual group, no member of a near-group can accurately determine the number of its membership at a particular point in time.

For example, most any university department member will tell you the number of other individuals who comprise the faculty of their department. It is apparent that if there are eight members in a department of psychology, each member will know each other member, his role, and the total number of members of the department. In contrast, in examining the size of gangs or near-group participation, the size increases in almost direct relationship to the lack of membership clarity. That is, the second- and third-level members are modified numerically with greater ease than the central members. Third-level members are distorted at times to an almost infinite number.

In one interview, a gang leader distorted the size and affiliations of the gang as his emotional state shifted. In an hour interview, the size of his gang varied from 100 members to 4,000, from five brother gangs or alliances to 60, from about ten square blocks of territorial control to include jurisdiction over the five boroughs of New York City, New Jersey, and part of Philadelphia.

Another characteristic of the gang is its lack of role definition. Gang boys exhibit considerable difficulty and contradiction in their roles in the gang. They may say that the gang is organized for protection and that one role of a gang is to fight. How, when, whom, and for what reason he is to fight are seldom clear. The right duties and obligations associated with the gang member's role in the gang vary from gang boy to gang boy.

One gang boy may define himself as a protector of the younger boys in the neighborhood. Another defines his role in the gang as "We are going to get all those guys who call us Spics." Still other gang boys define their participation in the gang as involuntarily forced upon them, through their being "drafted." Moreover, few gang members maintain a consistent function or role within the gang organization.

Definition of membership is vague and indefinite. A youth will say he belongs one day and will quit the next without necessarily telling any other gang member. I would ask one gang boy who came into my office daily whether he was a Balkan. This was comparable to asking him, "How do you feel today?"

Because of limited social ability to assume rights, duties, and obligations in constructive solidified groups, the gang boy attaches himself to a structure which requires limited social ability and can itself be modified to fit his monetary needs. This malleability factor is characteristic of the near-group membership. As roles are building blocks of a group, diffuse role definitions fit in adequately to the near-group which itself has diverse and diffuse objectives and goals. The near-group, unlike a true group, has norms, roles, functions, cohesion, size, and goals which are shaped by the emotional needs of its members.

GANG LEADERSHIP CHARACTERISTICS

Another aspect of near-groups is the factor of self-appointed leadership, usually of a dictatorial, authoritarian type. In interviewing hundreds of gang members, one finds that many of them give themselves some role of leadership. For example, in the Egyptian Kings, approximately five boys defined themselves as "war counselors." It is equally apparent that, except on specific occasions, no one will argue with this self-defined role. Consequently, leadership in the gang may be assumed by practically any member of the gang if he so determines and emotionally needs the power of being a leader at the time. It is not necessary to have his leadership role ratified by his constituents.

Another aspect of leadership in the gang is the procedure of "drafting" or enlisting new members. In many instances, this pattern of coercion to get another youth to join or belong to the gang becomes an end in itself, rather than a means to an end. In short, the process of inducing, coercing, and threatening violence upon another youth, under the guise of getting him to join, is an important gang leader activity. The gang boy is not truly concerned with acquiring another gang member, since the meaning of membership is vague at best; however, acting the power role of a leader forcing another youth to do something against his will becomes meaningful to the "drafter."

GANG FUNCTIONS

In most groups some function is performed or believed to be performed. The function which it performs may be a constructive one, as in an industrial organization, a P.T.A. group, or a political party. On the other hand, it may be a socially destructive group, such as a drug syndicate, a group of bookies, or a subversive political party. There is usually a consensus of objectives and goals shared by the membership, and their behavior tends to be essentially organized group action.

The structure of a near-group is such that not only do its functions vary greatly and shift considerably from time to time, but its primary function is unclear. The gang may on one occasion be organized to protect the neighborhood; on another occasion, to take over a particular territory; and on still another, it may be organized in response to or for the purpose of racial discrimination.

The function of near-groups, moreover, is not one which is clearly understood, known, and communicated among all of its members. There is no consensus in this near-group of goals, objectives, or functions of the collectivity—much near-group behavior is individualistic and flows from emotional disturbance.

A prime function of the gang is to

provide a channel to act out hostility and aggression to satisfy the continuing and momentary emotional needs of its members. The gang is a convenient and malleable structure quickly adaptable to the needs of emotionally disturbed youths, who are unable to fulfill the responsibility and demands required for participation in constructive groups. A boy belongs to the gang because he lacks the social ability to relate to others and to assume responsibility for the relationship, not because the gang gives him a "feeling of belonging."

Because of the gang youth's limited "social ability," he constructs a social organization which enables him to relate and to function at his limited level of performance. In this structure norms are adjusted so that the gang youth can function and achieve despite his limited ability to relate to others.

An example of this is the function of violence in the near-group of the gang. Violence in the gang is highly valued as a means for the achievement of reputation or "rep." This inversion of societal norms is a means for quick upward social mobility in the gang. He can acquire and maintain a position in the gang through establishing a violent reputation.

The following comments by members of the Egyptian Kings illustrate this point:

If I would of got the knife, I would have stabbed him. That would have gave me more of a build-up. People would have respected me for what I've done and things like that. They would say, "There goes a cold killer."

It makes you feel like a big shot. You know some guys think they're big shots and all that. They think, you know, they got the power to do everything they feel like doing.

They say, like, "I wanna stab a guy," and the other guy says, "Oh, I wouldn't dare to do that." You know, he thinks I'm acting like a big shot. That's the way he feels. He probably thinks in his mind, "Oh, he probably won't do that." Then, when we go to a fight, you know, he finds out what I do.

Momentarily, I started to thinking about it inside: den I have my mind made up I'm not going to be in no gang. Then I go on inside. Something comes up den here come all my friends coming to me. Like I said before, I'm intelligent and so forth. They be coming to me—then they talk to me about what they gonna do. Like, "Man, we'll go out here and kill this guy." I say, "Yeah." They kept on talkin' and talkin.' I said, "Man, I just gotta go with you." Myself, I don't want to go, but when they start talkin' about what they gonna do, I say, "So, he isn't gonna take over my rep. I ain't gonna let him be known more than me." And I go ahead just for selfishness.

The near-group of the gang, with its diffuse and malleable structure, can function as a convenient vehicle for the acting out of varied individual needs and problems. For the gang leader it can be a super-powered organization through which (in his phantasy) he dominates and controls "divisions" of thousands of members. For gang members, unable to achieve in more demanding social organizations, swift and sudden violence is a means for quick upward social mobility and the achievement of a reputation. For less disturbed youths, the gang may function as a convenient temporary escape from the dull and rigid requirements of a difficult and demanding society. These are only some of the functions the near-group of the gang performs for its membership.

NEAR-GROUP THEORY AND SOCIAL PROBLEMS

The concept of the near-group may be of importance in the analysis of other collectivities which reflect and produce social problems. The analysis of other social structures may reveal similar distortions of their organization. To operate on an assumption of individuals in interaction with each other, around some function, with some shared mutual expectation, in a particular normative system as always being a group formation is to project a degree of distortion onto certain types of collectivities. Groups are social structures at one end of a continuum; mobs are social structures at another end; and at the center are near-groups which have some of the characteristics of both, and yet are characterized by factors not found fully in either.

In summary, these factors may include the following:

1. Individualized role definition to fit momentary needs.

2. Diffuse and differential definitions of membership.

3. Emotion-motivated behavior.

4. A decrease of cohesiveness as one moves from the center of the collectivity to the periphery.

5. Limited responsibility and sociability required for membership and belonging.

6. Self-appointed and disturbed leadership.

7. A limited consensus among participants of the collectivities' functions or goals.

8. A shifting and personalized stratification system.

9. Shifting membership.

10. The inclusion in size of phantasy membership.

11. Limited consensus of normative expectations.

12. Norms in conflict with the inclusive social system's prescriptions.

Although the gang was the primary type of near-group appraised in this analysis, there are perhaps other collectivities whose structure is distorted by autistic observers. Their organization might become clearer if subjected to this conceptual scheme. Specifically, in the area of criminal behavior, these might very well include adult gangs varyingly called the "Mafia," the "National Crime Syndicate," and so-called International Crime Cartels. There are indications that these social organizations are comparable in organization to the delinquent gang. They might fit the near-group category if closely analyzed in this context, rather than aggrandized and distorted by mass media and even Senate Committees.

Other more institutionalized collectivities might fit the near-group pattern. As a possible example, "the family in transition" may not be in transition at all. The family, as a social institution, may be suffering from near-groupism. Moreover, such standardized escape hatches as alcoholism, psychoses, and addictions may be too prosaic for the sophisticated intellectual to utilize in escape from himself. For him, the creation and perpetuation of near-groups requiring limited responsibility and personal commitment may be a more attractive contemporary form for expressing social and personal pathology. The measure of organization or disorganization of an inclusive social system may possibly be assessed by the prevalence of near-group collectivities in its midst. The delinquent gang may be only one type of near-group in American society.

References

1. Cohen, Albert K., *Delinquent Boys* (Glencoe: The Free Press, 1955).
2. Bloch, Herbert, and Arthur Niederhoffer, *The Gang* (New York: The Philosophical Library, 1958).
3. Furman, Slyvan S., *Reaching the Unreached* (New York: Youth Board, 1952).

23.

Field Observations of Middle Class "Gangs"

Howard L. Myerhoff and Barbara G. Myerhoff

The sociological literature about gangs contains at least two sharply conflicting descriptions of the extent of gang structure and the nature of their values. In the most prevalent view, the gang is seen as a kind of primary group, highly structured, relatively permanent and autonomous, possessing a well-developed delinquent subculture which is transmitted to new members. The gang is interpreted as meeting strongly felt needs of its members and as providing a collectively derived solution to common problems of adjustment. Different writers who hold this view have stressed different problems, but nearly all have agreed that one of the most important functions of the gang is to establish close bonds of loyalty and solidarity between members of a tightly knit peer group.

Cohen[1] has identified the primary needs met by the gang as those of resolving status frustration for lower class boys, and providing an expression of masculine identification for middle class boys. Parsons[2] has also emphasized the achievement of sexual identity as a problem dealt with by delinquent behavior. Cloward and Ohlin,[3] following Merton's conception, have specified the discrepancy between aspirations toward success goals and opportunities for achieving them as the problem giving rise to gang behavior. Kvaraceus and Miller[4] have stressed the inherent

* The observations reported in this paper were carried out as part of a Youth Studies Center developmental project, which ultimately led to an action-research program concerned with the treatment of delinquent gangs. Both the developmental project and the action-research program, now in process, received support from the Ford Foundation. The authors would like to thank A. W. McEachern of the Youth Studies Center, University of Southern California, for his generous and valuable assistance, criticism, and encouragement. A shorter version of this paper was read at the annual meeting of the Pacific Sociological Association in Sacramento, April 1962.

[1] Albert K. Cohen, *Delinquent Boys: The Culture of the Gang* (Glencoe: Free Press, 1955).

[2] Talcott Parsons, "Certain Primary Sources and Patterns of Aggression in the Social Structure of the Western World," reprinted in Mullahy (Ed.), *A Study of Interpersonal Relations* (New York: Grove Press, Evergreen Edition, 1949).

[3] Richard A. Cloward and Lloyd E. Ohlin, *Delinquency and Opportunity: A Theory of Delinquent Gangs* (Glencoe: Free Press, 1961).

[4] William C. Kvaraceus and Walter B. Miller, *Delinquent Behavior: Culture and the Individual* (Washington, D.C.: National Education Association, 1959).

SOURCE. Howard L. Myerhoff and Barbara G. Myerhoff, "Field Observations of Middle Class 'Gangs,'" from *Social Forces*, Volume 42, March 1964 pp. 328–336. Reprinted with the permission of the University of North Carolina Press.

conflict between lower and middle class values and the delinquent's predisposition to the former in explaining gang behavior. Eisenstadt[5] and Bloch and Niederhoffer[6] have pointed to the gang as a collective response to the adolescent's striving toward the attainment of adulthood and the frustrations attendant on the transition from one age status to another. These authors identify different components of the gang subculture according to their interpretation of its function, but implicit or explicit in all these positions is the view of the gang as an integrated and relatively cohesive group.

A strikingly different interpretation of the structure of gangs describes them as informal, short lived, secondary groups without a clear-cut, stable delinquent structure. Lewis Yablonsky[7] has suggested a conceptualization of the gang as a "near-group," specifying the following definitive characteristics: diffuse role definitions, limited cohesion, impermanence, minimal consensus on norms, shifting membership, emotionally disturbed leaders, and limited definition of membership expectations. On a continuum of the extent of social organization, Yablonsky locates the gang midway between the mob at one end and the group at the other. The gang is seen as in a state of equilibrium, moving sometimes closer to one end of the continuum and sometimes the other, but never actually becoming completely disorganized like a mob or completely organized like a group. He contends that detached worker programs, by treating the gang as a true group, may actually make it one. When a detached

worker acknowledges a gang's leaders, recognizes its territory, membership, name, and purpose, he crystallizes its organization, lending it a structure which it did not previously have. This Yablonsky calls the "group-fulfilling prophecy."

The gangs he has observed are, in actuality, quite different from groups. They are "near-groups" which have a diffuse and malleable structure that enables them to meet the varied and individual needs of the members. For many gang members who are unable to meet the demands and responsibilities of more structured social organizations, it is the gang's very lack of organization and absence of expectations which constitute its primary sources of satisfaction. Youths affiliate with a gang not for a feeling of belonging and solidarity but because it is an organization within which they can relate to others in spite of their limited social abilities. The flexibility of gang organization means that it can meet diverse, momentary needs of the members who, accordingly, participate in it with varying intensity. Yablonsky suggests that in a gang there are a few core members, surrounded by a large number of peripheral members to whom the gang is much less important and who are more loosely attached to it.

James F. Short, Jr. objects to Yablonsky's description of the gang as a near-group on the grounds that he has overstated the case,[8] but agrees, never-

<hr>

[5] S. N. Eisenstadt, *From Generation to Generation: Age Groups and Social Structure* (Glencoe: Free Press, 1956).

[6] Herbert A. Bloch and Arthur Niederhoffer, *The Gang: A Study of Adolescent Behavior* (New York: Philosophical Library, 1958).

[7] Lewis Yablonsky, "The Delinquent Gang as a Near-Group," *Social Problems*, Vol. 7 (Fall 1959), pp. 108–117.

[8] In a recent article Pfautz raised the question of whether Yablonsky's "near-group" concept is necessary. He suggests that Yablonsky's findings could be more productively recast into the theoretical traditions of collective behavior in general and social movements in particular. Certainly, Pfautz's point that this would widen the theoretical relevance of Yablonsky's findings is well-taken. There are two reasons for the authors' preference for the near-group concept rather than a collective behavior orientation: first, an immediate concern with indicating the point by point similarity between these observations and

theless, that gangs do not have "the stability of membership, the tightly knit organization and rigid hierarchical structure which is sometimes attributed to them."[9] Most of the groups he has observed have the kind of shifting membership which Yablonsky described.

The supervisor of a large, long-lived detached worker program in Los Angeles with many years of gang experience there and in Harlem has given a description much like that of Yablonsky.[10] He observed that delinquent gangs seldom act as a corporate group and that most of their anti-social activities are committed in groups of two's or three's, or by a single person. He found communication between members to be meager and sporadic, reflecting the same limitations in social abilities that Yablonsky identified. In fact, one of the goals of his detached worker program is the structuring of gangs into social groups, encouraging cooperation and communication between members and a gradual assumption of social responsibilities. When successful, a detached worker is able to form a gang into a club which elects officers, collects dues, arranges activities, and eventually establishes non-delinquent norms and role expectations. Thus by substituting the satisfactions of membership in an organized social group for delinquent

activities, the program provides an aspect of socialization which gang members have not previously experienced. The program is able, in this way, to prepare gang members to meet the requirements and responsibilities of conventional, adult social life. The technique is apparently the self-conscious application of what Yablonsky has called "the group-fulfilling prophecy," and seems to be quite a successful one.

The field observations presented here are based on the experiences of a participant-observer who spent two weeks among several groups of deviant and non-deviant middle class youths in a suburb of Los Angeles. These observations are particularly pertinent to the prevailing conflicting interpretations of the extent of gang structure. The middle class youngsters described here were located through lists of "hangouts" provided by local police, school authorities, and probation officers. The observer "hung around" these places and when asked who he was, which was seldom, explained that he was a writer doing a series of articles on teenagers. The youngsters talked freely in front of and to the observer, and after a short time included him in many of their activities, such as house and beach parties, drag races, car club meetings, bull sessions, and bowling. Altogether, about eighty youngsters ranging in age between fifteen and eighteen were observed. All were Caucasian, most in high school, Protestant, and in appearance and manner readily distinguishable from the lower class boys and girls who occasionally mixed with them.

Impressions, activities, and conversations were recorded by the observer in a daily journal and roughly classified into the following categories: values and peer interactions, deviant activities, and group organization.[11] It should be

those reported by Yablonsky, regardless of the conceptual framework he uses in describing them, and second, the authors' feeling that in view of the fragmented and discontinuous state of the literature on the subject, it is at present more important to compare and relate studies of adolescent collective deviant activities to one another than to more general sociological issues and concepts. Harold W. Pfautz, "Near-Group Theory and Collective Behavior: A Critical Reformulation," *Social Problems*, Vol. 9 (Fall 1961), pp. 167–174.

[9] James F. Short, Jr., "Street Corner Groups and Patterns of Delinquency," A Progress Report from National Institute of Mental Health Research Grant, M-3301 (Chicago, March 1961), p. 20.

[10] Alva Collier, personal communication (Los Angeles, 1961).

[11] These field observations precisely conform to what Zelditch has called Type I information. This consists of incidents

kept in mind that these comments are observations, not findings. Many authors have lamented the dearth of speculation about as well as empirical observations of gangs, in both the middle and lower classes. Cohen and Short recently said about middle class delinquent subcultures: "The saddest commentary, however, is that we are faced with a poverty of speculation, without which there can be no meaningful research, without which, in turn, there can be no conclusions that are more than speculation."[12] These observations and comments lead to some of the speculation which must precede meaningful empirical research, and their greatest value may prove to be heuristic.

VALUES AND PEER INTERACTIONS

The youngsters observed, like most groups of teenagers, were rather uniform in dress and demeanor. Their self-possession and poise, along with elaborate grooming and expensive, well-tended clothes combined to give an impression of urbanity and sophistication beyond what would normally be expected of this age group. For most events, the girls wore tight capris, blouses or cashmere sweaters, silver fingernail and toenail polish, towering intricate coiffeurs, brush-applied iridescent lipstick, and heavy eye make-up. The boys, like the girls, were uniformly clean, and like them preferred their pants as tight as possible; levis were rarely seen. Usually an Ivy League shirt was worn outside the pants and over

this a nylon windbreaker. At beaches both boys and girls wore bikinis, and apparently no one without a deep and even tan ever dared appear. The overall impression fostered was one of careful, elegant casualness sustained in manner as well as appearance. The complete absence of the social and physical awkwardness usually associated with adolescence was indeed striking.

The content of conversation among these groups did not differ appreciably from what one would expect to find among most teenagers; it concerned clothes, dates, sex, school classes and activities, bridge, sports, and so forth. But no subject dominated the conversation as much as the car, which seemed an object of undying, one might say morbid, fascination. The majority of girls and boys owned their own cars and virtually all had access to a car, usually a late model American or foreign sports car. "Custom jobs" were not rare and cars were often "shaved," "chopped," "channeled," and "pinstriped." All were scrupulously clean and highly polished. The argot concerning the car was as elaborate and subtle as one might expect in view of its importance; such matters as "dual quads," "turning seven grand," "slicks," "3:7 trans ratio" were frequently discussed with great intensity. Driving skill and mechanical expertise were prized far above mere ownership of a desirable car.

The car, in fact, permeated every aspect of these youngsters' social life. The size of groups which gathered was usually limited by the number a single car could hold, and when several cars congregated, at drive-ins for example, youngsters demonstrated a distinct unwillingness to leave the car. Radios in cars were never off and all activities took place against a background of popular music. The car also affected

and histories, and treats as data the meanings assigned to and explanations given for activities as well as the behavior itself. Morris Zelditch, Jr., "Some Methodological Problems of Field Studies," *American Journal of Sociology*, Vol. 67 (March 1962), pp. 566–576.

[12] Albert K. Cohen and James F. Short, Jr., "Research in Delinquent Subcultures," *Journal of Social Issues*, Vol. 14, No. 3 (1958), p. 34.

the places frequented, with drive-in movies and restaurants preferred. After school and on weekends, many of these youngsters could be seen slowly cruising in their cars, up and down the neighborhood streets, greeting acquaintances, chatting, taking friends for short rides, all with an air of easy sociability. These cruises in manner and purpose were reminiscent of the Spanish late afternoon *Paseo,* in which young people stroll casually up and down streets closed off for that purpose. The cars were the location for nearly all social events engaged in by these youngsters. They were the site of bull sessions, drinking bouts, and necking parties. In all, the car provided a mobile parlor, clubhouse, dining room, and bedroom; it was at once the setting and symbol of much of adolescent deviant and non-deviant sociability and sexuality.

Several writers have emphasized the dominant role of the car in patterns of middle class deviance. Wattenberg and Balistrieri[13] found auto theft to be characteristic of "favored groups," older white boys who had better relations with peers and came from more desirable neighborhoods than did boys charged with other types of offenses. T. C. N. Gibbens[14] studied adolescent car thieves in London and also found them to be a "favored group," not because they lived in better neighborhoods but because they came from homes which were intact and affectionate. All these findings and impressions may be interpreted as supporting the contention of Parsons[15] and Cohen[16]

that the primary middle class problem to which delinquency is a response is the establishment of masculine identity. Indeed, the sexual significance of the car has been widely recognized. Gibbens comments that: "In the simplest cases joy-riding is of the common 'proving' type, in which an overprotected lad from a 'good' home commits an offense to prove his masculinity. . . . The daring act represents a bid for independence, and the car provides a feeling of power in which he feels so lacking. . . ."[17] Certainly, this view is corroborated by the observations of middle class youths offered here, among whom the car, if not a sufficient cause of masculinity, is at least a necessary condition for it.

In view of the importance of the car, it was not surprising to find that the only formal social organizations to which many of these youngsters belonged were car clubs, whose membership often transcended the class and age affiliations typical of the more informal gatherings. These clubs usually consist of about fifteen members and are devoted to the building and legal and illegal racing of cars. In order to be admitted, youngsters' cars must undergo rigorous police safety inspections and members may be expelled or excluded for too many traffic tickets. In marked contrast to the informal groups, these clubs are highly structured. Meetings are regular and frequent, membership is stable, leaders are elected for specified terms, and the clubs have names, plaques, and jackets. The meetings are conducted strictly according to Roberts' Rules of Order, fines are levied for infractions of rules, dues are collected, and events are planned in detail and in advance. A well-developed pattern of mutual aid and extensive cooperation has been established, and it is not

[13] William W. Wattenberg and James Balistrieri, "Automobile Theft: A 'Favored Group' Delinquency," *American Journal of Sociology,* Vol. 57 (May 1952), pp. 575–579.

[14] T. C. N. Gibbens, "Car Thieves," *British Journal of Delinquency,* 7–9 (1957–1959), pp. 257–265.

[15] Parsons, *op. cit.*

[16] Cohen, *op. cit.*

[17] Gibbens, *op. cit.,* p. 262.

unusual for members to pool money, skills, and time to build a car which is entered in races and rallies by the entire group. It is obviously no accident that the only object around which spontaneous, unsupervised yet structured groups form is the car.

DEVIANT ACTIVITIES

The deviant behavior of the groups observed varied greatly in seriousness. Some of their activities may be considered deviant only because technically illegal, such as curfew violation and beer drinking, while more serious infractions such as theft and narcotics are less common. The more serious deviant activities seemed to involve the least number of people at one time; youngsters were alone or with a friend or two on these occasions. The less serious infractions were not usually the purpose of a gathering but were rather incidental to another activity. These included spontaneous drag racing, drinking, and much sexual activity.

Of the more serious violations, theft was certainly the most common. Many boys spoke of frequent and regular stealing, often from employers. Ready access rather than need or desire seemed to determine the choice of stolen objects. These items were seldom traded or converted into cash. Great pride was evidenced in the cleverness with which the thefts were executed and a good performance seemed more important than the acquisition of goods. Several boys boasted about never having been caught although they had been engaging in this activity for years. The stolen goods were by no means small, inexpensive, or easily portable, but included such items as tires, car radios, phonographs, tape recorders, and television sets. Great care was taken in order to ensure that stolen goods were not missed. Thefts were timed so as to coincide with events such as inventories, and the filling of orders.

It is not possible on the basis of these observations to estimate the frequency of these thefts, but one can say with certainty that they were by no means uncommon. This phenomenon appears to be very similar to "white collar crime" and as such raises questions as to the generalizability of theories of delinquency causation based solely on socio-economic variables. As Wattenberg and Balistrieri have pointed out: "The point of impact of the concept of [white collar crime] lies in its assumption that the form of anti-social or illegal conduct rather than its frequency varies from . . . class to class in our society."[18] It may well be that the "white collar delinquent" engages in as many anti-social activities as do lower class youngsters, but a combination of factors, particularly the form of delinquency, interact to prevent these activities from coming to the attention of the authorities, or if apprehended, prevent the middle class youngsters from being officially handled and recorded. Indeed, there is already much evidence to suggest this is the case.[19]

The same discretion, judgment, and self-possession which characterized thefts was observed in the homosexual, and to a lesser degree, the heterosexual gatherings. These events were held in private homes and occasionally included slightly older boys from nearby colleges. They were not events which were likely to attract the attention of police or even parents. The homosexual youngsters often met one another at

[18] Wattenberg and Balistrieri, op. cit., p. 575.
[19] A. L. Porterfield, "Delinquency and Its Outcome in Court and College," American Journal of Sociology, Vol. 48 (1943), pp. 199–208; Ivan F. Nye and James F. Short, Jr., "Scaling Delinquent Behavior," American Sociological Review, Vol. 22 (1957), pp. 326–331.

small cabarets, coffee houses, and bars in which few lower class teenagers or adults were to be seen. They also met in several private clubs whose members were primarily upper and middle class teenage homosexuals. These youngsters were typically inconspicuous and did not indulge in egregious displays of homosexuality either in dress or manner. While in the clubs, many were openly solicitous and flirtatious, but upon leaving, their more conventional manners were resumed. The same caution was apparent among those who purchased and used narcotics, usually marijuana. It was smoked at small, quiet parties, rarely while driving or in public places. It was not unusual to hear these poised, well-dressed youngsters speak of stealing, using narcotics, and the advantages and disadvantages of their respective college choices in the same tone of voice and conversation.

The middle class group anti-social activities which *do* come to the attention of the authorities are of a rather different nature than those just described. Several examples of these were provided by a local probation officer assigned to the neighborhood. On one occasion, he recalled, a group of about ten boys went back and forth across a busy intersection between 5:30 and 6:30 in the evening, effectively bringing traffic to a complete standstill until dispersed by the police. Another time, a car full of boys drove slowly down a main shopping street spraying the well dressed shoppers with the contents of a fire extinguisher. One incident involved a group of boys who stole an old car and took it to a vacant lot and while one boy drove the car around in circles, the others threw stones at it, until it was nothing but a battered corpse.

There is a mischievous, often amusing overtone to all these incidents; they are not the kind likely to be thought malicious or violent. Rather, they are spontaneous and gratuitous, proving nothing but providing "kicks." This behavior is not the kind which is likely to seriously alarm parents or police. It has none of the grim overtones usually associated, correctly or not, with the activities of lower class gangs. In general, the non-violent nature of the deviant activities of these youngsters is salient, and personal aggression rare. The anti-social activities observed among these groups rarely took the form of open defiance of authority; manipulation rather than rebellion appeared to be the preferred technique for handling trouble with authorities. Cohen and Short have postulated just such a difference between lower and middle class delinquency:

. . . we are persuaded that further research will reveal subtle but important differences between working class and middle class patterns of delinquency. It seems probable that the qualities of malice, bellicosity, and violence will be underplayed in the middle class subcultures and that these subcultures will emphasize more the deliberate courting of danger . . . and a sophisticated, irresponsible, "playboy" approach to activities symbolic in our culture, of adult roles and centering largely around sex, liquor, and automobiles.[20]

How closely that description fits the middle class groups observed is readily apparent.

Interestingly enough, even while engaging in flagrant, frequent infractions of the law, these youngsters sustained the opinion that their activities would in no way interfere with their future plans. They did not define themselves as delinquents or even trouble makers and did not expect others to do so. More likely than not, upon graduating from high school and entering college, as most planned to do, these youngsters

[20] Cohen and Short, *op. cit.,* p. 26.

will leave their deviant activities behind without a trace in the form of official records, self-definition, or residues of unpleasant experiences with authorities. The police seemed to share this expectation. An incident was observed in which a boy was picked up for drinking and curfew violation. In the patrol car he expressed his concern lest the occasion jeopardize his chances for entering college. The officer, who had until that point been rather surly, hastened to reassure the boy that such a possibility was quite unlikely, and implied that nothing would come of the visit to the station.

The same expectations were shared by the people who worked at the places where these youngsters congregated— waitresses, life guards, theater managers—who did not feel that even as a group they constituted a serious nuisance. Their tolerance is no doubt increased by middle class youngsters' liberal spending habits which make it worth their while to put up with an occasional annoyance. But in addition their attitudes are affected by the usually pleasant relations they have with these boys and girls, whose interpersonal experiences with adults and peers are more harmonious and extensive than those observed among the more socially inadequate lower class gangs observed by Yablonsky and the supervisor of the detached worker program in Los Angeles. This difference in social ability is hardly surprising in view of the middle classes' traditional specialization in entrepreneurial activities. The techniques of smooth social relations are the bread and butter of the middle classes, and middle class teenagers, deviant and non-deviant alike, demonstrate remarkable agility in the manipulation of social situations. Their interpersonal skills enable them to control their social environment to a much greater degree than possible for lower class teenagers who have not had the opportunity to acquire and perfect these techniques.

GROUP ORGANIZATION

It can be seen that the groups observed, with the exception of disturbed leadership, precisely conform to Yablonsky's description of a near-group. Certainly, they do not qualify for the term "gang" as it is usually used, nor do they have well-developed delinquent values. On the contrary, the similarity between these youngsters' values and those of the adult, dominant society is conspicuous. Such a continuity has been suggested by Matza and Sykes[21] in a recent article in which they contend that the values underlying much juvenile delinquency are far less deviant than commonly portrayed, due to a prevailing oversimplification of middle class values. The authors argue that existing alongside the official, dominant values in society is another conflicting set which they call subterranean. These are values which are frequently relegated by adults to leisure time pursuits and are not ordinarily allowed to interfere with the regular course of a conventional life. Matza and Sykes point out that the content of these subterranean values has been described by Veblen in his portrayal of the "gentleman of leisure"—disdain for work, identification of masculinity with tough, aggressive behavior, and the search for thrills and adventures. The authors feel that the delinquent emphasizes a society's subterranean values but instead of relegating them to after-hours activities, he makes them a way of life, a code of behavior. The delinquent, then, has not

---

[21] David Matza and Gresham M. Sykes, "Juvenile Delinquency and Subterranean Values," *American Sociological Review*, Vol. 26 (October 1961), pp. 712–719.

evolved an original set of values but has only taken over one aspect of those held by most people along with their publicly proclaimed, respectable middle class values.

J. A. Pitt-Rivers[22] has suggested the concept "infra-structure" to describe what Matza and Sykes have referred to as subterranean values. The infra-structure is a set of values which exists alongside and in opposition to the official beliefs and behavior required by the formal systems of authority. It is not merely a set of separate beliefs held by one segment of the community but is that part of the social structure consisting of the personal, internalized version of officially endorsed values. The two systems are seen by Pitt-Rivers as interdependent, representing the private and public morals held simultaneously by everyone in the social system. The opposition of the value systems creates a structural tension or ambivalence which, though never really sharp enough to seriously endanger the social order, nevertheless provides a predisposition to deviance from officially prescribed behavior. The relation between the two systems is continuous, and while certain people or groups are more influenced by one system than the other, both affect all behavior to some degree.

In the light of the observations presented here, one may postulate that just as certain individuals and social groups are closer to one set of these values than the other, so are different age groups. Adolescence may be understood as a period in the life span of the individual when he is closer to deviant or subterranean values than he will be as an adult or has been as a child. Several authors have conceptualized adolescence as a period of license, a time for social and sexual exploration. Benedict[23] has pointed out the expectation that the adolescent will be irresponsible, though as an adult a few years later he can no longer be, and Erikson[24] has described adolescence as a psycho-social moratorium, set aside for experimentation in establishing an identity prior to the assumption of adult roles. One implication which can be drawn from these interpretations is that a teen-ager's "deviant behavior" may be in actuality a phase in his history when he is allowed and even expected to behave in accord with a set of subterranean values which do not disappear when he becomes an adult but instead are acted upon only on more appropriate occasions.

The adolescent in our culture, it is suggested, may be viewed as an aristocrat, a gentleman of leisure who, for a time, is not required to work but is allowed to play, explore, test limits, indulge his pleasures, and little else besides. This description of the delinquent as a kind of aristocrat closely resembles Finestone's characterization of the Negro teenage narcotic addict.[25] The "cat" is an individual who has developed an elaborate repertoire of manipulative techniques for dealing with the world, eschewing violence in favor of persuasion and charm. "He seeks through a harmonious combination of charm, ingratiating speech, dress, music, the proper dedication to his 'kick' and unrestrained generosity to make of his day to day life itself a gracious work of

---

22 J. A. Pitt-Rivers, *The People of the Sierra* (Chicago: University of Chicago Press, Phoenix Edition, 1961).

23 Ruth Benedict, "Continuities and Discontinuities in Cultural Conditioning," reprinted in Mullahy (Ed.), *A Study of Interpersonal Relations* (New York: Grove Press, Evergreen Edition, 1949).
24 Erik H. Erikson, *Childhood and Society* (New York: W. W. Norton, 1950).
25 Harold Finestone, "Cats, Kicks and Color," *Social Problems*, Vol. 5 (July 1957), pp. 3–13.

art."[26] The similarity between this depiction of the "cat" and the youngsters described here is indeed remarkable, especially in light of the differences between them in race, class, and circumstance.

There is, then, much reason to think that Matza and Sykes are justified in urging that delinquency might be better understood as an extension of the adult conforming world rather than as discontinuous with it. One advantage of this interpretation is that it allows for a single explanation of lower and middle class delinquency and thus avoids the inconsistency inherent in theories which specify the influence of socio-economic factors in the etiology of lower class delinquency and psychological factors in the etiology of middle class delinquency. It is likely that much may be gained by exploring the similarity between the delinquent and the rest of society rather than his deviance from it. Certainly these observations suggest that middle class deviants may differ from lower class delinquents not in the frequency of their anti-social activities, but only in the form which they take and the sophistication, social intelligence, judgment, and skill with which they are executed.

SUMMARY

These observations have raised several important issues concerning the structure and values of delinquent groups. It may be that the extent of gang structure is frequently exaggerated and that such groups may not be as cohesive, structured, and stable as they are commonly depicted. The groups described here manifested all but one of the characteristics (disturbed leadership) described by Yablonsky as those of a near-group. There is a coincidence of opinion based on

26 *Ibid.,* p. 5.

three sets of observations (Yablonsky's, the supervisor of a detached worker program in Los Angeles, and those reported in this paper) suggesting that the common conception of the gang as a highly organized primary group is not always accurate and may be the result of the gross exaggerations made possible by the dearth of empirical observations of gangs. Exaggeration may also have taken place in the extent of the differences between delinquent values and those of the dominant society. The observations reported in this paper are in accord with the suggestions of Matza and Sykes that the delinquent subculture is an extension of values held by most members of the society but indulged in less openly and less often. Certainly the behavior and beliefs of the middle class youngsters observed are not dramatically different from those of most conventional teenagers or adults.

In view of these three sets of observations, the following questions may be asked: (1) How often and to what extent are gangs primary groups with elaborate delinquent subcultures, and how prevalent are such groups when compared with the loosely structured, secondary, impermanent collectivities with little or no delinquent subculture such as those described here? (2) In view of the conflicting characterizations of the extent of gang structure and the nature of gang values, would not there be more scientific value in describing gangs in terms of at least these two variables rather than primarily on the basis of the content of their deviant activities? (3) To what extent, if any, does adult recognition, particularly in the form of the assignment of detached workers to gangs, legitimize and formalize these groups, lending them a cohesion and solidarity which they previously might not have had? (4) Has the emphasis on the deviant activities of these groups obscured their similarity to conventional teenagers and adults, thereby exaggerating the differences between delinquents and non-delinquents? And (5) would it not be more fruitful to examine the extent and nature of the similarities rather than differences between deviant and non-deviant teenagers and adults?

The action implications of these questions are far-reaching. If, as Yablonsky suggests, the gang meets different needs for different members, a uniform approach on a gang basis is inappropriate. More suitable would be an attempt to help individual members develop the interpersonal skills which would enable them to participate in structured, socially accepted groups. Or, by deliberately applying techniques such as Yablonsky's "group-fulfilling prophecy," gangs might be made into non-deviant clubs. And, if delinquent values are but a continuation of one aspect of the accepted value system subscribed to by most law abiding people, a program designed to integrate these values into a more appropriate place in deviant youngsters' lives (for example, by providing socially acceptable means of expressing aggression and seeking adventure) would be more honest and effective than attempts to eliminate them altogether.

At this stage, only one firm conclusion is justified. The variables in terms of which gangs can best be understood have not yet been identified and are not likely to be until widespread and systematic empirical observation is conducted. The impressions reported here suggest just how valuable and unsettling such observation may prove.

24.

Gang Members and Ecological Conflict *

Carl Werthman and Irving Piliavin

From the front seat of a moving patrol car, street life in a typical Negro ghetto is perceived as an uninterrupted sequence of suspicious scenes. Every well dressed man or woman standing aimlessly on the street during hours when most people are at work is carefully scrutinized for signs of an illegal source of income; every boy wearing boots, black pants, long hair, and a club jacket is viewed as potentially responsible for some item on the list of muggings, broken windows, and petty thefts that still remain to be cleared; and every hostile glance directed at the passing patrolman is read as a sign of possible guilt.

The residents of these neighborhoods regard this kind of surveillance as the deepest of insults. As soon as a patrolman begins to interrogate, the suspect can easily see that his moral identity is being challenged because of his dress, his hair style, his skin color, and his presence in the ghetto itself.

Negro gang members are constantly singled out for interrogation by the police, and the boys develop their own techniques of retaliation. They taunt the police with jibes and threaten their authority with gestures of insolence, as if daring the police to become bigots and bullies in order to defend their honor. Moreover, these techniques of retaliation often do succeed in provoking this response. When suspect after suspect becomes hostile and surly, the police being to see themselves as representing the law among a people that lack proper respect for it. They too begin to feel maligned, and they soon become defensively cynical and aggressively moralistic. From the point of view of a patrolman, night sticks are only used upon sufficient provocation, and arrests are only made with just cause.

* This paper is based on data gathered during two separate research projects. The study of the police was supported by Grant MH-06328 from the National Institute of Mental Mealth at the United States Public Health Service and administered by the Survey Research Center at the University of California in Berkeley. The study of delinquent street gangs was initiated by the Survey Research Center on a grant from the Ford Foundation and was later moved to the Center for the Study of Law and Society on the Berkeley campus where funds were made available under a generous grant from the Office of Juvenile Delinquency and Youth Development, Welfare Administration, U.S. Department of Health, Education, and Welfare in cooperation with the President's Committee on Juvenile Delinquency and Youth Crime.

SOURCE. David J. Bordua (ed.), *The Police*, New York: John Wiley and Sons, Inc., 1967, pp. 56–98. Original title, "Gang Members and the Police." (Editorial adaptations.) Reprinted with permission.

After studying the interaction between policemen and gang members for over a year, it became clear, at least to these observers, that behind the antagonism between these two groups lies a number of problems in the sociology of law. First, although the law and local custom overlap considerably in Negro ghettos, the disjuncture that remains brings the boys into conflict with the police, a conflict that has ecological as well as legal dimensions. Second, for a set of structural reasons to be discussed, the methods used by the police to locate suspects tend to undermine their legitimacy in the eyes of many ghetto residents. These cultural conditions affect the nature of expectations in face-to-face encounters as well as the way both parties perceive and evaluate each other's behavior. This chapter is therefore an attempt to analyze the way patrolmen and gang boys first perceive or construct their respective worlds and then respond to the situation created for them by the actions and expectations of the other.[1]

[1] The data on policemen were collected by Irving Piliavin, Scott Briar, and Roy Turner, who spent eighteen months observing and interviewing patrolmen and juvenile officers on daily patrols in Oakland and San Francisco. We are deeply indebted to Briar and Turner for the long hours they spent in the field on this project and for the many contributions they made to the analysis. The data on gang members were collected by Carl Werthman in a series of taped interviews with fifty-six "core" members of eleven "delinquent gangs" or "jacket clubs," plus observations and more informal conversations involving over one hundred members of these eleven gangs. The boys were drawn from the clientele of a delinquency-prevention program in San Francisco called Youth For Service, and we owe particular thanks to Orville Luster, Percy Pinkney, and the rest of the staff at this agency for helping us conduct this research out of their offices for a two-year period. Of the fifty-six boys interviewed on tape, thirty-seven were Negro, eleven were Mexican, and eight were Caucasian. This chapter is thus based primarily on a sample of Negro gang boys.

THE PERSPECTIVE OF THE GANG MEMBER

The Meaning and Uses of Streets

It is generally agreed that the transformation of city blocks and street corners into "hangouts," territories," or "turfs" invests the streets with a special meaning to the members of a lower-class juvenile gang. Although much has been made of the unusual patriotism associated with these places and the quasi-military fashion in which they are occasionally defended, there has been little systematic study of the way gang members actually put the streets to use.

Sherri Cavan has suggested that a house is a place where "activities which would be unlawful in public places such as poker games and nudity, and activities which would be a source of embarrassment in public places such as family arguments and love making can be freely engaged in.'"[2] On the basis of this criterion, the plots of public land used as "hangouts" by gang members must also be considered a sort of "home" or "private place." Activities such as poker games, arguments, love-making, drinking wine, and serious reading of comic books and newspapers are considered uniquely appropriate in this setting. As a rule, gang members use street corners for behavior that most ordinary adolescents would confine to a house or a car.

There are even occasions in the "home life" of gang members when the streets become functionally independent of all other settings. One function of expropriating hangout space in front of a doughnut shop or candy store is the ready access to a kitchen and to food. During the periods when entire days are spent in or around private

[2] Sherri Cavan, "Interaction in Home Territories," *Berkeley Journal of Sociology,* Vol. VIII, p. 18.

space, gang members typically purchase a doughnut and coffee every few hours. This is often supplemented at regular intervals by food and liquor obtained through extralegal channels. The boys typically know the precise time when all deliveries to grocery stories, bakeries, homes, and liquor stores are made. The unguarded truck appears to be the major source of an unconventional food supply. Goods obtained from shoplifting (a more dangerous enterprise) are also used to stave off hunger, but shoplifting seems more often reserved for luxuries such as clothes, party supplies, and an occasional sporting good. A diet provided from these sources can sustain a boy for days, with the addition of a little cheap wine and a daily ration of about ten cigarettes.

Since all routine life functions are at one time or another performed on the streets, the conventional standards of public decorum are considerably relaxed. Entrance into the private space or hangout is occasioned by a noticeable relaxation of physical posture. Shoulders slump, shirttails appear, and greetings are exchanged with an abandon that is only achieved by people who usually receive houseguests in the kitchen. A good deal of time is also spent combing hair in front of store windows and dancing to rock and roll (often without a partner and without music) as if completely absorbed in the privacy of a bedroom.

Yet as soon as the boys leave the street corner, they become self-consciously absorbed in the demands of a public role. They pay careful attention to uniform—either casually immaculate ("looking sharp") or meticulously disheveled ("looking bad")— and cover the territory in the characteristic hiking style ("walking pimp"). Most of the boys would no sooner start a poker game two blocks away from the privacy of the hangout than more

respectable citizens would think of making love in their front yards. Of course there are many notable exceptions to this rule, and on an irregular basis most boys do both.

The fact that gang members make relatively relaxed and private use of public streets does pose some problems for them, particularly when it comes to controlling the entrance of outsiders. People can take liberties in houses because a house is "an area of restricted entrance,"[3] and those who enter other people's houses either by accident or against the implicit consent of their occupants are potentially subjected to physical assault, legal action, or, at the very least, embarrassment.

With the exception of legal action, gang members also have these sanctions at their command. They use every means at their disposal to make outsiders accept the transparent walls they construct around the hangout. In practice, however, there are limits to the defensive measures that can be taken if one's private space is defined by most people, however innocently, as a public street corner.

Since practically every category of person who uses the public pathways is very nearly forced to violate whatever "rules of trespass" the gang members might like to make, it is easily understandable why the situation itself engenders some amount of bitterness among the boys. Over and above the negative feelings associated with this situational shortcoming, however, the gang members do recognize differences among those who actually or might potentially violate the boundaries of the hangout. Moreover, the feelings of hostility directed toward the various categories of outsiders can be ranked hierarchically.

The least disliked category of persons

[3] *Ibid.*, p. 18.

and those most accommodating to the claims made by a gang are the "familiars," mostly residents of the local neighborhood. They walk through even the most boisterous gatherings on private space as though they were not aware of its special character. This response to a potentially difficult situation is correctly interpreted by the boys as a sign that their claims to privacy are being politely accepted. The potential conflict between those who use this physical space as a living room and those who use it as a public thoroughfare is neatly resolved by having both parties studiously pretend to ignore the presence of the other. Occasionally a "familiar" will nod or smile at members of the club. At this time both parties seem to accept a definition of the situation as neighbors whose back doors are always open to one another's unannounced appearance.

More disliked and less accommodating are the "unfamiliars." These persons are not known to gang members, and thus there is no prior mutual understanding as to how the situation of potential conflict is to be resolved. Gang members communicate their claims on the hangout by calling an abrupt halt to verbal interchange in such a way as to suggest that a legitimate setting for private conversation has been rudely intruded upon. The members then begin to stare, and out of the hostile silence may come a wisecrack or a taunt. The boys are usually willing to accept a noticeable increase in walking pace and lowered eyes as sufficient implicit apology. An "unfamiliar" who continues to behave impolitely, either by refusing to hurry out of the space or by challenging the reality offered to him by the boys, becomes eligible for sanctions otherwise appropriate to a common housebreaker.

Usually, however, these illegal sanctions are not invoked. Gang boys have other less legally problematic ways of terrorizing casual observers, and one distinct class of favorites involves riding roughshod over the numerous rules of etiquette that organize routine behavior in public places. The boys may come within short range of a stranger, for example, and ask to "borrow" whatever the person happens to possess, be it tires from a used car salesman, a bicycle from a young boy, or money from practically anyone. This tactic constitutes a dramatic demonstration to most people of how much they are dependent on mundane conventions to maintain the assumption that one is usually safe around strangers. Similarly, the simple act of refusing to move when standing directly in the path of a passerby can destroy the faith of any witness in the orderly character of their immediate social world.

Although intentional violations of etiquette are obviously not crimes, they often succeed in doing considerable psychic damage to their targets. The stranger may give a gang boy money, walk around him if he is blocking the way, or pretend to ignore his antics altogether, but he will be apprehensive because he does not know what lies immediately ahead. With the threat of violence in the air, these situations become "disorganized."[4]

Yet as far as gang members are concerned, both "familiars" and "unfamiliars" share a single redeeming trait; neither can usually avoid trespassing on the street corner. They therefore cannot really be blamed for their presence since they are also the victims of an uncontrollable geographic factor—the awkward arrangement of streets. But there

[4] For a systematic discussion of this approach to the problem of "social disorganization" see Albert K. Cohen, "The Study of Social Disorganization and Deviant Behavior," in Robert S. Merton, Leonard Broom, and Leonard S. Cottrell, Jr., eds., *Sociology Today* (New York, Basic Books, 1959), pp. 474–83.

are other categories of persons who, like gang members, make something special out of public space. They are not forced for material reasons to violate the boundaries of the hangout. They make their own sets of social claims on access to the street corner.

The first of these special people are the members of rival gangs. Like the "familiars," they are willing to support the reality of claims to a private use of the street corner. Given the prestige system that exists among gangs, however, they have a vested interest (although rarely consummated) in obtaining unconditional rights of access both to the hang-out and to the larger "territory" of which it is a part. Next to the rumble, the "suprise attack" on a hangout is considered the ultimate declaration of all-out war. Admittedly these events are quite rare, but should a gang ever win a total victory in one of these wars, the symbol of their success would be unconditional access to the hangout.[5]

The police are the most despised and least accommodating threat to a gang's conception of a hangout. Like gang members, the police have a vested interest in imposing a set of normative claims on the people who use the streets. The very places that are defended like homes by gang members also constitute places of work or "beats" to the police, and the home-like uses to which gang members put the streets are often perceived as threats to the patrolman's task of maintaining the conventional rules that ordinarily govern be-

havior on them. Although the boys attempt either subtly or violently to convince outsiders that their behavior at the hangout is a strictly private affair, the police tend to insist with equal conviction that all behavior on public property is their legitimate concern. The relationship between gang members and policemen thus has its roots in an ecological conflict over claims to final authority in the same setting. The Chicago police apparently have a phrase that expresses this relationship. When they are annoyed at a gang for their behavior at a hangout, they will say "Gi'me that corner!"

In practice, the police usually do make some concessions to the boys and allow them a privileged use of the streets. Patrolmen often tolerate drinking and gambling at the hangout, activities that become suitable grounds for arrest in other parts of the neighborhood. Under no conditions, however, is the hangout considered a completely invulnerable shield against the authority of the police. It is typically under constant surveillance, and the police even stage periodic "shakedowns" as a reminder to the boys that final authority for their behavior on the streets rests with the public's official landlords. For example:

One time me and a couple of friends, we came down to the corner on Monday night because we was supposed to have our meeting. And we was standing there on the corner bullshitting like we always do, and there was only four of us. Then this cop on a motorcycle pulled over and walked over to us. I seen him before. He rides around the neighborhood a lot. He didn't say nothing. He just zipped down his jacket and there was his big old billy club. And then he started asking questions, identification, what were we doing, and all like that. And he searched us and got our names down on the book and everything. We wasn't doing anything except what we

---

[5] No conflict of this magnitude took place while this study was being done. However, some of the boys studied tell stories about an immediately preceding period in San Francisco gang history when these raids were not uncommon. In fact, a number of boys in the same neighborhood remember seeing a machine gun hidden in a park near the hangout that was used on at least two frequently mentioned occasions to defend the private space. These boys also claim that the machine gun was not used any place else.

usually do on that corner. (What's that?) Stand there bullshitting. They do anything to get our names on that book. You know. They want us to know they in charge.

Gang Boys and the Law

This ecological conflict thus has a legal dimension. The view of fighting held by gang boys, for example, is clearly a case in which the law and the mores conflict. The police are often called upon to break through layers of screaming girls in order to separate a pair of street-style gladiators, and one patrolman even suggested that the worst injuries he had sustained as an officer had been leg bites received from females on these occasions. Yet to gang boys, most of these fights are both honorable and necessary. They were either challenged, insulted, or hit first, and thus they are always bitter when penalized by the police.

Like that time that me and this kid from the Sabines was having this big fight up at school. He hit me during gym class. It was sort of accidental, but, see, I said something to him, and then he said something back and so we had this fight. The girls was going crazy. Jumping up and down and screaming and everything like they do. I guess this cop thought there was a riot going on or something cause he really came busting in there. Well, he grabbed us and threw us into the car and all that old shit. We tried to tell him what we was fighting about, but he wouldn't listen. Them cops is something else, man. What he expect us to do? Have one of them duals with guns or something?

There are other situations, however, in which the formal legal status of a disorder is more ambiguous, and these situations can cause trouble when both the police and the gang boys lay claims to the benefit of the doubt. For example, when strangers or "unfamiliars" are being treated to gross violations of etiquette or to other such attacks on

their faith in social order, the police quite naturally feel constrained to take action. Yet from a gang member's point of view, the legal issues involved in disorganizing a social situation are not always clear-cut. For example:

Last Sunday we went to see about buying a car. So we went down to a shop. We were out there parked, and this friend of mine was trying to con the guy into giving him some tires. He was standing there next to this Merc saying, "Why don't you give us the tires?" So the guy says, "No, I'm gonna sell it, and who'd want to buy a car with the tires gone?" So we were trying to open the door, but the guy wouldn't give us the keys to open the door. So there were about ten of us there, and it was in the daytime, and we was just messing around. You know, laughing and everything.

So finally this cop comes by. This fat slob. He was drunk when he got out of the car cause his shirt was out, man. So the dude gets out, and he comes up to me and he say, "What's wrong?" and I go, "What do you mean, what's wrong?" I wasn't trying to get smart with him. I was just saying it. And he goes, "Don't get smart! I was just asking you what's wrong?" I say, "I'm not trying to get smart!" So then he goes, "Now you are!" I didn't say nothing. I just shut up.

So he walks over to this other friend of mine and he goes, "What seems to be the trouble?" But my friend didn't say nothing. So he pulled out this club, and he came over to me and pushed me against the car and he goes, "So you're a smart guy huh?" So I say, "No." And then I smelled him. He must have been drinking wine cause I smelled it all over his breath so I knew he was drunk. So I moved away from him. But he goes, "Come over here!" I didn't want to get next to him 'cause I knew he was going to try something.

So after that, the jerk, he stands out in the middle of the street and he says, "Well, if there's any trouble and you want it settled, I'll settle it!" And he starts slapping the club on his hands and walking around to see who he can hit. So we start telling him there ain't no trouble or nothing. And the guy's older brother, he was twenty-one, he came out and said, "What's wrong?" And the cop goes, "Who's asking you? I'm asking the questions, not you!" Smart dude you know. We didn't want to offend him, 'cause we knew he was drunk. So he walked up to me again. I don't know what was wrong with the dude! He trying to do something! He says, "I'm gonna give you three minutes to get off the street!" He can't give you three minutes to get off the street when you're not doing nothing, right? So we were laughing.

After a few minutes we got in the car and started driving around. And the first thing you know he started following us. We went around the corner and stopped. And he throw me in the car and goes, "Now I'm taking you down to the station!" I say, "For what?" And he goes, "Because I told you to get out of here and you didn't do it!" So I tried to stick up for my rights, and I asked what he was taking me in for. I say, "Just 'cause I was on the street?" And he goes, "Yeah."

Finally, there is the issue of the role played by the police in protracted conflicts between gang boys and other segments of the community, particularly local store owners, school personnel, and Recreation Department officials. Much of the vandalism in low-income neighborhoods is directed at these targets, and the reasons for attack are often not hard to find. The following quote, for example, was taken from a Negro gang boy whose colleagues had just ransacked a local grocery store and been sent to jail.

I know why them cats did it, and I bet they ain't sorry. Even now. We used to go to this place all the time to buy cokes and stuff, and this Chinaman who run the place, he didn't like us. He'd sometime call us "boy" and "nigger" and be hollering that we stealing stuff, and when we start talking back to him, he'd quick turn around and start calling the cops. Then the

cops would come. You know, like they always do. About fifteen minutes or an hour late. And by that time we just be standing around in front of this place waiting on them. Well, one day we walked in and this Chinaman, he tell us he don't have no cokes. But we can see them. They just sitting there behind this glass. So then he says, "Okay." He gonna sell us the cokes. But he gonna charge us eighteen cents. So Leroy got mad and just grabbed one, and then the cops picked him up. They didn't do nothing to him. Just rode him around or something. But that made Leroy even madder so he went and wrecked the place. Man, you shoulda seen it. Glass all smashed. Cans all over the floor. They got Leroy and them. It was in the papers. But if they get out, I bet they gonna do it again.

The Situation of the Patrolman

As William Whyte observed some twenty-five years ago, the police and the gang boys do not always agree about *what* rules the police should enforce or about *how* they should enforce them. Whyte said:

The policeman is subject to sharply conflicting social pressures. On one side are the "good people" of Eastern City, who have written their moral judgements into the law and demand through their newspapers that the law be enforced. On the other side are the people of Cornerville, who have different standards and have built up an organization whose perpetuation depends upon freedom to violate the law.[6]

This conflict forces the patrolmen to make a decision about which set of standards to enforce, and Whyte's advice to them about this choice was unambiguous. "Under these circumstances," he said, "the smoothest course for the officer is to conform to the social

[6] William Foote Whyte, *Street Corner Society* (Chicago, The University of Chicago Press, 1943), p. 138.

organization with which he is in direct contact and at the same time to try and give the impression to the outside world that he is enforcing the law."[7]

From the point of view of a patrolman, however, this advice is not quite as helpful as it might sound since it still leaves unanswered the question of precisely what "conforming" to local standards involves. It is clear, for example, that the residents of most low-income communities, gang members included, expect the police to stand for *something*. The boys, in fact, are exceedingly contemptuous of patrolmen who know that legal standards are being broken but who are either too frightened or too cynical to act. If a patrolman tolerates all behavior, legal and illegal alike, he is likely to be defined by gang boys either as "chicken" or as "corrupt."

Man, you should have seen them cops out at the Point on Saturday night. Zeke, and Orville, and Percy (gang workers) and them were there. They can tell you. Five carloads of cops was there, lights flashing and everything. And everybody is just standing around after this party. Fights going on, girls screaming, everything. And then this cat pulls out a gun and starts firing. Man, he was five feet away from them cops and they stood there! Just stood there looking! Somebody coulda got killed or something. Or maybe they just didn't care. Maybe they was saying "Why not let them niggers go kill each other anyway. They ain't got no sense."

A patrolman can therefore compromise his legitimacy while maintaining order in one of two ways; either by visibly betraying his obligation to enforce *some* rules of law or by fullfilling these obligations in ways that conflict with the moral standards of the local population. If he is too legalistic, he runs the risk of being perceived as arrogant and unjust; but if he tailors his standards to the *practices* of the neighborhood rather than to its *ideals*, he is looked down upon for abdicating his responsibilities altogether. The gang boys are not without their own standards of fairness, and it is these standards that the patrolman must attempt to enforce.

A "good cop" is thus a man who can successfully handle a subtle and narrowly defined moral challenge. He must try to order the life of an ethnic lower-class community from within by holding people such as gang boys to their own ideals, however little these ideals may be reflected in behavior. As Whyte suggested,

Cornerville people and many of the officers believe that the policeman should have the confidence of the people in his area so that he can settle many difficulties in a personal manner without making arrests. . . . The policeman who takes a strictly legalistic view of his duties cuts himself off from the personal relations necessary to enable him to serve as a mediator of disputes in his area.[8]

Whyte's emphasis on mediation certainly applies to the way gang boys expect patrolmen to handle fights. In situations involving violence, it seems that the "good cop" functions as an arbitrator. He does not turn the boys over to a local school principal for "fighting after school," nor does he cart them away to the station. He isolates them in a squad car, talks the situation over with them, and then does what he can to achieve at least a semipermanent peace.

(Have you guys ever met any good cops?) Yeah, there was two studs out in Lakeview once, not the regular cops, who was pretty straight. Remember when he had that big fight at the playground and those guys from Hunters Point got hurt?

----

[7] *Ibid.*, p. 138.

[8] *Ibid.*, p. 136.

Mr. J. (the playground director) sent for the cops only they didn't take us in. They talked to us for about an hour. They asked us what we fighting about and why did we fight and could we use boxing gloves and did we know that fighting was against the law and all that. But they finally let us go, and they got Willie to take the Hunters Point boys home. They was *real* straight, those two. I think they must have lived out there or something, or maybe they was in a club once themselves.

Yet the task of being defined as a "good cop" in the process of handling routine "disorders" involves something more than arbitration. As we have seen, the act of badgering a used car salesman for free tires may be sufficiently annoying to prompt a patrolman to intervene; but if a patrolman makes categorical claims to final authority in these situations, his authority is likely to be challenged.

When gang boys are apprehended for disorganizing a social situation or for behaving badly at a hangout, a "good cop" will therefore remind them of their values while also suggesting that he could claim the right to use force. He responds to formally ambiguous legal situations with an artful ambiguity of his own, and his reward for this delicate maneuver is legitimacy.

Those two studs out in Lakeview wouldn't always be on our back for playing neither. We'd be standing on the corner pulling some kinda phoney shit, and they'd pull up to find out if we was up to something. But they talked to us nice. They wouldn't let us get away with nothing, and, I mean, them cats would bust you if they had to. But they talked to us nice.

Even with the best of intentions, then, it is not easy to be considered a "good cop." Not only must the gang boys be persuaded that a policeman understands and likes them, they must also

be convinced that he shares their conception of justice and is fully prepared to enforce it. In practice, most confrontations between patrolmen and gang members thus contain the possibilities of conflict—a conflict over whose conception of proper behavior *will* prevail, a conflict over whose conception *ought* to prevail, and therefore a conflict over whose moral identity is to remain publicly intact. Furthermore, the fact that most policemen are not defined as "good cops" cannot be accounted for simply by the wide variety of social and personal defects commonly attributed to them. For example, it may be true that the behavior of policemen is affected by a class and ethnic predisposition to prejudice towards Negros and a psychological predisposition to danger, violence, and authoritarianism, not to mention inadequate education, training, and pay. Yet there are also structural and situational contingencies associated directly with the process of law enforcement itself that make it difficult for even the most enlightened and saintly of policemen to avoid being seen as pariahs by a large segment of the ethnic poor, contingencies that are part and parcel of the methods used by the police.

THE PERSPECTIVE OF THE POLICE

Stated formally, the fundamental problem of police work is the location of a set of criminals that corresponds to a set of reported crimes. The primary resource needed to accomplish this objective is knowledge, and for obvious reasons this resource is limited. With the exception of those who the police can manage to witness in the act of breaking the law, little is generally known about the specific identities of people who have committed crimes in the past.

• • •

Most juvenile officers actually do begin their investigations by adopting the methods of their fictional colleagues in detective stories. All complaints from schools, parents, citizens, and other policemen about specific infractions believed to involve young people are referred to the juvenile detail, and work proceeds from the crime to a search for the offender.

• • •

In practice, the juvenile officer often proceeds directly to boys who have proven themselves capable of committing crime, and then he relies on his skills at interrogation. Although the officer may consult his files on the population of suspects and offenders located during previous investigations, these files are used largely as memory aides.[9] Most of this information is in his head.

The success of this method is suggested by the fact that over 90% of convicted juveniles confess, a rate that testifies both to the competence of juvenile officers at interrogation and the incompetence of gang boys at concealing information. Those boys who have unusual control over words, voice tones, facial expressions, and body muscles can sometimes manage to avoid conviction indefinitely unless they are apprehended at the scene of a crime. Yet these talents are rare. Some gangs contain no such talented members; others contain two or three. It is therefore rarely necessary for a juvenile officer to expend much time and energy collecting evidence in order to build his case against a boy.

Although the procedures used by juvenile officers are unquestionably efficient, the boys on permanent suspect lists do not appreciate the elegance of these techniques. As David Matza has pointed out, efficient enforcement systems contain agents who suspect, apprehend, and interrogate only a few possible candidates. Most of us—the happy few—are rarely if ever contacted or questioned. . . . Thus, even in those cases in which guilt is confessed, the subcultural delinquent may sense injustice becauce of selective procedures inherent in any efficient system of enforcement. He feels that cognizance is unevenly exercised.[10] This sentiment is often expressed as follows:

Every time something happens in this neighborhood, them mother fuckin' cops come looking for me! I may not be doing nothing, but if somebody gets beat or something gets stole they always be coming right to my place to find out what's going on!

Encounters

The techniques of interrogation used by juvenile officers can best be viewed as self-conscious variations in the posture adopted towards suspects. If an officer has not been able to compile a good list of suspects after interviewing a complainant, he may simply cruise the local neighborhood asking familiar boys for information. This style of interrogation is usually conducted in a casual, informal, and conspiratorial tone of voice. It is designed to suggest that nothing serious has happened, that the officer is merely curious about a particular incident, or that a "favor" from the boy being interrogated will someday be returned. As far as the boys are concerned, however, this posture is simply "sneaky."

Some cops may be nice when you meet them, but as soon as you turn your back they be keeping full tab on you. Like this

9 These files are often cross-indexed by name, nickname, race, and previous offense. Many juvenile bureaus also keep membership lists of gangs (if available) and a picture or sample of the club jackets currently in use.

10 David Matza, *Delinquency and Drift* (New York, John Wiley and Sons, 1964), p. 108.

juvenile officer, Sergeant K. and his buddy. Every time I see him in school the sucker come up to me real nice and start running down his shit. "How's it going? What you been doing?" He gets to interrogating my ass, man, like I done something wrong! And all the time he be coming on nice! You know, like, "It's just between you and me." All that old shit. He sometimes say, "No, we don't expect you to squeal on your friends or nothing. We just want a little help. You do us a favor, we do you a favor. You go on and tell me what boys was involved and I guarantee you I let you go home. Nothing gonna happen anyway. You know. It ain't really serious." All that old shit! And then they turn around and try to book you every damn chance they get! Some of them nice cops you got to watch real careful.

When a juvenile officer has compiled a more promising list of suspects, however, his approach to interrogation is likely to be decidely less flattering. After confronting a boy with a list of acquaintances, the officer may wait for a suspicious silence to follow a particular name; or he might accuse a suspect directly in the hope that, even if innocent, the boy might get rattled enough to produce the actual offender.

Yet a juvenile officer is likely to give his most deferential and endearing performance when he thinks he has finally located the culprit. By suggesting that the suspect is regarded as a "good boy" and will not be done any harm, the officer attempts to ease him into a confession.

Although a great many gang boys are tricked into confessions, the authority of a juvenile officer is rarely rejected because of the hypocrisy involved in his techniques of interrogation. Since it strikes the boys as reasonable that a juvenile officer would attempt to catch them for the crimes they actually do commit, these defeats are often taken philosophically. As one boy put it:

If you done something and you be lying and yelling when the boys from juvy come around and they catch you lying, well, what you gonna do? You gonna complain 'cause you was caught? Hell man, you can't do that. You did something, and you was caught, and that's the way it goes.

Yet the sense of injustice created by the actions of a juvenile officer does not necessarily disappear after a confession. In many cases, the equity of a disposition also becomes an issue.

Outcomes

The juvenile officer exercises a good deal of discretion in deciding how to process offenders, a discretion that far transcends the measure of ambiguity ordinarily involved in legal assessments of motivation and intent.[11] . . .

A "delinquent" is therefore not a juvenile who happens to have committed an illegal act. He is a young person whose moral character has been negatively assessed. And this fact has led some observers to conclude that the transformation of young people into official "delinquents" is best looked at as an organizational rather than a legal process since policemen, probation officers, and juvenile court judges often base their dispositions on a host of criteria that are virtually unrelated to the nature of the specific offense.[12]

The *magnitude of an offense*, of course, can become a factor in dispositions. One responsibly planned and willfully executed robbery, rape, or assault can ruin the moral status of a juvenile indefinitely. Since 90% of the crimes

[11] For a more complete discussion of police discretion in dealing with juveniles, see Irving Piliavin and Scott Briar, "Police Encounters with Juveniles," *The American Journal of Sociology,* Vol. LXX, No. 2 (Sept. 1964), pp. 209–211.

[12] The problem of discretion has been formulated and studied by Aaron Cicourel in these terms. See Aaron V. Circourel, *The Social Organization of Juvenile Justice* (forthcoming).

committed by juveniles are minor offenses, however, this criterion is only rarely used.

The number of *previous contacts with police* has a more important effect on dispositions. These contacts are typically recorded on easily accessible files, and these files contain everything from arrests and convictions to contacts made on the flimsiest of contingent grounds. If a boy confesses to a crime and is not known to the police, he is often released. If he is caught for a third or fourth time, however, the sum total of previous contacts may be enough to affect a judgment about his moral character adversely, regardless of the nature or magnitude of the present offense and regardless of the reasons he was previously contacted. . . .

• • •

There is even some evidence to suggest that assessments about the type and quality of *parental control* are even more important factors in dispositions than *any* of the offense-related criteria. One of the main concerns of a juvenile officer is the likelihood of future offense, and this determination is often made largely on the basis of "the kinds of parents" a boy happens to possess. Thus, the moral character of parents also passes under review; and if a house appears messy, a parent is missing, or a mother is on welfare, the probability of arrest increases. Similarly, a boy with a father and two older brothers in jail is considered a different sort of person from a boy whose immediate family is not known to the police. As Cicourel points out, these judgments about family life are particularly subject to bias by attitudes related to class.[13]

See, like if you or maybe one of your brothers, say both of you, been to Y.A.,* or your sister, every time they see you they get on your back. They know all your family. If they ever pick you up and look at your records, they automatically take you in. They see where your sister been to jail, your brother, or if you ever went to jail. And they start saying, "Your whole family is rotten. Your whole family is jailbirds." Shit like that. And this is what really make you mad, when they tell you your mother don't know how to read!

Although the family situation of a boy and his record of prior police contacts both enter into dispositions, the most important factor affecting the decision of juvenile officers is the *attitude* displayed by the offender, both during and after the confession itself. Cicourel, for example, found that juvenile officers were strongly influenced by the style and speed with which the offender confessed.[14] If a boy blurts out his misdeeds immediately, this behavior is taken as a sign that the boy "trusts" authority and is therefore "under control." If the boy proves to be a "tough nut to crack," however, he is viewed with suspicion. As soon as a juvenile is defined as "hardened," he is considered no less dangerous to society than the adult criminal.

Similarly, the boys who appear frightened, humble, penitent, and ashamed are also more likely to go free. They are often defined as "weak, troubled, and the victim of circumstances" but basically "good boys," an assessment of moral character that may win them a release.

• • •

Most of the juvenile officers we interviewed felt that the attitude of the

[13] Aaron Cicourel, "Social Class, Family Structure and the Administration of Juvenile Justice," Center for the Study of Law and Society, University of California at Berkeley, Working Paper, MS.

* The detention facilities administered by the California Youth Authority.

[14] Cicourel, *The Social Organization of Juvenile Justice, Loc. cit.*

offender was the major determinant of dispositions in 50% of their cases, and Nathan Goldman reports that "defiance on the part of a boy will lead to juvenile court quicker than anything else."[15]

It is hardly necessary to describe the way most gang boys feel about the equity of these dispositions. One only needs to imagine the look on a boy's face when he is told that he is about to spend a year in jail for an offense committed with a friend who was sent home when he promptly confessed.

• • •

The Situation of Suspicion

David Matza has pointed out that the policeman's methodological problem here "is similar in almost every respect to that faced by sociologists." Both must classify individuals by searching for the particular actors that best fit a set of social or legal categories, and both are typically forced to use indicators of the categories of persons they are looking for since true referents rarely exist.[16] . . .

Policemen develop indicators of suspicion by a method of pragmatic induction. Past experience leads them to conclude that more crimes are committed in the poorer sections of town than in the wealthier areas, that Negroes are more likely to cause public disturbances than whites, and that adolescents in certain areas are a greater source of trouble than other categories of the citizenry. On the basis of these conclusions, the police divide the population and physical territory under surveillance into a variety of categories, make some initial assumptions about the moral character of the people and places in these cate-

gories, and then focus attention on those categories of persons and places felt to have the shadiest moral characteristics. As one patrolman states:

If you know that the bulk of your delinquency problem comes from kids who, say, are from 12 to 14 years of age, when you're on patrol you are much more likely to be sensitive to the activities of juveniles in this age bracket than older or younger youth. This would be good law enforcement practice. The logic in our case is the same except that our delinquency problem is largely found in the Negro community and it is these youth toward whom we are sensitized.[17]

According to both gang members and patrolmen, residence in a *neighborhood* is the most general indicator used by the police to select a sample of potential law violators. Many local patrolmen tend to consider *all residents* of "bad" neighborhoods rather weakly committed to whatever moral order they make it their business to enforce, and this transforms most of the people who use the streets in these neighborhoods into good candidates for suspicion.

(Tell me something. Do you guys know anyone up on the hill who doesn't get rousted by the police?) Up on the hill? Everybody gets picked on cause of the reputation of Hunters Point.

(Everybody does?) They sure do. Everybody gets picked on. Even parents. All the time they holler, "You oughta know how to raise your kids! Don't you know how to raise your kids right?"

That's right, man. That's what's happening.

Although many patrolmen believe that some entire neighborhoods are morally inferior to others, they do not enforce their standards with the same

[15] Nathan Goldman, *The Differential Selection of Juvenile Offenders for Court Appearances*, National Council on Crime and Delinquency (1963), p. 106.

[16] See David Matza, "The Selection of Deviants," *MS*, p. 32.

[17] Irving Piliavin and Scott Briar, *op. cit.*, p. 212.

severity in all parts of "poor" neighborhoods. According to gang members, the "territory" contains both *safe spots* and *danger spots*. The danger spots tend to be public places of business, such as outdoor drive-in hamburger stands or pool halls, where a great many young people in the neighborhood often congregate and where fights and arguments frequently break out. The probability of being defined as suspicious by the police in these places is quite high, and thus physical presence is more of a risk than in other spots.

• • •

The one condition under which a hangout does become a relatively free place is during the brief periods when patrolmen regularize their appearances at the street corner. Gang members very quickly chart these regularities, and during the periods when they have "the cops figured out" they feel comparatively safe; however, these periods of relative freedom rarely last longer than a few weeks.

(When you guys were on the streets every night, do you think the police came around every night?) We seen the police every night. Not, you know, that they stop us every night, but I seen one every night. Sometimes it was O.K. like when we knew the main streets they'd be on and when they show up. . . . For a while they always be coming around 10:30 so we be waiting for them. So about that time somebody'd start looking out the door and say, "the heat coming!" So, you know, either everybody leave or the ones over eighteen stay. And then after they gone, then everybody just slide on back there and resume where they left off at.

Although the police seem to create a few "safe spots" within "bad neighborhoods," gang members report that the *boundaries of neighborhoods* are patrolled with great seriousness and severity. The police are seen as very hard on "suspicious looking" adolescents who have strayed from home territory.

(Do you guys stay mostly at Hunters Point or do you travel into other districts?) If we go someplace, they tell us to go on home. Because every time we go somewhere we mostly go in big groups and they don't want us. One time we was walking on Steiner Street. So a cop drove up and he say, "Hey! Hanky and Panky! Come here!" And he say, "You all out of bounds, get back on the other side of Steiner Street." Steiner Street is supposed to be out of bounds. (What's on the other side of Steiner?) Nothin' but houses.

Gang members interpret the policy of trying to stop them from traveling into other lower-class neighborhoods as a tactic to stop gang wars, and our research on the police suggests that the boys are right. The police do tend to see all sojourns into neighboring territories as potential attacks on rival gangs.

They don't want us to come out of Hunters Point to tell the truth. Because every time we come out, man, they think we going to fight. But that ain't always true, and it ain't us that always starts the stuff. We on our way home. And they gonna pick us up for fighting back.

In addition to preventing gang members from traveling into neighborhoods of the same class and ethnic status as their own, the police are equally as stringent about preventing the boys from crossing boundaries into neighborhoods of a higher status or a different color. Although the policy of the police is the same in both cases, they attribute different motives to the boys for wanting to enter higher-status areas. When gang members visit other lower-class neighborhoods, the police suspect them of instigating war; when they are found in middle- or upper-class neighborhoods, the police suspect them of intentions to commit robbery or rape.

Me and a friend of mine, we went to a girl's house name of, ah, no, I ain't gonna say her name. You might know her. She was stayin' in a white district. So when we was up there, I guess they saw we were colored. You know, not mostly colored people stay up there. It was about ten o'clock 'cause we was leaving the girl's flat. Just walked out the door. Comin' out the door, and here's the curb. We right there by the curb. Gonna go down the block. Cops come around the corner with an orange light. I believe they just sitting there waiting to nab us. They probably seen us go in there. They come and pull us out. Shake us down. *All* the way down, too, man. They shake us all the way down. And ask us what we doing over here. We tell them we came out to this girl's house. He say, "Where'd you stay?" I say, "Well, you just saw us come out the house 'cause I saw you you right around the corner." He say, "Well, she's colored." So they say, "Some girl got raped up here." Or something like that. Some old lie. Then he say, "Where you live?" I say, "Hunters Point." He say, "I'm gonna give you about ten or fifteen minutes to catch the bus, and if you're not off this corner, if I see you over here, I'll bust you." Just like that. If the police catch you walkin' with a white girl, boy, you in big trouble.

Race thus becomes a particularly salient indicator of "suspiciousness" when Negroes or Mexicans are found in white neighborhoods. Being a Negro per se (or being a Negro in a Negro neighborhood) is apparently not as important a criterion of suspiciousness as being a Negro who is "out of place."

If boys from Hunters Point or Fillmore (Negro neighborhoods in San Francisco) go in all white districts, the police will stop you and ask you where you from. If you say Fillmore or Hunters Point, they'll take you down to the station and run checks on you. Any burglaries, any purse snatchings, anything.

• • •

It is also possible to become a "sus-picious person" by *ecological contami-nation.* A boy who is standing near a friend who has landed in the situation of suspicion has a good chance of being drawn into the sample himself.

Remember that day on 44th Street? Remember what them cops did? They caught Arthur and the guys with a false I.D. They was buying beer and they got caught. So I walked into the store just to see what was happening. So they started talking to Arthur and them and they told them to get in the car. So then he points to me and say, "You! Get in the car!" And I said, "Damn! I didn't do nothing!" But he said, "Get in the car!"

In addition to the variety of *places* used to draw samples, however, the police also seem to rely on a number of physical or material *individual attri-butes.* Certain kinds of clothing, hair, and walking styles seem intrinsically to trigger suspicion. The general descrip-tion of these styles had best be left to the boys themselves.

(Why do you think the cops pick you up all the time?) Why do they pick us up? They don't pick everybody up. They just pick up on the ones with the hats on and trench coats and conks.* If you got long hair and hats on, something like this one, you gonna get picked up. Especially a conk. And the way you dress. Sometimes, like if you've got on black pants, better not have on no black pants or bends† or Levi's.

They think you going to rob somebody. And don't have a head scarf on your head. They'll bust you for having a head scarf.‡

---

* A "conk" is a hair straightening process used by Negroes that is similar in concept to the permanent wave.

† "Bends" are a form of the bell-bottom trouser which, when worn effectively, all but obscure the shoe from vision, thus creating the impression that the wearer is moving down the street with an alarmingly irresponsible shuffle.

‡ Head scarves (sometimes called "mammy rags") are worn by Negroes around the forehead to keep "conk jobs" in place.

(All right, so they bust you for clothes. That's one thing. Is there anything else?) The way you walk sometimes. If you walk pimp. Don't try to walk pimp. Don't try to be cool. You know. They'll bust you for that. (Could you tell me how you walk pimp? You know. You just walk cool like. Like you got a boss high.§ Like you got a fix or something. Last night a cop picked me up for that. He told me I had a bad walk. He say, "You think you're bad." You know.

• • •

It should not be construed from the above discussion that the process of locating a population of potential offenders always proceeds on such slim grounds. There are a variety of "scenes" that constitute much more obvious bases for investigation. However, since policemen rarely stumble on armed men standing over dead bodies, much of their activity involves a subtle and exceedingly tenuous reading of both appearances and events. For example, when dealing with people who possess the ecological and personal indicators of suspiciousness outlined above, patrolmen may turn a screwdriver into a "deadly weapon" and a scratch on the neck into evidence of rape.

Like you be walking. Just come from working on the car or something. And if you've got a screwdriver or something in your back pocket, hell, they may beat the shit outa you. They talk about you got a burglary tool or you got a deadly weapon on you.

Remember the time when we was getting ready to go up to the gym? We came home from school one day. He had some scratches on his neck, and the cop pull over and say, "Turn around!" The cop grabbed him. I didn't say nothing. I was walking. I got to the top of the stairs, and the cop holler "Turn around" at me too. So I turn around. And the cop look at my neck and he say, "Yeah. You too. You got scratches on your neck too." So he took us

§ "Boss" is a synonym for "good."

down to the police station. It seem like some girl way over in another district got raped. And the girl say, "I think they live over at Hunters Point and I scratched one of them on the neck." Some stuff like that.

Gang members are very much aware of their moral status in the eyes of the police. On most occasions, they are likely to know that the police have singled them out for interrogation because of the neighborhood they live in, because of their hair styles, or perhaps because they are temporarily "out of place." They know how the police operate, and they are particularly aware of the role played by judgments about moral character in this methodology.

As one might imagine, gang boys thus tend to regard their more or less permanent place in the situation of suspicion with considerable resentment, a resentment that quite often spills over into outrage. Although the boys do not pretend to be moral pillars of the community, they feel, and with considerable statistical justification, that they are much better people than the operation of the crime detection process would otherwise suggest. Not all trips to neighboring territories are undertaken for the purposes of attacking rival gangs or pillaging the houses of the white rich, and most of the time, as the boys put it, "we was just mindin' our own business when the cops came along." Similarly, their resentment at being picked up for the clothes they wear and the hair styles they sport has the same basis in logic. As one boy succinctly put the argument, "Hell man, them cops is supposed to be out catching criminals! They ain't paid to be lookin' after *my hair!*"

• • •

But the problems faced by the police in constructing efficient indicators of suspicion are every bit as tricky as those faced by the social scientist in the privacy of a laboratory. Not only is "suspiciousness" a rather vague and poorly defined category, we can also expect conclusions to be biased by the amount of illegal activity that is visible to the police. We still do not know, for example, how much of the petty crime committed by lower-class juveniles in public is also committed by middle-class youths behind such private barriers to official vision as homes and cars.[18]

In addition, the nature of the data that the police are exposed to is partly a function of the way patrols are organized. The police can only see what the structure of their beats makes it possible for them to see, and lower-class neighborhoods are patrolled with greater frequency and vigilance than neighborhoods in the suburbs. . . .

As one might expect, gang members make various kinds of attempts to avoid the situation of suspicion, and appearances are sometimes altered in order to minimize the prospects of becoming a target for interrogation.

When a large group of boys are congregating on the same street corner and a squad car appears on the horizon, the group often expands the physical space it was occupying and breaks up into subunits of two and three. Gang members seem to feel the police consider a large number of small conversations less suspicious than a single conversation in which many boys are involved.

• • •

When a police car appears, gang boys often attempt to position themselves near females if there are any close by. Gang members argue that the

police regard mixed couples with less suspicion than they do small groups of boys.

Sometimes we jump next to the little ladies. Like one time when we was waiting for a bus and it was after curfew, we saw the heat come cruisin' down the street. And there was this ugly old lady walkin' by the bus stop. Well I just step right up beside her and start tippin' down the street. She got scared but she didn't do nothin' but keep walkin'. You better off walkin' with a woman. They figure you're not gonna be gettin' into nothing if you with a girl.

Similarly, unmarried older boys will occasionally wear wedding rings in order to bolster their moral status in the eyes of the police. Next to walking beside a girl, gang members feel they can best improve their public image by having it assumed that they are married.

Man, I even took to wearing a finger chain so them cops would think I got an old lady. I figure they less likely to bust you for humbug if they know you got a wife.

Most gang members are also equipped with a battery of socially acceptable reasons for being on the streets. As Paul Goodman has noted, the police in America take a rather dim view of people who are on the streets "doing nothing."[19] . . .

If a cop sees you on the street, he'll say, "What are you doing out of school?" And you just say, "I'm looking for a job." And he'll say, "All right, but if I catch you around here again and you ain't got a job I'll throw you in jail."

As adolescence wears on, the consequences of being picked up by the police become more and more serious; and as months replace days as the unit

[18] For a thorough discussion of the emphasis placed on public places by patrol officers, see Arthur L. Stinchcombe, "Institutions of Privacy in the Determination of Police Administrative Practice," *The American Journal of Sociology,* Vol. LXIX, No. 2 (Sept. 1963), pp. 150–61.

[19] Paul Goodman, *Growing Up Absurd* (New York, Vintage Books, 1960), p. 130.

of sentence, the boys begin to alter their appearances in ways that imply ever increasing compromises with their preferred public identities. The first, and in some ways the most precious, article of clothing to disappear is the club jacket. Most gang members, however, do not decide to stop wearing their jackets all at once. They first decide to wear their jackets "inside out" so that club names on the back or nicknames on the front cannot be seen. Finally, the jackets are abandoned altogether.

When we was in high school, we had a club meeting and decided not to wear our jackets any more. It was just gettin' too hot. Everytime something happen, somebody say I saw a boy in a blue jacket and first thing you know, the cops be knockin' on your door. First we wore them inside out. You know, so no names or nothin' would show. But finally we just stopped wearing them at all.

For most boys, the last article of distinctive social identity to disappear is long hair.

Our whole club is getting this kind of haircut so we can see what they gonna say next. See practically all of us got these short ones. We all had our hair cut. I guess they gonna find something else to pick on now. Most times if you ain't got a hat on, they say, "Conk job! Get in the wagon! You a hood!"

At some point during adolescence, however, a gang boy becomes recognizable to patrolmen by *name*. And when this happens, there is no longer any real escape from constant surveillance by the police. Most of the techniques employed to dodge the situation of suspicion are rendered useless. Even if precautions are taken, the boys usually find they are still trapped. Their place in the situation of suspicion becomes permanent.

• • •

Encounters

As soon as a patrolman leaves his squad car to begin an interrogation his relationship with a gang boy enters a new but related phase. The gang member desires to be treated with civility and politeness. If he has not committed a crime (or if the interrogating officer is not expected to know about it), he expects the officer to treat him with the respect due any respectable member of the community.

On the other hand, the patrolman has considerable leeway in deciding what view of the suspect to communicate. He can decide to treat the boy with a bureaucratic impassivity and respect, sometimes even with relaxed friendliness; or he can decide to issue commands, back the boy against a wall, and frisk him. . . . To a large extent, therefore, the issue of whether the authority of the patrolman will be challenged hangs on whether this initial insult is compounded or dissipated during the course of interrogation.

Curiously enough, gang boys are often treated deferentially when they are actually caught in the act of violating a law. Patrolmen who are made suspicious by gang boys driving new cars, for example, usually begin their interrogations in a menacing tone of voice. Yet as soon as it becomes clear that the car is stolen, the ensuing interaction is often conducted in a calm and businesslike way. Some patrolmen offer the boys cigarettes as tranquilizers against uneasiness, and many of the boys obey the officer's commands without flinching. In short, when gang members are arrested for clear violations of law and are not insulted in the process, the legitimacy of the arresting officer is often granted without challenge.

This observation is not surprising once it is realized that the essence of suspicion is a frustrated desire for properly validated information.[20] Communicating negative judgments about the moral character of others is one of the job contingencies faced by patrolmen. But as soon as suspicion is either confirmed or disproved, the necessity to make assessments disappears. The professional policeman does not necessarily have contempt for people who commit crimes. On the contrary, he is better positioned than most of us to appreciate the ingenuity, skill, and courage often displayed by people who sometimes break the law.

• • •

The police expect law-abiding citizens to express their respect for the law by addressing its representatives with various gestures of deference.[21] It is desired that the suspect's physical presence communicate civility, politeness, penitence, and perhaps fear. In addition, the use of such terms as "Sir" and "Officer" are expected as indications that the humble status of the juvenile in the eyes of adult and legal authority is properly understood. If these deference gestures are forthcoming, the officer has no choice but to assume the suspect is innocent, in which case he usually lets him go. Gang members understand the logic of this gestural vocabulary very well.

(What responses seem to work for you when the cops pick you up?) If you kiss their ass and say, "Yes Sir, No Sir," and all that jazz, then they'll let you go. If you don't say that, then they gonna take you in. Like, "Yes *Sir!* No *Sir!*" But if you

[20] For an analysis of suspicion as an "awareness context" see Barney G. Glazer and Anselm L. Strauss, *Awareness of Dying* (Chicago, Aldine Publishing Company, 1965), pp. 47–64.
[21] For a systematic discussion of the role played by deference in maintaining the ceremonial integrity of routine social life, see Erving Goffman, "The Nature of Deference and Demeanor," *American Anthropologist,* Vol. 58 (June 1957), pp. 473–502.

stand up and say it straight, like "Yes Sir" and "No Sir" and all that, you cool.

• • •

Yet officers sometimes make their contempt for gang members even more explicit. Instances were observed, for example, of officers commenting on the "nice tan" of a Negro suspect or inquiring after the birth place of a Negro by asking, "Where were you born? Mississippi?" Not all officers utilize these tactics, but most Negro gang members believe that the great majority of police officers are prejudiced, and most can cite personal experiences to document this position.

Remember that time we was coming from the show? This cop car pulls up and these two cops jump out quick. The first stud says, "All right, God Damn you! All you black Africans up against the motherfucking wall!" All that shit. So we got up against the wall over there on Market Street. This long house. You know. So then they started. "Where all you ignorant sons of bitches coming from?" We say we coming from the show. "What show?" We say we coming from the Amazon. They say, "Yeah, we got a call there's a whole bunch of shit going on over there! I think I'll call all you mother fuckers in!" So nobody say nothing. So then he starts again. "What's your name? Let me see your I.D.!" Finally, this cop's buddy say, "You want to run them in Joe? They ain't really done nothing." So then Joe stops. He say, "Now all you black Africans pick up your spears and go home! I don't want you guys walking up the street!" Shit like that, man. You know. We wasn't doing nothing. We just coming up the street like we always do coming from the show. That shit happens all the time. There ain't a day that we don't get rousted like that.

When a gang boy finds himself placed in the situation of suspicion unjustly and then insulted in the following encounter as well, he must decide whether to swallow the insult by deferring to the patrolman or whether to defend his honor by challenging the authority of the interrogating officer. To display the ritual signs of deference means suffering the private torments associated with cowardice as well as the public humiliation involved in losing face, and thus most gang members, when faced with this situation, prefer to challenge the authority of the police.

• • •

OUTCOMES

If a juvenile being interrogated in the situation of suspicion refuses to proffer the expected politeness or to use the words that typically denote respect and if no offense has been discovered, a patrolman finds himself in a very awkward position. He cannot arrest the boy for insolence or defiance, since for obvious reasons no charges of this nature exist. The patrolman is thus faced with the choice of three rather unpleasant alternatives.

First, he can back down, allowing his authority to evaporate. If a patrolman allows his authority to escape, however, there is no guarantee that it can be recaptured the next day or any day thereafter. . . .

. . . If a patrolman does decide to back down, he must be careful to retreat strategically by withdrawing from the encounter without a public loss of face. This is usually done by communicating to the juvenile that his innocence is fortuitous, that he is the kind of person who *could* have committed an offense, and that he owes his release to the grouchy good graces of the interrogating officer. . . .

If a patrolman chooses to press his claims to authority, however, he has only two sanctions available with which to make these claims good. On the one hand, he can attempt an arrest.

• • •

On the other hand, there are a variety of curfew, vagrancy, and loitering laws that can be used to formally or officially prosecute the informal violation of norms governing deportment in the situation of suspicion.

I got arrested once when we were just riding around in a car. There was a bunch of us in the car. A police car stopped us, and it was about ten after ten when they stopped us. They started asking us our names and wanted to see our identification. Then they called in on us. So they got through calling in on us, and they just sit in the car and wait 'til the call came through. Then they'd bring back your I.D. and take another one. One at a time. They held me and another boy till last. And when they got to us it was five minutes to eleven. They told everybody they could go home, but they told us it didn't make no sense for us to go home because we was just riding around and we'd never make it home in five minutes. So they busted us both for curfew.

In addition to these laws, a boy can also be charged with "suspicion" of practically anything. When the police use suspicion as a charge, however, they usually try to make the specific offense as serious as possible. This is why the criminal records of many gang boys are often heavily laced with such charges as "suspicion of robbery" and "suspicion of rape."

• • •

Gang boys are aware that the police have a very difficult time making these illusory charges stick. They can always succeed in sending a boy to jail for a few hours or a few days, but most of these charges are dismissed at a preliminary hearing on recommendations from probation officers. Moreover, gang members also understand the power of probation officers, and by behaving better in front of these officials they can often embarrass the local authority of patrolmen by having decisions to arrest reversed over their heads. As far as the patrolmen are concerned, then, the boys can make a mockery of false charges as a sanction against impertinence in the situation of suspicion.

Perhaps more important, however, a patrolman's sergeant also knows that most trivial or trumped up charges are likely to be dropped, and thus the police department itself puts a premium on ability to command authority without invoking the sanction of arrest. . . .

It is largely for these reasons that many patrolmen prefer to settle a challenge to authority on the spot, an alternative that necessarily poses the prospect of violence. As William Westley has pointed out in the last analysis the police can always try to "coerce respect."[22]

They don't never beat you in the car. They wait until they get you to the station. And then they beat you when the first shift comes on and they beat you when the second shift comes on. I've seen it happen. I was right there in the next cell. They had a boy. His name was Stan, and they had beat him already as soon as they

[22] The above analysis of why policemen retaliate when the legitimacy of their authority is challenged differs somewhat from Westley's analysis of why a large percentage of the policemen he studied "believed that it was legitimate to use violence to coerce respect." Westley argues that disrespectful behavior constitutes a threat to the already low "occupational status" of policemen and therefore comes as a blow to their self-esteem. Westley's hypothesis would suggest, however, that those policemen who *accepted* their low occupational status would therefore allow their authority to be challenged. Although Westley's variables no doubt affect the behavior of patrolmen, there also seems to be more at stake than status as a workman when claims to authority are ignored. In a sense the patrolman whose authority has been successfully called into question has already abdicated a sizable chunk of his honor as well as his job. See William A. Westley, "Violence and the Police," *American Journal of Sociology*, Vol. LIX (July 1953).

brought him in. And then when they was changing shifts, you know, the detective came and looked on the paper that say what he was booked for, I think it was robbery or something like that, and they started beating on him again. See, the police are smart. They don't leave no bruises. They'll beat you somewhere where it don't show. That's the main places where they look to hit you at. And if it did show, your word wouldn't be as good as theirs. They can lie too, you know. All they have to say is that you was resisting and that's the only reason they need for doing what they do.

Resisting arrest is the one charge involving violence that seems uniquely designed to deal with improper deportment in the situation of suspicion. A policeman interviewed by Westley suggests that when the challenge to authority is not sufficiently serious to warrant this charge, the police may continue to provoke the suspect until the level of belligerence reaches proportions that legitimate invoking this category of offense.

For example, when you stop a fellow for a routine questioning, say a wise guy, and he starts talking back to you and telling you that you are no good and that sort of thing. You know you can take a man in on a disorderly conduct charge, but you can practically never make it stick. So what you do in a case like this is to egg the guy on until he makes a remark where you can justifiably slap him, and then if he fights back, you can call it resisting arrest.[23]

And from a gang member's point of view:

Another reason why they beat up on you is because they always have the advantage over you. The cop might say, "You done this." And you might say, "I didn't!" And he'll say, "Don't talk back to me or I'll go upside your head!" You know, and then

[23] *Ibid.*, p. 30.

they say they had a right to hit you or arrest you because you were talking back to an officer or resisting arrest, and you were merely trying to explain or tell him that you hadn't done what he said you'd done. One of those kinds of things. Well, that means you in the wrong when you get downtown anyway. You're always in the wrong.

• • •

On the street, of course, the issues involved in these encounters are by no means as clear-cut as the above analysis might suggest. Much of the interaction between gang members and policeman takes place in scenes that are almost totally chaotic and confused. . . .

• • •

When gang members find themselves *arrested* for insolence rather than for any other specific offense, they are doubly outraged. Not only have they been insulted, but their response to the insult has been the principal reason for their arrest. Under the circumstances, the legitimacy of the interrogating policeman is all but destroyed. The boys have a good word for the factors other than offense that often lead to their arrest. When asked, they will say they got "busted" for "humbug."

Like most people, the boys manage to construct a theory that allows them to "explain" the persistence of police harassment, but this theory is simply a version of their general belief that "everyone is always out for themselves." Most patrolmen are seen as corrupt, prejudiced, and sadistic opportunists who exploit their position of power over the boys in order to earn the respect of fellow officers, a theory that is usually formulated as follows:

Why do they pick us up? Just to be messing with somebody. To get more stripes, that's all, to get more stripes.

Similarly, the fact that patrolmen al-ways seem to demand respect is attributed largely to an idiosyncratic egomania that seems somehow to flourish in the profession of police work:

You know what cracks me up about them guys, them cops you know, they think you're supposed to do everything they say just 'cause they're cops. They don't even bother about the books. They just think that because they're cops you're supposed to respect them more than anybody else. Does it say that? Does it say in the books that you're supposed to respect them more than anybody else? No it don't! You're supposed to respect everybody, right? And you're supposed to treat everybody equal. They shouldn't be treated as though they were anything special. You should extend courtesy to them the same as you would to your family, the same as you would to your father and mother. I mean you don't have to go out of your way for them. I mean I don't even say "Sir" to my old man. He doesn't expect me to say "Sir!" What a bunch of phony dudes. One time I got arrested for gang activity and they put the cuffs on me, and the officer put them on pretty hard, and they was hurting my wrists. So I told the officer, I told him real nice, I say, "Officer, could you loosen these cuffs a little, they're cutting off my blood circulation." It was really my wine circulation. So he say, "Okay." And he come over there, and when I wasn't looking he squeezed them tighter.

But the above theory of arrogance and opportunism does not provide a basis for the total denial of police authority because it only applies to individuals rather than to the police as an occupational group. The boys continue to believe that patrolmen *should* treat them with respect and that arrests *should* be confined to behavior that is clearly against the law. This is why policemen who treat the boys deferentially and do not arrest them for "humbug" may still on occasion be considered "good cops."

Yet the gang boys continue to have experiences with patrolmen that contradict their conventional expectations about how the police should behave. Moreover, with the exception of the Black Muslims, no one has offered them a comprehensive explanation of their situation. The result is thus a diffuse frustration and fury that occasionally turns into a blind and explosive rage.

On September 28, 1966, for example, a white patrolman in the Hunters Point district of San Francisco spotted three Negro boys in an approaching car and became suspicious when the boys jumped out of the car and began running away. The officer claims he fired three shots in the air before hitting one of the boys in the back with a fourth. The boy was sixteen, and he died on a barren stretch of the rocky Hunters Point Hill just a few feet from his home. The car was reported stolen four hours after the boy was dead.

When the gang boys in the area saw the body, they began breaking windows, burning buildings, and looting stores. The uprising went on for twenty-four hours and only stopped when the National Guard arrived. The citizens of San Francisco responded to the outbreak of violence by attempting to find jobs for the youth at Hunters Point. As far as the general community was concerned, the cause of the riot was unemployment.

Yet it was no accident that the demonstration was triggered by an incident involving the police. Gang boys interpret the way the boundaries of their neighborhoods are patrolled as a conscious policy of confinement, and the police are looked upon as a foreign army of occupation. There are limits to what the natives will take from these troops, however, and there are times when more is needed to express rebellion than artful displays of insolence. These boys have been angry, bewildered, and resentful about the police for as long as they can remember, and they simply decided to strike back the only way they knew how.

Things don't change. Like day before yesterday. We were sitting down on the steps talking with Joe and them. So here comes the police, coming down there messing with people.

"Where do you live?" they say.

"Up on the Hill."

He say, "Where do you eat at?"

"Up on the Hill."

"Where do you sleep at?"

"Up on the Hill."

He say, "Where you get your mail at?" I say, "Up on the Hill."

He say, "Well don't you think you ought to be getting up the Hill right now!"

So we went up the Hill.

25.

The Function of Social Definitions in the

Development of the Gang Boy's Career

Carl Werthmann

The moral career of the lower class juvenile gang boy often begins at age 6, 7, or 8 when he is defined by his teachers as "predelinquent" for demonstrating to his friends that he is not a "sissy," and it ends between the ages of 16 and 25 when he either takes a job, goes to college, joins the Army, or becomes a criminal.[1] Although much of

NOTE. The research on which this paper is based was initiated by the Survey Research Center at the University of California in Berkeley on a grant from the Ford Foundation and was later moved to the Center for the Study of Law and Society on the Berkeley campus, where funds were made available under a generous grant from the Office of Juvenile Delinquency and Youth Development, Welfare Administration, U.S. Department of Health, Education, and Welfare, in cooperation with the President's Committee on Juvenile Delinquency and Youth Crime.

SOURCE. *Task Force Report: Juvenile Delinquency and Youth Crime, A Report by the President's Commission on Law Enforcement and Administration of Justice*, Washington, D.C.; U.S. Government Printing Office, 1967, pp. 155–170. (*Original title:* "The Function of Social Definitions in the Development of Delinquent Careers.") (Editorial adaptations.) Reprinted with permission.

[1] The concept of a moral career has been defined by Erving Goffman as "the regular sequence of changes that career entails in the person's self and in his framework of

his behavior during this period can be seen and is seen by him as a voluntary set of claims on one of the temporary social identities available to him as a lower class "youth," his final choice of an "adult" identity will depend in large measure on the way his moral character has been assessed, categorized, and acted upon by his parents, teachers, and officials of the law as well as on the attitudes and actions he has chosen in response. How the boys embrace these identities, how adults tend to define and treat them for doing so, and how the boys respond to these definitions and treatments is thus the subject of this paper.[2]

imagery for judging himself and others." See Erving Goffman, "The Moral Career of the Mental Patient," in *Asylums* (New York: Doubleday & Co., Inc., 1961), p. 128.

[2] The data on which this study is based consists of taped interviews with 56 "core" members of 11 "delinquent" gangs or "jacket clubs" plus observations and more informal conversations involving over 100 members of these 11 gangs. The boys were drawn from the clientele of a delinquency-prevention program in San Francisco called Youth for Service, and the research was conducted largely out of their offices for a 2-year period. Of the 56 boys interviewed on tape, 37 were Negro, 11 were Mexican,

THE IDENTITY MATERIALS OF THE DELINQUENT

Although the special conditions of youth as a status do not dictate, provoke, or account for "delinquent" behavior, these conditions constitute the structural possibilities that allow it to exist; and, as suggested by the fact that most gang boys leave the streets as soon as they are forced to make a living, one of these conditions concerns the way young people are related to the economy.[3] Since they are required by law to attend school until the age of 16 or thereabouts, they are virtually forced to remain financially dependent on their parents during these years, and this state of dependence diminishes the magnitude of their responsibilities considerably. They do not have to support themselves or a family, and the schools are equipped to run quite well, if not better, without them. Unlike adults, they are thus left relatively free to organize their lives around noneconomic pursuits. Looked at another way, however, they are also deprived of occupational categories and activities as ways to differentiate themselves from one another.

In the adult world, occupations are the major source of social identity. The jobs themselves are used to classify and rank, while the norms governing performance are the principal criteria by which competence and character are judged. In the world inhabited by youth, however, identities must be constructed from other materials; and on the whole, these materials are limited to the activities that take place in

schools and those engaged in and around them.[4] The school provides a number of instrumental training roles for those who wish to pursue them, but if a student is neither academically nor politically inclined, these roles are likely not to have much meaning. Particularly in elementary and junior high schools, it is not so much what you *do* that counts but rather what you *are*, since everyone tends to be doing about the same things.

In the absence of occupational titles, a rich vocabulary of identity categories tends to emerge, a vocabulary that often includes referents to physical or anatomical features, clothing styles, places, possessions, special membership groups, and a general relationship to the administration of schools.[5] In addition, each of

[4] Although the family can be seen as an important source of emotional support for the various contests that go on outside it, there is little important contribution it can make to the genesis of public identities since most young people do not spend time together in the same home.

[5] Just prior to the completion of this study, for example, the high school population of San Francisco had divided itself into four major groups. The lower and working class Negroes, Spanish-speaking minorities, and whites were referred to as "bloods," "barts," and "white shoes," respectively, while the fourth group, the "Ivy Leaguers," contained the middle and lower middle class segments of all three races. The relationship to schools implicit in this vocabulary is obvious, and all four groups were easily identifiable by uniform. The "bloods," "barts," and "white shoes" were further broken down into gangs by districts and each gang had its own jacket. Moreover, the district and gang distinctions took precedence over race in racially integrated districts so that the lower class Negroes and whites living in predominantly Spanish-speaking areas wore the "bart" uniform and were referred to by members of their own race as such.

In the city of Albany on the other side of the San Francisco Bay, the vocabulary adopted by the students in the all-white high school is devoid of ethnic references but certainly no less to the point; the students who congregate during recess on plots of land in the middle of the school have been entitled the "quadrangles"; the stu-

and 8 were Caucasian. This report is thus based primarily on a sample of Negro gang boys.

[3] To the extent that these conditions rule out the possibilities of deviance, they can be referred to as elements of "structural conduciveness." See Neil J. Smelser, *Theory of Collective Behavior* (New York: The Free Press of Glencoe, 1963), p. 15.

these categories tends to be associated with certain skills and attributes of character as well as with the activities in which these skills and character traits are generally displayed.

As Erving Goffman has elegantly made clear, however, there are certain skills and attributes of character, particularly those most prized by gang boys, that can only be claimed by aspirants to them in social situations where something of consequence is risked; and since the school facilities available for nonacademic character construction are generally limited to games, it is not surprising that boys who wish to play for higher stakes tend to use each other, the law, and sometimes even school officials in order to demonstrate their claims.[6]

It is impossible to prove that one is cool, courageous, or "smart," for example, without a situation in which there is something to be cool, courageous, or "smart" about, just as it is difficult to gain a reputation for being "tough" unless the skills involved are occasionally put to a test. In situations where it is possible to claim possession of these attributes, the reward won or utility gained, in addition to whatever material goods may be at stake, is an increment in status or reputation, a commodity that youth, like adults, spend a sizable amount of time attempting to obtain and protect. Conversely, the risks include the possibility of damaging the

body or the pocketbook as well as the chance of being shown to lack whatever skills or attributes of character the situation calls for. In addition, when the law is being used to prove possession of moral character, there is also the probability of being observed or discovered and thus sanctioned by the State. Goffman further suggests that risky situations should be entered voluntarily if a person wishes others to grant him possession of the desired attributes without any contingent doubts: and when this happens, he says, there is "action" to be found.[7]

Claiming title to these character traits can be more difficult than it may first appear, however, since risky situations do not arise very often in the course of an average day. In fact, as Goffman points out, most people manage to arrange their lives so that matters of consequence such as physical safety and a money supply are protected from unnecessary risk, although as a result these people encounter few situations in which the most heroic of social virtues can actually be claimed rather than assumed.

Yet if someone with an adult status actually decides he desires "action," there is always Las Vegas or a risky job, while a lower class gang boy is more or less forced to create his own. If he wishes to prove that he is autonomous, courageous, loyal, or has "heart," not only must he take a chance, he must also construct the situation in which to take it; and for most gang boys this means that risky situations must be made from whatever materials happen to be available on the streets and at schools.[8]

dents who meet in the parking lot outside the school are called just that, "parking lots"; and the remainder of the student body is referred to as "uncommitted," presumably because they occupy the territory between the parking lot and the quadrangle that surrounds the school on four sides.

[6] I am indebted to a recent unpublished paper by Goffman for much of the analysis of gang acitivity that follows. See Erving Goffman, "Where the Action Is: Or, Hemingway Revisited," Center For the Study of Law and Society. University of California, Berkeley, 1965.

[7] As Goffman puts it, "action" can be located "wherever the individual knowingly takes chances that are defined as voluntary, and whose conduct is perceived as a reflection on character." Goffman, op. cit., p. 48.

[8] It was largely on the basis of an argument such as this that Norman Mailer sug-

On the streets, the various activities defined by law as "thefts" provide perhaps the best examples of the way gang boys use laws to construct and claim identities. In order to become usable as identity materials, however, the situations in which laws against theft are broken must be carefully selected to insure that sufficient risk is present. Unlike the professional thief who takes pride in knowing how to minimize the occupational risks of his trade, most younger gang boys create risks where none need be involved.[9] Joyriding, for example, is ideally suited for this purpose since "cool" is required to get a stolen car started quickly; and once started, the situation contains the generous though not overwhelming risk of detection. Moreover, given the wide range of risky activities that can be engaged in once the cars are stolen, joyriding is viewed as an abundant source of the anxiety, excitement, and tension that accompanies the taking of risks for its own sake, a complex of emotions often referred to as "kicks."

(Did you guys do much joyriding?) Yeah. When I was about 13, I didn't do nothing but steal cars. The guy that I always stole with, both of us liked to drive so we'd steal a car. And then he'd go steal another car and we'd chase each other. Like there would be two in our car, two in the other car, and we'd drive by and stick out our hands, and if you touch them then they have to chase you. Or we'd steal an old car, you know, that have the running boards on it. We'd stand on that and kick the car going past. Kind of fun, but, uh, it's real dangerous. We used

to have a ball when we'd do that other game with the hands though.

In addition to joyriding which was almost always done at night, the younger gang boys I studied also located two risky daytime situations in which to engage in theft. On Saturday afternoons, they would delight in trying to steal hubcaps from a packed parking lot next to a local supermarket, and on special occasions, they enjoyed breaking into gum and candy machines located in a crowded amusement park. In the parking lot, the challenge consisted of making away with the hubcaps without being seen, while in the equally crowded amusement park, the risk consisted of darting through the customers and away from the police after making sure that the theft itself had been observed.

(What else did you guys used to do when you were in Junior High School?) Well, we would sometimes, three or four of us, maybe go to Playland and rob the machines. That would be a ball cause, see, what we'd do is maybe have two guys start fighting or maybe jump on a sailor or something like that. In the meantime, the other two guys would go back in there while the police was, you know, chasing the others, while we was back there breaking the machines open, you know. There was about five or six of them machines. So then the cops would always see us cause somebody would yell for them. So they would stop chasing the other guys and start chasing us. We had a lot of fun up there.

Even among the younger boys, however, thievery was sometimes undertaken for motives other than "kicks" or "fun." Shoplifting, for example, was viewed as a more instrumental activity, as was the practice of stealing coin changers from temporarily evacuated buses parked in a nearby public depot. In the case of shoplifting, most of the boys wanted and wore the various items

_____

gested "medieval jousting tournaments in Central Park" and "horse races through the streets of Little Italy" as delinquency prevention programs for the City of New York. See Norman Mailer, *The Presidential Papers* (New York: Bantam Books, 1964), p. 22.

[9] See Edwin H. Sutherland *The Professional Thief* (Chicago: The University of Chicago Press, 1937).

of clothing they stole; and when buses were robbed, either the money was divided among the boys or it was used to buy supplies for a party being given by the club.

Like we'd give a party on a Friday night. Well, we know the bread man come Thursday. And we know what time he gets there and what time he leaves, so we know what time to be there to get the bread. And then we know where to get the tuna fish and the Kool Aid. That's simple. Just walk into any store and steal that. I used to call everybody so they get up. Let's say two gonna go get the bread. The other two gonna go out to the streetcars cause early in the morning they just leave their money on the bus cause there ain't nobody around. Get some coffee at the Fire Department. So they go on and hit the streetcar and get the money, something like that.

Yet these thefts were not perceived as exclusively instrumental. Practically as soon as the gang was formed in elementary school, its identity system differentiated into "thieves" and "fighters," and both types of boys were perceived as performing some function for the group. Thus, even when the purpose of theft was defined as instrumental, the act itself was quickly communicated to the other gang members since it was a source of identification as well as party supplies.

Our club was organized. We had a mutual understanding between us. Everybody in the club had something good about them or something bad. Everybody had some kind of profession. Like Ray, he was the fighter, always throwing his weight around when we had a fight or something. Little Johnnie and Ronnie, they were what we called the thieves. They was the best! I mean those two could steal anything. Then, like Arnold couldn't spell his name. He couldn't spell Arnold. I mean, boy he needed help.

As the members of a gang get older,

their perception and use of theft become increasingly instrumental; and if they are still in the gang after graduating or getting expelled from high school, theft turns into a particular version of the "hustle." These hustles still involve risks, but the risks are no longer incurred exclusively for what can be demonstrated about the self by taking them. The possible sanctions faced are much more serious than they were in junior high school. Moreover, the boys now need the money. Without it they would find themselves hard pressed to sustain a daily round of socializing with ease. Thus, their relationship to the risky situation changes as both positive and negative outcomes become more consequential; and as this shift takes place, the actual thefts themselves are talked about less and less. Where a boy happens to be getting his money becomes his own private business, a policy that gradually evolves as attempts are made to cut down the probability of detection.

Yet the boys still do not see themselves as professional thieves, even after they have graduated from high school. As long as they can rely on their parents for room and board, the hustle is viewed as a transitory, impermanent, and part-time way of simply getting by. It is not conceived of as an "adult" training role, even though it is an instrumental relationship to the economic world. On the other hand, if the boys remain on the streets after 18, they are no longer stealing for "kicks."

The laws against theft are not the only materials used by gang boys to demonstrate moral character. On the streets, they also tend to use each other for this purpose, activities that Goffman has called "character games."

I assume that when two persons are in one another's presence it will be inevitable that many of the obligations of one will be the expectations of the other (and vice versa), in matters both substantive and ceremonial. Each participant will have a personal vested interest in seeing to it that in this particular case the rules the other ought to obey are in fact obeyed by him. Mutual dependence on the other's proper conduct occurs. Each individual necessarily thus becomes a field in which the other necessarily practices good or bad conduct. In the ordinary course of affairs, compliance, forebearance and the mechanisms of apology and excuse insure that showdowns don't occur. None the less, contests over whose treatment of the other is to prevail are always a possibility, and can almost always be made to occur. The participants will then find themselves committed to producing evidence that will cause a re-assessment of self at the expense of the assessment that will come to be made of the other. A "character game" results.[10]

Goffman further suggests that a claim to possess "honor" is what initiates most character games, honor defined as "the property of character which causes the individual to engage in a character contest when his rights have been violated and when the likely cost of the contest is high."[11] Like other forms of "action," then, character games are played at some risk but also presumably for some reward.

As Short and Strodtbeck have pointed out, fighting is perhaps the classic example of a gang activity that is best understood with this model.[12] After observing gang boys in Chicago for a number of years, these authors concluded that most fights take place either when a "rep" for toughness is suddenly challenged by a situation that the gang boy cannot avoid confronting or when a challenge to within-group rank appears, either from inside or outside the gang. In the first instance, the gang boy is handed a chance to appear "honorable," perhaps even a chance he did not want; while in the second instance, the boy will provoke a character contest to reaffirm or reclaim his status in the gang after it is challenged by a streetworker or another boy, sometimes during an absence in jail.

Although it is quite true that most older gang boys will only fight when their reputations or ranks are threatened, the younger boys can sometimes be found initiating fights even though they have not been provoked. These fights are consciously sought out or searched for in an attempt to build a reputation where none existed before, and the boys are referred to as "looking for trouble" because they are "coming up." In these situations, an attempt is often made to select the target carefully. Not any rival gang will serve as a suitable object on which to build a rep, and thus, as in the following case, a gang invading "rival territory" may decide to go home if the members cannot find boys who are big or important enough to prove a case.

Remember when them guys from Hunters Point came over looking for us? Man, it got real bad there. Cause when we made the papers, you know, everybody thought we was something. So then they all come lookin' for you. Gonna knock off the big boys. So a whole bunch of these little kids from Hunters Point came lookin' for us one night. They was coming up, and they figured they could beat us or something. (Did you fight?) No. We wasn't in the neighborhood that night. They found a bunch of guys their age but they wasn't interested in that. They just went home.

Particularly among younger boys, a great deal of bullying is apparently also

10 Goffman, op. cit. n.6, p. 60.
11 Goffman, op. cit. n.6, p. 63.
12 James F. Short, Jr., and Fred L. Strodtbeck, *Group Process and Gang Delinquency* (Chicago: The University of Chicago Press, 1965), pp. 248–264; also J. Short and F. Strodtbeck, "Why Gangs Fight," *Trans-Action*, 1, 1964.

inspired by attempts to build rather than protect reputations. For example, a schoolteacher in Washington, D.C., recently told me that her fourth grade class already contained a boy who had earned the nickname "tough cat," a nickname that was apparently achieved by beating up younger, older, bigger, and smaller boys virtually at random.[13] After the nickname was given to a single boy, it then became a free-floating identity aspired to by others in the class and could be claimed for the same activity. Once the boys get to high school, however, this sort of fighting tends to be perceived as "unfair."

When I was in Junior High some kids called me king of the school, and there was about seven of us. You know, we ran that school. Those girls, they kinda looked up to us. We didn't let nobody go with nothing. It ain't nothing now, but we all would get in front of the line—Get out the way, let us through— you know. There wasn't about seven of us. Want some money, just ask for it and they glad to give it to you cause they scared. It was just that we was seven bullies I guess. Cause we'd snap our fingers and they'd do what we tell them. See, that was when we was younger. The girls, they went for all that cause they didn't know no better than you. They liked to see somebody being bad then. Big show-offs. Somebody who's a lot of fun. See, they like that then. But now that you get older, they don't go for it so much no more.

There may be a parallel here between the apparently "senseless violence" engaged in by very young boys and the more serious instances of "random violence" some times found among gang boys at the very end of their "delinquent" careers. In the oldest gang I worked with, all of whose members were between 20 and 25, a few of the boys would occasionally stab strangers

miscellaneously, ostensibly for having received a "dirty look." Most of these stabbings seemed to occur when the boys were in the process of bragging about their past exploits and their virtually nonexistent "reps."

It is possible that for very young boys, the task of building a "rep" can involve creating an audience for this behavior where none previously existed, and this task may involve selecting targets miscellaneously in order to establish the rules. In the case of older boys, however, the instances of random violence seem to occur just after most of the real audience for this behavior abandons this source of identity for an occupation, at which point the boys who still wish to retain an identity by engaging in acts of violence may choose to imagine that this audience still exists. Although the consequences of these audience creation problems are clearly more serious among older boys than among younger ones, both tend to be defined as "disturbed" by their immediate audience of peers.

Regardless of whether fights are entered into voluntarily or involuntarily and regardless of whether they take place in situations that are imagined or real, the basic principle involved in this mode of identity construction seems to be clear: the fight is defined as a situation in which reputation or rank can be won or lost. Whether a particular fight will be entered into depends on the expected values of the various outcomes, and these values can vary considerably from boy to boy. It is no accident, for example, that situations involving violence are often perceived as "turning points" by ex-gang members when contemplating their past careers. Particularly among older boys, it is easy to see how reputations can get large enough so as not to be worth the risk of defending.[14] Similarly, in areas where it

[13] I am indebted to Ethel Rosenthal for this observation.

[14] I encountered two boys who dropped

is tacitly understood that certain affronts can only be revenged by attempting to kill the offender, the person offended may simply decide to leave town rather than run the risk of being sent to jail or killed in defense of his honor.[15]

In addition to fighting, there are also other activities in which gang boys use each other to claim and construct identities. The behavior described by Miller as "verbal aggression," also known variously as "ranking," "capping," or "sounding," seems to involve some of the same principles found in fights.[16] As Matza has pointed out, this activity amounts essentially to a process of testing status by insult, and thus honor is the quality of moral character at stake.[17] Goffman has called these encounters "contest contests," situations in which someone forces someone else "into a contest over whether or not there will be a contest."[18] Like fighting, it involves risk and can thus have a bearing on status. Unlike fighting, however, it is not engaged in to demonstrate toughness or courage but rather to display a type of verbal agility that gang boys call "smart."

Short and Strodtbeck have also suggested that the "utility-risk paradigm" might shed some light on the high percentage of illegitimate pregnancies that gang boys produce while engaged in another type of "interpersonal action" discussed by Goffman, namely "making

out."[19] Sexual activity sometimes begins very early among gang boys, and there is typically a great deal of it throughout a career. Most of the Negro boys claimed to have lost their virginity around the age of 8 or 9, and some were having intercourse regularly in junior high school. During most of the years spent in a gang, girls are seen primarily as objects for sexual play, and it is not until the age of 16 or older that they are sometimes treated with anything resembling respect. Ultimately, however, it is marriage that takes most boys out of the gang, thus providing one of the few available legitimate excuses for leaving the streets.[20]

Although Short and Strodtbeck suggest that two separate risks are involved in illegitimacy, the first being the probability of engaging in sexual intercourse with a given frequency and the second being the probability that these actions will eventuate in parenthood, only one of these risks is used as a source of identity. Success or failure at "making it" with a girl is socially risky since the outcome affects status in the gang, while it is doubtful that the risks involved in gambling without contraception are considered a source of pleasure independent of the act itself.

The gang boy thus aspires to an identity that puts him in a special relationship to risk. When he is around his friends, he often creates the situations in which he chooses to exist, an act of creation that involves selecting out certain features of the social environment and then transforming them into the conditions that allow him to define a self. In part, these risks are taken for their own sake since a reputation can

---

out of gang activity for this reason. In one case, the boy decided it was time to leave after he was shot at twice in 1 week from passing automobiles driven by members of different rival gangs.

[15] Claude Brown, *Manchild in the Promised Land* (New York: The Macmillan Co., 1965), p. 171.

[16] W. B. Miller, H. Geertz, and S. G. Cutter, "Aggression in a Boy's Street Corner Group," *Psychiatry* (November 1961), pp. 283–298.

[17] David Matza, *Delinquency and Drift* (John Wiley & Sons, 1964), pp. 42–44.

[18] Goffman, op. cit., p. 68.

[19] Short and Strodtbeck, *Group Process*, op. cit. n. 12, pp. 44–45, 249–250.

[20] Walter B. Miller, "The Corner Gang Boys Get Married," *Trans-Action*, vol. 1 (November 1963), pp. 10–12.

be built on this capacity alone and the emotional reward is a "kick." In part, there are also honor, courage, and loyalty involved, special attributes of moral character that can only be demonstrated in situations of risk. Taken together, however, these risks seem to represent a set of special claims to the status of "men," a status they are culturally and structurally forbidden to occupy until the "delinquent career" comes to an end. Why gang boys rather than others decide to take these risks is a difficult if not impossible question to answer. Yet it is possible to look at how the gang boy deals with the mechanisms that ordinarily prevent these risks from being taken.

THE GENESIS OF AUTONOMY

Although the absence of adult economic responsibilities can be seen as conducive to the development of unconventional identity formations among youth, young people are also politically dependent on adults. A person under age 18 is always in the legal custody of someone; and if he proves to be beyond control by parents, he can always be adopted by the State. In effect, this means that young people can be ordered to obey the rules established for them by their parents since the law can be appealed to if these commands are not obeyed.

In most instances, however, this parental power develops into authority. As a rule, young people simply assume that parents are a legitimate if sometimes difficult source of rules and thus obey them voluntarily.[21] Perhaps more important, it is precisely this authority relationship that allows at least the preadolescent to define himself as "a child."

[21] Max Weber, *The Theory of Social and Economic Organization*, translated by A. M. Henderson and Talcott Parsons (Glencoe: The Free Press, 1947).

He implicitly surrenders all autonomy and thus does not exercise whatever capacity he might have to make his own decisions. In return, he can afford to feel "protected."

In addition to establishing their own authority, parents also have a vested interest in endowing school teachers with a temporary "title to rule." This legitimacy is sometimes conferred in subtle ways but most techniques are easy to observe. Parents caution their offspring to behave and get good grades, then teachers are visited to determine whether these prescriptions are being obeyed. In instances where there is a dispute between teacher and child, parents rarely voice criticism to a son or daughter—however much the teacher may be castigated for ruining the future of the family in the privacy of a bedroom.

To further insure that the authority of school personnel is legitimated, boys and girls are made aware that these officials can and do inform parents of their misadventures. Parents, teachers, and other adult officials thus see to it that children are not allowed to segregate roles. Since parents typically have the ultimate power, they become the center of a communications network for other adult authorities. Whether the child is at school or on the streets, he is made to feel that none of his behavior can be hidden from his parents.[22]

The youngsters who define themselves as dependent do not mind being the subjects of this friendly conspiracy and most would feel very insecure without it. They often cannot tolerate a segregation of roles, even when the com-

[22] It is largely for this reason that vehicles for public transportation such as buses become scenes of mass confusion when children ride them unsupervised to and from school. The bus drivers do not have access to parents and the children know it.

munications network is broken by accident and thus they often feel the need to confess their sins in order to relieve themselves of the responsibility for hiding information. These "confessionals" are considered rewarding moments for parents who take pride in constructing leakproof systems of surveillance over their offspring. They are looked upon as indicators of "trust."

Precisely how this network of authority is cultivated and maintained remains something of a psychosocial mystery. Yet the fact remains that as long as parents can manage to have their ideals about the behavior of their offspring either aspired to or even vaguely achieved, there is precious little chance, as we will see, that policemen and probation officers will end up defining them as "delinquents," provided, of course, that the number of crimes committed is kept to some reasonable limit. Although I encountered a great many parents who had come to look upon the trip to jail as "routine" by the time their sons were 16, I found none who said that at an earlier point in life they had not hoped for something better. In practically every case, it was possible to locate a set of expectations that was perceived by parents either to have broken down or never to have developed, despite the fact that many had also come to view the news of "trouble" as a more or less "normal" event.

The situation that these parents find themselves in can perhaps best be described with a vocabulary developed by Harold Garfinkel for the analysis of how stable social activity systems are "constituted," become "disorganized," and are "reconstituted."[23] Garfinkel suggests that routine social activities are defined in the most fundamental sense of that word by a set of "constitutive" or "basic" rules, i.e., rules that are used to make behavior recognizable as an act or event in some known order of events. Unlike institutionalized norms (or "preferred rules" as Garfinkel calls them), the "basic" rules do not specify how a person is to act in an activity but only the range of possible acts he could perform as well as the social category of person he is if he takes part in them. As examples of "basic rules," Garfinkel cites those that "constitute" the game of tictactoe: "Play is conducted on a three by three matrix by two players who move alternatively. The first player makes a mark in one of the unoccupied cells. The second player, in his turn, places his mark in one of the remaining unoccupied cells. And so on. The term 'tictactoe player' refers to a person who seeks to act in compliance with these possible events as constitutively expected ones."[24]

Garfinkel further suggests that in order for an activity system to be "stable," the people involved in the activity must "trust" each other, "trust" defined as a condition in which the participants expect one another to act in compliance with the basic or constitutive rules. If these rules are violated, the activity is in danger of becoming "confused" or "disorganized" since people will find themselves without a context in which to interpret the meaning of the act committed by the violator and thus will not know how to respond to him. In addition, there is often a feeling that the condition of "trust" has been broken and the people who believe themselves to be participants in the activity are likely to get anxious, frustrated, or angry.

In groups such as families, friendships, and businesses where participants are quite committed to one another for

---

[23] Harold Garfinkel, "Some Conceptions of and Experiments with 'Trust' as a Condition of Stable Concerted Actions," MS.

[24] Garfinkel, op. cit. n. 23, p. 6.

personal, economic, and legal reasons, some attempt is usually made to "normalize" the situation. This can mean that there is a renewal of belief in the other person's commitment to the previous rules or that the rules will change, in which case an act or event that was not previously understood will come to be perceived as "normal" or "routine." If a "basic" rule is added or subtracted, however, the result is a new activity.

Following this conceptual scheme, we can see that where the participants in an activity include an "authority" as well as others who are seen as "subordinates," the set of basic rules establishing the activity will always include a rule which constitutes this relationship. From the point of view of a subordinate, moreover, this rule will be one that says: I choose to obey all the preferred rules or norms that are established for me in this activity by the category of person who is designated the authority, say a parent, a teacher, or perhaps even all adults.

In addition, we can predict that where an authority has a part in some activity, it will be important to him that his subordinates act in compliance with the basic rule establishing the source of preferred rules, or, put another way, that his subordinates "trust" him. From the point of view of the authority, moreover, the important issue about all acts becomes not whether they are being performed in accordance with a particular rule but whether they are being performed in accordance with the rule establishing who it is that properly establishes the rules themselves.

This problem is frequently and simply illustrated among the parents of pre-adolescent and "predelinquent" boys, many of whom are described as simply "out of control." In these cases, what the parents seem to be describing are situations in which no stable pattern of mutual expectations has developed at all. Whatever preferred rules they attempt to establish as a way of ordering the activities of the family are more or less randomly ignored by their offspring. In the neighborhood where this study was done, for example, there were always a certain number of boys on the streets who, from the point of view of their parents, had "suddenly disappeared." They were usually classified as "runaways" after failing to appear for 1, 2, or 3 consecutive nights, but since they only rarely proved to be more than 10 blocks away from their houses at any time and during an absence might even faithfully attend school, this classification was sometimes not adopted until a week of absence had elapsed. In some cases, the inability to predict an appearance was almost total. These parents could rarely count on their sons either to be at school, at home for meals, or sometimes even in bed. For example:

(How do you handle Melvin when he gets into trouble?) Well, we figure that weekends are the main times he looks forward to—parties and going out. So we'd say, "You can't go out tonight." You know, we'd try to keep him from something he really wanted to do. But he usually goes out anyway. Like one night we was watching TV, and Melvin said he was tired and went to bed. So then I get a phone call from a lady who wants to know if Melvin is here because her son is with him. I said, "No, he has gone to bed already." She says, "Are you sure?" I said, "I'm pretty sure." So I went downstairs and I peeked in and saw a lump in the bed but I didn't see his head. So I took a look and he was gone. He came home about 12:30, and we talked for a while. (What did you do?) Well, I told him he was wrong going against his parents like that, but he keeps sneaking out anyway. (What does your husband do about it?) Well, he don't do much. I'm the one who gets upset. My husband, he'll say something to Mel and then he'll just relax and forget about it. (Husband and wife laugh together.) There's little we can do, you know. It's hard to talk to him cause he just go ahead and do what he wants anyway.[25]

The initial response of most parents to this behavior is anger, a sense of betrayal, and a feeling that the family situation has become "disorganized." After a while, however, this lack of predictability becomes virtually "routine." Passing one of these mothers on the street, she might report that "Charles is gone again." Only wistfully would she ask me whether I had seen him or happened to know where he was. She already knew that by and large Charles made up his own mind when to come and go. Since she did not know where, however, she was curious.

Although it is often hard to judge how the absence of parental trust is perceived by the boys involved, in most cases it seems to be taken as a simple matter of fact. When the very young boys are asked why they "ran away," they often do not seem to know; and when they are asked on the streets why they do not return home, their answer

is usually, "because when I do I'll get a beating."

These children, most between the ages of 6 and 10, were the most puzzling people I met on this study. Their behavior always seemed to make perfect sense to them, but it also seemed to make so much sense that they could not produce accounts for it. Although they sometimes exhibited a touch of bravado, they were only rarely defensive, and most managed to carry themselves with what can only be described as miniature adult poise. When they were not in motion or suddenly running away, they assumed the posture of "little men," often shouldering their autonomy with great dignity but rarely with perfect ease.

These children are a testimony to the fact that basic rules about authority are not accepted automatically, even among the young. The assumption of dependence must be cultivated before it can be used as a basis for control, and this becomes quite clear when for some reason this assumption is never made. In these cases, the children often demonstrate a remarkable capacity to take care of themselves. In fact, one could argue that the preadolescent who does not conceive of himself as dependent on his parents also does not really conceive of himself as "a child," particularly when he loses his virginity at 8 and supports himself on lunch money taken from classmates. Once the authority rule is rejected, the family as an activity system becomes an entirely new game. Politically the child is not an adult, but sociologically it is hard to argue that he is still a child.[26]

---

[25] The family being described here is a classic example of a "disorganized" activity system since the son himself could rarely count on the appearance of his parents. Both worked, the father as a free-lance garage mechanic and the mother as an Avon saleslady, and both enjoyed taking spur-of-the-moment trips to Las Vegas. This meant that when the boy disappeared, he often returned to find his parents gone and vice-versa. Moreover, given the fact that random disappearances tend to stop around age 12, these family situations are often as unpredictable to sociologists as they are to the family members involved. The boy being discussed, for example, had an older brother on the honor roll at a local San Francisco high school during the same period that he asked his streetworker whether he could be admitted "voluntarily" to Juvenile Hall when he felt that his family situation was unmanageable at home, a desire that is not uncommon although rarely acted upon by the younger boys.

[26] Herb Gans notes the tendency among working class Italians in Boston to treat their children as "little adults." It could well be that the posture of the boys described in this paper is simply an exaggerated version of lower class socialization generally. See Herbert J. Gans, *The Urban Villagers* (New York: The Free Press of Glencoe, 1962), p. 59.

When the gang boy gets on in years, there is often a violent showdown with a father; and regardless of whether these fights are won or lost, most parents simply resign themselves to viewing "trouble" as "normal" or "routine."

My father don't get smart with me no more. He used to whup me, throw me downstairs, until I got big enough to beat him. The last time he touch me, he was coming downstairs talking some noise about something. I don't know what. He had a drink, and he always make something up when he start drinking. He was trying to get smart with me, so he swung at me and missed. I just got tired of it. I snatched him and threw him up against the wall, and then we started fighting. My sister grabbed him around the neck and started choking him. So I started hitting him in the nose and everything, and around the mouth. Then he pushed my mother and I hit him again. Then he quit, and I carried him back upstairs. Next morning he jump up saying, "What happened last night? My leg hurts." And all that old bullshit. He made like he don't know what had happened. And ever since then, you know, he don't say nothing to me.

Similarly, mothers also seemed to resign themselves quite quickly to the possibilities of future "trouble." Where there was no father in the house, they often placed the blame for their son's behavior on his absence. But even in situations where the father was present, they continued to offer what advice and support they could, once it became clear that punishment was no deterrent. On a day-to-day basis, whatever efforts at direction were exerted tended to be directed at keeping the boys in the house on weekday evenings, at least until they did their homework, and trying to get them home at a reasonable hour on Friday and Saturday nights. In most instances, however, even these attempts at control gradually broke down, particularly among the older boys and those who were either suspended or permanently out of school. As time wears on, a long unexplained absence from home as well as phone calls from the police become socially expected parts of the family activity system itself.

Well, like last week, you know. Last Saturday I came home about 4 o'clock and they got kind of excited. And they didn't say nothing that night. But the next morning they kept talking "where you been" and all this. And I told them where I had been and they said okay. They told me to stay in this weekend but they didn't say nothing about it this weekend so I went out last night and tonight. (When she tells you not to do something, do you go along with her or what?) Like you mean stay or something? Oh, if she say stay in, I talk to her about it for an hour or two and then she get mad and say, "Oh, get out of the house. Leave." That's what I been waiting for.

Not only is the assumption of autonomy the important issue at home, it also has important implications for the way gang boys are defined and treated by school officials as well as for the ways they often fight back. Most young people adopt a posture of deference in the presence of adult authorities because this posture is a taken-for-granted assumption about the self. To gang boys, however, this posture becomes a matter of choice. They can defer or not defer, depending on their mood, their audience, and their feelings about a teacher; and for many teachers, the very existence of the assumption that submissiveness is a matter of choice becomes sufficient grounds for the withdrawal of "trust."

AUTONOMY AND THE SCHOOLS

The posture of premature autonomy is carried directly into the schools and the result is the "predelinquent." As early as the first and second grade, his teachers find him wild, distracted, and utterly oblivious to their presumed authority. He gets out of chairs when he feels like it; begins fighting when he feels like it; and all of this is done as if the teacher were not present. Even the best teachers find him virtually unmanageable in groups, even though the best teachers also seem to like these boys.

Once the boys begin proving they are "tough," there seems to be little the school can do to stop them. If they are suspended, they come to school anyway; and if they are transferred from one class to another, they return to the first class or to whatever teacher they happen to like. The social system of the third grader is an arena of social life that very much needs to be explored. It is certainly the beginning of the "delinquent career," and in some respects it seems to be its wildest phase. The boys seem immune to sanctions, and thus bullying, theft, and truancy are often blatantly displayed. It is not really until the fifth or sixth grade that organized gangs begin to form, and, in a certain sense, it is not until this age that the boys can be brought under systematic group control. Most of my work was done with older boys, however, and thus this discussion must be confined to them.

Recent sociology on gang boys has been very hard on the schools. Cloward and Ohlin suggests that lower class delinquents suffer from unequal "*access* to educational facilities;"[27] Cohen points to their "*failures* in the classroom;"[28] and Miller and Kvaraceus argue that a "*conflict* of culture" between school administrators and lower class students is precipitating delinquent behavior.[29]

Although there are many differences between contemporary sociological portraits of the lower class juvenile delinquent, the same model of his educational problem is used by all authors. Regardless of whether the delinquent is ambitious and capable,[30] ambitious and incapable,[31] or unambitious and incapable,[32] the school is sketched as a monolith of middle class personnel against which he fares badly.

Yet data collected by observation and interview over a 2-year period on the educational performances and classroom experiences of lower class gang members suggests that pitting middle class schools against variations in the motivation and capacity of some lower class boys is at best too simple and at worst incorrect as a model of the problems faced by the delinquents.

First, some of the "trouble" that gang boys get into takes place on school grounds but outside the classroom. There is some evidence, for example, that gang boys tend to view the rules against fighting, smoking, and gambling the same way they view the laws against theft, as opportunities to demonstrate courage in situations that entail some risk. As suggested in the following quote, the boys sometimes sound thankful for these rules.

(What do you guys do when you cut school?) Well, like everybody, you know, everybody get together and say "Everybody cut Friday and we'll go to Luigi's house." So, you know, a lot of boys and girls go up there and we have a party. Drinking. Having a good time. Otherwise if we have a day off from school, you

27 Richard A. Cloward and Lloyd E. Ohlin, *Delinquency and Opportunity* (Glencoe: The Free Press, 1960), p. 102.
28 Albert K. Cohen, *Delinquent Boys* (Glencoe: The Free Press, 1965), p. 116.
29 Walter B. Miller and William C. Kvaraceus, "Delinquent Behavior: Culture and the Individual," National Education Association of the United States, 1959, p. 44. See also Walter Miller, "Lower Class Culture as a Generating Milieu of Gang Delinquency, *Journal of Social Issues,* vol. XIV, 1958.
30 Cloward and Ohlin op. cit. n. 27.
31 Cohen, op. cit. n. 28.
32 Miller, op. cit. n. 29.

know, during the weekend, and we gave that, it probably wouldn't be too much fun cause it'd be almost legal. You know, when I first went to Gompers, we used to be able to smoke in the halls cause the ends of the halls was all concrete. We used to be able to smoke there. I didn't hardly ever smoke there though. We used to go smoke in the bathroom. It seemed like, you know, smoking was better to me since I had to hide to do it. It seem like everything at that school, you have to do it backwards to make it seem more better to you.

Second, during middle adolescence when the law requires gang members to attend school, there seems to be no relationship between academic performance and "trouble." Gangs contain bright boys who do well, bright boys who do less well, dull boys who pass, dull boys who fail, and illiterates.

Finally, the school difficulties of these boys occur only in some classes and not others. Good and bad students alike are consistently able to get through half or more of their classes without friction. It is only in particular classes with particular teachers that incidents leading to suspension flare up. We thus need to see how the same gang boy may become a "troublemaker" in one classroom and an "ordinary student" in another. To do this, it is again worth using Garfinkel's scheme to look at the classroom as a place where a range of possible activities or "constitutive orders of events" can take place, including the most common and mutually related set known as "teaching and learning." This is not the only activity that can take place in classrooms, however, as suggested by the fact that many young people, including gang boys, tend also to see the classroom as a place to see friends, converse by written notes, read comic books, eat, sleep, or stare out the window. For example:

If I'm bored then I have to do some-

thing to make it exciting. First, second, and third ain't too bad because I get me two comic books and they last me three periods. (You read comic books for the first three periods?) Yeah. See in my first three periods I got typing, English, and some kind of thing—Social Studies I think. In them three periods I read comic books, and the next three periods I got Shop and I got Gym and then I got Math. Them last three periods I don't read comic books because I only bring two, and they only last three periods.

Friday we had a substitute in class named Mr. Fox, and I had a headache so I went to sleep. (Why were you sleeping? Were you out late the night before?) No, I wasn't. I just had a headache. And I went to sleep cause my head was hurting. They wasn't doing nothing but talking. About this and that, Sally and John, and I just went to sleep. The class wasn't doing nothing but fussing, fooling around, talking, so I went to sleep.

When it becomes clear to a teacher that he is in the presence of people engaged in activities other than "teaching and learning," there are a number of ways he can choose to respond to this observation. One thing he can do, for example, is decide to overlook whatever other activities besides "learning" are taking place and decide to "teach" with those people who show signs of wanting to learn. In these classrooms there is rarely "trouble."

(Have you ever had any good teachers, Ray?) Yeah, Mr. F. and Mr. T. in junior high school. (What made them good?) They just help you, you know. They didn't want you always working all the time. As long as you keep your voices down, you know, and don't be talking out loud and hollering, you could go on and talk in groups and have a good time. (They let you have a good time. Did they flunk you?) Yeah, they flunked me. But I mean it was my fault too cause they gave me all the breaks, you know. Anything I asked for, they gonna give me a break. But, you know, I just never do right anyway.

One possible danger of ignoring people who engage in activities other than "learning" is that these people will always be overlooked, even when they decide to enter the "learning" activity. When this happens, there is the possibility that the person overlooked will resent not being allowed to enter the activity.

Like this one stud, man, he don't try to help us at all. He just goes on rapping (talking) to the poopbutts (squares), and when we ask a question he don't even pay no attention. I don't think that's fair. We there trying to learn just like anybody else! (All the time?) Well, sometimes.

The teacher may also, if he wishes, agree to participate in the activities preferred by the other people in the classroom, in which case either a different order of events or some mixture of this order and "teaching" gets constituted. Activities such as "talking to friends," "having fun," and "horsing around" then become "normal" events that can go on at different times in the same room. In these classrooms also there is rarely "trouble."

Like my Civics teacher, he understands all the students. He know we like to play. Like, you know, he joke with us for about the first 15 minutes and then, you know, everybody gets settled down and then they want to do some work. He got a good sense of humor and he understand.

When confronted with activities other than "learning," however, there are also teachers who tend to feel not only that their rights to teach are being violated but also that the basic rule establishing their authority is being broken. In addition to perceiving that their honor has been challenged, these teachers are also

likely to conclude that "trust" is no longer warranted; and when these feelings are communicated to gang boys, the result is almost always defined as "getting smart." In some cases, the teacher will insult them in return; but in most cases he will resort to the imperative and begin to issue "commands." This is a sure sign to gang members that the teacher no longer trusts them to comply with the basic rule establishing his authority. Conversely, however, the boys tend to view these commands as abridgments of their own rights to autonomy, and thus the prospect of a "character contest" arises.

The teachers that get into trouble, they just keep pounding. You *do* this! You know, they ain't gonna ask you nice. You just do this or else, you know, I'm gonna kick you out of school. All that old foul action. Like in Math class, this teacher always hollers. He always raises his voice and hollers, "Do this work!" All that old shit. Everybody just looks at him. Don't say shit, and just sit down, talk, wait around, you know.

This breakdown of trust on the part of teachers does not always occur as one event in a developmental sequence as suggested by the examples quoted above. There are also teachers whose previous experience has led them to define their students as "untrustworthy" right from the start, and they will thus communicate this lack of trust on the first day of class. Similarly, by the time the boys have been through junior high school, they have experienced enough teachers to know that this category of person also cannot always be trusted to honor their claims to a choice about the activities they wish to engage in. Most gang boys will therefore test the limits of the classroom situation before making up their minds whether a teacher can be trusted. This is done by purposely violating a rule preferred by the teacher in such a way as to suggest that their participation in the classroom is a voluntary act and should be acknowledged as such with the proper amount of respect. If the teacher responds to this move by becoming either angry or afraid, the boys know they are dealing with someone who is either "tough," "smart," or "lame." On the other hand, if the teacher responds by acknowledging the right while insisting that the rules still be obeyed, he is considered "straight."

In addition to the issue of who decides what activities take place in classrooms, there are also other disputes that sometimes arise. For example, although the students may be willing to comply with the rule establishing the teacher as the source of preferred rules, they may also feel that there are limits to the kinds of things a teacher can legitimately make rules about. These issues are most likely to arise when teachers feel it is within their jurisdiction to make rules about the dress and physical appearance of the people engaged in the activity of "learning." To the extent, moreover, that a gang boy feels that his moral character has been reconstituted by the teacher because of the clothes he wears, he is likely to experience a grave sense of injustice.[33]

The teachers would start on the hair and go on down to the dress. Cause I was getting this scene a lot of times. Telling me to get a haircut.

"No, I'm sorry. I don't need one."

"Why don't you get a haircut?"

"Well, this is my hair, and I feel if you were to get it cut, you'd have to pay for my clothes also."

"Well, ain't nobody saying anything about your clothes. I mean, you're a nice dresser."

I said, "Well, then I wear my hair the way I want."

Other problems of a similar nature arise in classrooms, particularly those having to do with the grounds used by teachers to evaluate the student in his capacity as a "learner."[34] In all these cases, the basic sequence of events is the same. First, the boys behave in a variety of ways for a variety of reasons. If they are tired, they sleep; if they are bored, they read comic books; if they are energetic, they may feel like "having fun"; and if they do not yet trust the teacher, they may test him.

Second, this behavior is defined by the teacher. If he does not see it as part of the "teaching and learning" situation, he may tolerate or ignore it. If it is transformed into an "event" in the "teaching and learning" activity, the teacher either interprets it as a violation of a preferred rule or as a challenge to his authority. In both cases the moral character of the gang boy is likely to be reconstituted; but if the act is only considered a violation of a preferred rule, the teacher may ask a boy politely to stop. If it is viewed as a challenge to authority, however, the response will be sharper since the teacher will feel that his honor is at stake.

Finally, the boys themselves must decide how to act. If the request to stop is made politely, their own sense of honor is not offended and they are likely to cease whatever it is they are doing. If the teacher's retort is derogatory, however, the boys are likely to view the teacher's defense of his rights to authority as a violation of their own rights to autonomy and thus the character contest is on. If the boys do not concede the contest, they challenge the authority of the teacher directly, and this challenge tends to take one of three forms: it can be done subtly with a

[33] For a general discussion of the problems created by contingent or purposive infraction of irrelevant rules, see Erving Goffman, *Encounters* (Indianapolis: The Bobbs-Merrill Co., 1961), pp. 17–85.

[34] These issues are discussed in the author's M.A. thesis, "Delinquency and Authority," Dept. of Sociology, University of California, Berkeley, 1964.

demeanor suggesting insolence; it can be done directly with words; or it can be done forcefully with violence. All three methods are used in the encounter described below:

The first day I came to school I was late to class so this teacher got smart with me. He didn't know me by name. See a lot of people have to go by the office and see what class they in or something. Like there was a lot of new people there. So you know I was fooling around cause I know nothing gonna happen to you if you late. Cause all you tell them, you got the program mixed or something.

When I came into the class you know I heard a lot of hollering and stuff. Mr. H. was in the class too. He's a teacher, see. I guess he had a student teacher or something, you know, because he was getting his papers and stuff. So Mr. H. went out. Well, this new teacher probably wonder if he gonna be able to get along with me or something. Cause the class was kinda loud. When I walked in the class got quiet all of a sudden. Like they thought the Principal was coming in or something.

So I walk into class and everybody look up. That's natural, you know, when somebody walk into class. People gonna look up at you. They gonna see who it is coming in or something. So I stopped. You know, like this. Looked around. See if there was any new faces. Then a girl named Diane, she say, "Hey Ray!" You know, when I walk into class they start calling me and stuff. They start hollering at me.

I just smile and walk on. You know. I had my hands in my pockets or something cause I didn't have no books and I just walk into class with my hands in my pockets a lot of times. I mean I have to walk where I can relax. I'm not going to walk with my back straight. I mean you know I relax. (What were you wearing?) About what I got on now. I had a pair of black slacks and a shirt on. My hair was long and I had taps on my shoes. I had kinda boots on but they weren't real high boots. They came up to about here.

Then I looked over at the teacher. I see we had a new teacher. He was standing in front of the desks working on some papers and doing something. He looked at me. I mean you enter by the front of the classroom so when you walk into the classroom he's standing right there. You gotta walk in front of him to get to the seats. So then I went to sit down. Soon as I passed his desk he say, "Just go sit down." Just like that.

So I stop. I turn around and look at him, then I went and sat down. (What kind of look did you give him?) You might say I gave him a hard look. I thought you know he might say something else. Cause that same day he came he got to hollering at people and stuff. I don't like people to holler at me. He was short, you know, about medium build. He might be able to do a little bit. So I say to myself, "I better sit down and meditate a little bit."

So I went and sat down. I sat in the last row in the last seat. Then he say, "Come sit up closer." So I scoot up another chair or two. Then he tell me to come sit up in the front. So I sat up there.

Then you know a lot of people was talking. A lot of people begin telling me that he be getting smart all day. You know Stubby? He is a big square but he pretty nice. He told me how the teacher was. And Angela start telling me about how he try to get smart with her. He say, "This is where you don't pick out no boy friend. You come and get your education." I mean just cause you talk to a boy, that don't mean you be scheming on them or nothing. It just that you want to be friends with people.

Then he say something like, "You two shut up or I'll throw you out on your ear!" So he told me he'd throw me out.

So I say, "The best thing you can do is ask me to leave and don't tell me. You'll get your damn ass kicked off if you keep messing!"

Then he told me to move over on the other side. See I was talking to everybody so he told me to move away from everybody. And so I moved to the other side. He told me to move three times! I had to move three times!

And then he got to arguing with somebody else. I think at somebody else that came in the class. You know, a new person. So while he was talking to them, I left out. I snuck out of class.

So I walked out the class. Went out in the yard and started playing basketball. We were supposed to turn in the basketball out there so I took the ball through the hall on the way back in. I was gonna go back out there and play some more. See I had the ball and I passed by his class and I looked in. I seen him with his back turned an I didn't like him. That's when I hit him. I hit him with the ball. Got him! I didn't miss. Threw it hard too. Real hard!

Faced with behavior like this, a school administrator has a number of sanctions at his command. He can suspend the boys, alter their grades, and some are not above violence.[35] Yet most of these sanctions have little meaning to the boys, particularly during elementary and junior high school. When the boys are young, they simply assume they will graduate from high school, even if they flunk every course. In part, they know they will be passed on automatically every other semester since the school considers them a menace to the younger boys if they are left behind; and in part, they are simply too young to care much about time. For example:

(Did you ever flunk a grade?) No. I just never passed. Every other term I passed. Ha. Ha. Cause you see they had to pass me in the low seven. So in the high seven I flunk. So they pass me to low eight. Low eight I flunk. They pass me to the high eight. The high eight I flunk. And so on like that. (You can't flunk twice in the same grade. Is that it?) They see that you ain't gonna do it anyway so shit, they just go on and put you up in the next one. In high eight they

[35] Although a Principal may not feel that his school is demeaned by violence, he sometimes feels that he and his teachers are. This attitude often leads to the hiring of lower status specialists such as gym teachers and janitors to administer the beatings. Apparently these people are felt to be of sufficiently low status not to be offended by violence.

transferred me. That's when I moved. I went to Benjamin Franklin, and Mr. B., whatever you call him, he was Principal there. He said he was gonna try me out in high nine. So I went there and I flunked. And there was another Principal who came and took over. He took over cause Mr. B. got transferred some place else. He say after summer if I bring my birth certificate to prove I was 16, he was gonna transfer me to high school. So I brought it to him after the summer, and Mr. P., the Principal at the high school, he said he was gonna try me out and put me in my right place. (What's your right place?) High junior. (So you went from high nine to high junior?) Yeah. (How are you making out in high junior?) Well, I'm still trying to make it. Knocking me out some Z's and getting me some A's and B's.

It is only when the boys get to high school that the sanctions meted out by the school begin to matter, and by then it is sometimes too late. Before the high school years most boys simply assume that the future will take care of itself; but in the sophomore and junior years of high school, the future becomes the present. Graduating, finding a decent job, and marrying the right kind of girl all become problematic, and the boys thus develop some stake in passing courses. Yet here again, any increase in the subjective importance of sanctions also depends on the objective facts of a boy's situation, and these situations tend to vary directly with mental capacity. Many of the boys who are bright enough to graduate from high school make some attempt to do so, but the boys who are illiterate or consistently F students invariably fail. Consider this conversation between three boys who have all been in the same neighborhood gang since fifth grade. The gang began breaking up in the junior year of high school when some of the boys made a serious attempt to graduate. The first boy speaking is the vice president and the second boy speaking is the president. Notice the difference in the way they perceive their fates.

WERTHMAN. Do you guys think it is important to graduate from high school?

VICE PRESIDENT. Hell yeah! That's the most important thing in your life right now. If you ain't got no high school diploma, you ain't got shit! You oughta least have 1 or 2 years of college so you can say "I've been to college." I tell you, like if I was gonna get married like after I got out of school and my wife had a little more education than me, I'd rather feel embarrassed than marry her. Cause in the old days, all a man was supposed to be for was work and fighting wars. His woman was at home washing clothes and taking care of babies. OK. Then it was fine. Cause then she could go to school and get some education and help her husband. But now it's more the man's responsibility cause the ladies done lost respect like they done had back there. I mean they don't do as much for a man as they did back then. Now they depend on the man no matter what. They look for the man to do. And if the man can't do, well naturally she gonna get her ass out. She gonna get hip quick. Get her somebody that can. You know.

WERTHMAN. What about you, Charles, are you going to graduate from high school?

PRESIDENT. No comment. (What do you mean, "no comment?") I'm not saying nothing. (Why not?) Well, I mean if it wasn't too late I'd try and change it. But the way I see it now there's no need to even try to catch up cause I know I can't do it within these next 3 months. So I'm not even going to try. I plan on being a bum anyway. See, my uncle's a bum and he's making it.

WERTHMAN. How about you, Billy?

MEMBER. Me myself, I don't care if I don't get no job, if I'm a tramp or something. I can stay in the house and steal hub caps and sell them and get some food and pay the electricity and stuff. And that'd be all right because you don't have to pay no rent. (But what if you want to get married?) Well if you want to get married, man, you steal some hub caps and you get some food money and you can pay

the electricity and stuff. You ain't got to worry about paying the rent. (Do you think you will graduate from high school?) Hell no. They gonna kick me out any day now. If I go back tomorrow, I think I gonna get kicked out for good.

A gang boy's career as a "delinquent" in the schools is thus a somewhat problematic affair. It begins in earnest around the fourth or fifth grade when he comes to the attention of his teachers for paying no attention to them, beating up other students, and forcing his colleagues to surrender their lunch money. During junior high school the fights are better organized and the posture adopted towards teachers turns from unconcern to insolence. And in the last years of high school, the boys either graduate or depart, usually at the school's request. For most of these years, the school regards him as hopeless, and they suspend him regularly for his activities in the presence of other boys as well as for his attitude towards the authority of the school itself. Most of this behavior, however, is designed to claim an identity that the school itself cannot stamp out. What the boys do on the streets with one another is beyond the scope of their control although they punish it severely when it happens to take place on school grounds.

Whether the boys are given the chance to engage in character contests with teachers, however, is directly affected by the school itself since what is made of an act depends almost entirely on how it is defined and evaluated by the teacher, including the issue of whether or not the act is a violation of the basic authority rule. The boy is using the teacher to define himself as autonomous; and, like his behavior on the streets, he often creates or provokes the situation in which he then defends his honor. Yet if a teacher is willing to concede the fact that school is meaningless to some boys and therefore that other activities besides "teaching and learning" will necessarily go on in class, and if he is willing to limit the scope of his jurisdiction to the activity of "teaching and learning" itself, then his authority is likely to remain intact, regardless of how much it may be "tested." Whether or not he wishes to persuade the boys to join the learning process is another matter, but it is precisely at this point that we see the merits of defining authority, after Bertrand de Juvenel, as "the faculty of gaining another man's assent."[36]

●   ●   ●

CONTINGENCIES, RISKS, AND OPPORTUNITIES

There is some evidence to suggest that most gang boys have a conception of how and when their careers as "delinquents" will end. As Short and Strodtbeck have recently reported, most look forward to becoming stable and dependable husbands in well-run households, despite their reluctance to voice these expectations around one another and despite the fact that some become fathers out of wedlock along the way.[37] Similarly, although about half the boys interviewed by Short and Strodtbeck anticipate problems in securing "good paying honest jobs," their images of family life make it clear that the great majority expect to be holding down some kind of conventional occupation when they become "adults."[38] During

most of the years spent in gangs, however, these occupational concerns are neither salient nor relevant. The boys understand that as long as they are defined and define themselves as "youth," they are not the people they will someday become; and for this reason they have little difficulty identifying with two apparently conflicting sets of attitudes, values, and behavior patterns.

As we have seen, the issue of whether a particular career will come to the expected conventional end is often resolved in large measure by how a boy deals with a host of contingencies that arise before the end of the career arrives, particularly those associated with the way he is defined and acted upon by parents, teachers, policemen, probation officers, and judges of the juvenile court. At the early stages of the career, it is often difficult for the boys to make objective assessments of the risks they run in defining themselves since the implications of these acts for the way moral character is defined, evaluated, and acted upon are only known "after" the acts themselves have taken place. This is particularly true in the case of the police where many more rules are invoked to pass judgment on the offender than were actually involved in the offense, particularly since these judgments are often made on the basis of how he behaves in four different institutions at once. As Howard Becker has suggested, "deviance is not a quality of the act a person commits, but rather a consequence of the application by others of rules and sanctions to an 'offender';"[39] and there are many instances in which the criteria used to reconstitute moral character are simply seen by gang boys as arbitrary, unfair, or outright illegitimate.

Yet regardless of how a boy feels

[36] Bertrand de Juvenel, *Sovereignty: An Inquiry Into the Political Good,* translated by J. F. Huntington (Chicago: The University of Chicago Press, 1957), p. 29.
[37] Short and Strodtbeck, *Group Process,* op. cit. n.12, pp. 25–46.
[38] See James F. Short, Jr., Ramon Rivera, and Ray A. Tennyson, "Opportunities, Gang Membership, and Delinquency," *American Sociological Review* (February 1965), p. 60; see also Delbert S. Elliott, "Delinquency and Perceived Opportunity," *Sociological Inquiry* (Spring, 1962), pp. 216–228.

[39] Howard S. Becker, *Outsiders* (New York: The Free Press of Glencoe, 1963), p. 9.

about the rules that have been used to judge him, these judgements often alter the objective facts of his situation, and this requires him to make new decisions. He must decide, for example, whether to use his probation restrictions as an excuse to leave the gang or as a new and riskier source of identity material, just as he must decide how he feels about the fact that his parents may no longer trust him. By viewing the "delinquent career" as a more or less stable sequence of acts taken in risky social situations in order to claim an identity or define a self, often followed by changes in the rules and judgements that make up these situations, and followed again by new choices of the self in response to these changes, it is possible to see how a gang boy could arrive at the age of 18 or 21 to find that his situation makes it costly, painful, or difficult for him to take the conventional job that he always expected to take, particularly if the boy has come to view the conventional world as a place full of the kinds of people who have labeled him a "delinquent."[40]

This process can be seen quite clearly in the schools where the initial payoff in female acclaim for fights and risky character contests slowly vanishes during high school. The "big men" in 7th grade often become school rejects in the 10th or 11th, and thus they do pay a price for their early notoriety, only this price cannot always be foreseen.

Once a gang boy gets beyond the age of 18, moreover, his situation changes rather dramatically. Whether he likes it or not, he now has a choice to make about what identity system to enter. He could get married, get a job, and assume the status of a full-fledged "adult"; he could decide to postpone this decision in legitimate ways such as joining the Army and going to school at night; or he could decide to remain for a few more years as an elder statesman on the streets, in which case he will continue to make use of the identity materials available to youth.

The decision he makes at this point in his career will depend in part on his situation. If he managed to graduate from high school, he may well decide to go on to college; but if he was expelled from high school, he may feel either bitter or reluctant about going back to night school to get the high school degree. He knows that he has been administratively reborn in the eyes of the law, and thus the risks he takes by staying in the streets increase considerably since he now may be processed by the courts as an adult. On the other hand, if his status in the gang world is still high, he may not want to trade it right away for a low-paying blue-collar job; and he knows he will be rejected by the Army if he has a jail record of any kind.

In short, it is at this point in his career that the "opportunities" available to him will affect his behavior, his attitudes, and the decisions he makes about his life.[41] If there are no legitimate options open to him, options that at best would not make him suffer a sudden decrease in status and at worst would allow him not to face his ultimately dismal status-fate as an adult, then he may well decide to stay on the streets, despite the greater consequences involved in taking risks. He may adopt a "hustle," and he may also adopt a full-blown ideology along with it. Since

---

[40] This process has been described in somewhat different terms by Lemert as a transformation from "primary" to "secondary" deviance. See Edwin M. Lemert, *Social Pathology* (New York: McGraw Hill Book Co., 1951), p. 75.

[41] This view suggests that the various processes discussed by Cloward and Ohlin tend to affect outcomes of the transition between youth and adult status at the end of the delinquent career. See Cloward and Ohlin, *Delinquency and Opportunity*, op. cit. n.30.

he now views the conventional world as a place he is expected to enter, he tends to develop a "position" on it. Jobs become "slaves"; going to school becomes "serving time"; and in some cases the assumptions about marriage and getting a conventional job are replaced by fantasies about the quick and big "score." These are no longer the "delinquent boys" described by Cohen.[42] They are the self-styled aristocrats described by Finestone and Sykes and Matza.[43] They have an answer to everything, and they always "know the score."

After a few years of this existence, these boys are really at the end of their "delinquent" careers. Some get jobs, some go to jail, some get killed, and some simply fade into an older underground of pool rooms and petty thefts. Most cannot avoid ending up with conventional jobs, however, largely because the "illegitimate opportunities" available simply are not that good.

---

[42] Cohen, *Delinquent Boys*, op. cit. n.28.
[43] Harold Finestone, "Cats, Kicks, and Colors," *Social Problems*, vol. 5 (July 1957), pp. 3–13; G. M. Sykes and David Matza, "Techniques of Neutralization: A Theory of Delinquency," *American Sociological Review*, vol. 22 (December 1957), pp. 664–670.

26.

Violent Crimes in City Gangs

Walter B. Miller

The 1960's have witnessed a remarkable upsurge of public concern over violence in the United States. The mass media flash before the public a vivid and multi-varied kaleidoscope of images of violence. Little attention is paid to those who question the assumption that the United States is experiencing an unparalleled epidemic of violence, who point out that other periods in the past may have been equally violent or more so; that troops were required to subdue rioting farmers in 1790, rioting tax-protesters in 1794, rioting laborers in the 1870's and 1880's, and rioting railroad workers in 1877; that race riots killed fifty people in St. Louis in 1917 and erupted in twenty-six other cities soon after; that fifty-seven whites were killed in a slave uprising in 1831; that the Plug Uglies, Dead Rabbits, and other street gangs virtually ruled parts of New York for close to forty years; that rival bootleg mobs engaged in armed warfare in Chicago and elsewhere during the Capone era; and that the number killed in the 1863 draft riots in New York was estimated at up to

SOURCE. Walter Miller, "Violent Crimes in City Gangs," from *The Annals of the American Academy of Political and Social Science,* Volume 364, March 1966, pp. 97–112. Reprinted with permission.

1,000 men. Nevertheless, however much one may question the conviction that the United States today is engulfed in unprecedented violence, one can scarcely question the ascendancy of the *belief* that it is. It is this belief that moves men to action—action whose consequences are just as real as if the validity of the belief were incontrovertible.

Close to the core of the public imagery of violence is the urban street gang. The imagery evokes tableaux of sinister adolescent wolf packs prowling the darkened streets of the city intent on evil-doing, of grinning gangs of teen-agers tormenting old ladies in wheel-chairs and ganging up on hated and envied honor students, and of brutal bands of black-jacketed motorcyclists sweeping through quiet towns in orgies of terror and destruction. The substance of this image and its basic components of human cruelty, brutal sadism, and a delight in violence for its own sake have become conventionalized within the subculture of professional writers. The tradition received strong impetus in the public entertainment of the early 1950's with Marlon Brando and his black-jacketed motorcycle thugs, gathered momentum with the insolent and sadistic high-schoolers of *The Blackboard Jun-*

gle, and achieved the status of an established ingredient of American folklore with the Sharks and Jets of the *West Side Story.*

What is the reality behind these images? Is the street gang fierce and romantic like the Sharks and Jets? Is it a tough but good-hearted bunch of rough-and-ready guys like the "Gang that Sang Heart of my Heart"? Or is it brutal and ruthless like the motorcyclists in *The Wild Ones?* In many instances where an idea of interest engages both scholars and the public, most of the public embrace one set of conceptions and most scholars, another. This is not so in the case of the street gang; there is almost as much divergence within the ranks of scholars as there is between the scholars and the public.

One recent book on gangs contains these statements:

Violence [is] the core spirit of the modern gang. . . . The gang boy . . . makes unprovoked violence . . . [senseless rather than premeditated] . . . .the major activity or dream of his life. . . . The gang trades in violence. Brutality is basic to its system.[1]

Another recent work presents a different picture:

The very few [gang] boys who persist in extreme aggression or other dangerous exploits are regarded generally as "crazy" by the other boys. . . . Our conservative estimate is that not more than one in five instances of potential violence actually result in serious consequences. . . . For average Negro gang boys the probability of an arrest for involvement in instances of potential violence is probably no greater than .04.[2]

A third important work states:

In [a] second type [of delinquent gang or subculture] violence is the keynote. . . . The immediate aim in the world of fighting gangs is to acquire a reputation for toughness and destructive violence. . . . In the world of violence such attributes as race, socioeconomic position, age, and the like, are irrelevant.[3]

What is the reality behind these differences? The question is readily raised, but is not, unfortunately, readily answered. There exists in this area of high general interest a surprising dearth of reliable information. It is quite possible that discrepancies between the statements of scholars arise from the fact that each is referring to different kinds of gangs in different kinds of neighborhoods in different kinds of cities. We simply do not know. Lacking the information necessary to make general statements as to the nature of violence in the American city gang, it becomes obvious that one major need is a series of careful empirical studies of particular gangs in a range of cities and a variety of neighborhoods. The present paper is an attempt to present such information for the one inner-city neighborhood, "Midcity," in a major eastern city, "Port City."

WHAT ARE "VIOLENT" CRIMES?

The term "violence" is highly charged. Like many terms which carry strong opprobrium, it is applied with little discrimination to a wide range of things which meet with general disapproval. Included in this broad net are phenomena such as toy advertising on television, boxing, rock-and-roll music and the mannerisms of its performers, fictional private detectives, and modern

[1] L. Yablonsky, *The Violent Gang* (New York: The Macmillan Company, 1963), pp. 4, 6.
[2] J. F. Short and F. L. Strodtbeck, *Group Process and Gang Delinquency* (Chicago: University of Chicago Press, 1965), pp. 224, 258.
[3] F. A. Cloward and L. E. Ohlin, *Delinquency and Opportunity: A Theory of Delinquent Gangs* (Glencoe, Ill.: Free Press, 1960), pp. 20, 24.

art. Used in this fashion the scope of the term becomes so broad as to vitiate its utility severely. Adding the term "crimes" to the designation substantially narrows its focus. It is at once apparent that not all "violence" is criminal (warfare, football, surgery, wrecking cars for scrap), but it is less apparent to some that not all crime is violent. In fact, the great bulk of adolescent crime consists of nonviolent forms of theft and statute violations such as truancy and running away. In the present report "violent crimes" are defined as *legally proscribed acts whose primary object is the deliberate use of force to inflict injury on persons or objects, and, under some circumstances, the stated intention to engage in such acts.* While the scope of this paper prevents discussion of numerous complex issues involved in this definition, for example, the role of "threat of force" as criminally culpable, an idea of the kinds of acts included under the definition may be obtained directly by referring to Tables 3 and 4. Table 3 delineates sixteen forms of "violent" offenses directed at persons and objects, and Table 4 delineates fourteen legal categories. It is to these forms that the term "violent crimes" will apply.

CIRCUMSTANCES AND METHODS OF STUDY

Conclusions presented in subsequent sections are based on the research findings of an extensive study of youth gangs in "Midcity," a central-city slum district of 100,000 persons. Information was obtained on some 150 corner gangs, numbering about 4,500 males and females, aged twelve to twenty, in the middle and late 1950's. Selected for more detailed study were twenty-one of these gangs numbering about 700 members; selection was based primarily on their reputation as the "toughest" in the city. Study data of many kinds were obtained from numer-

ous sources, but the great bulk of data was derived from the detailed field records of workers who were in direct daily contact with gang members for periods averaging two years per gang. Seven of these gangs, numbering 205 members (four white male gangs, one Negro male, one white female, one Negro female) were subject to the most intensive field observation, and are designated "intensive observation" gangs. Findings presented here are based primarily on the experience of these seven, along with that of fourteen male gangs numbering 293 members (including the five intensive-observation male gangs) whose criminal records were obtained from the state central criminal records division.

Detailed qualitative information on the daily behavior of gang members in sixty "behavioral areas" (for example, sexual behavior, family behavior, and theft) was collected and analyzed; however, the bulk of the findings presented here will be quanitative in nature, due to requirements of brevity.[4] Present findings are based primarily on three kinds of data: (1) *Field-recorded behavior*—all actions and sentiments recorded for the seven intensive observation gangs which relate to assault (N = 1,600); (2) *Field-recorded crimes*—all recorded instances of illegal acts of assault and property damage engaged in by members of the same gangs (N = 228); and (3) *Court-recorded crimes*—all charges of assaultive or property damage offenses recorded by court officials for members of the fourteen male gangs between the ages of seven and twenty-seven (N = 138).

The analysis distinguishes four major characteristics of gangs: age, sex, race,

[4] Qualitative data on the nature of "violent" and other forms of gang behavior which convey a notion of its "flavor" and life-context will be presented in W. B. Miller, *City Gangs* (New York: John Wiley & Sons, forthcoming).

and social status. Of the seven intensive-observation gangs, five were male (N = 155) and two, female (N = 50); none of the fourteen court-record gangs was female. Five of the intensive-observation gangs were white (N = 127) and two, Negro (N = 78); eight of the court-record gangs were white (N = 169) and six, Negro (N = 124). The ethnic-religious status of the white gangs was multinational Catholic (Irish-Italian, with Irish dominant, some French, and Slavic). Social status was determined by a relatively complex method based on a combination of educational, occupational, and other criteria (for example, parents' occupation, gang members' occupation, gang members' education, and families' welfare experience).[5] On the basis of these criteria all gangs were designated "lower class." Three levels *within* the lower class were delineated and were designated, from highest to lowest, Lower Class I, II, and III. Gangs analyzed in the present paper belonged to levels II and III; the former level is designated "higher" status, and the latter, "lower." It should be kept in mind that the terms "higher" and "lower" in this context refer to the lowest and next-lowest of three intra-lower-class social-status levels.[6]

THE PATTERNING OF VIOLENT CRIMES IN CITY GANGS

Study data make it possible to address a set of questions central to any

[5] Details of this method are presented in *City Gangs*, op. cit.

[6] IBM processing of court-recorded offenses and preliminary analyses of field-recorded assault behavior and illegal incidents was done by Dr. Robert Stanfield, University of Massachusetts; additional data analysis by Donald Zall, Midcity Delinquency Research Project. Some of the specific figures in the tables may be slightly altered in the larger report; such alterations will not, however, affect the substance of the findings. The research was supported under the National Insti-

consideration of the reality of violent crime in city gangs. How prevalent are violent crimes, both in absolute terms and relative to other forms of crime? What proportion of gang members engage in violent crimes? Is individual or collective participation more common? Are those most active in such crimes more likely to be younger or older? white or Negro? male or female? higher or lower in social status? What forms do violent crimes take, and which forms are most prevalent? Who and what are the targets of violent crimes? How serious are they? How does violence figure in the daily lives of gang members?

The following sections present data bearing on each of these questions, based on the experience of Midcity gangs in the 1950's. The first section bears on the last of the questions just cited. What was the role of assaultive behavior in the daily lives of gang members?

Assault-oriented behavior

Approximately 1,600 actions and sentiments relating to assaultive behavior were recorded by field workers during the course of their work with the seven "intensive observation" gangs—a period averaging two years per gang.[7]

tute of Health's Grant M-1414, and administered by the Boston University School of Social Work.

[7] The definition of "violent crimes" used here would call for an analysis at this point of behavior oriented to both assault and property destruction. However, the type of data-processing necessary to an integrated analysis of these two behavioral forms has not been done for "property damage," so that the present section is based almost entirely on behavior involving persons rather than persons and property. Behavior involving property damage was relatively infrequent; 265 actions and sentiments were recorded, ranking this form of behavior forty-fifth of sixty forms; vandalistic behavior was about one-sixth as common as assaultive behavior, a ratio paralleled in officially recorded data (cf. Table 4). Most subsequent sections will utilize findings based on both assault and property damage.

This number comprised about 3 per cent of a total of about 54,000 actions and sentiments oriented to some sixty behavioral areas (for example, sexual behavior, drinking behavior, theft, and police-oriented behavior). Assault-oriented behavior was relatively common, ranking ninth among sixty behavioral areas. A substantial portion of this behavior, however, took the form of words rather than deeds; for example, while the total number of assault-oriented actions and sentiments was over two and a half times as great as those relating to theft, the actual number of "arrestable" incidents of assault was less than half the number of theft incidents. This finding is concordant with others which depict the area of assaultive behavior as one characterized by considerably more smoke than fire.

About one half (821) of the 1,600 actions and sentiments were categorized as "approved" or "disapproved" with reference to a specified set of evaluative standards of middle-class adults;[8] the remainder were categorized as "evaluatively neutral." There were approximately thirty "disapproved" assault-oriented actions for every instance of "arrestable" assault, and five instances of arrestable assault for every court appearance on assault changes. Males engaged in assault-oriented behavior far more frequently than females (males 6.3 events per month, females 1.4), and younger males more frequently than older.

Information concerning both actions and sentiments relating to assault—data

[8] Examples of *approved actions:* "acting to forestall threatened fighting" and "agreeing to settle disputes by means other than physical violence"; *disapproved actions:* "participating in gang-fighting" and "carrying weapons"; *approved sentiments:* "arguing against involvement in gang fighting" and "opposing the use of weapons"; *disapproved sentiments:* "defining fighting prowess as an essential virtue" and "perceiving fighting as inevitable."

not generally available—revealed both similarities and differences in the patterning of these two levels of behavior. Expressed sentiments concerning assaultive behavior were about one and a half times as common as actual actions; in this respect, assault was unique among analyzed forms of behavior, since, in every other case, recorded actions were more common than sentiments, for example, theft behavior (actions 1.5 times sentiments) and family-oriented behavior (actions 2.2 times sentiments). The majority of actions and sentiments (70 per cent) were "disapproved" with reference to adult middle-class standards; actions and sentiments were "concordant" in this respect, in that both ran counter to middle-class standards by similar proportions (actions, 74 per cent disapproved and sentiments, 68 per cent). This concordance contrasted with other forms of behavior: in sexual behavior, the level of disapproved action was substantially higher than that of disapproved sentiment; in family-oriented behavior, the level of disapproved sentiment, substantially higher than that of action.

Separate analyses were made of behavior oriented to "individual" assault (mostly fights between two persons) and "collective" assault (mostly gang fighting). With regard to individual assault, the number of actions and the number of sentiments were approximately equal (181 actions, 187 sentiments); in the case of collective assault, in contrast, there was almost twice as much talk as action (239 sentiments, 124 actions). Sentiments with respect both to individual and collective assault were supportive of disapproved behavior, but collective assault received less support than individual. Behavior *opposing* disapproved assault showed an interesting pattern; specific actions aimed to inhibit or forestall collective assault were over twice as common as actions opposing individual assault. Gang members thus appeared to be considerably more reluctant to engage in collective than in individual fighting; the former was dangerous and frightening, with uncontrolled escalation a predictable risk, while much of the latter involved relatively mild set-to's between peers within the "controlled" context of gang interaction.

Assault-oriented behavior, in summary, was relatively common, but a substantial part of this behavior entailed words rather than deeds. Both actions and sentiments ran counter to conventional middle-class adult standards, with these two levels of behavior concordant in this respect. Insofar as there did exist an element of assault-inhibiting behavior, it was manifested in connection with collective rather than individual assault. This provides evidence for the existence within the gang of a set of "natural" forces operating to control collective assault, a phenomenon to be discussed further.

Frequency of violent crime

The wide currency of an image of violence as a dominant occupation and preoccupation of street gangs grants special importance to the question of the actual prevalence of violent crimes. How frequently did gang members engage in illegal acts of assault and property damage? Table 1 shows that members of the five intensive-observation male gangs, on the basis of field records of known offenses, were involved in violent crimes at a rate of somewhat under one offense for each two boys per ten-month period, and that the fourteen male gangs, on the basis of court-recorded offenses, were charged with "violent" crimes at a rate of somewhat under one charge for each two boys

Table 1

FREQUENCY OF VIOLENT CRIMES BY MALE GANG MEMBERS
(BY RACE AND SOCIAL STATUS)

Race and Social Status	Five Intensive-Observation Gangs			Fourteen Court-Record Gangs		
	Number of Individuals	Number of Involvements[a]	Rate[b]	Number of Individuals	Number of Charges[c]	Rate[d]
White L.C. III	66	154	8.4	97	81	8.3
Negro L.C. III	—[e]	—	—	58	39	6.7
White L.C. II	50	40	1.5	72	10	1.4
Negro L.C. II	39	34	2.5	66	8	1.2
	155	228	4.7	293	138	4.7

L.C.III (8.4) = L.C.II (2.0) × 4.2   L.C.III (7.7) = L.C.II (1.3) × 5.9
White (5.4) = Negro (2.5) × 2.1   White (5.4) = Negro (3.8) × 1.4

[a] No incidents assault and property damage × number of participants.

[b] Involvements per 10 individuals per ten-month period.

[c] Charges on fourteen categories of assault and property-damage offenses (see Table 4).

[d] Charges per ten individuals ages seven through eighteen.

[e] Not included in study population.

during the twelve-year period from ages seven through eighteen.[9] The 228 "violent offense" involvements comprised 24 per cent of all categories of illegal involvements (assault 17 per cent, property damage 7 per cent), with assault about one-half as common as theft, the most common offense, and property damage about one-quarter as common. The 138 court charges comprised 17 per cent of all categories of charge (assault charges 11 per cent, property damage 6 per cent) with assault charges about one-third as common as theft, the most common charge, and property damage about one-fifth as common. The total number of "violence-oriented" actions and sentiments examined in the previous section comprised something under 4 per cent of actions and sentiments oriented to sixty behavioral areas (assault-oriented behavior, 3.2 per cent; property-damage-oriented, 0.5 per cent).

[9] Four types of "unit" figure in this and following tables. These are: (1) *Incidents:* An illegal incident is a behavioral event or sequence of events adjudged by a coder to provide a sound basis for arrest if known to authorities. Information as to most incidents was obtained from field records. In the case of assault incidents, this definition ruled out a fair number of moderately to fairly serious instances of actual or intended assault which involved members of the same gang or occurred under circumstances deemed unlikely to produce arrest even if known. (2) *Involvements:* Incidents multiplied by number of participants, for example, two gang members fight two others—one incident, four involvements. (3) *Court Appearances:* The appearance in court of a gang member on a "new" charge or charges (excluded are rehearings, appeals, and the like). (4) *Court Charges:* Appearances multiplied by number of separate charges, for example, an individual's being charged at one appearance with breaking and entering, possession of burglars' tools, and conspiracy to commit larceny counts as three "charges." The "violent crime" charges of Table 1 represent fourteen categories of offense involving actual or threatened injury to persons or objects. The fourteen offense designations appear in Table 4, and were condensed from forty categories of police-blotter designations.

These figures would indicate that violence and violent crimes did not play a dominant role in the lives of Midcity gangs. The cumulative figures taken alone—228 known offenses by 155 boys during a period of approximately two years, and 138 court charges for 293 boys during a twelve-year age span—would appear to indicate a fairly high "absolute" volume of violent crime. If, however, the volume of such crime is compared with that of other forms—with "violent" behavior, both actional and verbal, comprising less than 4 per cent of all recorded behavior, field-recorded "violent" offenses comprising less than one-quarter of all known offenses, and court charges of violent crimes less than one-fifth of all charges—violence appears neither as a dominant preoccupation of city gangs nor as a dominant form of criminal activity. Moreover, one should bear in mind that these rates apply to young people of the most "violent" sex, during the most "violent" years of their lives, during a time when they were members of the toughest gangs in the toughest section of the city.

Race and social status

The relative importance of race and social status is indicated in Table 1, with field-recorded and court-recorded data showing close correspondence. Of the two characteristics, social status is clearly more important. Lower-status gang members (Lower Class III) engaged in field-recorded acts of illegal violence four times as often as those of higher status (Lower Class II) and were charged in court six times as often. White and Negro rates, in contrast, differ by a factor of two or less. The finding that boys of lower educational and occupational status both engaged in and were arrested for violent crimes to a substantially greater degree than those of higher status is not particularly surprising, and conforms to much research which shows that those of lower social status are likely to be more active in criminal behavior. What is noteworthy is the fact that differences of this magnitude appear in a situation where status differences are as small, relatively, as those between Lower Class II and III. One might expect, for example, substantial differences between college boys and high school drop-outs, but the existence of differences on the order of four to six times between groups *within* the lower class suggests that even relatively small social-status differences among laboring-class populations can be associated with relatively large differences in criminal behavior.

Table 1 findings relating to race run counter to those of many studies which show Negroes to be more "violent" than whites and to engage more actively in violent crimes. Comparing similar-status white and Negro gangs in Midcity shows that racial differences were relatively unimportant, and that, insofar as there were differences, it was the whites rather than the Negroes who were more likely both to engage in and to be arrested for violent crimes. White gang members engaged in field-recorded acts of illegal violence twice as often as Negro gang members and were charged in court one and a half times as often. These data, moreover, do not support a contention that Negroes who engage in crime to a degree similar to that of whites tend to be arrested to a greater degree. The one instance where Negro rates exceed those of whites is in the case of field-recorded crimes for higher status gangs (white rate 1.5, Negro 2.5).[10] Court data, however, show that

the Negro boys, with a *higher* rate of field-recorded crime, have a slightly *lower* rate of court-recorded crime. An explanation of these findings cannot be undertaken here; for present purposes it is sufficient to note that carefully collected data from one major American city do not support the notion that Negroes are more violent than whites at *similar social status levels,* nor the notion that high Negro arrest rates are invariably a consequence of the discriminatory application of justice by prejudiced white policemen and judges.

Age and violent crime

Was there any relationship between the age of gang members and their propensity to engage in violent crimes? Table 2 shows a clear and regular relationship between age and offense-frequency. The yearly rate of changes rises quite steadily between the ages of 12 and 18, reaches a peak of about 9 charges per 100 boys at age 18, then drops off quite rapidly to age 22, leveling off thereafter to a relatively low rate of about 3 charges per 100 boys per year. The bulk of court action (82 per cent of 229 charges) involved assaultive rather than property-damage offenses. The latter were proportionately more prevalent during the 11–13 age period, after which the former constitute a clear majority.

The age-patterning of theft-connected versus nontheft-connected violence and of intended versus actual violence was also determined. Violence in connection with theft—almost invariably the threat rather than the use thereof—constituted a relatively small proportion

---

[10] This ratio obtains for males only; calculations which include the girls' gangs show higher rates for whites in this category as well as the others. Data on field-recorded crimes on the female gangs are not included in Table 1 for purposes of comparability with court data; there were

too few court-recorded offenses for females to make analysis practicable. At the time the field data were collected (1954–1957) Negroes comprised about 35 per cent of the population of Midcity; court data cover the years up to 1964, at which time Negroes comprised about 55 per cent of the population.

Table 2

FREQUENCY OF VIOLENT CRIMES BY AGE: 14 MALE GANGS $(N = 293)$:
COURT CHARGES $(N = 229)$

Age	Number of Individuals	Number of Charges[a]	Rate[b]	Assault Charges[c]	Rate	Property Damage Charges[d]	Rate
8	293	—	—	—	—	—	—
9	293	—	—	—	—	—	—
10	293	1	0.3	1	0.3	—	—
11	293	7	2.4	2	0.7	5	1.7
12	293	—	—	—	—	—	—
13	293	6	2.0	1	0.3	5	1.7
14	293	16	5.5	12	4.1	4	1.4
15	293	19	6.5	14	4.8	5	1.7
16	293	26	8.9	21	7.2	5	1.7
17	293	25	8.5	21	7.2	5	1.7
18	293	27	9.2	23	7.8	3	1.0
19	293	21	7.2	18	6.1	3	1.0
20	293	22	7.5	21	7.2	1	0.3
21	293	20	6.8	19	6.5	1	0.3
22	292	9	3.1	8	2.7	1	0.3
23	281	10	3.5	8	2.8	2	0.7
24	247	5	2.0	4	1.6	1	0.4
25	191	7	3.7	6	3.1	1	0.5
26	155	5	3.2	5	3.2	—	—
27	95	3	3.1	3	3.2	—	—

[a] Charges on fourteen categories of offense (see Table 4).
[b] Charges per 100 individuals per year of age.
[c] Categories 1, 3, 4, 5, 5, 7, 8, 9, 13, and 14, Table 4.
[d] Categories 2, 10, 13, 12, Table 4.

of all charges (14 per cent), occurring primarily during the 15–21 age period. Court action based on the threat or intention to use violence rather than on its actual use comprised about one-quarter of all charges, becoming steadily more common between the ages of thirteen and twenty, and less common thereafter. At age twenty the number of charges based on the threat of violence was exactly equal to the number based on actual violence.

These data indicate quite clearly that involvement in violent crimes was a relatively transient phenomenon of adolescence, and did not presage a continuing pattern of similar involvement in adulthood. It should also be noted that these findings do not support an image of violent crimes as erratically impulsive, uncontrolled, and unpredictable. The fact that the practice of violent crime by gang members showed so regular and so predictable a relationship to age would indicate that violence was a "controlled" form of behavior—subject to a set of shared conceptions as to which forms were appropriate, and how often they were appropriate, at different age levels.

Participation in assaultive crime

What proportion of gang members engaged in assaultive crimes?[11] During the two-year period of field observation, 53 of the 205 intensive-contact gang members (26 per cent) were known to have engaged in illegal acts of as-

[11] Findings do not include data on property damage. See footnote 7.

sault—50 out of 155 males (32 per cent), and 3 out of 50 females (6 per cent.) Male-participation figures ranged from 22 per cent for the higher status gangs to 42 per cent for the lower. "Heavy" participants (four or more crimes) comprised only 4 per cent (six males, no females) of all gang members. During the same period nineteen gang members (all males) appeared in court on assault charges—about 12 per cent of the male gang members. While there is little doubt that some gang members also engaged in assaultive crimes that were known neither to field workers nor officials, the fact that three-quarters of the gang members and two-thirds of the males were *not* known to have engaged in assaultive crimes during the observation period and that 88 per cent of the males and 100 per cent of the females did not appear in court ·on charges of assaultive crimes strengthens the previous conclusion that assault was was not a dominant form of gang activity.

A related question concerns the relative prevalence of individual and collective assault. One image of gang violence depicts gang members as cowardly when alone, daring to attack others only when bolstered by a clear numerical superiority. Study data give little support to this image. Fifty-one per cent of recorded assault incidents involved either one-to-one engagements or engagements in which a single gang member confronted more than one antagonist. As will be shown in the discussion of "targets," a good proportion of the targets of collective assault were also groups rather than individuals. Some instances of the "ganging-up" phenomenon did occur, but they were relatively infrequent.

The character of violent crime

What was the character of violent crime in Midcity gangs? Violent crimes,

like other forms of gang behavior, consist of a multiplicity of particular events, varying considerably in form and circumstance. Any classification based on a single system does not account for the diversity of violence. The following sections use five ways of categorizing violent crimes: (1) *forms of crime directed at persons* (distinctions based on age, gang membership, and collectivity of actors and targets); (2) *forms of crime directed at objects* (distinctions based on mode of inflicting damage); (3) *forms of crime directed at persons and objects* (based on official classifications); (4) *targets of crime directed at persons* (distinctions based on age, sex, race, gang membership, collectivity); and (5) *targets of crime directed at objects* (distinctions based on identity of object).

Table 3 (column 1) shows the distribution of eleven specific forms of field-recorded assault directed at persons. In three-quarters of all incidents participants on both sides were peers of the same sex. In 60 per cent of the incidents, gang members acted in groups; in 40 per cent as individuals. Fifty-one per cent of the incidents involved collective engagements between same-sex peers. The most common form was the collective engagement between members of different gangs; it constituted one-third of all forms and was three times as common as the next most common form. Few of these engagements were full-scale massed-encounter gang fights; most were brief strike-and-fall-back forays by small guerrilla bands. Assault on male adults, the second most common form (11 per cent), involved, for the most part, the threat or use of force in connection with theft (for example, "mugging," or threatening a cab-driver with a knife) or attacks on policemen trying to make an arrest. It should be noted that those forms of gang assault which most alarm the public were

Table 3

FORMS OF VIOLENT CRIME: FIELD-RECORDED OFFENSES:
SEVEN INTENSIVE-OBSERVATION GANGS $(N = 205)$: INCIDENTS $(N = 125)$

Person-Directed			Object-Directed		
	Number of Incidents	% Known Forms		Number of Incidents	% All Forms
1. Collective engagement: different gangs	27	32.9	1. Damaging via body blow, other body action	10	27.0
2. Assault by individual on individual adult, same sex	9	11.0	2. Throwing of missile (stone, brick, etc.)	10	27.0
3. Two-person engagement: different gangs	6	7.3	3. Scratching, marking, defacing, object or edifice	8	21.6
4. Two-person engagement: gang member, nongang peer	6	7.3	4. Setting fire to object or edifice	4	10.8
5. Two-person engagement: intragang	5	6.1	5. Damaging via explosive	1	2.7
6. Collective assault on same sex peer, nongang-member	5	6.1	6. Other	4	10.8
7. Threatened collective assault on adult	5	6.1		37	100.0
8. Assault by individual on group	4	4.9			
9. Assault by individual on female peer	4	4.9			
10. Participation in general disturbance, riot	3	3.6			
11. Collective assault on same-sex peer, member of other gang	2	2.4			
12. Other	6	7.3			
13. Form unknown	6	—			
	88	99.9			

rare. No case of assault on an adult woman, either by individuals or groups, was recorded. In three of the four instances of sexual assault on a female peer, the victim was either a past or present girl friend of the attacker. Only three incidents involving general rioting were recorded; two were prison riots

and the third, a riot on a Sunday excursion boat.

The character of violent crimes acted on by the courts parallels that of field-recorded crimes. Table 4 shows the distribution of fourteen categories of offense for 293 gang members during the age period from late childhood to early adulthood. Charges based on assault (187) were five and a half times as common as charges on property damage (42). About one-third of all assault charges involved the threat rather than the direct use of force. The most common charge was "assault and battery," including, primarily, various kinds of unarmed engagements such as street fighting and barroom brawls. The more "serious" forms of assaultive crime were among the less prevalent: armed assault, 8 per cent; armed robbery, 5 per cent; sexual assault, 4 per cent. Not one of the 293 gang members appeared in court on charges of either murder or manslaughter between the ages of seven and twenty-seven.

Table 4

FORMS OF VIOLENT CRIME: COURT-RECORDED OFFENSES: 14 MALE GANGS ($N = 293$): COURT CHARGES THROUGH AGE 27 ($N = 229$)

Offense	Number	Percentage
1. Assault and battery: no weapon	75	32.7
2. Property damage	36	15.7
3. Affray	27	11.8
4. Theft-connected threat of force: no weapon	22	9.6
5. Possession of weapon	18	7.9
6. Assault, with weapon	18	7.9
7. Theft-connected threat of force: with weapon	11	4 8
8. Assault, threat of	8	3.5
9. Sexual assault	8	3.5
10. Arson	6	2.5
11. Property damage, threat of	—	—
12. Arson, threat of	—	—
13. Manslaughter	—	—
14. Murder	—	—
	229	100.0

The use of weapons and the inflicting of injury are two indications that violent crimes are of the more serious kind. Weapons were employed in a minority of cases of assault, actual or threatened, figuring in 16 of the 88 field-recorded offenses and about 55 of the 187 court offenses.[12] In the 16 field-recorded incidents in which weapons were used to threaten or injure, 9 involved knives, 4, an object used as a club (baseball bat, pool cue), and 3, missiles (rocks, balls). In none of the 88 incidents was a firearm of any description used. The bulk of assaultive incidents, then, involved the direct use of the unarmed body; this finding accords with others in failing to support the notion that gang members engage in assault only when fortified by superior resources.

Serious injuries consequent on assault were also relatively uncommon. There were twenty-seven known injuries to all participants in the eighty-eight incidents of assault; most of these were minor cuts, scratches, and bruises. The most serious injury was a fractured skull inflicted by a crutch wielded during a small-scale set-to between two gangs. There were also two other skull injuries, three cases of broken bones, three broken noses, and one shoulder dislocation (incurred during a fight between girls). While these injuries were serious enough for those who sustained them, it could not be said that the totality of person-directed violence by Midcity gang members incurred any serious cost in maimed bodies. The average week-end of highway driving in and around Port City produces more serious body injuries than two years of violent crimes by Midcity gangs.

Data on modes of property damage similarly reflect a pattern of involve-

---

[12] On the basis of field-recorded data it was estimated that about one-quarter of "Affray" charges involved sticks or other weapons.

ment in the less serious forms. As shown in Table 3, in ten of the thirty-seven field-recorded incidents the body was used directly to inflict damage (punching out a window, breaking fences for slats); another ten involved common kinds of missle-throwing (brick through store window). Most of the "defacing" acts were not particularly destructive, for example, scratching the name of the gang on a store wall. Fire-setting was confined to relatively small objects, for example, trash barrels. No instance was recorded of viciously destructive forms of vandalism such as desecration of churches or cemeteries or bombing of residences. The one case where explosives were used involved the igniting of rifle cartridge powder in a variety store. Of the forty-two cases of court-charged property-destruction, only six involved arson; the actual nature of vandalistic acts was not specified in the legal designations.

Targets of violent crime

While much gang violence took the form of "engagements with" rather than "attacks on" other persons, additional insight may be gained by viewing the gang members as "actors," and asking: "What categories of person were targets of gang assaults, and what kinds of physical objects targets of damage?" One image of gang violence already mentioned sees the act of "ganging up" on solitary and defenseless victims as a dominant gang practice; another sees racial antagonism as a major element in gang violence. What do these data show?

Table 5 shows the distribution of 88 field-recorded incidents of assault for 13 categories of target, and 43 incidents of damage for 6 categories.[13]

Of 77 targets of assault whose identity was known, a substantial majority (73 per cent) were persons of the same age and sex category as the gang members, and a substantial majority (71 per cent), of the same race. One-half of all targets were peers of the same age, sex, and race category. On initial inspection the data seem to grant substance to the "ganging up" notion; 44 of 77 targets (57 per cent) were individuals. Reference to Table 3, however, shows that 34 of these incidents were assaults on individuals *by* individuals; of the remaining 10, 4 were adult males (police, mugging victims) and one, the female member of a couple robbed at knife point. The remaining 5 were same-sex peers, some of whom were members of rival gangs. There was no recorded instance of collective assault on a child, on old men or women, or on females by males. There was no instance of an attack on a white female by a Negro male. Partly balancing the five cases of collective assault on lone peers were three instances in which a lone gang member took on a group.

These data thus grant virtually no support to the notion that favored targets of gang attacks are the weak, the solitary, the defenseless, and the innocent; in most cases assaulters and assaultees were evenly matched; the bulk of assaultive incidents involved contests between peers in which the preservation and defense of gang honor was a central issue. Some support is given to the notion of racial friction; 30 per cent of all targets were of a different race, and racial antagonism played some part in these encounters. On the other hand, of thirty-three instances of collective assault, a majority (55 per cent) involved antagonists of the same race.

Physical objects and facilities suffering damage by gang members were largely those which they used and frequented in the course of daily life. Most

[13] Findings are based on field-recorded data only; official offense designations seldom specify targets.

Table 5

TARGETS OF VIOLENT CRIME: FIELD-RECORDED OFFENSES: SEVEN
INTENSIVE-OBSERVATION GANGS $(N = 205)$: INCIDENTS $(N = 125)$

Persons	Number of Incidents	% Known Targets	Objects	Number of Incidents	% All Targets
1. Groups of adolescents, other gangs, same sex, race	18	23.4	1. Stores, commercial facilities: premises, equipment	11	29.7
2. Groups of adolescents, other gangs, same sex, different race	12	15.5	2. Semipublic facilities: social agencies, gyms, etc.	10	27.0
3. Individual adults, same sex, same race	12	15.5	3. Automobiles	8	21.6
4. Individual adolescents, other gangs, same sex, same race	8	10.4	4. Public facilities: schools, public transportation, etc.	5	13.5
5. Individual adolescents, nongang, same sex, race	6	7.8	5. Private houses: premises, furnishings	3	8.1
6. Individual adolescents, nongang, different sex, same race	4	5.2		37	99.9
7. Individual adolescents, nongang, same sex, different race	4	5.2			
8. Individual adults, same sex, different race	4	5.2			
9. Individual adolescents, own gang	3	3.9			
10. Groups of adolescents, own gang	3	3.9			
11. Individual adolescents, nongang, same sex, different race	2	2.6			
12. Individual adults, different sex, same race	1	1.3			
13. Target unknown	11	—			
	88	99.9			

damage was inflicted on public and semipublic facilities, little on private residences or other property. There was no evidence of "ideological" vandalism (stoning embassies, painting swastikas on synagogues). Most damage was deliberate, but some additional amount was a semiaccidental consequence of the profligate effusion of body energy so characteristic of male adolescents (breaking a store window in course of a scuffle). Little of the deliberately inflicted property damage represented a diffuse outpouring of accumulated hostility against arbitrary objects; in most cases the gang members injured the possession or properties of particular persons who had angered them, as a concrete expression of that anger (defacing automobile of mother responsible for having gang member committed to correctional institution; breaking windows of settlement house after ejection therefrom). There was thus little evidence of "senseless" destruction; most property damage was directed and responsive.

Gang fighting

An important form of gang violence is the gang fight; fiction and drama often depict gang fighting or gang wars as a central feature of gang life (for example, *West Side Story*). The Midcity study conceptualized a fully developed gang fight as involving four stages: initial provocation, initial attack, strategy-planning and mobilization, and counterattack.[14] During the study period, members of the intensive-observation gangs participated in situations involving some combination of these stages fifteen times. Despite intensive efforts by prowar agitators and elaborate preparations for war, only one of these situations eventuated in full-scale conflict; in the other fourteen, one or both sides found a way to avoid open battle. A major objective of gang members was to put themselves in the posture of fighting without actually having to fight. The gangs utilized a variety of techniques to maintain their reputation as proud men, unable to tolerate an affront to honor, without having to confront the dangerous and frightening reality of massed antagonists. Among these were the "fair fight" (two cham-

[14] A description of the gang fight as a form of gang behavior is included in W. B. Miller, "Lower-Class Culture as a Generating Milieu of Gang Delinquency," *Journal of Social Issues,* Vol. XXXI, No. 4 (December 1957), pp. 17, 18.

pions represent their gangs *a la* David and Goliath); clandestine informing of police by prospective combatants; *reluctantly* accepting mediation by social workers.

Despite the very low ratio of actual to threatened fighting, a short-term observer swept up in the bustle and flurry of fight-oriented activity, and ignorant of the essentially ritualistic nature of much of this activity, might gain a strong impression of a great deal of actual violence. In this area, as in others, detailed observation of gangs over extended periods revealed that gang fighting resembled other forms of gang violence in showing much more smoke than fire.

THE PROBLEM OF GANG VIOLENCE

The picture of gang violence which emerges from the study of Midcity gangs differs markedly from the conventional imagery as well as from that presented by some scholars. How is this difference to be explained? The most obvious possibility is that Midcity gangs were somehow atypical of gangs in Port City, and of the "true" American street gang. In important respects the gangs were *not* representative of those in Port City, having been selected on the basis of their reputation as the "toughest" in the city, and were thus *more* violent than the average Port City gang. The possibility remains, in the absence of information equivalent in scope and detail to that presented here, that Port City gangs were atypical of, and less violent than, gangs in other cities. I would like in this connection to offer my personal opinion, based on ten years of contact with gang workers and researchers from all parts of the country, that Midcity gangs were in fact *quite* typical of "tough" gangs in Chicago, Brooklyn, Philadelphia, Detroit, and similar cities, and represent the "reality" of gang violence much more accurately than "the Wild Ones" or the Egyptian Kings, represented as the prototypical "violent gang" in a well-known television program.

Even if one grants that actual city gangs are far less violent than those manufactured by the mass media and that the public fear of gangs has been unduly aroused by exaggerated images, the problem of gang violence is still a real one. However one may argue that all social groups need outlets for violence and that gang violence may serve to siphon off accumulated aggression in a "functional" or necessary way, the fact remains that members of Midcity gangs repeatedly violated the law in using force to effect theft, in fighting, and in inflicting damage on property as regular and routine pursuits of adolescence. *Customary* engagement in illegal violence by a substantial sector of the population, however much milder than generally pictured, constitutes an important threat to the internal order of any large urbanized society, a threat which must be coped with. What clues are offered by the research findings of the Midcity study as to the problem of gang violence and its control?

First, a brief summary of what it *was*. Violence as a concern occupied a fairly important place in the daily lives of gang members, but was distinguished among all forms of behavior in the degree to which concern took the form of talk rather than action. Violent crime as such was fairly common during middle and late adolescence, but, relative to other forms of crime, was not dominant. Most violent crimes were directed at persons, few at property. Only a small minority of gang members was active in violent crimes. Race had little to do with the frequency of involvement in violent crimes, but social status figured prominently. The practice of violent crimes was an essentially transient phenomenon of male adolescence, reaching a

peak at the age when concern with attaining adult manhood was at a peak. While the nature of minor forms showed considerable variation, the large bulk of violent crime in Midcity gangs consisted in unarmed physical encounters between male antagonists—either in the classic form of combat skirmishes between small bands of warriors or the equally classic form of direct combative engagement between two males.

Next, a brief summary of what it was *not*. Violence was not a dominant activity of the gangs; nor a central reason for their existence. Violent crime was not a racial phenomenon—either in the sense that racial antagonisms played a major role in gang conflict, or that Negroes were more violent, or that resentment of racial injustice was a major incentive for violence. It was not "ganging up" by malicious sadists on the weak, the innocent, the solitary. It did not victimize adult females. With few exceptions, violent crimes fell into the "less serious" category, with the extreme or shocking crimes rare.

One way of summarizing the character of violent crime in Midcity gangs is to make a distinction between two kinds of violence—"means" violence and "end" violence. The concept of violence as a "means" involves the notion of a resort to violence when other means of attaining a desired objective have failed. Those who undertake violence in this context represent their involvement as distasteful but necessary—an attitude epitomized in the parental slogan, "It hurts me more than it does you." The concept of violence as an "end" involves the notion of eager recourse to violence for its own sake—epitomized in the mythical Irishman who says, "What a grand party! Let's start a fight!" The distinction is illustrated by concepts of two kinds of policeman—the one who with great reluctance resorts to force in order to make an arrest and the "brutal" policeman who inflicts violence unnecessarily and repeatedly for pure pleasure. It is obvious that "pure" cases of either means- or end-violence are rare or nonexistent; the "purest" means-violence may involve some personal gratification, and the "purest" end-violence can be seen as instrumental to other ends.

In the public mind, means-violence is unfortunate but sometimes necessary; it is the spectacle of end-violence which stirs deep indignation. Much of the public outrage over gang violence arises from the fact that it has been falsely represented, with great success, as pure end-violence ("senseless," "violence for its own sake") when it is largely, in fact, means-violence.

What are the "ends" toward which gang violence is a means, and how is one to evaluate the legitimacy of these ends? Most scholars of gangs agree that these ends are predominantly ideological rather than material, and revolve on the concepts of prestige and honor. Gang members fight to secure and defend their honor as males; to secure and defend the reputation of their local area and the honor of their women; to show

that an affront to their pride and dignity demands retaliation.[15] Combat between males is a major means for attaining these ends.

It happens that great nations engage in national wars for almost identical reasons. It also happens, ironically, that during this period of national concern over gang violence our nation is pursuing, in the international arena, very similar ends by very similar means. At root, the solution to the problem of gang violence lies in the discovery of a way of providing for men the means of attaining cherished objectives—personal honor, prestige, defense against perceived threats to one's homeland—without resort to violence. When men have found a solution to this problem, they will at the same time have solved the problem of violent crimes in city gangs.

---

[15] The centrality of "honor" as a motive is evidenced by the fact that the "detached worker" method of working with gangs has achieved its clearest successes in preventing gang fights by the technique of furnishing would-be combatants with various means of avoiding direct. conflict without sacrificing honor.

27.

Dimensions of Current Gang Delinquency

Thomas M. Gannon

It has often been observed that the gang of today is not like the gang of yesterday. The factual and mythical exploits described in Asbury's *The Gangs of New York* as well as the intriguing "natural histories" compiled by the "Chicago school"—Shaw, McKay, Thrasher, *et al.*—give accounts of gang behavior that differ in important respects from delinquency as it has been hypothesized to exist today.[1] Recent literature has focused on the "specialization" of current delinquent activity, the heightened use of lethal weapons in group conflict, and the emergence of more "retreatist" charateristics of gang

life, especially the use of narcotics. Theoretically, delinquency is seen as rooted less in community tradition and "fun," and more in frustration and protest or even in the serious business of achieving manhood.[2] There also appears to be a decline in large-scale gang conflict, the splintering of highly organized gangs into smaller cliques, and increased social skills and aspirations among many of the individuals involved in these groups.

The present research into the types of groups serviced by the street club workers of the New York City Youth Board found evidence of the beginnings of a more sophisticated type of delinquent group. The structure of these groups has been taking shape almost imperceptibly over the past several

SOURCE. Thomas M. Gannon, "Dimensions of Current Gang Delinquency" from *Journal of Research in Crime and Delinquency*, Volume 4, No. 2, January 1967, pp. 119–131. Reprinted with permission.

[1] Herbert Asbury, *The Gangs of New York* (New York: Alfred A. Knopf, 1927); Clifford R. Shaw, *The Jack Roller* (Chicago: University of Chicago Press, 1930); Clifford R. Shaw and Maurice E. Moore, *The Natural History of a Delinquent Career* (Chicago: University of Chicago Press, 1931); Clifford R. Shaw and Henry D. McKay, *Juvenile Delinquency and Urban Areas* (Chicago: University of Chicago Press, 1956); Frederic M. Thrasher, *The Gang* (Chicago: University of Chicago Press, 1936); *cf.* James F. Short, Jr. and Fred L. Strodtbeck, *Group Process and Gang Delinquency* (Chicago: University of Chicago Press, 1966), pp. 77–78.

[2] Albert K. Cohen, *Delinquent Boys: The Culture of the Gang* (New York: Free Press, 1955); Albert K. Cohen and James F. Short, Jr., "Research in Delinquent Subcultures," *Journal of Social Issues*, July 1958, pp. 20–37; Richard A. Cloward and Lloyd E. Ohlin, *Delinquency and Opportunity* (New York: Free Press, 1960); Walter B. Miller, "Lower Class Culture as a Generating Milieu of Gang Delinquency," *Journal of Social Issues*, July 1958, pp. 5–19; David J. Bordua, "Some Comments on Theories of Group Delinquency," *Sociological Inquiry*, Spring 1962, pp. 245–60; Gilbert Geis, *Juvenile Gangs* (Washington, D.C.: President's Committee on Juvenile Delinquency, 1965).

years in New York City and deserves explicit recognition and closer observation. The following analysis is based on a participant observation and questionnaire study of the Youth Board's street club project, the Council of Social and Athletic Clubs (CSAC).[3]

Questionnaries were sent to the entire CSAC staff; the personal interviews were used more as intepretative aids than as statistical data for the study. Specifically, over half the unit offices (55 per cent) were visited with concentration, and a third (33.6 per cent) of the workers were interviewed at length and accompanied on the job. Eighty of the 111 workers returned the questionnaire (72 per cent), and it is on these returns that the statistical findings are based.

To reconcile the various theoretical viewpoints on gang delinquency would require greater precision than the present study could attempt to obtain. Consequently, the different aspects of deviance analyzed have been grouped under the term "gang delinquency," avoiding for the moment the knotty problem of specifying the nature of subcultural or "contracultural" delinquency or the problem of defining delinquent subculture.[4] For our purposes, it seemed more important to delineate the broad structure and function of the groups now serviced by the Youth Board.

Gathering data entirely from the street workers has certain limitations. Kobrin has clearly indicated the value and unique contribution such data can have for sociological analysis. Nevertheless, from the viewpoint of the individual worker, it is easy to arrive at many misconceptions of the type of group the agency services, since he sees only a selected number of groups and their activity cannot be as easily defined in its natural environment as it might in a more controlled setting. In the end we would agree with Kobrin that "fruitful observation of such groups is possible only when the observer is accepted by the subjects in a role which they perceive as meaningful in relation to their needs and problems."[5]

Altogether, the eighty street workers who responded to the questionnaire serviced 113 groups directly and 109 groups indirectly. Over two-thirds of the street workers (66.3 per cent) serviced one group directly, whereas twenty-seven were assigned to two or three direct-service groups. Over two-fifths of the workers (46.3 per cent) provided indirect service to one group, one-fifth (21.3 per cent) to two groups, and 13.7 per cent to three or more groups. For practical purposes, indirect service means that the Youth Board worker keeps aware of the general activities of certain groups that are known to him, especially if these activities might involve conflict with his or another group. These boys may or may not participate in the worker's programs. Only one-fifth of the street workers today operate on a one-to-one relationship with a single delinquent group. In summary, the Youth Board is currently in contact with over 3,100 boys in the high delinquency areas of New York.

[3] The present investigation is part of a larger study of the changing role of street work and was undertaken while the author was a Research Associate with the New York City Youth Board. Appreciation is due Maude M. Craig and Mary Koval for their active support and critical suggestions during the course of the study, and to Erminie C. Lacey for tabulating the statistical data.

[4] Robert K. Merton, "The Socio-Cultural Environment and Anomie," *New Perspectives for Research on Juvenile Delinquency,* Helen L. Witmer and Ruth Kotinsky, eds. (Washington, D.C.: U.S. Children's Bureau, 1956).

[5] Solomon Kobrin, "Sociological Aspects of the Development of a Street Corner Group: an Exploratory Study," *American Journal of Ortho-psychiatry,* October 1961, p. 685. See also, Short and Strodtbeck, *op. cit. supra* note 1, pp. 8–10.

STRUCTURE AND ORGANIZATION OF THE GROUP

Traditionally, the Youth Board has distinguished four types of adolescent groups with which it has come into contact.

1. The *corner group* develops in a particular spot; its members usually grow up together and continue to hang around as a group, talking or engaging in some joint activity. Together they normally display little antisocial behavior.

2. The *social club* almost always organizes around some common interest (e.g. baseball, basketball, jazz) and, like the corner group, is seldom involved in any serious group delinquency.

3. The *conflict group* might begin either as a corner or social group, but becomes involved in serious conflict with other groups. This conflict may be due to the need for protection or the desire for aggression. As a rule the group has weapons and an organizational structure designed for conflict.

4. The *thoroughly delinquent and pathological group,* totally committed to continuous violent activity,[6] resembles what Short has called the "hustling" group organized for the purpose of economic gain through nonlegitimate means, or Cloward and Ohlin's "criminal gang" whose primary activities are centered around rational, systematic, economically-motivated criminal activity.[7]

The Youth Board has been mainly concerned with the third type of adolescent group. Fighting potential varies not only in degree from one gang to another, but also in the form of con-

flict. An aggressive gang is involved in considerable initiation of conflict with rival gangs and in reputation- and status-seeking. A defensive group, on the other hand, seeks to maintain its identity without initiating conflict with other groups. It will usually prefer to settle provocations through peaceful means and to employ violent retaliation for only the most severe attack. Even this retaliation will often be carried on without weapons and may be followed by increased self-isolation from other gangs in the community.

This distinction between aggressive (or "fighting") gangs and defensive gangs became important in the present study when we inquired into the types of groups presently receiving street service.[8] As Table 1 indicates, over half the workers (53.8 per cent) would describe their groups as defensive, less than one-sixth (15.0 per cent) as fighting gangs, and almost one-third (31.2 per cent) as corner-social. These findings substantiate those of the 1964 survey of the CSAC which found that the group serviced by the street workers were organized and structured to meet needs other than aggression.[9] All ag-

Table 1

DISTRIBUTION BY TYPE OF GROUPS SERVICED BY YOUTH BOARD

Type of Group	Number	Percent
Defensive	43	53.8
Fighting	12	15.0
Corner	18	22.5
Social	7	8.7
Total	80	100.0

[6] New York City Youth Board, *Reaching the Fighting Gang,* (New York: New York City Youth Board, 1960), pp. 14–16.

[7] J. F. Short, Jr., introduction to the abridged version of Thrasher, *op. cit. supra* note 1, p. xlvi; also Cloward and Ohlin, *op. cit. supra* note 2, p. 20.

[8] For a development of this distinction, see Thomas M. Gannon, S.J., "Emergence of the 'Defensive' Gang," *Federal Probation,* December 1966, pp. 44–48.

[9] Elliott Bovelle, George Beschner, James Norton, and Robert Rothenberg, eds., *Survey of the Street Club Project* (Research Report, New York City Youth Board, 1964), pp. 13–14.

gressive behavior is certainly not absent in the defensive, corner, and social groups, but fighting does not constitute their main activity.

Probing further the structure of the gangs, we find almost all of the workers (88.8 per cent) reporting that the distinction between "core" and "peripheral" membership was still valid for their groups and most indicated that the groups have splintered into smaller cliques numbering from three to fifteen members. These cliques are usually part of a larger, more loosely organized group of about thirty-five boys of which 28.0 per cent are core members.

Table 2

ETHNIC COMPOSITION OF THE GROUPS [a]

Ethnic Composition	Number	Percent
Puerto Rican	29	36.2
Negro	28	35.0
Negro and Puerto Rican	10	12.5
White	9	11.3
Negro and white	2	2.5
Puerto Rican and white	2	2.5
Total	80	100.0

[a] The boys range in age from thirteen to nineteen years, with the lower limit for the defensive gang closer to fifteen years of age. As indicated in Table 2, most of these groups (over four-fifths) are either Negro, Puerto Rican, or a combination of the two.

Over one-third of the workers (36.4 per cent) reported a relatively strong leadership in their groups, with a president, titles, and division of labor, while 63.6 per cent reported an informal leadership structure. Approximately one-half (53.3 per cent) indicated a significant relationship to some older or other group, with 40 per cent relating to an older group, 13.3 per cent to another group. Twenty-three per cent of the workers felt that their groups could be structurally classified as independent, self-contained units; 24 per cent said that their groups had splintered into smaller cliques with only a loose relationship to other groups. In terms of general group cohesion, however, more than half the workers (54.5 per cent) would label their groups loosely knit.

Regarding educational and employment status, the members of these groups—fighting or defensive—display very similar characteristics. During the fall and winter months the workers reported that less than half their boys are in school (46.4 per cent), just over one-quarter (27.4 per cent) are employed; the remainder (26.4 per cent) seem to do nothing. During the summer, the "do-nothing" rate increases slightly (32.4 per cent); the number in school understandably drops (12.6 per cent); and many more boys are employed (55.0 per cent). The increased rate of summer employment probably is due to the city's push for additional summer job opportunities as well as to the Youth Board's summer "crash programs."

The number of gang boys in school is impressive. Since these figures represent youngsters who are able to remain in school, there is reason to believe that the Youth Board is no longer working only with boys who "have left school at the minimum age . . . and who, while in school, were chronically truant."[10] However, the present findings indicate little variation in the number of those "seemingly doing nothing" reported in the 1964 CSAC survey (25 per cent versus 26.6 per cent). More interesting is the strong similarity (Table 3) between fighting and defensive groups. The social groups represent different patterns of school attendance and employment: 68.2 per cent are in school and 10.6 per cent are seemingly doing nothing during the school year; 76.9 per cent are employed and only 17.4

[10] New York City Youth Board, *op. cit. supra* note 6, p. 55.

Table 3

SCHOOL ATTENDANCE AND EMPLOYMENT

Type of Employment	Fighting Group	Defensive Group	Corner Group	Social Group	Fighting and Defensive
Winter and fall:					
Usually employed	27.6	27.4	28.0	21.2	27.4
In school	41.9	45.1	43.3	68.2	44.4
Seemingly doing nothing	30.5	27.5	28.7	10.6	28.2
Total	100.0	100.0	100.0	100.0	100.0
Summer months:					
Usually employed	54.5	55.3	61.3	76.9	55.0
In school	9.7	13.3	7.5	5.7	12.6
Seemingly doing nothing	35.8	31.4	31.2	17.4	32.4
Total	100.0	100.0	100.0	100.0	100.0

per cent do nothing during the summer.

GROUP FORMATION AND MAINTENANCE

Why do youngsters join and continue to belong to these groups? In order to understand this question, the worker must be able to perceive both the uniqueness of his group and the ways in which the group functions to satisfy the needs and solve the problems of its members. According to current theories of gang delinquency, it does not seem much fun to be a gang delinquent. Thrasher's boys enjoyed being chased by the police, shooting dice, skipping school, and rolling drunks. Miller's boys have a little fun and excitement, but it seems somewhat desperate. For Cohen, and Cloward and Ohlin, the gang boys are driven into deviance by grim economic stress, status deprivation, and psychological necessity. Individuals always try to solve their problems in a satisfactory manner; for adolescents, this often takes the form of a "group" solution. The choice of a group and its importance to the members will usually depend on the way in which they perceive its relevance to their own situation. What factors appear most relevant?

Since over two-thirds of the workers (68.4 per cent) reported that there had been more than one worker assigned to the group since the Youth Board began its service, it seemed more productive to inquire why the CSAC initiated service to these groups and why the workers felt the group remains together, than to inquire when the group first formed. Most of the workers (90.9 per cent) reported that their group first received service because of its history of aggressive antisocial behavior. Only 10.8 per cent mentioned increased problems in the area (other than gang fighting) and 4.1 per cent indicated that a growing narcotics problem brought the worker into the area. One worker reported that the group had requested a worker.

As Table 4 reveals, most of the workers (93.8 per cent) felt their group stayed together because they lived in the same area. The next most common (70 per cent) reason given for maintaining the group was the homogeneity of problems in school, home, or in the neighborhood. This gives more empirical substance to Cohen's observation that a delinquent subculture forms as a group solution to common problems of frus-

Table 4

REASONS GIVEN BY WORKERS FOR GROUP MAINTENANCE

Worker's Responses[a]	Number	Percent
Live in the same area	75	93.8
Have same problems in school, family, neighborhood, etc.	56	70.0
Are friends	55	68.8
Feel need for protection	49	61.3
Have same interests	48	60.0
Attracted by older delinquent group in the area	23	28.8
All use or experiment with narcotics	16	20.0
Want to fight	7	8.8
Other reasons (ethnic rivalry, delinquent tradition, etc.)	4	5.0

[a] Each worker may have one or more responses.

tration.[11] Strongly reminiscent of Thrasher's analysis, the third most common factor (68.8 per cent) contributing to group maintenance was the fact that the boys are friends. The need for protection was the reason for staying together for three-fifths of the groups with similarity of interests.

Comparing the fighting and defensive groups on these items, one finds that the fighting group is more often maintained because of the need for protection, because the boys have similar problems in school, family, or neighborhood, and because an older delinquent group is attractive to them. They are less often held together by similar interests or ethnic background.

We have already mentioned the current tendency for larger groups to split into smaller cliques. Short and Strodtbeck have pointed out in their study of delinquent groups:

"Data from a large, white street-corner group without *discernible delinquency specialization* . . . also suggest that "criminal cliques" may develop within such groups. In the observed case, a clique of eight boys formed exclusively around rationally directed theft activities—auto stripping, burglary, shoplifting, etc. This clique did not hang together on the corner, but met in one another's homes. When on the corner, they hung with members of the larger groups. They participated in the general hanging and drinking patterns, and in occasional altercations with various adults as part of this larger group, but not as a *distinguishable clique. Only in their pattern of theft activities were they a clique.*"[12]

Our own data indicate that over three-fourths (76 per cent) of the workers have observed such clique formation. Unlike the case referred to by Short and Strodtbeck, however, these cliques formed around a number of delinquent activities: narcotics (in first place), theft (second), and illicit sex (third), with small proportions indicating drinking and gambling.

PATTERNS OF DEVIANT BEHAVIOR

A distinction has been made between groups which the street workers service directly and those serviced indirectly. Although all the preceding statistics have referred exclusively to directly serviced groups, the distinction becomes useful when discussing patterns of deviance. Two-fifths of the workers indicated that the direct-service groups are more aggressive than the groups ser-

[11] Cohen, *op. cit. supra* note 2, pp. 132–33.

[12] Short and Strodtbeck, *op. cit. supra* note 1, p. 98.

viced indirectly; the same number reported lessened involvement in criminal activity; and two-thirds indicated a decrease in gang fighting in their direct-service group. Less than one-third (32.3 per cent), however, considered the direct-service groups more deviant and more than one-third saw the direct service groups as more formally organized.

The majority of workers (69.3 per cent) reported that the direct-service groups demanded more time and energy. This is understandable in view of the workers' assignments; most would feel that they were not doing their job properly if they devoted the same time to both types of groups. Still, one might expect that the directly serviced groups would display more reason for attention in terms of aggressiveness and overall deviance.

More specifically, how did the workers assess the group's deviance? Interviews with the workers, rather than replies to the research questionnaire, revealed that 62 per cent of the workers felt drinking to be the most prominent deviant characteristic; 47.6 per cent listed stealing (burglary, petty theft) in first place; only 18.4 per cent specified auto theft. Experimenting with narcotics was most commonly reported (68.2 per cent). (No distinction here was made between use of marijuana, glue-sniffing, "pep" pills, etc.) A much smaller number (14.3 per cent) indicated that a number of group members were addicted to more serious forms of narcotics. Thirty per cent listed gambling (cards, dice, numbers) as the most common deviance; 21.8 per cent, school problems (truancy, dropout, school adjustment); and 18.8 per cent, illicit sex activities.

When assessing these figures, it is important to recall that no attempt was made to discover the number of boys in each group who engaged in these activities. The findings of Short and Strodtbeck concerning the incidence of certain behavior among individual gang boys review this aspect in greater detail.[13] We were interested in a more general picture of the patterns of deviance perceived by the street workers as most characteristic of their groups. From this vantage point, most of the groups appear to have significant involvement in narcotics experimentation, excessive drinking, stealing, and gambling. Parallel to this, almost all workers reported that members of their group had been arrested at some time and/or had served time in a jail or reformatory.

On the other hand, it is also important to know what kinds of relatively "constructive" behavior these groups display. In enumerating the types of social activity most often pursued by the groups, hanging around on the street (socializing, group "bull-sessions," etc.) was most frequent (87.6 per cent); dating and dancing rated second (64.3 per cent); sports activities were third (46.2 per cent). An interesting subject for further research would be the degree to which factors of deviance and constructive activity were related within the same group, as well as the various clusters of deviance which tended to exist together in different group types.

The measure of social conflict in a community, and the amount of socially imposed frustration in achieving society's established goals and rewards, have long been viewed as significant indicators of deviance. Since all the youths serviced by the Youth Board come from neighborhoods which lack cohesiveness and unity and where transiency and instability become the over-riding features of social life, there are obvious and powerful pressures for

[13] Short and Strodtbeck, *op. cit. supra* note 1, pp. 87–93.

violent behavior.[14] As Cloward and Ohlin have observed:

. . . an unorganized community cannot provide access to legitimate channels to success-goals, and thus discontent among the youth with their life-chances is heightened. Secondly, access to stable criminal opportunity systems is also restricted, for disorganized neighborhoods do not develop different age-levels of offender or integration of carriers of criminal and conventional values. The young, in short, are relatively deprived of *both* conventional and criminal opportunities. Finally, social controls are weak in such communities. These conditions, we believe, lead to the emergence of conflict subcultures.[15]

One cannot reasonably expect an absence of group conflict in the day-to-day street corner activities of these youths. It is more relevant, therefore, to examine the form this group conflict assumes.

Over the past year, almost three-fourths (74.7 per cent) of the workers reported that their groups were involved in some conflicts with members of other groups even though there has been a parallel trend of decreasing gang fights (68.9 per cent). On analysis this is found to be an average of 3.1 conflicts per group. During the same period 59 per cent of the workers reported some serious intragroup conflicts (2.5 per group), and more workers (80.6 per cent) reported some serious conflicts with persons other than rival gang members. A "serious" conflict was defined as a fight with weapons between two or more members of opposing or allied groups or with individuals not

affiliated with a group, which results in serious injury and possible arrest.

The type of conflict most often reported by workers with fighting or defensive groups was serious conflict with other groups (Table 5); similar numbers report group involvement in serious conflict with persons other than gang members. The corner and social groups, however, seem to be involved in more conflicts with non-gang youths than in either intragroup or intergroup conflicts. As expected, the percentage of conflict involvement, as well as the number of conflicts reported per respondent, generally decreases from the fighting and defensive groups to the corner and social groups. These findings substantiate those of the 1964 CSAC survey which found a trend toward less group conflict over the preceding two-year period.

Any gang fight or intergroup conflict is almost always the result of provocation which mobilizes the groups or individuals within these groups. Provocations are usually exterior but, without an interior sensitivity to such situations, they would have little meaning. As the Sherifs observe:

"There may be cases in which the realistic basis for conflict is so overgeneralized by members as to justify aggression on anyone who is not a group member. . . . Still, realistic factors and the group basis of violence and aggression should be considered in formulating proposals of what to do to prevent occurrence."[16]

The current data show the rank order of provocations (Table 6): drinking, girls, neighborhood group differences, "sounding," individual membership reprisals, racial tension, and arguments over the price of drugs or liquor. These findings contradict those of the 1964

[14] Cf. "Delinquency in Youth Board Neighborhoods," Research Report, New York City Youth Board, August 1965; also "Socio-Economic Factors for the Twenty-Nine Youth Board Neighborhoods," Research Report, New York City Youth Board, November 1963.

[15] Cloward and Ohlin, *op. cit. supra* note 2, p. 172.

[16] Muzafer and Carolyn Sherif, *Reference Groups: Explorations into Conformity and Deviation of Adolescents* (New York: Harper & Row, 1964), p. 230.

Table 5

INCIDENCE OF CONFLICT REPORTED BY GROUP WORKERS

Number of Conflicts	Fighting Group		Defensive Group		Corner Group		Social Group		All Groups	
	No.	%	No.	%	No.	%	No.	%	No.	%
Serious conflicts with other groups										
Total responses	12	100.0	42	100.0	18	100.0	7	100.0	79	100.0
None	—	—	5	11.9	10	55.6	5	71.4	20	25.3
Some	12	100.0	37	88.1	8	44.4	2	28.6	59	74.7
Conflicts per group	79	6.6	136	3.2	24	1.3	2	0.3	241	3.1
Serious intragroup conflicts										
Total responses	12	—	42	—	17	—	7	—	78	—
None	2	11.7	10	23.8	14	82.4	6	85.7	32	41.0
Some	10	88.3	32	76.2	3	17.6	1	14.3	46	59.0
Conflicts per group	56	4.7	132	3.1	6	0.4	1	0.1	195	2.5
Conflicts with other persons										
Total responses	12	—	42	—	16	—	7	—	77	—
None	—	—	7	16.7	5	41.2	3	42.9	15	19.5
Some	12	100.0	35	83.3	11	68.8	4	57.1	62	80.6
Conflicts per group	80	6.7	233	5.5	32	2.0	9	1.3	354	4.6

Table 6

COMPARISON BETWEEN WORKER-REPORTED PROVOCATIONS TO
GROUP CONFLICT IN 1964 AND 1965 SURVEYS

Provocations to Conflict	Most often		Sometimes		Seldom	
	1964[a]	1965[a]	1964	1965	1964	1965
Drinking	40.6%	42.0%	46.9%	50.7%	10.9%	7.2%
Girls	26.6	34.8	39.1	40.6	20.3	24.6
Neighborhood group differences	37.5	34.8	34.4	31.9	10.7	7.3
Racial tension	45.3	30.6	34.4	24.2	31.3	45.2
Individual reprisals	25.0	21.2	56.7	50.0	21.9	28.8
"Sounding"	28.1	25.4	45.3	46.0	31.3	28.6
Price of liquor or drugs	18.8	9.4	34.4	29.7	51.6	60.9

[a] In this table, the total numbers for the 1964 survey were N = 64; for the 1965 study, the totals were as follows: drinking (N = 69), girls (N = 69); neighborhood group differences (N = 51), racial tension (N = 62), individual reprisals (N = 66), "sounding" (N = 63), price of liquor/drugs (N = 64).

CSAC survey which found that, in the preceding two years, nearly one-half of the group conflicts reported by the workers had developed because of racial tensions or involvement over girls. The present data, as well as the research staff's interview experience, does not support this emphasis on racial tension.

That such tension exists is unquestionable; whether it currently figures significantly in conflict provocations has not been determined.

As indicated in Table 7, the most common form of conflict reported by the workers was defensive fighting. The groups also tend to become involved in

Table 7

DISTRIBUTION OF TYPES OF CONFLICT OF YOUTH BOARD GROUPS

Forms of Conflict	Most Often		Sometimes		Seldom	
	No.	%	No.	%	No.	%
Spontaneous fights	27	40.3	25	37.3	15	22.2
Individual skirmishes	21	32.8	28	43.8	15	23.4
Defensive fighting	19	29.2	33	50.8	13	20.0
Planned rumbles	14	22.2	19	30.2	30	47.6
Japping attacks	13	20.3	28	43.8	23	35.9

individual skirmishes, spontaneous fighting, and "japping" attacks. It is interesting that planned rumbles rank fourth as one of the least common forms of group conflict.

The Sherifs have observed: "A major concern of every group studied which engaged in violence against other groups and their members was avoidance of conflict."[17] In their research findings, this concern was frequently discussed and translated into appropriate precautions just as observable as planning an attack and easier to observe than actual violence. The present data support these findings; over two-thirds (67.1 per cent) of the workers reported that boys in their groups often discussed with them their desire not to fight. More of the respondents (73.8 per cent) indicated that the boys often discussed getting out of the neighborhood. Understandably, defensive groups were more apt to discuss their desire not to fight than were fighting groups (71.4 per cent versus 58.3 per cent); the fighting groups, on the other hand, more often discussed getting out of the neighborhood (83.3 per cent versus 72.1 per cent).

The workers reported (Table 8) that discussions with the boys more often concerned getting ahead in life, getting a job as a youth worker or social worker, and questions about the danger of pregnancy of girl friends than the use of marijuana or how to get rid of a weapon.

IMPLICATIONS FOR GROUP NORMS

The shift in fighting patterns raises an interesting question about the function which conflict plays within the status system of the group. According to Matza, the distinctive feature of the "spirit" of delinquency is the celebration of prowess.[18] Prowess can add considerably to the adventurous element of life as well as to the success of one's reputation in the group. In this sense aggression is closely linked with the idea of prowess. The code of the "warrior" calls for aggressive manliness, a reluctance to accept a slight on one's honor. Such a code is reflected in the delinquent's esteem for "heart" (the ratio between bravery and fighting ability).

In the defensive group fighting skills continue to run high as a status symbol, but with the decrease in gang warfare a member's reputation tends to rest on his fighting *potential* rather than on his proved victories. With more of the boys interested in getting jobs, staying in school, and "getting ahead," status begins to be measured also in terms of a job, weekly salary, future plans, and one's involvement with the larger so-

[17] Sherif and Sherif, *op. cit. supra* note 16, p. 231.

[18] David Matza, "Subterranean Traditions of Youth," *Annals of the American Academy of Political and Social Science,* November 1961, p. 107.

Table 8

ISSUES DISCUSSED WITH WORKERS

	Yes		No or Not Sure	
Subject Discussed	No.	%	No.	%
How to get rid of a weapon	34	48.8	41	52.1
Pregnancy	64	81.0	15	19.0
Getting ahead in life	75	93.8	5	6.2
Getting out of the neighborhood	59	73.8	21	26.2
Desire not to fight	53	67.1	26	32.9
Use of marijuana	57	71.3	23	28.7
Getting job as youth or social worker	71	91.0	7	9.0

ciety. Given the fact that all these boys come from the lower-class culture where toughness is virtually connatural with social prestige, aggression and violence as motivating factors will never · be wholly absent. What is more surprising is the emergence of the desire to get ahead, to have a stake in society. This trend, which is reflected in all our data of the defensive group, runs counter to the fatalism and lack of concern with legitimate achievement attributed to the lower-class boy.[19]

DIMENSIONS OF SOCIAL DISABILITY

In his classic analysis of street-corner society, William Whyte comments:

The stable composition of the group and the lack of social assurance on the part of its members contribute toward producing a very high rate of social interaction within the group. The group structure is a product of this interaction. . . . Out of such interaction there arises a system of mutual obligations which is fundamental to group cohesion.[20]

Whyte attributes the corner boys' lack of social assurance to their limited range

of social experiences, with attendant rigidity in behavior.

While the workers in the present study report the existence of some deficiency in social skills (lack of social "know-how" and social assurance), the contributing factors appear slightly different. First, as Short and Strodtbeck point out, the lack cannot be attributed to the intensity and rigidity of interaction patterns with their own group.[21] The workers unanimously report that in their groups these patterns are not stable enough to produce rigidity. However, there can be little doubt that gang boys lack the variety of experience which increases their ability to adapt to new situations such as an organized athletic team or a new job.

Most of the workers (92.2 per cent) reported that their boys are able to move freely in the area, but only 36.4 per cent felt that these same boys could move freely outside their neighborhood. Seventy per cent considered that their groups spoke at least passable English; 64.9 per cent reported that their groups could be aware of appointment times if they wanted to be, and 37.7 per cent could keep track of money and save if they wished to purchase something.

Generally, 59.5 per cent felt that their boys showed increased interest in

[19] Miller, *op. cit. supra* note 2, p. 9; see also Arthur Pearl, "Youth in Lower Class Settings," *Problems of Youth,* Sherif and Sherif, eds. (Chicago: Aldine, 1965), pp. 89–109.

[20] William F. Whyte, *Street Corner Society* (Chicago: University of Chicago Press, 1955), p. 256.

[21] Short and Strodtbeck, *op. cit. supra* note 1, p. 218.

school and employment, which correlates with the school and employment rates mentioned earlier. Over half of the workers (55.4 per cent) indicated an overall increase in their group's social skills and over half (55.8 per cent) reported that their boys get along relatively well with their peers. Although quite favorable, this last finding indicates a certain ambivalence on the part of gang members regarding their own group; this ambivalence appears more revealingly in the boys' tendency (observed during interviews with them) to endorse such apparently conflicting statements as: "Friends are generally more trouble than they are worth" *and* "You can only be really alive when you are with friends."[22] When the underlying tone of aggression noted earlier is considered, it becomes clearer that the fear of threat seems to hang over even the closest of group friendships and further substantiation is given to the observations of Short and Strodtbeck that the gang is hardly the stable and rewarding web of relationships it is often assumed to be.[23]

SUMMARY

The present analysis has shown that the average group serviced by the New York City Youth Board's street workers is the defensive gang of about thirty-five members, ten of whom can be classified as "hard core." The group ranges in age from thirteen to nineteen years, is either Puerto Rican or Negro, and displays a rather loosely knit structure, informal leadership, and some relationship to an older or other group. More boys are in school or employed than are seemingly doing nothing. Aggression as a principal mechanism of group maintenance has considerably declined. Group cohesion has lessened while the group's tolerance for other forms of deviant behavior (e.g., use of narcotics) has increased. The boys seem most concerned with getting a job, getting ahead, or a girl friend's pregnancy, and express a stronger desire to stay away from fighting. Group conflicts most often are directed toward members of other groups. These are usually provoked by drinking, girls, and neighborhood group differences.

Aggressive skills continue to rank high as group status symbols. Similarly, the groups display extreme sensitivity to any kind of status threat. In terms of social skills, the boys now seem to do better than they did at the outset of the project. Many of the groups can function both within and outside the area. Nevertheless, to equate this increased social ability with middle-class adolescent styles of life would be a misconception of the still bleak and treacherous existence experienced by current delinquent groups.

[22] *Ibid.*, p. 221.
[23] *Ibid.*, p. 231.

section IV

Legal Processing of Delinquency

The materials of this section have been selected to give the student a conception of the nature and practice of the juvenile court movement, as well as some of the sociolegal problems that have developed since the first law defining juvenile delinquency was passed by the Illinois legislature in 1899. The juvenile court movement grew out of the conviction that youthful offenders should not receive the same treatment as adults. The fundamental idea of this first juvenile court law was that the state, with a judge assuming the role of a parent, should extend its protective arm to children in order to "cure" and "save" rather than to punish. The court was to recognize the individuality of the child and adapt its procedure accordingly.

Since that time, many problems have arisen about the juvenile court's relationship to other courts, the legality of its procedure, and the rules of evidence. Part of this difficulty may be viewed as resulting from the diversity, jurisdiction, and functioning of the juvenile court systems in the various states.

Not all youths who commit delinquent acts come to the attention of the courts and the correctional agencies. Police officers are often permitted considerable latitude in deciding which juveniles come to the attention of the courts and are thereby officially identified as delinquents. The study by Piliavin and Briar shows that the social judgment made by police officers in labeling a juvenile "a delinquent" is influenced by race, prior offense records, grooming, and demeanor instead of by the kind of offense he has committed.

Dunham's article presents two idealized conceptions of the juvenile court—the social agency and the legalistic conceptions—and discusses the conflict between these two contradictory orientations. Caldwell's article reviews the history and characteristics of the juvenile court; it discusses the events and forces that produced it and the consequences for the court's philosophy and operation. Basic questions are raised concerning the future of the court, with particular emphasis placed on the need to differentiate clearly the judicial function of the court from the casework function.

The selection by Tappan reflects the concern expressed by many authorities regarding the Court's functions. Tappan accepts the basic goals of the juvenile court movement, but opposes the continuing expansion of the functions of the juvenile court. He strongly objects to the vagueness of the definitions of offenses for which the courts may try children, since this factor makes possible serious interference with the individual's liberties. He enumerates what he considers to be minimal protections of due process, and refers to the dangers involved in practices such as informal probation and the unofficial handling of cases.

With respect to the functions of the court, the question is often raised why probation is administered by the court whereas other forms of correctional treatment are administered by separate agencies. The administrative, casework, and welfare functions associated with adjudication are performed directly by probation personnel as a part of the court. The current practice is for the court to decide how the juvenile is to be processed—whether he is to be placed on probation or is to be committed to an institution.

Diana discusses present-day probation in contrast to what, in his view, are some unsubstantiated claims about the way probation operates in practice. A significant discrepancy which emerges is that experienced workers in the field do not have as well-defined views of what constitutes probation as do those who are writing in this area. The discrepancy between probation in theory and probation in actual practice remains as much a problem in our own day as in the previous decade when these problems were set forth.

As Paul Tappan has pointed out, the vague character of juvenile court statutes has resulted in the juvenile court's assuming responsibility for many children who, he believes, should not be processed through the courts. Moreover, the "flexibility" of the court, originally thought to facilitate the treatment process, not only has failed in this regard but, indeed, has resulted in a denial of constitutional rights for children.

Two landmark legal decisions, *In re Gault* (1967), and *Kent v. United States* (1966), have in an important sense changed the structure of the court. Alan Neighbor discusses the ruling of the Supreme Court, and the misconceptions regarding the scope of the Gault decision. The implications of these decisions for the probation officer is discussed by Cayton. In the final selection, Coxe analyzes the controversy over the lawyer's role in the adjudication and disposition process and points out some of the effects of the Gault ruling on institutional populations.

28.

Police Encounters with Juveniles

Irving Piliavin and Scott Briar

As the first of a series of decisions made in the channeling of youthful offenders through the agencies concerned with juvenile justice and corrections, the disposition decisions made by police officers have potentially profound consequences for apprehended juveniles.[1] Thus arrest, the most severe of the dispositions available to police, may not only lead to confinement of the suspected offender but also bring him loss of social status, restriction of educational and employment opportunities, and future harassment by law-enforcement personnel.[2] According to some criminologists, the stigmatization resulting from police apprehension, arrest, and detention actually reinforces deviant behavior.[3] Other authorities have suggested, in fact, that this stigmatization serves as the catalytic agent initiating delinquent careers.[4] Despite their presumed significance, however, little empirical analysis has been reported regarding the factors influencing, or consequences resulting from, police actions with juvenile offenders. Furthermore, while some studies of police encounters with adult offenders have been reported, the extent to which the findings of these investigations pertain to law-enforcement practices with youthful offenders is not known.[5]

* This study was supported by Grant MH-06328-02, National Institute of Mental Health, U. S. Public Health Service.

[1] Richard D. Schwartz and Jerome H. Skolnick, "Two Studies of Legal Stigma," *Social Problems*, 10 (April, 1962), 133–142.

[2] Sol Rubin, *Crime and Juvenile Delinquency* (New York: Oceana Publications, 1958); B. F. McSally, "Finding Jobs for Released Offenders," *Federal Probation*, 24 (June, 1960), 12–17; Harold D. Lasswell and Richard C. Donnelly, "The Continuing Debate over Responsibility: An Introduction to Isolating the Condemnation Sanction," *Yale Law Journal*, 68 (April, 1959), 869–899.

[3] Richard A. Cloward and Lloyd E. Ohlin, *Delinquency and Opportunity* (Glencoe, Ill.: Free Press, 1960), pp. 124–130.

[4] Frank Tannenbaum, *Crime and the Community* (New York: Columbia University Press, 1936), pp. 17–20; Howard S. Becker, *Outsiders: Studies in the Sociology of Deviance* (New York: Free Press of Glencoe, 1963), chaps. i and ii.

[5] For a detailed accounting of police discretionary practices, see Joseph Goldstein, "Police Discretion Not To Invoke the Criminal Process: Low Visibility Decisions in the Administration of Justice," *Yale Law Journal*, 69 (1960), 543–594; Wayne R. LaFave, "The Police and Non-enforcement of the Law—Part I," *Wisconsin Law Review*, January, 1962, pp. 104–137; S. H. Kadish, "Legal Norms and Discretion in the Police and Sentencing Processes,"

SOURCE. Irving Piliavin and Scott Briar, "Police Encounters with Juveniles," from *The American Journal of Sociology*, Volume 70, September 1964, pp. 206–214. Copyright © 1964, University of Chicago Press. Reprinted with the permission of the University of Chicago Press.

The above considerations have led the writers to undertake a longitudinal study of the conditions influencing, and consequences flowing from, police actions with juveniles. In the present paper findings will be presented indicating the influence of certain factors on police actions. Research data consist primarily of notes and records based on nine months' observation of all juvenile officers in one police department.[6] The officers were observed in the course of their regular tours of duty.[7] While these data do not lend themselves to quantitative assessments of reliability and validity, the candor shown by the officers in their interviews with the investigators and their use of officially frowned-upon practices while under observation provide some assurance that the materials presented below accurately reflect the typical operations and attitudes of the law-enforcement personnel studied.

The setting for the research, a metropolitan police department serving an industrial city with approximately 450,000 inhabitants, was noted within the community it served and among law-enforcement officials elsewhere for the honesty and superior quality of its personnel. Incidents involving criminal activity or brutality by members of the department had been extremely rare during the ten years preceding this

study; personnel standards were comparatively high; and an extensive training program was provided to both new and experienced personnel. Juvenile Bureau members, the primary subjects of this investigation, differed somewhat from other members of the department in that they were responsible for delinquency prevention as well as law enforcement, that is, juvenile officers were expected to be knowledgeable about conditions leading to crime and delinquency and to be able to work with community agencies serving known or potential juvenile offenders. Accordingly, in the assignment of personnel to the Juvenile Bureau, consideration was given not only to an officer's devotion to and reliability in law enforcement but also to his commitment to delinquency prevention. Assignment to the Bureau was of advantage to policemen seeking promotions. Consequently, many officers requested transfer to this unit, and its personnel comprised a highly select group of officers.

In the field, juvenile officers operated essentially as patrol officers. They cruised assigned beats and, although concerned primarily with juvenile offenders, frequently had occasion to apprehend and arrest adults. Confrontations between the officers and juveniles occurred in one of the following three ways, in order of increasing frequency: (1) encounters resulting from officers' spotting officially "wanted" youths; (2) encounters taking place at or near the scene of offenses reported to police headquarters; and (3) encounters occurring as the result of officers' directly observing youths either committing offenses or in "suspicious circumstances." However, the probability that a confrontation would take place between officer and juvenile, or that a particular disposition of an identified offender would be made, was only in part determined by the knowledge that an offense

---

Harvard Law Review, 75 (March, 1962), 904–931.

[6] Approximately thirty officers were assigned to the Juvenile Bureau in the department studied. While we had an opportunity to observe all officers in the Bureau during the study, our observations were concentrated on those who had been working in the Bureau for one or two years at least. Although two of the officers in the Juvenile Bureau were Negro, we observed these officers on only a few occasions.

[7] Although observations were not confined to specific days or work shifts, more observations were made during evenings and weekends because police activity was greatest during these periods.

had occurred or that a particular juvenile had committed an offense. The bases for and utilization of non-offenses related criteria by police in accosting and disposing of juveniles are the focuses of the following discussion.

SANCTIONS FOR DISCRETION

In each encounter with juveniles, with the minor exception of officially "wanted" youths,[8] a central task confronting the officer was to decide what official action to take against the boys involved. In making these disposition decisions, officers could select any one of five discrete alternatives:

1. Outright release.
2. Release and submission of a "field interrogation report" briefly describing the circumstances initiating the police-juvenile confrontation.
3. "Official reprimand" and release to parents or guardian.
4. Citation to juvenile court.
5. Arrest and confinement in juvenile hall.

Dispositions 3, 4, and 5 differed from the others in two basic respects. First, with rare exceptions, when an officer chose to reprimand, cite, or arrest a boy, he took the youth to the police station. Second, the reprimanded, cited, or arrested boy acquired an official police "record," that is, his name was officially recorded in Bureau files as a juvenile violator.

Analysis of the distribution of police disposition decisions about juveniles revealed that in virtually every category of offense the full range of official disposition alternatives available to officers was employed. This wide range of discretion resulted primarily from two conditions. First, it reflected the reluctance of officers to expose certain youths to

the stigmatization presumed to be associated with official police action. Few juvenile officers believed that correctional agencies serving the community could effectively help delinquents. For some officers this attitude reflected a lack of confidence in rehabilitation techniques; for others, a belief that high case loads and lack of professional training among correctional workers vitiated their efforts at treatment. All officers were agreed, however, that juvenile justice and correctional processes were essentially concerned with apprehension and punishment rather than treatment. Furthermore, all officers believed that some aspects of these processes (e.g., judicial definition of youths as delinquents and removal of delinquents from the community), as well as some of the possible consequences of these processes (e.g., intimate institutional contact with "hard-core" delinquents, as well as parental, school, and conventional peer disapproval or rejection), could reinforce what previously might have been only a tentative proclivity toward delinquent values and behavior. Consequently, when officers found reason to doubt that a youth being confronted was highly committed toward deviance, they were inclined to treat him with leniency.

Second, and more important, the practice of discretion was sanctioned by police-department policy. Training manuals and departmental bulletins stressed that the disposition of each juvenile offender was not to be based solely on the type of infraction he committed. Thus, while it was departmental policy to "arrest and confine all juveniles who have committed a felony or misdemeanor involving theft, sex offense, battery, possession of dangerous weapons, prowling, peeping, intoxication, incorrigibility, and disturbance of the peace," it was acknowledged that "such considerations as age, attitude and prior

---

[8] "Wanted" juveniles usually were placed under arrest or in protective custody, a practice which in effect relieved officers of the responsibility for deciding what to do with these youths.

criminal record might indicate that a different disposition would be more appropriate."[9] The official justification for discretion in processing juvenile offenders, based on the preventive aims of the Juvenile Bureau, was that each juvenile violator should be dealt with solely on the basis of what was best for him.[10] Unofficially, administrative legitimation of discretion was further justified on the grounds that strict enforcement practices would overcrowd court calendars and detention facilities, as well as dramatically increase juvenile crime rates—consequences to be avoided because they would expose the police department to community criticism.[11]

In practice, the official policy justifying use of discretion served as a demand that discretion be exercised. As such, it posed three problems for juvenile officers. First, it represented a departure from the traditional police practice with which the juvenile officers themselves were identified, in the sense that they were expected to justify their juvenile disposition decisions not simply by evidence proving a youth had committed a crime—grounds on which police were officially expected to base their dispositions of non-juvenile offenders[12]—but in the *character* of the youth. Second, in disposing of juvenile offenders, officers were expected, in effect, to make judicial rather than ministerial decisions.[13] Third, the shift from the offense

to the offender as the basis for determining the appropriate disposition substantially increased the uncertainty and ambiguity for officers in the situation of apprehension because no explicit rules existed for determining which disposition different types of youths should receive. Despite these problems, officers were constrained to base disposition decisions on the character of the apprehended youth, not only because they wanted to be fair, but because persistent failure to do so could result in judicial criticism, departmental censure, and, they believed, loss of authority with juveniles.[14]

DISPOSITION CRITERIA

Assessing the character of apprehended offenders posed relatively few difficulties for officers in the case of youths who had committed serious crimes such as robbery, homicide, aggravated assault, grand theft, auto theft, rape, and arson. Officials generally regarded these juveniles as confirmed delinquents simply by virtue of their involvement in offenses of this magnitude.[15] However, the infraction committed did not always suffice to determine the appropriate disposition for some serious offenders;[16] and, in the case of minor offenders, who comprised over 90 per cent of the youths against

9 Quoted from a training manual issued by the police department studied in this research.

10 Presumably this also implied that police action with juveniles was to be determined partly by the offenders' need for correctional services.

11 This was reported by beat officers as well as supervisory and administrative personnel of the Juvenile Bureau.

12 In actual practice, of course, disposition decisions regarding adult offenders also were influenced by many factors extraneous to the offense per se.

13 For example, in dealing with adult violators, officers had no disposition alter-

native comparable to the reprimand-and-release category, a disposition which contained elements of punishment but did not involve mediation by the court.

14 The concern of officers over possible loss of authority stemmed from their belief that court failure to support arrests by appropriate action would cause policemen to "lose face" in the eyes of juveniles.

15 It is also likely that the possibility of negative publicity resulting from the failure to arrest such violators—particularly if they became involved in further serious crime—brought about strong administrative pressure for their arrest.

16 For example, in the year preceding this research, over 30 per cent of the juveniles involved in burglaries and 12 per cent of the juveniles committing auto theft received dispositions other than arrest.

whom police took action, the violation per se generally played an insignificant role in the choice of disposition. While a number of minor offenders were seen as serious delinquents deserving arrest, many others were perceived either as "good" boys whose offenses were atypical of their customary behavior, as pawns of undesirable associates or, in any case, as boys for whom arrest was regarded as an unwarranted and possibly harmful punishment. Thus, for nearly all minor violators and for some serious delinquents, the assessment of character—the distinction between serious delinquents, "good" boys, misguided youths, and so on—and the dispositions which followed from these assessments were based on youths' personal characteristics and not their offenses.

Despite this dependence of disposition decisions on the personal characteristics of these youths, however, police officers actually had access only to very limited information about boys at the time they had to decide what to do with them. In the field, officers typically had no data concerning the past offense records, school performance, family situation, or personal adjustment of apprehended youths.[17] Furthermore, files at police headquarters provided data only about each boy's prior offense record. Thus both the decision made in the field—whether or not to bring the boy in—and the decision made at the station—which disposition to invoke—were based largely on cues which emerged from the interaction between the officer and the youth, cues from

which the officer inferred the youth's character. These cues included the youth's group affiliations, age, race, grooming, dress, and demeanor. Older juveniles, members of known delinquent gangs, Negroes, youths with well-oiled hair, black jackets, and soiled denims or jeans (the presumed uniform of "tough" boys), and boys who in their interactions with officers did not manifest what were considered to be appropriate signs of respect tended to receive the more severe dispositions.

Other than prior record, the most important of the above clues was a youth's *demeanor*. In the opinion of juvenile patrolmen themselves the demeanor of apprehended juveniles was a major determinant of their decisions for 50–60 per cent of the juvenile cases they processed.[18] A less subjective indication of the association between a youth's demeanor and police disposition is provided by Table 1, which presents the police dispositions for sixty-six youths whose encounters with police were observed in the course of this study.[19] For purposes of this analysis, each youth's demeanor in the encounter was classified as either co-operative or unco-operative.[20] The results clearly

---

[17] On occasion, officers apprehended youths whom they personally knew to be prior offenders. This did not occur frequently, however, for several reasons. First, approximately 75 per cent of apprehended youths had no prior official records; second, officers periodically exchanged patrol areas, thus limiting their exposure to, and knowledge about, these areas; and third, patrolmen seldom spent more than three or four years in the juvenile division.

[18] While reliable subgroup estimates were impossible to obtain through observation because of the relatively small number of incidents observed, the importance of demeanor in disposition decisions appeared to be much less significant with known prior offenders.

[19] Systematic data were collected on police encounters with seventy-six juveniles. In ten of these encounters the police concluded that their suspicions were groundless, and consequently the juveniles involved were exonerated; these ten cases were eliminated from this analysis of demeanor. (The total number of encounters observed was considerably more than seventy-six, but systematic data-collection procedures were not instituted until several months after observations began.)

[20] The data used for the classification of demeanor were the written records of observations made by the authors. The classifications were made by an independent judge not associated with this study. In classifying a youth's demeanor as

Table 1

SEVERITY OF POLICE DISPOSITION BY YOUTH'S DEMEANOR

Severity of police disposition	Youth's demeanor		Total
	Co-operative	Unco-operative	
Arrest (most severe)	2	14	16
Citation or official reprimand	4	5	9
Informal reprimand	15	1	16
Admonish and release (least severe)	24	1	25
Total	45	21	66

reveal a marked association between youth demeanor and the severity of police dispositions.

The cues used by police to assess demeanor were fairly simple. Juveniles who were contrite about their infractions, respectful to officers, and fearful of the sanctions that might be employed against them tended to be viewed by patrolmen as basically law-abiding or at least "salvageable." For these youths it was usually assumed that informal or formal reprimand would suffice to guarantee their future conformity. In contrast, youthful offenders who were fractious, obdurate, or who appeared nonchalant in their encounters with patrolmen were likely to be viewed as "would-be tough guys" or "punks" who fully deserved the most severe sanction: arrest. The following excerpts from observation notes illustrate the importance attached to demeanor by police in making disposition decisions.

1. The interrogation of "A" (an eighteen-year-old upper-lower-class white male accused of statutory rape) was assigned to a police sergeant with long experience on the force. As I sat in his office while we waited for the youth to arrive for questioning, the sergeant expressed his uncertainty

as to what he should do with this young man. On the one hand, he could not ignore the fact that an offense had been committed; he had been informed, in fact, that the youth was prepared to confess to the offense. Nor could he overlook the continued pressure from the girl's father (an important political figure) for the police to take severe action against the youth. On the other hand, the sergeant had formed a low opinion of the girl's moral character, and he considered it unfair to charge "A" with statutory rape when the girl was a willing partner to the offense and might even have been the instigator of it. However, his sense of injustice concerning "A" was tempered by his image of the youth as a "punk," based, he explained, on information he had received that the youth belonged to a certain gang, the members of which were well known to, and disliked by, the police. Nevertheless, as we prepared to leave his office to interview "A," the sergeant was still in doubt as to what he should do with him.

As we walked down the corridor to the interrogation room, the sergeant was stopped by a reporter from the local newspaper. In an excited tone of voice, the reporter explained that his editor was pressing him to get further information about this case. The newspaper had printed some of the facts about the girl's disappearance, and as a consequence the girl's father was threatening suit against the paper for defamation of the girl's character. It would strengthen the newspaper's position, the reporter explained, if the police had information indicating that the girl's associates, particularly the youth the sergeant was about to interrogate, were persons of disreputable character. This

co-operative or unco-operative, particular attention was paid to: (1) the youth's responses to police officers' questions and requests; (2) the respect and deference—or lack of these qualities—shown by the youth toward police officers; and (3) police officers' assessments of the youth's demeanor.

stimulus seemed to resolve the sergeant's uncertainty. He told the reporter, "unofficially," that the youth was known to be an undesirable person, citing as evidence his membership in the delinquent gang. Furthermore, the sergeant added that he had evidence that this youth had been intimate with the girl over a period of many months. When the reporter asked if the police were planning to do anything to the youth, the sergeant answered that he intended to charge the youth with statutory rape.

In the interrogation, however, three points quickly emerged which profoundly affected the sergeant's judgment of the youth. First, the youth was polite and co-operative; he consistently addressed the officer as "sir," answered all questions quietly, and signed a statement implicating himself in numerous counts of statutory rape. Second, the youth's intentions toward the girl appeared to have been honorable; for example, he said that he wanted to marry her eventually. Third, the youth was not in fact a member of the gang in question. The sergeant's attitude became increasingly sympathetic, and after we left the interrogation room he announced his intention to "get 'A' off the hook," meaning that he wanted to have the charges against "A" reduced or, if possible, dropped.

2. Officers "X" and "Y" brought into the police station a seventeen-year-old white boy who, along with two older companions, had been found in a home having sex relations with a fifteen-year-old girl. The boy responded to police officers' queries slowly and with obvious disregard. It was apparent that his lack of deference toward the officers and his failure to evidence concern about his situation were irritating his questioners. Finally, one of the officers turned to me and, obviously angry, commented that in his view the boy was simply a "stud" interested only in sex, eating, and sleeping. The policemen conjectured that the boy "probably already had knocked up half a dozen girls." The boy ignored these remarks, except for an occasional impassive stare at the patrolmen. Turning to the boy, the officer remarked, "What the hell am I going to do with you?" And again the boy simply returned the officer's gaze. The latter then said, "Well, I guess we'll just have to put you away for a while." An arrest report was then made out and the boy was taken to Juvenile Hall.

Although anger and disgust frequently characterized officers' attitudes toward recalcitrant and impassive juvenile offenders, their manner while processing these youths was typically routine, restrained, and without rancor. While the officers' restraint may have been due in part to their desire to avoid accusation and censure, it also seemed to reflect their inurement to a frequent experience. By and large, only their occasional "needling" or insulting of a boy gave any hint of the underlying resentment and dislike they felt toward many of these youths.[21]

PREJUDICE IN APPREHENSION AND DISPOSITION DECISIONS

Compared to other youths, Negroes and boys whose appearance matched the delinquent stereotype were more frequently stopped and interrogated by patrolmen—often even in the absence of evidence that an offense had been committed[22]—and usually were given

[21] Officers' animosity toward recalcitrant or aloof offenders appeared to stem from two sources: moral indignation that these juveniles were self-righteous and indifferent about their transgressions, and resentment that these youths failed to accord police the respect they believed they deserved. Since the patrolmen perceived themselves as honestly and impartially performing a vital community function warranting respect and deference from the community at large, they attributed the lack of respect shown them by these juveniles to the latters' immorality.

[22] The clearest evidence for this assertion is provided by the overrepresentation of Negroes among "innocent" juveniles accosted by the police. As noted, of the seventy-six juveniles on whom systematic data were collected, ten were exonerated and released without suspicion. Seven, or two-thirds of these ten "innocent" juveniles were Negro, in contrast to the allegedly "guilty" youths, less than one-third of whom were Negro. The following incident

more severe dispositions for the same violations. Our data suggest, however, that these selective apprehension and disposition practices resulted not only from the intrusion of long-held prejudices of individual police officers but also from certain job-related experiences of law-enforcement personnel. First, the tendency for police to give more severe dispositions to Negroes and to youths whose appearance corresponded to that which police associated with delinquents partly reflected the fact, observed in this study, that these youths also were much more likely than were other types of boys to exhibit the sort of recalcitrant demeanor which police construed as a sign of the confirmed delinquent. Further, officers assumed, partly on the basis of departmental statistics, that Negroes and juveniles who "look tough" (e.g., who wear chinos, leather jackets, boots, etc.) commit crimes more frequently than do other types of youths.[23] In this sense, the police justified their selective treatment of these youths along epidemiological lines: that is, they were concentrating their attention on those youths whom they believed were most likely to commit delinquent acts. In the words of one highly placed official in the department:

If you know that the bulk of your delin-

illustrates the operation of this bias: One officer, observing a youth walking along the street, commented that the youth "looks suspicious" and promptly stopped and questioned him. Asked later to explain what aroused his suspicion, the officer explained, "He was a Negro wearing dark glasses at midnight."

[23] While police statistics did not permit an analysis of crime rates by appearance, they strongly supported officers' contentions concerning the delinquency rate among Negroes. Of all male juveniles processed by the police department in 1961, for example, 40.2 per cent were Negro and 33.9 per cent were white. These two groups comprised at that time, respectively, about 22.7 per cent and 73.6 per cent of the population in the community studied.

quent problem comes from kids who, say, are from twelve to fourteen years of age, when you're out on patrol you are much more likely to be sensitive to the activities of juveniles in this age bracket than older or younger groups. This would be good law-enforcement practice. The logic in our case is the same except that our delinquency problem is largely found in the Negro community and it is these youths toward whom we are sensitized.

As regards prejudice per se, eighteen of twenty-seven officers interviewed openly admitted a dislike for Negroes. However, they attributed their dislike to experiences they had, as policemen, with youths from this minority group. The officers reported that Negro boys were much more likely than non-Negroes to "give us a hard time," be uncooperative, and show no remorse for their transgressions. Recurrent exposure to such attitudes among Negro youth, the officers claimed, generated their antipathy toward Negroes. The following excerpt is typical of the views expressed by these officers:

They (Negroes) have no regard for the law or for the police. They just don't seem to give a damn. Few of them are interested in school or getting ahead. The girls start having illegitimate kids before they are sixteen years old and the boys are always "out for kicks." Furthermore, many of these kids try to run you down. They say the damnedest things to you and they seem to have absolutely no respect for you as an adult. I admit I am prejudiced now, but frankly I don't think I was when I began police work.

IMPLICATIONS

It is apparent from the findings presented above that the police officers studied in this research were permitted and even encouraged to exercise immense latitude in disposing of the juveniles they encountered. That is, it was within the officers' discretionary authority, except in extreme limiting cases, to decide which juveniles were to come to the attention of the courts and correctional agencies and thereby be identified officially as delinquents. In exercising this discretion policemen were strongly guided by the demeanor of those who were apprehended, a practice which ultimately led, as seen above, to certain youths (particularly Negroes[24] and boys dressed in the style of "toughs") being treated more severely than other juveniles for comparable offenses.

But the relevance of demeanor was not limited only to police disposition practices. Thus, for example, in conjunction with police crime statistics the criterion of demeanor led police to concentrate their surveillance activities in areas frequented or inhabited by Negroes. Furthermore, these youths were accosted more often than others by officers on patrol simply because their skin color identified them as potential troublemakers. These discriminatory practices—and it is important to note that they are discriminatory, even if based on accurate statistical information —may well have self-fulfilling consequences. Thus it is not unlikely that frequent encounters with police, particularly those involving youths innocent of wrongdoing, will increase the hostility of these juveniles toward law-enforcement personnel. It is also not unlikely that the frequency of such encounters will in time reduce their significance in the eyes of apprehended juveniles, thereby leading these youths to regard them as "routine." Such responses to police encounters, however, are those which law-enforcement personnel perceive as indicators of the serious delinquent. They thus serve to

vindicate and reinforce officers' prejudices, leading to closer surveillance of Negro districts, more frequent encounters with Negro youths, and so on in a vicious circle. Moreover, the consequences of this chain of events are reflected in police statistics showing a disproportionately high percentage of Negroes among juvenile offenders, thereby providing "objective" justification for concentrating police attention on Negro youths.

To a substantial extent, as we have implied earlier, the discretion practiced by juvenile officers is simply an extension of the juvenile-court philosophy, which holds that in making legal decisions regarding juveniles, more weight should be given to the juvenile's character and life-situation than to his actual offending behavior. The juvenile officer's disposition decisions—and the information he uses as a basis for them —are more akin to the discriminations made by probation officers and other correctional workers than they are to decisions of police officers dealing with non-juvenile offenders. The problem is that such clinical-type decisions are not restrained by mechanisms comparable to the principles of due process and the rules of procedure governing police decisions regarding adult offenders. Consequently, prejudicial practices by police officers can escape notice more easily in their dealings with juveniles than with adults.

The observations made in this study serve to underscore the fact that the official delinquent, as distinguished from the juvenile who simply commits a delinquent act, is the product of a social judgment, in this case a judgment made by the police. He is a delinquent because someone in authority has defined him as one, often on the basis of the public face he has presented to officials rather than of the kind of offense he has committed.

[24] An unco-operative demeanor was presented by more than one-third of the Negro youths but by only one-sixth of the white youths encountered by the police in the course of our observations.

29.

The Juvenile Court: Contradictory Orientations in Processing Offenders

H. Warren Dunham

EVENTS AND FORCES FORMING THE JUVENILE COURT

The historical origin of the juvenile court is, no doubt, sufficiently familiar to the readers of this symposium to warrant but a brief recapitulation. While the first law defining juvenile delinquency was passed by the Illinois legislature in April 1899,[1] and the juvenile court itself began functioning in June of that year, its founding had been amply anticipated by certain legalistic precedents in equity and criminal law. More specifically, from the English courts of chancery or equity, the principle of *parens patriae* had evolved in the case of *Eyre v. Shaftsbury* in 1772.[2] This principle, which enabled the court to act in lieu of parents who were deemed unwilling or unable to perform their proper parental functions, paved the way for the juvenile court to assume jurisdiction of dependent and neglected children. Even before this decision, however, the doctrine that the

state under certain conditions had to act as a protector of minors had long been a part of the common law.[3]

But it is in dealing with delinquent children that the criminal-law origins of the juvenile court are of significance. It had long been an accepted principle of the common law that a child under seven years of age could not commit a criminal act because he could not have *mens rea,* a guilty mind.[4] From here, it was logical next to question the responsibility of children above seven years of age, and in so doing, the juvenile court law has been regarded merely as extending the application of a common-law principle.

Another development anticipating the juvenile court was the inauguration of probation as a device for dealing with offenders. This practice, initiated in Boston in 1841,[5] which included from the beginning adult as well as juvenile

[1] Ill. Laws 1899, p. 131.
[2] 2 P. Wms. 103, 24 Eng. Rep. 659 (Ch. 1722).

[3] See H. H. Lou, *Juvenile Courts in the United States* 3 (1927).
[4] See Rollin M. Perkins, *Criminal Law* 729–732 (1957).
[5] See Helen D. Pigeon, *Probation and Parole in Theory and Practice* 85 (1942).

SOURCE. H. Warren Dunham, "The Juvenile Court: Contradictory Orientations in Processing Offenders," from *Law and Contemporary Problems,* Volume 23, No. 3, Summer 1958, pp. 508–527. From a symposium, *Sentencing,* Copyright © 1958, Duke University. Reprinted with permission.

offenders, early highlighted some of the special protections that a child needed when brought before a court of law.

One other development which paved the way for the juvenile court was the establishment of special institutions for confining child offenders. The first institution for juvenile delinquents, the House of Refuge, in New York City, opened on January 1, 1825, and by 1860, sixteen of such institutions had been opened in the United States.[6] These responded to the need long felt by the reform element in American society that a child who had been convicted of violating a law should not be confined with hardened adult criminals in jails and penitentiaries, where, it was believed, only further demoralization and corruption could ensue. Even so, up to the first quarter of the twentieth century, children were still being punished by incarceration in institutions designed for adults.

Thus, it is seen that early legal precedents, the development of probation, and the establishment of special institutions for juvenile offenders anticipated the first juvenile court in Illinois, which was to become the prototype for legal tribunals dealing with children whose behavior or situation indicated positive state intervention. The concept of the juvenile court spread quickly and was favorably received throughout the country. Indeed, by 1923, all states, with the exception of Connecticut and Wyoming, had enacted legislation defining a juvenile delinquent and establishing a special court for hearing children's cases; and by the early 1940's, even the two hold-out states had come into compliance with this trend.

While these historical events define the establishment of the juvenile court, in a broader cultural sense it can be regarded as the product of such social forces as our humanitarianism, on the one hand, and the growth of cities, on the other. The force of humanitarianism is well symbolized in the personalities of those women, Jane Addams and Julia Lathrop in Illinois, who agitated for the first juvenile court law. The high principles and unselfish motives which fired these women played a positive role in giving to the juvenile court, from its inception, the stamp of a social agency for dealing with a maladjusted child, rather than that of a punitive court attempting to exact retribution.

The rapid growth of cities, which characterized not only the United States, but the world in the nineteenth century, was also a significant factor. In 1800, there was no city with a population of 100,000 in the United States, but by 1900, there were thirty-seven.[7] This urbanization was a product of the factory system plus improvements in agricultural technology. The cities grew not so much through natural increase, as through vast movements of people thereto from rural areas and from various European countries seeking jobs, opportunities, and a new life.

Most of these European migrants faced new and untested situations in the slum environments of our large cities. Their children, often caught in the conflict between European peasant values and the values reflected in American institutions, responded in delinquent ways and began to flood the jails, reformatories, and courts. Their parents, handicapped by language difficulties, were unable to comprehend or cope with these situations, and this tended

[6] See N. K. Teeters and J. O. Reinemann, *The Challenge of Delinquency* 429–447 (1950).

[7] See U. S. Dep't of State, Census Office, *Second Census of the United States* (1801); U. S. Dep't of Commerce, Bureau of the Census, *Statistical Abstract of the United States* (1957).

to foster certain unforeseen functions of the emerging juvenile court, such as aiding the process of immigrant family adjustment, serving as an educational agency in American values, and often protecting the child from demoralizing home situations.

Definitions

Some difficulty has been experienced in determining exactly what the juvenile court is and what a juvenile delinquent is. The difficulty in defining the juvenile court stems from the fact that it is usually attached to a probate or county court and is generally of limited jurisdiction. Thus, while each state now has a juvenile court, its organization and the policies governing it vary markedly throughout the country. While most large cities have a court presided over by a special judge that is devoted exclusively to the processing of cases involving children, many rural counties merely have the probate judge change hats when hearing children's cases. In some jurisdictions, the juvenile court judge is appointed; in many other jurisdictions, he is an elected official. A few judges have looked upon the juvenile court judgeship as a career; others have seen it merely as a step in an upward political climb. Some judges take a human, personal interest in the children brought before them; others merely handle the cases within the framework of the law. Some juvenile courts, particularly those in large cities, have a staff of trained professionals, probation officers, social workers, psychologists, statisticians; others have hardly any. In some juvenile courts, the probation officers are trained social workers; in others, their professional training is minimal. In some juvenile courts, these professionals are under civil service and have tenure; in others, they are largely personal and political appointments. Some juvenile courts

work closely with the numerous social agencies dealing with children; others have little or no contact with such agencies.

Three types of juvenile courts which have emerged in the various states have been identified. First, in most counties, other courts have jurisdiction over juvenile cases as well, and when hearing such cases they are referred to as juvenile courts. Second, there are some juvenile courts which are separate and divorced completely from other courts; these are usually found in counties with large cities. Finally, some juvenile courts are tied to special courts that handle selected social-problem cases, such as divorce and truancy, although there also has been a tendency to place such social-problem cases in juvenile courts which have an independent organization—a practice that has engendered certain support for a so-called family court.

A recent survey shows that in some forty states, jurisdiction is overlapping between the general criminal and juvenile courts. It is noted that the provision for alternate authority is related to the seriousness of the offense and/or the maturity of the child-defendant. The interpretive remarks on this matter are most relevant:[8]

Practice belies the motives which have supported the child welfare movement, revealing the limitations of our humanitarianism. More specifically, it points up the emphasis which our legal system continues to place upon incapacitation and deterrence—the protection of the public even at the expense of the child. In part, it may reflect too, the feeling that a fuller and more careful hearing should be given to serious cases than the juvenile court ordinarily provides.

When one turns to the definition of

[8] Tappan, "Children and Youth in the Criminal Court," 261 *Annals* 128, 132 (1947).

a juvenile delinquent, there is not so much variation as in the case of the juvenile court. All states have laws which, although varying in wording, show a common core of agreement in this regard. Thus, a child is uniformly considered delinquent if he acts in such a way as to violate a local ordinance or state law. In addition, most states further include such acts or conditions as "habitual truancy from school," "knowingly associating with thieves, vicious or immoral persons," "incorrigibility," "beyond control of parent or guardian," and "growing up in idleness and crime." These are only a few of the thirty-four items commonly found in the laws defining juvenile delinquency in the several states.[9]

In general, state laws defining delinquency have moved from the specific to the generic. Accordingly, the legislation that established the juvenile court in Illinois defined a delinquent as "any child under the age of sixteen years who has violated any law of the state or any city or village ordinance."[10] This concise statement contrasts markedly with the later New York legislation which defines a delinquent as:[11]

. . . a child over seven and under sixteen years of age (a) who violates any law of . . . this state or any ordinance of the city of New York, or who commits any act which if committed by an adult would be an offense punishable otherwise than by death or life imprisonment; (b) who is incorrigible, ungovernable, or habitually disobedient and beyond the control of his parents, guardian, custodian or other lawful authority; (c) who is habitually truant; (d) who without just cause and without the consent of his parent, guardian or other custodian deserts his home or place of abode; (e) who engages in any occupa-

tion which is in violation of the law; (f) who begs or who solicits alms or money in public places; (g) who associates with immoral or vicious persons; (h) who frequents any place the maintenance of which is in violation of law; (i) who habitually uses obscene or profane language; or (j) who so deports himself as wilfully to injure or endanger the morals or health of himself or others.

Another observable trend has been the strengthening of the role of the juvenile court by assuring it wider jurisdiction over children's cases and by emphasizing that the child is not on trial for a specific crime. But some decisions contain language to the effect that the child's constitutional rights are to be assured through right of appeal —even though this right is seldom exercised in the juvenile court;[12] and this matter has provided one of the principal foci for criticism of the juvenile court. Some judges and lawyers have maintained that the juvenile court in operation practically subverts the "due process" clause of the constitution in its zeal to apply the doctrine of *parens patriae*.

In addition to the generally diffuse manner in which they define delinquency, state laws differ markedly with respect to fixing the maximum legal age of a delinquent, varying from sixteen to twenty-one, with seventeen being the most common.

In summary, then, it should be noted that juvenile delinquency is a broad generic term which embraces many diverse forms of antisocial behavior of the child and which is defined somewhat differently in the various states, even though a converging tendency may be observed in the various laws.

It is only to be expected that these differences in court organization and

[9] See Frederick B. Sussman, *Law of Juvenile Delinquency: The Laws of the Forty-Eight States* 20 (1950).
[10] Ill. Laws 1899, p. 137.
[11] N.Y.C. Dom. Rel. Ct. Act § 2(15).
[12] Herbert A. Bloch and Frank T. Flynn, *Delinquency: The Juvenile Offender in America Today* 353 (1956).

in the definition of delinquency have made for wide variations in juvenile court policies and practices. Some juvenile courts are rigid, others are flexible; some are authoritarian, others are permissive; some are dictatorial, others are democratic. These contrasts are reflected in the number of cases heard unofficially in comparison with those heard officially, as well as in the use of various dispositions and the differences among juvenile court judges in the use of the dispositions available to them. But above all, they are reflected by the dominance of the image, as either a legal or social agency, that the juvenile court has of itself.

THE SOCIAL-AGENCY IMAGE OF THE COURT

Juvenile courts in the United States run the gamut from the authoritarian legalistic tribunal at one extreme to the permissive, social-agency type of organization at the other. While there is no one juvenile court which coincides completely with either of these idealized poles, it could probably be demonstrated that those which are an adjunct to another court correspond more closely to the legalistic image and those which have a completely independent organization, with a full-time judge, tend to adhere to the social-agency image. In this part, an attempt will be made to delineate the ideal social-agency image of the juvenile court. In so doing, those influences that were crucial in molding this image, the general character of this image, and some of its unanticipated consequences will be identified.

In the social-agency image, the purposes of the juvenile court are to understand the child, to diagnose his difficulty, to treat his condition, and to fit him back into the community. These purposes are held, to a greater or lesser degree, by the personnel that constitutes the juvenile court organization. More difficult, however, is the unraveling of all the tangible and intangible influences that have gone into constructing this social-agency image. In this connection, five influences have been selected which, in the judgment of the writer, have been primarily responsible for the evolution of this image and for its development at the expense of the juvenile court's more legalistic role. These are and have been: (1) the aggressive social-work orientation of the United States Children's Bureau; (2) the broadening jurisdiction of the juvenile court to include not only neglected and dependent children, but all matters of a legal nature involving children; (3) the gradual professionalization of social work; (4) various court decisions involving delinquency; and (5) the growing prospects of treatment through the increased acceptance by social workers of psychoanalysis, which has provided techniques for getting at the roots of conflict which supposedly produce delinquency. While each one of these influences has played its specific role, it would be quite difficult to assess their respective weights. It is sufficient merely to note that collectively they interacted and mutually reinforced an image of the juvenile court as a social-agency institution of independent status.

Thirteen years after the first juvenile court was established in Illinois, the Children's Bureau was created and lodged in the United States Department of Labor.[13] The appointment of Julia Lathrop, an early proponent of the first juvenile court law, as its first head was a significant factor in enabling the emerging profession of social work to exercise a powerful influence

[13] 37 Stat. 79 (1912), 42 U.S.C. § 191 (1952); 37 Stat. 737 (1913), 5 U.S.C. § 616 (1952).

over the development of the juvenile court. This influence has been reflected in the collection of statistics, the development of model juvenile court laws, the promulgation of standards for measuring juvenile court operation, the initiation of studies of juvenile court cases, the encouragement of juvenile courts to institute treatment services, the calling of national conferences of practicing professionals dealing with the problem, the emphasis on the need of probation officers with case-work training, and the attempts to construct educational and experience standards for those persons who would enter juvenile court work. All of these efforts and others have helped so to orient the juvenile court as to enable it to construct an image of itself as a social-work agency, designed primarily to meet the needs of the child. When Julia Lathrop left the Bureau in 1921, the high standards which she had set and the high ideals of child care and welfare for which she strived were carried forward by the distinguished social workers that followed her—Grace Abbott, 1921–1933, Katherine Lenroot, 1934–1951, and Martha Eliot, 1951–1956.

In short, the Children's Bureau, during its comparatively short history, has been most successful in shaping the image of the juvenile court as an agency for seeking the welfare of the child. Its failures, if they may be so termed, have been primarily of a negative nature—that is, it has failed to recognize that high ideals without sufficient knowledge are not enough, with the consequence that the social-agency image, which is at present the dominant image, has led to certain unanticipated consequences and unresolved dilemmas which have often placed the child in situations that are harmful rather than helpful to him. One commentator probably had these matters in mind when he noted that

"the plight of the youngster has been increased by the deprivation of these [public hearings, trial by jury, right of appeal] and other ordinary elements of due process that are assured in the criminal court."[14]

The second influence, the broadening jurisdiction of the juvenile court, was a natural outgrowth of the reform spirit which dominated its founding. This helped, again, to emphasize the often-quoted characteristic of the juvenile court—that the child before it is not being tried for a crime, but rather that the court is acting in lieu of the parent and, as a benevolent one, by inquiring into the development and circumstances surrounding his maladjustment in order to determine the course of action that will best meet his needs and insure his continued welfare. This tendency of the juvenile court to deal with all cases involving children, however, has resulted in an obscuring and sloughing over of the differences between the delinquent and the dependent or neglected child and in a dealing with every child as if he were maladjusted or presented some kind of problem. Social workers, in fact, in their conception of juvenile courts, unwittingly reflect this obscuring tendency:[15]

The purpose of the juvenile court is not to inflict a penalty on a child but to save him from further delinquency and from neglect. Its success, therefore, depends upon a comprehensive understanding of all significant aspects of the case. . . . If treatment is to be directed to causes and adapted to the needs of the individual, the child himself must be studied—his physical condition, his mental capacities, his personality and the driving forces of his conduct.

[14] Tappan, *supra* note 8, at 130.
[15] K. F. Lenroot and E. O. Lundberg, *Juvenile Courts at Work—A Study of the Organization and Method of Ten Courts* 88, 94 (U.S. Children's Bureau, Dep't of Labor Pub. No. 141, 1925).

It seems only too clear. The purpose of the juvenile court is not to determine whether the child has committed any act for which he should be held; rather it is to get at the causes of his misbehavior in order that he can be given treatment appropriate to his needs.

The growth and establishment of social-work practice on a professional level has been a third influence that has helped to strengthen the social-agency image of the juvenile court. During the forty years following the birth of the juvenile court, the growth of social work was rapid. In the colleges and universities, social work, often lodged in sociology departments, gradually broke away to form independent departments; in some universities, it emerged as a full-fledged, degree-granting graduate professional school. The professional organizations for social workers kept pace. The American Association of Social Workers, an outgrowth of the National Social Workers Exchange, was founded in 1921, the American Association of Medical Social Workers in 1918, the National Association of School of Social Workers in 1919, the American Association of Psychiatric Social Workers in 1926, the American Association of Group Workers in 1946, and the Social Work Research Group in 1949. Within the last three years, all of these groups have joined to form the National Association of Social Workers. These professional organizations not only have helped to support the hands of those strategically placed workers in the Children's Bureau, but also have served as pressure groups in various communities to bring about the appointment of the type of juvenile court personnel that would strengthen the social-agency image of the court.

The fourth influence here—certain court decisions—have also helped to move the juvenile court toward a so-cial-agency image. The constitutionality of the legislation creating the juvenile court was quick to be tested. In one of the earliest of these cases, *Commonwealth v. Fisher,* the defendant attacked the juvenile court and its procedures, claiming that he had been deprived thereby of certain of his constitutional rights. The court stated in part:[16]

> The last reason to be noticed why the act should be declared unconstitutional is that it denies the appellant a trial by jury. Here again is the fallacy that he was tried by the court . . . and no act of the legislature can deny this right to any citizen, young or old, minor or adult, if he is to be tried for a crime against the commonwealth. But there was no trial for any crime here, and the act is operative only when there is to be no trial. The very purpose of the act is to prevent a trial. . . .

And so it went. Decision after decision helped to mold an image of the juvenile court that departed farther and farther from traditional legal principles. At the time, various criticisms were leveled at these decisions. One charge was "socialism"; another, more reasoned, was that they were merely in keeping with a certain popular support that the new laws enjoyed. In any event, these decisions provided solid support for interpreting the laws to the end of converting the juvenile court into a kind of social agency.

Perhaps the most outstanding influence impelling the juvenile court towards its social-agency self-image has been the early recognition that a child brought before the court must be treated for his problem, rather than be punished for his crime. This attitude supposedly opened the door for "scientific justice," where the child before the juvenile court would be studied in a total fashion—biological, psychological, and sociological; a diagnostic judgment

[16] Commonwealth v. Fisher, 213 Pa. 48, 53, 62 Atl. 198, 200 (1905).

made; and a treatment prescribed which would meet unfulfilled needs, secure his protection, and insure his return to social and psychological health. Thus, individualization of treatment was to be achieved in the juvenile court by the convergence of the enthusiastic support of reformers, the scientific advances in psychology and psychiatry, and the dominant individualistic theme of our culture.

With this initial treatment-orientation, the medical analogy was quick to appear in the literature, aided and abetted particularly by the development of psychoanalysis, with its varieties and the application of its insights into the delinquent child.[17] From the study of neuroses and their emotional manifestations, it was, then, but a short jump to the viewing of delinquent behavior as a symptom of some underlying emotional conflict.[18] When this occurred, it followed that each case must be studied carefully and completely to reach the source of the conflict in the child's personality that could account for the "acting-out"— even though socially disapproved—behavior, and adequate provisions, psychiatric and/or case-work, made for its correction. As the doctor restores the physically sick child to health, so, it was urged, would the clinical team of psychiatrist, psychologist, and social worker restore the delinquent child to behavioral health, where those unpleasant "acting-out" symptoms would disappear.

[17] See, e.g., A. Aichhorn, *Wayward Youth* (1935).
[18] It should be emphasized that the claim is not advanced that delinquency is *never* the outgrowth of some emotional condition. It cannot, however, *explain* all delinquent behavior, as some of the uncritical adherents of the medical analogy seem to imply. The sole purpose here is to show the manner in which "treatment" philosophy has molded the social-agency image of the juvenile court.

As has been pointed out above, this treatment viewpoint has been present from the very beginning, despite the fact that no technique for treating delinquent behavior had been adequately formulated and tested. Even today, with the many advances of the basic sciences, such techniques are but imperfectly understood and do not, as many sophisticated therapists have recognized, meet expectations.[19] In study after study, this fact has been demonstrated. The fact remains, however, that during the fifty-nine years since the founding of the juvenile court, the clamor concerning the need for treatment, nature of treatment, correct treatment procedure, and treatment facilities has continued to fill the pages of the professional journals, newspaper supplements, and professional lectures on delinquency to various community groups.

While treatment has been discussed here primarily in terms of the application of psychiatric and case-work techniques, the inference should not be drawn that these are the only activities regarded as treatment by the juvenile court. The fact of the matter is that under the impact of the treatment philosophy held by professionals, every action that the juvenile court takes is regarded as "treatment." Whether the juvenile court sends the child to the reformatory or the clinic, places him on probation or in a foster home, dismisses him with a lecture or without a lecture—all is rationalized as treatment, especially by those professionals who have a deep need to view the juvenile court as an agency for treatment and never for punishment of the child.

[19] See Peck, "Why Does a Young Delinquent Resist Treatment?" *The Child,* Nov. 1951, p. 35; Lippman, *Treatment of Juvenile Delinquents,"* in *National Conference of Social Work, Proceedings* 317 (1945).

The social-agency image of the juvenile court has had a dynamic quality—that is, it has been growing and expanding since the birth of the juvenile court in Illinois—and it is reflected in annual reports of various juvenile courts, in numerous publications of the Children's Bureau, in certain court decisions, and in many articles in professional and semiprofessional social-work journals. For example, here is a statement from an annual report of 1925:[20]

Or as the statute now reads, "The court from time to time may adjourn the hearing and inquire into the habits, surroundings, conditions and tendencies of the child so as to enable the court to render such order or judgment as shall best conserve the welfare of the child and carry out the objects of this act." As a result of this enactment the justices have been enabled to scrap once and for all the old legal trial of children with its absurd and obsolete limitations of testimony and to inquire into the causes of the children's neglect or delinquency untrammelled by narrow rules of evidence.

It is significant to note that the writer has no difficulty in considering delinquency and neglect together and is perfectly willing to throw out the "narrow rules of evidence" and the "absurd and obsolete limitations of testimony" in order to get at the "real causes" of the child's difficulty. It is difficult to refrain from observing, however, that it seems extremely relevant, if only in the interest of fair play, to establish the fact as to whether or not the child committed a particular act that would make him delinquent under the existing statute.

In this same report, the judge writes of the future of the court:[21]

We prefer to think of it as a definite arm of the government engaged in the task of protecting and correcting the handicapped children of the community and of supervising their social adjustments, but not extending its functions over matters which could be administered by other departments of state or even by semi-public agencies without invoking judicial action. . . . Even now the court is seeking to treat every case, in which its assistance is invoked, to the end that the cause of the disease or disorder complained of may be removed and that its patients may be restored to perfect moral health. As time goes on its facilities for helping its patients and of achieving their social adjustments will be developed and improved. . . . In short the court of tomorrow, as we picture it, will resemble in many respects the ideal which we are struggling, more or less imperfectly, to obtain today. It will administer the law faithfully and conscientiously but at the same time its emphasis will be laid more and more on the exercise of social justice by which alone the children who come before it may be readjusted, safeguarded and developed into future assets for the State.

This judge, only too clearly, has been willing to have his legal training modified or supplemented, as the case may be, by certain conceptions and values derived from a social-work point of view.

Perhaps no clearer formulation of this social-agency image of the juvenile court is provided than a statement by the Wayne County Juvenile Court made over fifteen years ago:[22]

The average citizen thinks of the Juvenile Court in terms of a criminal court for young boys and girls, and believes that the Detention Home is a jail to which these boys and girls are sentenced.

These misconceptions overlook the great progress which society has made in the past one hundred years in dealing with delinquent children. For it is as recent as that, that children of tender years who violated the criminal laws were locked

---

[20] Children's Court of the City of New York, Ann. Rep. 16 (1925).

[21] *Id.* at 31.

[22] The Wayne County Juvenile Court 1–2 (n.d.),

up in the same jails, were tried by the same prosecutors and judges, and in many cases received the same punishment, as hardened adult criminals. Often the punishment consisted of many years' imprisonment, and even, in a few instances, death. The protest by socially-minded people against this treatment by the criminal courts of juvenile offenders on the same basis as adult offenders, resulted in the Juvenile Court movement. Progressive people realized that the administration of social justice, at least so far as children are concerned, should not be based on theories of retribution and revenge, but rather on the principles of reformation and correction. They felt that children, by the very reason of their immature years, cannot and should not be held as strictly accountable for their acts as are adults.

The Juvenile Court is the outcome of this agitation for social justice for children. It is the first legal tribunal where the law works side by side with the sciences which deal with human behavior. The Court adopted the social case-work method, by which the child is treated individually in relation to his whole environment. It is in this procedure that the Juvenile Court differs from the criminal courts, where an accused person is sought to be convicted of and punished for having committed a particular crime. The juvenile delinquents who are brought before the Juvenile Court are not regarded as criminals, irrespective of the misconduct or offense with which they are charged. They are considered to be boys and girls who have become maladjusted and, perhaps through no fault of their own, have expressed their normal feelings and emotions in delinquent ways. The Court recognizes that these children need its special care, protection and understanding; and through proper supervision and guidance, it endeavors to divert the forces of delinquent behavior into normal and satisfactory channels.

This statement, which appears to be largely for public-relations purposes, epitomizes the spirit and aspirations of the juvenile court set in a social-agency framework. It goes almost without saying that there will be great disparity between actual practice and this pollyanna view of what the juvenile court aspires to be.

Within this social-agency framework, the juvenile court ideally should function in the following manner: A complaint would be made to the juvenile court's intake desk by the police, a social agency, a neighbor, a parent, or a socially minded citizen. If the behavior difficulty could not be resolved with the complainant, process would issue and the child would be brought in. The child and its parents would be questioned by a social worker, and if the child could be released to its parents, this would be done; otherwise, the child would be held at a detention home pending a thorough social study of the case. In this latter event, the child himself would be variously viewed as maladjusted, having a problem, in trouble, or an example of need frustration or a type of "acting-out" behavior. A social worker then would be assigned to the case to make the required social study.

Preliminary study of the case might indicate to the worker that the child's difficulty was not very deep-seated and that the case could be handled unofficially with a preliminary hearing and dismissed to the best interests of the child and others who were involved. On the other hand, preliminary inquiry might indicate the need for a complete social study; and, if so, the study would continue and might include thorough physical, psychiatric, and psychological examinations, as well as a thorough developmental picture of the child in his family and/or other social situation. The social investigation would logically lead to some diagnostic formulation involving the nature of the problem and the probable roots of the difficulty. On the basis of this formulation, some plan of treatment would be outlined which, of course, might include "institutional treatment." At this point, again, a decision would be made as to whether the case could be handled unofficially and recommended treatment carried out by the juvenile court clinic, child-guidance agency, a family agency, or a private psychiatrist, or whether the case should he handled officially and brought before the juvenile court judge, with the understanding that he would see that the recommended treatment was carried out. In either case, treatment would continue if the subject proved willing to accept it. If, however, he did not, more stringent measures would probably be recommended; in fact, the plan might include any one of the several dispositions, euphemistically called "treatments," that have been traditionally open to the juvenile court judge—namely, dismissal, supervised probation, foster-home placement, or institutional commitment. The juvenile court might also insist that the child be given psychiatric treatment by some independent agency. At this point, social-work supervisors, now termed probation officers, would take over and follow the child through the prescribed course. In the ideal social-agency-type juvenile court, however, the great majority of the cases would tend to be handled "unofficially."

As the juvenile court has moved in the direction of perfecting its social-agency image, several unforeseen consequences have emerged. For example, court decisions have helped mold this image as, one after another, they have affirmed that private hearings, the introduction of social-study material, the absence of a defense attorney, and the lack of trial by jury do not constitute a denial of due process because the child is not being tried for a crime. Accordingly, those legal safeguards which have been the cornerstone of Anglo-Saxon jurisprudence for centuries are not available to the child in the juvenile court because he is considered not to be responsible for his act up to a specified age, depending upon the state law, but rather is regarded as "having a problem." The disposition of the child in the juvenile court is, thus, almost entirely dependent upon the wisdom of the judge.

Another consequence of this emerging social-agency image of the juvenile court has been an attempt, particularly noticeable in the first six postwar years, to hold parents responsible for the delinquent acts of their child. The underlying reasoning is this: Social workers, via their varieties of psychoanalytic orientations, have regarded the home as the fundamental source of the love and security necessary to shape the child into a mature adult. When the child is not given this love and security, he experiences a feeling of frustration and unfulfilled needs, which leads to distorted and ambivalent reactions to one or both parents, and some resultant deep-seated conflict or splintering of his ego. The parents, in turn, owing to their own inadequacies or because of the emotional state of the child, are able to provide nothing but the most erratic and inconsistent discipline and supervision. In such a family atmosphere, accordingly, the child may begin to "act out" his conflicts in delinquent ways. Now, this all-too-brief statement of the asserted psychological roots of delinquency in the family setting has been sold to certain juvenile court judges, with the result that schools for parents have been started, and parents have been summoned into juvenile court and, in some instances, given jail sentences because they have, from this perspective, been adjudged responsible for the delinquencies of their child.[23]

Another consequence of the juvenile court's assumption of the role of a social-work agency is that the original differences among the conditions of dependency, neglect, and delinquency have gradually become obscure, and the juvenile court has approached each child as a young person who has a problem and needs help, regardless of his basic condition. It is but a step from this obfuscation to the general notion that the underlying cause of these diverse conditions is the same, despite the lack of evidence to support such a position.

A final consequence of this adherence to a social-agency orientation by the juvenile court—and perhaps the most telling one—is the moral confusion it occasions in both the child and his parents. In the popular mind, a court is an instrument for securing justice between persons and for securing the rights of the person charged with a specific criminal act by the state. When, however, the juvenile court fails directly to advert to the fact that a particular illegal act has been committed by the child and, in its zeal to "treat" the child, completely glosses over this matter, the final disposition of the child's case is very likely to seem to him confusing and even unjust. And his parents, in turn, will reflect this confusion, because on their social level, they cannot very easily accept the view that the child by virtue of his behavior is "sick" and needs "treatment," but rather are committed to the view that

the court is there for justice and for punishing a person who has done something that is wrong.

One critic perceives this situation very clearly when he notes the lack of understanding of parents as to the function of a psychiatric clinic to which the juvenile court referred their children's cases. He points out that when cases brought before the juvenile court on charges of incorrigibility were referred to the clinic, the parents and the child considered the clinic action a part of the punishment for the offense instead of a means of treatment.[24] Moreover, this attitude on the part of the child and his parents will continue to exist and plague the "treatment" process, because it will generally be impossible for the juvenile court to convey its "scientific" orientation to people whose morality is framed exclusively in terms of right and wrong.

It is also cogent to inquire how far we can carry certain theories of treatment of criminal behavior, on both juvenile and adult levels, without undermining the concept of legal responsibility; for it should be clear that a popular acceptance of the idea that no one is responsible for what he does would lead to chaos. Here, confusion is attributable to the deterministic character of science—the attempt to explain given behavior by isolating the interrelated factors antecedent to it—under which the doctrine of scientific responsibility replaces that of legal responsibility.[25] So, when the juvenile court attempts to help the child by "treating" his "disorder," it is literally using the child to collect data to substantiate certain theories of child be-

---

[23] Space does not permit consideration of this problem in greater detail. The statutes have generally given judges authority to proceed against a parent or other adult where it can be shown that he has directly contributed to the delinquency of the child. See Teeters and Reinemann, *op. cit. supra* note 6, at 200–206.

[24] O'Keefe, "Mental Hygiene Facilities for the Juvenile Delinquent," *Federal Probation,* June 1948, pp. 31–35.

[25] See Green, "The Concept of Responsibility," 33 *J. Crim. L. & Criminology* 392–394 (1943).

havior and to foist on him some inadequately tested notions about treatment of juvenile misconduct, while, at the same time, chipping away at the concept of legal responsibility.

THE LEGAL IMAGE OF THE COURT

It has been observed that the true social-agency image of the juvenile court tends to emerge only in those few highly organized, independent juvenile courts to be found in large cities. The juvenile court as established by law in the great majority of states, however, is a part of a court of general jurisdiction and, as such, is part of a county court system. With such legal status, therefore, one can well appreciate the furious character of the conflict that has been occasioned by efforts to convert the juvenile court into a type of social agency, with traditional legal procedures de-emphasized or eliminated and various treatments introduced in order "to cure" the child. The conflict has, in fact, been continuous, and in recent years it has become even sharper as various studies have indicated both that many basic legal rights are being denied the child and his parents and that there may be a great gap between conception and execution of successful treatment of a "maladjusted" child. Thus, it has been observed that "measured by any reasonable standards the juvenile courts have failed to live up to the high expectations held by the early reformers."[26]

The conventional response to such observations has been that the juvenile court fails precisely because the community cannot or is unwilling to provide the necessary resources and facilities to do a first-rate job. Statements to the effect that there are not enough

[26] Bloch and Flynn, *op. cit. supra* note 12, at 317.

properly trained probation officers, the judge is only part-time and has failed to grasp the juvenile court idea, detention facilities are inadequate, there are not sufficient treatment facilities in the juvenile court or community, there is a need for more psychiatric time, the people comprising the community must be educated to the function of the juvenile court, and the salary scale is inadequate are to be found scattered throughout the literature. While any one or all of these shortcomings may exist with respect to any particular juvenile court, however, there is no evidence convincingly to show that if these defects were remedied, juvenile courts in general would be able to do a better job in preventing recidivism in children who had once been found to be delinquent. In fact, much of the evidence appears to be exactly to the contrary.[27] Even so, ameliorative measures might still be justified on the ground that the juvenile court would be able to perform its social-control function more adequately and more humanely.

What, then, are some of the central issues in this conflict between the social-agency and the legalistic orientations of the juvenile court?

First, the problem of the extent of jurisdiction of the juvenile court has been debated on two fronts: what

[27] See W. Healy and A. Bronner, *Treatment and What Happened Afterward* (1939); E. Powers and H. Witmer, *An Experiment in the Prevention of Juvenile Delinquency: The Cambridge Somerville Youth Study* (1951); Dunham and Knauer, "The Juvenile Court and Its Relation to Adult Criminality," 32 *Social Forces* 290 (1954); Diana, "Is Casework in Probation Necessary?," *Focus*, Jan. 1955, p. 1; Adamson and Dunham, "Clinical Treatment of Male Juvenile Delinquency: A Case Study in Effort and Result," 21 *Am. Socio. Rev.* 312 (1956); R. W. England, "What Is Responsible for Satisfactory Probation and Post Probation Outcome?," 47 *J. Crim. L., C. & P.S.* 667 (1957).

relationship does it bear to other courts; and what type of cases should legitimately come before it? The problem of the relationship of the juvenile court to other courts was considered in the often-quoted case of *People v. Lattimore*. There, the Illinois Supreme Court reviewed and affirmed the criminal court conviction of the defendant while she was still a ward of the juvenile court, upholding the lower court's jurisdiction in these words:[28]

The Juvenile Court is a court of limited jurisdiction. The legislature is without authority to confer upon an inferior court the power to stay a court created by the constitution from proceeding with the trial of a cause jurisdiction of which is expressly granted to it by the constitution. . . . It was not intended by the legislature that the juvenile court should be made a haven of refuge where a delinquent child of the age recognized by law as capable of committing a crime should be immune from punishment of violating the criminal laws of the state, committed by such child subsequent to his or her being declared a delinquent child.

The problem is still widely debated, however, and generally arises in one form or another when a child of juvenile-court age commits a capital offense. One solution has been to make the juvenile court independent by creating state-wide juvenile courts systems, as has been done in Connecticut, Rhode Island, and Utah. But it will take more time to determine where this system has improved the administration of juvenile justice.[29]

With respect to the types of cases that should come before it, there has been a tendency throughout its history for the juvenile court to assume jurisdiction over most cases involving children—often, it is asserted, more than it could satisfactorily handle. Thus, adoption, unmarried mothers, mother's pension, and sometimes divorce cases have been lodged in the juvenile court, as it has extended its aegis over cases of dependency and neglect as well as delinquency. As noted above, this tends to confuse the juvenile court's function.

The practice of handling cases unofficially is another matter about which much controversy has raged over the years. This practice is extremely variable among juvenile courts, as certain juvenile courts handle no cases unofficially, while others may handle the bulk of their cases in this manner. The arguments advanced in support of the practice is that it is in keeping with the juvenile court's basic treatment philosophy; it keeps the child from having a court record; it enables professional opinion other than that of the judge to influence the case; and it saves the time and energy of the judge for the more serious cases. On the other hand, it is argued that the practice conduces inefficiency in that it diverts judicial attention to cases that should be handled by other agencies; it weakens the juvenile court's authority in the more serious cases; and it confuses any criteria which attempt to distinguish between court and noncourt cases and discourages other agencies from developing and devoting their resources to the prevention of delinquency. It almost goes without saying that the practice makes meaningless any attempt to report statistical comparisons between communities as to the frequency of delinquency.

Another problem confronting every juvenile court judge is that of balancing the welfare of the child, in accordance with the juvenile court's basic philosophy, against the protection of the community. This issue has not been

---

[28] People v. Lattimore, 119 N.E. 275, 362 Ill. 206 (1935).
[29] See Rubin, "State Juvenile Court: A New Standard," *Focus*, July 1951, p. 103.

articulated very clearly in the past, but recently it has received greater attention as it has been brought more sharply into focus.[30] While it might be argued, in the spirit of Adam Smith's economic theory, that securing the welfare of the child will insure best the welfare of the community, this is not likely to have much appeal to those persons who have been injured in some fashion by the acts of a child. They may demand retribution and even revenge, which to them is justice. In fact, it is extremely doubtful that the aims of protecting and securing the welfare of the child can ever be completely realized until a sizable majority of the people in any community understands and accepts, the basic philosophy of the juvenile court. This widespread lack of public rapport accounts for the perennial charge that the juvenile court is "coddling young criminals." Even if the necessary public understanding were brought about, however, the issue would still have to be faced as to how to deal most effectively with delinquent behavior in achieving both the welfare of the community and that of the child.

Another problem, as yet not adequately explored, concerns the limitations of individualized treatment within an authoritative court setting. While it has been accepted by many enlightened persons that punishment per se secures no beneficial results to the person or to the community, it is also becoming increasingly clear that our treatment techniques do not accomplish what we would like. In this area, however, our knowledge is quite deficient. We cannot well distinguish between those cases that might benefit from some form of psychotherapy and

those cases that will not. Nor can we distinguish between those cases in which delinquency will, in any event, be arrested and those in which help is needed. Then, too, no matter what "treatment" disposition the court may use—probation, foster-home placement, referral to a treatment clinic, or commitment to an institution—the fact remains that it is likely to be viewed by the child and his parents as punishment and not treatment, although these devices probably afford a more individualized and progressive scheme of punishment than various kinds of treatment per se. There is, finally, some doubt as to the validity of one assumption of treatment philosophy seldom mentioned in the literature—the assumption that the child facing the therapist is either not thinking or, if he is, he is freely entering into cooperation with the therapist to achieve a cure. With delinquents, nothing could be farther from reality. For quite often, the delinquent "patient" is not only thinking, but thinking of how he can beat this "rap"; and in trying to do so, he will not hesitate to attempt to manipulate the therapist, who will have to be steeped in a knowledge of the delinquent's world if he is not to be duped.

These issues must all be resolved if the juvenile court is to fulfill a valid legal function.[31] Ideally, the juvenile court would be independent of other courts, with its jurisdiction carefully defined by law. The law would, for the guidance of the juvenile court, carefully and precisely define the specific acts for which a child could be held as a delinquent. At the intake desk, a complaint would be registered with the appropriate evidence to sup-

---

[30] See *Standards for Specialized Courts Dealing with Children* 2 (U. S. Children's Bureau, Dep't of Health, Education and Welfare Pub. No. 346, 1954).

[31] In constructing this legal image, the focus here is primarily on delinquency cases and excludes other kinds of cases handled by juvenile courts.

port the contention that an act of delinquency had been committed. The gathering of such evidence would be primarily a police task, in which assistance might perhaps be rendered by a probation officer of the juvenile court. The probation officer, the police, and the juvenile court referee would decide whether or not the evidence was sufficient to warrant a delinquency petition. If not, the child would be dismissed with a warm, friendly attitude; if the evidence was sufficient, however, the child would be held either in the custody of his parents or guardian or in a detention home for a juvenile court appearance.

When brought before the juvenile court, after a very short detention period, the first task of the judge would be to inform the child and his parents of all their legal rights according to law, particularly their right to legal counsel and appeal. The judge would then hear the evidence and find whether or not the child had committed a delinquent act. The judge, before determining the disposition of the case, would then confer with those professional members of his staff who had worked on the case to determine if some consensus had been reached among them as to which available disposition would serve best to secure both the welfare of the child and protection for the community. He would then pronounce the disposition that had been decided in consultation. Such dispositions, even though mild and humane, would bear a punishment and not a treatment label. The atmosphere of the juvenile court at all times would be formal, dignified, and authoritative. The judge, as representative of community authority, would always attempt to impress the child and his parents with the gravity of the situation and the consequences that would likely ensue if such act or acts were repeated. Such a juvenile court would

have no facility for clinical treatment of the child, for it would be recognized that treatment can be carried on only when a case is not being adjudicated. Nor would it indulge in the unofficial handling of cases. For it should be clear that if no delinquent act has been committed, the taking of any action with reference to the child is a violation of his rights, unless the child and/or his parents request help—and in that event, he and/or they would be referred to the most appropriate available agency.

CONFLICT OF IMAGES—A NEW OPPORTUNITY

The proponents of these two images —the social-agency and the legalistic —which have here been delineated have been engaged in ideological battle over the juvenile court during its sixty years of existence. To be sure, the social-agency image has been the more dominant and aggressive, although in recent years, the balance has swung back somewhat toward the legalistic image.[32] The conflict of these images, however, still clearly appears in juvenile court attitudes and the decisions of the various judges as they seek to cope with the cases before them. A slight ironical twist may be seen when an eminent judge describes the juvenile court as comparable to a hospital or clinic where the "sick" patient is diagnosed, hospitalized, treated, and discharged,[33] while a well-known

[32] See, e.g., Paul W. Tappan, *Comparative Survey on Juvenile Delinquency* (1952); Killian, "The Juvenile Court as an Institution," 261 *Annals* 89 (1949). Over thirty years ago, Eliot saw the need to separate judicial and treatment functions. See Eliot, "The Project Problem Method Applied in Indeterminate Sentence, Probation, and Other Re-educational Treatment," in *The Child, the Clinic and the Court* 102 (1925).

[33] P. W. Alexander, "Of Juvenile Court Justice and Judges," in *N.P.P.A. Yearbook* 187, 192 (1947).

social worker states that the juvenile court is first a court where legal responsibility is established specifically by law with respect to certain behavior and conditions of children and adults.[34]

The clash of these two images in the history of the juvenile court has been of crucial significance, because it tends to force a re-examination of all theories concerning the etiology of delinquent behavior, as well as theories concerning the most effective ways of handling delinquents to produce the desired results. It has brought the juvenile court to what one critic, drawing an analogy from the field of mechanics, has termed "dead center," where no force can move it either way and it slowly grinds to a dead stop![35] Whether "dead center" or some other phrase best describes the present situation of the juvenile court, however, is beside the point; the fact still remains that the juvenile court has not demonstrated the accomplishments which would justify the faith of its founders. But the present situation of the juvenile court might well afford a unique opportunity —that is, the opportunity to sponsor and encourage scientific research inquiries to answer some of the pressing questions that this clash of images has produced. Both the spirit and tradition of the juvenile court make it possible to do this.

Lack of space limits a detailed discussion here, and so only a few problems suitable for research can be suggested. There is a great need to determine how the juvenile court can be made most effective, both as an instrument of social control in the community and as an instrument for arresting delinquent behavior in youth. Let us consider this experiment: We hear from many sources that a delinquent child needs psychological treatment and not punishment. Therefore, let us set up a well-equipped clinic, with the best-qualified personnel that it is possible to obtain, even at the expense of paying them salaries somewhat higher than the prevailing scales in the community. When such a clinic is established, from the signed complaints coming to the juvenile court, one child would go to the clinic for appropriate treatment and one would go to the juvenile court, which would function exclusively as a legal tribunal, using the dispositions available to it. The clinic would only take enough cases to insure an adequately sized sample, previously agreed upon. Two to three years after treatment, a follow-up study would be made on both juvenile court and clinic cases, primarily to determine if the subjects still continued their delinquent behavior or were in any way dependent problems for the community. The writer strongly suspects that there would be no significant differences in outcome between the juvenile court and clinic cases because of the almost universally overlooked fact that clinic treatment may be useful in only certain types of cases. If the clinic succeeded with certain kinds of cases, they might be hidden in the figures and would be balanced by those cases in which a favorable adjustment would have been effected regardless of the disposition made. This suggests that successfully treated cases are those that would recover if nothing were done.

There is need also to determine the relative merits of the different disposals available to the juvenile court and the kind of cases that might respond most appropriately to each. Similarly, there is need to determine, if possible, the significance of the impact of the court experience upon the child: Will it be more crucial to certain children coming

[34] Alice Scott Nutt, *The Juvenile Court and the Public Welfare Agency in the Child Welfare Program* (U. S. Children's Bureau, Dep't of Health, Education and Welfare Pub. No. 327, 1949).

[35] McCrea, "Juvenile Courts and Juvenile Probation," 3 *N.P.P.A.J.* 385 (1957).

from some segments of society than to other children from other segments? In evaluating each study, a two-faceted standard would be employed: does the child continue his antisocial behavior as an adult; and/or does the child continue to have a socially unacceptable dependent status as an adult?

These research suggestions are only a few of the tacks that the juvenile court might pursue to help ease itself from its present static position. Research might also promote the divestiture of the built-in egocentric protective mechanisms that are found in certain juvenile courts and direct attention once again to the problem of the child and the task of transforming the juvenile court into an effective agency for the social control of youth.

There would hardly seem to be any dispute among professionals in the criminological field that a philosophy of treatment and reformation is of a morally higher order than is a philosophy of punishment; there is less certainty, however, about the views of the general public on this matter. But regardless of public attitudes, the question of how far and under what circumstances the reward-penalty system of a society can be modified is most crucial. For it would seem that in any kind of social structure, there will always be certain persons who cannot and will not be accommodated. Some of these persons will be so-called criminals, and the central sociological task is to discover, if possible, what their minimum number should be and then to determine the best social arrangements to keep their number at this level. With respect to juvenile delinquents, this probably represents the

"hard core" which fails to respond to any therapeutic approach.

The juvenile court, most markedly of all our agencies for handling socially aberrant individuals, has adhered to the philosophy of treatment and reformation, with the lofty ideal of safeguarding, almost at any cost, the welfare of the child. While this ideal is eminently praiseworthy and expressive of the humanitarian quality of American culture, the question can, however, and should be raised as to whether the existing social-agency-type juvenile court has succeeded in creating the most appropriate conditions for arresting a child's misconduct and for providing him with those personality strengths that will enable him to adjust to the community in a socially acceptable manner. This is a question, it is submitted, that merits the most careful and thoughtful examination.

In this paper an attempt has been made to portray two idealized conceptions of the juvenile court—the social-agency and the legalistic—the nature of the conflict between them, and the resultant state of rigidity into which it has become frozen. While the social-agency image has been the most dominant and aggressive, the legalistic image still remains with us in many juvenile courts, hidden in the traditions of the criminal law. The future of the juvenile court hinges upon our capacity to analyze carefully the issues in this conflict in order that we may devise the type of institutional procedure—in conformity with our existing knowledge—that will best insure both protection for the community and essential personality strengths for our youth.

30.

The Juvenile Court: Its Development and
Some Major Problems

Robert G. Caldwell

On July 1, 1899, the first juvenile court in the world[1] began its legal existence in Chicago, Illinois.[2] This event has been widely acclaimed as a revolutionary advance in the treatment of delinquent and neglected children and as the beginning of a new era in the cooperation of law, science, and social work in the field of child welfare. In fact, according to some writers, it foreshadows the time when all offenders, both juvenile and adult, will be treated individually through scientific and case work processes instead of punished by the methods of criminal law.[3]

LEGAL ROOTS OF THE COURT

The juvenile court owes a great deal to American ingenuity and enterprise, but it also has legal roots that can be traced back to principles that are deeply embedded in English jurisprudence. These principles are to be found in the differential treatment which was given to children by the English courts through the application of common law and equity doctrines for the protection of innocence and dependency.

One of the legal roots of the juvenile court is the principle of equity or chancery that originated because of the rigidity of the common law and its failure to provide adequate remedies in

[1] There is some difference of opinion as to whether the first juvenile court was established in the United States. It is said, for example, that children's courts were introduced by ministerial order in South Australia in 1889 and later legalized under a state act in 1895, but it is generally agreed that the United States should be given credit for having the first real juvenile court. There is also some dispute as to whether Chicago, Illinois, or Denver, Colorado, had the first juvenile court in the United States, but preference is generally given to Chicago, since the law approved in Colorado on April 12, 1899, was essentially a truancy law although it did contain some of the features of a juvenile court law. See Lou, *Juvenile Courts in the United States* 13–23 (1927); Lindsey, "Colorado's Contribution to the Juvenile Court," *The Child, the Clinic, and the Court* 274–289 (Addams ed. 1925); Clarke, *Social Legislation* 375–377 (1957).

[2] For easy reference to the first juvenile court act, see 2 Abbott, *The Child and the State* 392–401 (1938).

[3] Lou, *op. cit. supra* note 1, at 2; Pound, "The Juvenile Court and the Law," *Yearbook*, 1944, 1–22 (Nat'l Prob. Ass'n, 1945); Chute, "Fifty Years of the Juvenile Court," *Yearbook*, 1949, 1–20 (Nat'l Prob. and Parole Ass'n, 1950); Winnet, "Fifty Years of the Juvenile Court: An Evaluation," 36 *A.B.A.J.* 363–366 (1950).

SOURCE. Robert G. Caldwell, "The Juvenile Court: Its Development and Some Major Problems," from *Journal of Criminal Law, Criminology and Police Science*, Volume 51, January-February 1961, pp. 493–511. Copyright © 1961, The Williams and Wilkins Company, Baltimore, Maryland.

deserving cases. Eventually the chancellor, who was the head of England's judicial system, was held responsible for giving greater flexibility to the law in such cases and for balancing the interests of litigants in a more equitable manner as measured by the merits of the individual case. Since equity was thus dispensed by the Council of Chancery, the terms "equity" and "chancery" came to be used interchangeably. Through this system of equity the king acted as *parens patriae,* or as "father of his country," in exercising his power of guardianship over the persons and property of minors, who were considered wards of the state and as such entitled to special protection. Although originally equity was used chiefly to protect dependent or neglected children who had property interests, its action prefigured the protective intervention of the state through the instrumentality of the juvenile court in cases of delinquency.

The other legal root of the juvenile court is the presumption of innocence thrown about children by the common law. According to its doctrines a child under the age of 7 is conclusively presumed incapable of entertaining criminal intent and therefore of committing a crime. Between the ages of 7 and 14, a child is presumed to be incapable of committing a crime, but the presumption may be rebutted by showing that the offender has enough intelligence to know the nature of his act. After the age of 14, children, like adults, are presumed to be responsible for their actions. Thus the creation of the juvenile court involved the extension of the principle that children below a certain age cannot be held criminally responsible—a principle that has a long history in the common law.[4]

HISTORICAL BACKGROUND OF THE COURT

In America, where English jurisprudence was introduced by the early colonists, such tendencies as the increase in the complexity of social relationships, the growth of humanitarianism, and the rise of the social sciences contributed to the expansion of the area in which the child received differential treatment by law.[5] Thus in order to protect children from confinement in jails and prisons, institutions for juvenile offenders were opened in New York in 1825, in Boston in 1826, and in Philadelphia in 1828. Gradually such institutions were constructed in other parts of the country. The foster-home movement, originating in New York in 1853 with the establishment of the Children's Aid Society, which specialized in the placement of destitute and deserted children, soon spread to other states. Chicago as early as 1861 provided for a commission to hear and determine petty cases of boys from 6 to 17. Suffolk County (Boston) in 1870 and New York in 1877 instituted separate hearings for children, and then in 1892 New York created separate dockets and records as well as separate trials for juveniles under 16. By the enactment of a statute in 1869, Massachusetts stipulated that an agent of the State Board of Charities should attend the trials of children, protect their interests, and make recommendations regarding them to the judge. Between 1878 and 1898 Massachusetts established a state-wide system of probation and thus initiated a movement that eventually carried this method of correction into every state in the United States. The years of the nine-

---

[4] Lou, *op. cit. supra* note 1, at 1–12; Clarke, *op. cit. supra* note 1, at 372–374; Sussman, *Law of Juvenile Delinquency* 15,

16 (1959); Pound, *op. cit. supra* note 3, at 4–8. See also Pound, "The Rise of Socialized Criminal Justice," *Yearbook,* 1942, 1–22 (Nat'l Prob. Ass'n, 1942).

[5] Caldwell, *Criminology* 360 (1956).

teenth century also saw the enactment of laws for the regulation of child labor, the development of special services for handicapped children, and the growth of public education.[6]

As this brief summary of some of the important changes in the field of child welfare indicates, there was a growing acceptance of public responsibility for the protection and care of children, but as yet there was no legal machinery by which juvenile offenders could be handled, not as criminals according to the regular procedure of the criminal court, but as wards of the state who were in need of special care, protection, and treatment. Meanwhile, however, Chicago welfare and civic organizations, notably the Chicago Woman's Club and the Catholic Visitation and Aid Society, were setting the stage for the appearance of exactly this kind of machinery. As a result of their persistent agitation, a spirited campaign was begun for the establishment of a juvenile court, and under the leadership of such organizations as the State Board of Charities and the Chicago Bar Association, this campaign was eventually successful in creating the world's first juvenile court.[7]

An examination of the historical background of this court shows that many varied influences helped to pro-

duce the climate in which it had its origin. In fact, its establishment may well be considered a logical and exceedingly important development in a much broader movement for the expansion of the specialized treatment given to children in an increasingly complex society. Although the idea of the juvenile court combined the already existing elements of institutional segregation, probation supervision, foster-home placement, separate judicial hearings, and an approach that emphasized the rehabilitation of the juvenile offender, even so, as Tappan explains, it did constitute a significant achievement in judicial integration by providing for a more systematic and independent handling of children's cases.[8]

THE FIRST JUVENILE COURT

The Juvenile Court of Cook County, the first of its kind in the world, was established in Chicago by a state law approved on July 1, 1899. This law, entitled "An Act to Regulate the Treatment and Control of Dependent, Neglected, and Delinquent Children," provided for the establishment of a juvenile court in all counties with a population of over 500,000, but since only Cook County had a population of that size, it alone received such a court. In other counties circuit and county courts were to handle cases arising under the law. The juvenile court was given jurisdiction over children under the age of 16 years who were adjudged to be dependent, neglected, or delinquent, and it was to have a special judge (chosen by the circuit court judges from among their number at such times as they should determine), a separate court room, separate records, and an informal procedure, which meant that such important parts of the

[6] Chute, *op. cit. supra* note 3, at 2, 3; Sussman, *op. cit. supra* note 4, at 11–14; Teeters and Reinemann, *The Challenge of Delinquency* 282–286 (1950); Tappan, *Comparative Survey of Juvenile Delinquency* (Part I, North America) 14–16 (United Nations Department of Economics and Social Affairs, 1958); Block and Flynn, *Delinquency: The Juvenile Offender in America Today* 307–312 (1956).
[7] Lathrop, "The Background of the Juvenile Court in Illinois," and Hurley, "Origin of the Illinois Juvenile Court Law," *The Child, the Clinic, and the Court* 290–297, 320–330 (Addams ed. 1925); 2 Abbott, *op. cit. supra* note 2, at 330, 331; Chute, *op. cit. supra* note 3, at 3, 4; Lou, *op. cit. supra* note 1, at 20, 21; Sussman, *op. cit. supra* note 4, at 13, 14.

[8] Tappan, *op. cit. supra* note 6, at 14, 15.

criminal court trial as the indictment, pleadings, and jury (unless the jury was demanded by an interested party or ordered by the judge) were to be eliminated. A summons, unless it proved to be ineffectual, was to be used instead of a warrant in all cases, and the court was given authority to appoint probation officers, who were to serve without compensation. The juvenile court act was to be construed liberally so that the care, custody, and the discipline of the child should approximate as nearly as possible that which should be given by his parents.[9]

If one bears in mind the following facts about the first juvenile court law, it may help him to acquire a better perspective of the juvenile court movement in the United States:

1. The first court was not to be a new or independent tribunal but merely a special jurisdiction in the circuit court.

2. The juvenile court was to be a special court and not an administrative agency. As Dean Pound has said, "It was set up as a court of equity, with the administrative functions incidental to equity jurisdiction, not as a criminal court, and not, as might have happened later, as an administrative agency with incidental adjudicating functions."[10]

3. The law did not stipulate that juvenile delinquents should be "treated" and not punished. It merely provided that the child should receive approximately the same care, custody, and discipline that his parents should give to him.[11]

4. A juvenile delinquent was simply defined as "any child under the age of 16 years who violates any law

of this State or any city or village ordinance."[12]

5. In all trials under the law any interested party might demand, or the judge might order, a jury of six to try the case.[13]

In effect, then, the first juvenile court law established the status of delinquency as "something less than crime."[14] In doing this it made two fundamental changes in the handling of juvenile offenders that are especially noteworthy. First, it raised the age below which a child could not be a criminal from 7 to 16 and made a child who was alleged to be delinquent subject to the jurisdiction of the juvenile court. Secondly, it placed the operation of the court under equity or chancery jurisdiction and thereby extended the application of the principle of guardianship, which had been used to protect neglected and dependent children, to all children, including juvenile delinquents, who were in need of protection by the state. These two changes, in modified form, remain as essential characteristics of all juvenile court legislation.[15]

TRENDS IN THE JUVENILE COURT MOVEMENT

Geographical Expansion

After Illinois had taken the initiative, other states soon followed her example and established juvenile courts. In fact, within ten years twenty states and the District of Columbia enacted juvenile court laws. By 1920 all except three states had done so, and in 1945, when Wyoming took action, the list of states having juvenile court laws was finally complete. Today

---

[9] 2 Abbott, *op. cit. supra* note 2, at 392–401.

[10] Pound, *op. cit. supra* note 3, at 5.

[11] 2 Abbott, *op. cit. supra* note 2, at 400, 401.

[12] *Id.* at 393.

[13] *Ibid.*

[14] Tappan, *op. cit. supra* note 6, at 14.

[15] Caldwell, *op. cit. supra* note 5, at 360, 361.

all states, the District of Columbia,[16] and Puerto Rico have some kind of juvenile court legislation,[17] and the movement has had considerable success in other countries.[18]

Jurisdictional Extension

While the juvenile court movement was spreading, the jurisdiction of the court itself was being extended. In general, the definition of juvenile delinquency was broadened, and the types of nondelinquency cases (such as those involving illegitimacy, mental and physical defectives, etc.) under the jurisdiction of the court were increased. Furthermore, the tendency was to raise the upper age level of the children subject to the authority of the court from 16 to 17 or 18, and for some cases in a few states, to 21. In addition, the juvenile court was given jurisdiction over adults in certain cases involving children—for example, in cases in which an adult had contributed to the delinquency of a juvenile.[19]

---

[16] There are no federal juvenile courts. Children under 18 who violate a federal law not punishable by death or life imprisonment may be transferred to a state juvenile court or proceeded against as juvenile delinquents in a federal district court. Sussman, *op. cit. supra* note 4, at 76.

[17] Sussman, *op. cit. supra* note 4, at 15, 65–76; Caldwell, *op. cit. supra* note 5, at 361.

[18] See Smith, *Juvenile Court Laws in Foreign Countries* (U. S. Children's Bureau Publication No. 328, Washington, D.C.: U. S. Government Printing Office, 1951); Clarke, *op. cit. supra* note 1, at 377–383; *Int'l Com. of the Howard League for Penal Reform, Lawless Youth: A Challenge to the New Europe* (London: George Allen and Unwin, Ltd., 1947); Watson, *British Juvenile Courts* (London: Longmans, Green and Co., 1948); Henriques, "Children's Courts in England," 37 *J. Crim. L. & C.* 295 (1946); Sellin, "Sweden's Substitute of the Juvenile Court," 261 *Annals* 137 (Jan. 1949); Pihlblad, "The Juvenile Offender in Norway," 46 *J. Crim. L., C.&P.S.* 500 (1955).

[19] Caldwell, *op. cit. supra* note 5, at 361.

Increase in Court's Influence

Then, too, after the creation of the juvenile court, it began to exert an increasing influence on the principles and methods used in the adjustment of many other family problems and in the handling of adolescent and adult offenders. For example, some cities, like Cincinnati, Philadelphia, and Wilmington, Delaware, established special courts, called family or domestic relations courts, with jurisdiction over cases involving all kinds of family problems, such as delinquency, dependency, neglect, adoption, illegitimacy, nonsupport, and crimes by members of a family against one another. In effect, the operation of these courts means that many of the principles and methods of the juvenile court are being applied to an increasing variety of social problems. Moreover, special courts for adolescents have been set up in certain cities, like Chicago, Philadelphia, and New York, in which an attempt is being made to combine some of the principles and methods of the juvenile court with those of the criminal court in proceedings against youthful offenders who are above the juvenile court age but below the age of 21. A much more systematic and inclusive program for dealing with this type of offender is represented by the various youth authorities that have been created in such states as California and Minnesota. In their emphasis upon individual diagnosis and treatment these programs, too, reflect to some extent the spreading influence of the philosophy of the juvenile court. Finally, it may be said that this influence can also be seen in the use of presentence investigation and probation in the cases of adult offenders in our criminal courts.[20]

---

[20] No attempt will be made in this article to discuss the development of family and adolescent courts and the various youth

The increasing complexity of American society has contributed significantly to these trends in the juvenile court movement. Such interrelated factors as industrialization, urbanization, the unprecedented movement of populations, the amazing utilization of natural resources, the rapid accumulation of inventions and discoveries, and the acceleration of transportation and communication have tended to undermine the family and the neighborhood and, forcing our communities to find additional sources of social control, have given considerable impetus to the establishment of juvenile courts and sent into them an increasing number and variety of cases. In the meantime, other influences have more specifically affected the philosophy and methods of the juvenile court. Thus social workers, under the aggressive leadership of such organizations as the United States Children's Bureau, the National Probation and Parole Association, and various other associations now united into the National Association of Social Workers, have joined with psychiatrists in stressing the importance of case work training and treatment services in the operation of the juvenile court, and the efforts of a comparatively few well-organized, big-city juvenile courts at conventions and conferences have served to focus and intensify these in-

fluences. The resulting tendency has been to picture juvenile delinquency as symptomatic of some underlying emotional condition, which must be diagnosed by means of the concepts and techniques of psychiatry, psychology, and social work, and for which treatment, not punishment, must be administered through the efforts of a team of psychiatrists, psychologists, and social workers. Surprisingly enough, the legal profession, also, has contributed to this tendency through important court decisions regarding the juvenile court that have stressed its social service functions and minimized its legal characteristics. The total effect of all this has been to place increasing emphasis on the treatment of the individual and to give decreasing attention to his legal rights and the security of the community. Thus the balance between rights, on the one hand, and duties and responsibilities, on the other, which every court must seek to maintain, has been upset as the juvenile court has been pushed more and more into the role of a social work agency.

CHARACTERISTICS OF THE JUVENILE COURT

Although the juvenile court has had an uneven development and has manifested a great diversity in its methods and procedures, nevertheless, certain characteristics have appeared which are considered essential in its operation. As early as 1920, Evelina Belden of the United States Children's Bureau listed the following as the essential characteristics of the juvenile court: (1) separate hearings for children's cases, (2) informal or chancery procedure, (3) regular probation service, (4) separate detention of children, (5) special court and probation records, and (6) provision for mental and physical examinations.[21] Of course, many so-called

authorities. However, a considerable bibliography about these subjects now exists. See for example, Teeters and Reinemann, op. cit. supra note 6, at 344–383, 762–765; Block and Flynn, op. cit. supra note 6, at 459–507; Caldwell, op. cit. supra note 5, at 378–385; Tappan, Delinquent Girls in Court (1947); Beck, Five States (1951); Ludwig, Youth and the Law (1955); Tappan, "The Young Adult Offender under the American Law Institute's Model Penal Code," 19 Fed. Prob. 20 (Dec. 1955); Youngdahl, "Give the Youth Corrections Program a Chance," 20 Fed. Prob. 3 (March 1956); Tappan, "Young Adults under the Youth Authority," 47 J. Crim. L., C.&P.S. 629 (1957); Melson, Delinquency and the Family Court," 23 Fed. Prob. 13 (March 1959).

[21] Beldin, Courts in the United States Hearing Children's Cases 7–10 (U. S.

juvenile courts have few of these characteristics, and others possess them in varying degrees. However, in the opinion of many observers, if a court does not have them, it cannot claim to be a juvenile court.

A few years ago, Katharine Lenroot, then chief of the United States Children's Bureau, presented a summary of standards for the juvenile court which indicate the characteristics that many now believe the court should have. These standards call for the following:

1. Broad jurisdiction in cases of children under 18 years of age requiring court action or protection because of their acts or circumstances.

2. A judge chosen because of his special qualifications for juvenile court work, with legal training, acquaintance with social problems, and understanding of child psychology.

3. Informal court procedure and private hearings.

4. Detention kept at a minimum, outside of jails and police stations and as far as possible in private boarding homes.

5. A well-qualified probation staff, with limitation of case loads, and definite plans for constructive work in each case.

6. Availability of resources for individual and specialized treatment such as medical, psychological, and psychiatric services, foster family and institutional care, and recreational services and facilities.

7. State supervision of probation work.

8. An adequate record system, providing for both legal and social records and for the safeguarding of these records from indiscriminate public inspection.[22]

These standards form much of the basis of the *Standard Juvenile Court Act,* the latest edition of which was issued by the National Probation and Parole Association in 1959,[23] and to a great extent they have been incorporated in the *Standards for Specialized Courts Dealing with Children,* which was prepared by the United States Children's Bureau in 1954.[24]

THE PRESENT STATUS OF THE COURT

In the United States the juvenile court varies greatly from one jurisdiction to another, manifesting at present all stages of its complex development. And it should not be overlooked that its philosophy, structure, and functions are still in the process of evolution. Rarely is the court a distinct and highly specialized one, and in the more rural counties it is largely of a rudimentary nature. Usually it is part of a court with more general jurisdiction, the judges holding sessions for juveniles at regular or irregular intervals.[25] Since there is this great diversity, no simple description of the juvenile courts of the United States can be given. However, it is possible to indicate in general terms their present status with respect to certain important features.

Children's Bureau Publication No. 65, Washington, D.C.: U. S. Government Printing Office, 1920).

[22] Lenroot, "The Juvenile Court Today," 13 *Fed. Prob.* 10 (Sept. 1949).

[23] *A Standard Juvenile Court Act* (rev. ed.; New York: Nat'l Prob. and Parole Ass'n, 1959). This act is the product of the efforts of the National Probation and Parole Association and the United States Children's Bureau together with others who want to promote greater uniformity and higher standards in the juvenile courts of America. Its various editions have been published in the hope that they might be used as models in the preparation and amendment of state laws. For the provisions of the 1959 edition of this act and comments on its various sections see 5 *Nat'l Prob. and Parole Ass'n Jour.* 323–391 (1959).

[24] *Standards for Specialized Courts Dealing with Children* (U. S. Children's Bureau Publication No. 346, Washington, D.C.: U. S. Government Printing Office, 1954).

[25] Tappan, *op. cit. supra* note 6, at 15, 24.

Philosophy of the Court

In the words of Tappan, the juvenile court and its methods are "by no means a mere direct borrowing from chancery and common law," but, on the contrary, have emerged largely from "the philosophy and techniques of modern casework and, more particularly, the ideologies of the child-welfare movement concerning the rights of children and the devices that should be used to meet their needs." In fact, "the operations of the specialized juvenile court reflect the contemporary impact of case-work oriented probation officers, administrative social agency procedures, and other non-legal (if not distinctly anti-legal) forces far more than they do the influence of either chancery or common law, modern or ancient."[26]

Although generalizations about anything as complex as the juvenile court are always hazardous, it appears that the following are important elements in the court's philosophy:

1. THE SUPERIOR RIGHTS OF THE STATE. The state is the "higher or ultimate parent" of all the children within its borders. The rights of the child's own parents are always subject to the control of the state when in the opinion of the court the best interests of the child demand it. If the state has to intervene in the case of any child, it exercises its power of guardianship over the child and provides him with the protection, care, and guidance that he needs. This is an adaptation of the ancient doctrine of *parens patriae,* by which all English children were made wards of the Crown.[27]

2. INDIVIDUALIZATION OF JUSTICE. A basic principle in the philosophy of the juvenile court is the recognition that people are different and that each must be considered in the light of his own background and personality. The court, therefore, must adapt its actions to the circumstances of the individual case by ascertaining the needs and potentialities of the child and coordinating the knowledge and skills of law, science, and social work for the promotion of his welfare. This means the balancing of interests in an equitable manner by administrative rather than adversary methods within a flexible procedure such as that provided by chancery. Dean Pound has called this "individualized justice."[28]

3. THE STATUS OF DELINQUENCY. The state should try to protect the child from the harmful brand of criminality. In order to accomplish this the law created the status of delinquency, which is something less than crime and is variously defined in different states. However, this still does not satisfy some students of the court who advocate the removal of even the "delinquency tag," which they claim is just another harmful label, and assert that delinquency acts have no significance except as symptoms of conditions that demand investigation by the court.[29]

4. NONCRIMINAL PROCEDURE. By

---

[26] *Id.* at 9. There is a difference of opinion regarding the extent to which the principles of equity and the criminal law contributed to the origin of the juvenile court. See Mack, "Legal Problems Involved in the Establishment of the Juvenile Court," *The Delinquent Child and the Home* 181 (Breckinridge and Abbott eds. 1912); Pound, *Interpretations of Legal History* 134, 135 (1923); S. and E. T. Glueck, "Historical and Legislative Background of the Juvenile Court," *The Problem of Delinquency* 258, 259 (Glueck ed. 1959); Lou, *op. cit. supra* note 1, at 2–7.

[27] Mack, *op. cit. supra* note 26, at 181–187; Lou, *op. cit. supra* note 1, at 2–9; Schramm, "Philosophy of the Juvenile Court," 261 *Annals* 101 (June 1949).

[28] Pound, "The Future of Socialized Justice," *Yearbook,* 1946, 6 (Nat'l Prob. Ass'n 1947); Schramm, *op. cit. supra* note 27, at 103, 104; Lou, *op. cit. supra* note 1, at 2–5; Block and Flynn, *op. cit. supra* note 6, at 317, 318; *Standards for Specialized Courts Dealing with Children, op. cit. supra* note 24, at 1, 2.

[29] Mack, *op. cit. supra* note 26, at 189; Sussman, *op. cit. supra* note 4, at 20; Tappan, *op. cit. supra* note 6, at 14, 15.

means of an informal procedure the juvenile court functions in such a way as to give primary consideration to the interests of the child. In general the courts have held that the procedure of the juvenile court is not criminal in nature since its purpose is not to convict the child of a crime, but to protect, aid, and guide him, and that, therefore, it is not unconstitutional if it denies him certain rights which are guaranteed to an adult in a criminal trial.[30]

5. REMEDIAL, PREVENTIVE, AND NON-PUNITIVE PURPOSE. The action of the juvenile court is to save the child and to prevent him from becoming a criminal. It seeks to provide him with about the same care and protection that his parents should give him. Although, as we have explained, the first juvenile court law did not stipulate that the child should not be punished, many subsequent court decisions and most of the literature on the subject insist that the substitution of treatment for punishment is an essential element in the philosophy of the court.[31]

Geographical Area Served by the Court

The county is the geographical area served by most juvenile courts in the United States, but for some the jurisdictional unit is the town, the city, the borough, or the judicial district. Since the county is the conventional unit of state government and of many private organizations, its use as the jurisdic-

tional area for the court has obvious advantages in the coordination of the court's work with that of other agencies interested in child welfare. However, most counties cannot afford to maintain courts at modern standards, and even if they could, the volume of work would not justify the necessary expense.[32] In some states this problem could be solved by making the area served by the juvenile court the same as the judicial district served by other courts in the state and thereby enable one juvenile court to take care of the cases of two or more counties. Utah, Connecticut, and Rhode Island have pushed beyond this and, establishing state systems of juvenile courts, have created larger jurisdictional districts within their borders.[33]

Types of Juvenile Courts

There are about 3000 juvenile courts in the United States, although actually many are only slightly different from criminal courts. In referring to the inferior quality of many juvenile courts, Lowell Carr has said, "In well over 2000 counties in the United States nobody has ever seen a well-staffed, modern juvenile court in action."[34] Even New York City, a wealthy community with relatively high welfare standards, has fallen considerably short of the ideal level of performance set for the juvenile court.[35]

Juvenile courts in the United States may be classified into these three types: (1) "designated courts," such as municipal, county, district, and circuit courts which have been selected or

---

[30] Clarke, *op. cit. supra* note 1, at 410; Lou, *op. cit. supra* note 1, at 10. For a convenient digest of some of the important cases regarding the constitutionality of the juvenile court, see *The Problem of Delinquency* 334–506 (Glueck ed. 1959).

[31] Mack, *op. cit. supra* note 26, at 190; *Int'l Com. of the Howard League for Penal Reform, op. cit. supra* note 18, at 9–21; *Standards for Specialized Courts Dealing with Children, op. cit. supra* note 24, at 1; Chute, *op. cit. supra* note 3, at 1; Lou, *op. cit. supra* note 1, at 7; Hurley, *op. cit. supra* note 7, at 328; Clarke, *op. cit. supra* note 1, at 410–415.

[32] Carr, "Most Courts Have To Be Substandard," 13 *Fed. Prob.* 29 (Sept. 1949).

[33] Sussman, *op. cit. supra* note 4, at 25; Larson, "Utah's State-Wide Juvenile Court Plan," 13 *Fed. Prob.* 15 (June 1949).

[34] Carr, *op. cit. supra* note 32, at 31. See also Dobbs, "Realism and the Juvenile Court," 31 *Focus* 104 (July 1952).

[35] Tappan, *op. cit. supra* note 6, at 15, 16. For a careful study of New York's juvenile courts, see Kahn, *A Court for Children* (1953).

designated to hear children's cases and while so functioning are called juvenile courts; (2) independent and separate courts whose administration is entirely divorced from other courts; and (3) coordinated courts, which are coordinated with other special courts such as domestic relations or family courts. The great majority of the juvenile courts are "designated courts," and even many of the separate and independent ones are presided over by judges from other courts so that their separateness and independence may be more nominal than real.[36]

Jurisdiction of the Court

All juvenile courts have jurisdiction in delinquency cases, and almost all of them have jurisdiction in cases of dependency and neglect as well. In addition, some have authority to handle other problems such as feeble-mindedness, adoptions, illegitimacy, and guardianship. Although the definition of delinquency varies from state to state, in most states the violation of a state law or municipal ordinance (an act which in the case of an adult would be a crime) is the main category of delinquency. Yet in all states delinquency is more than this, including such items as habitual truancy, incorrigibility, waywardness, and association with immoral persons.

Juvenile court laws differ also with respect to the age of the children over whom the court has jurisdiction. The laws of most states do not specify any lower age limit, merely providing that children under a certain age are subject to the jurisdiction of the court. Most states make 18 the upper age limit; some set it at 16 or 17; and a few put it as high as 21. In some states the upper age limit differs according to the sex of the child. Many states permit the juvenile court, after it has once acquired jurisdiction over the child, to retain jurisdiction until he has reached 21.

In many states the juvenile court does not have exclusive jurisdiction over all delinquency cases but has only concurrent jurisdiction with the criminal court, delinquency cases being handled by either court. Often, however, such concurrent jurisdiction is limited by law to cases of children above a specified age or to cases involving certain offenses or to certain counties. Furthermore, in many states certain offenses, for example, murder, manslaughter and rape, are entirely excluded from the jurisdiction of the juvenile court, and in these states children charged with such offenses are tried in the criminal court.

The jurisdiction of the court is affected in still another way by the provision in most states that it may exercise authority over adults in certain cases involving children. Thus in many states the juvenile court may require a parent to contribute to the support of his child, or it may try adults charged with contributing to the delinquency, neglect, or dependency of a child.[37]

The Judge and the Probation Officer

Although the effectiveness of the juvenile court depends to a very large degree upon the efficiency of its personnel, relatively few courts have staffs that are especially qualified for their work. In most juvenile courts the judges have been appointed or elected on the basis of their general qualifications for judicial work, and they divide their time between adult and juvenile cases. Only in a very few courts has the judge been selected because he has some specialized training or experience in the handling of children's problems. Often,

[36] Teeters and Reinemann, op. cit. supra note 6, at 295–297.

[37] Sussman, op. cit. supra note 4, at 18, 19, 26–28.

however, a referee is appointed to assist the judge in the performance of his juvenile court duties. Although considerable progress has been made in improving the quality of probation in some parts of the country, the great majority of courts are still without the services of a sufficient number of well-qualified and adequately paid workers.[38]

Procedure of the Court

Police action initiates the procedure in most delinquency cases, but often it begins with action by a parent or other private person or with a referral by a social agency or another court. In recent years, about 50 percent of the delinquency cases have been handled informally or unofficially, that is, without an official record or hearing, but with the judge or someone else, such as a probation officer, taking the necessary steps to dispose of the case. The types of cases that are handled in this way vary greatly from court to court, but the tendency seems to be to reserve official hearings for older children and those brought before the court on serious charges.

When a case is handled officially, a petition (which is merely a statement containing important facts of the case, such as the names and addresses of the child and his parents or guardian and the cause of the action) is filed in the court, and the case is then scheduled for a hearing. If the child is not being held in detention and his presence is required, a summons ordering him to appear, or in some cases a warrant for his arrest, is issued. In most

jurisdictions a prehearing investigation is conducted so that both the hearing and the disposition of the case can be based on the facts so obtained. Some jurisdictions, however, require that the child must be adjudged delinquent before his case is investigated. In these jurisdictions the hearing is held first, and if the child is found to be delinquent, the court is adjourned, the investigation is completed, and the information is then used by the court in the disposition of the case. Unfortunately, inadequacy of personnel and excessive case loads often prevent the investigation from being more than a superficial inquiry.

Juvenile court hearings are usually less formal than trials in the criminal court, but the degree of informality varies considerably throughout the country. Privacy, however, characterizes most hearings; only persons who are definitely connected with the case are permitted to attend. Seldom is a prosecuting attorney or a counsel for the defense present during the hearing, and although jury trials are permitted in many jurisdictions, usually juries are not used. However, the right of appeal in one form or another is available in most jurisdictions.[39]

Disposition of Cases

After the hearing, the case may be disposed of in one of several ways. The case may be dismissed; a court order may be issued stipulating that the child be examined and treated by a physician, psychiatrist, or psychologist or placed in a hospital or some other institution or agency for whatever care may be necessary; the child may be placed on probation or in a

[38] Lenroot, *op. cit. supra* note 22, at 14, 15; Killian, "The Juvenile Court as an Institution," 261 *Annals* 92 (Jan. 1949); Teeters and Reinemann, *op. cit. supra* note 6, at 313–319; Tappan, *op. cit. supra* note 6, at 13; Davis, "The Iowa Juvenile Court Judge," 42 *J. Crim. L., C.&P.S.* 338 (1951).

[39] Sussman, *op. cit. supra* note 4, at 29–37; *Nat'l Conference on Prevention and Control of Juvenile Delinquency, Report on Juvenile Court Laws* 6, 7 (Washington, D.C.: U. S. Government Printing Office, 1947).

foster home; or he may be committed to a correctional institution. According to the United States Children's Bureau, almost half of all delinquency cases disposed of by the juvenile courts during 1957 were dismissed, adjusted, or held open without further hearing, and about one-fourth were placed on probation.[40]

Cooperation with Other Agencies

The success of the juvenile court depends to a great extent upon the work of other agencies, such as the police, schools, clinics, churches, welfare organizations, and correctional institutions, and it in turn can significantly contribute to the success of these other agencies. It should be obvious, then, that the court should play an important part in promoting greater coordination among the law-enforcement and welfare agencies of the community and in the establishment of a delinquency prevention program. Some courts have coordinated their work very closely with other agencies, but many have done very little to foster this relationship.[41]

CRITICISMS OF THE JUVENILE COURT

Ever since the juvenile court was established over sixty years ago, it has been severely criticized by both its friends and its enemies.[42] At first much of the criticism questioned the constitutionality of the court, but as one judicial decision after another supported the court, the attack against it shifted toward its modification or improvement. In fact, today few critics would have the temerity to advocate the abolition of the court, and it seems, as Dr. William Healy has said, that "the juvenile court is here to stay."[43] However, since so many well-informed persons have joined in the criticism, several of the important questions raised by them require our examination.

1. *Has the juvenile court dealt effectively with juvenile delinquency?* This question is so complex that perhaps any discussion of it can succeed in only raising other perplexing questions. It is true that various statistical attempts have been made to evaluate the effectiveness of the juvenile court. Several of these show that from about one-fourth to over two-fifths of older juveniles and adult offenders have previously been dealt with by the court.[44] Another study, made by the Gluecks, revealed that 88.2 percent of the juveniles included in their analysis again became delinquent within five years after the end of their official treatment by the juvenile court of Boston, and that 70 percent of them were actually convicted of serious offenses.[45]

However, studies such as these have not been conclusive. Not only have comparatively few courts been carefully studied, but also the findings of the investigations have not been con-

---

[40] Sussman, *op. cit. supra* note 4, at 45–50; *United States Children's Bureau, Juvenile Court Statistics,* 1957, 2 (Statistical Series, No. 52, 1959).

[41] Schramm, *op. cit. supra* note 27, at 104, 105; *Nat'l Conference on Prevention and Control of Juvenile Delinquency, Report on Juvenile Court Administration* 18–20 (Washington, D. C.: U. S. Government Printing Office, 1947); Breckinridge, *Social Work and the Courts* 231–240 (1934).

[42] Much of the discussion of the criticisms of the juvenile court presented here is an adaptation of that contained in the author's text, *Criminology,* published by the Ronald Press Co. in 1956. See pp. 370–378.

[43] Healy, "Thoughts about Juvenile Courts," 13 *Fed. Prob.* 18, 19 (Sept. 1949).

[44] Sutherland, *Principles of Criminology,* 316, 317 (1947).

[45] S. and E. Glueck, *One Thousand Juvenile Delinquents* 167 (1934). For opposing views regarding this study, see Sheldon Glueck's and Harry L. Eastman's articles in *Yearbook,* 1934, 63–103 (Nat'l Prob. Ass'n, 1934).

sistent. Besides, there are all kinds of juvenile courts, many being such in name only, and an evaluation of one is hardly a fair appraisal of others. Then, too, the cases covered by the investigations often do not constitute a representative sample of those coming before the court, and the recidivism noted is only that of which there is a record. Actually no one knows how much undetected delinquency and crime there is among those who have been previously handled by the court. Furthermore, the court is only one part of a very complex culture, with which it is inextricably and functionally related, and no one, therefore, knows to what extent influences other than (and perhaps even in spite of) that of the court caused the improvement in those who subsequently did not become recidivistic.

But suppose it could be proved that the juvenile court has failed, should delinquents be tried in the criminal court? Certainly no informed person would be in favor of this. Is the solution, then, "bigger and better" juvenile courts? To this question no simple answer can be given. Most counties have too few people to justify, others too little wealth to afford, better juvenile courts. Besides, large segments of our population are already restive under the burden of heavy taxation. Should taxpayers be asked to contribute more for the improvement of our juvenile courts? Should some of the funds that are now being spent for other purposes, for example, for the operation of public schools, be diverted to the development of the juvenile courts?[46]

But even the "biggest" and the "best" court could do little to change the conditions that are causing crime and delinquency. No systematic science

46 Caldwell, *op. cit. supra* note 5, at 371.

of human behavior exists, and the knowledge that we do have requires the support of public opinion if it is to be used most effectively. Furthermore, how much judicial regulation will a community tolerate? If a community is to preserve certain rights and privileges, how much regulation should it tolerate? Obviously, questions of this kind can be considered only as they are related to other values in our culture.

Still other questions must be raised. What is meant by a "better" or the "best" juvenile court? What criteria should be used to measure the quality of a court? There is considerable disagreement regarding these questions. Some claim that the provisions of the *Standard Juvenile Court Act* should be used as the criteria for evaluating a juvenile court, but others would refuse to endorse such a proposal. However, in spite of the fact that so many difficulties interfere with attempts to evaluate the effectiveness of the juvenile court, certain steps can be taken now to improve the quality of its work. Some of these will be mentioned later in the discussion of the problems of the court.

2. *What types of cases should be handled by the juvenile court?* Like the first question, this one is too broad to be examined thoroughly in an article of this kind, but reference to a few specific situations will indicate why it has been raised.

After the juvenile court was established it became the one agency in most communities which could provide some kind of social service for the increasing number of children who needed care and protection, and so it tended to assume responsibility for a growing volume of cases. Moreover, this tendency was accelerated by the passage of laws that stipulated that certain types of children were to be cared for at public expense. In general the court did not resist this tendency, and in some communities court officials actually encouraged it so that they might gain in power and influence. And once the court had assumed responsibility for certain cases, it tended to keep this responsibility even after the need for doing so had disappeared. As a result, the juvenile court has become a catchall for a great variety of cases requiring public attention.

As educational facilities and child welfare services have developed throughout the country, there has developed an increasing demand for the transfer of certain cases from the jurisdiction of the court to that of the schools and welfare agencies. However, it is ·difficult to determine just what criteria could be employed in dividing the cases between the court and other agencies. Some who speak for the welfare agencies say that the juvenile court could exercise functions that are primarily judicial and pertain to law enforcement, while the welfare agencies could exercise functions that are primarily administrative.[47] But this suggested standard is not sufficiently precise to indicate exactly where the line is to be drawn. Undoubtedly it would mean the transfer of many neglect and dependency cases to welfare agencies, but opponents have stressed the complexity of the situation. Neglect, dependency, and delinquency are often interrelated, and delinquency cases involve much administrative work. Besides, many neglect and dependency cases require the exercise of authority supported by the law. In many instances only the court has sufficient authority to enforce decisions and to protect the rights of children and parents, and depriving the court of its administrative duties would unnecessarily complicate the handling of every delinquency case.

The suggestion that certain cases, such as truancy and incorrigibility, be transferred from the juvenile court to the school has likewise stirred up a controversy. Those in favor of the transfer have argued that schools are in close contact with children and their families, have a great deal of information about them, and are already doing a considerable amount of work with them through the efforts of visiting teachers, counselors, clinicians, and parent-teachers' associations; that children should not be exposed to court experience, with its stigmatizing and traumatic implications, except as a last resort; and that the schools would develop more effective programs for the prevention of delinquency if they were not permitted to shift so many of their responsibilities to the court. On the other side of the controversy, many have contended that the personnel of the schools are already overworked and underpaid and should be relieved of some of their responsibilities instead of being given more; that schools do not have enough authority to handle many of the cases; that the stigma of a law-enforcement agency would be attached to the schools if they had to handle delinquency cases; and that many children are not attending school or are in private and parochial schools and thus beyond the authority of public educational officials.

Actually there is much merit in the arguments on both sides of this controversy. Some of the work of the

[47] See, for example, Nutt, "The Responsibility of the Juvenile Court and the Public Welfare Agency in the Child Welfare Program," *Yearbook*, 1947, 206 (Nat'l Prob. and Parole Ass'n, 1948). See also Nutt, "The Future of the Juvenile Court as a Case Work Agency," *Yearbook*, 1939, 157 (Nat'l Prob. Ass'n, 1939); Nutt, "Juvenile Court Function," *Yearbook*, 1942, 94 (Nat'l Prob. Ass'n 1942); Geiser, "The Court as a Case Work Agency," *Yearbook*, 1942, 105 (Nat'l Prob. Ass'n, 1942); Mead, "The Juvenile Court and Child Welfare Services," *Yearbook*, 1947, 224 (Nat'l Prob. and Parole Ass'n, 1948).

court can be safely transferred to educational and welfare agencies, but many administrative duties must be retained by it. Just where the line will be drawn will probably have to be worked out on a local basis through the judicious balancing of needs and resources and the development of greater cooperation among courts, schools, and welfare agencies.[48]

Apart from this, however, other critics of the court have insisted that older juveniles who commit serious crimes, such as murder, manslaughter, rape, and robbery, should not be dealt with in the juvenile court but should be tried in the criminal court. In fact, many states have laws giving the criminal court either original or exclusive jurisdiction over such cases. Opponents of this policy have branded it as reactionary and in violation of the philosophy of the court. According to this philosophy, they explain, the court should have exclusive jurisdiction over all children requiring judicial action, should guide and protect those who come before it, and should not stigmatize or punish them or hold them up as examples for others.

In reply to this argument, those who believe that older juveniles charged with serious offenses should be tried in the criminal court contend: (1) that the upper age limit of children, especially those charged with serious

crimes, over whom the juvenile court should have jurisdiction is a debatable subject; (2) that although the juvenile court uses words like "guidance," "care," and "protection," the fact is that it, too, resorts to punitive methods in handling children; (3) that the public, regardless of what the philosophy of the court may be, looks upon the court as a place where violators of the law are sentenced and punished; (4) that one measure of the support that courts and the law receive is the intensity of the feeling that law-abiding citizens have against law violators; and (5) that failure to punish serious violators not only encourages others to commit crimes but also discourages law-abiding citizens from supporting law-enforcement agencies.

In this controversy, also, there is much to be said in favor of both sides. Certainly no court can exist apart from the community in which it functions and to which it must look for support, and to hold that the court should try to ignore the deep feelings and strong desires of the people whose values it is called upon to enforce is a highly unrealistic and arbitrary attitude. It is partly because of this fact that the *Standard Juvenile Court Act* includes a provision that juveniles 16 years of age or older charged with serious crimes may be tried in the criminal court if the juvenile court deems this to be in the best interest of the children and the public.[49] However, if the case of a youthful serious offender is heard in a juvenile court, then this should be done according to clearly defined rules of procedure, and he should be protected from arbitrary action and abuse of authority just as the adult felon is in the criminal court.

There has also been some recognition of the limitations of the juvenile court for dealing with older and more

[48] Eliot, "Case Work Functions and Judicial Functions: Their Coordination," *Yearbook,* 1937, 252 (Nat'l Prob. Ass'n, 1937); Pound, *op. cit. supra* note 3, at 14, 15; Schramm, "The Juvenile Court Idea," 13 *Fed. Prob.* 21 (Sept. 1949); *Controlling Juvenile Delinquency* (U. S. Children's Bureau Publication No. 301, Washington, D. C.; U. S. Government Printing Office, 1943); Hyatt, "The School, the Juvenile Court, and the Social Attitude," *Yearbook,* 1931, 49 (Nat'l Prob. Ass'n, 1931); Harper, "School and Court Relationships Concerning Behavior Problems," *Yearbook,* 1932 and 1933, 163 (Nat'l Prob. Ass'n, 1933); Taber, "The Judge and the Schools," *Yearbook,* 1944, 41 (Nat'l Prob. Ass'n, 1945).

[49] *A Standard Juvenile Court Act, op. cit. supra* note 23, § 13.

serious offenders in states where the pressure has been to raise the upper age limit of the court and to give it exclusive jurisdiction over all children. For example, in California where the court had exclusive jurisdiction to the age of 18 and concurrent jurisdiction to the age of 21, a special study commission in 1949 recommended that the juvenile court judge should be required to decide specifically whether a juvenile over 16 charged with a crime could be better handled by the juvenile court or by a criminal court.[50]

3. *Are the rights of the child and his parents protected in the juvenile court?* As the juvenile court has developed it has become increasingly dominated by the ideas and methods of child welfare and case work authorities. Contributing to this tendency have been the occupancy of many juvenile court positions by persons who have been trained in social work or who are in agreement with its principles, the very infrequent presence of attorneys in the court, the inadequate legal training of many of its judges and referees, the general exclusion of the public and the press from its hearings, and the rarity of appeals from its decisions. As a result of this departure of the juvenile court from some of the most basic concepts of justice in our culture, there has appeared a growing controversy over whether the rights of the child and his parents are being endangered by the increase in the authority and administrative functions of the court.[51] In this controversy, criticism has been directed especially

against (1) broad definitions of delinquency, (2) unofficial handling of cases, (3) prehearing investigations, and (4) extreme informality of procedure.[52]

In general these aspects of the court have been defended by the claim that they facilitate preventive and nonpunitive action by the court. Thus advocates of a broad definition of delinquency contend that it permits the court to act in situations which warrant its intervention without becoming entangled in technical disputes over the meaning of terms. In conformance with this point of view, some states have broadened the definition of delinquency by substituting a few general categories of delinquency for a number of specifically defined acts. The laws of some other states and the *Standard Juvenile Court Act*[53] have gone beyond this and do not define delinquency at all. Instead, without using the term delinquency, they merely describe certain situations and classifications of children over which the court has jurisdiction. This avoidance of the "delinquency tag," it is argued, enables the court to help and protect the child without stigmatizing him in any

---

[50] Tappan, *op. cit. supra* note 6, at 8.

[51] *Id.* at 2. Administrative functions of the court include such activities as investigation of cases, planning for the care of children, supervision of probationers, and foster-home placement. These are to be contrasted with the court's judicial functions, which refer to such matters as adoption and guardianship and decisions regarding custody and commitment.

[52] See Tappan, *Juvenile Delinquency* 195–223 (1949); Schramm, *op. cit. supra* note 48, at 19–23; Pound, *op. cit. supra* note 4, at 1–22; Waite, "How Far Can Court Procedure Be Socialized without Impairing Individual Rights?" 12 *J. Crim. L. & C.* 339 (1921); Rubin, "Protecting the Child in the Juvenile Court," 43 *J. Crim. L., C.&P.S.* 425 (1952); Kahn, *op. cit. supra* note 35, at 95–135; Nunberg, "Problems in the Structure of the Juvenile Court," 48 *J. Crim. L., C.&P.S.* 500 (1958); Herman, "Scope and Purposes of Juvenile Court Jurisdiction," 48 *J. Crim. L., C.&P.S.* 590 (1958); Diana, "The Rights of Juvenile Delinquents: An Appraisal of Juvenile Court Procedure," 47 *J. Crim. L., C.&P.S.* 561 (1957); Allen, "The Borderland of the Criminal Law: Problems of 'Socializing' Criminal Justice," 32 *Soc. Serv. Rev.* 107 (1958).

[53] *A Standard Juvenile Court Act, op. cit. supra* note 23, at 8.

way. The unofficial handling of cases has been justified on the grounds that official court action is not needed in many situations, that it enables the court to assist children who, although not yet within its jurisdiction, are in danger of becoming so, and that the official label of delinquency should be avoided as much as possible. Prehearing investigations should be used, it is asserted, because they provide important facts for the hearings and thus allow the hearings themselves to be utilized as part of the treatment process. Extreme informality of procedure is favored by those who believe that only by minimizing all rules can the philosophy of the juvenile court gain full expression. They maintain that rules are not important anyway since the state is not bringing action against a defendant, as it would in a criminal trial, but is rather acting as a guardian of the child, and that therefore we need not be concerned about protecting the child from possible harm.

However, a number of important points have been stressed on the other side of the controversy, and an examination will now be made of some of these. Broad definitions of delinquency and the unofficial handling of cases, it is contended, channel an increasing number of children not having serious problems into courts which, by general admission, are overloaded, understaffed, and inadequately equipped for preventive work. Handling by these courts not only gives such children the appearance of being seriously delinquent in the eyes of the public, and thus actually defeats the alleged purpose of this practice, but also exposes them to the danger of being treated as if they were serious delinquents or, what is worse, of being indiscriminately committed to correctional institutions when perhaps they are suffering only from neglect or dependency. More-

over, even when the court can engage in extensive preventive work, this activity may discourage the development of other agencies better organized and equipped to do this work.

Besides, it is argued, where is the child who does not have a problem? With little effort hundreds of children who have problems can be found in any community and brought into court. And if the court is not vigilant, it may be used by parents as a weapon against children in situations where the parents themselves are to blame. Thus the family is given a crutch at a time when it should be encouraged to strengthen itself through its own efforts—and other agencies can assist the family to do this far more effectively than can the court.

Furthermore, it is asserted, the situation is not improved by the use of the prehearing investigation. Too often this tends to become the hearing itself—a process during which the facts are gathered and the decision regarding disposition is reached even before the court has determined whether the child is delinquent. Indeed, his mere presence in court may be interpreted as presumptive evidence of his delinquency, and this may be easily inflated to conclusive evidence if some personal problem in his history can be discovered and dilated upon by the probation officer. If the hearing has been conducted with an extremely informal procedure, the child will find that the decision can be overturned only with great difficulty. If, as its advocates claim, the prehearing investigation is not to be used to acquire evidence against the child, then there is no sound reason why the investigation should not be postponed until after the child has been adjudged delinquent. Here another point needs to be stressed. The court cannot be certain that a problem child will become a delinquent child, and besides, its own ineptitude may convert a problem into delinquency.

Moreover, it is urged, the rights of the child and his parents are especially endangered if the case is handled with extreme informality, because then there is no attorney to guard against the abuse of authority, no set of rules to ward off hearsay and gossip, no way of breaking through the secrecy of the hearing, and often no appeal from the court's decision. The child and his parents have even less protection if the case is handled unofficially, for in such a procedure very few legal checks limit the court's discretion, and redress at law becomes difficult since no official record exists upon which the child can plead his case. The situation can be worse if broad definitions of delinquency are used, because these leave the term vague and fuzzy, and under them all children tend to be pooled indiscriminately as wards of the state without an opportunity to marshal evidence against a specific charge. If these children are then processed through unofficial handling or informal hearings from which many, if not most, of the limitations of due process have been removed, they are largely at the court's discretion, which too frequently may be only the expression of the judge's prejudice. How ironical it is that this situation is justified in the name of equity, especially since the court of equity has always had its rules and formality for the same reason that rules and formality should be present in the juvenile court, that is, to check the abuse of power and to protect the rights of the individual.

Finally, it is protested, euphemistic terminology, such as "hearing" instead of "trial," or "disposition" instead of "sentence," should not be allowed to conceal the fact that the nature of the entire procedure in the juvenile court may be little different from that of a criminal court. In fact, it may be worse, for it may abandon the principles upon which justice is based under the guise of promoting a superior justice. It is understandable, therefore, why Carr has said, "No man is wise enough or good enough to be trusted with arbitrary power—even the arbitrary power to prejudge the case of some delinquent child in the juvenile court."[54]

These, then, are some of the points that have been stressed by those who are opposed to broad definitions of delinquency, unofficial handling of cases, prehearing investigations, and extreme informality of procedure. That they are impressive ones is evidenced by the fact that an increasing number of thoughtful writers have demanded greater protection for the child and his parents in the juvenile court. And Tappan, in dismay over the seriousness of the situation, has asked, "Who is to save the child from his saviors?"[55]

This analysis of the criticisms of the juvenile court clearly shows that we are dealing with questions of emphasis and fine distinctions in a process which involves the balancing of the best interests of both the individual and society. It also indicates some of the social, philosophical, legal, and operational problems that confront the juvenile court. In the consideration of these problems, we shall be able to maintain a better sense of proportion if we remember these facts: (1) Although the general tendency has been toward the operation of the juvenile court as an administrative agency with great emphasis on social service functions, this type of operation has not been achieved to any great extent except in the comparatively few highly-organized, independent courts in our large cities; but,

[54] Carr, *Delinquency Control* 240 (1950).

[55] Tappan, *op. cit. supra* note 52, at 208.

it must be added, these courts have been exerting a disproportionate influence in the establishment of standards and goals in the juvenile court movement. (2) Many courts, instead of taking action themselves, are already referring a large number of cases to schools and welfare agencies. (3) Many courts that have few of the essential characteristics of the juvenile court are nevertheless effectively handling cases because of the wisdom of the judge and the support of interested citizens. (4) Many courts, regardless of what can be done in their behalf, will remain "substandard courts" even when measured by the most moderate criteria—a fact which becomes increasingly apparent since these courts have shown little improvement despite the unprecedented prosperity of this country. (5) Many communities will have to continue to send their neglect and dependency cases and some of their truany cases to the juvenile court simply because they do not now have, and may never have, any other agency able to assume this responsibility. (6) The majority of the alleged delinquents appearing in the juvenile court do not contest the allegations brought against them and are actually delinquent, although, of course, this does not mean that these children are not entitled to all necessary legal protection.

Since the juvenile court in the United States is a functioning part of an increasingly complex culture, it must share in all the social problems, including delinquency, that this type of society tends to produce. To the extent that the juvenile court operates effectively to rehabilitate juvenile offenders and to deter others from becoming delinquent, it functions as an agency of prevention and contributes somewhat to social reorganization. But obviously it can remove only some of the conditions that are causing the delinquency

with which it is dealing, and it has virtually no control over industrialization, urbanization, and other such powerful forces that are transforming and disorganizing American society— including the juvenile court itself—and piling up social problems faster than we can handle them.

Although there has been considerable debate about how the juvenile courts can improve their staffs, lower their case loads, and reduce their other operational problems, most students of the court agree that certain changes can be made now to accomplish these objectives. Many communities can and should spend more money on their courts, and others should use their present expenditures more effectively. Many courts should have judges who are better trained in both the law and the social sciences, larger jurisdictional areas, and a stronger position in their state's judicial system.[56] All courts should closely coordinate their operations with those of welfare and law-enforcement agencies. And everywhere the public should be told more about the court and encouraged to support its work.

It is recognized, of course, that all the problems of the court are interrelated and interacting and that many of them are beyond its control. However, there are major problems of a philosophical and legal nature with which the court can deal directly and which are contributing materially to

---

[56] The way in which the position of the juvenile court in the state's judicial system is to be strengthened will be affected by the surrounding social and political conditions. According to the Standard Juvenile Court Act, if the court is not part of a state system of juvenile courts, it should be set up within the existing judicial structure as a separate division at the level of the highest court of general trial jurisdiction. Sussman, *op. cit. supra* note 4, at vii. See also Rubin, "State Juvenile Court: A New Standard," 30 *Focus* 103 (July 1951).

its operational difficulties. The juvenile court, like all courts, must try to balance the interests of the individual and society in the adjudication of its cases. In the United States social relationships are being torn apart by conflicts, and agencies of social control subverted by divisive influences. The ensuing confusion is blurring the sense of right and wrong, diluting basic loyalties, endangering many cherished rights, and sweeping away duties and responsibilities essential for the security of the community. The juvenile court can help to reduce this confusion if its philosophical and legal foundations are strengthened. The proposals advanced below are designed to do this by casting the court in a more realistic role, protecting the rights and clarifying the duties of those coming before it, and enabling it to effect a better balance between the rights of the child and his parents and the security of the community.

PROPOSALS REGARDING THE COURT'S PHILOSOPHY AND LEGAL BASIS

Philosophy of the Court

The roots of most of the controversy over the juvenile court are to be found in the dual role that it plays in attempting to function both as a court of law and as a social service agency. In fact, many writers on the subject believe that the basic problem confronting the court involves a decision as to which of its two functions, the legal or the social service, is to predominate.[57]

The juvenile court was established

[57] See for example, Baker, "The Functions of the Juvenile Court," 24 *Case and Con.* 449 (Nov. 1917); Long, "The Juvenile Court and Community Resources," *Yearbook*, 1940, 24 (Nat'l Prob. Ass'n, 1940); Eastman and Cousins, "Juvenile Court and Welfare Agency: Their Division of Function," 38 *A.B.A.J.* 575–577, 623 (1952); Nunberg, *op. cit. supra* note 52, at 500.

as a court, albeit a special one, and in structure, function, and procedure it remains essentially a court.[58] Therefore, efforts should be made to strengthen its true, or judicial, nature and to retain and develop only that part of its social service function that is necessary for the administration of individualized justice.

As a court, even in the administration of this type of justice, it must not only express the values of the society in which it functions but also reinforce these values. Dean Pound, a friend of the juvenile court, clearly recognized this when he said:

If we work out a system of making penal treatment fit the crime, we risk losing sight of the individual delinquent in pursuit of system. If we look only at the individual delinquent, we risk losing system in pursuit of individual treatment and lose objectivity which is demanded when we are constraining the individual by the force of politically organized society. It comes down to the reconciling of the general security with the individual life, which as I have said, is a fundamental problem of the whole legal order.[59]

In other words, no court, not even the juvenile court, can be just a therapeutic agency. It is, and must be, a moral agency as well. And when a child is adjudicated a delinquent by the court, he is, and of necessity must be, stigmatized as a violator of the moral values of his society. This is what the people want and expect of any agency such as a court which is established to protect and strengthen their values. In fact, the court must act in this way if it is to promote the rehabilitation of the child. If it did otherwise, it would flaunt the very values to which the child must learn to adjust and for which he

[58] Both legal scholars and social welfare authorities have recognized this fact. See, for example, Pound, *op. cit. supra* note 3, at 5; Nutt, *op. cit. supra* note 47, at 212.

[59] Pound, *op. cit. supra* note 4, at 15.

must develop a loyalty. This is not to ignore the fact that values change and that considerable confusion regarding moral standards exists in the United States. The point is that the court cannot avoid its responsibility as a moral agency. It must do what it can to reduce this confusion. It must devote itself to the interests of the delinquent and respect his rights, but it must also take its stand with the community and insist that he learn to discharge his duties and assume his responsibilities as a member of society, thus giving encouragement and support to law-abiding citizens and helping to maintain the public sense of justice. The way in which the court does this will, of course, depend upon the facts of the case as they are revealed and evaluated in the process of "individualized justice."

Furthermore, in the disposition of the delinquency case the court forces the child to submit to its authority by placing him on probation, by committing him to a correctional institution, or by dealing with him in some other similar way. And by no stretch of the imagination can what actually happens to the child during this process be called merely treatment. Thus the action of the court involves both community condemnation of antisocial conduct and the imposition of unpleasant consequences by political authority—the two essential elements of punishment.[60] It is, therefore, highly unrealistic to say that the court treats, but does not punish, the child. What it really does is to emphasize treatment in a correctional process which includes, and of necessity must include, both treatment and punishment.

This conclusion tends to be supported by several other facts. There is no systematic science of human behavior,

and the concepts and techniques of treatment are still largely inadequate. Moreover, as Dunham has explained, neither the child nor his parents are inclined to view his behavior as symptomatic of a sickness that needs treatment, but instead "are committed to the view that the court is there for justice and for punishing a person who has done something that is wrong."[61] Besides, the stipulation that the court should act as a parent in protecting and caring for the child does not rule out the necessity and desirability of punishment. Here again Dean Pound had a clear understanding of the nature of the court. "Juvenile probation," he said, "is not a mode of penal treatment nor a substitute for punishment. It is a mode of exercising the authority of the state as *parens patriae*. It may be conceded that the parent may have at times to administer what common law called reasonable correction to the child. No doubt there is often a corrective element in judicial treatment of juvenile offenders. But the spirit is that of the parent rather than that of the ruler."[62]

This modification of the philosophy of the juvenile court is superior to that generally accepted in several important respects. First, it clearly recognizes the necessity of balancing the interests of the delinquent and the community in the process of "individualized justice." Second, it provides a practical basis of action which can be accepted without conflict by both law-enforcement officers and court personnel. Third, by honestly admitting that the court must not only treat but also punish, this modified philosophy dispels the cloud of hypocrisy now enveloping the juvenile court, and gives it a position in society

[60] Hart, "The Aims of the Criminal Law," 23 *Law and Contemp. Prob.* 401 (1958).

[61] Dunham, "The Juvenile Court: Contradictory Orientations in Processing Offenders, 23 *Law and Contemp. Prob.* 520 (1958).

[62] Pound, *op. cit. supra* note 4, at 16.

where it can be respected by all law-abiding citizens. Finally, by revealing the true nature of the court, this modified philosophy brings the possibility of the abuse of power out into the open where it can be clearly understood and effectively controlled.

Jurisdiction of the Court

The jurisdiction of the juvenile court should be limited to (1) delinquency cases, and (2) those dependency and neglect cases in which a decision must be made affecting the legal status of the child, his custody, or the rights of his parents. All other dependency and neglect cases should be handled by administrative agencies without court action, and truancy should be dealt with by the schools.[63] This proposal is made in recognition of the fact that the juvenile court is essentially a court and not an administrative agency, and that, therefore, it suffers from inherent limitations in welfare work. Furthermore, the considerable increase in the number of welfare agencies and public services during the past few decades not only makes this transfer of responsibilities possible but also leaves the court with a greater capacity to handle the growing volume of delinquency cases.

The court should deal with children who can be shown to be delinquent by the application of specific, sharply defined criteria, and not with children who have problems according to the opinions of teachers, clergymen, and social workers—however sincere these beliefs may be. Juvenile delinquency, therefore, should be defined as the violation of a state law or city or town ordinance by a child whose act if committed by an adult would be a crime. This simple, specific definition eliminates all the references to such vague conditions as "being ungovernable" or "growing up in idleness" which clutter up our statutes on delinquency and invite loose interpretation and abuse of authority. Thus it will prevent the juvenile court from moving into areas where other agencies can render more effective service, and at the same time it will protect children and their parents from indiscriminate handling by the court without regard for the cause of action in the case.

The juvenile court should have original and exclusive jurisdiction over all children between the ages of 7 and 18 who are alleged to be delinquent, except in cases where a child is charged with a minor traffic offense or where a child of 16 or over is charged with a serious felony, such as murder, armed robbery, or rape. In the cases involving minor traffic offenses, there is no need of special handling. They can be adequately dealt with by a police or traffic court, and thus the burden on the juvenile court can be reduced.[64] In the cases where children 16 or over are charged with serious felonies the criminal court should have original jurisdiction but with authority to transfer such cases to the juvenile court if in the opinion of the judge this would be in the best interests of both the child and the community. The criminal court should have the authority to act first in these. cases, because it, more than the juvenile court, is held responsible for the security of society and is organized and administered especially for this purpose. As Ludwig has emphasized, "Making treatment of all criminal behavior of young offenders, regardless of its seriousness or triviality, depend

---

[63] This is essentially the proposal made by Sol Rubin in his book, *Crime and Juvenile Delinquency* 60–63 (1958). See also Nutt, *op. cit. supra* note 47, at 213; Hanna, "Dependency and Neglect Cases in the Juvenile Court," *Yearbook,* 1941, 136 (Nat'l Prob. Ass'n, 1941).

[64] See *Standards for Specialized Courts Dealing with Children, op. cit. supra* note 24, at 29, 30.

solely upon the individual need of the offender for rehabilitation may well lead our impressionable young community to conclude that fracturing someone's skull is no more immoral than fracturing his bedroom window."[65] This point is particularly important since a large and increasing percentage of serious crimes are being committed by young people. Thus the handling of a large percentage of these young offenders in the juvenile court—a court which is not primarily concerned with the public sense of justice and security —will make the criminal law increasingly inoperative and cause additional confusion regarding our code of morality and the importance of vigorous law enforcement. This in turn may contribute to the growth of indifference and cynicism regarding the duties and responsibilities of citizenship and to an already alarming trend toward the centralization of power in the hands of a few who, under the guise of science and treatment, often seek to impose their own values upon an increasingly disorganized people. To make matters worse, what is hailed as humanitarianism is frequently just public indifference regarding the way in which delinquents and criminals are handled.

The case of an adult charged with an offense against a child should be handled not in the juvenile court but in the criminal court. This will place these cases in a court better designed to assure protection of all fundamental rights in a criminal proceeding[66] and will help the public to understand that the juvenile court is a special court for children and not in any sense of the word a criminal court.

Procedure of the Court

Through its intake procedure the juvenile court should carefully screen all cases brought to its attention so as to eliminate those that do not require the attention of the court or any other agency and to insure the referral of as many other cases as possible to agencies that are better equipped than the court to provide curative and preventive treatment. The cases that are accepted by the court should receive official handling. If a case is not in need of official handling, it should not be handled by the court at all, but should be referred to some other agency. Too often unofficial handling is merely the haphazard, ineffective disposition of cases by understaffed, overloaded courts, which is justified under the guise of avoiding the "delinquency tag."[67]

The court should establish the fact of delinquency in a case before an investigation of the case is made. Prehearing investigations are not only an encroachment upon the rights of the child who has not yet been proved delinquent, but are costly in time, energy, and money in the cases of those who are discharged as not delinquent.

The procedure during the hearing should be informal but based upon sufficient rules to insure justice and consistency. The child and his parents should be fully informed regarding their legal rights. These should include the right to be represented by counsel, to have a clear explanation of the allegations against the child, to cross-examine hostile witnesses, to summon witnesses in the child's defense, to have protection against irrelevant and hearsay testimony and compulsory self-incrimination, to have a hearing before a jury if this is desired, to have proof of delinquency by at least a preponderance

---

[65] Ludwig, *op. cit. supra* note 20, at 311.
[66] *Id.* at 151.

[67] Tappan, "Unofficial Delinquency," 29 *Neb. L. Rev.* 547 (1950); Herman, *op. cit. supra* note 52, at 596; Sussman, *op. cit. supra* note 4, at 29, 30; Rubin, *op. cit. supra* note 63, at 66–68; *Standards for Specialized Courts Dealing with Children, op. cit. supra* note 24, at 43–45.

of convincing evidence, and to have access to a higher court for the purpose of an appeal. In addition, every juvenile before the court should be given the opportunity to have a public hearing if he so desires, and if he prefers a private one, members of the press should be admitted to the hearing but should not be permitted to publish the name of the child or any identifying data regarding him without the permission of the court. Their mere presence, however, should exert a wholesome and restraining influence on the court's operations.[68]

Disposition of Cases

The disposition of the case should be made by the judge after a study of the investigation report and consultation with the probation officer and other specialists who have worked on the case. However, simply because the judge must turn to specialists for assistance in his disposition of the case does not mean that it might be better to have the disposition made entirely by a panel of "experts." In the first place this incorrectly suggests that there is a type of knowledge that the judge does not have, cannot understand, and can never acquire. This not only grossly exaggerates the amount of knowledge we now have regarding human behavior but also greatly underestimates the intelligence and skill of the majority of our judges. If a particular judge is so incompetent or stubborn that he cannot, or will not, benefit by having the assistance of specialists, then the solution lies in his removal from office, not in unnecessarily complicating the machinery of the court by the creation of a panel of "experts." And if the judge

is so overworked that he does not have time to analyze carefully the facts contained in the investigation report and to consult with specialists about the various aspects of the case, then the answer is to be found in the appointment of more judges. There is no short cut or cheap way to "individualized justice," and the mere existence of a juvenile court does not insure its achievement.

Furthermore, the facts of adjudication and disposition cannot be examined as if they existed apart from each other. These facts exist in the life of a single child who must be seen in his entirety —developing from what he was to what he will be. They must be assembled creatively in the mind of one person who has the authority to balance the interests of both the individual and the community and who is held responsible by the community for this function. The facts of a case can be seen in a variety of ways, depending upon the relation of the examiner to the facts, and the mind is easily misled into seeing only one side of this picture. The judge who decides that a child is a delinquent should make this decision to intervene in the child's life not only in full knowledge of what will happen to the child as he is subjected to the available social services but also in deep awareness of being held responsible for the entire procedure. Only in such a process of sober deliberation can the knowledge of the facts be creatively transformed into a wise decision. The division of authority among the members of a panel fragmentizes the facts of the case and dilutes the sense of responsibility regarding the interests of the child and his relationship to the community.[69]

[68] Tappan, "Treatment Without Trial," 24 *Social Forces* 308 (March 1946); Cappello, "Due Process in the Juvenile Court," 2 *Catholic U. L. Rev.* 90 (1952); Geis, "Publicity and Juvenile Court Proceedings," 30 *Rocky Mt. L. Rev.* 101 (1958).

[69] Kahn, *op. cit. supra* note 35, at 277; Hall, "The Youth Correction Authority Act, Progress or Menace," 28 *A.B.A.J.* 317 (1942); Frank, *Courts on Trial* ch. 4 (1949).

These proposals are not advanced with any desire to convert the juvenile court into a criminal court but rather with full recognition of both its great potentialities and its inherent limitations. The juvenile court must be seen as a court—not as an administrative agency, but as a court—designed to protect the child from the traumatic experiences of a criminal trial and to provide more flexible machinery for balancing the interests of the child and the community in the light of the most recent knowledge regarding human behavior. It is not, however, especially equipped to do welfare work, and so wherever possible it should be divested of jurisdiction over cases in which the child is simply in need of aid. On the other hand, it is a court, and its action does necessarily stigmatize the child. Therefore, its jurisdiction and procedure should be governed by simple, specific rules so that while the child is receiving guidance and protection, his rights and the security of the community are not neglected.

The foregoing proposals have sought to strip away those excrescences that have interfered with the expression of the true nature of the juvenile court, but they have left it with all the characteristics which are essential to its functioning and growth. Delinquency as a status different from that of crime, judges carefully selected on the basis of both their legal and social science training and knowledge, separate hearings as informal and private as are consistent with the protection of rights,

availability of resources, such as medical, psychological, and psychiatric services, that can be used to make the investigation of cases more effective, regular probation service by an adequate number of well-trained officers, separate detention of children, special and confidential court and probation records—all these and more remain intact and are given a deeper meaning by a more realistic philosophy.

It is recognized that not all these proposals can immediately be put into effect everywhere. It is believed, however, that they do represent desirable goals toward which all juvenile courts should be directed so that they will become more effective agencies of social control.

But, as Dean Pound wisely counseled, "the law is not equal to the whole task of social control. Delinquency presents a problem far too complex to be dealt with by any single method. Hence in this field cooperation is peculiarly called for and is called for in a very wide field. If a socialized criminal justice is to achieve all that it may, we must be thinking about more than cooperation of judge and probation officer and social worker. These must cooperate, or at least be prepared to cooperate with the community organizer, the social engineer, the progressive educator, the social coordinator, the health officer, the clergyman, and the public-spirited promoter of legislation."[70]

[70] Pound, *op. cit. supra* note 4, at 13, 14.

31.

Treatment Without Trial

Paul Tappan

During the past generation there have developed in the court procedures of this country a series of novel institutional devices breaking with legal tradition and looking toward a more "socialized" processing of offenders. These devices are largely a hybrid product of court and case work methods. Some of them it is the purpose of this paper to consider. In general they are characterized by one or both of the following: (1) informal, unofficial probation supervision or institutional remand before a hearing is held, and (2) hearings in which there is no determination as to guilt of an offense, where personality factors and the "total situation" determine adjudication.

The purposes behind the emerging procedural methods appear fairly clear and, on their face at least, "progressive" and laudable. The desire is to avoid the stigma which grows out of court contact and adjudication and, particularly where the offense involved is of no great seriousness, to prevent the sentencing to an offender's status and to formal correction. The aim, too, is to break with the legal approach of adjudging defendants on the proof of a given criminal act, holding it more

scientifically appropriate to determine through social and biological information whether a case needs treatment and, if so, what sort is required. To the socially minded it may appear absurd to concentrate attention upon a criminal act when it is itself merely a symptom or end product of character drives conditioned through extended experience. The need, it may be claimed, is to view rather the area of true significance—the defendant's total personality —in order to deal correctly with the case. Statutes which define the elements of a crime and establish a fixed penalty conceived by a legislature as punishment appropriate to the seriousness of that act appear as absurd relics of a classical criminology in an age when social science points toward individualization, prevention, and rehabilitation. Furthermore, the experimental courts of today rest largely on the shoulders of probation departments which have fostered the development of the new procedures. They would extend the philosophy and practice of case work in dealing with what are basically conduct problems, avoiding the "legal technicalities" which may slow or prevent the application of

SOURCE. Paul W. Tappan, "Treatment Without Trial," from *Social Forces*, Volume 24, March 1946, pp. 306–311. Reprinted with the permission of the University of North Carolina Press.

needed therapy based on social diagnosis and prescription for the peculiar needs of the case. The prevailing philosophy of these courts has been expressed ably by its advocates.[1]

The growth of an idea and its institutional entrenchment are well illustrated by the continuing crystallization in our courts of these new procedures. The methods used are rather numerous and varied in detail, but they fall into one or the other of the two general categories referred to above. For the most part they have originated in nonstatutory or extra-legal procedures, avoiding therefore the hazard of invalidation by appellate decisions. Some have received statutory formulation. By and large, however, the legal specifications under which the experimental courts operate do not sanction that full flowering of novel procedure which case work philosophy has brought into actual court custom. Indeed, under the statutes many of the existing practices are invalid; some of the informal administrative procedures are clearly violative of due process.

Let us review briefly the evolution of some of these devices employed to circumvent the traditional methods of criminal trial (wherein the issue of guilt is determined by the court and penalties are graded to the offense). Their origins lie in the children's court movement in which has developed a series of peculiarities in processing, today quite generally diffused throughout the country at this level of tribunal. Their emergence may be understood in part as a result of the rationalizing principle of the state as *parens patriae*, protector to the child, associated with the belief that deprivation of proce-

dural rights is unimportant when the court is attempting to treat and protect the child. Its purpose is clinical and rehabilitative. There has been small danger of defendant's contesting the validity of the procedural methods employed: neither the naive child nor his distraught parent are wont to challenge the procedures, and no attorney or prosecutor is present generally to raise the issue. If the right of review is permitted, it is discouraged and often condemned as a legal device to undo the progressive work of the court.[2] Chiefly the following differentiating characteristics mark the children's court methodology:

1. *Intake.* Basic information is sought by a probation officer at intake on the background of the case—family data; educational, economic and recreational history; conduct of the child; and other germane matters.

2. *Unofficial treatment.* Probation personnel (known in the New York Children's Court as the Adjustment Bureau) may apply informal supervision to cases in which the intake officer believed that social therapy was needed but which did not appear to require court hearing and adjudication. (It should be noted that an extremely elastic discretion may be employed at intake in directing the case to unofficial treatment or to court. When—as is the widely prevailing condition today —the operative philosophy of probation departments favors informal case work without a hearing, this "treatment without trial" becomes a popular practice.)

3. *Pre-adjudication investigation.* Reversing the procedure traditional in our criminal courts, at the juvenile level a social investigation on each case is undertaken by a probation officer *prior to*

---

[1] See, for example, Pauline V. Young, *Social Treatment in Probation and Delinquency* (1937); Herbert H. Lou, *Juvenile Courts in the United States* (1927); Belle B. Beard, *Juvenile Probation* (1934).

[2] See Benedict S. Alper, "Forty Years of the Juvenile Court," *American Sociological Review* (April, 1941), p. 230.

a hearing, and the information obtained therefrom is made available later at the hearing. This is unorthodox procedure in two chief respects: It applies to all cases whether or not the defendant is later adjudicated. (It tends, of course, to lead to adjudication in commonly establishing the foundation therefor in the discovery of social problems deemed to need treatment.) Also, in preceding the hearing, it allows in evidence matters which would be considered prejudicial, incompetent, and irrelevant for purposes of proof in the usual criminal trial.

4. *Interim dispositions.* During the period of social investigation a temporary disposition of the case must be made by adjourning to a later date and either paroling the defendant to home or agency or remanding him to an institution. The period of interim disposition is usually several weeks. In effect it constitutes a phase of treatment without trial when the child is either incarcerated (often with others already found to be delinquent, sometimes with convicted adult criminals[3]) or held under the restricted liberty of probation-scrutiny.

5. *Adjudication based on the total situation.* As noted above, the information from reports of probation investigation is available at the hearing. Thereby social data come to determine not only the treatment methods to be employed (as in the criminal court) but very largely whether or not the defendant is to be adjudicated a delinquent. Hence his guilt of a specific offense comes to be considered irrelevant, court decision being predicated upon the social and personal problems appearing in the history of the defendant and his family.

6. *Omnibus statutes.* The wide lati-

tude of discretion possible in adjudication is supported and extended by the statutes defining the recalcitrant child so broadly as to facilitate the easy status-fixing of delinquency.[4] Where, in accordance with the provisions of the statutes, a hearing is held before treatment is applied, it is scarcely a "trial" in the usual sense since guilt of specific enumerated offenses need not be proven to adjudicate. Rather, rumor of the needs of the defendant and/or his family may be a matter of primary moment to the children's court's decision. Again it is treatment without trial.

The procedures which evolved in the children's courts have come to be applied in the more recently emerging tribunals for adolescents. The variations in age-coverage of the children's court statutes in different jurisdictions are significant here. A large proportion of the states provide for children's court control over the delinquent up to the age of 18, some as high as 21. A few, including New York, end jurisdiction at 16. The trend has been generally upward throughout the country.

The result has been a drive to develop special facilities for the adolescent who otherwise must traverse the trial routes taken by adult criminals. New York City in its Adolescent Courts in Brooklyn and Queens, its citywide Wayward Minor Court for girls, and its Youthful Offender divisions of the County Courts, has provided special tribunals and methods of processing for the recalcitrant youth over 16. Similarly,

---

[3] See Leonard V. Harrison and Pryor M. Grant, *Youth in the Toils* (1938).

[4] Under the Federal Juvenile Court Act which has now been in operation for six years, such pre-hearing investigations are also conducted and reports submitted to the court at the hearing. As in the state courts, the procedures used are largely extra-legal in permitting adjudication based in part upon untested hearsay of probation reports. In the federal courts, however, many protections to the defendant's interests exist which are absent in the courts of the states.

Chicago, Philadelphia, and other cities have established courts to deal particularly with young offenders over the juvenile age.[5] For the most part these tribunals apply procedures comparable to those previously developed in the children's courts and they justify their use by analogy. It should be noted in passing, however, that there are several clear differences which should distinguish adolescent from juvenile procedures: The children's courts are often —as in New York—civil, whereas the adolescent courts are a part of the criminal court system. Also, the same standards of behavior cannot justifiably be applied to adolescent and child. Too, the facilities of the children's courts for treatment are generally more numerous, varied, and qualitatively superior to those of the adolescent courts—a significant matter in determining the sorts of cases in which jurisdiction should be taken by a court.

These courts for adolescents, too, operate under broad statutes which define the recalcitrant or wayward youth in most general fashion, thus facilitating adjudication when the court may wish to apply treatment to the case before it.[6] Pre-hearing investigations, interim procedures—often with temporary institutional disposition—and adjudication based on general hearsay information concerning personality and social background appear again at this

[5] See particularly the following: *Young People in the Courts of New York State*, Leg. Doc. 55 (1942); Paul W. Tappan, *Court for Wayward Girls* (1946); Worthington and Topping, *Specialized Courts Dealing with Sex Delinquency* (1925).

[6] See New York Statutes: the Wayward Minor Act, chapter 873, laws of 1945, recently expanding the terms of the original statute and permitting, particularly, remands without consent. See also the Youthful Offender Act, chapter 549, laws of 1943, recently repealed in its application to the Special Sessions Court, chapter 873, laws of 1945.

level—though somewhat more fearfully than in the children's courts. Here the individuals processed are adults under the criminal law and the large variations from due process could more easily lead to invalidation of the court methods. "Consent" of the defendant to the investigation before hearing has usually been required. There is formal statutory enunciation of defendant's rights, including the provision that his statements during investigation may not be used against his interest at the trial. Yet these matters are taken as a most *pro forma* matter. Indeed, under the new Wayward Minor Act in New York the requirement of consent for interim remands of two weeks has been abandoned so that such commitments may be made automatically. In some of the experimental courts the adolescent's consent to investigation and special hearing virtually assures adjudication of the status of offender but with more lenient treatment than could be expected from the criminal court to which the case would otherwise go. Thus the defendant is presented with a choice of consenting to an investigation by an officer of the court on the basis of which adjudication is most probable, to be followed by probation supervision; or, protesting his innocence, he risks conviction in an ordinary criminal court where the judge may impose a harsher penalty of commitment. This selection would test severely the preferences of many defendants innocent of law-violation.

These recent experimental methods of treatment without trial outlined above which have taken hold at the children's level and entered the adolescent range somewhat tentatively have come to appear in our adult criminal courts as well. Here they have emerged in at least two forms. The idea of "pre-adjudication conciliation" has been applied unofficially in the Magistrates' Courts of New York City, though never very largely used. It has been chiefly a matter of attempting informal probation treatment of social problems and conciliatory efforts between defendants and complainants when the offense alleged was minor and/or no complaint would issue. Considerably more formalized has been the device adopted elsewhere of applying probation where certain offenses are alleged without the requirement of arraignment or of adjudication.[7] The accused party is confronted with an option not unlike that of the defendant in the adolescent courts: he may accept unofficial treatment, without however going through trial and conviction for an offense at all, or he may stand trial with the danger of conviction and possible incarceration. One would dislike to be "taken in" "on suspicion" and confronted with this choice.

These various methods of applying court treatment without a full and fair judicial trial of the issue of guilt of a particular offense, despite their seductive rationale, appear to the writer to be peculiarly hazardous and unnecessary. Though criticism of methods used in experimental courts has sometimes been attacked as "technical" and reactionary, nevertheless the techniques which develop crescively through unthoughtful adoption in our social institutions do need careful inspection to test their effectiveness and their wider consequences. Novel experimental devices must be tried to be sure, yet permanent crystallization is to be avoided of methods which are based on error or which lead to excessive in-

justice. Existing or developing institutions may be "progressive" or "reactionary" depending upon the directions of their development and their effects.

In general denial of the validity of the current procedures, the writer maintains that they resemble too closely in some respects the philosophy of the Star Chamber. For their greatest fault is in failing to give to the defendant some of the most basic protections of due process which inhere in our modern legal system. Under our constitutions and laws the defendant deserves at very least (1) a definite charge of a particular offense, (2) the right to be confronted by the witnesses from whom is derived the evidence on which he is convicted, (3) a (real) right to counsel and appeal, and (4) conviction only upon a preponderance of credible, competent, relevant evidence. (In a criminal court such evidence should, of course, be convincing beyond a reasonable doubt.) These rights are assured even in the administrative tribunals of today; their disappearance from our criminal and quasi-criminal courts should not be tolerated.

The view is expressed by some criminologists that the issue of a particular criminal act is unimportant, particularly in dealing with the young where the general objective is to accomplish preventive and rehabilitative results; that general conduct, personality, and social problems are sufficient to justify adjudication and/or treatment at this level; and that broad statutes are needed to give the necessary latitude, the free play to court discretion. The difficulties with this approach are basic: Where no specific and clear-cut offense categories are established most anyone can be adjudicated to a status carrying stigma and potentially damaging treatment by the correctional agencies of criminal and quasi-criminal courts. The

[7] See *Attorney General's Survey of Release Procedures*, Vol. II, pp. 113–115, for the development of assorted practices of this sort under the statutes of Massachusetts, Rhode Island, Kentucky, and Maine.

utmost of discretion is left in the hands of judicial and probation personnel unhampered by statutory definitions or limitations, undirected save by a very general principle of treating, reforming, rehabilitating. Unfortunately the personnel of our courts cannot be omniscient or omnicompetent. Indeed, they vary tremendously in their views on conduct, morality, treatment methods, and in their personal biases. Too they tend to, lean toward punitive and correctional treatment and, in the experimental courts, toward broadening their functions to treat all manner of social problems. The result may often be damaging when individuals innocent of any serious wrongdoing or real law violation are subject to the rather crude tools of correctional treatment such as those available to our courts. As the author has said elsewhere:

. . . the court system is not designed to deal with problems which are not directly associated with law violation. The philosophies of courts, commitment institutions and probation bureaus are preponderately correctional and punitive. Their rôles have been clearly assigned in the mind and reactions of the defendant by the stereotypes of the cop, the criminal court, the reform school, and the probation officer. Similarly the public attitude toward these institutions and the adolescents subjected to them renders it wholly unrealistic for the courts to attempt to operate as general social agencies: they bear the indelible stamp of public stigma and ostracism. *Thus the frame of reference within which the court may legitimately and effectively operate is narrowly limited by public and institutional definition.* Attempts therefore at comprehensive social work are sheer folly; the problems of domestic relations, psychological pathology, occupational maladjustments, etc. are not within the sphere of appropriate function. This is the more obviously true when no offense has been shown—haphazard manipulation by the unskilled or partially trained probation officer in areas of specialized therapy adds

misapplied treatment to the injustice of court and institutional contact. Even when an offense has been proven, far greater success in treatment could be achieved by the referral of problems requiring trained and non-correctional specialized assistance to proper public and private agencies. (Yet, the adolescent courts are far from attaining a nice integration with the varied social agencies of the city, though the fault is not wholly their own.) In addition to the inappropriateness of crimino-legal handling of general social problems, the absurdity of this trend is enhanced by the insufficiency of personnel in the courts. Where, for optimum results, they should work experimentally and intensively on a carefully selected sample of favorable probation risks to insure creative individualization and reformation, the expansive drive in some courts toward problem-solving for all-comers has resulted in attenuated, inexact, and ineffectual service. The proper sphere of social agencies and behavior clinics should not be usurped by the courts, however benevolent the motivation. It appears clear that the work of crime prevention must be performed, if at all, *before* court contact and by non-court agencies. *The personnel of correctional court and institution is not equipped to do a noncorrectional job.*[8]

Within the present limitations of our knowledge in the fields of psychology, sociology, and biology, our guesses must be quite tentative concerning treatment methods. Nevertheless we can and should use the training of specialists in these fields to recommend and apply therapy to the unadjusted who go through our courts. It is a different matter entirely, however, to attempt to apply these still-infantile sciences through non-specialists, who make up our court personnel for the most part, to determine on the basis of personality or total situation whom the court should adjudicate, whom it should treat. The idea that the function of law is

[8] Paul W. Tappan, *The Adolescent in Court* (1946).

to provide officials with convenient and general tools by which they may convict and treat those known to be criminals, or believed to require treatment, is a very cynical notion. Held by a few officials of our criminal courts, it is even more out of place at the children's or adolescents' level. The best and safest criterion justifying court action is the commission of an act in violation of a rule of law specifically defining the conduct to be avoided. Such a criminal act expresses—as no vague standard of recalcitrance or "moral depravity" can—a clear, definite, and relevant foundation for court action. It may well be argued that the offense categories should be increased to include specific forms of misconduct appearing in youth which, if untreated, would lead into crime of a more serious nature. If so, these must come into legal definition and delimitation so as to avoid the injustices flowing from an uninstructed judicial latitude. The present law and practice encourage abuse by the generality and variability of principles applied. The result is that these experimental courts appear either to operate on a presumption of guilt or to assume guilt to be irrelevant. A most progressive step, then, for the courts desiring to deal as effectively as possible with the young would be the clear statutory enunciation of the conduct-categories to be tabooed. This would mean that adjudication should occur only if and when such conduct is clearly shown by legitimate evidence.

Closely associated with the problem of the general statutes and free discretion which now obtain in these courts is the method so widely use of holding pre-adjudication investigations with reports to the court at the hearing. If adjudication of the offender status should be based—as the author has maintained—on proof of guilt of a particular offense, there is no sound reason for requiring an investigation until after the hearing—and then, of course, only for those cases which are adjudicated. This more traditional procedure would provide at least three distinct advantages over the present method:

1. It would save from court correctional devices those cases which do not merit adjudication legally, cases which are now treated with inappropriate methods due to the expansionist drives within these tribunals toward general social problem-solving.

2. It would make unnecessary the use of parole and remand during rather extended periods of social investigation when no hearing has been held. It is certainly impossible in good law or sound sense to assume a defendant to be guilty of an unproven charge or to justify his treatment without trial during an interim disposition. Errors can be and frequently are made in these courts, as in adult criminal courts, through arrests of and complaints against innocent parties. Too, often when the complaint is made by parents, the fault and problem lies with them not their child; in these cases to impose institutional remands or to adjudicate, as we often do, and apply treatment that is at least partially correctional, punitive, and non-specialized does unnecessary injustice.

3. It would result in a considerably more efficient utilization of the all-too-limited probation resources available in these courts. Under the suggested procedure numerous investigations would not be required: the time thus saved could be devoted to the more creative and rehabilitative work of supervision in cases that had been carefully selected by legal process for social treatment. To reiterate, social investigations should be made *after* adjudication in order that the court may apply therapy as

nicely adjusted to the individual requirements of the cases as possible. To be sure, the suggested change in procedure would require that more witnesses be used at hearings to determine the relevant facts and adjudication would be made more difficult. However, difficulty in eliciting proof of specific offenses is no justification for holding as offenders all who are brought into court. Rather, the elimination of many who do not deserve adjudication could be a great positive gain in preventing that development of delinquencies which occurs so often among the young who have been exposed to the correctional facilities of our courts.

Since the adoption in our adolescent courts of the procedures referred to has been rationalized by their prior institutionalization at the children's court level, it is significant to note that these devices have come under serious criticism by the judiciary of that children's court system. Chief Justice W. B. Cobb of the Domestic Relations Court in New York City has recently attacked with vehemence the unofficial treatment of the adjustment bureau, the use of prehearing investigations for purposes of adjudication, and extended remands without a hearing. He condemns them as legally and socially invalid.[9] The reasoning which denounces them must apply as vigorously in the adolescent and adult courts where mild misconduct or complete innocence may lead today to criminal court treatment.

In conclusion it should be noted that our system of law as it is constituted

[9] W. Bruce Cobb, Address delivered on February 6, 1945 before a Joint Meeting of the Committees of the Court of Domestic Relations, of the Association of the Bar, and the County Lawyers Association.

today and within its appropriate methods of application does permit of full and sound individualization of treatment based on the findings and theories of the social sciences. Just treatment of the alleged offender requires this sort of processing. (1) The charge of a specific, statutorily defined offense. (2) A hearing of the issue at the earliest meeting of the court at which witnesses may be summoned with full protection of the defendant's rights of due process (including an attorney, relevant and competent testimony in his presence, adjudication only on convincing proof, and appeal). (3) Where court contact with a case indicates that the individual is not guilty of an offense but does require treatment, he should be referred to those public or private social agencies which may deal in a specialized way with his problem, thereby assuring most effective treatment without stigma. Much of this could be done at Intake. (Indeed, one of the most useful functions of these specialized tribunals could well be to act as agencies of referral to more specialized social facilities in order that individual and community problems may be met more effectively.) (4) A probation investigation into the background of the adjudicated offender to determine on the basis of his prior history, conduct, and character what methods of therapy may best be applied to re-condition him and protect society. (5) In the case of adjudicated offenders after receipt of the probation report and any other information available which is relevant to disposition, the court should dispose of the case with careful attention to adjusting treatment methods to the needs of the case, avoiding institutionalization wherever possible.

32.

What is Probation?

Lewis Diana

SUMMARY OF HISTORICAL DEVELOPMENT OF PROBATION

Some authorities trace the roots of probation to the middle ages when such devices as the benefit of clergy and the law of sanctuary made it possible either to avoid or at least to postpone punishment.[1] It is more likely that there was not any continuous linear development of probation, although one can point to various forerunners such as the judicial reprieve, by which the court suspended the imposition or execution of a sentence, and the practice of releasing an offender on his own recognizance. Consequently, probation was probably more directly an outgrowth of the different methods in England and America for suspending sentence.

Under the common law the courts of England had for many years bound over petty offenders to sureties or released them on their own recognizance even without sureties.[2] Such practices were also common in some of the American colonies, especially Massa-

chusetts, which in 1836 recognized by law the releasing of minor offenders with sureties. In 1869 this same state also authorized the placement, after investigation, of youthful offenders in private homes under the supervision of an agent of the state.

Credit for the first use of the term probation goes to John Augustus, a Boston shoemaker, who apparently became interested in befriending violators of the law, bailed many of them out of jail, and provided them with sympathetic supervision. This was as early as 1841. It was not until 1878, however, that the first probation law was passed, Massachusetts again taking the lead. In that year the mayor of Boston was given the power to appoint probation officers, and only two years later, in 1880, the law was extended to apply to other communities within the state. Then in 1891 Massachusetts passed a second law, which required the extension of probation to the criminal courts. By 1900, though, only five states— Massachusetts, Missouri, Rhode Island, New Jersey, and Vermont—recognized probation legally.[3] By 1933 all states

[1] Halpern, "Probation," *Encyclopedia of Criminology* 388 (Philosophical Library, New York, 1949).

[2] United Nations, Department of Social Affairs, *Probation and Related Measures* 16 (1951).

[3] Barnes and Teeters, *New Horizons in Criminology* 760 (2d ed., Prentice-Hall, New York, 1955).

SOURCE. Lewis Diana, "What Is Probation?", from *Journal of Criminal Law, Criminology and Police Science*, Volume 51, July-August 1960, pp. 189–204, Copyright © 1960, The Williams and Wilkins Company, Baltimore, Maryland.

except Wyoming had juvenile probation laws, and all but thirteen states had adult probation laws. This latter group had been cut to five states by 1950: Mississippi, Nevada, New Mexico, Oklahoma, and South Dakota.[4]

The variety of legislation governing probation in the United States may have stemmed (1) from the Supreme Court's denial in the *Killits* case that there existed any inherent judicial power to suspend sentence or any other process in the administration of the criminal code and (2) from the different points of view which developed concerning the practice of probation. The result, in the United States at any rate, has been to give to the courts a fairly wide discretion in the use of probation.

It remains to be said that with the creation of the Cook County Juvenile Court in 1899, probation as a principle and as a practice received great momentum. Great hopes have since been pinned upon it.

DEFINITIONS OF PROBATION

Probation as a Legal Disposition Only

One point of view sees probation simply as a suspension of sentence by the court. Since sentence is not imposed, the offender remains in the community until the length of the sentence has expired, unless, of course, in the meantime he has engaged in any conduct that would warrant carrying out the sentence. This system leaves everything to the probationer and makes of probation a simple policing procedure. Therefore, it implies two things to the probationer: another chance, and the threat of punishment should he fail to improve his behavior.

In point of time this view has been expressed by authors, mostly with a legal background, writing in the first

[4] *Ibid.*

decade of the twentieth century. I have found no references to it after 1908 when Judge McKenzie Cleland put it this way: probation is a plan "of suspending over offenders the maximum sentence permitted by law" and of allowing them "to determine by their subsequent conduct whether they should lose or retain their liberty . . . with the full knowledge that further delinquency meant . . . severe punishment."[5]

Probation as a Measure of Leniency

In a review of the literature I found but one author who took this approach to probation.[6] However, it probably best represents the general lay point of view, as well as that of most probationers. This fact presents a basic problem to professional personnel, who view probation as a form of treatment. Many offenders, however, especially among juveniles, feel their acts are unfortunate slips, and while possibly inexplicable, they are, in the final analysis, choices between right and wrong, choices which the offenders feel capable of controlling. Consequently, in their own minds they are not sick persons or necessarily even the products of undesirable environments and so certainly in no need of treatment.

Probation as a Punitive Measure

This again represents a view which has found little acceptance in the literature, especially during the last fifty years. I discovered only one writer who made punishment the *dominant* note in his theory of probation. According to Almy, probation must be presented to the probationer as a form of punishment, one which permits him to escape

[5] Cleland, "New Gospel in Criminology; Municipal Court of Chicago," 31 *McClure's* 358–362 (June 1908).
[6] Smith, A. C., "Does Probation Aid or Prevent Crime?," 125 *Annals* 242 (1926).

commitment and its stigma but one which also makes other demands. If these demands are not met, then the probationer can expect to receive the same type of punishment as other offenders.[7] The assumption underlying such a view is that it is the certainty of punishment which deters.

Probation as an Administrative Process

It is likely that the earlier ideas of reform and rehabilitation attached to probation came about as a reaction to the various abuses associated with the imprisonment of children. As a result, a great deal of sentiment was tied to the concept of probation in its beginnings. This sentiment, together with the goal of reform or rehabilitation, formed the nucleus of the conception of probation as an administrative process. Essentially what probation consists of under this conception is the execution of concrete measures aimed at helping the offender stay out of further trouble. The ultimate goal of complete rehabilitation in this approach, however, was something which was more hoped for than worked for. In this respect it is a fairly negative approach consisting mainly of things done for the offender in the *hope* that they will *somehow* deter him from a further career in crime. Thus, arranging for medical treatment, making appointments for the administration of tests, effecting school transfers, seeking employment for the offender, checking on his activities, and so on constitute the major content of probation under this viewpoint.

Slightly more than thirty per cent of the authors writing in this field have seen the administrative process as the major framework of probation.[8] Most of these, however, date from 1902 to 1920. Since 1935, only two writers have espoused this concept. This fact may indicate the close identification of the correctional field with social work, which was largely administrative in the earlier years. Later, changing concepts and techniques in social work quickly found their way into child welfare and juvenile court probation services. The newer approaches represented by casework and its psychoanalytic foundations have not found unanimous approval, however.

Thus, Dr. Philipp Parsons of the Department of Sociology, University of Oregon, has stated:

In the rehabilitation field . . . research and administration become the all important factors. Research consists in getting the facts of a given situation, and administration consists in devising programs adapted to the facts and in carrying out these programs by whatever techniques the conditions may make practical. . . .

. . . changing conditions, economic, political, and social, have shifted the major emphasis in remedial work from individuals and families to groups and conditions. Training for remedial work, therefore, must be built upon a base of research, organization, and administration rather than upon the case work which was the foundation of social work training in the past generation.

. . . rehabilitating convicted persons in connection with a scientific system of penology . . . is primarily an administrative job and also primarily a job for men.[9]

The process of probation which follows an administrative pattern is illustrated in an article by Jessie Keys. Writing in *World's Work* in 1909, Miss Keys stated that the search for ultimate causes is not the least important work

[7] Almy, "Probation as Punishment," 24 *Survey* 657 (1910).
[8] All of the available literature since 1900 has been reviewed.

[9] Parsons, P. A., "Qualifying Workers for the Correctional Field," *Yearbook, Nat'l Probation and Parole Ass'n* 66–86 (1938).

of the juvenile court. These causes were usually felt to be parental neglect or parental vice or both. To illustrate she cited the case of a boy who had a mania for stealing pocket knives:

His father and paternal grandfather had been master mechanics. After his father died his mother led an irregular life and neglected the boy. His hereditary instincts came to the surface. Since his mother refused to help him gratify his desire for mechanics, he undertook to gratify it in any way he could.[10]

Unlike modern casework, no attempt was made during the boy's probation to help him "verbalize" and express his feelings and so come to a personal solution based on the untapped resources of his deeper personality. Instead: "We went to his mother and she awoke to her responsibility. We talked to the boy firmly and found him willing to work. Finally, we found a position for him."[11]

The probation process not only included finding work for the boy but also included telling the mother how to keep her house clean and giving her other directives. It literally forced the boy into a certain mold, by the use of pressure, and sometimes intimidation, to do what he was told was right. Thus the probation officer attempted to produce what was not ordinarily a part of the boy's pattern of behavior.

In 1910 Maude E. Miner, Secretary of the New York Probation Association, reported that probation for the convicted girl consisted of a process of character building through discipline and correction. These were applied by obtaining employment for the girl, visiting her home, getting the cooperation of her parents, providing needed medical care, and bringing her into contact with beneficial influences such as churches and clubs.[12]

In 1911 the Illinois law on adult probation provided that certain categories of first offenders could be placed on probation. The court was obliged to impose certain conditions designed both to protect the community and to give the probationers some "sensible practical aid." These conditions included paying court costs, supplying bond, supporting dependents, and making regular reports to the probation officer.[13] Obviously, under such circumstances probation could be little else than administrative.

From a figure well known in corrections, C. L. Chute:

The probation officer must investigate all offenders and must keep himself informed concerning their conduct and condition. He must report on each case at least once every month to the court and must use all suitable methods not inconsistent with the conditions imposed by the court, to aid persons on probation and to bring about improvement in their conduct and condition.[14]

Or:

The probation officer helps a man to get and keep a job, finds him wholesome amusement, looks after his leisure hours and generally backs him up to playing a man's part in the world much as the special war agencies kept up the morale of the army.[15]

The supposed therapeutic effects of administrative techniques are illustrated in an article by Platt:

[10] Keys, "Cases of the Children's Court," 18 *World's Work* 11612 (1909).
[11] *Ibid.*

[12] Miner, "Probation Work for Women," 36 *Annals* 27 (1910).
[13] "New Illinois Law on Adult Probation," 26 *Survey* 18 (1911).
[14] Chute, "Probation a Federal Need," 43 *Survey* 775 (1920).
[15] "Emptying the Jails: Probation System in New York City," 100 *The Independent* 40 (1919).

Get a boy into a good club, give him duties and see what happens—interest, pride, loyalty, ambition, cooperation, social teamwork, social sense, all will probably soon follow.[16]

In 1919 no less an authority than the sub-committee of the National Conference of Social Work summed up this point of view by reporting that the office of the probation officer is administrative. It may have its authority beyond the court but accountability to the court is, in the final analysis, the foundation of probation service.[17]

Probation as Social Casework Treatment

Reinemann has defined probation as follows:

Legally, in the case of an adult offender, probation is the suspension of sentence during a period of freedom, on condition of good behavior. In the case of a delinquent child, the juvenile court uses probation as a form of *case disposition* which allows the child to live at liberty in his own home or in the custody of a suitable person, be it a relative, a friend of the family, or a foster home, under supervision of an agent of the court and upon such conditions as the court determines. *Socially, probation is a form of treatment* administered by probation officers on a case work basis."[18] (Emphasis added.)

The dichotomy between adult and juvenile probation seemingly is disappearing. In any event definitions of probation as a legal disposition are rarely found in current literature. On the contrary, the bulk of the literature —between eighty-five and ninety per cent of it since 1940—views probation

as some form of treatment, more often than not as casework treatment.

Casework and its foster parent, psychiatry, have had extensive influence in the juvenile court movement. This influence is illustrated by the broad scope of many of our juvenile court laws, by the shunting aside, in the rising tide of a clinical ideology, of legal precedents in favor of loose and informal procedures, by the indeterminate sentence, by the emphasis on the total situation of an offender, by the absorption with emotional problems, and by the prevailing adherence to a psychoanalytic theory of causation.

The point of view which identifies probation with casework treatment is difficult to analyze. It cannot be presented as a consistent or well-defined approach and appears, rather, to represent an attitude or state of mind in lieu of a technique or substantive theory. In any event the literature presenting probation as casework treatment generally defines probation as the *application* of casework principles and techniques in dealing with the offender. But what is casework?

Taber describes it this way:

Case work . . . may be defined as a process of attempting to understand the needs, impulses and actions of an individual and of helping him to recognize these in a way that is satisfying to himself and yet in accord with the demands of social living.

. . . treatment cannot be forced upon another person . . . . To help another person we must accept him as he is with an honest respect for his capacity as well as regard for his need to solve his own problem with whatever help the worker can give him. The case worker is concerned with assisting the individual to realize his own capacities to the fullest extent, as well as to orient him to the resources existing within his environment which will provide a satisfying outlet. In short, change

[16] Platt, "Does Punishment Pay?," 55 *Survey* 605–607 (1926).
[17] Parsons, H. C., "Probation and Parole; Report of the Sub-Committee," *Nat'l Conference of Social Work* 113 (1919).
[18] Reinemann, "Probation and the Juvenile Delinquent," 261 *Annals* 109 (1949).

to be·effective depends upon the individual's willingness to help himself. . . . He must be assisted in finding his own way at his own pace. . . .

Every phase of behavior has a different meaning for each individual, and treatment if it is to be effective must be differentiated according to the individual's need. . . . There are no formulas which we can readily apply . . . but we can sharply define in a warm but objective manner the alternatives which confront a delinquent in order that he may redirect his behavior if he has the strength and will to do so.[19]

Most concepts of casework also include assumptions concerning the nature and causes of delinquent behavior:

Delinquent behavior and other forms of conflict are generally compensating substitutes for experiences and impulses which the individual fears to recognize and dares not express. The tension resulting creates frustration and fear. Whether or not the release takes the form of a criminal act is purely fortuitous and is dependent upon the attitudes and tensions operating at the time. . . .

If we accept the fact that the probation officer's work concerns itself with helping the man under supervision to bring to conscious expression his underlying emotional conflicts and thus rid those deep-seated unknown drives of their tension and potency, and if we recognize that the probationer's moral decisions must be his own, not the probation officer's, then is the generic problem of interpretation with which the probation officer is faced any different from that which must be met by the case worker?[20]

Miss Genevieve Gabower, formerly Director of Social Work in the Juvenile Court, Washington, D. C., refers to casework in this way:

The worker sees a need for giving service in the case of a child where either the solicitude or the indifference of the parents, or a combination of extremes of the two operates as a barrier to his growth and development. He can be of service by developing and maintaining a relationship of continuing interest and acceptance and thus assisting in establishing stability. Case work . . . through this kind of relationship . . . may operate as a medium through which the youth can find that he has ability to conform to community standards.[21]

In other words, from Miss Gabower's point of view, the relationship which by some is described *as* casework is here presented only as an instrument of casework. But what casework is, is still not explained.

One thing is certain, however: the casework point of view represents a shift in emphasis from the social conditions of behavior to individual behavior itself, especially such behavior as can be approached from the standpoint of the "dynamics" of psychoanalytic mechanisms. The shift has been from a social to a clinical frame of reference. Crime and delinquency are acts containing social implications, but it is chiefly the individual personality which interests the caseworker. Thus, Miss Louise McGuire, also one-time Director of Social Work in the Juvenile Court, Washington, D. C., states: "Back of the overt acts are the motives. These latter are our concern and the basis of case work treatment."[22]

Miss McGuire's article represents an attempt to delineate casework into three phases: (1) social inquiry into the total situation of the client; (2)

[19] Taber, "The Value of Casework to the Probationer," *Yearbook, Nat'l Probation and Parole Ass'n* 167–179 (1940).

[20] Reeves, "Administrative Procedures and Case Work Services," *Yearbook, Nat'l Probation and Parole Ass'n* 180–192 (1940).

[21] Gabower, "Motivating the Delinquent to Accept Treatment," *Yearbook, Nat'l Probation and Parole Ass'n* 207–219 (1940).

[22] McGuire, "Essentials of Case Work with Delinquents," *Yearbook, Nat'l Probation and Parole Ass'n* (1935).

social diagnosis, that is, inquiry into the relationships and attitudes of the client; and (3) social casework treatment. In this last phase there are three objectives: (1) to induce right notions of conduct (responsible behavior) in the client; (2) to induce motives which will assure loyalty to good norms of conduct; and (3) to develop the client's latent abilities.

To achieve these objectives casework treatment is divided into two sections: mechanistic devices and deep therapy. The former consist in the utilization of the resources of community agencies. The latter, deep therapy, refers to the process of changing the attitudes of the probationer, giving him insight through interpretation.[23]

This essentially clinical approach is supported by most other writers outside the academic disciplines of criminology and sociology. Hagerty, for example, has said, "We offer as our major premise that solution of the crime problem involves chiefly the study and personality treatment of the individual offender."[24] He goes on to define casework as an aid in the restoration of self-support and self-respect in the "client."

More recently Hyman S. Lippman, Director of the Amherst H. Wilder Child Guidance Clinic, St. Paul, Minnesota, has declared that casework on the part of the probation officer is the essential ingredient in his "treatment" of delinquency.[25] While not defining casework, Lippman does specify *relationship* as the major contribution of a probation officer and the interview as his main tool. The unconscious conflicts

of the neurotic delinquent of course, "are deeply imbedded, and can *only* be brought to light by the psychiatrist trained in psychoanalytic techniques."[26] (Emphasis added.)

David Crystal, Executive Director, Jewish Social Service Bureau Rochester, N. Y., sees probation as a treatment process of the entire family. But the process is curiously enough still described in clinical terms as the focus of casework is:

1. How does the probation officer help the probationer accept the conditions of his current reality?

2. How does and can the family relate to the probationer in terms of the new experience?

(*a*) Can they express honestly their feelings of guilt, of anticipated reprisal, of uncertainty about the impact this will have on their future lives?

(*b*) Will they require special help from a worker other than the probation officer, in a different kind of agency in the community? Can they now or later accept the need for help?

(*c*) Is the total responsibility for change to be lodged exclusively on the offender, or can the family see change as a reaction not to one but multiple causes and that they too are part of the change, externally and internally, by their physical presence and concrete offering of shelter and food and job and by the attitude with which these visible and tangible things about the family are given?[27]

Henry J. Palmieri, Director of Social Services of the Juvenile Court of the District of Columbia, declares probation is a casework service and a method of treatment which "is no longer an ideal" but "a reality."[28] However, he defines neither casework nor treatment but assumes their identity with probation.

---

23 *Ibid.*
24 Hagerty, "The Delinquent as a Case Problem," *Yearbook, Nat'l Probation and Parole Ass'n* (1935).
25 Lippman, "The Role of the Probation Officer in the Treatment of Delinquency in Children," 12 *Federal Probation* 36 (1948).

26 *Id.* at 37.
27 Crystal, "Family Casework in Probation," 13 *Federal Probation* 47–53 (1949).
28 Palmieri, "Probation Is Treatment," 13 *Federal Probation* 20 (1949).

Glover outlines four basic principles of treatment without, however, specifying how they are effected: (1) treatment based on consent of the offender; (2) treatment planned for the individual; (3) treatment planned around the offender's own situation; and (4) treatment planned to redirect the offender's emotions.[29]

The strong clinical orientation of casework seeking to induce proper motives, to aid in the achievement of insight and self-respect, and to change attitudes of the offender may be worthwhile and desirable. But the aims and the orientation do not define the process of casework. *How* is insight produced? *How* are interpretations given? *How* are attitudes changed? *How* is relationship established? The answers to these questions are rarely mentioned in the literature, and casework continues to be defined in broad and general terms as, for example, "an art in which knowledge of the science of human relations and skill in relationship are used to mobilize capacities in the individual and resources in the community appropriate for better adjustment between the client and all or any part of his total environment."[30]

One of the most recent and well-known texts defines casework as follows: "Social casework is a process used by certain human welfare agencies to help individuals to cope more effectively with their problems in social functioning."[31]

The elements, then, which are said to comprise the principles of casework invariably stamp it as a clinical process for the most part. It is often stated, for example, that casework implies that the probation officer has a respect for individual differences and that he should have not only a natural desire to serve others but also an understanding of the processes that develop personalities. The probation officer *accepts* and the client then may show "movement" because for the first time he is seen able to talk freely and naturally to another person about himself and how he feels. The worker understands and conveys that understanding to the "client," thereby relieving the "client's" anxieties and stimulating a more constructive outlook.

Biestek explains a casework relationship on the basis of seven needs of the client. "The caseworker is *sensitive* to, *understands,* and appropriately *responds* to these needs" and "the client is somehow *aware* of the caseworker's sensitivity, understanding, and response."[32] The seven needs of the client embody corresponding principles:[33]

The need of the client	The name of the principle
1. To be treated as an individual.	1. Individualization.
2. To express feelings.	2. Purposeful expression of feelings.
3. To get sympathetic response to problems.	3. Controlled emotional involvement.
4. To be recognized as a person of worth.	4. Acceptance.
5. Not to be judged.	5. Nonjudgmental attitude.
6. To make his own choices and decisions.	6. Client self-determination.
7. To keep secrets about self.	7. Confidentiality.

[29] Glover, "Probation: The Art of Introducing the Probationer to a Better Way of Life," 15 *Federal Probation* 8 (1951).

[30] Bowers, "The Nature and Definition of Social Casework: Part III," 30 *J. Soc. Casework* 417 (1949).

[31] Perlman, *Social Casework, A Problem-Solving Process* (Chicago, University of Chicago Press, 1957).

[32] Biestek, *The Casework Relationship* 17 (Chicago, Loyola University Press, 1957).

[33] Reproduced from Biestek, *op. cit. supra* note 32, at 17.

Casework thus attempts to formalize, standardize, and professionalize the display and exercise of warmth, sympathy, respect, and understanding, all of which are considered to be basic elements in therapeutic treatment of the individual. In probation, also, any punitive quality in the process has been removed, and the goal has become not merely the elimination of the probationer's anti-social conduct but, whenever possible, the improvement of his personality and the achievement of a more nearly perfect total adjustment. What probation is, therefore, must include the means by which those goals are realized. This casework usually does by simply stating casework *as* the means or process. There have been attempts at clarification, but the field defies synthesis.

Miss Witmer has pointed out that:

. . . social work is a very specific system of organized activities based on a body of values and technical rules which are becoming increasingly well-formulated. . . . it has a definite function to perform. It is not a vague, indeterminate method of doing good or promoting welfare, or even of helping people out of trouble, indistinguishable from psychiatry at one end and uplift work at the other. . . .

. . . social case work centers around helping individuals with the difficulties they encounter in a particular group relationship. . . .[34]

Miss Witmer also suggests that while probation presently involves the use of casework, it is mainly executive and diagnostic, centering on changes in the environment of the offender. Such casework "lacks the sharpness of focus and precision of method which perception of specific function has given to case work in other fields."[35] But in my ex-

perience, at least, this "sharpness of focus and precision of method" of casework in other fields is more an attribute of casework in the literature than of casework in the field. What is specific and precise in any other agency is not mentioned. It appears that it is the field or area of operation of these other agencies that is more or less precise and not necessarily their techniques.

Miss Witmer denies the similarity of casework and psychiatry or therapy but nevertheless states its aims in therapeutic terms: "Modern case work works with the client rather than on his behalf" since the sources of difficulty are supposedly known only to the "client."[36] However, the caseworker assumes the existence of underlying or unconscious conflicts and so is practically committed to a psychotherapeutic point of view. Where this is denied, superficial distinctions are usually drawn between casework and therapy, such as the fact that in therapy it is the "client" himself who seeks the therapist, or that in therapy one delves more deeply into the unconscious and there is a more intense emotional involvement of "client" and therapist. There is convincing evidence, however, that points to the emergence of casework, and certainly of psychiatric social work, as another therapeutic profession.

The dominant theoretical note in casework is sounded by psychoanalysis. Acceptance of a psychoanalytic view will, of course, influence notions of what makes a criminal a criminal or a delinquent a delinquent. The major assumptions fall back on the emotional problems of the individual offender; consequently, illegal behavior is seen primarily as a symptom of an emotional illness, and the offense itself is not considered to be very important, especially in delinquency. Parallel with this as-

[34] Witmer, "Social Case Work in the Field of Juvenile Probation," *Yearbook, Nat'l Probation and Parole Ass'n* 153–166 (1941).
[35] *Ibid.*

[36] *Ibid.*

sumption, which is accepted by many caseworkers as a sound and accurate summary of the facts, is the habit of looking for emotional problems in all cases before the court. This ignores the real possibility that many of the problems of offenders arise from the hazards common to all people in learning to live with themselves and others. Also, to most people, appearing before a court of law is a new experience. When a person has not had time to cope with such a new situation, it is conceivable that he may present the appearance of maladjustment. In any event, life is such that most, if not all, people have emotional and other problems, and whether or not they are offenders, they generally adjust without services based on any nebulous clinical ideology.

Casework must be numbered among the victims of much of the epidemic dogma and naïveté that is psychoanalysis. Too many correctional workers have become dizzy on a diluted psychoanalytic approach. They allow its glib and fanciful formulations to explain difficult problems. It is all neatly done, since little thought and no proof are necessary. Ready-made proof exists: whatever the problem, it is the result of emotional conflicts originating in the oral, anal, phallic, and other erotic stages of development, and the dynamic interplay of id, ego, and superego. The criminal and the delinquent, too, as each and all of us, end up as the appendage to the penis. It is the tail that twirls the tiger.

As matters now stand the probation officer or caseworker grounded in a psychoanalytic approach tends to look at a case through the lenses of his "trained" preconceptions of the client's emotional life. He is likely, therefore, to ignore the group processes from which that emotional life is nourished. Obeisance and abject devotion to the illusory and presumptuous claim of psychoanalytic theory to absolute knowledge of the dynamics of human behavior may lead to a great deal of dialectical ingenuity but not to much progress in the treatment of the problem of crime and delinquency.

In conclusion, probation as casework concentrates not so much on crime and delinquency as on criminals and delinquents, and not so much on criminals and delinquents as on criminals and delinquents with emotional problems. In general, as Sutherland has pointed out,[37] casework in probation follows psychiatric conceptions in that insight by the probationer into the reasons for his behavior is the chief goal of treatment. A person with such insight is felt to be unlikely to repeat his delinquent activities. The primary method consists of intensive interviews through which the probation officer not only comes to understand the probationer but the probationer, to understand himself. An identification with the probation officer then helps the offender emulate his behavior until finally the point is reached where the probationer becomes independent of this identification and can carry on normal and socially acceptable behavior on his own.

Probation as a Combination of Casework and Administration

This point of view regarding probation does not, as it might suggest, constitute a catch-all for those approaches which do not fit the categories discussed thus far. From this standpoint probation is represented both by casework functions and by administrative or executive procedures. Where casework is paramount, administrative functions are supplementary. Where administrative duties are indicated as the primary plan of approach, casework skills and tech-

[37] Sutherland, *Principles of Criminology,* 399–400 (Philadelphia, J. B. Lippincott Co., 4th ed., 1947).

niques, however defined, must be utilized in the performance of those duties. In other words, some cases may be felt to require intensive interviews more than anything else. But in the course of most cases there are, practically without exception, other things to be done as well: arranging a transfer of schools, scheduling medical and other appointments, and so on. Other cases may be felt to call for mainly administrative functions, such as those just mentioned, plus limited and superficial contacts with the probationers. But in performing those functions and in making those contacts, a casework approach must be applied. In this respect the utilization of casework techniques is usually manifested in the attitude taken toward the probationer.

Murphy illustrates this school of thought:

> Probation officers have another task, that of controlling, guiding and rehabilitating probationers. Here they are called upon to make accurate personality diagnoses and plan comprehensively to improve the probationers' environment and economic life, to adjust delicate family problems, find employment, provide for necessary medical treatment and health assistance, determine recreational needs and social needs, stimulate spiritual and moral improvement. . . . Patterns of behavior can be changed only when attitudes, loyalties and group relationships can be altered or recreated.[38]

In summary, then, this point of view sees probation as the simultaneous application of casework and administrative functions, but in specific cases it is more one than the other. Whichever is paramount in any particular case, the other is complementary. About twenty per cent of the literature reviewed supports this approach to probation.

[38] Murphy, "Training For and On the Job," *Yearbook, Nat'l Probation and Parole Ass'n* 93–108 (1938).

WHAT IS PROBATION?

With the exception of the first three categories (legal, punitive, merciful), all views emphasize the treatment aspects of probation. In the literature reviewed only five per cent of the writers thought of probation wholly as a legal disposition or as a measure of either punishment or leniency. In fact, in the literature of the past thirty years such views receive no mention at all. Therefore, notions of probation as either casework or administration, or a combination of the two, are prominent. These leading approaches overlap considerably so that their differentiation consists almost solely in their respective points of emphasis. Thus, all three would agree that probation is a legal disposition and that probation is not to be thought of as mere leniency or as mere punishment; but in the first instance, it is viewed as basically casework treatment; in the second, administrative supervision; and in the third, both of these. Each, however, contains elements of the other. So in all cases probation is seen as a social as well as a legal process, as a method of supervision and guidance in which all available community resources are used, and as a process which should aim at the total adjustment of the offender. The casework approach overshadows the rest by far, so that in phrasing a composite definition derived from the literature it should receive its obvious prominence.

As culled from the professional literature, then, probation may be thought of as the application of modern, scientific casework to specially selected offenders[39] who are placed by the courts

[39] It is standard practice to accept for probation only those offenders whose cases have been investigated and found to meet the requirements of favorable prognosis set up by the individual courts. Therefore, offenders placed on probation may be thought of as specially selected.

under the personal supervision of a probation officer, sometimes under conditional suspension of punishment, and given treatment aimed at their complete and permanent social rehabilitation.

Probation in Reality

What is depicted in the literature does not often represent a very real or accurate representation of what exists in reality. The result of abject worship at the holy shrine of psychoanalysis has not been the development of scientifically validated techniques for the treatment of offenders on probation.[40] In fact, few probation officers, either in the literature or in the field, give a clear and specific description of what they mean by treatment, casework or otherwise. Probation officers, whether trained in schools of social work or not, frequently express the opinion that just about anything that is done in the way of investigation of cases, bringing into play any of the skills one may have acquired in training or by his experiences, comes under the heading of casework treatment. This would include any service, advice, counseling, or surveillance.

Undoubtedly part of the difficulty lies in the fact that the field of social work seems to have no well-defined and consistent theory which it can call its own. Casework can mean anything from "working with an offender" to helping a "client" to "grow" or to achieve insight, helping him to help himself, a form of therapy, or a "method which recognizes the individual's inner capacity as to the key to his adjustment, and the necessity of his participating in the process of rehabilitation."[41]

How these things are accomplished, however, is rarely specified except in terms of an *administrative* process. So the probation officer will be told, ideally, that he must have a plan of treatment, that his attitude toward the offender must be non-punitive, and that he will try to "win the confidence" of the probationer and overcome the resistance of parents, or of husband or wife, as the case may be. The constructive kind of relationship that the probation officer thus aims for apparently is to be gained through frequent and periodic contacts at the office of the probation officer or at the offender's home or even school, in the case of a juvenile. In addition, the probation officer will be acquainted with most, if not all, of the resources of the community and will hold frequent conferences with the offender's employer, school principal, teacher, or school social worker and refer the offender to any one of a number of other agencies which might help him on his road to readjustment.

It is interesting, then, to compare such a description of probation as casework treatment with what probation officers actually do. At the Juvenile Court of Allegheny County in Pittsburgh, Pennsylvania, it was found that more than half the probation officers did active work with only thirty to forty per cent of their caseload. Even if telephone conversations and correspondence with an offender, members of his family, and others are counted as contacts, sixty-four per cent of the staff had fewer than six contacts with a child over a period of one year.[42] As a matter of fact more than half the probation officers considered that the most important part of their work consisted of their contacts with a child and others during the investigation period prior to the hearing.

40 See Cressey," The Nature and Effectiveness of Correctional Techniques, 23 *Law & Contemp. Prob.* 754-771 (1958).
41 Taber, *op. cit. supra* note 19.

42 All the figures and information in this section were obtained from the Juvenile Court, Pittsburgh, Pa., in 1951, when the author was a probation officer of the court.

Half of the probation officers reported they did no planning on *any* of their cases, one-fourth indicated that they approached from five to ten per cent of their caseload with a plan in mind, and the remaining fourth said this was true in forty to fifty per cent of their cases. Thirty-five per cent of the probation staff felt that many of the children under their supervision at any one time could probably get along *without any* probation service at all, and ninety-five per cent felt that some of the children under their supervision could adjust without it.

Analysis of a sample of 540 probation records for this court (up to 1951) showed that the total number of personal contacts with each probationer averaged less than five in an average probation period of sixteen and one-half months. In other words, each probationer generally got to see his probation officer about once every three months. Only six per cent received more than five visits at home during the probation period, and nearly eighty-four per cent received only *one* home visit. Similarly, seventy-eight per cent of the probationers had but one interview in the probation office during the average probation period of sixteen and one-half months. Yet the number of delinquents on probation who later became criminals was less among those who had the *fewest* contacts with their probation officers. Since the majority of the delinquents received a minimum of attention while they were on probation and yet did not later become criminals (as of ten years later), this apparent adjustment must be attributed to factors other than treatment received on probation.

Supervision in seventy-six percent of the cases consisted *entirely* of routine reporting, and only ten per cent of the cases were handled with a definite plan of treatment. How it could be other-

wise would be difficult to conceive after a glance at the duties of the probation officers of this court (Table 1).

The duties outlined in Table 1 take, on an average, from three and one-half to four and one-half days of a five-day week. The time remaining *may* then be devoted to supervising offenders placed on probation, i.e., checking on their activities either by conducting personal interviews or by having the probationer and his parents fill out forms sent by mail; getting progress reports from school or place of employment or institution; and helping the offender get employment, club membership, and so on.

To what extent such a system as this applies to other courts I cannot say, except for the dozen or so with which I am personally familiar and among which, for the most part, a similar situation exists. As late as 1957 members of the staff of the juvenile court in Pittsburgh, Pennsylvania, informed me that the situation at that time remained the same as presented here. The Family Court of the State of Delaware is one exception. The counselors of that court prepare no pre-hearing or pre-sentence reports as such, nor do they usually appear in court at the initial hearing. On the contrary, the judges refer cases which they continue for ninety days to members of the probation staff for counseling. The results of the counseling then help the judges make a final disposition at the end of the ninety-day period.

However, even with such a procedure the offender who is referred to the staff receives, on the average, one-half hour per week of counseling, or a total of six hours for the ninety-day period.

Returning to the juvenile court in Pittsburgh, Pennsylvania, it is significant that only fourteen per cent of probationers in the sample studied received what their probation officers called

Table 1

Duties	Details	
Pre-hearing investigations.	Average five per week, consuming about two-thirds of probation officer's time.	Get statements from: complainants, offender, offender's mother and father, and any other interested party. Compile personal history of offender. Describe offender's environment—home visit. Get reports from school, other agencies active, past or present, with offender or family. Arrange for physical examination of offender.
Prepare report for judge.		Dictation.
Conference with supervisor.		Diagnose behavior and personality of offender. Plan of treatment, if any.
Prepare case summaries for psychologist, psychiatrist, other agencies, institutions. Arrange institutional, foster home placement. Make appointments for testing, clothing issue, medical care, etc. Release assigned cases from detention home.	Involves about 20% of cases.	Correspondence. Phone calls.
Presentation of cases in court.	One day per week set aside for this.	Notify by letter all persons to appear; file petitions; prepare old cases continued and those reappearing on new charges.

casework treatment. A comparison of the results of their work with those of the officers not qualified for casework showed no difference in the recidivism rates of their charges. It is also interesting to note that in the two courts with which I have been associated the probationers who were referred to psychiatrists for treatment had the highest recidivism rate of all!

It is fairly certain that most probation, however it may be conceived in the literature or in the field, still amounts to little more than administrative supervision. But in order to compare the views of the professional personnel represented in the literature with the views of those whose work actually determines what is probation, I asked twenty of the most experienced probation officers from eight courts, including officers both trained and not trained in schools of social work, to write me their answers to the following questions:

1. How would you define probation? Generally speaking, of what does it consist in practice?

2. Is casework an essential part of probation? If so, how would you define casework?

3. What are the aims of probation?

4. What do you believe probation *should* be ideally?

The following are the verbatim replies to question (1) which I received:

1. Probation is a kind of status the child obtains as a result of the court hearing.

2. Probation is a suspended sentence to begin with, as a basis for providing

supervision. In practice it is a continuation of a suspended case, to see if the child does all right. There is no intention of doing anything, though most probation officers won't admit it. Probation is putting a threat over the head of a child. Authority puts weight back of probation. You can see this with our success with neglected and delinquent cases which other agencies have given up. We're the policemen back of the agencies.

3. What it simmers down to is police work. There is no planning, but giving supervision to prevent violations or repetition of delinquent behavior.

4. Probation is an instrument of the court. The child is under the jurisdiction of the court. There are certain areas in which he is expected to function in a certain way. This consists of periodic reports made by the youngster or his family to the probation officer, or the probation officer's contacts with the family and the child, or any collateral contacts, the purpose of the contacts being to determine the child's ability to adjust in the community and to offer additional assistance in a supportive way to help the child adjust.

5. Probation is to help instill in a boy enough confidence in himself to make an adjustment in society, with the knowledge that he can always call on the probation officer for information and advice when needed.

6. Probation consists of the contacts which a probation officer has with a boy after the court hearing. It is also supervision to see how the boy adjusts in the home and the community. Through probation we try to select what boys have to abide by and to explain to them the negative and the positive sides of a situation, explaining limitations and the need to face them.

7. Probation means that the court feels that whatever a child has done he can adjust at home under the supervision of his parents. We look the parents and the home over and decide whether they can handle the supervision. The probation officer merely gives support to that supervision, like a doctor who prescribes. He isn't going to go to your home and make you take the medicine, but if he feels the patient needs to go to the hospital, he goes.

8. Probation is comparable to commitment; that is, it is handled through a court order. But it is not leniency. Probation can be as severe as commitment. Probation is not only law but also a mutual relationship in which we are trying to get children to accept limits.

9. Probation is a period of time during which a child is expected to realize he has made a mistake and that he must be careful to avoid repetition while he is on probation. This realization may or may not be with the help of the probation officer.

10. Probation is using the material brought out by investigation, the causes as well as the effects of antisocial or asocial behavior on the part of delinquents brought to the court. It is taking that and trying to determine from it the particular mores or standards that have been operating in the growing period of the delinquent and trying to arrive at standards or mores which will fit that child and his family and be satisfactory to society, and using all these in a plan thought best in terms of adjustment.

Probation is not something which comes after the court hearing. When a child becomes known to us, he is thought of as being on probation. There is no reason to wait for the hearing. We try to work with a child as soon as we get him. Finally, probation can only be successful if the basic family make-up is considered. What caused a child to be delinquent must be changed.

11. Primarily we are a court of rehabilitation when it comes to the delinquent. When we put a child on probation we are saying to him, "You have run afoul of the rules of society and this is the court's offer to you to try to prove you can live in society without continuing that type of behavior. It is not only probation on the part of the child but also on the part of the parents, because adult behavior often lies behind a child's behavior. The child has to show he no longer needs supervision other than his own family.

12. Probation has a Latin derivation and means the act or process of giving a chance or trial. It is comparable to repairing damage done to an automobile. You repair it and give it another trial rather than let it run in its poor condition.

13. Probation is the period after a child has been brought to the court's attention as a result of a behavior problem. During this period there is an opportunity to see whether, with the help of the worker, his attitudes and activities can be reorganized so that he can make a better adjustment and conduct himself in a more acceptable manner.

It is a two-way thing. It is not just a period. The child must have someone interested in him, to guide him. Interviews with him may be of a general nature or be related to his specific behavior.

14. Probation is working with a child and his family on the problems presented at the court hearing. For the worker it is almost the role of confidant and adviser.

15. Probation is a helping service to a person with a problem. The problem itself may be adjusted or the person is helped to make an adjustment to the problem. Probation is also a means of keeping in touch with a person in order to prevent further difficulty.

16. Probation has its legal aspects. But it is also helping a child adjust to society and its requirements, which is the chief aim of probation. It should be a constructive experience.

17. Probation is helping a child fit into the school, home and community, fitting him into their standards.

18. In practice probation consists in meeting emergencies as they arise instead of routine treatment, which time doesn't allow.

19. When a child comes to the court and a problem is presented, you are not putting him on probation for punishment but to find causes and remedies. Probation means not only working with a child but also considering all the surrounding factors.

20. Probation is helping the individual to adjust. You utilize your own skills and the community resources within the scope and functions of the agency.

Only one of the above statements mentions the idea that punishment is even an aspect of probation, and the concept of leniency is omitted by all twenty probation officers, though it is implied by some. Four offer a partly legal definition, while none specifically presents the view that probation is essentially either an administrative process or a combination of administrative and casework. Partly this may be attributed to the fact that most personnel in the field probably do not express themselves in the same way as do professional authors who are not primarily workers but administrators and teachers. In this respect perhaps the most significant thing of all is the fact that, although certain cliches appear, *in not one definition is casework itself mentioned.* Yet in reply to the second question, "Is casework an essential part of probation?", fourteen probation officers gave an unqualified *yes.* Five of the others felt casework was essential to probation but limited time precluded its use. Only one answered *no.*

Definitions of casework itself were even more general and vague than the definitions of probation. The explanation which was offered most contained such phrases as "helping people to help themselves," "helping a person make an adjustment," "changing a person's attitudes," "establishing a mutual relationship," "working with a person," and "the ability to work with people." Sixteen of the twenty responses fell into such a classification. Two probation officers felt probation *is* casework and that the definition of casework is about the same as the definition of probation. The remaining two expressed the opinion that almost anything that is done in the way of investigation of cases can be thought of as casework.

Obviously there is no consensus or standardization of opinion concerning probation among these twenty experienced workers, nor have they any clear conception of what casework is. I suspect such a situation is general.

When the aims of probation were considered, half the probation officers said the "total adjustment" of the offender was the chief goal. Five believed "complete rehabilitation" was the end pursued, and four thought that adjustment with respect to the particular problem presented was the purpose of probation. Only one officer stated that supervision alone was the real aim of probation. If the two terms "total adjustment" and "complete rehabilitation" are considered synonomous for all practical purposes, then fifteen of the twenty probation officers concurred on this, the highest goal of probation.

With respect to what probation *should* be, thirteen probation officers felt probation should consist of casework treatment. The remaining seven believed casework is not a general process and therefore should be applied only to those cases which indicate a need for that type of treatment. (Yet in answer to the second question all but one believed casework *is* essential to probation.)

It may well be that few correctional personnel are really aware of whatever techniques they use, and it is very highly probable that only a small percentage of the total are qualified caseworkers. It is also highly probable, and certainly seems to be the case from this writer's experience, that the image that many probation officers have of themselves is a picture of a warm and understanding though objective person, a kind of watered-down or embryonic clinician. In any event the influence of a clinical, casework ideology, along with its confused and contradictory elements, has been pervasive. Convention papers, the literature and supervisors are filled with this ideology, so that it is constantly before the probation officer. It

is no more than could be expected, then, if the probation officer feels that whatever he does and however he does it, it *is* treatment.

CONCLUSION

A review of the literature reveals the predominance of the view that probation is a process of casework treatment, and this point of view seems to be shared by probation personnel in the field. However, casework is usually described in general, vague and nebulous language characterized by an abundance of cliches and a lack of clarity and specificity.

Seen from an operational point of view probation appears to be quite different from its ideal, casework conceptions. Probation varies from rare instances of intensive individual treatment, however defined, to simply noncommitment.

Actually, then, probation may be defined as a legal disposition which allows the offender his usual freedom during a period in which he is expected to refrain from unlawful behavior. Operationally, probation is primarily a process of verifying the behavior of an offender (1) through periodic reports of the offender and members of his family to the probation officer and (2) by the incidence or absence of adverse reports from the police and other agencies. Secondarily, probation is a process of guiding and directing the behavior of an offender by means of intensive interviewing utilizing ill-defined casework techniques.

Finally, it can be said that probation in practice is a gesture toward conformity to the school of thought which combines administrative and casework procedures. For the most part, however, probation remains an administrative function with the statement Healy and Bronner made thirty-four years ago still quite accurate: "probation is a term that gives no clue to what is done by way of treatment."[43]

Beyond the Clinical Horizon

Current conceptions of the causation, prevention, and treatment of crime and delinquency center almost exclusively on the offender himself, in spite of the fact that, logically, the offender himself is only part of the problem. Most contemporary thinking is based upon observations made only under certain highly selective conditions—in courts, institutions and schools. Behavior related to other less accessible, though perhaps more important situations—for example, family behavior, behavior in the gang, in the play group, and an analysis of the societal setting of such behavior—are relegated to an academic and professional purgatory in the current craze and obsession with psychodynamics. Whatever the merits of psychodynamics, the picture remains unbalanced. Correctional workers and litérateurs have an obligation to examine and question the basic assumptions of a psychoanalytically ridden and prejudiced clinical profession. They ought to consider, for example, whether the social system itself should be investigated as a basic variable in anti-social behavior and whether the correctional workers should become active in promoting fundamental social reform or reorganization. These and other pertinent questions are largely ignored and most likely will continue to be ignored so long as those in corrections are held in an apparently hypnotic grip of obsession with behavior problems and psychodynamics.

The theories which have dominated, and continue to dominate, practitioners are psychiatric in origin. Insight by the

[43] Healy and Bronner, *Delinquents and Criminals, Their Making and Unmaking,* 82 (New York, The Macmillan Co., 1926).

probationer into the reasons for his behavior is the major goal of treatment. A person with such insight is considered to be unlikely to repeat his deviant behavior as he becomes independent of his identification with the probation officer. At that point, supposedly, the offender can carry on normal and socially acceptable behavior on his own.

Concerning the nature and causes of delinquent behavior, most casework concepts include assumptions involving emotional tensions which result in maladjustment. However, the resolution of the inner conflicts which generate such tensions offers no guarantee of relief from criminality. Neither does the existence of such tensions invariably lead to criminal or delinquent behavior.

Despite an apparently increasing emphasis in psychiatry upon group processes in treating individual cases, the focus still remains the resolution of the individual's disorder or conflicts. As yet there exists no theory or technique for treating the *group* relationships of the individual. The New York City Youth Board's Street Club Project is a step in that direction but with the disadvantage, perhaps, of channeling the energies of gang members into strictly middle-class pursuits. There is also an underlying assumption that *all* members of the individual's relevant group need treatment or assistance.

The conclusion must be that an exclusively clinical approach to the criminality of behavior, relying as it does on the dynamics of intrapsychic phenomena, will continue to yield disappointing results. So, too, will any approach favoring a group etiology if it fails to make the basis of its approach an appraisal of the total society.

The clinical approach of psychiatry and casework views the individual offender, or his behavior, as abnormal when in fact such behavior may accurately reflect the character of group life. Given certain particular patterns of life, criminal and delinquent behavior may be the type of adjustment to those patterns one would expect.

It may be the character of our societal organization itself that produces personalities which cannot assume responsible attitudes.[44] And such personalities need not take shape only as criminals and delinquents but may be reflected in other types of irresponsibility of which the law takes little or no notice. In fact the more perverse and dangerous forms of personality deviation symbolized by aggression and an irrepressible urge to dominate others are those which reach their ultimate forms of expression *within* the existing institutional structure. Since positions of power attract such aggressive and egocentric types, we often view the spectacle of criminals prosecuting criminals! It is a matter of what types of anti-social or abnormal behavior the society will tolerate. Excesses of power and avarice are in conformity with our standards if displayed by those on the way up, or by those already there. It might be profitable, or at least interesting, to put some promising doctoral candidate on the track of executives in business, labor, religion, and government, and of professional caseworkers, psychiatrists, and psychoanalysts. How do they compare in personality and background with our delinquents and criminals? In many cases I should venture to guess that the similarities would be remarkable indeed!

The problems we face today, in this and in other fields, may be the result of a number of factors which we will never be able to put together into a meaningful theory. We must try at any rate. We may start at almost any point, perhaps with the observation that many of the

individual's functions in life have been passed onto the state. The modern American is materially relatively secure, but he is personally insecure and anxious. With the tremendous ballooning of authority, he has been compelled to submit to a complex form of institutional control, and he finds many of his once acceptable outlets for aggression effectively taken away. His is a situation of maximum stimulation of aggressive drives and minimum outlet for their expression. Such a condition deprives individual energies of much constructive force. On the contrary, our contemporary condition intensifies anxiety, enhances the development of dominant attitudes which are themselves abnormal and irrational, and encourages individually irresponsible behavior which may nonetheless be socially acceptable. For in America there is no organized protest against an asocial condition. Instead there are orgies of random activities, of lust for sex and payola, of ambitions tuned to success, the special talent, as someone put it, of those who have no talent, or of crime—all manifestations of boundless energy, but with no real power within.

The American character is essentially egotistical and asocial, ever striving to find its own peculiar niche, a spot which, in the end, may prove to be inimical to his very nature. His social relations are fluid and formless. No one is more addicted to the concept "community" and yet so indifferent to it in reality, no one so willing and ready to separate himself from every social mooring, to run wherever the fortunes of dollars and status happen to drag him. Freedom in America is the right to break away. And when he is not climbing up in society, or running away from it, he is taking the criminal's path of running straight into it. The tantalizing promises of success are still held out to him, his appetites keyed up to

[44] Comfort, *Authority and Delinquency in the Modern State* (London, Routledge and Kegan Paul, 1950).

the breaking point by the hucksters' din, only to be disappointed and disillusioned by the stark realities. Crime may often be his revenge for the dashing of hopes, promises, and ambitions bred from and nourished in a criminal philosophy of life.

The American temperament is a criminal temperament sprung from an undisciplined individualism. The exaltation, the deification of success selects those who can manipulate, "put one over" on someone, who can circumvent the law, who can literally "get away with murder."

The American temper also continues to persist in the illusion of classlessness so that social energy among us is wasted either in aimless, diffuse, excess sociability or, with no social ideal or movement to give conscious direction to our frustrations and discontents, in anti-social behavior. Rather than becoming socially conscious or revolutionary, we become Masons or criminals. This inability to identify oneself consistently with one's particular class results in a sociological dualism that casts doubt in one's own mind as to what he really is and disrupts the achievement of balance and stability of character. The conflict deepens, too, when, unaware of his fundamental class relationship to his society, he feels drawn to it directly. But that society, dedicated to a bourgeois existence, has never been imbued with and has never produced a real spirit of solidarity among its people. It has produced little that is socially substantial; it has produced only a philosophy of every man for himself.

But the clinician will, I suspect, for some time to come continue to see the anti-social man as a sick man. He will urge more and better clinics and more and better trained caseworkers, psychologists, and psychiatrists. It would be worthwhile to investigate to what extent the clinical professions attract people with a basic impulse to direct and control the lives of others. It is certainly not improbable that, in many cases, the therapist or counselor gains a great deal more in ego support from the therapeutic situation than does the patient! In fact, what has been said above may apply to clinical personnel in whom hostility and the compulsion to dominate others may appear as the other side of the coin. And the remainder of us will probably continue to rely on the very institutions which threaten to, or already have, eclipsed the possibility of much more enlightenment. It may be time to look to extra-institutional means by which individual behavior may be rationally developed and controlled, for institutions alone, I suspect, have not all the power we have attributed to them. In any event, in the final analysis, as Comfort has said, ". . . a statement of the desirable pattern of individual conduct makes nonsense without an extension of the description to cover the type of society in which such conduct is possible."[45]

Social scientists apparently fear the prospect of viewing their fields in political terms. But if the institutional ethics of power are not examined and attacked, if need be; if, instead of disentangling ourselves from the decayed and decaying elements of our society we, on the contrary, continue to identify with them and invest our future in their fortunes, then our prospects are dark indeed.

[45] *Ibid.*

33.

The Gault Decision: Due Process and
the Juvenile Courts

Alan Neigher

On May 15, 1967, the Supreme Court of the United States ruled that juvenile courts must grant to children many of the procedural protections required in adult criminal trials by the Bill of Rights. In this, the *Gault*[1] decision, the Supreme Court for the first time considered the constitutional rights of children in juvenile courts.

It is not questioned that *Gault* will have a major impact on the future of juvenile courts in this country, many of which having for years operated under a philosophy that made ordinary procedural safeguards seem evil. It is submitted, however, that the *Gault* decision is neither a panacea for children in trouble nor an onerous burden for juvenile law enforcement officers. The decision will hopefully protect young people from being given indeterminate "correctional" sentences for making allegedly obscene phone calls that no one thinks necessary to verify. The decision may make life a bit more difficult for

SOURCE. Alan Neigher. "The Gault Decision: Due Process and the Juvenile Courts" from *Federal Probation*, Volume 31, December 1967, pp. 8–18. Reprinted with permission.

[1] *In Re Gault*, 387 U.S. 1 (1967).

judges and probation officers. It is clear that at the very least, *Gault* will grant some semblance of consistent legal protection to the child.

But there are some popular misconceptions concerning the scope of *Gault*. As an example, the front page of the May 16, 1967, *New York Times* headlined an otherwise excellent summary of the decision as follows: "High Court Rules Adult Code Holds in Juvenile Trials . . . Finds Children Are Entitled to the Basic Protections Given in Bill of Rights."[2] But the decision does not accord to juveniles all of the protections of the Bill of Rights. All juvenile courts —with the exception of the District of Columbia—are, in fact, state courts. The Bill of Rights has not yet been made applicable in its entirety to state criminal proceedings. Further, the *Gault* decision was limited to but a few Bill of Rights issues. This must be kept in mind, although, as will be later noted, the decision was as significant for what it *suggested* as it was for what it actually held as binding legal precedent.

Thus, before the decision may be discussed in terms of its implications for

[2] *New York Times*, May 16, 1967, p. 1, col. 1 (city ed.).

453

the juvenile courts, a brief examination is in order as to what the "basic protections" of the Bill of Rights are, and whether these protections have been extended to state (and thereby juvenile) proceedings.

BILL OF RIGHTS AND THE FOURTEENTH AMENDMENT

The Bill of Rights[3] means the first Ten Amendments to the newly written Federal Constitution, proposed to the state legislatures by the First Congress in 1789. The Bill of Rights was intended to be a series of limitations on the three *federal* branches: The Congress, the Executive, and the Judiciary. These proposed limitations were a practical political necessity, to mollify local concern over the sanctity of state autonomy in many areas of the law, and thereby speed ratification by the necessary nine state legislatures.

Of these Ten Amendments, six are not directly related to the criminal process. These are the First, Second, Third, Seventh, Ninth, and Tenth. Left for consideration, therefore, are the Fourth, Fifth, Sixth, and Eighth Amendments. And of these four, the Fourth and Eighth were not at issue in *Gault* and will be treated briefly.

Before these Amendments are discussed, the Fourteenth Amendment must be considered because it is closely related to the concept of federalism and because it affects not only those Amendments related to the criminal process, but also the entire Ten Amendments and their applicability to the states.

The Bill of Rights was expressly in-

[3] For excellent summaries of the entire Constitution from which much of the following material on the Bill of Rights is drawn, see Antieau, *Commentaries on the Constitution of the United States (1960)*, and The Younger Lawyers Committee of the Federal Bar Association, *These Unalienable Rights* (1965).

tended to be a check on federal power. There was nothing in the original Constitution to prevent the states from formulating their own systems of criminal administration, and indeed, the Tenth Amendment provides that "The powers not delegated to the United States by the Constitution; nor prohibited by it to the States, are reserved to the States respectively, or to the people."

After the Civil War, almost a century after the ratification of the Constitution (which included the Bill of Rights), Amendments Thirteen, Fourteen, and Fifteen were enacted, largely for the benefit of the newly emancipated slaves. Amendment Thirteen abolished slavery; Amendment Fifteen provided that race, color, or previous condition of servitude shall not be a disability for voting.

Amendment Fourteen was written partly to assure fair and equitable treatment on the part of state authorities to the newly emancipated. For our purposes, its most pertinent part in Section 1, which provides: ". . . No State shall make or enforce any law which shall abridge the privileges or immunities of citizens of the United States; nor shall any State deprive any person of life, liberty, or property, *without due process of law;* nor deny to any person within its jurisdiction the equal protection of the laws."

Thus, the "due process" clause of the Fifth Amendment was made applicable to the states. However, the vague and sweeping concept of due process was slow in making its impact felt on the states which had been left virtually autonomous in formulating criminal procedures. But in recent years, on a case-by-case basis, the Supreme Court has made *some* of the Bill of Rights protection binding on the states through the due process clause of the Fourteenth Amendment. Of those protections now applicable to the states included are several under those Amendments not relevant to the criminal process (especially freedom of speech under the First Amendment), and these need not be considered here.

The Fourth Amendment was largely a reaction to the Writs of Assistance issued in the colonies prior to the Revolution, which gave British revenue officers nearly unlimited authority to search private dwellings and to seize goods. Consequently, the Fourth Amendment reflects the Founders' jealous regard of the right to privacy—to be secure against unreasonable invasion of one's person, property, and home. The Fourth Amendment now applies in full to both federal and state authorities.

The Fourth Amendment provides for the security of people "in their persons, houses, papers, and effects against unreasonable searches and seizures." The laws pertaining to warrants—for both search and arrest—are too technical to be set out here. Suffice it to say that, as to searches and seizures of property, unless there is consent, individuals and their possessions or dwellings cannot be searched or seized without a warrant, except when this is justified by the surrounding circumstances and is done in a reasonable manner.

The Fourth Amendment prohibits unwarranted and unreasonable arrests, but it does not require that the police obtain a warrant for every arrest. The police may arrest without a warrant where the arresting officer actually sees the commission of a misdeameanor or a felony; also, the arresting officer may arrest without a warrant when he has "probable cause" to believe a felony has been committed. Probable cause is difficult to define precisely, but it may generally be stated that it is the existence of such facts and circumstances as would lead a reasonable person to believe that the suspect to be arrested is guilty of the offense.

Where a warrant must be obtained, it must specifically describe the person to be arrested. A general warrant—one that is to be filled in at the arresting officer's convenience—is not valid. An arrest made pursuant to an invalid warrant is unlawful. A warrant for either arrest or search and seizure may be issued only by a magistrate or judge; police officers have no authority to issue warrants.

THE FIFTH AMENDMENT

The First Congress included a specific provision regarding grand jury indictments as the first clause of the Fifth Amendment. The purpose of the provision is to insure that persons will not be brought to trial arbitrarily when there is no reasonable basis for believing they are guilty of a crime, and that those who are brought to trial will be adequately informed of the charges against them. The Supreme Court has held that the due process clause of the Fourteenth Amendment does not require a state to provide grand jury indictment, so long as the state provides other means of insuring justice to the accused.

The next clause provides that no person "shall . . . be subject for the same offense to be twice put in jeopardy of life or limb." The Founders' sense of fair play led them to include in the Fifth Amendment the concept that the Government should not be able to harass and persecute a man by trying him repeatedly for the same offense. The double jeopardy prohibition has not yet been binding on the states. However, the states are bound by the due process clause of the Fourteenth Amendment; thus, successive trials which flaunt the principles of justice and fair play are not permitted.

The Fifth Amendment next provides that no person "shall be compelled in any criminal case to be a witness against himself. . . ." The history of inquisition and torture in the Old World gave the Founders ample reason to provide against the idea that a man should be forced to incriminate himself by his own words. The privilege has two aspects: (1) the right to be free from coercion designed to extract a confession; and (2) the right to remain silent without having an inference of guilt drawn from that silence.

Freedom from coerced confessions has long been recognized as basic to due process and neither federal nor state governments may extract a confession by force. Force need not be physical; mental coercion such as threats or interrogation to the point of exhaustion would make a confession coerced, and thereby invalid.

The second aspect of the privilege against self-incrimination is the right to remain silent. This is the right invoked by those who "take the Fifth." This right, too, has recently been extended to apply to the states under the Fourteenth Amendment. A criminal defendant has the right to refuse to testify entirely; his failure to take the stand may not even be commented upon by the prosecution in either the federal or state courts. A witness, on the other hand, must take the stand if called, and must claim the privilege one question at a time. The privilege applies not only to criminal trials, but extends also to those before congressional committees, grand juries, and administrative agencies.[4]

The privilege against self-incrimination was highly relevant to the Gault decision.

Following the self-incrimination provision appears the most sweeping con-

cept of American jurisprudence: that no person shall "be deprived of life, liberty or property without due process of law." We have seen that the "due process" concept was later duplicated in the Fourteenth Amendment.

If there exists a legal concept not susceptible of precise definition it is due process. It means justice; it means judicial fair play. It is perhaps the very essence of our constitutional tradition. It is both "substantive" and "procedural" —it prohibits the making of laws that are unfair in themselves, and it prohibits unfair application of the law.

Due process applies to Congress in its law-making authority, and forbids laws that are arbitrary or unreasonable. And when the Executive Branch exercises a law-making or rule-making function, it, too, must exercise substantive due process.

Procedural due process requires that the laws, once made, be applied fairly. It means that an individual has the right to be fairly heard before he stands to lose life, liberty, or property. It requires a fair trial in a criminal case and a hearing by an impartial tribunal in a property case.

Procedural due process considerations were at the heart of the Gault decision.

THE SIXTH AMENDMENT

The Sixth Amendment is of particular importance to the Gault decision. Of the entire Bill of Rights, it is the one most particularly concerned with the rights of an accused in a Federal criminal trial. The text of the Sixth Amendment follows:

In all criminal prosecutions, the accused shall enjoy the right to a speedy and public trial, by an impartial jury of the State and District wherein the crime shall have been committed, which District shall have been previously ascertained by law, *and to be informed of the nature and cause of the accusation; to be confronted with the wit-*

---

[4] The privilege has one notable exception: A person has no right to remain silent if a statute (federal or state) gives him immunity from prosecution—that is, if the government is prevented from prosecuting him on the basis of his testimony.

nesses against him; to have compulsory process for obtaining witnesses in his favor, *and to have the assistance of Counsel for his defense.* [Emphasis added.]

The right to a jury trial in criminal prosecutions was considered so important to the Founders that they included the right in the main body of the Constitution as well as in the Bill of Rights: Article III, Section 2, commands that the "Trials of all Crimes, except in Cases of Impeachment, shall be by Jury. . . ."

The Sixth Amendment establishes the basic requirement that the accused be tried by the traditional jury of 12. On the other hand, the states are *not* required to provide trial by jury, although many do by virtue of their own constitutions. Some states provide for juries of 8 or 10, rather than 12. However, the Fourteenth Amendment mandate that the states provide due process requires that whatever form of trial the states do provide must be fair.

Not "all criminal prosecutions" by the Federal Government require jury trials. Military trials, criminal contempt proceedings, or petty offenses punishable by small fines or short periods of imprisonment may be conducted without juries. When the right to jury trial applies, this right may be waived, and the defendant may be tried by a judge alone, where both the defendant and the Government so agree, with the consent of the trial judge.

The Sixth Amendment further provides that "the accused enjoy . . . a speedy and public trial." The history of the Inquisition and the Court of the Star Chamber was not lost on the Founding Fathers. These Courts were notorious for their practices of detaining accused persons for long periods, and interrogating witnesses in secret. The Sixth Amendment provided against these abuses by insuring that the accused has the right to defend himself

while witnesses and evidence are still available. The wisdom of this protection is readily apparent if one considers the anxiety involved in a prolonged criminal prosecution. Thus, if an accused is not afforded a speedy trial, he may not be tried at all. As to what constitutes a "speedy trial" suffice it to say that standards of reasonableness must govern. The right to a speedy trial has not yet been held binding upon the states under the Fourteenth Amendment, although an obvious prolongment would probably violate due process.

The right to a *public* trial is a basic right under due process, and this right does extend to defendants in trials conducted by the states. The presence of the public and representatives of the press acts as a guarantee that the court will proceed appropriately. The Supreme Court has not yet determined whether all trials must be freely open to the public or whether circumstances will permit a limitation on the type of spectators allowed.

The next protection afforded under the Sixth Amendment is the right to an impartial jury. The definition of "impartial" as used here has two aspects. First, there must be an opportunity for a cross section of the community to serve as jurors. Exclusion because of race, religion, national origin, or economic status violates the defendant's Sixth Amendment rights, whether the trial be federal or state. The cross-section concept does *not* require that every jury be composed of all the various racial, religious, ethnic, or economic groups of the community. It does prohibit court officials from *systematically* excluding any of these groups.

Second, the right to an impartial jury also involves the problem of publicity surrounding the trial. The First Amendment guarantees of free speech and freedom of the press must be balanced against the accused's right to be accorded a jury that will consider his case with an open mind. Modern communications techniques have added great complexity to this problem. The Supreme Court held in the case of Dr. Sam Sheppard that due process is violated where widespread newspaper publicity saturates the community so as to make it virtually impossible to find a panel of impartial jurors.

The Sixth Amendment next requires that a person be tried by "an impartial jury of the State and District wherein the crime shall have been committed, which District shall have been previously ascertained by law." This provision insures that a person will be tried only in that area where the crime was committed—where evidence and witnesses should be readily available, unless circumstances dictate that an impartial trial can only be had elsewhere. It is also required that Congress define in advance the boundaries of the Districts in which crimes shall be tried. The Supreme Court has not yet dealt with the issue of whether the due process clause of the Fourteenth Amendment limits the states in determining where trials for state offenses may be held.

Of great relevance to the *Gault* decision is the next phrase of the Sixth Amendment, which provides that the accused shall enjoy the right "to be informed of the nature and cause of the accusation." Thus, the accused must be informed of the charges against him sufficiently in advance of the court proceedings to allow him a reasonable opportunity to prepare a defense. Also, such notice must specify the alleged misconduct with reasonable particularity. Again this guarantee obtains, whether the trial be federal or state.

The second clause of the Sixth Amendment also was critical to the *Gault* decision. It provides that the accused shall enjoy the right "to be confronted with the witnesses against him." The philosophy underlying this clause is that the accused should be met by his accusers face-to-face, and be able to subject the testimony of the witnesses against him to cross-examination. The right to confrontation is a basic due process protection and applies to state, as well as to federal, courts.

The Sixth Amendment next provides that an accused be entitled to have the court compel witnesses to appear and testify if they are unwilling to come voluntarily. A refusal to so compel witnesses to testify on behalf of the accused violates the right to a fair trial, and consequently offends the due process clause. Although the Supreme Court has not dealt directly with the issue, it does not seem likely that such a basic fair trial protection would fail to be held binding on the states under the Fourteenth Amendment.

Finally, the Sixth Amendment provides that the accused shall "have the assistance of counsel for his defense." There was no right to counsel prior to the enactment of the Bill of Rights, and the accused had to rely on the graces of the trial judge to act as his counsel. The inclusion of this right in the Sixth Amendment reflected the belief of the Founders that most defendants are vastly unprepared to protect themselves against the resources of the state's prosecution machinery. The accused today in both federal and state proceedings has the right to counsel in felony cases, and in misdemeanor cases where the accused is in jeopardy of incarceration. In such cases, the recent *Escobedo* and *Miranda* decisions have extended the right to counsel beyond the trial stage; the accused is now entitled to counsel when the investigation focuses upon him so as to attempt to elicit incriminating statements. The reader should note that it is at this point, also, that the Fifth Amendment's privilege against self-incrimination attaches.

THE EIGHTH AMENDMENT

Statutes prohibiting excessive bail and cruel and unusual punishment had been enacted in precolonial England and in the constitutions of a number of colonies. These prohibitions were reflected in the Eighth Amendment which reads: "Excessive bail shall not be required, nor excessive fines imposed, nor cruel and unusual punishment inflicted."

It has not been definitely settled whether the provisions of the Eighth Amendment are applicable to the states under the Fourteenth Amendment.

Bail is a mechanism designed to insure the appearance of a defendant in court; by posting bail, the defendant undertakes to guarantee his appearance in court or else forfeit a sum of money. The amount of bail required is generally set by the magistrate who commits an arrested person to custody. Not every accused person is entitled to bail—military personnel and those accused of capital crimes are generally denied such release. But where the accused is entitled to bail, the Eighth Amendment requires that it not be "excessive." Such factors as the defendant's criminal history, the seriousness of the crime and ability to pay are relevant to the issue of excessiveness. There is generally no right to bail after conviction pending appeal; requests for such bail are left largely to the discretion of the trial judge.

As to the excessive fine provision, it is generally left to Congress to prescribe the limits of fines and to the trial courts to decide what fine should be imposed in a particular case. The Supreme Court has refused to review fines levied by the lower federal courts.

There are no precise standards as to what constitutes cruel and unusual punishment. The death penalty is not of itself cruel and unusual; what is forbidden by very early tradition of Anglo-American law is the infliction of unnecessary pain in the execution of the death sentence.

It is apparent that the Eighth Amendment, like its companions, leaves many problems unanswered, especially because the Eighth Amendment's prohibitions are not yet binding on the states. The law of bail—especially as it applies to the indigent accused—is in a state of re-evaluation. There are those who have argued, in the wake of the Chessman case, that long delay in execution is cruel and unusual punishment; indeed, there are many who argue that by modern standards, the death penalty is itself cruel and unusual punishment.

It is not pretended that the above summary of certain of the Bill of Rights criminal protections is an authoritative treatise. Indeed, entire volumes have been written on some individual Amendments. It is only hoped that the reader be informed of these protections so that the *Gault* decision might be placed in its proper constitutional perspective.

THE CASE OF THE "LEWD AND INDECENT" PHONE CALL

Gerald and another boy were taken into custody in the morning of June 8, 1964, by the Sheriff of Gila County, Arizona. The police were acting upon a verbal complaint from a Mrs. Cook, a neighbor of the boys, that she received a lewd and indecent phone call. Both of Gerald's parents were at work that morning and no notice of the police action was left at their home. Gerald's mother learned of his being taken to the Children's Detention House only after Gerald's older brother went to look for him at the home of the other boy. At the detention Home, the mother and brother were told "why Jerry was there" and that a hearing would be held the next day at 3 o'clock.

A petition praying for a hearing was filed on June 9 by an Officer Flagg which recited that "said minor is under the age of 18 years and in need of protection of this Honorable Court [and that] said minor is a delinquent minor." The petition was not served on the Gaults and they first saw it 2 months later.

On June 9, a hearing was held in the chambers of Juvenile Judge McGhee with Gerald, his mother, his brother and the probation officers being present. No formal or informal record of this hearing was made. Judge McGhee questioned Gerald about the telephone calls without advising him of a right to counsel or a privilege against self-incrimination. There is conflicting testimony as to Gerald's answers. Both Officer Flagg and Judge McGhee stated that Gerald admitted making at least one of the indecent remarks while Mrs. Gault recalled that her son only admitted dialing Mrs. Cook's number.

Gerald was released from the detention home without explanation on either the 11th or the 12th (again the memories of Mrs. Gault and Officer Flagg conflict) pending further hearings; a hearing was held before Judge McGhee on June 15th. Mrs. Gault asked that Mrs. Cook be present but was told by the Judge that "she didn't have to be present." Neither the Gaults nor Officer Flagg remembered any admission by Gerald at this proceeding of making the indecent remarks, though the judge did remember Gerald's admitting some of the less serious statements. At the conclusion of the hearing, Gerald was committed as a juvenile delinquent to the State Industrial School "for the period of his minority [6 years] unless sooner discharged by due process of law."

No appeal is permitted under Arizona law in juvenile cases. Gerald filed a writ of habeas corpus with the Supreme Court of Arizona which was referred to the Superior Court for hearing. Among other matters, Judge McGhee testified that he acted under a section of the Arizona Code which defines a "delinquent child" as one who (in the judge's words) is "habitually involved in immoral matters." The basis for the judge's conclusion seemed to be a referral made 2 years earlier concerning Gerald when the boy allegedly had "stolen" a baseball glove "and lied to the Police Department about it." No petition or hearing apparently resulted from this "referral." The judge testified that Gerald had violated the section of the Arizona Criminal Code which provides that a person who "'in the presence of or hearing of any woman or child . . . uses vulgar, abusive or obscene language, is guilty of a misdemeanor. . . .'" The penalty for an adult convicted under this section is a fine of $5 to $50, or imprisonment for not more than 2 months.

The Superior Court dismissed the habeas corpus petition, and Gerald sought review in the Arizona Supreme Court on many due process grounds. The Arizona Supreme Court affirmed the dismissal of the petition.

The appellants, in their appeal to the United States Supreme Court, did not raise all of the issues brought before the Supreme Court of Arizona. The appeal was based on the argument that the Juvenile Code of Arizona is invalid because, contrary to the due process clause of the Fourteenth Amendment, the Juvenile is taken from the custody of his parents and committed to a state institution pursuant to proceedings where the Juvenile Court has virtually unlimited discretion, and in which the following basic rights are denied: Notice of the charges; right to counsel; right to confrontation and cross-examination; privilege against self-incrimination; right to a transcript of the proceedings; and right to appelate review.

These were the questions before the Supreme Court in the *Gault* decision. The Court explicitly noted that other issues passed upon by the Supreme Court of Arizona, but not presented by the appellants to the Supreme Court of the United States, would not be considered. This is consistent with the Court's strict practice of reviewing—if it chooses to review at all—only those issues actually presented to it.

THE DECISION

The *Gault* decision was handed down May 15, 1967, a little over 5 months after its oral argument was heard by the Supreme Court. Mr. Justice Fortas wrote the opinion for the majority which was, in effect, 8 to 1. Justice Fortas was joined by Chief Justice Warren and Justices Brennan, Clark, and Douglas. Mr. Justice Black concurred with the result but argued that juveniles in jeopardy of confinement be tried in accordance with all of the Bill of Rights protections made applicable to the states by the Fourteenth Amendment.[5] Mr. Justice White concurred with the majority except for Part V concerning self-incrimination, confrontation, and cross-examination which he felt need not be reached, since the decision would be reversed on other grounds.[6] Mr. Justice Harlan concurred in part and dissented in part: he concurred with the majority insofar as it held that Gerald was deprived of due process of law by being denied adequate notice, record of the proceedings, and right to counsel; he dissented on the grounds that the other procedural safeguards imposed by the Court might discourage "efforts to find more satisfactory solutions for the problems of juvenile crime,

and may thus now hamper enlightened development of juvenile courts."[7]

Only Mr. Justice Stewart dissented in full. Although acknowledging the shortcomings of many of the juvenile and family courts, he maintained that the procedural safeguards imposed by the decision would abolish the flexibility and informality of juvenile courts and would cause children again to be treated as adults.[8]

In summary form, the decision held as follows:

Notice of Charges[9]

A petition alleging in general terms that the child is "neglected, dependent or delinquent" is sufficient notice under Arizona law.[10] It is not required that the petition be served upon the parents. No facts need be alleged in the initial petition; the Arizona Supreme Court held that such facts need not be alleged until the close of the initial hearing. No petition at all was served upon Gerald or his parents prior to the initial hearing.

The Arizona Supreme Court rejected Gerald's claim that due process had been denied because of failure to provide adequate notice on the following grounds: that "Mrs. Gault knew the exact nature of the charge against Gerald from the day he was taken to the detention home"; that the Gaults had appeared at the two hearings "without objection"; that advance notice of the specific charges or basis for taking the juvenile into custody and for the hearing is not necessary because "the policy of the juvenile law is to hide youthful errors from the full gaze of the public and bury them in the graveyard of the forgotten past."

---

[5] *In Re Gault, supra* note 1, at 59–64.
[6] *Id.* at 64–65.

[7] *Id.* at 65–78.
[8] *Id.* at 78–81.
[9] *Id.* at 31–34.
[10] Ariz. Rev. Stat. Ann. tit. 8, §222 (1955).

The Supreme Court rejected these arguments, noting that the "initial hearing" in this case was in fact a hearing on the merits of the case. The Court stated that even if there was validity to the practice of deferring specific notice on the grounds of protecting the child from the public eye, it must yield to the due process requirement of adequate notice. Therefore, a hearing where a youth's freedom and the parent's right to custody are in jeopardy may not be held unless the child and his parents or guardian be first notified in writing of the specific issues that must be met at that hearing. Such notice must be given at the earliest practicable time and sufficiently in advance of the hearing to permit preparation. Mere "knowledge" of the kind Mrs. Gault allegedly had of the charges against Gerald does not constitute a waiver of the right to adequate notice because of its lack of particularity.

Right to Counsel[11]

The Arizona Supreme Court had held that representation of counsel for a minor is discretionary with the trial judge. The Supreme Court disagreed, noting that neither probation officer nor judge can adequately represent the child. Since a proceeding where a child stands to be found "delinquent" and subject to loss of liberty is comparable in gravity to an adult felony prosecution, the juvenile needs the assistance of counsel for the same reasons underlying the inclusion of the right in the Sixth Amendment: The juvenile—even less than the average adult criminal defendant—is not prepared to cope with the complexities of the law or of building an adequate defense. Thus, the due process clause of the Fourteenth Amendment requires that in state proceedings which may result in commitment the child and his parent must be

notified of the child's right to be represented by counsel. If they are unable to afford a lawyer, one must be appointed for them.[12]

The Court discounted the holding of the Arizona Supreme Court that since Mrs. Gault knew that she could have appeared with counsel, her failure to do so was a waiver of the right. Notification of the right to counsel plus "specific consideration" of whether to waive the right must precede a valid waiver. Without being expressly advised of the right (and Mrs. Gault was not so advised) there can be no "'specific consideration" and thus, no waiver.

Self-Incrimination, Confrontation, and Cross-Examination.[13]

It will be recalled that at the June 9 hearing, Judge McGhee questioned Gerald about the telephone calls without advising him of his right to counsel or his right to remain silent. The judge and Officer Flagg stated that Gerald admitted making at least one of the indecent remarks; Mrs. Gault recalled only that her son admitted dialing Mrs. Cook's number. The Arizona Supreme Court rejected Gerald's contention that

---

[11] In Re Gault, supra note 1, at 34–42.

[12] The Court emphasized as "forceful" the Report of the President's Commission on Law Enforcement and Administration of Justice, The Challenge of Crime in a Free Society, pp. 86–7 (hereinafter cited as NAT'L CRIME COMM'N REPORT) (1967), which recommended: "Counsel should be appointed as a matter of course wherever coercive action is a possibility without requiring any affirmative choice by child or parent." In Re Gault, supra note 1, at 38–40 n. 65. Also cited was HEW, Standards for Juvenile and Family Courts, Children's Bureau Pub. No. 437-1966, p. 57 (1966) (hereinafter cited as Standards) which states: "As a component part of a fair hearing required by due process guaranteed under the 14th Amendment, notice of the right to counsel should be required at all hearings and counsel provided upon request when the family is financially unable to employ counsel." In Re Gault, supra note 1, at 39.

[13] Id. at 42–57.

he had a right to be advised that he need not incriminate himself, saying that the "necessary flexibility for individualized treatment will be enhanced by a rule which does not require the judge to advise the infant of a privilege against self-incrimination."

The Supreme Court rejected this view and held that any admissions that Gerald allegedly made were improperly obtained in violation of the Fifth Amendment's privilege against self-incrimination. The Court traced the history underlying the privilege, and observed: "One of its purposes is to prevent the State, whether by force or by psychological domination, from overcoming the mind and will of the person under investigation and depriving him of the freedom to decide whether to assist the State in securing his conviction." The court implied that no less than the freedom from coerced confessions is the importance of the reliability of the admission or confession. Such reliability, especially as to alleged admissions or confessions from those of Gerald's age, must undergo careful scrutiny, for, in the Court's words: "It would indeed be surprising if the privilege against self-incrimination were available to hardened criminals but not to children. The language of the Fifth Amendment, applicable to the States by operation of the Fourteenth Amendment, is unequivocal and without exception. And the scope of the privilege is comprehensive."[14]

The State of Arizona argued that the

Fifth Amendment provides only that no person "shall be compelled in any *criminal case* to be a witness against himself" and should therefore not apply through the Fourteenth Amendment to state juvenile proceedings. The Supreme Court held that the privilege is not based upon the *type* of proceeding in which it is involved, "but upon the nature of the statement or admission made, the exposure which it invites." Since the privilege may be invoked in a civil or administrative proceeding, the court noted that it would make no difference whether juvenile proceedings are deemed "civil" or "criminal." The court took the opportunity to express its disapproval with these labels, and noted that in over half of the states, juveniles may be placed in adult penal institutions after a finding of delinquency.[15] The Court stated: "For this purpose, at least, commitment is a deprivation of liberty. It is incarceration against one's will, whether it is called 'criminal' or 'civil.' And our Constitution guarantees that no person shall be 'compelled' to be a witness against himself when he is threatened with deprivation of his liberty. . . ."

The Court noted that "special problems may arise with respect to waiver of the privilege by or on behalf of children, and that there may well be some differences in technique—but not in principle—depending upon the age of the child and the presence and competence of parents." And as special care must be taken before the privilege is validly waived, so also must admissions obtained without the presence of counsel be subject to the greatest scrutiny. Here we see the Fifth Amendment's self-incrimination provision to be vitally interwoven with the Sixth Amendment's right to counsel.

[14] The Court cited to this point *Standards, supra* note 12, at 49, for authority that prior to a police interview, the child and his parents should be informed of his right to have legal counsel present and to refuse to answer questions. This provision of the *Standards* also suggests that the parents and child be informed of their right to refuse to be fingerprinted, but the Court refused to express any opinion as to fingerprinting as this issue was not before the Court. *In Re Gault, supra* note 1, at 49.

[15] HEW, *Delinquent Children in Penal Institutions,* Children's Bureau Pub. No. 415–1964, p. 1 (1964).

The "confession" of Gerald, made without counsel, outside of the presence of his parents, and without advising him of his right to remain silent served as the basis for Judge McGhee's finding of delinquency. Since this "admission" or "confession" was obtained in violation of those rights noted above, the Supreme Court searched for another basis on which the judgment might rest. There was none to be found. There was no sworn testimony. The complainant, Mrs. Cook, did not appear. The Arizona Supreme Court held that "sworn testimony must be required of all witnesses" including those related to the juvenile court system. The Supreme Court held that this is not sufficient: In the absence of a valid confession adequate to support the determination of the Court, confrontation and sworn testimony by witnesses available for cross-examination were essential for a finding of "delinquency" and a subsequent order depriving Gerald of his liberty.[16] The court made it clear, therefore, that an adjudication of "delinquency" or a commitment to an institution is invalid unless the juvenile is afforded the same protections respecting sworn testimony that an adult would receive in a criminal trial.

Appellate Review and Transcript of Proceedings.[17]

The Supreme Court did not specifically decide whether there is a right to appellate review in a juvenile case[18] or whether juvenile courts are required to provide a transcript of the hearings for review, because the decision of the Arizona Supreme Court could be reversed on other grounds. Notwithstanding its failure to rule directly on this issue, the Court pointed out the undesirable consequences of the present case, where: no record of the proceedings was kept; no findings or grounds for basing the juvenile court's conclusions were stated; and the reviewing courts were forced to reconstruct a record while Judge McGhee had the "unseemly duty of testifying under cross-examination as to the events that transpired in the hearings before him."[19]

EPILOGUE

It should be evident to the reader that the legal precedents handed down by the *Gault* decision are neither numerous nor complex. At any proceeding where a child may be committed to a state institution, that child and his parent or guardian must be given notice in writing of the specific charges against the child sufficiently in advance of the proceedings to permit adequate preparation. The child and his parent must be

---

[16] For this point, the Court again cited *Standards, supra* note 12, at 72–73, which states that all testimony should be under oath and that only competent material and relevant evidence under rules applicable to civil cases should be admitted into evidence. Also cited was, *e.g.,* Note, "Rights and Rehabilitation in Juvenile Courts," 67 Colum. L. Rev. 281, 336 (1967): "Particularly in delinquency cases, where the issue of fact is the commission of a crime, the introduction of heresay—such as the report of a policeman who did not witness the events—contravenes the purpose underlying the Sixth Amendment right of confrontation." (Footnote omitted.) *In Re Gault, supra* note 1, at 56–57, n. 98.

[17] *Id.* at 57–59.

[18] The Supreme Court has yet to hold that a state is required to provide any right to appellate review, *Griffin v. Illinois,* 351 U.S. 12, 18 (1956).

[19] The Court cited, *e.g., Standards, supra* note 12, at 8, which recommends "written findings of fact, some form or record of the hearing" "and the right to appeal." It recommends verbatim recording of the hearing by stereotypist or mechanical recording. *Id.* at 76. Finally, it urges that the judge make clear to the child and family their right to appeal. *Id.* at 78. Also cited was, *e.g.,* NAT'L CRIME COMM'N REPORT, *supra* note 12, at 86, which states that "records make possible appeals which, even if they do not occur, import by their possibility a healthy atmosphere of accountability." *In Re Gault, supra* note 1, at 58–69, n. 102.

notified of the child's right to be represented by counsel, and if financial considerations so require, counsel must be appointed for them. The child and his parents or guardian must be advised of the child's right to remain silent. Admission or confessions obtained from the child without the presence of counsel must undergo the greatest scrutiny in order to insure reliability. In the absence of a valid confession, no finding of "delinquency" and no order of commitment of the child for any length of time may be upheld unless such finding is supported by confrontation and sworn testimony of witnesses available for cross-examination.

If indeed the *Gault* decision were significant only for the black-letter law, summarized above, the demands made upon our juvenile judges and probation officers would be rather easy to comply with. The few mandates of *Gault* would eventually become implemented (with, of course, varying degrees of enthusiasm). However, the decision cannot be read solely in the light of its few binding precedents.

Some may recall that it was the same Justice Fortas who wrote for the majority in the *Kent*[20] decision, which a year prior to *Gault* considered the requirement for a valid waiver of "exclusive" jurisdiction of the juvenile court of the District of Columbia so that a youth could be tried in the District's adult criminal court. The essence of *Kent* was that the basic requirements of due process and fairness be met in such a proceeding. But although confined to the narrow issue of waiver proceedings, *Kent* was a prologue to *Gault* insofar as it expressed disenchantment with the course of juvenile justice in this country, which was expressed in an often-quoted sentence: "There is evidence . . . that there may be grounds for concern that the child receives the worst of both worlds: that he gets neither the protections accorded to adults nor the solicitous care and regenerative treatment postulated for children.[21]

With this warning, an alert was sounded in *Kent* for what would become in *Gault* an indictment of the juvenile courts. Despite the limitation of issues actually adjudicated in the decision, *Gault*, taken as a whole, is a comprehensive note of concern over the administration of juvenile justice in this country. Part II of the decision[22] dealing largely with background and history contains 41 footnotes citing materials covering the entire ambit of juvenile justice, from custody to treatment, from probation to psychiatric care, and including numerous books, studies, and articles critical of virtually every aspect of the juvenile process. In Part II the parens patriae doctrine—the concept of the state assuming the role of substitute parent—was challenged on both historical grounds ("its meaning is murky and its historic credentials are of dubious relevance") and on legal grounds ("[T]he constitutional and theoretical basis for this peculiar system is—to say the least—debatable."). The nomenclature attached to "receiving homes" or "industrial schools" did not, in the Court's view, alter the practical reality that these are institutions of confinement where juveniles may for years be deprived of their liberty. The Court was careful to note that the "substitute parents" of the early reformers' ideology have, in fact, become guards, state employees, and fellow juveniles incarcerated for offenses ranging in scope from "waywardness" to rape and murder.

It is therefore apparent to the reader of Part II of the *Gault* decision that the

---

[20] *Kent v. United States,* 383 U.S. 541 (1966).

[21] *Id.* at 556, citing Handler, "The Juvenile Courts and the Adversary Systems: Problems of Function and Form," 1965 WIS. L. REV. 7 (other citations omitted).

[22] *In Re Gault, supra* note 1, at 12–31.

case was not, as the narrow scope of its holding might wrongly suggest, decided in the abstract. Part II was a harsh and critical prelude to the decision. It was tempered with concern for a system of justice that the Court suggests has fallen short of its early hopes and aspirations, and it was laced with documentation of these failings. It is submitted that the marked distaste for the course of juvenile justice in this country, which permeated the decision, was of itself a prologue (as *Kent* was for *Gault*) for further decisions by the Supreme Court extending the due process clause into other aspects of juvenile proceedings. To speculate on the direction of such hypothetical extensions would be indeed foolish. As noted earlier, the Supreme Court selects only a small fraction of those cases submitted to it for review, and of these, only those issues necessary to dispose of a case are actually adjudicated (the appellate review and transcript issue in *Gault* is an example).

For those who are understandably concerned with the present, the *Gault* decision leaves many questions unanswered. Mr. Justice Fortas wrote in *Gault* that "neither the Fourteenth Amendment nor the Bill of Rights is for adults alone." But if indeed they are not for adults only, the Fourteenth Amendment and the Bill of Rights are not yet for children completely. The *Gault* decision did not cover the procedures or constitutional rights applicable to the pre-judicial of post-adjudicative stages of the juvenile process.[23] Thus, the body of law now pertaining to the rights of the adult criminal suspect when he is first brought into custody does not yet apply to the juvenile suspect. It is yet to be decided whether the Fourth Amendment's prohibitions

against unreasonable searches and seizures, protections made fully binding upon the states, will affect the kind of evidentiary matter admissible against the child in an adjudicatory proceeding. The Fifth Amendment's right to a grand jury indictment and the double jeopardy prohibition have not yet been made fully binding upon the states by the Supreme Court, and their relevance to juvenile proceedings are uncertain.

One may ponder whether prolonged confinement in a "receiving home" pending a hearing on the merits would violate the Sixth Amendment's guarantee of a *speedy* trial, if this right is held to be firmly binding upon the states. The Sixth Amendment's guarantee to a *public* trial, which is binding upon the states, may have significant implications for juvenile hearings, which have by statute in a large proportion of the states been closed to the public. The Sixth Amendment's guarantee that the accused be entitled to have the court compel witnesses to appear and testify, a right closely related to the right of confrontation, has potential relevance to juvenile hearings, and cannot be ignored (although this right is not yet firmly binding upon the states under the Fourteenth Amendment).

One might further consider the Eighth Amendment and its prohibitions against cruel and unusual punishment, excessive fines, and excessive bail. If any or all of the Eight Amendment is eventually made binding upon the states, how will the course of juvenile justice be affected? Is it cruel and unusual punishment to deny to a child those safeguards not considered by *Gault* and then subject that child to confinement in an institution of limited treatment facilities? Does unconditional relegation to a "receiving home" pending a hearing infringe on the prohibition against excessive bail?

That these issues may legitimately be

[23] *Id.* at 13.

framed, in the light of the Supreme Court's refusal in *Gault* to accept the traditional noncriminal label attached to juvenile proceedings is, in the writer's opinion, the greatest significance of the decision. It is not possible to even speculate as to the extent to which the Supreme Court is prepared to go in according to juveniles the procedural safeguards available to adults in criminal proceedings. All that is clear is that the sweeping, intangible concept of due process has at last been officially introduced to our juvenile courts.

34.

Relationship of the Probation Officer and
the Defense Attorney After Gault

Charles E. Cayton

The Supreme Court's decision of *In Re Gault*[1] in the spring of 1967 plunged the juvenile court system into a period of dramatic change. Juveniles accused of delinquency received some of the most basic of due process rights—to notice, to counsel, to confrontation and cross-examination, and the privilege against self-incrimination. Without requiring them, the Court strongly emphasized the rights to appellate review and to a transcript of proceedings in the *Gault* opinion itself,[2] and has begun to consider cases challenging other aspects of current juvenile court procedure.[3]

SOURCE. Charles E. Cayton, "Relationship of the Probation Officer and the Defense Attorney After Gault" from *Federal Probation*, Volume 32, March 1970, pp. 8–13. Reprinted with permission.

[1] 387 U.S. 1.

[2] At 387 U.S. 58.

[3] A Nebraska case, raising the issues of jury trials and the proper standard of proof in delinquency hearings, was recently dismissed by the Supreme Court on jurisdictional grounds. Dissenting from the per curiam opinion, Justices Black and Douglas argued strongly for jury trials in delinquency hearings, and, implicitly at least, for the full application of the procedural rights of the Bill of Rights to delinquency hearings. See *DeBacker v. Brainard*, No. 15 October Term, 1969, decided November 12, 1969.

The *Gault* decision is apparently only the beginning of the Supreme Court's intervention on behalf of the legal part of the sociolegal blending of approaches in the modern juvenile court. This article reports on the results of a study of a local juvenile court system in California, designed to examine a key dimension of the changes touched off by *Gault*—the developing relationship between probation officers and attorneys in juvenile court.

CALIFORNIA AND GAULT

Just prior to the Gault decision the California legislature had before it bills which dramatically increased the legal rights of juveniles, going beyond what the Supreme Court did in *Gault*. What the California legislation essentially proposed was to extend the right to counsel and the privilege against self-incrimination far back into the prehearing and law enforcement stages. It was to juvenile justice what *Miranda v. Arizona*[4] was to adult criminal cases. Subsequently passed and signed by the Governor during the 1967 session, the key bill, AB 1095, was introduced with wide

[4] 384 U.S. 436 (1966).

bipartisan sponsorship on March 16, 1967, 2 months before the *Gault* decision.

It may seem ironic and somewhat surprising that California should steal a march on the Supreme Court in "handcuffing the police." Yet as early as 1961 California had written into its Juvenile Court Law most of the rights announced in *Gault*. Thus for juveniles California compressed into 6 years a revolution which took the Supreme Court 25 years, from *Powell* v. *Alabama*[5] to *Miranda* v. *Arizona*. Attorneys for all accused juveniles, indigent or not, were now a real possibility at every significant stage of juvenile proceedings, from arrest through disposition, for a system which had arrested over 303,000 juveniles statewide only the year before.[6] Miranda-like warnings were required at the time of arrest, at probation intake, and at all delinquency hearings.

REACTION IN A CALIFORNIA COUNTY

Officials at the study site, a Southern California county, reacted quickly to implement the new legislation. Waiver forms were prepared containing language designed to warn juveniles of their new rights at the police and probation intake stages, so that intelligent and voluntary waivers could be made. If he desired, the juvenile could retain counsel, or have counsel appointed, and he had the right to remain silent. The juvenile court judge and the referee hearing cases in the county began to observe the new procedure in their hearing rooms. The juvenile caseload of the public defender's office in the county soon doubled and a second referee was added to the system to handle the increase in contested cases.

At the same time, the officials in the county responsible for making the changes attempted to retain as many as possible of the traditional features of juvenile proceedings. The intake probation officers were still responsible for making filing decisions. The investigating probation officer still prepared, in a single report, the materials which formed the basis of his recommendations to the hearing officer as to findings on the charges and an appropriate dispositional plan. Hearings were *not* bifurcated—the referee or judge still had both aspects of the investigating probation officer's report available *prior* to the hearing—and the preponderance of the evidence rule remained in effect.

Contrary to the practice adopted in a neighboring county, the decision was made *not* to introduce prosecuting attorneys into contested hearings in a systematic fashion. Nor did the county decide to staff the juvenile court with a legal officer from the probation department to formally present cases. The hearing was conducted, from start to finish, by the judge or one of his referees. The stage was set, then, for the systematic introduction of a new social position—that of defense attorney—into the social structure of a local juvenile court system[7] at the same time the county, in making the change, was attempting to retain the traditional features of juvenile court practice to as great a degree as possible.

To measure new role relationships, depth interviews of the occupants of the significant social positions making up this local juvenile court system were

---

[5] 287 U.S. 45 (1932).

[6] California Department of Justice, Bureau of Criminal Statistics, *Crime and Delinquency in California in 1966* (Sacramento, California, 1967), p. 180.

[7] A 1960 study conducted in California by the Governor's Special Study Commission found that in most counties lawyers appeared in juvenile courts in less than 1 percent of the cases. Governor's Special Study Commission on Juvenile Justice, Report of the Commission, *A Study of the Administration of Juvenile Justice in California*, Part II (Sacramento, California, 1960), p. 12.

conducted in the summer of 1968, after the new procedures had been in effect roughly 1 year. Those interviewed, approximately 40 in all, included members of the youth bureaus of the city police and county sheriff's departments, of the intake and investigation sections of the county probation department, of the public defender's office in the county, private attorneys, the juvenile court referees, and the juvenile court judge. Several days were spent observing delinquency hearings, especially contested hearings.

THREE ATTORNEY ROLES

Attorneys, faced with a new kind of client, and working in an unfamiliar setting, had no consistent approach to their roles in the juvenile court system. At one extreme they were "advocates" who patterned their behavior after their roles in adult criminal cases:

There is no substantial difference between the position of a defendant in juvenile court from that of a defendant in adult court as far as I'm concerned. I know there is all this talk about rehabilitation, but in practice, if you look at what happens after a case is over and the kid is in CYA, it's just like a jail. So you can't pay any attention to the theory. It's just there to make people feel better. You can say: "I'm really sending you to jail in your own interest." This is poppycock! I fight for whatever the kid wants. Of course, I have to be reasonable. I can't ask for probation when it is impossible, but I try to get the best deal for a kid, just like I do in my defenses in adult court.

At the other extreme, attorneys took a rehabilitative stance, a distinctly different, even an opposite, approach from the style of the "advocate":

The two systems [adult and juvenile] are in no way comparable. You are in two different ball games. If the probation officer determines that a juvenile is a suitable client for juvenile court then I tell the kid to level completely with them. The juvenile court is a non-adversary system designed to rehabilitate these minors. This is the whole purpose and philosophy of the Juvenile Court Law. I don't want these kids to get the idea that they are beating a rap. When they do something wrong, they ought to face it while they are young and can do something about it. I treat them like they are my own kids and this is what the Code says you should do: Give them the treatment their parents ought to be giving them.

Most attorneys, however, had mixed feelings about the proper approach to juvenile court practice.

A third role type, essentially a mixture of the advocate and rehabilitative approaches, was the most popular role. For these attorneys, an advocacy style held little incentive when there were no juries in juvenile court and they appeared frequently before the same hearing officer. Adult court was a place where attorneys could shoot for a hung jury even if they had an otherwise hopeless defense. This did not work in juvenile court. In adult court attorneys could plead for mercy to enlist the judge's support, or cite statutory provisions during sentencing hearings to help, or at least impress their clients. In juvenile court they sounded like "pitchmen," they could not cite penalty provisions, and they did not know enough about the various detention facilities to be effective. At the same time, most attorneys felt that there really was not as much at stake in juvenile court for their clients anyway. At most the juvenile would have a misdemeanor on a confidential record. All these factors lessened their incentive to be advocates.

Still, several of these attorneys held the "advocacy" approach just below the surface. On minor offenses such as truancy or runaways they recommended to their clients that they admit the offense. Even here, some had mixed feelings. As one attorney said: "I never feel right in recommending that a client admit to something." If the offense was serious, with commitment to a detention facility likely, these attorneys made it a policy to recommend silence about the offense. As one public defender said: "I can't see allowing a kid to confess himself into CYA; that's not m/ job."

For most attorneys, then, the proper approach to juvenile court lay in an ambiguous area between the two extremes of advocacy and rehabilitation. These attorneys were only partial advocates. Since in most juvenile cases there was not as much at stake legally as in adult criminal cases, and because juvenile cases were heard informally without a jury, it often was in the interest of the minor to admit the offense. In adult court you kept your client silent and made the district attorney prove his case. In approaching a juvenile hearing an attorney had to take a rehabilitative approach, acting as an adviser rather than an advocate. On the other hand, one had to be careful that the juvenile did not admit to something he did not do. In this situation, the attorney permitted the minor to talk to the intake and investigating probation officers only about matters unconnected with the offense. At the hearing itself, there was no prosecutor to take "potshots" at in the hope of influencing the judge and jury. Faith in the fairness of the judge or referee had to carry the day, rather than legal fencing. Attorneys usually went along with the probation officer's disposition recommendations even when they disagreed with them.

Under the best circumstances, this mixing of stances worked well. Still, practicing in the juvenile court system could be very frustrating, as the following attorney's comment shows:

You have to be prepared for anything in juvenile court. As an attorney you may go out to the Hall prepared to defend your client on a specific issue. However, once you are there it is possible that the hearing may develop into a trial for some quite different issue. The petition can be amended right there in court, if it hasn't already been changed before. If they can't get him on an armed robbery charge, they can amend it to petty theft and if that doesn't work, they can amend it to malicious mischief. The galling thing about this is that it may not make one whit of difference for the sentence a kid receives which charge he is convicted of.[8] The ground rules are constantly changing. For a long time I didn't know whom or what I was fighting.

PROBATION OFFICERS AND ATTORNEYS

The probation officers had a similar range of approaches to their relationships with attorneys. Some saw attorneys in a "Perry Mason" light:

Probation officers and lawyers take quite different approaches. We get more involved with the child and what he is while the lawyer is interested only in the tech-

---

[8] This situation was characterized by a phrase often used by the probation officers: "A 602 is a 602!" Section 602 of the California Juvenile Court Law, and a common provision in most states, provides, in part: "Any person under the age of 21 years who violates any law of this State or of the United States or any ordinance of any county of this State defining crime . . . is within the jurisdiction of the juvenile court, which may adjudge such person to be a ward of this court."
Thus, any law violation, from a minor to a very serious offense, brings a juvenile within the jurisdiction of the juvenile court. Once within this jurisdiction, the legal degree of the seriousness of the violation tends to be of lesser importance than the casework factors—home, family, and personal needs—in determining disposition, which may include removal from the home even for an offense which would be considered a minor one if committed by an adult. Such "incarceration" under the concept of individualized justice puzzles many offense-oriented attorneys, as this outburst suggests.

nical questions of the law. Sure, attorneys try to affect my filing and disposition recommendations. That's their job. If they didn't do that, they wouldn't be earning their fees. They try all the Perry Mason tricks—the rosy picture of the family, the bad guys in the police station, the momentary lapse theory, the effect of the record on the young juvenile. However, I simply listen and give their views no weight. You can't con an attorney. You end up giving them all this information and then they turn around and stab you in the back. They are either going to cooperate with you or not.

At the same time, all the probation officers felt that minors were incapable of deciding whether to ask for an attorney. This put officers with a "Perry Mason" image of attorneys in the difficult position of being asked for advice in making the waiver decision. Refusal to "help" interfered with rapport during intake, while a more positive response forced the probation officer temporarily into the unfamiliar and essentially undesired role of legal advisor and gave his subsequent intake relationship overtones of "prosecution."

Probation officers who viewed attorneys more sympathetically, many of whom they considered to be "almost social workers," saw the Miranda-like warnings and the presence of attorneys as a clarifying force. Once the "technical" issues were removed from the interview, the intake and investigation process could get down to the essentials —discovering the needs of the offender. Moreover, the increased presence of attorneys in juvenile cases reinforced a tendency to make filing decisions based on a juvenile's environmental and personal needs, leaving the attorney the task of battling the case made "against" the juvenile by the police.

Since the juvenile could have a defence attorney "on his side" to balance any overzealous police action, relations with the probation officer were much freer. If an occasional aggressive defense attorney tried to allow the juvenile to escape needed treatment on a legal technicality, the referee, a lawyer himself, would take care that tactics of this sort did not interfere with a proper decision. The probation officer's major stake in a juvenile case, and the whole thrust of his training and interests related to the dispositional phases, and since it was the rare attorney who had the resources and training to challenge competently a given dispositional recommendation, attorneys in the juvenile court system were not felt to be a threat.

In contrast to these two general approaches to attorneys, some of the intake and investigating officers saw great similarity between their own roles and those of attorneys. Such officers viewed themselves as having above average knowledge of the law and hence could give "sound" legal advice in the warning and waiver process. Giving this advice was consistent with a "helping" role, though it tended to force the juvenile's perception of the police in the unfavorable direction of prosecutors. In dealing directly with a juvenile's attorney (usually a private attorney) at intake, these probation officers established a relationship which approached the "plea-bargaining" or "charge-negotiation" interchange so characteristic of defense attorney-district attorney relationships in adult criminal cases.[9]

While the probation officer in fact faced the attorney in a distinctly inferior position vis-a-vis technical knowledge of the rules of evidence in such an interchange, there were elements that could

[9] "Plea-bargaining" refers to the system in which defendants trade a plea of guilty for a reduction in the charges against them. See Donald J. Newman, *Conviction: The Determination of Guilt or Innocence Without Trial* (Boston: Little, Brown and Co., 1966).

put the probation officer in an equal, if not superior position. Since the police generally appeared as "prosecutors," at least in absentia, the attorney and the intake officer were drawn toward common ground in discussing a given juvenile's problems. The civil rule of a preponderance of the evidence, in effect at the hearings, made the potential outcome of a filing decision much less uncertain for the probation officer, even if the evidence was somewhat shaky. Added to this was the fact that the intake officer had much greater control over disposition outcomes, which often were decisive in a juvenile case where so far as the charges were concerned the legal degree of seriousness meant little. Moreover, if an attorney really did his homework and seemed to be genuinely concerned to work out a good dispositional framework for a minor and his family, an informal closure of the case, without a court hearing, was the better course anyway.[10]

WHO IS THE PROSECUTOR IN JUVENILE COURT?

A curious and symptomatic feature of the responses of the personnel interviewed in this local juvenile court system was revealed by their answers to the question of who now "prosecutes" in juvenile court. Put another way, the question was: Against whom is a defense attorney "defending" his clients

[10] Informal disposition of arrested juveniles, by police, probation departments, and juvenile courts settled most cases in California in 1966. While a total of 303,020 juvenile arrests were made, only 37,344 petitions were received by the State's juvenile courts. The courts dismissed 6,978 of these petitions. Formal court action therefore occurred in only 30,366 cases, or only slightly more than 10 percent of the total number of juvenile arrests. Compiled from statistics published in California, Department of Justice, Bureau of Criminal Statistics, *Crime and Delinquency in California in 1966* (Sacramento, 1967), pp. 29, 46, 180, 183, 200, 202.

in a juvenile delinquency proceeding? The most appropriate answer is, of course, to say "nobody prosecutes because nobody has to defend; all parties are acting on behalf of an accused juvenile." Yet this response glosses over the confusion of roles in juvenile court brought on legally by *Gault* and practically by the increased juvenile court activity of defense attorneys.

In spite of this, and possibly a surprise for many, the classic answer still foreclosed discussion in some instances, even for some of the attorneys who read and faithfully adhered to the words of the opening section of the California Juvenile Court Law:

> The purpose of this chapter is to secure for each minor under the jurisdiction of the juvenile court such care and guidance, preferably in his own home, as will serve the spiritual, emotional, mental, and physical welfare of the minor and the best interests of the state: . . . to secure for him custody, care, and discipline as nearly as possible equivalent to that which should have been given by his parents.

On the other hand, such an answer did not and could not settle the matter of "prosecution" in the juvenile court system. It was a major assumption of the *Gault* opinion that juvenile offenders needed legal defense and that this defense could be adequately provided neither by the probation officer nor by the juvenile court judge. Thus a consciousness of prosecutor roles developing in the county's juvenile court was understandable. What had perhaps been latent before now became manifest, despite the fact that the district attorney still remained out of juvenile proceedings.

When police officers were asked "who prosecutes?" they replied "the probation officer—he files the petition." When probation officers and referees were asked, they replied "the case was prepared by the police." When the defense attorneys were asked, they replied "the probation officer and the referee—the probation officer prepares the case and the referee presents it in court." Most important, there was substantial agreement, however reluctant, among all the officials interviewed that the district attorney would eventually have to take over formal investigation and presentation of the State's side in delinquency cases. Thus, the search for a prosecutor, if not a conscious desire for one, seemed to be a major symptom of the structural change put in motion in the county by the *Gault* decision and by the California legislature's amendments to the Juvenile Court Law.

ROLE AMBIGUITY AND SOCIAL CHANGE

The lack of clear role definitions tends to place a strain on organizational structures and the incumbents of the positions making up an organization.[11] If the experience of this county juvenile court system is any indication, the positions of juvenile probation officer at intake and the defense attorney practicing in juvenile court now suffer from a rather serious condition of role ambiguity.[12] Such a condition can have

important consequences for the social effectiveness of an organization as a whole and the personal effectiveness of the role performers. Miscues and misunderstandings develop and the jurisdictional boundaries of social interaction become confused. Important and necessary relationships for an organization may be broken off. The confusion and shifting of definitions of the social self required of attorneys and probation officers and others[13] may lead to cynicism, alienation from the goals of the organization, or even personality dislocation.[14]

Role ambiguity is at its greatest for the probation officer, who may find himself in a field of expectations defining him as simultaneously a "social worker," a "prosecutor," and even a "defense attorney," depending upon the circumstances of the defendant, the behavior of the police during the arrest process, and the approach a defense attorney takes to him. A defense attorney must simultaneously perform as a "social

[11] For one theory of role strain, see W. J. Goode, "A Theory of Role Strain," 25 *American Sociological Review* 483–496 (1960). "Role theory" is an important body of concepts linking anthropology, psychology, social psychology, and sociology. It has been little applied to the study of legal institutions. See Bruce J. Biddle and Edwin J. Thomas, *Role Theory* (New York: John Wiley & Sons, Inc., 1966).

[12] Role ambiguity may be formally defined as the existence of multiple roles for a single role sector of a social position. The sector probation officer—attorney is such a sector. Of course, a defense attorney committed strongly and clearly to an "advocacy" approach, or alternatively to a "rehabilitative" approach does not suffer from this condition. The great majority of attorneys and probation officers studied had no such clear role conceptions, however, nor did most probation officers have

clear role definitions for attorneys. A closely related, though not identical, variable is "degree of role consensus." See Neal Gross, Ward S. Mason, and Alexander W. McEachern, *Explorations in Role Analysis: Studies of the School Superintendency Role* (New York: John Wiley & Sons, Inc., 1958).

[13] Another dimension of role relationships examined was the defense attorney—referee relationship in juvenile court. Defense attorneys were asked if they ever made an objection in court to the line of questioning of defendants or witnesses used by a judge or referee in "cross-examination." They said that they rarely did this, wouldn't recommend it, and that if they did the referee (or judge) would turn right around and rule on his own actions anyway. Juvenile court judges and referees were seen as having the mixed role of prosecutor-judge, a fact which was both a source of humor and frustration for the attorneys.

[14] The relationship between self and role is discussed in Theodore R. Sarbin, "Role Theory," in Gardner Lindzey, ed., *Handbook of Social Psychology*, Vol. I (Cambridge, Massachusetts: Addison-Wesly Publishing Company, 1954), pp. 223–258.

worker" and as an "advocate," a difficult combination probably more appropriate to the traditional roles of probation officers.[15]

What roles our society eventually works out for probation officers and defense attorneys in the juvenile court system generally, and particularly in their own interaction during intake, needs more time and further study. It is not too much to suppose at the moment, however, that there is a close connection between the role ambiguity discovered here and the strikingly consistent expectation in this local system that prosecutors would soon be a general phenomenon in juvenile courts. This may only be a symptom of further social change.

Of course, juvenile probation officers do have certain role relationships which are free from ambiguity. For example, "carrying" officers seem free from role ambiguity in their role relationships with probationers. Here the probation officer's formula is "You have been found delinquent, let's do something about it." This is the ground rule of his subsequent interaction with a probationer and it enables him to direct this relationship over the course of a juvenile's probation period. Defense attorneys have many role relationships in the adult criminal legal system which are relatively unambiguous.

At the same time, it may be that role ambiguity will persist as a fact of certain roles in the juvenile court system, just as it did before *Gault* for the juvenile court judge and the probation officer who had to perform sociolegal role combinations.[16] Yet nowhere in our

society does the need seem greater to have clear and consistent role definitions than in the legal system, where the consequences for defendants from official role performances are so great and the public's understanding and acceptance of the objectives and performances of legal institutions so critical.

The adult court system, which contains both the positions of prosecutor and probation officer, performing their roles at relatively isolated points in the process, may yet prove to be the model for the future of the juvenile court. The greater the pressure from role ambiguity on the role relationship of probation officers and defense attorneys, the more intense may be the pressure for breaking off this relationship prior to a delinquency hearing, and for transferring the roles of the intake probation officer to the convenient and available alternative of prosecuting attorney.

LESSONS FOR THE FUTURE

The *parens patriae* doctrine, which casts the juvenile court and through it the state into the role of surrogate parents for juvenile offenders, has sustained and rationalized a separate juvenile court system for the 70 years of its life. Its advocates saw in it the possibility that the best features of criminal due process could be informally respected while maintaining, in a branch of the civil courts, a flexibility consistent with rehabilitative rather than punitive justice.

With the *Gault* decision the Supreme Court has heavily qualified the capacity of the *parens patriae* doctrine to remain a sufficient rationale for a separate juvenile court. At the same time, the Court failed to state a new philosophy

---

[15] It was precisely this combination that the Supreme Court found distasteful in *Gault*. In the developing attorney role style for juvenile court the shoe would seem to be on the other foot.

[16] A tendency pointing in this direction is the relatively low level of role involvement which public defenders have for their juvenile caseloads. See Anthony Platt, How-

ard Schechter, and Phyllis Tiffany, "In Defense of Youth: A Case Study of the Public Defender in Juvenile Court," 43 *Indiana Law Journal* 619–640 (Spring 1968).

for juvenile courts to follow. As it does in most cases, the Supreme Court stayed strictly with the concrete case, making it quite clear that while some of the important due process rights of persons accused of crimes now applied to juvenile courts, these courts could and should continue to proceed informally and adapt their methods to the nature and situations of their defendants.

What happens now depends to a great extent on how probation officers and attorneys work out their role relationships. The right to counsel in juvenile delinquency proceedings means much more than mechanical adherence to the procedural technicalities of the law. It means that the occupants of a social position which is a major force in the adult legal system have moved bodily into the social structure of juvenile justice. Defense attorney-probation officer roles hold the key to the future shape of that structure.

The intake officers and the defense attorneys are the only ones with a truly intimate relationship to accused juveniles prior to a delinquency hearing. At the hearing itself their arguments form the major basis of the hearing officer's decisions. Neither a "Perry Mason" image of attorneys by probation officers nor an aggressive advocacy stance by defense attorneys holds much hope for the future. Nor does the replacement, by prosecuting attorneys, of the intake functions of probation departments for juvenile courts now performed by individual probation officers in many jurisdictions.

Probably it is too much to expect that all attorneys will accept the rehabilitative approach of some of the attorneys interviewed in this study, just as we cannot expect probation officers to welcome attorneys with open arms. What is very hopeful is the degree to which the interviews showed attorneys adopting only a partial advocacy approach to juvenile court and the fact that some probation officers had enough confidence to approach attorneys as partners rather than adversaries. Only in this relationship can the two meet on relatively common ground. Sharing common aims as joint counselors to a minor and his family, each has something to offer the other. The defense attorney's greatest stumbling block is the disposition plan and this is the probation officer's great strength. The probation officer, untrained in the law, can learn much from the attorney that can sharpen his precision so far as the adjudicatory phases of casework are concerned. Both have a common interest in keeping prosecutors out of juvenile court.

Rescuing the separate juvenile court from its current limbo will not be an easy task. What this study illustrates is that the task must begin at the very basic level of attorney and probation officer roles in intake. Clearly, the responsibility for taking the initiative in establishing constructive relationships with attorneys rests with individual probation officers and their departments. They have the greatest stake in the question of whether the juvenile court takes the full step to the adult court pattern. If a stable and effective attorney-probation officer role can be worked out that step need not be taken.

35.

Lawyers in Juvenile Court

Spencer Coxe

The term "right to counsel" is ambiguous. It may mean merely the right to have counsel present in court, or it may mean the right to be furnished with counsel, by court appointment if necessary. The right of a juvenile to have counsel *present* in delinquency proceedings antedates the landmark *Gault* decision of the United States Supreme Court.[1] In most jurisdictions, including Pennsylvania (the only state with which the author is familiar), this right had already been recognized either by statute or by judicial decision. The right of a juvenile to have counsel *furnished* was not firmly established as a constitutional principle until *Gault*.

The *Gault* decision will give tremendous impetus to the trend toward provision of counsel, not only because of the explicit "right" to counsel" ruling, but because it is now clear that delinquency proceedings are adversary in nature and are governed by rules and concepts that require a lawyer for both parties. And because the Supreme Court has now laid down the principles by which juvenile proceedings must be conducted, lawyers now have an understandable and meaningful role to play. (The extent of this role and its limitations have not yet been defined.)

Already the trend is clear. In Philadelphia, only about 5 per cent of the children appearing in juvenile court had been represented by counsel in the period immediately preceding 1967. At present, close to 40 per cent of the children are represented.

As the trend toward representation of juveniles gathers momentum, it may be helpful to review the situation that led to the *Gault* decision and to take another look at the controversy over lawyers in juvenile court.

First, *Gault* has cleared away the myth that juvenile court judges are kindly uncles who take the place of the wise and loving parent. The cruel fact is now out in the open: the juvenile court plays the same role as the criminal court. The basic task of each is to remove wrongdoers from society so that they can trouble us no more and so that their punishment will deter others. With respect to both adults and children, there is much talk of rehabilitation, but most of it is hypocrisy, as demonstrated by (1) the nature of the institutions in which we confine the troublemakers,

SOURCE. Spencer Coxe, "Lawyers in Juvenile Court," from *Crime and Delinquency*, Volume 13, No. 4, October 1967, pp. 488–493. Reprinted with permission.

[1] *In the Matter of Gault*, 35 U.S. Law Week 4399 (U.S. Sup. Ct. 15 May 1967).

(2) the small amount of money we are willing to spend on probation staffs and remedial services, and (3) our unwillingness to mount a meaningful attack on the causes of crime and delinquency. In short and in general, delinquency proceedings are essentially punitive and are invoked for the sake of protecting society, not the child.

This fact of life admitted, it follows that a child charged with delinquency should have the right to counsel at every stage of the proceedings, for exactly the same reason that an adult accused of crime should have this assistance—namely, that the child, like the adult, is threatened with loss of liberty and with a damaging stigma. Indeed, a child may suffer more than an adult. The adult is more likely to be able to pick up life's threads after imprisonment; a child may find his emotional and economic future ruined by commitment in the formative years.

Second, the due process rights now guaranteed by *Gault* will remain essentially meaningless without the presence of a lawyer. A child denying the commission of an act of delinquency has a better chance of being treated fairly if the delinquency proceeding is adversary, and for this a lawyer is essential. Indeed, if an adult is unable to defend himself against a criminal charge without the help of a lawyer, a child is less able to avail himself of his rights—his right to be informed of the charges against him, his right to cross-examine witnesses, his right to have hearsay evidence excluded, and his right not to be forced to incriminate himself.

RESISTANCE BY THE SYSTEM

In a notable Philadelphia incident antedating *Gault*, eight children were adjudicated delinquent at a hearing which lasted approximately fifteen minutes. The defendants were not informed of the charges. At the hearing, there was no testimony whatsoever that any of the children had committed the act which had brought them into court. Neither they nor their parents were permitted to say anything in court. They were all committed indefinitely, several to a penal institution. At later rehearings, with counsel present, six were discharged. Some of the rehearings lasted three or four hours per child. Herein is the key to the "problem" of counsel, as the courts see it—in Philadelphia, at any rate. With counsel present as a general rule, it is impossible for one judge to "hear" seventy cases a day, as had been traditional. Counsel, therefore, threatens to break down the system, which requires a judge to get through as many cases as possible in a day. The job traditionally is conceived in arithmetical rather than human terms: how to dispose of x number of cases in y number of hours with z number of judges. The court and its probation staff have not welcomed lawyers because lawyers upset the arithmetic. A symbol of the resistance to lawyers has been the absence in the Philadelphia courtrooms of any table for defense counsel.

Another reason for hostility to lawyers is the human desire of judges to play God. The typical juvenile court act, with its lack of procedural safeguards and substantive standards defining delinquency, has permitted judges a freedom that exists nowhere else in the law. The same judges that had free rein before *Gault* are still sitting, and it would be naive to suppose that all of them are now willing to accept meekly the Supreme Court's reminder that they are servants rather than masters of due process. Indeed, in suburban Delaware County, at least one judge has made it quite clear that he intends to ignore *Gault* until his *own* Supreme Court tells him differently.

Thus, our third point is that the presence of a lawyer, playing an adversary role, is the best single means of insuring that a juvenile court judge will focus solely on deciding the case before him according to law and will not be swayed by secondary considerations such as the size of the list awaiting disposition or his faith in his own wisdom.

Demonstration of the need for counsel is only the first step. Two other important considerations remain—first, the availability of counsel; second, the role of counsel in juvenile court proceedings. Bar associations, programs financed by the 1964 Economic Opportunity Act, probation staffs, juvenile court judges, and the social work profession ought to be as zealous in seeing that free counsel is furnished to indigent juvenile defendants as they are when adults are accused of crime. We still have a long way to go. Even in Philadelphia, where a system of free legal assistance for juveniles is more highly developed than in most jurisdictions, over one-half of the children still appear without lawyers. Compare this with the criminal courts, where essentially *no* adult accused of crime appears in court without a lawyer. The brute fact is that close to 10,000 children whose families are unable to pay a lawyer's fee come under the Philadelphia court's jurisdiction each year.

The number of juvenile cases is roughly equal to the number of adult criminal cases. The meager support of the OEO and the generous volunteer services of lawyers are totally inadequate. The magnitude of the problem makes it a community responsibility.

ROLE IN ADJUDICATION

The role of counsel should be basically the same as in criminal cases; namely, to present the defendant's situation in the best possible light at every stage of the proceedings, beginning in the police station. This does not imply that the lawyer will regard his client

the way he would regard an adult accused of crime, or that his technique in dealing with the child's case will be the same. A sensitive lawyer will recognize that his role is not necessarily to help a kid beat the rap. A sensitive lawyer, like a sensitive judge or a sensitive social worker, knows when confession is good for the soul. But he also has reason to doubt the truth of many confessions which are prompted by fear of the police, fear of parents, or fear of other children. Therefore, counsel must often insist that the state prove its case.

What if the lawyer is insensitive? That is a risk, but it would appear that a child accused of delinquency stands a lot better chance of constructive interest and sympathy from a lawyer who is ethically bound to serve his interests than from a harried probation worker or from a judge who has already had fifty kids before him that day and five thousand in the past year.

We hear the argument that lawyers and adversary proceedings are apt to inflate a child's ego and harm him. Being neither a social worker nor a psychologist, I should perhaps refrain from evaluating this argument. But it does not impress me as much as the argument that children have a very keen sense of justice and are likely to be turned against society by being put through some kind of impersonal process without having someone, *at* their side and *on* their side, who can and will speak for them without being intimidated.

ROLE IN DISPOSITION

Another controversial question is whether the lawyer has any role to play in the disposition of the case. It is sometimes argued that a lawyer's services may be appropriate on behalf of a child who denies committing the offense which brings him into court, but that the lawyer's skill is irrelevant and its exercise obstructionist where the child admits the offense or has been found to have committed it, so that the only task remaining for the court is to decide what to do with him.

This thesis is unacceptable. In the first place, the distinction between adjudication and disposition is often nonexistent. In many jurisdictions the two steps are simultaneous and interwined. For example, in the *Gault* case, the hearing judge in Arizona apparently based his adjudication of delinquency, and also the commitment to the State Industrial School, on a statement in the probation report about "habitual involvement in immoral matters." The parents were unaware of the existence of the report or the charge until after the case had been decided. The *Gault* decision has not automatically brought an end to this confusion between adjudication and disposition; Supreme Court decisions are not self-executing.

Second, disposition like adjudication is supposed to be based on relevant evidence—evidence, for example, about the child's home life, his school record, and previous contacts with the police. In the production-line justice that has typified proceedings in most metropolitan juvenile courts, a judge's decision to commit a child to an institution rather than send him home may be grounded on little more than intuitions hastily arrived at on the basis of no information or scanty information. A long "police record," if subject to a lawyer's cross-examination, may turn out to reflect more upon the police than upon the child. School attendance records may also be misinterpreted; I have seen a damning "truancy" record evaporate under skillful analysis by the child's lawyer. Similarly, probation officers' reports based on neighbors' statements may be unreliable and certainly should have no immunity from a lawyer's challenge.

Third, without a legal advocate for the child, the judge not only may misapprehend the child's background and needs, but also may be unable to assess the merits of alternative dispositions. A lawyer can investigate and present the possibilities of supervision at home or with relatives. He may, before the hearing, make arrangements for the friendly help of a minister or for psychiatric care. In Pennsylvania we have found that judges may even be unaware of the nature of institutions to which they commit children. For example, most of them apparently have not known until recently that the State Correctional Institution at Dallas is a prison for "adults and juveniles declared to be and committed as defective delinquents,"[2] not a training school. At this institution, children spend a large part of their waking hours in prison cells. At the most they get one and a half hours of schooling a day, and some receive no schooling at all.

If counsel is needed at the dispositional phases, it follows that he must be furnished with all the information available to the judge. This principle was recognized by the Supreme Court in *Kent*,[3] at least with respect to the issues presented in that case. The Court stated that the right to counsel in juvenile court and the right to a hearing on waiver to criminal court are "meaningless—an illusion, a mockery—unless counsel is given an opportunity to function." Elaborating this, the Court stated that, "as a condition to a valid waiver order, petitioner was entitled to a hearing, including access by his counsel to the social records and probation or similar reports which presumably are considered by the court."

There may be occasions when the

[2] American Correctional Association, *Directory, Correctional Institutions and Agencies*, 1966 ed., p. 47.

[3] Kent v. United States, 383 U.S. 541.

parents should not have access to probation staff reports, but withholding the reports from inspection by counsel is not justified. Lawyers, as a group, may be trusted not to divulge inappropriate material to the child or his parents.

RESULTS

What do we know empirically about the effect of having comprehensive legal representation of juveniles? I pointed out above that in Philadelphia the percentage of juveniles represented by counsel has increased from 5 per cent to nearly 40 per cent since the summer of 1966. What has been the effect of this upon children and upon the community? It is too early to answer the question definitively. However, a few tentative conclusions can be drawn from the experience in Philadelphia. Some interesting information is available from an unpublished report of the Community Legal Service's Office for Juveniles.[4]

First, the provision of lawyers in a significant percentage of cases has resulted in a dramatic change in the pre-hearing custody policy. In the past, it was found "necessary" to confine large numbers of children for long periods of time before their hearing, and, despite much official hand-wringing, the situation became worse and worse. Chronic overcrowding of the Youth Study Center became the rule, with an average of fifty-three children sleeping on the gym floor each night. Now, as the result of test cases brought by CLS lawyers, the practice of holding children in detention before a court hearing merely upon the authority of a probation officer has been discontinued. Con-

sequently the Youth Study Center is now operating consistently at less than capacity. Also contributing to the depopulation of this facility has been legal action to compel a drastic reduction in post-hearing detention of children—sometimes up to three years—pending an opening in an institution providing appropriate treatment. The reduction has been accomplished by legal action to compel the release of children or their admission into other facilities. It is surprising how institutions will do what they "can't" when they have to. An important function of lawyers is to compel welfare services to do their jobs.

Second, the number of children being committed to institutions has dropped markedly as the proportion of children represented by counsel has risen. At the same time, significant numbers of children improperly committed in the past are being released on writs of habeas corpus. One can conclude from this only that juvenile facilities have been traditionally overcrowed largely because of unnecessary commitments. Stated bluntly, the presence of lawyers willing to fight for their clients is preventing judges from dumping children into institutions because they don't know what else to do and are too harried or callous to find another solution. It cannot be argued that the reduction is being effected by the release of children who should really be confined, for re-arrest of those represented by the CLS office has been at the unusually low rate of 2.6 per cent. (Admittedly the figure for one year's operation is not conclusive.)

A third dramatic by-product of large-scale representation is the creation of a staggering backlog of some 7,000 cases awaiting disposition. This is to be expected when one considers that in the pre-*Gault* days an average of fewer than two judges per court day disposed of 12,000 cases a year, and it was not un-

---

[4] Community Legal Services, Inc., is a non-profit charitable corporation whose purpose is to provide legal services for the indigent. It is funded 90 percent by a grant from the Office of Economic Opportunity and 10 per cent by the contributions of the members of the Philadelphia bar in the form of volunteer legal services.

common for one judge to "hear" 100 cases in a day. Nobody loves a backlog. Nonetheless, because of the backlog (and the lawyers who created it), the county court now finds it possible to do what was heretofore "impossible"— namely, to assign additional judges to the Juvenile Division. Five judges are now assigned each court day, instead of the customary two.

Thus, the tentative evidence seems to vindicate those of us who for years have been urging an abandonment of the *parens patriae* doctrine as hopelessly outdated by the harsh realities of modern life. The reality is that the state *cannot* be a good parent. If it cannot give love, it can at least give justice. The role of the lawyer is to see that it does.

section V

Treatment and Prevention

The treatment and prevention of juvenile delinquency is a difficult process. The difficulty stems from the fact that there is no consensus about what to prevent and treat, or how to accomplish these objectives. In terms of the psychiatric approach, Hakeem points out that delinquency is not viewed as behavior that is learned in the process of association, facilitated by certain self-conceptions and social processes, and supported by the definition of the situation. Rather, delinquency is but a *symptom* of psychopathology or some deeply embedded personality disturbance, although the literature reveals many contradictory statements and little data to substantiate the claims made by those advocating the psychiatric approach to delinquency treatment and prevention. In assessing the contradictions of psychiatry regarding delinquency prevention. Hakeem concludes that the limitations on data should be kept in mind.

Cressey, on the other hand, maintains that behavior, attitudes, beliefs, and values are not only the products of groups but are also the properties; therefore, attempts to change individual behavior should be directed at groups, and he discusses the application of Sutherland's theory of differential association to treatment.

An approach that has been widely used in New York City and elsewhere is the detached-worker movement. This movement actually began in Chicago in the late 1920s and was advanced by Thrasher in his study of gangs. The workers present themselves as friendly adults who provide guidance and assistance to adolescent groups. The worker must offer his services within a framework of values that reflects the adolescent group's orientation to the world—one that may be in conflict with the larger society. Walter Miller describes a detached-worker program that was carried out in Boston between the years 1954 and 1957 and evaluates the impact of this stratagem to achieve a significant reduction in delinquency.

Empey and Rabow discuss the effects of group counseling as a strategy for inducing behavioral change in delinquent probationers in Provo, Utah. This interesting experiment was guided by a behavioral theory that considers delinquency as a group phenomenon and views the task of rehabilitation as one of changing the shared delinquent characteristics. Treatment strategy is concerned with the total social system in which treatment must operate.

The Highfields Project illustrates an attempt by an institutional correctional system to develop and articulate connections between formal group therapy activities and other aspects of the total operation of the institution.

Although custody remains an important function which society ascribes to the juvenile correctional institution, another important goal is treatment and prevention. At the present time, all facilities for children give lip service to the treatment ideal, although the extent to which this goal is integrated into the organizational structure may be minimal. Polsky's analysis of the social structure in a private treatment institution for delinquent boys raises important questions concerning the extent to which treatment can take place in institutions. The informal social system he describes creates a powerful reference group for the inmates which effectively challenges and negates the staff's values and treatment efforts.

The article by Robinson and Smith, "The Effectiveness of Correctional Programs," analyzes findings from the major rehabilitation programs in California which were designed to measure five correctional alternatives. The authors conclude that there is no evidence to support claims that one correctional alternative is superior to another.

The selection by Sol Rubin raises fundamental questions concerning commitment to institutions when it is clear that the treatment available in these institutions is limited. Rubin maintains that the only basis for incarceration should be a concern for public safety. In every instance, alternatives to commitment should be explored in the community.

In the final selection, "The Future of Juvenile Institutions," Amos discusses some of the program changes that must be accepted and implemented, and the directions institutions should take in the future.

36.

A Critique of the Psychiatric Approach to
the Prevention of Juvenile Delinquency

Michael Hakeem

THE POWERFUL INFLUENCE
OF PSYCHIATRY

Psychiatrists, psychologists, social workers, and other psychiatrically oriented personnel have been powerfully influential in the work on the prevention of juvenile delinquency. The ideology of the psychiatric approach has had widespread acceptance. Psychiatrists and others who share their persuasion are much sought after for help with the problem. Their counsel is attended to eagerly. In turn, these practitioners have been more than generous with their advice.

To illustrate how widely the psychiatric approach has permeated public thinking, reference can be made to the final report of the New York Temporary State Commission on Youth and Delinquency. A large number of hearings were held by this body. All aspects of delinquency were discussed. Participants were from many walks of life. Psychiatrists, judges, school officials, social workers, legislators, and representatives of the general public testified. Hundreds of people were heard. The report concludes: "The emphasis placed on personality development, with its related problems of physical health, as the major immediate causative factor in delinquent behavior emerges as a striking characteristic of this inquiry." It is pointed out that the psychiatric orientation predominated also in the deliberations on prevention. The influence of this approach was likewise observed in the discussions on the correction of delinquents, where the emphasis was on "psychiatrically oriented treatment whether in clinic, hospital or training school" (39).

THE MODEST INFLUENCE
OF SOCIOLOGY

The influence of sociology in policies and practices relating to the prevention of delinquency has been modest in comparison with that of psychiatry. As a matter of fact, sociologists, especially those in criminology and corrections, have, in the main, subscribed to the psychiatric ideology. Furthermore, when sociologists have joined in deliberations looking toward the institution

SOURCE. Michael Hakeem, "A Critique of the Psychiatric Approach to the Prevention of Juvenile Delinquency," from *Social Problems,* Volume 5, No. 3, Winter 1957–1958, pp. 194–205. Reprinted with the permission of the Society for the Study of Social Problems and the author.

of practical measures for the prevention of delinquency, they have advocated, more often than not, the selfsame proposals which psychiatrists put forth. Sociologists have not often made recommendations distinguishable from those of the adherents of the psychiatric approach. It seems that sociologists have just not been able to convert their theories and research findings into propositions usable in the prevention of delinquency.

It is true that there have been some notable exceptions to this generalization, but they remain exceptions. Now, here is a discipline, psychiatry, which represents a portentous challenge to both the theory and practice of sociology in the prevention of delinquency. How have sociologists reacted? Generally speaking, they have not critically examined this alternative approach. Instead, they have frequently hailed and promoted its emergence and dominance almost as vigorously as have the psychiatrists. It is not surprising, incidentally, that an examination of psychiatric literature on delinquency reveals a negligible influence of sociological thinking.

Sometimes it is argued that social caseworkers, who work so intimately with psychiatrists, represent the sociological frame of reference in work with delinquents, and therefore sociologists are not needed. But social caseworkers do not represent sociology. Social caseworkers are almost completely committed to the psychiatric approach. Kahn, a social work educator, has noted that social work is not substantially influenced by social science and makes limited use of its knowledge (24).

Psychiatrists and social workers view the social case history through the frame of reference provided by the psychiatric, particularly the psychoanalytic, approach. They do not interpret social factors sociologically. Social data are viewed as the raw material for incorporation into psychological explanations. For example, Friedlander, who holds that the primary factors leading to antisocial behavior are "purely psychological" ones, sees environmental factors as important only insofar as they affect the parents' psychological rearing of the child (13). Schmideberg views social conditions as "the trigger or catalyst which brings into play various psychological phenomena which have their origin largely in the period of infantile development" (32). Most commonly, there is an even more clear-cut adherence to the fallacy of reductionism, as illustrated in the following statement by Bovet: "If a social factor is to become a criminal force, it must set in motion a number of psychological processes" (6, p. 20).

The point is that cultural conflict, group affiliations, social interaction, role, status, cultural norms, self-conception, and dozens of other sociological concepts are not viewed as providing, in their own right, a framework for analyzing behavior. They are most often seen, if they are seen at all, only as phenomena which may affect the psychological processes and psychopathology of the individual.

THE CONCEPT OF PRE-DELINQUENCY

Psychiatry, in its approach to the prevention of delinquency, proceeds on the basis of a number of assumptions. The claim is made that there exists a condition variously designated "pre-delinquency," "potential delinquency," or, in the psychoanalytic jargon, "latent delinquency." The position is taken that children afflicted with this condition will become delinquent unless there is remedial intervention. The contention is that such children can be identified at a very early age—even in earliest infancy—by psychiatrists and associated personnel. Once detected, they should be psychiatrically treated. Such treatment, preferably in a clinic, will prevent future delinquency. That is the series of assumptions subscribed to by the International Group of Experts on the Prevention of Crime and the Treatment of Offenders (30), the United Nations European Social Welfare Seminar (37), the United Nations itself (28), the Senate Subcommittee to Investigate Juvenile Delinquency (23), the United States Children's Bureau (19, p. 9), and the World Health Organization (6, pp. 55–56).

These agencies are taking their cues from psychiatrists and psychiatrically oriented specialists. For the assumptions are precisely the ones which these practitioners have been proclaiming. A typical example is provided by Banay, a psychiatrist who has long worked in corrections. He gives the following advice, referring to the prevention of delinquency:

If children were intelligently examined and treated [only under the supervision of a qualified psychiatrist] during the course of their school attendance it would be no difficult matter to predict which ones, upon graduation, would be likely to continue to have emotional difficulties resulting in deviant behavior. The most seriously disordered children could be treated and trained in special clinics (4).

The principle has been put in countless ways and it has been promulgated by countless psychiatrists. But only rarely has psychiatric zeal in this matter reached as high a pitch as it did in a declaration made by a renowned British psychiatrist and psychoanalyst, Dr. Edward Glover. He submitted a memorandum to the Royal Commission on Capital Punishment, on behalf of the Institute for the Scientific Treatment of Delinquency, which averred:

"If sufficient trouble were taken pathological cases liable to commit murder could be detected during early childhood; in other words pathological murder is potentially preventable . . ." (27, p. 492). Following is an excerpt from the dialogue between the chairman of the Commission and Dr. Glover on this point:

Do you think that that is only theoretically true, or do you think there is also some practicable way of setting about doing it?—I am quite convinced that there is a practicable way. It may require elaborate organisation [of psychiatric facilities] but it is practicable, that is beyond doubt . . . . I have no hesitation in saying that the crux of the whole approach to the problem of murder and the problem of prevention or punishment lies in an adequate attack at the right point. The right point is theoretically at any age, from birth upwards, but in practice between the ages of 2½ and 8. There should be an adequate service of child guidance, including the use of batteries of tests; and we feel fairly convinced that although you would not recognise all the potential murderers, that would be a foolish claim, you would strike seriously to the root of the problem of murder and its prevention.

You mean that by means such as those you could at least to a large extent eliminate that class of murderers who are murderers because they suffer from some form of mental disease?—From that age, yes. I could not say that would apply to all cases of murder, because mental stress is a thing which operates at all times of life.

Can you at that age identify those who have these potentialities in them?—That can now be done quite rapidly. There are so-called projective techniques of examination which are valuable, because they eliminate subjective bias on the part of the examiner and of the case examined. They have now arrived at a state of, not perfection, but adequacy, so that it is possible to take a child who is to all appearances merely an inhibited child, without any history of bad behaviour, and discover that he is potentially violent. I do not myself use these projective techniques, but I would like to see them widely employed to enable the diagnosis of potentially delinquent children to become effective (27, p. 501).

How did the Commission react to this attribution of extraordinary prescience to the projective tests? Did it probe skeptically for evidence? It did nothing of the sort. Rather, it asked for more details on the proposed procedures for carrying out the recommendations of Dr. Glover. And he obliged with a vast scheme for examining children in the schools, for "screening" the potential pathological murderers, for certifying suspected cases to local health officials, and for referring them to clinics for psychiatric observation, treatment, and surveillance (16).

Dr. Glover would place heavy emphasis on projective tests, and he cited the Rorschach as an example. This, of course, is the most widely used projective test. Now, it happens that the status of the Rorschach test—its usefulness, its reliability, and its validity— continue to be subjects around which swirls endless controversy. These are so far from being settled matters that the results of the Rorschach test should not be used as a basis for reaching decisions about people, and they should not be allowed to enter in any serious way into deliberations looking toward the disposition of cases.°

° Clinicians are quick to point out that they use the Rorschach results only as one part of a large array of information. Even if this were true, there are no scientific conclusions on the relative weight which should be assigned to them. In the deliberations of clinicians on any given case, scientifically standardized and demonstrable controls are not used to ensure that the Rorschach will not play a greater or lesser role than is thought desirable. Actually, it has been reported that some practitioners do depend exclusively on the Rorschach (12, p. 221). In either event, if the Rorschach is unreliable and invalid, its use as a basis for disposition of cases is unjustified.

Psychologists' evaluations of the Rorschach test range from unquestioning acceptance to outright rejection. It might be revealing to cite authorities whose views are at odds with Dr. Glover's enthusiasm. A psychologist, who is a specialist in the construction and evaluation of personality tests, recently stated that the Rorschach is "very unreliable and almost completely lacking in validity as far as the measurement of good or poor adjustment and emotional stability are concerned" (12, p. 134). Indeed, he takes as jaundiced a view of the Rorschach as he does of graphology, palmistry, and astrology and rules them all out as methods for determining personality characteristics. He even goes so far as to impugn the "critical acumen and scientific outlook" of psychiatrists and psychologists who would accept the Rorschach test, so certain is he that it is not a scientifically valid instrument (12, p. 225).

In an elaborate and comprehensive survey of statistical research on the Rorschach, Cronbach concluded:

So widespread are errors and unhappy choices of statistical procedures that few of the conclusions from statistical studies of the Rorschach test can be trusted. . . . Perhaps ninety per cent of the conclusions so far published as a result of statistical Rorschach studies are unsubstantiated . . . (9).

Wallen has described what he regards as severe defects in the Rorschach. He points out that examiners vary in their interpretation of the same record, that different examiners may obtain different records from the same client, and that any given record is only one of the possible records that a subject could produce (38). Finally, Benton, in a review of experimental and clinical data on the Rorschach, found that "current Rorschach practice is built on extremely shaky foundations." The use of the Rorschach test proceeds on the basis of assumptions which are largely unverified, according to him. His review led him to conclude that "the basic validity of the Rorschach personality sketch as an indicator of the important personality trends in the individual is yet to be established." As a matter of fact, Benton found that the personality of the examiner may play a decisive role in the subject's performance on the test (5).

THE SYMPTOMS OF PRE-DELINQUENCY

It is one of the basic tenets of the psychiatric approach that delinquent acts are symptoms. Delinquency is not viewed as behavior that is learned in the process of association, that is facilitated by certain self-conceptions, that is the outcome of social processing, that is supported by the definition of the situation. Delinquency is not explainable in its own right, according to the explicit or implicit psychiatric view of the matter. Delinquency is but a symptom—a surface symptom of psychopathology or some deeply hidden personality disturbance. Not only is it a symptom; it is "the hurt child's cry for help" (10). Children, clinicians say, do not, of course, consciously seek psychiatric treatment or other help when they are disturbed enough to need or want it. Their delinquency "is often their way of indirectly pointing up their need for help" (29).

Pre-delinquency, according to psychiatric reasoning, fits into the same framework. The child manifests certain personality traits and behavior that are taken for portents of delinquency. As has been mentioned, the psychiatrists insist that they can identify and treat such children and thereby stem the impending misfortune.

To illustrate the psychiatric ideology

in the prevention of delinquency, the personality traits and behavior regarded as symptomatic of maladjustment and oncoming delinquency, and the operation of a program calculated to identify and treat potential delinquents, reference can be made to a demonstration project sponsored by the United States Children's Bureau (35). This project covered one area in St. Paul, Minnesota, and was conducted from 1937 to 1943. It was directed by a psychiatrist, and the staff included caseworkers, group workers, psychologists, and others. A total of 1,466 children were registered for service. Of these, 739 received group work services and 727 received individualized services. However, casework permeated the whole treatment program (35, p. 57). The range in age was from three to twenty-two years and the median age was twelve. The project staff worked closely with community agencies. Parents, schools, churches, neighborhood organizations, parent-teachers associations, playground associations, the police, and social agencies were urged to refer children to the project. These groups were told that "any behavior exaggerated beyond what was normal for the child's age and sex might prove the forerunner of difficulty and should be weighed as a possible indication that some of the child's needs were not being satisfactorily met" (35, p. 47). Such behavior was regarded as a sign that the child "had called for help" (35, p. 13). That the project aimed squarely at the prevention of delinquency can be seen from the following rationale:

Service before the child has firmly established a pattern of behavior that is socially unacceptable . . . has a much greater opportunity to meet his needs than service brought to him at the point when, because of some antisocial act, the whole community is aroused (35, p. 13).

Four hundred and thirty-two cases were selected for a detailed analysis of the causes of maladjustment and of the treatment needed. These cases received intensive or limited treatment. The staff judged the outcome of treatment in these cases and found that 18 per cent showed "major improvement," 65 per cent, "partial improvement," and 17 per cent, "no improvement" (35, p. 72).

A long list of personality traits and types of behavior regarded as symptoms calling for the referral of children for expert diagnosis and treatment was prepared. Each symptom was described in a sentence or two, usually containing nothing more than examples of the behavior referred to (35, pp. 178–182). This list is presented below (35, pp. 47–48).

Bashfulness
Boastfulness
Boisterousness
Bossiness
Bullying
Cheating
Cruelty
Crying
Daydreaming
Deceit
Defiance
Dependence
Destructiveness
Disobedience
Drinking
Eating disturbances
Effeminate behavior (in boys)
Enuresis
Fabrication
Failure to perform assigned tasks
Fighting
Finicalness
Gambling
Gate-crashing
Hitching rides
Ill-mannered behavior
Impudence
Inattentiveness
Indolence

Lack of orderliness
Masturbation
Nailbiting
Negativism
Obscenity
Overactivity
Over-masculine behavior (in girls)
Profanity
Quarreling
Roughness
Selfishness
Sex perversion
Sex play
Sexual activity
Shifting activities
Show-off behavior
Silliness
Sleep disturbances
Smoking
Speech disturbances
Stealing
Stubbornness
Sullenness
Tardiness
Tattling
Teasing
Temper displays
Tics
Timidity
Thumbsucking
Truancy from home
Truancy from school
Uncleanliness
Uncouth personalities
Underactivity
Undesirable companions
Undesirable recreation
Unsportsmanship
Untidiness
Violation of street-trades regulations
Violation of traffic regulations

NORMALITY AND DEVIATION IN PRE-DELINQUENT BEHAVIOR

A large number of criticisms could be leveled at the St. Paul study. It violates some of the most elementary canons of research design. It does not even utilize a control group. That this is a crucial error in a research purporting to experimentally test the merit of a particular sort of treatment has been demonstrated amply in researches that have found mental patients, delinquents, and other types of subjects to show essentially the same kind and amount of improvement whether or not they receive treatment. For example, a recent survey of a large number of reports involving several thousand cases of neurotic children concluded that those who did not receive psychotherapy improved just as much as those who did (25). In regard to delinquents, Adamson and Dunham have shown that the general outcome for those receiving and those not receiving psychotherapy is the same (2). The point is that there is no evidence that it is· the treatment which brought about the alleged changes in the children of the St. Paul project. There is certainly good reason to believe that the children would have "improved" without treatment. And there is no evidence that simpler and less costly methods could not have yielded whatever results are claimed to have accrued from the methods used.

Ignoring other defects and turning to the items of behavior designated as precursors of delinquency, it must be said that it is at this point that the ideology of the psychiatric approach to the prevention of delinquency collapses. The kinds of behavior which are generally supposed to indicate predelinquency and which are said to require clinical treatment have not issued from valid research operations. Rather, they rest on the untested preconceptions of the adherents of the psychiatric ideology. Furthermore, research has not yet reduced these personality traits and behavior to reliably and validly measurable units. And it certainly has not been scientifically determined which traits, at what ages, in what degree, for what duration, in relation to what other traits, in what

configurations, and under what conditions, are indicative of future delinquency.°

That the staff of the St. Paul project was itself confused about the gravity of the behavior which should necessitate professional attention is shown by its discrepant references on this point. In one place, it is stated that the concern is with personality and behavior problems "however mild" (35, p. 3). Elsewhere, concern is expressed if these problems are "exaggerated" (35, p. 47). In another place, the reference is to "faint signals," and there it is noted in passing that these should be rated as equal in importance to behavior whose seriousness would be too great to ignore (19, p. 9). Whether mild or serious, faint or exaggerated, there have not been established scientific standards of normality in these characteristics and no objectively formulated yardstick for gauging their deviations has been developed. The St. Paul study provides no evidence whatsoever that

° *Unraveling Juvenile Delinquency*, the study by the Gluecks in which delinquents and non-delinquents are compared, has been widely pointed to as evidence of the attainment of the state of knowledge which is here denied. This study does not constitute refutation of the position taken here. The Gluecks' predictive attempts have not been satisfactorily validated to date. Further, the strong bias of the Gluecks in favor of a psychological explanation of delinquency led them to minimize some of the most significant findings of their study, namely, the operation of sociological factors, and to exaggerate the impact of psychological factors which their findings indicate to be of far less significance. Reckless has rearranged the factors in the study by the Gluecks and has shown that their own data provide evidence of the overwhelmingly greater importance of sociological than of psychological factors. See Walter C. Reckless, *The Crime Problem* (New York: Appleton-Century-Crofts, 2nd ed., 1955), 74–78. See also the two critical evaluations of the Glueck study, one by Rubin, and the other by Reiss, in the *American Journal of Sociology* for September, 1951.

would dispel any suspicion which one might be disposed to entertain that referral could have taken place on the basis of the referring adult's prejudices, peculiarities, whims, or private philosophy regarding children's behavior.

Even if deviations were measurable with complete scientific objectivity and were fully treatable, this would still be almost completely irrelevant to the prevention of delinquency. For example, suppose a child were discovered to evince a bothersome quantum of aggression, a characteristic which many clinicians insist is one of the cardinal signs of pre-delinquency. Should measures be taken to reduce the aggression? But aggression is not a trait that eventuates only in wanton rape and plunder. It can be quite handy in managing a corporation. Some generals have been aggressive. Some aggressive people have become noted explorers. Some have gone into medicine and law. Some have specialized in psychiatry. Some have entered teaching, as any student and any faculty member could attest. Aggression can find many happy uses.

THE PSYCHIATRIC "TOWER OF BABEL"

There is no better way to illustrate that labeling some children "pre-delinquent" is arbitrary and even whimsical and that the designation is dependent on the biases and preconceptions of the psychiatric personnel than to point to the vast confusion and conflict which prevail in psychiatry when it comes to a consideration of children's behavior and personality traits.

Some psychiatrists are fully aware of this state of affairs and have been frank in discussing it. Ackerman has dubbed the subject of diagnosis in child psychiatry a "Tower of Babel." He says that even within the same clinic there are differences in diagnostic concepts and

practices (1). Balser has written, "We have no exact data or scientific standards relating to norms and deviations in adolescent behavior" (3, p. 265). Josselyn has pointed out that "in this era of microscopic evaluation of personality, and particularly of childhood, there is a tendency to establish a yardstick for normalcy so finely calibrated no child can be measured by it and be adjudged psychologically healthy" (21). Senn has called attention to the existence of differences among psychiatrists in judging a child's normality and need for treatment and explains this by saying that psychiatry is "relatively young and unscientific" (33).

To be more specific, consider the long list of behavioral and personality traits which were given sinister significance in the St. Paul project. Practically every one of these items has been regarded as perfectly normal by some psychiatrists and other reputable experts on the development and rearing of children. Some regard them as normal even when exhibited in extreme form. Some, who do not designate them as normal or abnormal, simply state that they are worthy of nothing more than indifference.

Take "bashfulness," for example. A psychiatrist recently felt impelled to make an eloquent defense of a child's right to be bashful. Further, she makes it clear that a child's chances of winning out in any argument about the matter are nil: "If a child is not sufficiently shy he is considered unpleasantly bold, a state indicative of problems. If he is shy, something is wrong" (21). While she decries this dilemma, she devises one of her own which is bound to prove equally ensnaring. In discussing "truancy from school," another item which appears in the above list, she takes a dim view of the emotional condition of a child who truants. But she has an equally gloomy perspective of the child who does not: "The child's acceptance of school attendance and of returning to his home at prescribed hours indicates how fearful he is of giving up what little security he has and how dangerous the world beyond his immediate environment seems" (22). Take "masturbation," as a third example. A psychiatrist has advised parents that "almost all children should be permitted to set their own pace concerning masturbation" (20, p. 101). Take the matter of "overt homosexual practices," which is included under "sex perversion." One psychiatrist says that the period from roughly ten to fifteen years of age is a "homosexual phase." He further advises that the overt homosexual activities of this period may be thought of as rehearsals for heterosexuality (17).

Take "bullying," as a fifth example. One psychiatrist interprets this as a normal aspect of the group activity of children. "They will pick on one individual, and they are merciless." Instead of seeing this as requiring the psychiatric therapy of the bullies, he recommends that parents of the hapless victim explain to him that "these things do happen, that he must learn to take it, and that, if he does, they will respect him" (3, p. 267). Take "daydreaming," as an additional illustration. Clothier reports that "typical daydreams of the adolescent girl are phantasies of being raped, of acting as a prostitute, or of having a baby like the Virgin Mary without sex relations"* (8). Take "shifting activities." One psychiatrist

---

* These daydreams, which would appear bizarre to most people, are considered to be normally characteristic of the adolescent girl by Clothier. On the other hand, the daydreams that aroused concern in the St. Paul study are a most innocuous variety, as can be seen from the description of them: "Indulgence in pleasant reveries characterized by withdrawal of attention more or less completely from external sources" (35, p. 178).

maintains, referring to adolescent behavior, that the only predictable thing about it is its unpredictability (20, p. 56). Consider together such items as "ill-mannered behavior," "uncouthness," "roughness," "defiance," and "indolence." One psychiatrist claims, as do many others, that the adolescent may normally become "greedy, sloppy, disorderly, rough, impolite; he may lose interest in active work, become difficult in school, unsocial, moody, withdrawn" (36).

Take "stealing," to push the point still further. This has been viewed as "practically normal" for the child of eight or nine (18). Take "overactivity." Gesell and his associates, in their well-known studies on the development of normal children, found that the eleven-year-old boy is characterized by "incessant bodily activity and expenditure of energy." They noted that even when he was seated the activity of a boy at this age is "so constant that one almost becomes seasick watching him" (14, p. 73). Take "obscenity." To again draw on Gesell's observations, it was discovered that the twelve-year-old boy greatly enjoys "dirty jokes." "He not only understands them, but tells them with great relish, and laughs uproariously" (14, p. 123). Take "untidiness." It is unmistakably clear from Gesell's descriptions that children between ten and sixteen are extraordinarily messy, and there is only very slow, and most of the time very spotty, improvement during this period (14, pp. 322–323). Take "temper displays." Gesell found the boy of ten to exhibit unexpected periods of "frenzy." "He verily yells, strikes out, kicks furiously, and even bites!" (14, p. 332). Even in boys eleven years of age, Gesell observed "undercurrents of irritability, belligerence, and argumentativeness . . . . His anger has new intensity and depth" (14, p. 332). Take, finally, "sex perversion," which is said to apply to adolescents. Markey, a psychiatrist in a juvenile court, lists a number of sex perversions ranging from voyeurism to incest. In discussing these, he asserts that "any of these acts can appear in adolescents who give promise of good psychosexual health." He further takes the position that "any act which is expressed while growth is taking place is in itself relatively unimportant" (26).

Certainly these citations, drawn from a much larger number that could be assembled, incontrovertibly show that if the psychiatrically oriented staff of the St. Paul project was worried about the traits listed above, other specialists do not share their concern; if some psychiatrists see these traits as deviations, others see them as normal; if some see them as symptoms of pre-delinquency, others see them as signs of healthy personality development.

THE CACOPHONY IN CHILD-REARING ADVICE

While some psychiatrists are threatening parents with the horrendous eventualities in store for children who exhibit traits that other psychiatrists regard as eminently normal, still others are engaged in urging parents to take a view toward these traits that is diametrically opposed to that counseled by the alarmists. English, a well-known child psychiatrist, for example, presents a list of various types of behavior, all of which have been repeatedly implicated as symptoms of pre-delinquency and all of which were used in the St. Paul project, and tells parents that they should "certainly not worry" about them. He reassures parents that these are "entirely natural manifestations of childhood" (11, p. 275). But no sooner does he proffer this consoling reassurance than he, as have many other psychiatrists, calls attention to a kind of behavior which he apparently regards

as *really* ominous, namely, good behavior—in fact, exemplary behavior. The child who actually merits the parent's concern, according to English, is not the child who manifests the traits that have been so often viewed as calling for psychiatric treatment at the earliest possible moment. Rather, it is the "extremely good child" who should prove disquieting. This is the child, who, in the words of English, "always obeys [his father] without protest, strives to please him in every way, is meticulous about his clothes and belongings, and delights in bringing home an all A report card" (11, p. 276).

Not only do some psychiatrists advise parents to ignore or at least not to worry about the behavior and characteristics that other psychiatrists insist should occasion apprehension; some harshly rebuke parents for being concerned about the very traits that others have painstakingly instructed and warned them to get exercised about. For example, Senn thinks a parent who would worry about such behavior in a child is himself in need of assistance or therapy (34, pp. 45–46). Another psychiatrist makes his impatience with parents who worry about such behavior perfectly plain in the following angry outburst: "We cannot be too harsh against parents who become unduly alarmed over such symptoms" (31).

While parents are thus being buffeted about; while "pre-delinquents" are increasingly being summoned to the clinics and hospitals; while the clinicians are haranguing parents with their value judgments, which they commonly mistake for scientific dicta, regarding children's behavior; and while practically every tenet about child rearing held by some psychiatrists is being opposed by others, the voices of those few authorities who plead for caution, restraint, and the exercise of professional responsibility get all but lost in the raging din.

A fundamental postulate underlying the mental health movement, which, in the psychiatric scheme of things, encompasses the prevention of delinquency, is that if children were reared and handled in accordance with the recommendations and advice of psychiatry, they would be spared delinquency, maladjustment, mental illness, and other misfortunes. This rests on the premise that knowledge of what child-rearing practices will lead to this end has been scientifically established and is agreed upon by the experts. The evidence adduced here should go a long way in showing this to be largely an illusion.

More than this, some psychiatrists, the unheard voices already referred to, have frankly and explicitly disclaimed any such knowledge and agreement. Bruch, for example, denies that the three assumptions she considers to underlie the education of parents on child rearing have been validated. She lists these unvalidated assumptions as follows:

(1) That there is a body of knowledge about best techniques of child care, (2) that they can and should be taught to parents (and this has been done with the fervor and intensity of advertising and publicity campaigns), and (3) that their application will prevent the development of emotional maladjustment and produce good mental health in the coming generation (7).

Senn, reviewing the trends in research on child development since the turn of the century and examining the research of the past ten years, finds that the various child-rearing practices that have been widely disseminated and advocated "did not develop from the appearance of large bodies of scientific data which had been arrived at by careful research" (34, p. 43). Ginsburg,

reviewing the present status of the mental hygiene movement, observes that it has "flowered . . . without benefit of a sound body of scrutinized and validated facts." He further concludes: ". . . we do not have an adequate definition of mental health . . . . The notion of normality (the 'normal mind,' the 'healthy personality,' etc.) is based to a large degree and often solely on the value system of the author using the term . . ." (15). Finally, Bovet, who surveyed the psychiatric aspects of juvenile delinquency for the World Health Organization, and whose report has already been referred to, sets forth the following reflection:

It must be rare for decisions with serious coercive consequences to be taken with so little supporting evidence as in the case of juvenile delinquency. The inquirer who seeks by reading or discussion to ascertain current opinions on juvenile delinquency must be struck by the following two facts: first, each point of view, whether calmly or forcibly expressed, is based on a deep-rooted conviction; and secondly, it is impossible to demonstrate objectively the validity of any one opinion* (6, pp. 10-11).

CONCLUSIONS

Certain conclusions are inescapable. Psychiatry has great prestige and power in the work on the prevention of juvenile delinquency. This status is not justified if it is assumed to rest on psychiatry's positive contributions to this work. Nor is it justified if it is assumed to emerge from the demonstrated reliability and validity of psychiatric knowledge and premises.

Psychiatric knowledge regarding personality development has not been em-

---

* Bovet himself forgets all this in the remainder of his report and makes the same kind of incautious and unsubstantiated recommendations and statements that motivated his bleak observation. All of the "unheard voices" quoted above likewise forget their reservations in other writings.

pirically verified to the point where it can be applied to the prevention and therapy of juvenile delinquency. On the other hand, the zealousness of psychiatrists in making unsubstantiated claims and their success in winning support and in implementing their views seem boundless.

Sociologists should examine the claims of psychiatry more cautiously than they have been prone to do. There is reason to believe that correctional sociologists have done almost as much as psychiatrists and their adherents to advance the claims and practices of psychiatry, as much by their reluctance to view it critically as by their eagerness to support it actively.

Sociologists should explore their own concepts and research and determine how best these can contribute to practical programs in the understanding and prevention of delinquency and in the correction of delinquents. They should view psychiatric theories, research, and claims with the same scientific caution and sophistication that they are increasingly applying to their own discipline. Certainly they should resist the psychiatric aura that has come to dominate practical measures in corrections and before which many laymen, correctional administrators, legislators, and members of welfare boards stand agape.

References

1. Ackerman, Nathan W., "Psychiatric Disorders in Children—Diagnosis and Etiology in Our Time," in Paul H. Roch and Joseph Zubin, eds., *Current Problems in Psychiatric Diagnosis* (New York: Grune and Stratton, 1953), 220–221.

2. Adamson, LaMay, and H. Warren Dunham, "Clinical Treatment of Male Delinquents: A Case Study in Effort and Result," *American Sociological Review*, 21 (June, 1956), 312–320.

3. Balser, Benjamin H., "The Adolescent," in John P. Hubbard, ed., *The Early Detection and Prevention of Disease* (New York: McGraw-Hill, 1957).

4. Banay, Ralph S., *Youth in Despair* (New York: Coward-McCann, 1948), 186, 196.

5. Benton, Arthur L., "The Experimental Validation of the Rorschach Test," *British Journal of Medical Psychology*, 23 (Parts I and II, 1950), 55.

6. Bovet, Lucien, *Psychiatric Aspects of Juvenile Delinquency*, Monograph Series, No. 1 (Geneva: World Health Organization, 1951).

7. Bruch, Hilde, "Parent Education or the Illusion of Omnipotence," *American Journal of Orthopsychiatry*, 24 (October, 1954), 724.

8. Clothier, Florence, "The Unmarried Mother of School Age as Seen by a Psychiatrist," *Mental Hygiene*, 39 (October, 1955), 639.

9. Cronbach, Lee J., "Statistical Methods Applied to Rorschach Scores: A Review," *Psychological Bulletin*, 46 (September, 1949), 425.

10. Dorsey, John M., "The Use of the Psychoanalytic Principle in Child Guidance Work," in K. R. Eissler, ed., *Searchlights on Delinquency: New Psychoanalytic Studies* (New York: International Universities Press, 1949), 137.

11. English, O. Spurgeon, and Constance J. Foster, *Fathers Are Parents, Too: A Constructive Guide to Successful Fatherhood* (New York: G. P. Putnam's Sons, 1951).

12. Eysenck, H. J., *Sense and Nonsense in Psychology* (Middlesex: Penguin Books, 1957).

13. Friedlander, Kate, *The Psycho-Analytical Approach to Juvenile Delinquency: Theory: Case-Studies: Treatment* (New York: International Universities Press, 1947), 274–275.

37.

Changing Criminals: The Application of the Theory of Differential Association

Donald R. Cressey

Sociological theories and hypotheses have had great influence on development of general correctional policies, such as probation and parole, but they have been used only intermittently and haphazardly in reforming individual criminals. Since sociology is essentially a research discipline, sociologist-criminologists have devoted most of their time and energy to understanding and explaining crime; leaving to psychiatrists and others the problem of reforming criminals. Even the sociologists employed in correctional work have ordinarily committed themselves to nonsociological theories and techniques of reformation, leading the authors of one popular criminology textbook to ask just what correctional sociologists can accomplish which cannot be accomplished by other professional workers.[1]

Perhaps the major impediment to the application of sociological theories lies not in the nature of the theories themselves but, instead, in the futile attempt to adapt them to clinical use. Strictly speaking, the now popular policy of "individualized treatment" for delinquents and criminals does not commit one to any specific theory of criminality or any specific theory of reformation, but, rather, to the proposition that the conditions considered as causing an individual to behave criminally will be taken into account in the effort to change him. An attempt is made to diagnose the cause of the criminality and to base the techniques of reform upon the diagnosis. Analogy with the *method* of clinical medicine (diagnosis, prescription, and therapy) is obvious. However, by far the most popular interpretation of the policy of individualization is that the *theories,* as well as the methods, of clinical medicine must be used in diagnosing and changing criminals. The emphasis on this clinical principle has impeded the application of sociological theories and, it may be conjectured, success in correctional work.

The adherents of the clinical principle consider criminality to be an individual defect or disorder or a symp-

[1] Harry Elmer Barnes and Negley K. Teeters, *New Horizons in Criminology* (New York: Prentice-Hall, 1951), p. 644.

SOURCE. Donald R. Cressey, "Changing Criminals: The Application of the Theory of Differential Association," from *The American Journal of Sociology*, Volume 61, September 1955, pp. 116–120. Copyright © 1955, University of Chicago Press. Reprinted with the permission of the University of Chicago Press.

tom of either, and the criminal as one unable to canalize or sublimate his "primitive," antisocial impulses or tendencies,[2] who may be expressing symbolically in criminal behavior some unconscious urge or wish arising from an early traumatic emotional experience,[3] or as a person suffering from some other kind of defective trait or condition.

In all cases the implication is that the individual disorder, like a biological disorder, should be treated on a clinical basis. An extreme position is that criminality actually is a biological disorder, to be treated by modification of the physiology or anatomy of the individual. However, the more popular notion is that criminality is analogous to an infectious disease like syphilis—while group contacts of various kinds are necessary to the disorder, the disorder can be treated in a clinic, without reference to the persons from whom it was acquired.

Sociologists and social psychologists have provided an alternative principle on which to base the diagnosis and treatment of criminals, namely, that the behavior, attitudes, beliefs, and values which a person exhibits are not only the *products* of group contacts but also the *properties* of groups. If the behavior of an individual is an intrinsic part of groups to which he belongs, attempts to change the behavior must be directed at groups.[4] While this principle is generally accepted by sociologists, there has been no consistent or organized effort by sociologist-criminologists to base techniques or principles of treatment on it. Traditionally, we have emphasized that sociologists can make unique contributions to *clinical* diagnoses, and we have advocated the development of a "clinical sociology" which would enable us to improve these diagnoses.[5] But here we reach an impasse: if a case of criminality is attributed to the individual's group relations, there is little that can be done *in the clinic* to modify the diagnosed cause of the criminality. Moreover, extra-clinical work with criminals and delinquents ordinarily has merely extended the clinical principle to the offender's community and has largely ignored the group-relations principle. For example, in the "group work" of correctional agencies the emphasis usually is upon the role of the group merely in satisfying the needs of an individual. Thus the criminal is induced to join an "interest-activity" group, such as a hiking club, on the assumption that membership in the group somehow will enable him to overcome the defects or tendencies considered conducive to his delinquency.[6] Similarly, in correctional group therapy the emphasis is almost always on the use of a group to enable the individual to rid himself of undesirable psychological disorders, not criminality.[7] Even

[2] Sheldon and Eleanor T. Glueck, *Delinquents in the Making* (New York: Harper and Bros., 1952), pp. 162–163; see also Ruth Jacobs Levy, *Reductions in Recidivism through Therapy* (New York: Seltzer, 1941), pp. 16, 28.

[3] Edwin J. Lukas, "Crime Prevention: A Confusion in Goal," in Paul W. Tappan (ed.), *Contemporary Correction* (New York: McGraw-Hill Book Co., 1951), pp. 397–409.

[4] Cf. Dorwin Cartwright, "Achieving Change in People: Some Applications of Group Dynamics Theory," *Human Relations*, 4 (1951), 381–392.

[5] See Louis Wirth, "Clinical Sociology," *American Journal of Sociology*, 27 (July, 1931), 49–66; and Saul D. Alinsky, "A Sociological Technique in Clinical Criminology," *Proceedings of the American Prison Association*, 64 (1934), 167–178.

[6] See the discussion by Robert G. Hinckley and Lydia Hermann, *Group Treatment in Psychotherapy* (Minneapolis: University of Minnesota Press, 1951), pp. 8–11.

[7] See Donald R. Cressey, "Contradictory Theories in Correctional Group Therapy Programs," *Federal Probation*, 18 (June, 1954), 20–26.

in group-work programs directed at entire groups, such as delinquent gangs, emphasis usually is on new and different formal group activities rather than on new group attitudes and values.

The differential association theory of criminal behavior presents implications for diagnosis and treatment consistent with the group-relations principle for changing behavior and could be advantageously utilized in correctional work. According to it, persons become criminals principally because they have been relatively isolated from groups whose behavior patterns (including attitudes, motives, and rationalizations) are anticriminal, or because their residence, employment, social position, native capacities, or something else has brought them into relatively frequent association with the behavior patterns of criminal groups.[8] A diagnosis of criminality based on this theory would be directed at analysis of the criminal's attitudes, motives, and rationalizations regarding criminality and would recognize that those characteristics depend upon the groups to which the criminal belongs. Then, if criminals are to be changed, either they must become members of anticriminal groups, or their present pro-criminal group relations must be changed.[9]

The following set of interrelated principles, adapted in part from a more general statement by Dorwin Cartwright,[10] is intended as a guide to specific application of the differential association theory to correctional work. It is tentative and directs attention to areas where research and experimentation should prove fruitful. Two underlying assumptions are that small groups existing for the specific purpose of reforming criminals can be set up by correctional workers and that criminals can be induced to join them. The first five principles deal with the use of anticriminal groups as *media* of change, and the last principle emphasizes, further, the possibility of a criminal group's becoming the *target* of change.

1. If criminals are to be changed, they must be assimilated into groups which emphasize values conducive to law-abiding behavior and, concurrently, alienated from groups emphasizing values conducive to criminality. Since our experience has been that the majority of criminals experience great difficulty in securing intimate contacts in ordinary groups, special groups whose major common goal is the reformation of criminals must be created. This general principle, emphasized by Sutherland, has been recognized and used by Gersten, apparently with some success, in connection with a group therapy program in the New York Training School for Boys.[11]

2. The more relevant the common purpose of the group to the reformation of criminals, the greater will be its influence on the criminal members' attitudes and values. Just as a labor union exerts strong influence over its members' attitudes toward management but less influence on their attitudes toward say, Negroes, so a group organized for recreational or welfare purposes will have less success in influencing criminalistic

[8] Edwin H. Sutherland, *Principles of Criminology* (Philadelphia: J. B. Lippincott Co., 1947), pp. 6–9, 595, 616–617.
[9] Cf. Donald R. Taft, "The Group and Community Organization Approach to Prison Administration," *Proceedings of the American Prison Association*, 72 (1942), 275–284; and George B. Vold, "Discussion of *Guided Group Interaction in Correctional Work* by F. Lovell Bixby and Lloyd W. McCorkle," *American Sociological Review*, 16 (August, 1951), 460–461.
[10] Cartwright, *op. cit.*

[11] Sutherland, *op. cit.*, p. 451; Charles Gersten, "An Experimental Evaluation of Group Therapy with Juvenile Delinquents," *International Journal of Group Psychotherapy*, 1 (November, 1951), 311–318.

attitudes and values than will one whose explicit purpose is to change criminals. Interesting recreational activities, employment possibilities, and material assistance may serve effectively to attract criminals away from pro-criminal groups temporarily and may give the group some control over the criminals. But merely inducing a criminal to join a group to satisfy his personal needs is not enough. Probably the failure to recognize this, more than anything else, was responsible for the failure of the efforts at rehabilitation of the Cambridge-Somerville Youth Study workers.[12]

3. The more cohesive the group, the greater the members' readiness to influence others and the more relevant the problem of conformity to group norms. The criminals who are to be reformed and the persons expected to effect the change must, then, have a strong sense of belonging to one group: between them there must be a genuine "we" feeling. The reformers, consequently, should not be identifiable as correctional workers, probation or parole officers, or social workers. This principle has been extensively documented by Festinger and his co-workers.[13]

4. Both reformers and those to be reformed must achieve status within the group by exhibition of "pro-reform"

[12] See Margaret G. Reilly and Robert A. Young, "Agency-initiated Treatment of a Potentially Delinquent Boy," *American Journal of Orthopsychiatry*, 16 (October, 1946), 697–706; Edwin Powers, "An Experiment in Prevention of Delinquency," *Annals of the American Academy of Political and Social Science*, 261 (January, 1949), 77–88; Edwin Powers and Helen L. Witmer, *An Experiment in Prevention of Delinquency—the Cambridge-Somerville Youth Study* (New York: Columbia University Press, 1951).
[13] L. Festinger et al., *Theory and Experiment in Social Communication: Collected Papers* (Ann Arbor: Institute for Social Research, 1951).

or anticriminal values and behavior patterns. As a novitiate, the one to be reformed is likely to assign status according to social position outside the group, and part of the reformation process consists of influencing him both to assign and to achieve status on the basis of behavior patterns relevant to reformation. If he should assign status solely on the basis of social position in the community, he is likely to be influenced only slightly by the group. Even if he becomes better adjusted, socially and psychologically, by association with members having high status in the community, he is a therapeutic parasite and not actually a member until he accepts the group's own system for assigning status.

5. The most effective mechanism for exerting group pressure on members will be found in groups so organized that criminals are induced to join with noncriminals for the purpose of changing other criminals. A group in which criminal A joins with some noncriminals to change criminal B is probably most effective in changing criminal A, not B; in order to change criminal B, criminal A must necessarily share the values of the anticriminal members.

This process may be called "retroflexive reformation"; in attempting to reform others, the criminal almost automatically accepts the relevant common purpose of the group, identifies himself closely with other persons engaging in reformation, and assigns status on the basis of anticriminal behavior. He becomes a genuine member of this group, and at the same time he is alienated from his previous pro-criminal groups. This principle is used successfully by Alcoholics Anonymous to "cure" alcoholism; it has been applied to the treatment of psychotics by McCann and Almada; and its usefulness in criminology has been demonstrated by

Knopka.[14] Ex-convicts have been used in the Chicago Area Projects, which, generally, are organized in accordance with this principle, but its effect on the ex-convicts, either in their roles as reformers or as objects of reform, appears not to have been evaluated.

6. When an entire group is the target of change, as in a prison or among delinquent gangs, strong pressure for change can be achieved by convincing the members of the need for a change, thus making the group itself the source of pressure for change. Rather than inducing criminals to become members of pre-established anticriminal groups, the problem here is to change antireform and pro-criminal subcultures, so that group leaders evolve from among those who show the most marked hospitality to anticriminal values, attitudes, and behavior. Neither mere lectures, sermons, or exhortations by correctional workers nor mere redirection of the activities of a group nor individual psychotherapy, academic education, vocational training, or counseling will necessarily

change a group's culture. If the subculture is not changed, the person to be reformed is likely to exhibit two sets of attitudes and behaviors, one characteristic of the agency or person trying to change him, the other of the subculture.[15] Changes in the subculture probably can best be instigated by eliciting the co-operation of the type of criminal who, in prisons, is considered a "right guy."[16] This principle has been demonstrated in a recent experiment with hospitalized drug addicts, whose essentially antireform culture was changed, under the guise of group therapy, to a pro-reform culture.[17] To some extent, the principle was used in the experimental system of prison administration developed by Gill in the Massachusetts State Prison Colony.[18]

[14] Freed Bales, "Types of Social Structure as Factors in 'Cures' for Alcohol Addiction," *Applied Anthropology*, 1 (April-June, 1942), 1–13; Willis H. McCann and Albert A. Almada, "Round-Table Psychotherapy: A Technique in Group Psychotherapy," *Journal of Consulting Psychology*, 14 (December, 1950), 421–435; Gisela Knopka, "The Group Worker's Role in an Institution for Juvenile Delinquents," *Federal Probation*, 15 (June, 1951), 15–23.

[15] See Edwin A. Fleishman, "A Study in the Leadership Role of the Foreman in an Industrial Situation" (Columbus: Personnel Research Board, Ohio State University, 1951) (mimeographed).
[16] See Hans Riemer, "Socialization in the Prison Community," *Proceedings of the American Prison Association*, 67 (1937), 151–155.
[17] James J. Thorpe and Bernard Smith, "Phases in Group Development in Treatment of Drug Addicts," *International Journal of Group Psychotherapy*, 3 (January, 1953), 66–78.
[18] Howard B. Gill, "The Norfolk Prison Colony of Massachusetts," *Journal of Criminal Law and Criminology*, 22 (September, 1937), 389–395; see also Eric K. Clarke, "Group Therapy in Rehabilitation," *Federal Probation*, 16 (December, 1952), 28–32.

38.

The Impact of a "Total-Community" Delinquency Control Project

Walter B. Miller

THE MIDCITY PROJECT: METHODS AND CLIENT POPULATION

The Midcity Project conducted a delinquency control program in a lower-class district of Boston between the years 1954 and 1957. A major objective of the Project was to inhibit or reduce the amount of illegal activity engaged in by resident adolescents. Project methods derived from a "total community" philosophy which has become increasingly popular in recent years and currently forms the basis of several large-scale delinquency control programs.[1] On the assumption that delinquent behavior by urban lower-class adolescents, whatever their personality

[1] The principal current example is the extensive "Mobilization for Youth" project now underway in the Lower East Side of Manhattan. Present plans call for over 30 separate "action" programs in four major areas of work, education, community, and group service. The project is reported in detail in "A Proposal for the Prevention and Control of Delinquency by Expanding Opportunities," New York City: Mobilization for Youth, Inc. (December 1961), and in brief in "Report on Juvenile Delinquency," Washington, D.C.: Hearings of the Subcommittee on Appropriations, 1960, pp. 113–116.

characteristics, is in some significant degree facilitated by or actualized through certain structural features of the community, the Project executed "action" programs directed at three of the societal units seen to figure importantly in the genesis and perpetuation of delinquent behavior—the community, the family, and the gang.

The community program involved two major efforts: (1) the development and strengthening of local citizens' groups so as to enable them to take direct action in regard to local problems, including delinquency, and (2) an attempt to secure cooperation between those professional agencies whose operations in the community in some way involved adolescents (e.g., settlement houses, churches, schools, psychiatric and medical clinics, police, courts and probation departments, corrections and parole departments). A major short-term objective was to increase the possibility of concerted action both among the professional agencies themselves and between the professionals and the citizens' groups. The ultimate objective of these organizational efforts

SOURCE. Walter B. Miller, "The Impact of a 'Total-Community' Delinquency Control Project," from *Social Problems*, Volume 10, No. 2, Fall 1962, pp. 168–191. Reprinted with the permission of the Society for the Study of Social Problems and the author.

was to focus a variety of diffuse and uncoordinated efforts on problems of youth and delinquency in a single community so as to bring about more effective processes of prevention and control.[2]

Work with families was conducted within the framework of a "chronic-problem-family" approach; a group of families with histories of repeated and long-term utilization of public welfare services were located and subjected to a special and intensive program of psychiatrically-oriented casework.[3]

Work with gangs, the major effort of the Project, was based on the detached worker or area worker approach utilized by the New York Youth Board and similar projects.[4] An adult worker is assigned to an area, group, or groups with a mandate to contact, establish relations with, and attempt to change resident gangs. The application of this method by the Midcity Project incorporated three features not generally included in earlier programs: (1) All workers were professionally trained, with degrees in casework, group work, or both. (2) Each·worker but one devoted primary attention to a single group, maintaining recurrent and intensive contact with group members over an extended time period. (3) Psychiatric consultation was made available on a regular basis, so that workers

were in a position to utilize methods and perspectives of psychodynamic psychiatry in addition to the group dynamics and recreational approaches in which they had been trained.

Between June 1954 and May 1957, seven project field workers (five men, two women) maintained contact with approximately 400 youngsters between the ages of 12 and 21, comprising the membership of some 21 corner gangs. Seven of these, totaling 205 members, were sùbjected to intensive attention. Workers contacted their groups on an average of 3.5 times a week; contact periods averaged about 5 or 6 hours; total duration of contact ranged from 10 to 34 months. Four of the intensive service groups were white males (Catholic, largely Irish, some Italians and Canadian French); one was Negro male, one white female, and one Negro female. All groups "hung out" in contiguous neighborhoods of a single district of Midcity—a fairly typical lower-class "inner-city" community.[5]

[5] The term "lower class" is used in this paper to refer to that sector of the population in the lowest educational and occupational categories. For the purposes of Project statistical analyses, those census tracts in Midcity were designated as "lower class" in which 50% or more of the adult residents had failed to finish high school, and 60% or more of resident males pursued occupations in the bottom five occupational categories delineated by the 1950 United States Census. Nineteen of the 21 census tracts in Midcity were designated "lower class" by these criteria. Within lower class, three levels were distinguished. "Lower-class 3" included census tracts with 80% or more of adult males in the bottom five occupational categories and 70% or more of the adults in the "high-school non-completion" category; "Lower-class 2" included tracts with 70–80% males in low occupations and 60–70% adults not having completed high school; "Lower-class 1," 60–70% low occupation males, 50–60% high-school non-completion. Of the 6,500 adolescents in Midcity, 17.5% lived in Lower-class 3 tracts; 53.1% in Lower-class 2, and 20.4% in Lower-class 1. The remaining 8.8% were designated "middle class." Project gangs de-

[2] See Lester Houston and Lena DiCicco, "Community Development in a Boston District," Boston: on file United Community Services of Boston, 1956.

[3] See David M. Austin, "The Special Youth Program Approach to Chronic Problem Families," *Community Organization Papers*, New York City: Columbia University Press, 1958. Also, Joan Zilbach, "Work with Chronic Problem Families: A Five-Year Appraisal," Boston: on file Judge Baker Guidance Center, 1962.

[4] A brief description of the background of this method appears on p. 406 of Walter B. Miller, "The Impact of a Community Group Work Program on Delinquent Corner Groups," *The Social Service Review*, 31 (December 1957), pp. 390–406.

The average size of male groups was 30, and of female nine. All intensive service groups, as well as most of the other known groups, were "locality-based" rather than "emergent" or "situationally organized" groups.[6] This meant that the groups were indigenous, self-formed, and inheritors of a gang tradition which in some cases extended back for 50 years or more. This kind of gang system in important respects resembled certain African age-class systems in that a new "class" or corner-group unit was formed every two or three years, recruiting from like-aged boys residing in the vicinity of the central "hanging" locale.[7] Thus the

total corner aggregate in relatively stable residential areas generally consisted of three to five age-graded male groups, each maintaining a sense of allegiance to their corner and/or traditional gang name, and at the same time maintaining a clear sense of identity as a particular age-graded unit within the larger grouping.

Girls groups, for the most part, achieved their identity primarily through their relations with specific boys' units, which were both larger and more solidary. Each locality aggregate thus included several female groups, generally bearing a feminized version of the male group name (Bandits-Bandettes; Kings-Queens).

ACTION METHODS WITH CORNER GANGS

The methods used by Project workers encompassed a wide range of techniques and entailed work on many levels with many kinds of groups, agencies, and organizations.[8] Workers con-

---

rived primarily from Lower-class 2 and 3 areas; studied gangs comprised approximately 16% of the adolescent (13–19) Lower-class 2 and 3 population of the study area—roughly 30% of the males and 4% of the females.

[6] Beyond this crude distinction between "locality-based" gangs and "other" types, a more systematic typology of Midcity gangs cannot be presented here. Karl Holton also distinguishes a locality-based gang ("area gang") as one type in Los Angeles County, and includes a classic brief description which applies without modification to the Midcity type. Karl Holton, "Juvenile Gangs in the Los Angeles Area," in *Hearings of the Subcommittee on Juvenile Delinquency*, 86th Congress, Part 5, Washington, D.C.: (November 1960), pp. 886–888. The importance of the "locality-based" typological distinction in this context is to emphasize the fact that Project gangs were *not* "emergent" groups organized in response to some common activity interest such as athletics, or formed around a single influential "magnetic" youngster, or organized under the influence of recreational or social work personnel. The gang structure pre-existed the Project, was coordinate with and systematically related to the kinship structure, and was "multi-functional" and "versatile" in that it served as a staging base for a wide range of activities and served a wide range of functions, both practical and psychological, for its members.

[7] The age-class system of Midcity closely resembles that of the Otoro of Central Sudan as described by Asmarom Legesse; "[Some East African Age-] Class Systems," Special Paper, Graduate School of Education, Harvard University, May 1961, and

S. F. Nadel, *The Nuba*, London: Oxford University Press, 1947, pp. 132–146. The Otoro age-class system, "one of the simplest . . . in eastern Africa" is in operation between the ages of 11 and 26 (in contrast to other systems which operate during the total life span), and comprises five classes formed at three-year intervals (Class I, 11–14; II, 14–17; III, 17–20; IV, 20–23; V, 23–26). The Midcity system, while less formalized, operates roughly between the ages of 12 and 23, and generally comprises four classes with new classes forming every two to four years, depending on the size of the available recruitment pool, density of population, and other factors. (Class I [Midgets] 12–14; II [Juniors] 14–16; III [Intermediates] 16–19; IV [Seniors] 19–22.) Otoro age classes, like Midcity's, are "multi-functional" in that they form the basis of athletic teams, work groups, and other types of associational unit.

[8] Project "action" methods have been described briefly in several published papers; David M. Austin, "Goals for Gang Workers," *Social Work*, 2 (October 1957), pp. 43–50; Ethel Ackley and Beverly Fliegel, "A Social Work Approach to Street-Corner Girls," *Social Work*, 5 (October

ceptualized the process of working with the groups as a series of sequential phases, on the model of individual psychotherapy. Three major phases were delineated—roughly, relationship establishment, behavior modification, and termination. In practice workers found it difficult to conduct operations according to the planned "phase" sequence, and techniques seen as primarily appropriate to one phase were often used during another. There was, however, sufficiently close adherence to the phase concept as to make it possible to consider specific techniques as primarily associated with a given phase.

Phase I: Contact and Relationship Establishment

During this phase workers sought out and located resident corner gangs and established an acceptable role-identity. Neither the location of the groups nor the establishment of a viable basis for a continued relationship entailed particular difficulties.[9] This phase included considerable "testing" of the workers; the youngsters put on display a wide range of their customary behaviors, with particular stress on violative forms—watching the worker closely to see whether his reactions and evaluative responses fell within an acceptable range. The workers, for their part, had to evince suffi-

cient familiarity with and control over the basic subcultural system of lower-class adolescents and its component skills as to merit the respect of the groups, and the right to continued association.

A major objective in gaining entrée to the groups was to establish what workers called a "relationship." Influenced in part by concepts derived from individual psychotherapy, Project staff felt that the establishment of close and meaningful relationships with group members was a major device for effecting behavior change, and was in fact a necessary precondition of all other direct service methods. The workers' conception of a "good" relationship was complex, but can be described briefly as a situation in which both worker and group defined themselves as contained within a common orbit whose major conditions were mutual trust, mutual affection, and maintenance of reciprocal obligations. The workers in fact succeeded in establishing and maintaining relationships of just this type. Considering the fact that these alliances had to bridge both age (adult-adolescent) and social status (lower class-middle class) differences, they were achieved and maintained with a surprising degree of success.[10]

Phase II: Behavior Modification via Mutual Activity Involvement

The behavior modification phase made the greatest demands on the skills, resourcefulness, and energy of the workers. Workers engaged in a wide variety of activities with and in behalf of their groups. The bulk of these activities, however, centered around three major kinds of effort: (1) Organizing groups and using these

---

1960), pp. 27–36; Walter B. Miller, "The Impact of a Community Group Work Program on Delinquent Corner Groups," *op. cit.*; and "Preventive Work with Street-Corner Groups: Boston Delinquency Project," *The Annals of the American Academy of Political and Social Science*, 322 (March 1959), pp. 97–106, and in detail in one unpublished report, David Kantor and Lester Houston, *Methods of Working with Street Corner Youth*, 1959, mimeo, 227 pp., on file Harvard Student Volunteers Project.

[9] Extensive discussion of the specific techniques of contact, role-identity establishment and relationship maintenance is included in Kantor and Houston, *ibid.*

[10] Research methods for categorizing worker-group relationships according to intensity and intimacy will be cited in future reports.

as the basis of involvement in organized activities; (2) Serving as intermediary between group members and adult institutions; (3) Utilizing techniques of direct influence.

The workers devoted considerable effort to changing group relational systems from the informal type of the street gang to the formal type of the club or athletic team, and involving the groups so reorganized in a range of activities such as club meetings, athletic contests, dances, and fund-raising dinners. In most cases this effort was highly successful. Clubs formed from the corner groups met regularly, adopted constitutions, carried out extensive and effective club activities. Athletic teams moved from cellar positions to championships in city athletic leagues. One group grossed close to a thousand dollars at a fund-raising dance.

Project use of the "organized group and planned activities" method was buttressed by rationale which included at least five premises. (1) The experience of learning to operate in the "rule-governed" atmosphere of the formal club would, it was felt, increase the group members' ability to conduct collective activities in an orderly and law-abiding fashion. (2) The influence of the more lawfully oriented leaders would be increased, since authority-roles in clubs or teams would be allocated on different bases from those in the corner gang. (3) The need for the clubs to rely heavily on the adult worker for advice and facilitation would place him in a strategic position to influence group behavior. (4) The need for clubs to maintain harmonious relations with local adults such as settlement house personnel and dance hall owners in order to carry out their activity program, as well as the increasing visibility of the organized group, would put a premium on maintaining

a public reputation as non-troublesome, and thus inhibit behavior which would jeopardize this objective. (5) Active and extensive involvement in lawful and adult-approved recreational activities would, it was felt, substantially curtail both time and energy potentially available for unlawful activity. This devil-finds-work premise was taken as self-evidently valid, and was reinforced by the idleness-boredom explanation frequently forwarded by group members themselves—"We get in trouble because there's nuthin to do around here." On these grounds as well as others, the use of this method appeared amply justified.[11]

In performing the role of intermediary, workers proceeded on the premise that gang members were essentially isolated within their own adolescent slum world and were either denied, or lacked the ability to seek out, "access" to major adult institutions. This blocked access, it was felt, prevented the youngsters from seeking prestige through "legitimate" channels, forcing them instead to resort to "illegitimate" forms of achievement such as thievery, fighting, and prostitution. On this assumption, the Project aimed deliberately to open up channels of access to adult institutions—particularly in the areas of education and employment.

In the world of work, Project workers arranged appointments with employment agencies, drove group members to job interviews, counseled them as to proper demeanor as job applicants and as employees, urged wavering workers not to quit their jobs.

[11] Further elaboration of the rationale behind the "group-organization-and-activity" method, as well as some additional detail on its operation, is contained in David Austin, "Goals for Gang Workers," *op. cit.*, p. 49, and Walter B. Miller, "*The Place of the Organized Club in Corner-Group Work Method,*" Boston: on file Special Youth Program, mimeo, 7 pp. (November 1956).

Workers also contacted business firms and urged them to hire group members. In the area of education, workers attempted to solidify the often tenuous bonds between group members and the schools. They visited teachers, acted to discourage truancy, and worked assiduously—through means ranging from subtle persuasion to vigorous argument—to discourage the practice of dropping out of school at or before the legally permissible age. Workers arranged meetings with school personnel and attempted to acquaint teachers and other school staff with the special problems of corner youngsters. Every effort was made to arrange scholarships (generally athletic) for those group members for whom college seemed a possibility.

Workers also acted as go-between for their youngsters and a variety of other institutions. They arranged for lawyers in the event of court appearances, and interceded with judges, probation officers, correctional officials, and parole personnel. They obtained the use of the recreational facilities and meeting places in settlement houses and gyms which would not have considered admitting the rough and troublesome gang members in the absence of a responsible adult sponsor. They persuaded local storekeepers and businessmen to aid the groups in their money-raising efforts. They arranged for the use or rental of dance halls, and solicited radio stations to provide locally famous disc-jockeys to conduct record hops. They organized meetings between gang members and local policemen during which both sides were given the opportunity to air their mutual grievances.

During later stages of the Project, workers brought together the clubs of the corner gangs and the adult organizations formed by the Project's Community Organization program, and gang members and community adults served together on joint committees working in the area of community improvement. One such committee exerted sufficient pressure on municipal authorities to obtain a $60,000 allocation for the improvement of a local ball field; another committee instituted an annual "Sports Night" during which most of the community's gangs—some of whom were active gang-fighting enemies—attended a large banquet in which city officials and well-known sports figures made speeches and presented awards for meritorious athletic achievement.

Thus, as a consequence of the workers' activities, gang members gained access to a wide variety of legitimate adult institutions and organizations—schools, business establishments, settlement houses, municipal athletic leagues, public recreational facilities, guidance services, health facilities, municipal governmental agencies, citizens groups, and others. It could no longer be said that the groups were isolated, in any practical sense, from the world of legitimate opportunity.[12]

While Project methods placed major

[12] Project research data made it possible to determine the relative amount of worker effort devoted to various types of activity. The frequency of 12 different kinds of activity engaged in by workers toward or in behalf of group members ("worker functions") was tabulated for all seven workers. Of 9958 recorded worker functions, 3878 were executed in connection with 22 organizations or agencies. Of these "institutionally-oriented" functions, workers acted in the capacity of "intermediary" for group members 768 times (19.8%), making "intermediation" the second most frequent type of "institutionally-oriented" worker function. The most frequent function was the exercise of "direct influence" (28.7%), to be discussed in the next section. Thus about one-half of all institutionally-oriented worker activity involved two functions—acting as intermediary and engaging in direct influence efforts. Of the 768 intermediary functions, 466 (60.7%) were exercised in connection with six kinds of organizations or groups—business organizations, schools, social welfare agencies, families, and other gangs.

stress on changing environmental conditions through organization, activity involvement, and opening channels of access, workers were also committed to the use of methods designed to induce personality change. The training of most workers had involved exposure to the principles of, and some practice in the techniques of, psychodynamic psychotherapy, and serious consideration was given to the possibility of attempting some form of direct application of psychotherapeutic principles, or techniques based on "insight" therapy. After much discussion workers decided that the use of techniques appropriate to the controlled therapist-patient situation would not be practicable in the open and multi-cliented arena of the corner gang world, and arrangements were made to utilize this approach through indirect rather than direct means.

Psychodynamic methods and individual treatment approaches were utilized in two ways. First, a contract was made with a well-known child-psychiatry clinic, and workers consulted with psychodynamically trained psychiatrists on a regular basis. During these sessions the psychiatrists analyzed individual cases on the basis of detailed case summaries and recommended procedures for the workers to execute. In this way the actual operating policies of the workers were directly influenced by the diagnostic concepts and therapeutic procedures of psychodynamic psychiatry. Second, in cases where the workers or the psychiatric consultants felt that more direct or intensive therapy for group members or their families was indicated, arrangements were made to refer these cases either to the psychiatric clinic or to local casework or family-service agencies.

Another type of direct influence technique utilized by the workers was "group-dynamics"—a method which combined approaches of both psychodynamic and small-group theory. As adult advisors during club meetings, during informal bull-sessions, and in some instances during specially arranged group-therapy sessions, workers employed the specific techniques of persuasion and influence developed out of the group-dynamics approach (indirect suggestion, non-directive leadership, permissive group guidance, collective reinforcement). Sessions based on the group-therapy model were generally geared to specific emergent situations—such as an episode of sexual misbehavior among the girls or an upsurge of racial sentiment among the boys.[13]

The direct-influence technique which operated most consistently, however, was simply the continued presence with the group of a law-abiding, middle-class-oriented adult who provided active support for a particular value position. This value stance was communicated to the youngsters through two principal devises—advice and exemplification. The worker served as counsellor, advisor, mentor in a wide range of specific issues, problems, and areas of behavioral choice as these emerged in the course of daily life. Should I continue school or drop out? Can we refrain from retaliatory attack and still maintain our honor? How does one approach girls? How does one handle an overly romantic boy? Should I start a pimping operation? In all these issues and many more—sometimes broached by the worker, more frequently by the youngsters—the workers put their support—often subtle but nonetheless consistent—behind the law-abiding versus the law-violating choice, and, to a lesser extent, the middle-class-oriented over the

[13] A description of the use of group-dynamics techniques by Project workers is included in A. Paul Hare, "Group Dynamics as a Technique for Reducing Intergroup Tensions," Cambridge, Mass.: Harvard University, unpublished paper, 1957, pp. 14–22.

lower-class-oriented course of action in regard to long-term issues such as education, occupation, and family life.[14]

But the continued association of worker and group engaged a mechanism of influence which proved in many ways more potent than advice and counsel. The fact of constant association, and the fact that workers became increasingly accepted and admired, meant that they were in a particularly strategic position to serve as a "role-model," or object of emulation. A strong case can be made for the influencive potency of this device. Adolescents, as they move towards adult status, are often pictured as highly sensitive to, and in search of, models of estimable adult behavior, and as particularly susceptible to emulation of an adult who plays an important role in their lives and whom they respect and admire. It appeared, in fact, that gang members were considerably more impressed by what the workers *were* than by what they said or did. The youngsters were particularly aware that the workers were college people, that they were responsible spouses and parents in stable mother-father families, that they were conscientious workers under circumstances which afforded maximum opportunities for goofing-off. The workers' statuses as college people, "good" family people, and responsible workers constituted an implicit endorsement of these statuses, and the course of action they implied.

In some instances the admiration of group members for their worker approached hero-worship. One group set up a kind of shrine to their worker after his departure; on a shelf in the corner store where they hung out they placed his photograph, the athletic trophies they had won under his aegis,

and a scrap-book containing accounts of the many activities they had shared together. Visitors who knew the worker were importuned to relay to him a vital message—"Tell him we're keepin' our noses clean. . . ."

Phase III: Termination

Since the Project was set up on a three-year "demonstration" basis, the date of final contact was known well in advance. Due largely to the influence of psychodynamic concepts, workers were very much concerned about the possibly harmful effects of "termination," and formulated careful and extensive plans for effecting disengagement from their groups. During the termination phase the workers' efforts centered around three major areas: scheduling a gradual reduction in the frequency of contact and "services" so as to avoid an abrupt cut-off; preparing the groups emotionally for the idea of termination by probing for and discussing feelings of "desertion" anger and loss; and arranging for community agencies to assume as many as possible of the services workers had provided for the groups (e.g., recreational involvement, counseling, meeting places for the clubs).

Despite some difficult moments for both workers and group members (one worker's car was stolen during the tearful farewell banquet tendered him by his group the night before he was to leave for a new job in another city; group members explained this as a symbolic way of saying "Don't leave Midcity!"), termination was effected quite successfully; workers moved off to other involvements and the groups reassumed their workerless position within the community.

In sum, then, the methods used in the Project's attempt to inhibit delinquent behavior were based on a sophisticated rationale, utilized both so-

---

[14] For the frequency of use of "direct influence" techniques, see footnote 12.

ciocultural and psychological concepts and methods, encompassed an unusually wide range of practice techniques, and were executed with care, diligence, and energy by competent and professionally trained workers. It was impossible, of course, to execute all planned programs and methods as fully or as extensively as might have been desired, but in overall perspective the execution of the Project showed an unusually close degree of adherence to its ambitious and comprehensive plan of operation.[15] What, then, was the impact of these efforts on delinquent behavior?

THE IMPACT OF PROJECT EFFORTS

The Midcity Project was originally instituted in response to a community perception that uncontrolled gang violence was rampant in Midcity. Once the furor attending its inception had abated, the Project was reconceptualized as a "demonstration" project in community delinquency control.[16] This meant that in addition to setting up methods for effecting changes in its client population, the Project also assumed responsibility for testing the efficacy of these methods. The task of

evaluating project effectiveness was assigned to a social science research staff which operated in conjunction with the action program.[17] Since the major effort of the Project was its work with gangs, the evaluative aspect of the research design focused on the gang program, and took as a major concern the impact of group-directed methods on the behavior of target gangs. However, since the focal "client" population of the group-work program (gang members) was a subpopulation of the larger client population of the overall project ("trouble"-prone Midcity adolescents), measures of change in the gangs also constituted a test of the totality of control measures utilized by the Project, including its community organization and family-service programs.

The broad question—"Did the Project have any impact on the behavior of the groups it worked with?"—has, in effect, already been answered. The above description of Project methods shows that workers became actively and intensively involved in the lives and activities of the groups. It is hardly conceivable that relatively small groups of adolescents could experience daily association with an adult—especially an adult committed to the task of

[15] A previous report, "Preventive Work with Street-Corner Groups: Boston Delinquency Project," *op. cit.*, p. 106, cited certain factors which made it difficult to execute some project methods as fully as might have been desired. With greater perspective, derived both from the passage of time and increased knowledge of the experience of other projects, it would now appear that the Midcity Project was relatively less impeded in this regard than many similar projects, especially in regard to difficulties with police, courts, and schools, and that from a comparative viewpoint the Project was able to proceed relatively freely to effect most of its major methods.

[16] Events attending the inception of the Midcity Project are cited in "The Impact of a Community Group Work Program on Delinquent Corner Groups," *op. cit.*, and in Walter B. Miller, "Inter-Institutional Conflict as a Major Impediment to Delinquency Prevention," *Human Organization*, 17 (Fall 1958), pp. 20–23.

[17] Research methods were complex, utilizing a wide range of techniques and approaches. A major distinction was made between "evaluative" (measurement of impact) and "informational" (ethnographic description and analysis) research. No detailed account of research methods has been published, but brief descriptions appear in "The Impact of a Community Group Work Program on Delinquent Corner Groups," *op. cit.*, pp. 392–396, and "Preventive Work with Street-Corner Groups: Boston Delinquency Project," *op. cit.*, pp. 99–100, *passim*. A somewhat more detailed description of one kind of content analysis method used in an earlier pilot study, and modified for use in the larger study, appears in Walter B. Miller, Hildred Geertz, and Henry S. G. Cutter, "Aggression in a Boys' Street-Corner Group," *Psychiatry*, 24 (November 1961), pp. 284–285.

changing their behavior—without undergoing some substantial modification. But the fundamental *raison d'etre* of the Project was not that of demonstrating the possibility of establishing close relationships with gangs, or of organizing them into clubs, or of increasing their involvement in recreational activities, or of providing them with access to occupational or educational opportunities, or of forming citizens' organizations, or of increasing inter-agency cooperation. These objectives, estimable as they might be, were pursued not as ends in themselves but as means to a further and more fundamental end —the inhibition and control of criminal behavior. The substantial effects of the Project on nonviolent forms of behavior will be reported elsewhere; this paper addresses itself to a central and critical measure—the impact of the Project on specifically violative behavior.[18]

The principal question of the evaluative research was phrased as follows: *Was there a significant measurable inhibition of law-violating or morally disapproved behavior as a consequence of Project efforts?* For purposes of research procedure this question was broken down into two component questions: (1) To what extent was there a measurable reduction in the actual or expected frequency of violative behavior by Project group members during or after the period of Project contact? and (2) To what extent could

observed changes in violative behavior be attributed to Project activity rather than to other possible "causative" factors such as maturation or police activity?[19] Firm affirmative answers to the first question would necessarily have to precede attempts to answer further questions such as "Which methods were most effective?"; the value of describing what the workers did in order to reduce delinquency would evidently depend on whether it could be shown that delinquency had in fact been reduced.

Following sections will report three separate measures of change in patterns of violative behavior. These are: (1) disapproved forms of customary behavior; (2) illegal behavior; (3) court appearance rates. These three sets of measures represent different methods of analysis, different orders of specificity, and were derived from different sources. The implications of this for achieved results will be discussed later.

Trends in Disapproved Behavior

A central form of "violative" behavior is that which violates specific legal statutes (e.g., theft, armed assault). Also important, however, is behavior which violates "moral" norms or ethical standards. Concern with such behavior is of interest in its own right (Was there a reduction in morally violative behavior?) as well as in relation to illegal behavior (Were developments in the areas of illegal and immoral behavior related or independent?). The relationship between immoral and illegal behavior is highly complex; most behavior which violates legal norms also violates moral

[18] Detailed analyses of changes in "nonviolative" forms of behavior (e.g., frequency of recreational activities, trends in "evaluatively neutral" behaviors) as well as more generalized "change-process" analyses (e.g., "structural" changes in groups—factions, leadership; overall patterning of change and relations between changes in violative and non-violative patterns) will appear in Walter B. Miller, *City Gangs: An Experiment in Changing Gang Behavior,* John Wiley and Sons, in preparation.

[19] The "study population" toward which these questions were directed was the 205 members of the seven corner gangs subjected to "intensive service" by workers. Unless otherwise specified, the term "Project Groups" will be used to refer to this population.

norms (overtime parking is one example of an exception), but much immoral behavior seldom results in legal action (homosexual intimacy between women; failure to attempt to rescue a drowning stranger).

Designating specific forms of behavior as "illegal" presents a relatively simple task, since detailed and fairly explicit criminal codes are available; designating behavior as "immoral" is far more difficult, both because of the multiplicity of moral codes in American society, and because many important moral norms are not explicitly codified.[20] In addressing the question —"Did the Project bring about a decrease in morally violative behavior?", at least four sets of moral codes are of relevance—those of middle-class adults, of middle-class adolescents, of lower-class adults, and of lower-class adolescents.[21] While there are large areas of concordance among these sets, there are also important areas of noncorrespondence. The method employed in this area was as follows:

A major source of data for Project research was a large population of "behavior sequences" engaged in by group members during the study period. These were derived from a variety of sources, the principal source being the detailed descriptive daily field reports of the workers.[22] All recorded behavioral

events involving group members were extracted from the records and typed on separate data cards. These cards were coded, and filed in chronological order under 65 separate categories of behavior such as drinking behavior, sexual behavior, and theft. A total of 100,000 behavior sequences was recorded, coded, and filed.

Fourteen of the 65 behavior categories were selected for the purpose of analyzing trends in immoral behavior.[23] These were: theft, assault, drinking, sex, mating, work, education, religion, and involvement with courts, police, corrections, social welfare, family, and other gangs. Seventy-five thousand behavioral sequences were included under these fourteen categories.

A separate set of evaluative standards, based primarily on the workers' own values, was developed for each of the fourteen areas. The workers as individuals were essentially oriented to the value system of middle-class adults, but due largely to their training in social work, they espoused an "easier" or more permissive version of these standards. In addition, as a result of their experiences in the lower-class community, their standards had been further modified to accommodate in some degree those of the adolescent gangs. The workers' standards thus comprised an easier baseline against which to measure change since they were considerably less rigid than those

---

[20] A brief discussion of the complexities of the "multiple-moral-norm" system of the United States is contained in William C. Kvaraceus, Walter B. Miller, et al., *Delinquent Behavior: Culture and the Individual*, Washington, D.C.: National Education Association of the United States, 1959, pp. 46–49.

[21] This four-type distinction is very gross; a range of subsystems could be delineated within each of the four cited "systems."

[22] 8870 pages of typescript records were subjected to coding. Of these, 6600 pages were self-recorded field reports by workers; 690 pages were worker reports to the Project Director; 640 were field reports and interviews by research staff; 150 were tape-recorded transcriptions of group interaction.

A brief description of the principles of the data-coding system, based on the concept of the "object-oriented-behavior-sequence," is included in Ernest Lilienstein, James Short, et al., "Procedural Notes for the Coding of Detached Worker Interviews," Chicago: University of Chicago Youth Studies Program (February 1962), pp. 2–7.

[23] These fourteen were selected because they included the largest numbers of recorded events, and because they represented a range of behaviors along the dimension "high violative potential" (theft, assault) through "low violative potential" (church, family-oriented behavior).

which would be applied by most middle-class adults.

Listings were drawn up for each of the fourteen areas which designated as "approved" or "disapproved" about 25 specific forms of behavior per area. A distinction was made between "actions" (behavioral events observed to occur) and "sentiments" (attitudes or intentions).[24] Designations were based on three kinds of information: evaluative statements made by the workers concerning particular areas of behavior; attitudes or actions workers had supported or opposed in actual situations; and an attitude questionnaire administered to each worker. Preliminary listings were submitted to the workers to see if the items did in fact reflect the evaluative standards they felt themselves to espouse; there was high agreement with the listings; in a few instances of disagreement modifications were made.

A total of 14,471 actions and sentiments were categorized as "approved," "disapproved," or "evaluatively neutral." While these data made possible detailed and extensive analysis of differential patterns of behavior change in various areas and on different levels, the primary question for the most general purposes of impact measurement was phrased as—"Was there a significant reduction in the relative frequency of *disapproved actions* during the period of worker contact?" With some qualifications, the answer was "No."

Each worker's term of contact was divided into three equal phases, and the relative frequency of disapproved

24 Examples of approved and disapproved actions and sentiments in the area of drinking are as follows: *Approved action:* "refusal to buy or accept liquor"; *disapproved action:* "getting drunk, going on a drinking spree"; *approved sentiment:* "stated intention to discontinue or reduce frequency of drinking"; *disapproved sentiment:* "bragging of one's drinking prowess."

actions during the first and third phase was compared.[25] During the full study period, the 205 members of the seven intensive analysis groups engaged in 4518 approved or disapproved actions. During the initial phase, 785 of 1604 actions (48.9%) were disapproved; during the final phase, 613 of 1364 (44.9%)—a reduction of only 4%.

Of the fourteen behavior areas, only one ("school-oriented behavior") showed a statistically significant reduction in disapproved actions. Of the remaining thirteen, ten showed decreases in disapproved actions, one no change, and two (church- and social-agency-oriented behavior) showed increases. Of the seven analysis groups, only one (white, male, younger, higher social status) showed a statistically significant reduction. Of the remaining six, five showed decreases in disapproved actions, one no change, and one (white, male, older, lower social status) an increase.[26]

The unexpected degree of stability over time in the ratio of approved to

25 Selected findings in regard only to disapproved actions are reported here. Future reports will present and analyze trends in both actions and sentiments, and in approved, disapproved and evaluatively neutral forms, and the relations among these.

26 Chi-square was used to test significance. For all fourteen behavior areas for all seven groups, chi-square was 4.57 (one d.f.), which was significant between the .02 and .05 level. However, almost all the "change" variance was accounted for by the single area which showed a significant reduction (chi-square for "school" was 14.32, significant beyond the .01 level). The other 13 behavior areas, accounting for 91.6% of the evaluated actions, showed a reduction of only 2.3%. Chi-square was 1.52 (one d.f.) which fails of significance. Chi-square for the one significant change group (Junior Outlaws) was 9.21, significant at the .01 level. However, omitting the one "significant change" behavior area (school) from consideration, chi-square for the remaining 90% of Junior Outlaws behavior areas was 3.19—which fails of significance at the .05 level.

disapproved actions is all the more noteworthy in view of the fact that one might have expected the area of moral behavior to have felt the most direct impact of the workers' presence. One clue to the stability of the change figures lies in the fact that there was a good correspondence between the degree of change in disapproved actions and the social status of the group; in general, the lower the group's social status, the smaller the reduction in disapproved actions.[27]

Trends in Illegal Acts

The central question to be asked of a delinquency control program is—"Does it control delinquency?" One direct way of approaching this question is to focus on that "target" population most directly exposed to program action methods and ask "Was there a decrease in the frequency of crimes committed by the target population during the period of the program?" Under most circumstances this is difficult to answer, owing to the necessity of relying on records collected by police, courts, or other "official" agencies. The drawbacks of utilizing official incidence statistics as a measure of the actual occurrence of criminal behavior have frequently been pointed out; among these is the very complex process of selectivity which governs the conversion of committed crimes into official statistics; many crimes are never officially detected; many of those detected do not result in an official arrest; many arrests do not eventuate in court action,

and so on. At each stage of the conversion process, there is a multiplicity of factors relatively independent of the commission of the crime itself which determines whether or not a crime will be officially recorded, and in what form.

The Midcity Project was able to a large extent to overcome this difficulty by the nature of its base data. Because of their intimate daily association with gang members, workers were in a position both to observe crimes directly and to receive reports of crimes shortly after they occurred. The great majority of these never appeared in official records.[28]

The research question in the area of illegal behavior was phrased: "Was there a significant decrease in the frequency of statute violations committed by Project group members during the period of worker contact?" As in the case of disapproved actions, the answer was, with some qualifications, "No." Methods and results were as follows.

Every statute-violating act committed by a Project group member during the course of the contact period was recorded on an individual record form. While the bulk of recorded acts were derived from the workers' field reports, information was obtained from all available sources, including official records. Very few of the crimes recorded by official agencies were not also recorded

[27] Rank-difference correlation between "reduction in disapproved actions" and "lower social status" was —.82. The fact that this kind of association (the lower the social status the less change) appeared frequently in analyses of specific forms of behavior attests to the strength of the influence of group social status on patterns of delinquency and vulnerability to change efforts.

[28] The availability to the Project of both official and unofficial statistics on crime frequency made it possible to derive "conversion ratios" showing the proportion of crimes recorded by official agencies to those recorded by the Project. These ratios will be reported in greater detail in *City Gangs, op. cit.*; in brief, ratios of "Project-recorded" to "court-appeared" offenses were as follows. For all categories of offense for both sexes, 15% of known crimes resulted in court action. For males only this ratio was 16%; fewer than 1% of recorded female crimes were court processed. The highest ratio was in the case of theft-type offenses by males; about 25% were court processed. About 10% of male drinking and assaultive offenses resulted in court appearance.

by the Project; many of the crimes recorded by the Project did not appear in official records. During the course of the Project, a total of 1005 legally violative acts was recorded for members of the seven intensive analysis groups. Eighty-three per cent of the 205 Project group members had committed at least one illegal act; 90% of the 150 males had been so involved. These figures alone show that the Project did not prevent crime, and there had been no expectation that it would. But did it "control" or "inhibit" crime?

Offenses were classified under eleven categories: theft, assault, alcohol violations, sex offenses, trespassing, disorderly conduct, truancy, vandalism, gambling violations, and "other" (e.g., strewing tacks on street, killing cats).[29] Each worker's term of contact was divided into three equal phases, and the frequency of offenses during the initial and final phase was compared.

Seven hundred and fifty-two of the 1005 offenses were committed during the initial and final phases. Of these, 394 occurred during the initial phase, and 358 during the final—a reduction of 9.1%. Considering males only, however, 614 male crimes accounting for 81.6% of all offenses showed an *increase* of 1.3% between initial and final phases. In order to localize areas of greater and

lesser change, a distinction was made between "major" and "minor" types of offense, in which theft, assault, and alcohol offenses, accounting for 70.5% of all male offenses, were categorized as "major." On these major offenses the male groups showed an increase of 11.2%—the older male groups showing an increase of 4.7%, and the younger an increase of 21.8%.

In sum, then, it could not be said that there was any significant reduction in the frequency of known crimes during the course of the Project. The modest decrease shown by the total sample was accounted for largely by the girls and by minor offenses; major offenses by boys, in contrast, increased in frequency during the course of the Project, and major offenses by younger boys increased most of all.[30]

Trends in Court Appearances

The third major index to Project impact was based on court appearance statistics. The principal research question in this area was phrased: "Did the Project effect any decrease in the frequency with which Project group members appeared in court in connection with crimes?"[31] The use of court-

---

[29] Determination of illegality was based on the offense classifications of the Massachusetts Penal Code. The complexities of definition of the various offense categories cannot be detailed here, but most categories represent higher-level generality definitions than those of the code. For example, the category "theft" is used here to include all forms of unlawful appropriation of property, thus subsuming the more than 30 distinctions of the Penal Code, e.g., robbery, armed, unarmed; larceny, grand, petty; burglary, etc.). Non-theft auto violations are included under "other" since so few were recorded; similarly, narcotics violations, a major form of crime from a "seriousness" point of view, are included under "other" since virtually no instances were recorded.

[30] None of these changes proved significant on the basis of chi-square. Chi-square for the largest change, the increase of 21.8% for the younger males, was 3.32, which is just below the .05 level. More detailed analyses of these trends, broken down according to type of offense, sex, age, etc., will be presented in *City Gangs, op. cit.*

[31] Phrasing the question in this way was one of the devices used to accommodate the difficulties in using statistics compiled by official agencies. This phrasing takes the court appearance itself as an essentially independent index of impact; it does not assume any systematic connection between frequency of court appearance and frequency of criminal behavior. Having separate measures of Project-recorded and court-processed crimes (see footnote 28) makes possible separate computations of these ratios. Further, since court-appeared crime rather than committed crime can be

appearance data made it possible to amplify and strengthen the measurement of impact in three major ways. (1) It permitted a considerable time-extension. Previous sections describe trends which occurred during the actual period of worker contact. Sound determination of impact makes it necessary to know how these "during" trends related to trends both preceding and following the contact period. Post-contact trends become particularly important in light of the "negligible change" findings of the "during-contact" period, which raise the possibility that the real impact of the Project may have occurred following the workers' departure, as a kind of delayed reaction response. (2) The data were compiled by agencies which were essentially independent of the Project. Although the Project made every attempt to recognize, accommodate to, and correct for the possibility of in-project bias,[32] exclusive reliance on data collected primarily by those in the employ of the Project would admit the possibility that the objectives or values of Project staff would in some way prejudice results. Despite some contact between Project and court personnel, the operations of the courts were essentially independent of those of the Project, and the likelihood that the various courts in which group members appeared would be influenced in any consistent way by Project values or objectives was extremely small. (3) It made possible the application of time-trend measures to groups other than those taken by the Project as ob-

seen, from one perspective, as the more serious social problem, Project impact on the likelihood of appearance itself can be taken as one relatively independent measure of effectiveness.

[32] The technical and methodological devices for accommodating to or correcting for the possibility of in-project bias will be detailed in future reporting.

jects of change. The inclusion of a control population as part of the basic evaluative design was of vital importance. Despite the detail obtainable through the continued and intimate contact of group and worker, it would have been difficult to know, without a control population, the extent to which the experience of Project group members during the contact period was a response to worker influence rather than a variety of other possible influencing factors.

Court appearance data were processed in three different ways. The first made these data directly comparable with the other "during-contact" measures by asking—"Was there a significant decrease in the frequency with which Project group members appeared in court in connection with crimes during the contact period?" The second exploited the time-extension potentialities of the data by asking—"How did the frequency of court appearance during the contact period compare with frequency preceding and following this period?" The third utilized a control population and asked—"Did the court-appearance experience of gang members worked with by a delinquency control project for various periods between the ages of 14 and 19 differ significantly from the experience of similar gang members not so worked with?"

CONTACT PERIOD TRENDS. Names of the 205 members of the Project's intensive contact groups were submitted to the state's central criminal records division. Court appearance records were returned for all group members with court experience. These records contained full court appearance and correctional commitment data for the sixteen-year period from 1945 to 1961 —at which time older group members averaged 23 years of age, and younger, 21. It was thus possible to process the full sample as an age cohort in regard to court experience between the ages of 7 and 23, and including the period of Project contact. Each appearance in court on a new count for all male group members was tabulated.[33] "During-contact" appearance trends were analyzed in the same fashion as disapproved and illegal actions. The contact term for each group was divided into three equal phases, and the frequency of appearances during the initial and final phase was compared.

Trends in court-appeared offenses were essentially the same as trends in illegal actions. Group members appeared in court in connection with 144 offenses during the contact period. Fifty-one appearances occurred during the initial period and 48 during the final —a decrease of 5.8%. However, categorizing offenses as "major" and "minor" as was done in the case of illegal actions showed that for major offenses (theft, assault, alcohol), 31 appearances occured during the initial phase and 35 during the final—an increase of 12.9%.[34] There was, therefore, no significant decrease in the frequency with which group members appeared in court during the term of worker contact. Neither the slight decrease in all-offense trends nor the increase in major offense trends proved statistically significant. The fact that these "during-

contact" court appearance trends, involving 155 offenses, closely paralleled illegal act trends, involving 1005 offenses, served to corroborate both sets of trends, and to reinforce the finding of "negligible change" in legally violative behavior for the period of worker contact.

BEFORE-DURING-AFTER TRENDS: PROJECT GROUPS. In order to place the "during-contact" offense trends in a broader time perspective, it was necessary to compare them to rates preceding and following the contact period. Since group members were of different ages during the contact period, data were processed so as to make it possible to compare the court experience of the several groups at equivalent age periods. The average age of each group was determined, and the number of court appearances per group for each six-month period between the ages of 7 and 23 was tabulated. One set of results is shown in Table 1. The frequency curve of yearly court appearances resembled a normal distribution curve, skewed to the right. Appearance frequency increased gradually between the ages of 7 and 16, maintained a high level between 16 and 20, and dropped off quite rapidly after 20.

The period of maximum frequency of court appearances coincided, in general, with the period of worker contact. Although no single group remained in contact with a worker during the full period between ages 16 and 20, each of the groups experienced contact for periods ranging from one to two and a half years during this period. It could not be said, then, that frequency of court appearance during the contact period was appreciably lower than during the pre-contact period; on the contrary, groups achieved a peak of appearance frequency during the period of Project service efforts.

Another way of describing these

---

[33] Out of 145 "during-contact" court appearances, only one involved a girl. Since 155 illegal acts involved females, this supports the frequently reported finding that females are far less likely to be subjected to official processing for crimes than males. All following figures, therefore, refer to males only.

[34] Neither of these changes was statistically significant, testing with chi-square and Fisher's Exact Test. The three "major" offenses showed differing trends—with "theft" showing some decrease (23 to 19), "assault" remaining about the same (5 to 6) and "alcohol" showing a considerable increase (3 to 10). "Minor" crimes decreased from 20 to 13. These trends will be reported and analyzed more fully in future reports.

Table 1

NUMBER OF COURT APPEARANCES FOR YEAR:* AGES 7-23. PROJECT AND CONTROL
GROUPS

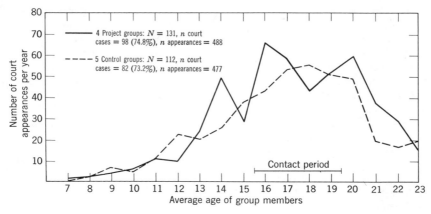

* On new charges, all offenses.

trends is by examining appearance frequency by six-month periods. During the six months preceding contact there were 21 appearances; during the first six months of contact there were 29, and during the last, 27. In the six months following termination appearances rose to 39, dropped to 20 for the next six months, and rose to 39 for the next. Thus, eighteen months after project termination, appearance frequency was at its highest point for the total adolescent period.

The yearly appearance curve (Table 1) does, however, show two rather prominent dips—one at age 15, the other at 18. The dip at 15 could not have been related to the Project, since contact had not yet begun. The dip at 18, however, occurred at a time when each of the three older groups was in contact with workers, and thus admits the possibility of worker influence.[35] It is also possible that the

[35] This "dip" phenomenon—a lowering of the frequency of violative behavior during the "middle" phase of worker contact —was also noted in connection with a

post-20 decline may have represented a delayed action effect. Thus, looking at the period of worker contact as one phase within the overall period of adolescence, it would appear that the presence of the workers did not inhibit the frequency of court appearances, but that a dip in appearance frequency at age 18 and a drop in frequency after age 20 may have been related to the workers' efforts.

COMPARISON OF PROJECT AND CONTROL GROUP TRENDS. Extending the examination of offense trends from the during-contact period to "before" and "after" periods, while furnishing important additional information, also raised additional questions. Was it just coincidental that the 16 to 19 peak in court appearances occurred during the contact period—or could the presence of the workers have been in some way

somewhat different kind of processing of illegal acts reported in "Preventive Work with Street-Corner Groups: Boston Delinquency Project," *op. cit.*, p. 100. Currently available data make it possible to amplify and modify the interpretation presented in the earlier paper.

responsible? Was the sharp decline in frequency of appearances after age 20 a delayed action result of worker effort? To clarify these questions it was necessary to examine the court appearance experience of a control population—a set of corner gangs as similar as possible to Project gangs, but who had *not* been worked with by the Project. The indexes reported so far have provided information as to whether significant change occurred, but have been inconclusive as to the all-important question of cause-and-effect (To what extent were observed trends related to the workers' efforts?). The use of a control population entailed certain risks—primarily the possibility that service and control populations might not be adequately matched in some respects—but the unique potency of the control method as a device for furnishing evidence in the vital area of "cause" outweighed these risks.

Each of the Project's seven intensive service groups was matched with a somewhat smaller number of members of similarly organized corner gangs of similar age, sex, ethnic status, and social status. Most of these groups hung out in the same district as did Project groups, and their existence and membership had been ascertained during the course of the Project. Since the total membership of the Control groups was not known as fully as that of Project groups, it was necessary in some instances to match one Project group with two Control groups of similar status characteristics. By this process, a population comprising 172 members of 11 corner gangs was selected to serve as a control population for the 205 members of the seven Project gangs. Court appearance data on Control groups were obtained, and the groups were processed as an age cohort in the same manner as Project groups.

The court appearance frequency curves for Project and Control groups are very similar (see Table 1). If the two dips in the Project curve are eliminated by joining the peaks at 14, 16, and 20, the shape of the two curves becomes almost identical. Both curves show a gradual rise from ages 7 to 16 or 17, maintain a high level to age 20, and drop rapidly between 20 and 23. Table 2 compares Project and Control groups according to the number of *individuals* per year per group to appear in court, rather than according to the number of *appearances* per year per group. On this basis, the similarity between Project and Control curves becomes even more marked. The dip at age 14 in the Project appearance curve (Table 1) flattens out, and both Project and Control groups show a dip at age 18, making the Project and Control curves virtually identical.[36]

The unusual degree of similarity between the court appearance curves of Project and Control groups constitutes the single most powerful piece of evidence on Project impact obtained by the research. The fact that a group of similar gangs not worked with by the Project showed an almost identical decrease in court appearance frequency between ages 20 and 23 removes any reasonable basis for attributing the post-20 decline of Project groups to worker efforts. Indeed, the high degree of overall similarity in court appearance experience between "served" and

[36] The implications of these court-appearance frequency trends transcend their utility as a technique for "controlling" for worker influence. One implication will be cited in footnote 43; more detailed interpretation and analysis, with special attention to the relative influence of worker activity and subcultural forces on the shape of the curves, will be included in *City Gangs, op. cit.* Also included will be greater detail on the process of locating, selecting, matching, and processing the control population.

Table 2

NUMBER OF INDIVIDUALS APPEARING IN COURT PER YEAR: * AGES 7-23. PROJECT AND CONTROL GROUPS

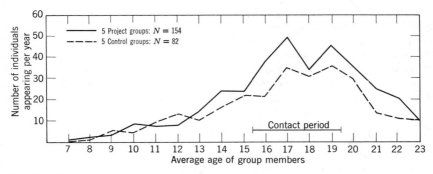

* At least once, on new charges, all offenses.

"unserved" groups makes it most difficult to claim that anything done by the Project had any significant influence on the likelihood of court appearance.

Project and Control groups show equally striking similarities in regard to three additional measures—the proportion of individuals who had appeared in court by age 23, the proportion who had re-appeared, and the number of appearances per individual. Of 131 members of four male Project groups, 98, or 74.8%, had appeared in court at least once by age 23. The fact that 75% of the members of gangs worked with by social workers had nevertheless appeared in court by age 23 would in itself appear to indicate very limited Project impact. This finding, however, still admits the possibility that appearance frequency might have been even higher in the absence of the workers, or conversely, that the high figure was in some way a consequence of the workers' efforts. Both of these possibilities are weakened by the Control cohort figures. Of 112 members of five male groups *not* worked with by the Project, 82, or 73.2%, had

appeared in court by age 23—almost exactly the same percentage shown by Project groups.[37]

The possibility still remains that Project group members, once having appeared in court, would be less likely than Control members to *reappear*. This was not the case. Of 98 members of Project groups who appeared in court at least once, 72, or 73.5%, appeared at least once again; of 82 Control group members who appeared at least once, 61, or 74.3%, appeared at least once

[37] The finding of negligible difference in court appearance frequency between Project and Control groups parallels the findings of the Cambridge-Somerville Youth Study—one of the few delinquency control projects to report findings of careful evaluative research (Edwin Powers and Helen Witmer, *An Experiment in the Prevention of Delinquency,* New York: Columbia University Press, 1951). It was found that 29.5% of a 325-boy treatment group had appeared in court by the time the oldest boys were 21, as compared with 28.3% of a 325-boy control group (p. 326). Despite differences in methods (Cambridge-Somerville used primarily individually focused counseling) and client populations (Cambridge-Somerville boys were less delinquent), the degree of similarity between the two projects in treatment and control outcomes is striking.

more. A further possibility exists that while similar proportions of *individuals* might have appéared in court, Project group members might have made fewer *appearances* per individual. However, Project and Control groups were also similar in this respect. Ninety-eight Project members who appeared in court between the ages of 7 and 23 appeared 488 times, or 5.0 appearances per individual. Eighty-two Control males appeared 447 times, or 5.4 appearances per individual. These figures, while not as close to identity as the outcome figures, fail to show a statistically significant difference. The unusual degree of closeness in all these court appearance measures for male Project and Control groups provides a firm basis for concluding that Project impact on the likelihood of court appearance was negligible.

Summary of "Impact" Findings

It is now possible to provide a definite answer to the principal evaluative research question—"Was there a significant measurable inhibition of law-violating or morally disapproved behavior as a consequence of Project efforts?" The answer, with little necessary qualification, is "No." All major measures of violative behavior—disapproved actions, illegal actions, during-contact court appearances, before-during-after appearances, and Project-Control group appearances—provide consistent support for a finding of "negligible impact."

There was a modest decrease, during the period of worker contact, in the frequency of disapproved actions in 14 areas of behavior—but much of this reduction was due to a decrease in a single area—school-oriented behavior. The overall change in the other 13 areas was only −2.3%.[38] The total

number of illegal actions engaged in by group members also decreased slightly, though not significantly, during the course of the Project. Most of this reduction, however, was accounted for by minor offenses; major offenses showed a slight increase. Similarly, while there was a small decrease in the frequency of all categories of court-appeared offenses, major offenses showed an increase. Examining the group members' court appearance trends between the ages 7 and 23 showed that court appearances were most frequent during the age-period when Project workers were with the groups. The possibility that a pronounced decrease in court appearance frequency after age 20 represented a delayed response to the Project was weakened by the fact that a similar decline occurred in the case of a set of similar gangs not worked with by the Project, and which, in fact, showed extremely similar court appearance trends both before, during, and after the age period during which Project groups were in contact with workers.

The fact that the various measures of impact are mutually consistent increases confidence in the overall "negligible impact" finding. Not only do the several indexes delineate similar trends in regard to the direction and magnitude of change (e.g., "during-period" change in disapproved actions, −4.0%; in illegal actions, −9.1%; in court appearance frequency, −5.8%), but also show a high degree of internal consistency in other respects. For example, the rank position of the five male groups in the degree of reduction in violative

truancy brought about by the fact that many of the earlier period truants had, by Project termination, passed the age at which school attendance was compulsory, thus ending their truancy. This possibility will be tested as part of a detailed analysis of change trends in each behavior area.

---

[38] It is possible that the decrease in disapproved school-oriented actions was due largely to a decrease in the frequency of

behavior shown by the three major indexes was very similar.[39]

Two previous papers reporting impact findings of the Midcity Project conveyed the impression of a limited but definite reduction in delinquency.[40] Why does the present report support a different conclusion? In the first place, present findings are based on new data not available in 1957 and 1959, as well as on more extensive analysis of data then available. Both previous papers stated that reported results were preliminary, and cited the possibility of modification by future analysis.[41] Second, present data focus more directly on the specific experience of a specific target population; some of the previous impact findings were based on less focused indexes of general community trends, in which the behavior of the Project's target groups was not as directly distinguishable. Third, the "before" and "after" time extension made possible by the use of court data shows some previously reported trends to have been relatively temporary fluctuations. Fourth, the use of a control population made it possible to anchor results more firmly by showing that important observed trends were common to both Project and non-Project groups, thus making possible a better determination of the extent to which "during" Project variation was in fact related to the workers' efforts.

THE EFFICACY OF PROJECT CONTROL METHODS

Which of the Project's methods were "tested" by the "negligible impact" findings? This complex question can be addressed only briefly here. It is evident that it was those methods which were most extensively employed or successfully executed which were shown most directly to have been least effective in inhibiting delinquency. Fifteen separate methods or techniques were cited earlier in connection with the three major programs (Community Organization, Family Service, Gang Work) of the Midcity Project. Of these, seven could be designated as extensively employed or successfully executed: establishment of district citizens' council; locating and contacting adolescent corner gangs; establishing relationships with gang members; effecting formal organization and involvement in organized recreational activity; provision of access to adult institutions; provision of adult role-model. It is to these seven methods that the "negligible impact" finding applies most directly. Of these, "recreation" is already recognized quite widely to be of limited effectiveness as an exclusive method; "relationship" is still seen in many quarters as quite effective; "adult role-model" was also found, by the Cambridge-Somerville Project, to have had little effect. Of two aspects of "access-provision"—enabling youngsters to avail themselves of existing opportunities, and altering larger societal institutions so as to create new opportunities—the Project achieved the former but exerted limited systematic effort in regard to the latter, so that this aspect of access-provision was only minimally tested.

[39] Rank-difference correlation coefficients were as follows: disapproved acts and illegal acts $+.80$; disapproved acts and court appearances $+.87$; illegal acts and court appearances, $+.97$. Even with the small N of 5, the good correspondence between disapproved acts and court appearances is impressive, since the data for the two rank series were derived from completely independent sources.

[40] "The Impact of a Community Group Work Program on Delinquent Corner Groups," *op. cit.*, pp. 390–406, and "Preventive Work with Street-Corner Groups: Boston Delinquency Project," *op. cit.*, pp. 97–106.

[41] It is similarly possible that some of the results cited here will be modified in the final Project report, especially in areas where more extensive internal analysis will enable fuller interpretations of reported trends.

Six methods could be characterized as less extensively employed or implemented with only moderate success: formation of citizens' groups; coordination of efforts of youth groups and adult citizens' groups; coordination of family-service agencies; treatment of "chronic problem" families; psychodynamic counseling and therapy; group dynamics. Some of these programs continued beyond the Project's three year demonstration period, but there is as yet no evidence available that any of these have had an impact on delinquency substantially different from that of the "best-tested" methods.

Two final methods—effecting concerted effort between citizens' groups and professional agencies, and coordinating the varied efforts of professional agencies themselves—were implemented only minimally. It is to these methods, then, that the "negligible impact" finding has least applicability. However, this failure of effectuation, especially in the area of inter-agency cooperation, was achieved only after extensive expenditure of effort, which might suggest that the cost of implementing this type of method, whose potential impact on delinquency is as yet undetermined, might not be commensurate with the degree of delinquency reduction it could perhaps produce.

In addition, granting that some of the Project's methods were tested less fully than others, the fact that all 15 (and others) were applied concurrently and in concert also constituted a test of the "synergism" concept—that the simultaneous and concerted application of multiple and diverse programs on different levels will produce an impact greater than the summed impact of the component programs. Thus the total-community–multiple-programs approach, as executed by the Midcity Project, also fell within the category of methods best tested by the finding of "negligible impact."

In evaluating the significance of these "negligible impact" findings three considerations should be borne in mind. The first concerns the scope and nature of the question to which "negligible impact" is an answer, the second the level on which the answer is presented, and the third the value of the Project to delinquency control as a larger enterprise.

The phrasing of the principal evaluative research question tests the effectiveness of the Project against a single and central criterion—the measurable inhibition of explicitly violative behavior of a designated target population. The Project had considerable impact in other areas. To cite only two of these: the establishment of the control project and the spread of knowledge as to its existence had a calming effect on the adult community. Pre-Project gang activities in Midcity had activated a sense of fear among many adults, and a feeling of helplessness in the face of actual and potential violence. Simple knowledge of the existence of the Project served to alleviate the community's sense of threat, in that there was now an established locus of responsibility for gang crime. The fact that *something* was being done was in itself important quite independent of the possible effectiveness of what was being done.

The Project was also instrumental in establishing new delinquency-control organizations, and left the community a legacy of organizations and programs which it had either brought into being or taken primary responsibility for. Among these were the District Community Council organized by Project staff, the project for providing direct service to "chronic problem" families, an annual sports award dinner for the youth of the community, and a permanent program of area work administered by the municipal government.

The organizational plan of this latter enterprise was drawn up before Project termination, so that the municipal delinquency control bureau, once established, was able to extend the general approach of the Project to the entire municipal area.[42] While the value of these organized enterprises must also be measured against the same "impact on delinquency" criterion which was applied to the Project, it is clear that their existence was one tangible product of the Project.

A second consideration concerns the "level" of the reported findings. Data presented in connection with each of the major indexes to impact are at the most gross analytical level—that is, they neither specify nor analyze systematically the internal variation of the reported trends in three important respects—variations among the several groups, variations among the several behavior areas, and finer fluctuations over time. The finding of "negligible impact" encompasses, most accurately, *all* analyzed forms of behavior of *all* analyzed groups for extended periods. Internal analyses not reported here show that some groups showed considerable change in some areas, and that some areas showed considerable change for some groups. Further, while initial and final levels of violative behavior in many instances showed little difference, a good deal of turbulence or fluctuation characterized intervening periods. The flat "negligible impact" statement, then, by concealing a considerable degree of internal variability, obscures the fact that there was differential vulnerability to change in different areas and for different groups. Fuller analyses of these variations, along with the methods associated with

greater and lesser vulnerability, will furnish specific policy guides to more and less strategic points of intervention.

A final consideration concerns the "value" of the Project in the face of its "negligible inhibition of delinquent behavior" outcome. There can be an important distinction, obscured by the term "evaluation" between the "effect" of an enterprise and its "value." The Midcity Project was established to test the possible effectiveness of its several approaches. These were in fact tested, and the Project was thus successful in the achievement of its "demonstration" objective. The evaluation model used here, based on multiple indexes to change, and using the "behavioral event" as a primary unit of analysis, can be applied in other instances where the impact of a specific change enterprise is at issue. Even more important, perhaps, is the fact that the process of gathering and analyzing the great bulk of data necessary to furnish a sound answer to the question of impact also produced a large volume of information of direct relevance to basic theoretical questions as to the origins of gangs and of gang delinquency. These findings also bear directly on a further question of considerable importance— "Why did the Project have so little impact on delinquency?"—a question to be addressed in some detail in future reports.[43]

[42] See D. Austin, "Recommendations for a Municipal Program of Delinquency Prevention," mimeo, 7 pp., United Community Services of Boston, 1957.

[43] Factors accounting for the limited impact of Project efforts will be treated in detail in *City Gangs, op. cit.* The explanatory analysis will forward the thesis that culturally derived incentives for engaging in violative behavior were far stronger than any counterpressures the Project could bring to bear. This explanation will derive from a general theory of gang delinquency whose central proposition, to be expanded at length, will be that patterned involvement in violative behavior by gangs of the Midcity type occurs where four cultural "conditions" exist concurrently—*maleness, adolescence, urban residence,* and *low-skill laboring class status.* Each of these condi-

tions is conceptualized as a particular type of subcultural system—each of whose "demanded" sets of behavior, taken separately, contribute some element of the motivation for engagement in gang delinquency, and whose concerted operation produces a subcultural milieu which furnishes strong and consistent support for customary involvement in criminal behavior. Data on "impact" presented here document the influence of two of these conditions—age status and social status. Court appearance frequency trends (Tables I and II) would appear to indicate that the single most important determinant of the frequency of that order of criminal behavior which eventuated in court appearance for Midcity male gangs was *age*, or more specifically, movement through a series of age-based subcultural stages. Commission of criminal acts of given types and frequency appeared as a required concomitant of passing through the successive age-stages of adolescence and a prerequisite to the assumption of adult status. The influence of these age-class demands, on the basis of this and other evidence, would appear to exceed that of other factors—including conditions

of the family, school, neighborhood or job world; police arrest policies, sentencing, confinement, probation and parole policies, and others. Data on *social status* (e.g., footnote 27, *passim*) along with much additional data not reported here, indicate a systematic relationship between social status *within* the lower class, and delinquency. 1. Within the 21-gang sample of the Midcity study, crime was both more prevalent and more serious among those whose social status, measured by occupational and educational indexes, was lowest. 2. Relatively small differences in status were associated with relatively large differences in patterned behavior; as lower status levels were approached, delinquency incidence increased exponentially rather than linearly; this indicates the necessity of making refined intra-class distinctions when analyzing the social "location" of criminal behavior. 3. Groups of lower social status showed the least reduction in violative forms of behavior; this lower vulnerability to change efforts would indicate that violative behavior was more entrenched, and thus more central to the subcultural system.

39.

The Provo Experiment in Delinquency Rehabilitation

LaMar T. Empey and Jerome Rabow

Despite the importance of sociological contributions to the understanding of delinquent behavior, relatively few of these contributions have been systematically utilized for purposes of rehabilitation.[1] The reason is at least partially inherent in the sociological tradition which views sociology primarily as a research discipline. As a consequence, the rehabilitation of delinquents has been left, by default, to people who have been relatively unaware of sociological theory and its implications for treatment.

This situation has produced or perpetuated problems along two dimensions. On one dimension are the problems engendered in reformatories where

authorities find themselves bound, not only by the norms of their own official system, but by the inmate system as well. They are unable to work out an effective program: (1) because the goals of the two systems are incompatible; and (2) because no one knows much about the structure and function of the inmate system and how it might be dealt with for purposes of rehabilitation.[2] Furthermore, the crux of any treatment program has ultimately to do with the decision-making process utilized by delinquents in the community, *not* in the reformatory. Yet, the deci-

* The inception and continuation of this experiment were made possible through the co-operation of the Judge (Monroe Paxman) and staff of the Third District Juvenile Court, a voluntary group known as the Citizens' Advisory Council, and Utah County Officials. Evaluation is supported by the Ford Foundation. Grateful acknowledgment is made to all involved.

[1] Donald R. Cressey, "Changing Criminals: The Application of the Theory of Differential Association," *American Journal of Sociology*, 61 (July, 1955), p. 116.

[2] Daniel Glaser maintains that the prison social system has not received the study it merits. Most writing about prisons, he says, is "impressionistic," "moralistic," "superficial," and "biased," rather than "systematic" and "objective." "The Sociological Approach to Crime and Correction," *Law and Contemporary Problems*, 23 (Autumn, 1958), p. 697; see also Gresham M. Sykes and Sheldon Messinger, "The Inmate Social System," in *Theoretical Studies in Social Organization of the Prison*, Social Science Research Council, March, 1960, pp. 5–19; and Lloyd W. McCorkle and Richard Korn, "Resocialization Within Walls," *The Annals of The American Academy of Political and Social Science*, 293 (May, 1954), pp. 88–98.

SOURCE. Lamar T. Empey and Jerome Rabow, "The Provo Experiment in Delinquency Rehabilitation," from *American Sociological Review*, Volume 26, October 1961, pp. 679–695. Reprinted with the permission of the American Sociological Association and the authors.

sions which lead to success in "doing time" in the reformatory are not of the same type needed for successful community adjustment. Existing conditions may actually be more effective in cementing ties to the delinquent system than in destroying them.[3]

The second dimension of the problem has to do with the traditional emphasis upon "individualized treatment."[4] This emphasis stems from two sources: (1) a humanistic concern for the importance of human dignity and the need for sympathetic understanding;[5] and (2) a widespread belief that delinquency is a psychological disease and the offender a "*sick*" person.[6] If, however, sociologists are even partially correct regarding the causes for delinquency, these two points of view overlook the possibility that most persistent delinquents do have the support of a meaningful reference group and are

[3] Sykes and Messinger, *op. cit.*, pp. 12–13; Richard McCleery, "Policy Change in Prison Management," *Michigan State University Political Research Studies*, No. 5, 1957; Richard A. Cloward, "Social Control in the Prison," in *Theoretical Studies in Social Organization of the Prison, op. cit.*, pp. 20–48; Stanton Wheeler, "Socialization in Correctional Communities," *American Sociological Review*, 26 (October, 1961).

[4] Cressey, *op. cit.*, p. 116.

[5] For example, see John G. Milner, "Report on an Evaluated Study of the Citizenship Training Program, Island of Hawaii," Los Angeles: University of Southern California School of Social Work, 1959, p. 4. Irving E. Cohen implies that anything which interferes with the establishment of "confidence, sympathy and understanding" between adult and offender interferes with the effectiveness of the individualized approach. See "Twilight Zones in Probation," *Journal of Criminal Law and Criminology*, 37, No. 4, p. 291.

[6] Michael Hakeem, "A Critique of the Psychiatric Approach to Juvenile Delinquency," in *Juvenile Delinquency*, edited by Joseph S. Roucek, New York: Philosophical Library, 1958. Hakeem provides a large bibliography to which attention can be directed if further information is desired. See also Daniel Glaser, "Criminality Theories and Behavioral Images," *American Journal of Sociology*, 61 (March, 1956), pp. 433–444.

not, therefore, without the emotional support and normative orientation which such a group can provide. In fact, a complete dedication to an individualistic approach poses an impasse: How can an individual who acquired delinquency from a group with which he identifies strongly be treated individually without regard to the persons or norms of the system from whom he acquired it?[7]

A successful treatment program for such a person would require techniques not normally included in the individualized approach. It should no more be expected that dedicated delinquents can be converted to conventionality by such means than that devout Pentecostals can be converted to Catholicism by the same means. Instead, different techniques are required for dealing with the normative orientation of the delinquent's system, replacing it with new values, beliefs, and rationalizations and developing means by which he can realize conventional satisfactions, especially with respect to successful employment.

This does not suggest, of course, that such traditional means as probation for dealing with the first offender or psychotherapy for dealing with the disturbed offender can be discarded. But it does suggest the need for experimental programs more consistent with sociological theory, and more consistent with the sociological premise that most *persistent* and *habitual* offenders are active members of a delinquent social system.[8]

[7] Cressey, *op. cit.*, p. 117. LaMay Adamson and H. Warren Dunham even imply that the clinical approach cannot work successfully with habitual offenders. See "Clinical Treatment of Male Delinquents: A Case Study in Effort and Result," *American Sociological Review*, 21 (June, 1956), p. 320.

[8] One program consistent with this premise is the Highfields Residential Group Center in New Jersey. Modern penology is indebted to it for the development of many

This paper presents the outlines of a program—the Provo Experiment in Delinquency Rehabilitation—which is derived from sociological theory and which seeks to apply sociological principles to rehabilitation. Because of its theoretical ties, the concern of the Experiment is as much with a systematic evaluation and reformulation of treatment consistent with findings as with the administration of treatment itself. For that reason, research and evaluation are an integral part of the program. Its theoretical orientation, major assumptions, treatment system, and research design are outlined below.

THEORETICAL ORIENTATION

With regards to causation, the Provo Experiment turned to a growing body of evidence which suggests two important conclusions: (1) that the greater part of delinquent behavior is not that of individuals engaging in highly secretive deviations, but is a group phenomenon—a shared deviation which is the product of differential group experience in a particular subculture,[9] and (2)

that because most delinquents tend to be concentrated in slums or to be the children of lower-class parents, their lives are characterized by learning situations which limit their access to success goals.[10]

Attention to these two conclusions does not mean that emotional problems[11] or "bad" homes[12] can be ignored. But only occasionally do these variables lead by themselves to delinquency. In most cases where older delinquents are involved other intervening variables must operate, the most important of which is the presence of a delinquent system—one which supplies status and recognition not normally obtainable elsewhere. Whether they are members

unique and important aspects. See Lloyd W. McCorkle, Albert Elias, and F. Lovell Bixby, *The Highfields Story: A Unique Experiment in the Treatment of Juvenile Delinquency*, New York: Henry Holt and Co., 1958; H. Ashley Weeks, *Youthful Offenders at Highfields*, Ann Arbor: University of Michigan Press, 1958; and Albert Elias and Jerome Rabow, "Post-Release Adjustment of Highfields Boys, 1955–1957," *The Welfare Reporter*, January, 1960, pp. 7–11.

[9] Richard A. Cloward and Lloyd E. Ohlin, *Delinquency and Opportunity: A Theory of Delinquent Gangs*, Glencoe, Ill.: The Free Press, 1960; Albert K. Cohen, *Delinquent Boys—The Culture of the Gang*, Glencoe, Ill.: The Free Press, 1955; Albert K. Cohen and James F. Short, Jr., "Research in Delinquency Subcultures," *The Journal of Social Issues*, 14 (1958), pp. 20–37; Solomon Kobrin, "The Conflict of Values in Delinquency Areas," *American Sociological Review*, 16 (October, 1951), pp. 653–661; Robert K. Merton, *Social Theory and Social Structure*, Glencoe, Ill.: The Free Press, 1957, Chapters 4–5; Walter B. Miller, "Lower Class Culture as a

Generating Milieu of Gang Delinquency," *The Journal of Social Issues*, 14 (1958), pp. 5–19; Clifford R. Shaw, *Delinquency Areas*, Chicago: University of Chicago Press, 1929; Clifford R. Shaw, Henry D. McKay, et al., *Juvenile Delinquency and Urban Areas*, Chicago: University of Chicago Press, 1931; Edwin H. Sutherland, *Principles of Criminology*, 4th ed., Philadelphia: Lippincott, 1947; Frank Tannenbaum, *Crime and the Community*, Boston: Ginn and Co., 1938; F. M. Thrasher, *The Gang*, Chicago: University of Chicago Press, 1936; William F. Whyte, *Street Corner Society*, Chicago: University of Chicago Press, 1943.

[10] Richard A. Cloward, "Illegitimate Means, Anomie, and Deviant Behavior," *American Sociological Review*, 24 (April, 1959), pp. 164–176; Cloward and Ohlin, *op. cit.*; Robert K. Merton, "Social Conformity, Deviation, and Opportunity-Structures: A Comment on the Contributions of Dubin and Cloward," *American Sociological Review*, 24 (April, 1959), pp. 177–189; Robert K. Merton, "The Social-Cultural Environment and Anomie," *New Perspectives for Research on Juvenile Delinquency*, edited by Helen Kotinsky, U. S. Department of Health, Education and Welfare, 1955, pp. 24–50; Merton, *Social Theory and Social Structure*, *op. cit.*

[11] Erik H. Erikson, "Ego Identity and the Psycho-Social Moratorium," *New Perspectives for Research on Juvenile Delinquency*, *op. cit.*, pp. 1–23.

[12] Jackson Toby, "The Differential Impact of Family Disorganization," *American Sociological Review*, 22 (October, 1957), pp. 505–511; and F. Ivan Nye, *Family Relationships and Delinquent Behavior*, New York: John Wiley and Sons, 1958.

of a tight-knit gang or of the amorphous structure of the "parent" delinquent subculture,[13] habitual delinquents tend to look affectively both to their peers and to the norms of their system for meaning and orientation. Thus, although a "bad" home may have been instrumental at some early phase in the genesis of a boy's delinquency, it must be recognized that it is now other delinquent boys, not his parents, who are current sources of support and identification. Any attempts to change him, therefore, would have to view him as more than an unstable isolate without a meaningful reference group. And, instead of concentrating on changing his parental relationships, they would have to recognize the intrinsic nature of his membership in the delinquent system and direct treatment to him as a part of that system.

There is another theoretical problem. An emphasis on the importance of the delinquent system raises some question regarding the extent to which delinquents are without any positive feeling for conventional standards. Vold says that one approach to explaining delinquency ". . . operates from the basic, implicit assumption that in a delinquency area, delinquency is the normal response of the normal individual— that the non-delinquent is really the 'problem case,' the nonconformist whose behavior needs to be accounted for."[14] This is a deterministic point of view suggesting the possibility that delinquents view conventional people as "foreigners" and conventional norms and beliefs as anathema. It implies that delinquents have been socialized entirely in a criminal system and have never internalized or encountered the

blandishments of conventional society.[15]

Actually, sociological literature suggests otherwise. It emphasizes, in general, that the subparts of complex society are intimately tied up with the whole,[16] and, specifically, that delinquents are very much aware of conventional standards; that they have been socialized in an environment dominated by middle-class morality;[17] that they have internalized the American success ideal to such a degree that they turn to illegitimate means in an effort to be successful[18] (or, failing in that, engage in malicious or retreatist activities);[19] that they are profoundly

13 Cohen and Short, Jr., op. cit., p. 24.
14 George B. Vold, "Discussion of Guided Group Interaction in Correctional Work by F. Lovell Bixby and Lloyd W. McCorkle," American Sociological Review, 16 (August, 1951), p. 460.

15 As Glaser points out, sociologists have tended to be deterministic and to ally themselves with psychiatrists in the struggle against classical legalists and religious leaders over the free will versus determinism issue. He labels this struggle as a "phony war," involving polemics more than reality. However, he says the war is losing its intensity because of a declining interest in metaphysical issues and a recognition of the importance of voluntaristic rather than reflexive conceptions of human behavior. Contrary to their protestations, the determinists, for example, recognize that humans are aware of alternative possible courses of behavior and make deliberate choices between them. See "The Sociological Approach to Crime and Correction," op. cit., pp. 686–687.
16 Sutherland, it will be recalled, maintained that "While criminal behavior is an expression of general needs and values, it is not explained by those general needs and values since non-criminal behavior is an expression of the same needs and values." Op. cit., pp. 6–7, italics ours. The accuracy of the statement would hinge on the definition of "needs" and "values." See also David J. Bordua, Sociological Theories and Their Implications for Juvenile Delinquency, U. S. Department of Health, Education and Welfare, 1960, p. 8, and Robin M. Williams, Jr., American Society, New York: Alfred A. Knopf, 1955, Chapter 11.
17 Cohen, op. cit., p. 133.
18 Merton, Social Theory and Social Structure, op. cit.
19 Cloward, op cit., and Cloward and Ohlin, op. cit. See also Robert Dubin, "Deviant Behavior and Social Structure: Continuities in Social Theory," American Sociological Review, 24 (April, 1959), pp. 147–164.

ambivalent about their delinquent behavior;[20] and that in order to cope with the claims of respectable norms upon them, they maintain a whole series of intricate rationalizations by which to "neutralize" their delinquent behavior.[21]

This suggests that delinquents are aware of conventional structure and its expectations. In many conventional settings they can, and usually do, behave conventionally. But it also suggests that, like other people, they are motivated by the normative expectations of their own subsystem. Consequently, when in the company of other delinquent boys, they may not only feel that they have to live up to minimal delinquent expectations but to appear more delinquent than they actually are, just as people in church often feel that they have to appear more holy than they actually are.

If this is the case, the problem of rehabilitation is probably not akin to converting delinquents to ways of behavior and points of view about which they are unaware and which they have never seriously considered as realistic alternatives. Instead, the feeling of ambivalence on their parts might be an element which could be used in rehabilitation.

An important sociological hypothesis based on this assumption would be that the ambivalence of most habitual delinquents is not primarily the result of personality conflicts developed in such social *microcosms* as the family but is inherent in the structure of the societal

macrocosm. A delinquent subsystem simply represents an alternative means for acquiring, or attempting to acquire, social and economic goals idealized by the societal system which are acquired by other people through conventional means.

If this hypothesis is accurate, delinquent ambivalence might actually be used in effecting change. A rehabilitation program might seek: (1) to make conventional and delinquent alternatives clear; (2) to lead delinquents to question the ultimate utility of delinquent alternatives; and (3) to help conventional alternatives assume some positive valence for them. It might then reduce the affective identification which they feel for the delinquent subsystem and tip the scales in the opposite direction.

MAJOR ASSUMPTIONS FOR TREATMENT

In order to relate such theoretical premises to the specific needs of treatment, the Provo Experiment adopted a series of major assumptions. They are as follows:

1. Delinquent behavior is primarily a group product and demands an approach to treatment far different from that which sees it as characteristic of a "sick," or "well-meaning" but "misguided," person.

2. An effective program must recognize the intrinsic nature of a delinquent's membership in a delinquent system and, therefore, must direct treatment to him as a part of that system.

3. Most habitual delinquents are affectively and ideologically dedicated to the delinquent system. Before they can be made amenable to change, they must be made anxious about the ultimate utility of that system for them.

4. Delinquents must be forced to deal with the conflicts which the demands

[20] Cohen, *Delinquent Boys, op. cit.,* p. 133; Cohen and Short, *op. cit.,* p. 21. See also John I. Kitsuse and David C. Dietrick, "Delinquent Boys: A Critique," *American Sociological Review,* 24 (April, 1959), p. 211.
[21] Gresham M. Sykes and David Matza, "Techniques of Neutralization: A Theory of Delinquency," *American Sociological Review,* 22 (December, 1957), pp. 664–670.

of conventional and delinquent systems place upon them. The resolution of such conflicts, either for or against further law violations, must ultimately involve a community decision. For that reason, a treatment program, in order to force realistic decision-making, can be most effective if it permits continued participation in the community as well as in the treatment process.

5. Delinquent ambivalence for purposes of rehabilitation can only be utilized in a setting conducive to the free expression of feelings—both delinquent and conventional. This means that the protection and rewards provided by the treatment system for *candor* must exceed those provided either by delinquents for adherence to delinquent roles or by officials for adherence to custodial demands for "good behavior." Only in this way can delinquent individuals become aware of the extent to which other delinquents share conventional as well as delinquent aspirations and, only in this way, can they be encouraged to examine the ultimate utility of each.

6. An effective program must develop a unified and cohesive social system in which delinquents and authorities alike are devoted to one task—overcoming lawbreaking. In order to accomplish this the program must avoid two pitfalls: (*a*) it must avoid establishing authorities as "rejectors" and making inevitable the creation of two social systems within the program; and (*b*) it must avoid the institutionalization of means by which skilled offenders can evade norms and escape sanctions.[22] The occasional imposition of negative sanctions is as necessary in this system as in any other system.

7. A treatment system will be most effective if the delinquent peer group is used as the means of perpetuating

the norms and imposing the sanctions of the system. The peer group should be seen by delinquents as the primary source of help and support. The traditional psychotherapeutic emphasis upon transference relationships is not viewed as the most vital factor in effecting change.

8. A program based on sociological theory may tend to exclude lectures, sermons, films, individual counseling, analytic psychotherapy, organized athletics, academic education, and vocational training as primary treatment techniques. It will have to concentrate, instead, on matters of another variety: changing reference group and normative orientations, utilizing ambivalent feelings resulting from the conflict of conventional and delinquent standards, and providing opportunities for recognition and achievement in conventional pursuits.

9. An effective treatment system must include rewards which are realistically meaningful to delinquents. They would include such things as peer acceptance for law-abiding behavior or the opportunity for gainful employment rather than badges, movies, or furlough privileges which are designed primarily to facilitate institutional control. Rewards, therefore, must only be given for realistic and lasting changes, not for conformance to norms which concentrate upon effective custody as an end in itself.

10. Finally, in summary, a successful program must be viewed by delinquents as possessing four important characteristics: (*a*) a social climate in which delinquents are given the opportunity to examine and experience alternatives related to a realistic choice between delinquent or non-delinquent behavior; (*b*) the opportunity to declare publicly to peers and authorities a belief or disbelief that they can benefit from a change in values; (*c*) a type of social

[22] McCorkle and Korn, *op. cit.*, pp. 88–91.

structure which will permit them to examine the role and legitimacy (for their purposes) of authorities in the treatment system; and (*d*) a type of treatment interaction which, because it places major responsibilities upon peer-group decision-making, grants status and recognition to individuals, not only for their own successful participation in the treatment interaction, but for their willingness to involve others.

THE TREATMENT SYSTEM[23]

The Provo Program, consistent with these basic assumptions, resides in the community and does not involve permanent incarceration. Boys live at home and spend only a part of each day at Pinehills (the program center). Otherwise they are free in the community.[24]

HISTORY AND LOCALE. The Provo Program was begun in 1956 as an "in-between" program designed specifically to help those habitual delinquents whose persistence made them candidates, in most cases, for a reformatory. It was instigated by a volunteer group of professional and lay people known as the *Citizens' Advisory Council to the Juvenile Court*. It has never had formal ties to government except through the Juvenile Court. This lack of ties has permitted considerable experimenta-

tion. Techniques have been modified to such a degree that the present program bears little resemblance to the original one. Legally, program officials are deputy probation officers appointed by the Juvenile Judge.

The cost of treatment is financed by county funds budgeted through the Juvenile Court. So near as we can estimate the cost per boy is approximately one-tenth of what it would cost if he were incarcerated in a reformatory. Research operations are financed by the Ford Foundation. Concentrated evaluation of the program is now in its second year of a six-year operation. Because both the theoretical orientation and treatment techniques of the program were in developmental process until its outlines were given final form for research purposes, it is difficult to make an objective evaluation of the over-all program based on recidivism rates for previous years, especially in the absence of adequate control groups. Such an evaluation, however, is an integral part of the present research and is described below.

Relations with welfare agencies and the community, per se, are informal but extremely co-operative. This is due to three things: the extreme good will and guiding influence of the Juvenile Court Judge, Monroe J. Paxman,[25] the unceasing efforts of the Citizens' Advisory Council to involve the entire county as a community, and the willingness of city and county officials, not only to overcome traditional fears regarding habitual offenders in the community, but to lend strong support to an experimental program of this type.

Community co-operation is probably enhanced by strong Mormon traditions.

[23] Except for the community aspects, the above assumptions and the treatment system are similar to those pioneered at Highfields. See McCorkle, Elias, and Bixby, *op. cit.* The Provo Program is especially indebted to Albert Elias, the present director of Highfields, not only for his knowledge about treatment techniques, but for his criticisms of the Provo Experiment.

[24] The idea of a community program is not new. The Boston Citizenship Training Group, Inc., a non-residential program, was begun in 1934–1936. However, it is for younger boys and utilizes a different approach. A similar program, initiated by Professor Ray R. Canning in Provo, was a forerunner to this experiment. See "A New Treatment Program for Juvenile Delinquents," *Journal of Criminal Law and Criminology*, 31 (March-April, 1941), pp. 712–719.

[25] Judge Paxman is a member of the Advisory Council of Judges to the National Council on Crime and Delinquency and is a member of the symposium preparing a work entitled, *Justice for the Child*, Chicago: University of Chicago, 1962.

However, Utah County is in a period of rapid transition which began in the early days of World War II with the introduction of a large steel plant, allied industries, and an influx of non-Mormons. This trend, both in industry and population, has continued to the present time. The treatment program is located in the city of Provo but draws boys from all major communities in the county—from a string of small cities, many of which border on each other, ranging in size from four to 40,000. The total population from which it draws its assignees is about 110,000.

Despite the fact that Utah County is not a highly urbanized area, when compared to large metropolitan centers, the concept of a "parent" delinquent subculture has real meaning for it. While there are no clear-cut gangs, per se, it is surprising to observe the extent to which delinquent boys from the entire county, who have never met, know each other by reputation, go with the same girls, use the same language, or can seek each other out when they change high schools. About half of them are permanently out of school, do not participate in any regular institutional activities, and are reliant almost entirely upon the delinquent system for social acceptance and participation.

ASSIGNEES. Only habitual offenders, 15–17 years, are assigned to the program. In the absence of public facilities, they are transported to and from home each day in automobiles driven by university students. Their offenses run the usual gamut: vandalism, trouble in school, shoplifting, car theft, burglary, forgery, and so forth. Highly disturbed and psychotic boys are not assigned. The pre-sentence investigation is used to exclude these people. They constitute an extremely small minority.

NUMBER IN ATTENDANCE. No more than twenty boys are assigned to the program at any one time. A large number would make difficult any attempts to establish and maintain a unified, cohesive system. This group of twenty is broken into two smaller groups, each of which operates as a separate discussion unit. When an older boy is released from one of these units, a new boy is added. This is an important feature because it serves as the means by which the culture of the system is perpetuated.

LENGTH OF ATTENDANCE. No length of stay is specified. It is intimately tied to the group and its processes because a boy's release depends not only upon his own behavior, but upon the maturation processes through which his group goes. Release usually comes somewhere between four and seven months.

NATURE OF PROGRAM. The program does not utilize any testing, gathering of case histories, or clinical diagnosis. One of its key tools, peer group interaction, is believed to provide a considerably richer source of information about boys and delinquency than do clinical methods.

The program, per se, is divided into two phases. Phase I is an intensive group program, utilizing work and the delinquent peer group as the principal instruments for change. During the winter, boys attend this phase three hours a day, five days a week, and all day on Saturdays. Activities include daily group discussions, hard work, and some unstructured activities in which boys are left entirely on their own. During the summer they attend an all-day program which involves work and group discussions. However, there are no practices without exceptions. For example, if a boy has a full-time job, he may be allowed to continue the job in lieu of working in the program. Other innovations occur repeatedly.

Phase II is designed to aid a boy after release from intensive treatment in Phase I. It involves two things: (1) an attempt to maintain some reference group support for a boy; and (2) community action to help him find employment. Both phases are described below.

PHASE I: INTENSIVE TREATMENT

Every attempt is made in Phase I to create a social system in which social structure, peer members, and authorities are oriented to the one task of instituting change. The more relevant to this task the system is, the greater will be its influence.

SOCIAL STRUCTURE. There is little formal structure in the Provo Program. Patterns are abhorred which might make boys think that their release depends upon *refraining* from swearing, engaging in open quarrels or doing such *"positive"* things as saying, "yes sir," or "no sir." Such criteria as these play into their hands. They learn to manipulate them in developing techniques for beating a system. Consequently, other than requiring boys to appear each day and work hard on the job, there are no formal demands. The only other daily activities are the group discussions at which attendance is optional.

The absence of formal structure helps to do more than avoid artificial criteria for release. It has the positive effect of making boys more amenable to treatment. In the absence of formal structure they are uneasy and they are not quite sure of themselves. Thus, the lack of clear-cut definitions for behavior helps to accomplish three important things: (1) It produces anxiety and turns boys towards the group as a method of resolving their anxiety. (2) It leaves boys free to define situations for themselves: leaders begin to lead, followers begin to follow, and manipulators begin to manipulate. It is these types of behavior which must be seen and analyzed if change is to take place. (3) It binds neither authorities nor the peer group to prescribed courses of action. Each is free to do whatever is needed to suit the needs of particular boys, groups, or situations.

On the other hand, the absence of formal structure obviously does not mean that there is no structure. But, that which does exist is informal and emphasizes ways of thinking and behaving which are not traditional. Perhaps the greatest difference lies in the fact that a considerable amount of power is vested in the delinquent peer group. It is the instrument by which norms are perpetuated and through which many important decisions are made. It is the primary source of pressure for change.

THE PEER GROUP. Attempts to involve a boy with the peer group begin the moment he arrives. Instead of meeting with and receiving an orientation lecture from authorities, he receives no formal instructions. He is always full of such questions as, "What do I have to do to get out of this place?" or "How long do I have to stay?", but such questions as these are never answered. They are turned aside with, "I don't know," or "Why don't you find out?" Adults will not orient him in the ways that he has grown to expect, nor will they answer any of his questions. He is forced to turn to his peers. Usually, he knows someone in the program, either personally or by reputation. As he begins to associate with other boys he discovers that important informal norms do exist, the most important of which makes *inconsistency* rather than *consistency* the rule. That which is appropriate for one situation, boy, or group may not be appropriate for another. Each merits a decision as it arises.

Other norms center most heavily about the daily group discussion sessions. These sessions are patterned after the technique of "Guided Group Interaction" which was developed at Fort Knox during World War II and at Highfields.[26] Guided Group Interaction emphasizes the idea that only through a group and its processes can a boy work out his problems. From a peer point of view it has three main goals: (1) to question the utility of a life devoted to delinquency; (2) to suggest alternative ways for behavior; and (3) to provide recognition for a boy's personal reformation and his willingness to reform others.[27]

Guided Group Interaction grants to the peer group a great deal of power, including that of helping to decide when each boy is ready to be released. This involves "retroflexive reformation."[28] If a delinquent is serious in his attempts to reform others he must automatically accept the common purpose of the reformation process, identify himself closely with others engaged in it, and grant prestige to those who succeed in it. In so doing, he becomes a genuine member of the reformation group and in the process may be alienated from his previous pro-delinquent groups.[29] Such is an ideal and long-term goal. Before it can be realized for any individual he must become heavily involved with the treatment system. Such involvement does not come easy and the system must include techniques which will impel him to involvement. Efforts to avoid the development of formal structure have already been described as one technique. Group processes constitute a second technique.

Before a group will help a boy "solve his problems" it demands that he review his total delinquent history. This produces anxiety because, while he is still relatively free, it is almost inevitable that he has much more to reveal than is already known by the police or the court. In an effort to avoid such involvement he may try subterfuge. But any reluctance on his part to be honest will not be taken lightly. Norms dictate that no one in the group can be released until everyone is honest and until every boy helps to solve problems. A refusal to come clean shows a lack of trust in the group and slows down the problem-solving process. Therefore, any recalcitrant boy is faced with a real dilemma. He can either choose involvement or relentless attack by his peers. Once a boy does involve himself, however, he learns that some of his fears were unwarranted. What goes on in the group meeting is sacred and is not revealed elsewhere.

A second process for involvement lies in the use of the peer group to perpetuate the norms of the treatment system. One of the most important norms suggests that most boys in the program are candidates for a reformatory. This is shocking because even habitual delinquents do not ordinarily

---

[26] See F. Lovell Bixby and Lloyd W. McCorkle, "Guided Group Interaction and Correctional Work," *American Sociological Review*, 16 (August, 1951), pp. 455–459; McCorkle, Elias, and Bixby, *The Highfields Story, op. cit.;* and Joseph Abrahams and Lloyd W. McCorkle, "Group Psychotherapy on Military Offenders," *American Journal of Sociology*, 51 (March, 1946), pp. 455–464. These sources present a very limited account of techniques employed. An intimate knowledge would require attendance at group sessions.

[27] Other goals relating to the emphasis upon group development, the role of the group therapist, and the nature of the therapeutic situations have been described briefly elsewhere. See *The Highfields Story, op. cit.*, pp. 72–80.

[28] Cressey, *op. cit.*, p. 119.

[29] Vold maintains that guided group interaction assumes that there is something wrong inside the individual and attempts to correct that. He is right in the sense that it emphasizes that an individual must accept responsibility for his own delinquencies and that no one can keep him out of prison unless he himself is ready to stay out. Vold, in our opinion, is incorrect if his remarks are taken to mean that the group does not discuss groups and group processes, what peers mean to a boy or how the orientations of delinquent groups differ from those of conventional society. *Op. cit.*, p. 360.

see themselves as serious offenders.[30] Yet, the tradition is clear; most failures at Pinehills are sent to the Utah State Industrial School. Therefore, each boy has a major decision to make: either he makes serious attempts to change or he gets sent away.

The third process of involvement could only occur in a community program. Each boy has the tremendous problem of choosing between the demands of his delinquent peers outside the program and the demands of those within it. The usual reaction is to test the situation by continuing to identify with the former. Efforts to do this, however, and to keep out of serious trouble are usually unsuccessful. The group is a collective board on delinquency; it usually includes a member who knows the individual personally or by reputation; and it can rely on the meeting to discover many things. Thus, the group is able to use actual behavior in the community to judge the extent to which a boy is involved with the program and to judge his readiness for release. The crucial criterion for any treatment program is not what an individual does while in it, but what he does while he is *not* in it.

The fourth process involves a number of important sanctions which the group can impose if a boy refuses to become involved. It can employ familiar techniques such as ostracism or derision or it can deny him the status and recognition which come with change. Furthermore, it can use sanctions arising out of the treatment system. For example, while authorities may impose restrictions on boys in the form of extra work or incarceration in jail, the group is often permitted, and encouraged, to explore reasons for the action and to help decide what future actions should be taken. For example, a boy may be placed in jail over the week-end and told that he will be returned there each week-end thereafter until his group decides to release him. It is not uncommon for the group, after thorough discussion, to return him one or more week-ends despite his protestations. Such an occurrence would be less likely in an ordinary reformatory because of the need for inmates to maintain solidarity against the official system. However, in this setting it is possible because boys are granted the power to make important decisions affecting their entire lives. Rather than having other people do things to them, they are doing things to themselves.

The ultimate sanction possessed by the group is refusal to release a boy from the program. Such a sanction has great power because it is normative to expect that no individual will be tolerated in the program indefinitely. Pinehills is not a place where boys "do time."

AUTHORITIES. The third source of pressure towards change rests in the hands of authorities. The role of an authority in a treatment system of this type is a difficult one. On one hand, he cannot be seen as a person whom skillful delinquents or groups can manipulate. But, on the other hand, he cannot be perceived permanently as a "rejector." Everything possible, therefore, must be done by him to create an adult image which is new and different.

Initially, authorities are probably seen as "rejectors." It will be recalled that they do not go out of their way to engage in regular social amenities, to put boys at ease, or to establish one-to-one relationships with boys. Adult behavior of this type is consistent with the treatment philosophy. It attempts to

[30] Delinquents are like other people: The worst can never happen to them. See also Mark R. Moran, "Inmate Concept of Self in a Reformatory Society," unpublished Ph.D. dissertation, Ohio State University, 1953.

have boys focus upon the peer group, not adults, as the vehicle by which questions and problems are resolved.

Second, boys learn that authorities will strongly uphold the norm which says that Pinehills is not a place for boys to "do time." If, therefore, a boy does not become involved and the group is unwilling or unable to take action, authorities will. Such action varies. It might involve requiring him to work all day without pay, placing him in jail, or putting him in a situation in which he has no role whatsoever. In the latter case he is free to wander around the Center all day but he is neither allowed to work nor given the satisfaction of answers to his questions regarding his future status.

Boys are seldom told why they are in trouble or, if they are told, solutions are not suggested. To do so would be to provide them structure by which to rationalize their behavior, hide other things they have been doing, and escape the need to change. Consequently, they are left on their own to figure out why authorities are doing what they are doing and what they must do to get out of trouble.

Situations of this type precipitate crises. Sometimes boys run away. But, whatever happens, the boy's status remains amorphous until he can come up with a solution to his dilemma. This dilemma, however, is not easily resolved.

There is no individual counseling since this would reflect heavily upon the integrity of the peer group. Consequently, he cannot resolve his problems by counseling with or pleasing adults. His only recourse is to the group. But since the group waits for him to bring up his troubles, he must involve himself with it or he cannot resolve them. Once he does, he must reveal why he is in trouble, what he has been doing

to get into trouble or how he has been abusing the program. If he refuses to become involved he may be returned to court by authorities. This latter alternative occurs rarely, since adults have more time than boys. While they can afford to wait, boys find it very difficult to "sweat out" a situation. They feel the need to resolve it.

As a result of such experiences, boys are often confused and hostile. But where such feelings might be cause for alarm elsewhere, they are welcomed at Pinehills. They are taken as a sign that a boy is not in command of the situation and is therefore amenable to change. Nevertheless, the treatment system does not leave him without an outlet for his feelings. The meeting is a place where his anger and hostility can be vented—not only against the program but against the adults who run it. But, in venting his confusion and hostility, it becomes possible for the group to analyze, not only his own behavior, but that of adults, and to determine to what end the behavior of all is leading. Initial perceptions of adults which were confusing and provoking can now be seen in a new way. The treatment system places responsibility upon a boy and his peers for changing delinquent behavior, not upon adults. Thus, adult behavior which was initially seen as rejecting can now be seen as consistent with this expectation. Boys have to look to their own resources for solutions of problems. In this way they are denied social-psychological support for "rejecting the rejectors," or for rejecting decisions demanded by the group. Furthermore, as a result of the new adult image which is pressed upon them, boys are led to examine their perceptions regarding other authorities. Boys may learn to see authorities with whom they had difficulties previously in a new, non-stereotyped fashion.

WORK AND OTHER ACTIVITIES

Any use of athletics, handicrafts, or remedial schooling involves a definition of rehabilitation goals. Are these activities actually important in changing delinquents? In the Provo Experiment they are not viewed as having an inherent value in developing non-delinquent behavior. In fact, they are viewed as detrimental because participation in them often becomes criteria for release. On the other hand, work habits are viewed as vitally important. Previous research suggests that employment is one of the most important means of changing reference from delinquent to law-abiding groups.[31] But, such findings simply pose the important question: How can boys be best prepared to find and hold employment?

Sociologists have noted the lack of opportunity structure for delinquents, but attention to a modification of the structure (assuming that it can be modified) as the sole approach to rehabilitation overlooks the need to prepare delinquents to utilize employment possibilities. One alternative for doing this is an education program with all its complications. The other is an immediate attack on delinquent values and work habits. The Provo Experiment chose the latter alternative. It hypothesized that an immediate attack on delinquent values, previous careers, and nocturnal habits would be more effective than an educational program. Sophisticated delinquents, who are otherwise very skillful in convincing peers and authorities of their good intentions, are often unable to work consistently. They have too long believed that only suckers work. Thus concentration is upon work habits. Boys are employed by the city and county in parks, streets,

and recreation areas. Their work habits are one focus of group discussion and an important criterion for change. After release, they are encouraged to attend academic and vocational schools should they desire.

THE STARTER MECHANISM:
PUTTING THE SYSTEM IN MOTION

There are both theoretical and practical considerations relative to the purposeful creation of the social structure at Pinehills and the process by which it was developed. The foregoing discussion described some of the structural elements involved and, by inference, suggested the means by which they were introduced. However, the following is presented as a means of further clarification.

The first consideration involved the necessity of establishing structure which could pose realistically and clearly the alternatives open to habitually delinquent boys. What are these alternatives? Since in most cases delinquents are lower-class individuals who not only lack many of the social skills but who have been school failures as well, the alternatives are not great. Some may become professional criminals, but this is a small minority. Therefore, most of them have two principal choices: (1) they can continue to be delinquent and expect, in most cases, to end up in prison; or (2) they can learn to live a rather marginal life in which they will be able to operate sufficiently within the law to avoid being locked up. Acceptance of the second alternative by delinquents would not mean that they would have to change their entire style of living, but it does mean that most would have to find employment and be willing to disregard delinquent behavior in favor of the drudgery of everyday living.

Until these alternatives are posed

[31] Glaser, "A Sociological Approach to Crime and Correction," *op. cit.*, pp. 690–691.

for them, and posed in a meaningful way, delinquents will not be able to make the necessary decisions regarding them. The need, therefore, was for the type of structure at Pinehills which could pose these alternatives initially without equivocation and thus force boys to consider involvement in the rehabilitative process as a realistic alternative for them.

By the time delinquents reach Pinehills they have been cajoled, threatened, lectured, and exhorted—all by a variety of people in a variety of settings: by parents, teachers, police, religious leaders, and court officials. As a consequence, most have developed a set of manipulative techniques which enable them to "neutralize" verbal admonitions by appearing to comply with them, yet refraining all the while from any real adherence. For that reason, it was concluded that *deeds*, not *words*, would be required as the chief means for posing clearly the structural alternatives open to them.

Upon arrival the first delinquents assigned to Pinehills had every reason to believe that this was another community agency for which they possessed the necessary "techniques of neutralization." It was housed in an ordinary two-story home, and authorities spent little time giving instructions or posing threats. It must have seemed, therefore, that Pinehills would not constitute a serious obstacle for which they could not find some means to avoid involvement.

The following are examples of happenings which helped to establish norms contrary to this view. After attending only one day, a rather sophisticated boy was not at home to be picked up for his second day. Instead, he left a note on his front door saying he was at the hospital visiting a sick sister. Official reaction was immediate and almost entirely opposite to what he expected.

No one made any efforts to contact him. Instead, a detention order was issued by the court to the police who arrested the boy later that evening and placed him in jail. He was left there for several days without the benefit of visits from anyone and then returned to Pinehills. Even then, no one said anything to him about his absence. No one had to; he did not miss again. Furthermore, he had been instrumental in initiating the norm which says that the principal alternative to Pinehills is incarceration.

A second occurrence established this norm even more clearly. After having been at Pinehills for two months and refusing to yield to the pressures of his group, a boy asked for a rehearing in court, apparently feeling that he could manipulate the judge more successfully than he could the people at Pinehills. His request was acted upon immediately. He was taken to jail that afternoon and a hearing arranged for the following morning. The judge committed him to the State Reformatory.[32] Since that time there has never been another request for a rehearing. In a similar way, especially during the first year, boys who continued to get in serious trouble while at Pinehills were recalled by the court for another hearing and assigned to the reformatory. These cases became legendary examples to later boys. However, adults have never had to call attention to them; they are passed on in the peer socialization process.

Once such traditions were established, they could be used in yet another

[32] Co-operation of this type between the Juvenile Courts and rehabilitative agencies is not always forthcoming. Yet, it also reflects two things: (1) the fact that Judge Paxman sentences only those boys to Pinehills who are habitual offenders; and (2) the fact that it is his conviction that rehabilitation must inevitably involve the Court's participation, both in posing alternatives for boys and in determining the effectiveness of various approaches.

way. They became devices by which to produce the type of uncertainty characteristic of social settings in which negative sanctions should be forthcoming but do not appear. The individual is left wondering why. For example, not all boys who miss a day or two at Pinehills now are sent to jail. In some cases, nothing is said to the individual in question. He is left, instead, to wonder when, and if, he will be sent. Likewise, other boys who have been in serious trouble in the community are not always sent to the State Reformatory but may be subjected to the same kind of waiting and uncertainty. Efforts are made, however, to make it impossible for boys to predict in advance what will happen in any particular case. Even adults cannot predict this, relying on the circumstances inherent in each case. Thus, both rigidity and inconsistency are present in the system at the same time.

The same sort of structural alternatives were posed regarding work. Boys who did not work consistently on their city jobs, where they were being paid, were returned to Pinehills to work for nothing. At Pinehills, they were usually alone and had to perform such onerous tasks as scrubbing the floor, washing windows, mowing the lawn, or cutting weeds. They might be left on this job for hours or weeks. The problem of being returned to work with the other boys for pay was left to them for their own resolution, usually in the group. So long as they said nothing, nothing was said to them except to assign them more work.

This type of structure posed stark but, in our opinion, realistic alternatives. It was stark and realistic because boys were still living in the community, but for the first time could sense the omnipresence of permanent incarceration. However, another type of structure less stringent was needed by which

boys could realistically resolve problems and make choices. Since, as has been mentioned, peer-group decision-making was chosen as the means for problem-resolution, attention was focused upon the daily group meetings as the primary source of information. It became the focal point of the whole treatment system.

The first group, not having any standards to guide it (except those which suggested resistance to official pressures), spent great portions of entire meetings without speaking. However, consistent with the idea that deeds, not words, count, and that a group has to resolve its own problems, the group leader refused to break the silence except at the very end of each meeting. At that time, he began standardizing one common meeting practice: he summarized what had been accomplished. Of silent meetings he simply said that nothing had been accomplished. He did point out, however, that he would be back the next day—that, in fact, he would be there a year from that day. Where would they be, still there? The problem was theirs.

When some boys could stand the silence no longer, they asked the group leader what they might talk about. Rather than making it easy for them he suggested something that could only involve them further: he suggested that someone might recite all the things he had done to get in trouble. Not completely without resources, however, boys responded by reciting only those things they had been caught for. In his summary, the leader noted this fact and suggested that whoever spoke the next time might desire to be more honest by telling all. Boys were reluctant to do this but, partly because it was an opportunity to enhance reputations and partly because they did not know what else to do, some gave honest recitations. When no official action was taken against them, two new and important norms were introduced: (1) the idea that what is said in the meeting is sacred to the meeting; and (2) that boys can afford to be candid—that, in fact, candor pays.

The subsequent recitals of delinquent activities ultimately led to a growing awareness of the ambivalence which many delinquents feel regarding their activities. In the social climate provided by the meeting some boys began to express feelings and receive support for behavior which the delinquent system with its emphasis on ideal-typical role behavior could not permit.

Eventually, the meeting reached a stage where it began to discuss the plethora of happenings which occurred daily, both at Pinehills and elsewhere in the community. These happenings, rather than impersonal, easily speculated-about material, were urged as the most productive subject matter. For example, many boys had reached the stage of trying devious rather than direct methods of missing sessions at Pinehills. They came with requests to be excused for normally laudatory activities: school functions, family outings, and even religious services. But, again adults refused to take the traditional course of assuming responsibility and making decisions for boys. Boys were directed to the meeting instead. This not only shifted the responsibility to them, but provided the opportunity to develop five important norms: (1) those having to do with absences; (2) the idea that the place for problem-solving is in the meeting; (3) that everyone, not just adults, should be involved in the process; (4) that if a boy wants the meeting to talk about his problems, he has to justify them as being more important than someone else's; and (5) that any request or point of view has to be substantiated both by evidence and some relevance to the solution of delinquent problems.

It became obvious that even simple requests could be complicated. Boys found themselves using their own rationalizations on each other, often providing both humorous and eye-opening experiences. The climate became increasingly resistant to superficial requests and more conducive to the examination of pressing problems. Boys who chose to fight the system found themselves fighting peers. A stubborn boy could be a thorn in the side of the whole group.

The daily meeting summaries took on increased importance as the leader helped the group: (1) to examine what had happened each day; (2) to examine to what ends various efforts were leading—that is, to examine what various boys were doing, or not doing, and what relevance this had for themselves and the group; (3) to suggest areas of discussion which had been neglected, ignored, or purposely hidden by group members; and (4) to describe the goals of the treatment system in such a way that boys could come to recognize the meaning of group discussions as a realistic source of problem-resolution.

The structural lines associated with the meeting eventually began to define not only the type of subject matter most relevant to change, but the general means for dealing with this subject matter. However, such structure was extremely flexible, permitting a wide latitude of behavior. Great care was taken to avoid the institutionalization of clear-cut steps by which boys could escape Pinehills. Problem-solving was, and still is, viewed as a process—a process not easily understood in advance, but something which develops uniquely for each new boy and each new group.

Finally, in summary, the Pinehills system, like many social systems, has some rigid prerequisites for continued membership. The broad structural outlines carefully define the limits beyond which members should not go. However, unlike most extreme authoritarian systems, there is an inner structure, associated with the meeting, which does not demand rigid conformity and which instead permits those deviations which are an honest expression of feelings.

The admission of deviations within the structural confines of the meeting helps to lower the barriers which prevent a realistic examination of their implications for the broader authoritarian structure, either at Pinehills or in society at large. Boys are able to make more realistic decisions as to which roles, conventional or delinquent, would seem to have the most utility for them.

This brief attempt to describe a complex system may have been misleading. The complexities involved are multivariate and profound. However, one important aspect of the experiment has to do with the theoretical development of, and research on, the nature of the treatment system. Each discussion session is recorded, and efforts are made to determine means by which treatment techniques might be improved and ways in which group processes can be articulated. All would be very useful in testing theory which suggests that experience in a cohesive group is an important variable in directing or changing behavior.

PHASE II: COMMUNITY ADJUSTMENT

Phase II involves an effort to maintain reference group support and employment for a boy after intensive treatment in Phase I. After his release from Phase I he continues to meet periodically for discussions with his old group. The goal is to utilize this group in accomplishing three things: (1) acting as a check on a boy's current behavior; (2) serving as a law-abiding reference group; and (3) aiding in the solution of new problems. It seeks to continue treatment in a different and

perhaps more intensive way than such traditional practices as probation or parole.

Efforts to find employment for boys are made by the Citizens' Advisory Council. If employment is found, a boy is simply informed that an employer needs someone. No efforts are taken by some well-meaning but pretentious adult to manipulate the boy's life.

These steps, along with the idea that delinquents should be permitted to make important decisions during the rehabilitative process, are consistent with structural-functional analysis which suggests that in order to eliminate existing structure, or identification with it, one must provide the necessary functional alternatives.[33]

APPROPRIATENESS OF TECHNIQUES

Many persons express disfavor with what they consider a harsh and punitive system at Pinehills. If, however, alternatives are not great for habitual delinquents, a program which suggests otherwise is not being honest with them. Delinquents are aware that society seldom provides honors for *not* being delinquent; that, in fact, conventional alternatives for them have not always promised significantly more than delinquent alternatives.[34] Therefore, expectations associated with the adoption of conventional alternatives should not be unrealistic.

On the other hand it should be remembered that, in terms familiar to delinquents, every effort is made at Pinehills to include as many positive

[33] Edwin M. Schur, "Sociological Analysis in Confidence Swindling," *Journal of Criminal Law, Criminology and Police Science*, 48 (September-October, 1957), p. 304.
[34] Gwynn Nettler has raised a question as to who perceives reality most accurately, deviants or "good" people. See "Good Men, Bad Men and the Perception of Realty," paper delivered at the meetings of the American Sociological Association, Chicago, September, 1959.

experiences as possible. The following are some which seem to function:

1. Peers examine problems which are common to all.

2. There is a recurring opportunity for each individual to be the focal point of attention among peers in which his behavior and problems become the most important concern of the moment.

3. Delinquent peers articulate in front of conventional adults without constraint with regard to topic, language, or feeling.

4. Delinquents have the opportunity, for the first time in an institutional setting, to make crucial decisions about their own lives. This in itself is a change in the opportunity structure and is a means of obligating them to the treatment system. In a reformatory a boy cannot help but see the official system as doing things to him in which he has no say: locking him up, testing him, feeding him, making his decisions. Why should he feel obligated? But when some important decision-making is turned over to him, he no longer has so many grounds for rejecting the system. Rejection in a reformatory might be functional in relating him to his peers, but in this system it is not so functional.

5. Delinquents participate in a treatment system that grants status in three ways: (a) for age and experience in the treatment process—old boys have the responsibility of teaching new boys the norms of the system; (b) for the exhibition of law-abiding behavior, not only in a minimal sense, but for actual qualitative changes in specific role behavior at Pinehills, home or with friends; and (c) for the willingness to confront other boys, in a group setting, with their delinquent behavior. (In a reformatory where he has to contend with the inmate system a boy can gain little and lose much for his willingness to be candid in front of adults about peers, but at Pinehills it is a primary source of prestige.) The ability to confront others often reflects more about the *confronter* than it does about the *confronted*. It is an indication of the extent to which he has accepted the reformation process and identified himself with it.[35]

6. Boys can find encouragement in a program which poses the possibility of relatively short restriction and the avoidance of incarceration.

7. The peer group is a potential source of reference group support for law-abiding behavior. Boys commonly refer to the fact that their group knows more about them than any other persons: parents or friends.

RESEARCH DESIGN

An integral part of the Provo Experiment is an evaluation of treatment extending over a five-year period. It includes means by which offenders who receive treatment are compared to two control groups: (1) a similar group of offenders who at time of sentence are placed on probation and left in the community; and (2) a similar group who at time of sentence are incarcerated in the Utah State Industrial School. Since it is virtually impossible to match all three groups, random selection is used to minimize the effect of sample bias. All three groups are drawn from a population of habitual delinquents who reside in Utah County, Utah, and who come before the Juvenile Court. Actual selection is as follows:

The Judge of the Court has in his possession two series of numbered en-

---

[35] Support for this idea can be found in a recently developed matrix designed to measure the impact of group interaction. See William and Ida Hill, *Interaction Matrix for Group Psychotherapy*, mimeographed manuscript, Utah State Mental Hospital, Provo, Utah, 1960. This matrix has been many years in development.

Table 1

SELECTION OF TREATMENT AND CONTROL GROUPS

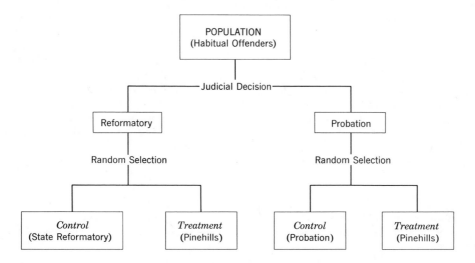

velopes—one series for selecting individuals to be placed in the *probation* treatment and control groups and one series for selecting the *reformatory* treatment and control groups. These series of envelopes are supplied by the research team and contain randomly selected slips of paper on which are written either *Control Group* or *Treatment Group*.

In making an assignment to one of these groups the Judge takes the following steps: (1) After hearing a case he decides whether he would ordinarily place the offender on probation or in the reformatory. He makes this decision as though Pinehills did not exist. Then (2) he brings the practice of random placement into play. He does so by opening an envelope from one of the two series supplied him (see Table 1). For example, if he decides initially that he would ordinarily send the boy to the reformatory, he would select an envelope from the *reformatory* series and depend upon the designation therein as

to whether the boy would actually go to the reformatory, and become a member of the *control* group, or be sent to Pinehills as a member of the *treatment* group.

This technique does not interfere with the judicial decision regarding the alternatives previously available to the Judge, but it does intercede, after the decision, by posing another alternative. The Judge is willing to permit the use of this alternative on the premise that, in the long run, his contributions to research will enable judicial decisions to be based ultimately on a more realistic evaluation of treatment programs available.

In order to make the comparison of treatment and control groups more meaningful, additional research is being conducted on the treatment process. Efforts are made to examine the problems involved in relating causation theory to intervention strategy, the role of the therapist in Guided Group Interaction, and the types of group interaction that seem most beneficial. Finally, a detailed examination is being made of the ways in which boys handle "critical incidents"[36] after release from treatment as compared to the way they handled them prior to treatment.

SUMMARY AND IMPLICATIONS

This paper describes an attempt to apply sociological theory to the treatment of delinquents. It concentrates not only upon treatment techniques, *per se*, but the type of social system in which these techniques must operate. The over-all treatment system it describes is like all other social systems in the sense that it specifies generalized requirements for continued membership in the system. At the same time, however, it also legitimizes the existence of a subsystem within it—the meeting—which permits the discussion and evaluation of happenings and feelings which *may* or *may not* support the over-all normative structure of the larger system.

The purposeful creation of this subsystem simply recognized what seemed to be two obvious facts: (1) that the existence of contrary normative expectations among delinquent and official members of the over-all system would ultimately result in the creation of such a subsystem anyway; and (2) that such a system, not officially recognized, would pose a greater threat, and would inhibit to a greater degree, the realization of the over-all rehabilitative goals of the major system than would its use as a rehabilitative tool.

This subsystem receives not only official sanction but grants considerable power and freedom to delinquent members. By permitting open expressions of

anger, frustration, and opposition, it removes social-psychological support for complete resistance to a realistic examination of the ultimate utility of delinquent versus conventional norms. At the same time, however, the freedom it grants is relative. So long as opposition to the demands of the larger system is contained in the meeting subsystem, such opposition is respected. But continued deviancy outside the meeting cannot be tolerated indefinitely. It must be seen as dysfunctional because the requirements of the over-all treatment system are identified with those of the total society and these requirements will ultimately predominate.

At the same time, the over-all treatment system includes elements designed to encourage and support the adoption of conventional roles. The roles it encourages and the rewards it grants, however, are peer-group-oriented and concentrate mainly upon the normative expectations of the social strata from which most delinquents come: working- rather than middle-class strata. This is done on the premise that a rehabilitation program is more realistic if it attempts to change normative orientations towards lawbreaking rather than attempting (or hoping) to change an individual's entire way of life. It suggests, for example, that a change in attitudes and values toward work *per se* is more important than attempting to create an interest in the educational, occupational, and recreational goals of the middle class.

The differences posed by this treatment system, as contrasted to many existing approaches to rehabilitation, are great. Means should be sought, therefore, in addition to this project by which its techniques and orientation can be treated as hypotheses and verified, modified, or rejected.

36 John C. Flanagan, "The Critical Incident Technique," *Psychological Bulletin*, 51 (July, 1954), pp. 327–358.

40.

The Highfields Project

H. Ashley Weeks

The Highfields Project for the Short-Term Treatment of Youthful Offenders inaugurated in New Jersey has been in operation since July 5, 1950. This report is an attempt to measure and evaluate various aspects of the Highfields Project for the first several years of its life.

The Short-Term Treatment of Youthful Offenders Program evolved from the need felt by many New Jersey judges for a new law to permit them to make definite sentences of not more than three months to the existing New Jersey facilities such as the reformatories and training schools. These judges believed that such a law would act as a deterrent to many boys—it would demonstrate to delinquent boys that commitment and incarceration for a much longer period would be their lot if they did not mend their ways. The judges felt that many delinquent boys were not yet serious enough offenders to warrant their being sent to the New Jersey State Home for Boys at Jamesburg or to one of the state's reformatories for an indeterminate period of confinement. Such boys had demonstrated that their misbehavior was serious enough to raise doubts in the minds of the judges as to

whether they could be placed or continued on probation with safety to the community and protection to themselves. Juvenile court judges are frequently loath to commit a boy to an institution which he is not likely to leave short of a year. They feel, with justification, that a boy often becomes worse when he is kept too long in an institution.[1] . . .

THE PROPOSED PROGRAM

The New Jersey program for the short-term treatment of youthful offenders[2] originally included these points:

Boys, while still officially on probation, would live, work, and play together in a unit which would house only a few boys at any one time.

Small groups of boys—not more than ten in any one group—would meet each day with the director, a trained guided group interactionist, in sessions

---

[1] There is much evidence to show that the longer the stay in a correctional institution the more likely a person is to fail on parole when he is released.

[2] Cf. F. Lovell Bixby, "Short Term Treatment of Youthful Offenders," *Focus*, 30 (March 1951), pp. 33–36.

SOURCE. H. Ashley Weeks, "The Highfields Project," from *Youthful Offenders at Highfields*, Ann Arbor: The University of Michigan Press, 1958, pp. 1–5, 7–10, 20–24, 118–128. Copyright © 1958, The University of Michigan Press. Reprinted with permission.

designed to uncover their problems and help them begin to solve them.

The boys would live as nearly normal lives as possible. There would be no outward symbols of incarceration, force, or even control. There would be no officers or guards. The personnel would consist only of the director, who would be responsible for establishing and maintaining a therapeutic climate, a man and his wife to supervise housekeeping and to assume the role of houseparents, and a handyman or jack-of-all-trades to assist the boys in developing their hobbies and in making themselves useful around the place.

There would be no formal educational program, but boys would listen to the radio and read newspapers and magazines and other material. This material would be thoroughly discussed and would give the residents a chance to evaluate and interpret together the information and opinions with which these mass media continually bombard us all.

The boys would work on some constructive project, not for vocational training but to gain work experience, and they would be paid a small wage for this work.

There would be hobby and craft projects in which all would participate. Each boy would be expected to select and finish one such project during his residency, whether it be "writing a short story, building a radio cabinet, overhauling a gasoline engine, or almost anything else that the individual feels he would like to do."

The boys would be allowed to go to local villages, accompanied by an adult, to shop, attend the movies, have a soda, or indulge in other approved activities of interest to them. On Sundays, religious activities and experiences would be available in the nearby community churches. There would be many opportunities to maintain community contacts. Periodically, during their short stay, they would be granted furloughs home. These would be in the nature of test situations and would also furnish experiences that could be discussed in the group sessions.[3]

As actually established, the project embodies some changes in the original plan as proposed by Dr. Bixby. The guided group interaction sessions are not held every night, but only five nights during each week. Usually, there are no sessions Thursday and Saturday nights. So far as is known, there is no specific discussion session in which the boys evaluate and interpret the information they have received from the mass media. Of course, certain attitudes and expressions received from their reading or listening are often brought forward in the sessions and aired and analyzed there, but this as observed by the writer is more by happenstance than design. Nor is there any hobby or craft program in which all participate. Boys can and do carry on projects, but again it is because of an individual interest and not by design. With these exceptions the program is very similar to the one Dr. Bixby originally conceived.

Certain criteria for the kind of residents were set up. In the first place, it was decided to limit the project to delinquent boys sixteen and seventeen years of age. Boys under this age would have to have school facilities provided for them in accordance with the state law, and those over seventeen are beyond the age when they may be handled as juveniles by the courts of the state. It was also decided to limit the project to first-commitment boys, that is, boys who had not formerly been committed to a state industrial school or other place of confinement. It was reasoned that boys who had had former

[3] Cf. *Focus*, pp. 35–36.

institutional experience might be so conditioned in their behavioral reactions that it would be difficult for them to participate wholeheartedly and freely in the guided group interaction sessions.[4] The kind of resident to be sent to Highfields was further limited by the exclusion of known sexual perverts and feebleminded and/or psychotic boys.

Before Highfields began to accept boys, discussions were held with the judges of the four large northeastern counties which have separate juvenile courts. It was explained to them that Highfields was not necessarily a substitute for either probation or incarceration, but a third choice. Whenever a judge had a boy before him who was sixteen or seventeen years of age and met the other criteria, the judge could consider whether the short-term treatment afforded at Highfields might be preferable to commitment or regular probation. A specialized facility such as Highfields would be helpful when he was in doubt. He could still place a boy on probation provided the boy would agree to spend a relatively short term (up to four months) under the treatment program.[5] If he decided a boy was suitable for Highfields, he could ascertain whether a bed was available there, and if it was he could see whether a boy would volunteer to go to Highfields. If a bed was not available, the former choice was still possible—incarceration or probation. . . .

[4] From time to time these criteria have been disregarded in the interest of a particular boy.

[5] Judges are loath to institutionalize a delinquent if they can possibly avoid it. This can be seen from the fact that boys often have long histories of delinquency and court appearances without commitment. They frequently are placed on probation again and again, or continued on probation. The ordinary delinquent has three or more official prior delinquencies before he is committed to a state institution. This is true not only in New Jersey but elsewhere.

ORIGINAL RESEARCH DESIGN

In order to secure the information needed to evaluate the program proposed by Dr. Bixby, it appeared that there were three basic questions which should be answered:

1. Do delinquents participating in the short-term treatment program show a higher, the same, or a lower recidivist rate than boys participating in other kinds of treatment programs?

2. Do delinquents participating in the short-term treatment program change their expressed attitudes, values, and opinions toward their families, law and order, and their own outlook on life?

3. Do delinquents participating in the short-term treatment program change their basic personality structures or at least the overt manifestations of their personalities?

These questions were based on certain theoretical considerations. It is generally assumed that correctional training, whether punitive or therapeutically oriented, changes and improves the overt behavior of the person undergoing the training. The lay public as well as the professionals at work in the field hope that the experiences persons have in correctional facilities will be reflected in an improvement in the behavior they exhibit after they are released. As Dr. Bixby has written: "The objective of all correctional procedures is the permanent protection of society through the rehabilitation of the greatest possible number of convicted offenders."[6] Recidivist rates, then, should be a general measure of the effectiveness of a correctional program.

But recidivism is not the sole measure of effectiveness. Persons who have

[6] "A Plan for the Short-Term Treatment of Youthful Offenders" (mimeographed), p. 1.

experienced correctional training may be favorably affected by the treatment only to have the good effects discounted by the fact that they are returned to the same family, the same neighborhood, and the same detrimental social groupings and influences which contributed to their antisocial behavior in the first place. But whether or not they subsequently get into further trouble with the law, the treatment they receive, if effective, should alter their attitudes, values, and opinions, and this alteration should be observable at the time they leave the treatment facility. We felt that the short-term treatment program should especially bring about changes in values, attitudes, and opinions. Guided group interaction sessions, we believed, should encourage the participants to recognize their problems in terms of their behavior, attitudes, and values and allow them to explore alternative solutions to their problems.

Fundamentally, attitudes and values serve to motivate certain kinds of behavior and inhibit other kinds. A person who despises the police, feels that laws are totally unfair or apply only to the other fellow, and is antagonistic toward or has no respect for his family or other authority, must be motivated differently from one who has opposite attitudes and values. Of course, some specific values may be held which are similar for the lawbreaker and the law-abider; but when this is the case, the object toward which the values are directed is probably narrower and more restricted for the lawbreaker than it is for the law-abider. In other words, the lawbreaker may have a feeling of loyalty, may uphold the norms of the group, but the object of this loyalty is restricted, for example, to his gang or individual members of it and not to society as a whole. The true gang delinquent growing up in high-delinquency areas is motivated certainly by many of the same values as are prevalent in the larger society, but these values are restricted and operate only in reference to his own in-group and fail to operate in reference to what he considers the out-group—the group, as he sees it, which is against him and repressive in its actions toward him.

In the third place, there are persons who, because of adverse conditions in their life histories, become psychologically maladjusted. These persons frequently engage in delinquent behavior because of their deep-seated anxieties and perplexities. Many delinquents have distorted conceptions of reality. For example, although this is not always verbalized, boys—and girls too—often feel that all adults are against them, that they are alone in a hostile world, and that they must battle to retain their personal significance. Treatment, to be effective, must change these basic personality manifestations in order to give a more realistic picture of society.[7]

In order to insure meaningful answers to the questions we were asking, an experimental design was called for. Therefore, we advocated securing pre- and post-information on each boy sent to the short-term treatment project and like information on boys who were handled in other ways. These other ways might include release with no further action by the court, probation, committal to a training school or reformatory, or even to a jail or other local place of incarceration. Theoretically, at least, samples of boys similar in every way to those sent to the short-

[7] We think of these two types as (1) the social deviant or gang delinquent and (2) the psychologically maladjusted. They are essentially the same types that Dr. Richard L. Jenkins calls the adaptive and the maladaptive delinquent. See his "Adaptive and Maladaptive Delinquency," *The Nervous Child,* Vol. 6.

term treatment facility could be drawn from those handled in each of these other ways, and comparisons made between them and the boys experiencing the short-term treatment program.

New Jersey has an excellent Diagnostic Center at Menlo Park, and it was suggested that all boys be screened at the Center and complete diagnostic workups on each boy be obtained when he first came to the attention of the court and again when he was discharged from whatever treatment he had been undergoing. Comparisons could then be made in terms of the changes revealed between the two workups and the particular treatment accorded the various groups of boys.

As the research plan was discussed with the judges of the four separate juvenile courts, it appeared that the great majority of boys would probably be committed to Annandale Farms, the New Jersey State Reformatory for Males, if there were no room for them at Highfields. It could be assumed that if Highfields did not exist almost all of the more serious delinquents as old as sixteen or seventeen would be sent to the reformatory at Annandale. Thus, it was decided for research purposes to use as a control group boys of the same ages as those eligible for Highfields who were committed to this reformatory. The control group would, of course, be selected according to the other criteria established for Highfields eligibility: it would be composed of boys who had not previously been in a state correctional institution, who did not appear to be feebleminded or psychotic, and who were not known sexual perverts. . . .

THE RESEARCH

During the spring of 1951 the following policy, initiated with the co-operation of the juvenile courts and parole offices, became the standard operating procedure carried on for the remainder of the study. Each time a judge decided to send a boy to either Highfields or Annandale, his office notified the research division at New York University and one of the staff traveled to the probation office or parental school of the respective court, where the tests were administered. Each time a boy was released from Highfields the director notified the research office and a member of the staff went to the respective probation office and administered the same tests as were given before. When a boy in the control group was released from Annandale the institution parole officer notified the district parole officer that the boy was in the control sample. This officer in turn notified the research office and arrangements were made to meet with the parolee and administer the tests. In this way almost all of the boys were tested just before they went to their respective facilities and just after they were released.[8] A few boys from counties which do not have a full-time juvenile court, such as Burlington, Monmouth, and Mercer, were first tested after they arrived at Highfields and shortly before they were released from there.[9] No procedure was established whereby the research office was notified when boys were sent to one or the

[8] Without the co-operation, interest, and awareness on the part of the judges of the juvenile court or the probation and parole officers and the superintendent of the reformatory of the necessity for this procedure, the research staff would have had much more difficulty than it encountered. We recognize that the procedure added to their already heavy burdens and we are exceedingly grateful.

[9] By far the greatest number of boys were sent to Highfields from the four counties with full-time juvenile courts; only relatively few were sent from all other counties of the state. Boys at Annandale from other than the juvenile court counties were selected for the control sample in about the same proportion as they were found in the Highfields population.

other facility from these counties. Occasionally, through some unusual contingency, the research office was not notified when boys were sent to Highfields or to Annandale by the four larger counties. With Highfields boys this did not appreciably delay the testing because we were informed that the boy had arrived and the tests had not been given, but in the case of Annandale the information was not so readily forthcoming. For this reason, about every two or three months during the course of the study we checked the records at Annandale and tested any boy who had not hitherto been tested. In this way, we secured as complete a sample as possible of all boys who met our criteria.

Because it was believed there might be a fictitious inflationary "halo" reflected in the results of the tests taken so soon after release from either facility, each boy who was still available (that is, still on probation or parole or had not joined the armed services) was called in to his probation or parole office and was given all the tests a third time, after he had been back in his community six months or more.[10]

The administration of these tests and the filling in of the interview schedule took, on the average, somewhat over two hours on the first contact. The post-test could be administered in much less time because it was not

necessary to interview again; and then, too, the boys knew the staff and there was no problem of establishing rapport. However, it should be mentioned that often the boys were somewhat more resistant to filling in the post-test, especially when, as originally was the case, we asked them to do so before they had had a chance to get home and see their families and friends. When this was discovered, we arranged the post-test a day or so after the boy had been home.

In addition to the testing, we have, through co-operation of the probation and parole offices, kept in touch with each boy over the length of the study. Periodically, we received reports from the respective offices on each boy's adjustment. If he got into further trouble and was returned to the court and recommitted to any correctional facility we were immediately notified.

For the purposes of this study the following definition of a recidivist, or failure, was adopted. A recidivist is one who, for any reason, was returned to court and/or violated probation or parole and as a result was committed to an institution. When we speak of failures or recidivists, we mean only boys who, subsequent to their first stay in either Highfields or Annandale, have been committed a second time. This commitment may be in Annandale, as is the case with most of the boys in our sample who have failed, or in a jail for a period of thirty days or longer, or penal institution in another state. Boys who have been called in to the probation or parole office or even brought before the court and admonished or warned but were not recommitted but continued on probation or parole are not failures by this definition.

Beginning November 1, 1951, and continuing until January 1953, another phase of the research was designed and

---

[10] This was not carried on after the first year or so, for several reasons. First, almost all of the boys tested were those making favorable adjustments, as many of those who failed on probation or parole had done so before the end of a six-month period and were recommitted. Second, by examining the various test scores it could not be seen that the boys changed much from the first post-test to the second. And finally, it added another burden to the probation and parole staffs to call these boys in. Often it was difficult to find a time when they could be tested. No boy was post-post-tested after November 1952.

carried out.[11] This was an attempt to ascertain whether persons who know a boy intimately see any changes in him after he has been out of his respective facility for six weeks or more.

The procedure for this phase of the research was as follows:

1. At the time the boy was first interviewed—before he entered High-fields or Annandale—he was asked if he had any objections to our talking about him with (1) one of his parents or his guardian or another relative, (2) a boy or girl friend, (3) the proprietor of the place where he "hung out," (4) a policeman or other representative of the law, and (5) his probation officer. If he had no objections (very few objected) we asked for names and addresses.

2. Each of the persons suggested was interviewed in order to find out about the boy's behavior and the interviewee's attitudes toward it at the time he got into his present trouble.

3. After the boy had been out of either facility for two months, each of these persons was interviewed again and was asked the same type of questions concerning the boy's behavior as at the first interview. A comparison of the pre- and post-interview shows whether they think the boy's behavior has changed or whether opinions and attitudes toward the boy have altered. It was felt that these interviews would also indicate whether there were any unusual community situations which would make it especially difficult for the boy to adjust.

No boys committed to Annandale were pre-tested after February 1954, and no boys sent to Highfields after

[11] This addition to the study was made possible by a grant-in-aid from the Rockefeller Foundation, to whom we are exceedingly grateful.

April of this same year. It was necessary to cut off the Annandale cases earlier than the Highfields ones because of the longer commitment period of the reformatory boys. Few boys, unless recalled by the committing judge, are released from Annandale earlier than twelve months. Therefore, boys committed through February 1954 would not leave Annandale before the end of January 1955; and because we wished to allow at least a six-month period after release to ascertain whether or not a boy made good, none could be included who would not be out of the institution for at least six months by the end of August 1955. The same reasoning was applied to the Highfields cases. Boys at Highfields stay as long as four months. All of the boys admitted to Highfields through April 1954, therefore, would normally be released by the last of August and would have been on probation in their communities for at least six months by the end of February 1955. The main reason for the earlier six-month cut-off date for the Highfields boys was that many more Highfields than Annandale boys had to be processed. It was also felt that numerically enough boys were in the Highfields sample and nothing would be gained by extending the time. Both groups of boys were finally followed up until October 1955.

From February 1951, when the first boys were tested, to the last of April 1954, two hundred and thirty-three boys were sent to Highfields by the courts, an average of about sixty-one boys a year.

From this beginning date to the end of January 1954, the same courts committed one hundred and twenty-two boys to Annandale. Nearly three-quarters of the boys sent to Highfields came almost equally from two of the most populous counties. One of these counties committed very few boys to Annandale—only three—whereas the second county committed almost two-thirds of the Annandale sample. This discrepancy in commitment rates was an indication that the Highfields and Annandale samples might not be exactly comparable.[12]

CONCLUSION

What answers can be given to the three questions which were proposed to guide this research?

1. Do delinquents participating in the short-term treatment program show a higher, the same, or a lower recidivist rate than boys participating in other kinds of treatment programs?

2. Do delinquents participating in the short-term treatment program change their expressed attitudes, values, and opinions toward their families, law and order, and their own outlook on life?

3. Do delinquents participating in the short-term treatment program change their basic personality structures or at least the overt manifestation of their personalities?

Answer to the First Question

There is no doubt that the Highfields Program for the Short-Term Treatment of Youthful Offenders is effective with a large proportion of the boys who are sent to the project. The data show that over the length of this study, when all the boys sent to the project by the counties of New Jersey are included, sixty-three in every hundred

[12] When we began the Highfields research, fifteen boys had already been there and were released at the end of their treatment or sent back to the court as unsuitable for residence at Highfields. These boys are not, of course, included in our analysis. It should be pointed out, however, that the results would not be altered in any significant way if they were.

Highfields boys, in contrast to only forty-seven in every hundred Annandale boys, complete their treatment and do not get into further difficulty serious enough to require that they be reinstitutionalized.

This better over-all record of the total two hundred and twenty-nine boys sent to Highfields appears to be due in the main to the large difference between the relative number of Negro boys from the two facilities with successful outcomes. There is very little difference in the relative number of white boys from the two facilities with successful outcomes, but fifty-nine in every hundred Highfields Negroes as compared with only thirty-three in every hundred Annandale Negroes complete their stay and do not get into further difficulty.

There is no reason to believe from the data available that this large discrepancy is accounted for by differences in the backgrounds of Negro boys sent to the two facilities. When the number of background variables related to outcome are held constant, Highfields still has relatively more Negro boys with low and high scores who are successful than does Annandale. Nor is the difference accounted for by the disproportionate number of white and Negro boys sent to either facility by each county. A comparison of the counties has shown that the county which sends the most Negroes to Annandale also sends the most Negroes to Highfields. In this county the proportion of boys with successful outcomes is basically the same as it is for all the counties which send boys to Highfields: about three in every five white and Negro boys complete their treatment period at Highfields and get into no further difficulty after release, whereas about the same ratio of Annandale white boys but only three in every ten Annandale Negro boys complete their stay and get into no further difficulty after release.

It must be remembered that boys are sent to Highfields while they are officially on probation to the court from which they are sent.[13] Because this is the case, boys can be sent back to the court if, in the opinion of the director, they are failing to adjust. About one-fifth of the boys, during the length of this study, have been declared unsuitable for residence. These include boys who ran away from Highfields (some within a few days or even a few hours after they first arrived), boys who found that the group and the program offered too great a threat to them, and boys who were so disruptive that they threatened the stability of other boys and the group as a whole. The majority of these boys were returned to the court within the first few weeks they were at the project. They cannot be

[13] The fact that boys sent to Highfields are officially on probation should not be construed to mean that they are less serious delinquents than boys sent to Annandale. Probation is an integral part of the Highfields program. There is little doubt that almost all of the boys in the Highfields sample would have been sent to Annandale or a similar facility, rather than placed on probation, if Highfields were not in existence.

The original research design included the drawing of a second control group from boys placed on probation. This plan was abandoned because of the impossibility of securing a sample of boys on probation which would be reasonably similar to the Highfields sample. It was not possible to find enough boys sixteen to seventeen years of age on probation with the same frequency of prior delinquencies and serious kinds of delinquencies as those of the Highfields boys, to say nothing of the similarity of many other background variables. There is every reason to believe that boys sent to Highfields are more like boys of the same age sent to Annandale than they are to boys placed on probation. All available information points to the fact that the great majority of Highfields boys are serious delinquents and have long histories of delinquency.

considered to have really experienced the Highfields program.

The elimination of the boys who have been returned to the court results in an even more striking contrast between the success rates for Highfields and Annandale boys. More than three-quarters (seventy-seven per cent) of the Highfields boys who completed treatment have been successful. In other words, for every hundred boys who complete residence in the respective facility, the Highfields program rehabilitates twenty-eight more than does the traditional program of caring for such boys.

Furthermore, a separate comparison of the success rates for white and Negro boys from the two facilities shows that Highfields has a higher success rate than Annandale for each group. Eight in every ten Highfields white boys are successful, whereas only six in every ten Annandale white boys are successful. Highfields Negroes succeed at more than double the rate of Annandale Negroes: seven out of ten Negroes are successful after their Highfields treatment, but only slightly over three in ten Negroes are successful after their Annandale stay.

When the differential in length of time after release is held constant the rates for Highfields boys are even more favorable than they are when time is not considered. Eight Highfields boys in every ten are successful a year after being released (there is no difference between whites and Negroes), whereas only five Annandale boys in every ten are likewise successful at the end of the same period of time. Seventeen more Highfields white boys in every hundred and almost fifty more Negro boys in every hundred are rehabilitated twelve months after release than Annandale white and Negro boys.

There is no reason to believe that

these differences in success rates are due to the fact that Highfields may get a "better type" of boy. The expectancy tables constructed on the basis of background variables found to be related to outcome for white and Negro boys have shown that the differences in the relative number of adverse background variables for Highfields and Annandale boys do not account for the differences in outcome.

The simple fact is that all boys who complete their stay at Highfields have a better chance of being successful than do boys who complete their stay at Annandale, and this is especially the case for Highfields Negro boys.

A word of caution is in order here. The fact that Negroes at Highfields appear to profit so much more than they do at Annandale does not necessarily indicate that Highfields-type facilities should be established solely for Negroes or that a higher proportion of Negroes should be sent to the present Highfields project. From the data collected, it cannot be concluded that Negroes would profit to the same extent if a facility were established for them alone or if a higher proportion of them were sent to the present facility. It appears that the success of the Negroes sent to Highfields may be related to the ratio of Negroes to whites there. At present, it is rare that there are, at any one time, more than four or five Negroes at the project in a total of eighteen to twenty boys. If the number were increased to eight or nine the whole acceptance and integration of the Negroes into the group might be different. This integration and acceptance is a fundamental aspect of the program at Highfields. A facility solely for Negroes would not allow the give-and-take between the white and Negro boys both in the guided group interaction sessions and in all their daily living experiences. In our opinion, the fact that white and Negro boys can discuss their common problems together is an important factor in the relatively low failure rate of the Negro boys who have been at Highfields.

Not only are higher proportions of Highfields than Annandale boys successful, but as time has passed since Highfields first opened in 1950 the proportion of boys who are successful has tended to increase. Also as time has gone by, relatively fewer boys have been returned to the court as unsuitable for residence. Of the eighty-five boys who entered Highfields during the last year of the study—from April 1953 to April 1954—only eight were sent back to the court as unsuitable for residence; and of those who completed their treatment nine out of ten had not got into further difficulty requiring institutional care, although every boy had been released and back in his community for more than a year. Sixteen of the seventy-seven boys who completed treatment during this period were Negroes, and every one of them had a successful outcome. In fact, all but two Negro boys have had successful outcomes after Highfields treatment since April 1952. Of course, a few more failures can be expected as the boys are out longer, but the data indicate that the great majority, over three-quarters, of the boys who fail do so within the first year after release. It appears certain that as the Highfields program has become stabilized and traditions have crystallized, it has become even more effective than it was at first.

Answer to the Second Question

There is very little evidence that Highfields boys, over the length of their treatment, change their attitudes toward family and toward law and order, and their outlook toward life, so far as the eight scales used to measure these attitudes show.

Highfields white boys showed no appreciable change on six of the eight scales. They became more favorable on the scale measuring attitude toward obeying the law, and less favorable on the scale measuring attitude toward law enforcement.

Annandale white boys also did not show many changes from pre- to post-test. On five of the eight scales there were no appreciable changes. They became more favorable on the scale measuring attitude toward general authority and less favorable on the scale measuring attitude toward law enforcement. Annandale white boys were more inclined to mark the neutral category on the post-test than they were on the pre-test on the scale measuring attitude toward the family.

On five of the eight scales Highfields Negro boys showed no appreciable difference from pre- to post-test. On three of the scales—attitude toward parental authority, attitude toward law enforcement, and attitude toward behavior norms—Highfields Negro boys became more unfavorable on the post-test than they were on the pre-test.

The Annandale Negro boys showed the greatest tendency to change. On only three of the eight scales did these boys show relatively no difference between pre- and post-test responses. These scales were: attitude toward law enforcement, attitude toward general authority, and attitude indicating acceptance of others. On five of the scales the Annandale Negro boys moved in a favorable direction and on one, attitude toward parental authority, they moved unfavorably.

Although there does not appear to be much evidence that Highfields or Annandale white or Negro boys change their responses on the eight scales, there is evidence that the attitude responses of the boys are related to outcome.

Actually, the pre-test responses of all white boys sent to either Highfields or Annandale on five of the scales significantly differentiate the boys who are likely to be successful from those who are likely to be unsuccessful. These scales are: attitude toward family, attitude toward parental authority, attitude toward obeying the law, attitude toward acceptance of others, and attitude toward behavior norms. On each of these scales boys with more favorable attitudes are more likely to have successful outcomes than boys with less favorable attitudes. An expectancy table constructed on the basis of the cumulative effect of these attitude variables, makes clear that white boys in both Highfields and Annandale who have low scores (zero or one) are much more likely than those with high scores to have successful outcomes; but *there is no appreciable difference between the success rates of Highfields and Annandale white boys who fall in the same score group, whether low or high.*

Only two of these scales show a relationship with outcome for Highfields and Annandale white boys who have completed their stay at either of the facilities: attitude toward obeying the law and attitude toward behavior norms. An expectancy table constructed on the basis of these two scales shows that Highfields white boys with no adverse attitude variables are more likely to be successful than those with one or more variables. This table does not discriminate for Annandale white boys who have completed treatment.

The attitude responses of all Negroes sent to either Highfields or Annandale show a significant relationship with outcome on three of the scales. These same scales also discriminate for only the Negro boys who complete their stay in either of two facilities. The scales which differentiate are: attitude toward family, attitude toward acceptance of others, and attitude toward behavior norms.

On the attitude toward family scale, Negro boys with less favorable attitudes are more likely than those with more favorable attitudes to have successful outcomes; this is especially pronounced for the Highfields Negroes. On the other two scales Negroes with more favorable attitudes are more likely than those with less favorable attitudes to have successful outcomes, as is the case with the white boys. The expectancy table constructed on the cumulative effect of these three scales shows very little discrimination for all Negroes sent to Highfields, but discriminates significantly for all Negroes sent to Annandale. The expectancy table based on these same scales discriminates for both Highfields and Annandale Negroes who have completed treatment. Negro boys with low scores who have completed treatment in either facility are more likely to be successful than those with high scores, but *Annandale Negroes with either low or high scores have lower success rates than do Highfields Negroes.*

Actually, there is much more discrimination on these scales than the above discussion of the expectancy tables would indicate. We have discussed only the pre-test responses on the attitude scales which discriminate in the same direction for boys in both facilities. In addition, some of the other scales show a relationship between the pre-test and/or post-test responses of the boys and outcome. A given scale may discriminate for Highfields boys but not for Annandale boys, or vice versa, or discriminate in opposite ways for boys in the two facilities.

It is interesting that on six of the eight scales the highest success rate is found for the Annandale Negro boys whose post-test responses fall in the most favorable categories. An expec-

tancy table based on Annandale Negroes' post-test responses shows that boys with low scores have much higher success rates than boys with high scores. Only for Annandale Negroes is there this consistency. In all other groups the highest success rate is likely to be found in any of the three categories. This may indicate that few Annandale Negroes can succeed unless they have favorable attitudes, but that Highfields Negroes can hold favorable or unfavorable attitudes and still succeed because they have learned to live with their attitudes without undue disturbance.

Answer to the Third Question

There is no evidence that Highfields white or Negro boys change much from pre- to post-test, judging from the overall responses they made to the ten scales adapted from the Army's Psychoneurotic Screening Adjunct to measure the boys' personality structure.

Highfields white boys show an overall difference in response of as much as ten percentage points between pre- and post-tests on only one scale; and Highfields Negro boys show this much difference on but two. The white boys shift in the direction of better adjustment, whereas the Negroes shift toward poorer adjustment on one of the scales and toward better adjustment on the other.

Annandale white and Negro boys shift at least ten percentage points between pre- and post-tests on more scales than do Highfields white and Negro boys. Annandale white boys show an over-all difference in response of as much as ten percentage points between pre- and post-tests on five of the ten scales; Annandale Negro boys show this much over-all difference in response on three scales. Two of these scales are the same as those on which the Annandale white boys shift, but none is the same as those on which the Highfields

Negroes shift. On one of the scales the Annandale Negroes shift in the direction of poorer adjustment, but on the other two scales the shift is toward better adjustment. On all five scales the Annandale white boys shift in the direction of better adjustment.

There is no consistent relationship between the boys' responses to either the pre- or post-test and outcome. The scales on which there is the most change from pre- to post-test are not necessarily the scales which show the greatest relationship between the boys' responses and outcome. A number of the scales which showed a relationship between boys' pre-test responses and outcome do not show the same relationship between the boys' post-test responses and outcome.

According to the analysis of the Miale-Holsopple Sentence Completions given to a sample of Highfields and Annandale boys, Highfields boys tend to change from pre- to post-test more than Annandale boys, and in a different way. But, as Dr. Holsopple writes: "There is no reason to suppose that the primary goals or basic drives of either group were substantially changed. With the Annandale group on the one hand, the goals remained distorted to unclear, the/ drives unrecognized or unaccepted. In contrast, among the Highfields group, there was movement toward a clearer view of primary goals and substantially increased acceptance of primary drives."

These changes, however, do not appear to be related to outcome. Just about as many Highfields as Annandale boys whose tests were analyzed have unsuccessful outcomes. It would be worth knowing whether the boys who change the most and in a favorable direction on these tests are the ones who are most likely to be successful. This cannot be ascertained from this analysis because it was done for the group of boys in each sample rather than for the individual boys making up the respective samples.

This research points out the fact that a higher proportion of Highfields than Annandale boys succeed and that this is true even when the background variables which are related to their success or failure are held constant. It has shown that it is possible, by using background and attitudinal variables, to differentiate boys who are likely to have high and low success rates even before they enter the respective facility. It has not shown that the boys' attitudes as measured by the tests change appreciably during their residence and treatment. It may well be that the instruments used in this research do not get at the kinds of changes which the Highfields white and Negro boys undergo during their period of treatment. When almost three more Highfields than Annandale white boys in every ten and five more Highfields than Annandale Negroes in every ten who complete their treatment succeed, there must be some explanation for it.

Highfields rehabilitates this high proportion of boys in a four-month period, whereas most other facilities keep boys at least three times as long. Not only is this fact important in itself, but it is important because Highfields is relatively much less expensive per boy treated than is the conventional facility. The "yearly per capita cost" of the residential aspects of the Highfields and Annandale programs, as figured by the state, is about the same, but this is misleading because it does not take into consideration the total number of boys who have experienced the Highfields program during the course of a year.[14] On a strict per capita basis the

[14] The yearly per capita cost on current maintenance while in the institutions was $1,413.95 for Highfields and $1,479.75 for Annandale during 1953 (see: *Mental Defi-*

Highfields program costs one-third as much as the traditional program for each boy treated. Because of the differential in the outcome rates, this cost differential would be much greater if it took into consideration the number of boys each facility rehabilitated.

It is hoped that research will continue at Highfields so that the many facets of the program can be explored and better understood. It would be very worthwhile to know which boys at Highfields change, how this change takes place, and what form it takes.

ciency in New Jersey, 1953). These per capita costs are figures on the basis of the number in the facility at the end of the fiscal year and not the total number treated during a year.

41.

The Cottage Social Structure

Howard W. Polsky

Out of the actor's interaction on the stage, mutual expectations and concerns arise. Patterns emerge that come alive in the performance of the social roles fostered by the action of the entire company. The full implications of the confrontations within and between the main and supporting actors gradually unfold before the audience.

Cottage 6 boys as a rule interact among themselves than with other cottages. And within the cottage, subgroup members have higher rates of internal confrontation than with the rest of the cottage. Carrying this progression farther, it follows that within a subgroup, clique members have higher interaction rates than nonclique members. Thus, at different levels the boys regard themselves as varying units of solidarity, who possess shared interests, attitudes, and activities that separate them from outsiders.

In this chapter we extend our examination of patterned social relations: subgroup, clique, and role formations; consensus of intracottage stratification; and, finally, the emergent social structure.

SOURCE. Howard W. Polsky, "The Cottage Social Structure," *Cottage Six*, New York: Russell Sage Foundation, 1962, Chapter 5, pp. 69–88. Reprinted with permission.

THE FORMATION OF SUBGROUPS AND CLIQUES

Subgroups and cliques are established in the cottage by boys in relatively close contact. Cliques are usually composed of roommates. One clique consisted of Red Leon, Steve Davis, and Lenny Wolf; Perry Yearwood, Chuck Small, and Ronny Miles made up another. Chet Ellins once remarked, "Two or three boys in a bedroom usually make up a group and decide they are going to raise hell, so they go around and stir up the other rooms."

Bedroom and dining-hall clusters reinforce one another, as indicated in Diagram 1.

If the observer repeatedly sees boys clustered together, he postulates that such configurations are relatively stable. Behavior is regularized by comprehension of what one's intimates have done, are doing, and are likely to do. The tables are labeled according to salient group and intergroup characteristics similar to cottage differentiation in Chapter 2. Table III dominates the cottage; I is a middle group; IV and V represent the lowest strata. Tables III and I appear to be more cohesive than the low subgroups, IV and V, where there was likely to be shifting between them.

Bedroom:	A	B	C	D	E	F	G
	Red Leon	Drake	Small	Ellins	Petane	Kahn	Lane
	Davis	Little	Miles	Parker	Stein	Dane	
	Wolf	Parma	Yearwood	Kranz	Rabin	Colorado	

Dining-Hall Table:	I		III		IV		V	
	Ellins ⎱ D Parker ⎰		Davis ⎱ Red Leon ⎬ A Wolf ⎰		Kahn ⎱ Dane ⎬ F Colorado ⎰		Stein ⎱ E Rabin ⎰	
	Miles ⎱ Yearwood ⎬ C Small ⎰		Drake ⎱ Parma ⎬ B Little ⎰		Petane E		Kranz D Lane G	

DIAGRAM 1.   BEDROOM AND DINING-HALL CLUSTERS

Boys in the same cliques participate in similar activities. One evening the observer was struck by subgroup differences at a dance. Attending were most of the boys from Tables III and I. Remaining in the cottage watching television were almost all the boys from IV and V (including new arrivals). At the dance, Rabin, a low-status boy, was isolated from the other Cottage 6 boys. He sat alone in the corner, depressed, watching his cottagemates dance with their girls.

Continued observation of interaction results in quick and sure definition of the main subgroups but the subtle relations within them, the clique differentiation, takes longer. Some boys, too, are in transition from one clique to another or are temporarily disaffected from their clique.

Once formed, however, cliques are consolidated by intensity of contact and the exclusion of outclique boys. This is variously manifested. In the food line Red Leon hit Rick Kahn and was joined by Artie, Drake, and Little, who also slugged him. Rick fled. In another instance, the boys at Table III looked over at Table I and burst into infectious laughter. The joke seemed to be a secret that Perry tried to unlock, but Table III refused to give him the key.

Tables III and I, however, generally stuck together and harassed outsiders.

Throughout one evening, Steve Davis hit Rick Kahn continually with a short leather strap. The latter implored Steve to cut it out, and although Kahn became quite angry, Steve continued to badger him. Later, Colorado tussled with Davis and backed down. Foster came in and began teasing and harassing both Kahn and Colorado, punching them sometimes quite hard. Of course, Foster never tangled with Davis or vice versa.

The social barrier between Tables IV and V, on the one hand, and Tables III and I on the other, is relatively impenetrable. When a boy from IV or V approached Table III or I, he took a calculated risk. Table III especially permitted no nonsense from boys sitting at these tables and in a crude way kept them in their place.

The following type of incident occurred hundreds of times. Petane went over to Table III and asked for the sugar. Davis simply pushed it a little; he did not pick it up and give it to Petane, which would have been the convenient and courteous gesture; he just touched it, implying that he gave Petane permission to borrow the sugar.

This relationship is in sharp contrast to the semi-permeable boundary between Tables III and I. Once when Davis was fooling with Miles, the latter told him that he acted just like a three-year-old. Davis curtly said, "What did you say? Take that back." Miles playfully countered, "OK, you act just like a twenty-five-year-old [after a pause] baby." Davis and Miles continued to exchange friendly taps.

High-status boys arrange birthday and going-away parties for members of their clique. They collect money from all the boys in the cottage and selected staff. Low-status boys' birthdays, on the contrary, are often ignored by friends and staff. After the boys leave Hollymeade, clique contact is maintained by correspondence and trysts in the city.

Status differences were crystallized to the extent that Rick Kahn's bedroom was ignominiously known as the "punk room." A new boy moves out of this room as soon as he can. It is uninvitingly and sparsely furnished and has a transitory unwanted character like its inhabitants.

CONSENSUS ON COTTAGE CLIQUES AND STATUSES

Social organization refers to human action insofar as the actor takes into account the actions of others. The boys in Cottage 6 achieved a stable consensus concerning their positions in the social system. Once the cliques and roles are differentiated, group consensus helps to freeze the status quo, as indicated by Steve Davis:

QUESTION. Did you, Red Leon, and Wolf always share the same room?
ANSWER. No. When I first came in, I roomed with two other boys. Then I started buddying around with Leon and finally moved into the end room. In there was me, Red Leon, and Wolf. Then it was the big room.
QUESTION. What do you mean by the big room?
ANSWER. What I mean by the big room is, we were about the only guys around the cottage who were considered big around the campus—me, Leon, and Lenny Wolf. All the kids considered us the tough-

est, me and Red Leon especially. But we never really looked for trouble.

Low-status members are equally aware of the cottage dichotomy. Len Stein told the observer that the cottage was broken down into two groups; the so-called *big crowd* and a *small crowd*. Davis' and Small's rooms contained the big crowd. When asked about Drake, Stein said that Drake, Parma, and Little were in the big crowd too. In the small crowd were Rick, Colorado, and Al Dane. Stein, Rabin, and Petane also fell into the small crowd.

A clever boy like Chet Ellins can specify differences (or roles) within the cliques. Kahn, Colorado, Petane, Werner, Stein, Rabin, and Dane were "bushboys" in Chet's words, "guys that go out and do the bigger guys' bidding because they just want to live . . . they want to become part of the group, but they're not even close enough to it yet . . . the shoe shiners and sox washers." Chet tabbed Werner as the most disliked boy because "he came up as a wise guy and everyone realizes he is just a punk. He feels he's getting accepted into the group, but I don't really think so." The interview continues:

QUESTION. Which guys clique together, Rabin and Petane, or Rick Kahn and Al Dane?
ANSWER. Just the way you named it off. Rabin and Petane are in a clique because they were in Cottage 5 together, living with each other. That's their private clique. Kahn and Dane were roommates, so they're together. But in Kahn's case he would drop Dane very quickly if he could get into one of the other groups. But since he can't, he's Dane's best friend, and I think it works both ways.

The boys' social positions were recognized by the cottage staff. Bill Milber, veteran cottage counselor, confirmed Chet's statement that Petane, Rabin,

Kahn, Dane, and Chase were "practically unnoticed by the top bunch of fellows . . . just outsiders." On the other hand, Ellins and Miles "came from a cottage [7] where they were top dogs and took the same position in 6. Miles was popular, gay, jolly, and a bully who kept the little fellows in line. Chet Ellins was quiet, the man behind the scenes."

Milber filled in the cottage picture: "There were boys in the middle range (Lane, Kranz, Parker) who were not at the top but they were not treated as bushboys either. Lane, for example, was popular. He was never in the cottage. He worked on the farm and as he passed the girls' cottages, he delivered lots of notes from them to the guys in the cottage."

Milber noted that some of the bushboys were strange, thus corroborating the boys' judgments: "Rick Kahn was a peculiar person. He had nasty ways, bullying the new boys who came in." In turn, he was bullied by the older ones, doing the dirty work for them. Not until the older boys left, did Rick assume any position of importance. But even then, he was rather unsociable and kept pretty much to himself—a "punk" to the very end.

Thus, the observer's growing familiarity with the cottage was sustained by the consensus of boys and cottage attendant staff. The clear recognition of the status structure is an important factor for pressuring boys to adjust to it. If one is viewed as a "punk," he must adapt to this cottage (and usually institutional) definition or take the consequences of defying it. The same is true of the dominant leaders. In order to live up to their reputation they frequently gave demonstrations of their authority.

This omnipresent delineation in the members' minds of subgroups and cliques (and roles) contributes to the perpetuation of the cottage subculture.

The reaction of old residents to newcomers is reflected in Foster's comment: "This cottage isn't like it used to be. Now they have a bunch of babies and queers." New boys who serve as sitting ducks for the older boys, await their turn to become metamorphosed into preying hawks for boys arriving after them. After all, persistent identification with the aggressor can lead under favorable circumstances to autonomous aggression.

COTTAGE CLIQUES AND ROLES

Assumption of a cottage role depends partially upon a boy's background and personality. The most important factor determining role assumption is the network of roles available to the boy from which he must select. Role behavior within the cottage is schematized below according to patterned transactions within and between the cliques, the most intense subgroup unit: (a) toughs (leadership), (b) "con-artists," (c) quiet types, (d) bushboys (or punks), and (e) scapegoats. Each of these roles can be seen to contribute to a complementary system of selves made relatively fixed through continued interaction. Their coordinated functioning in the daily life of Cottage 6 surrounds these disturbed delinquents with a well nigh irresistible social system.

a.   The Leadership Clique: Toughs

Every group creates a unique style. A delinquent group ranges from a casual collaboration of a hundred youngsters to a tightly knit structure. The function of leadership is to maintain the status quo. In order to maintain this equilibrium, the leader inculcates new members with group standards, delegates work and play "tasks," and eliminates or isolates unfit members. The group attacks, and defends itself from rival groups; resolves internal conflicts;

and accommodates itself to the requirements of its milieu.

In the personality, the governing ego assumes responsibility for the integration of individual roles and the actualization of plans. In his studies of group psychology, Freud noted that a group is united because its members project their superegos onto the leader.[1] The aggression pattern in Cottage 6 is maintained primarily by the leaders and diffused throughout the cottage. A sociological perspective of authoritarianism, however, must go beyond the analysis of individual egos to a delineation of social positions institutionalized by the boys' cumulative interaction.

The present cottage leadership inherited an aggressive tradition. According to Milber, who had entered the cottage as a counselor several years previously, former cottage parents were concerned mainly with control: "An old Irishman, who was very strong and strict, actually kept the cottage on an even keel." There had been no cottage parents in Cottage 6 for a short period prior to Milber's arrival. During this interim, the boys themselves had taken over, led by Red Leon, Wolf, Steve Davis, the "elder boys of the cottage—the top echelon" to use Milber's phrase.

A transitional period occurs when the older boys are departing and new boys are gaining control. This shifting of leadership results in a series of dramatic challenges and fights. After the dust has settled, the role of leadership is taken over by the upwardly mobile boys. . . . The observer asked Davis what occurred after he "took over" and he replied, "There were other guys who would fight

me, but I never really had a fight with anybody else. I mean there is nobody I can think of who would fight me."

An example of a smooth ascendancy to power was the arrival of Foster, an established tough, in Cottage 7. Even before entering Cottage 6 he was close to the top group there. A leader in "7," he was a bullying, unstable boy, skillful in athletics and gambling. Red Leon had just left Hollymeade. Since Foster was close to the leadership in "6," Steve Davis and Wolf, he was accepted automatically. The boys had looked forward to his coming in, and when he arrived, he went into Steve's room. According to Chet Ellins, "He sort of took over Red Leon's position, not as leader actually, but as Steve's and Wolf's roommate."

The boys were acutely sensitive about leadership status. Artie Parma said that Werner might try to take over, and some of the boys planned to talk to Werner before they left the cottage. "Talk to Werner" is a euphemism for putting Werner in his subservient place. The other person Artie mentioned was Colorado because "he was acting up lately."

In initiating, organizing, and controlling group action, the leaders set the cottage tone. If Steve Davis deigned to cooperate with the cottage parents, the others fell in line. At dinner one evening, John Raines prompted the boys to turn in their dishes and silverware. None of the boys at any of the tables moved because Davis was still drinking his coffee. Then Davis finished his coffee and slowly rose from the table. Only then did the rest of the boys follow suit, moving slowly away from the table. After telling John, "I guess everyone was waiting for me to finish my coffee," Davis brought his chair to the center of the dining room as was the custom, but at a snail's pace. The other boys figuratively and literally followed in his footsteps.

[1] See Freud, Sigmund, *Group Psychology and the Analysis of the Ego*, International Psychoanalytic Library, London, 1922; and Redl, Fritz, "Group Emotion and Leadership" in *Small Groups*, edited by Paul Hare, E. F. Borgatta, and R. F. Bales, Alfred A. Knopf, Inc., New York, 1955.

Steve Davis "supervised" the boys in the cottage. While he was watching television one evening after a party, he asked if anyone was cleaning up the mess. Someone told Davis that it was Rick's turn to clean up. Steve, not taking his eyes off television, yelled, "Okay, let's get it all cleaned up!" Steve's authority was never *directly* challenged.

Indirect limitations to the leader's control were evident, however, when he asserted his dominance over several boys. For example, Steve was watching the Goldbergs on television one evening, and some of the others wanted to see the Whirly Birds. When Davis got up to get a rag to clean the set, someone tried to change the channel. Davis became angry and told him to leave the channel as it was. Later, Davis hit Parker, who suggested that they switch programs. Chet Ellins then suggested that they all look at something else. Davis remained adamant, but later he and the boys tacitly compromised by seeing the Black Swan.

The leader, too, has the highest status with the staff. Steve Davis was influential in the dining hall. The "toughs" were recognized throughout Hollymeade. Some of the adults, including Milber, had worked out an accommodating approach toward them. Adults seldom interfered with internal aggression.

This example demonstrates how the leadership was able to structure internal activities of the cottage. The boys from Tables IV and V wanted to play baseball with Cottage 5. There was little response from Tables I and III, so the idea fizzled out. Fifteen minutes later the idea was renewed. This time most of the boys from Table III, notably Foster, spoke up for it. The alcove resounded with enthusiasm and the boys played ball after supper.

The leaders received numerous material and psychic rewards. They moved around more freely on the campus than others. At the end of his stay, Davis was eating breakfast with the girls in their cottage. When discovered, this caused much consternation at Hollymeade, because it indicated the extent to which some boys were able to manipulate rigid rules.

The cottage leadership can be viewed somewhat as a solar system with Davis, Wolf, and Red Leon (later replaced by Foster) as the sun and the first perimeter of satellites—Parma, Drake, and Little—revolving around them; and the rest of the cottage around all six.

Positions are based on ability to fulfill clique standards. Artie Parma, George Little, and Gary Drake, who occupied the same room, were all subservient to Steve Davis and Red Leon. The three were frequently found in Davis' room, rarely the reverse.

George Little, the most insecure of the satellite trio, was a volatile, anxious boy brimming with hostility. His obsequious currying of favor contributed to his low prestige. Davis thought Little "was just a nudge in the cottage, and everybody had to get used to him. Sometimes guys just blew up and hit him a few times." Davis tolerated Little because Red Leon used him as a bushboy and protected him. When Red Leon left Hollymeade, Davis banished Little from Table III. Little's anxiety rose markedly, and he became much more difficult to handle.

Followers like Artie Parma, Gary Drake, and George Little were mainly on the defensive in the leadership group. Once Artie knocked Red Leon's spoon off the table by mistake. Red curtly ordered him to pick it up. Artie appeared to the observer overly contrite and apologetic for a member of the same subgroup.

Artie was Davis' personal valet. The two were inseparable; Steve gave the orders, and Art jumped to carry them out. Drake, the third of the subsidiary triumvirate, went out of his way to take risks in order to become part of the group. For example, if the boys wanted beer, Drake would go into town for it. So that the top boys would not think of him as a scrounger, he would offer to lend his jacket, which he had not even worn himself since it came from the dry cleaner.

Overt aggression became less frequent after the leaders had consolidated their position. They increased their distance from newcomers. "As the younger and new boys came in from other cottages, things grew worse," Davis complained. "We—Red Leon, Wolf, and I —stayed pretty much to ourselves. There were no fights, no kangaroo courts, and no more riots. In the beginning everything is fights, and after time goes on, things start slowing down. You fight less and think about leaving Hollymeade and taking care of yourself."

Steve Davis' "slowing down" (as evidenced by the absence of major rumbles or kangaroo courts) did not preclude his continued control over the cottage. The delinquent leader does not need to establish his dominance every moment. He exudes aggression; it is implicit in every gesture. Past aggression results in the expectation, more effective than action, that if the occasion arose, Davis could conquer any opponent. Contrariwise, the "punk" in the cottage need not be humbled every day to be "status-bound."

The group "gives" to the leader his sense of power and prestige. What does the leader give to the group? Frequently more material goods than he receives. The leaders are adept at securing food, odds and ends, and cigarettes; the last named are a scarce commodity at Hollymeade. Steve Davis worked off-grounds and always had cigarettes, which he doled out to his friends. But more important, the leaders give security to the weaker boys in the sense of not oppressing them every moment. They "permit" them to exist.

The delinquent leader sets the tone of the cottage. Steve Davis claimed, "If they leave me alone, I will leave them alone." The hitch is that he constantly rationalized his aggression by projecting onto others his insecurities and inadequacies. *They* always wanted to attack *him*, so he literally beat them to the punch. A breach of a group standard sets in motion controls that swing the offender back to the standard and also keeps it alive in the minds of the other group members.

Red Leon usually provoked Davis into anti-social activities. After Leon left Hollymeade, Davis maintained his position with waning violence. Davis eventually was permitted to work off-grounds. He "went steady" with a Hollymeade girl and participated less in anti-social activities. During his last months at Hollymeade, he had a stabilizing influence upon the cottage. Periodically, top-clique boys, sparked by Steve Davis, were inspired to repair the cottage. However, this urge lasted only a couple of days and did not serve to increase the boys' collective sense of self-esteem.

b. "Con-Artists"

Several characteristics of the "con-artists" differentiated them from the rest of the Cottage 6 boys. In addition to expert ranking and pride in conniving, they were boastful about their athletic prowess and sexual exploits. Chuck Small, Perry Yearwood, and Ronny Miles occupied the same bedroom. The reader recalls that Chuck was mercilessly ranked out by the other two. Chet Ellins was close to this group. Jim Parker, a depressed and introverted boy, was in the clique, but not of it. He was literally and figuratively a "quiet type."

The playful, witty, uninhibited interactions of the con-artists made them fun to be with a times. At a fire drill, the usual kidding went on about the uselessness of the exercise. One of the boys suggested that they find matches and start a fire. Chet elaborated on the idea. Edna said she should not be standing outside because of her cold. Ronny countered, "Why don't you stay inside and burn?" During a meal Ronny turned around and pointed to the horse tattooed on his arm. He said he was going to make some clouds so that the horse would look as though it were taking off. He wanted something fantastic on his arm. Chet said at this point, "Why don't you put your face on it?"

This clique gambled extensively. No one trusted the other; each told the observer privately that the other would "stick a knife" in him if his back were turned. The "con-men" had fashioned a small conniving subsociety in which each stoutly believed that his best friends were incorrigible double-crossers. Of all the cliques, the one made up of con-men is the most manipulative and exploitative. They believe in grasping what they can and in deceiving anyone who stands in their way.

The most stable boy in this group was Ellins, who became much less closely associated with the others during the last months of his stay at Hollymeade. He participated less in gambling and excursions to the girls' cottages. Previously he had been one of the leading instigators of deviant activities at the institution.

Chuck Small, who never reformed at Hollymeade, was quite another con-artist. Among adults he projected an image of wanting to change. This picture, however, was inconsistent with the role he played in the cottage; he never ceased stealing and "conning"

money and services from peers and lower-echelon staff. His role changed only at the end of his stay when he became a tough guy in addition to being a con-man. Miles and Yearwood also bullied, manipulated, and ranked young, weak boys like Rabin until they departed.

c.   "Quiet Types"

According to Steve Davis, "quiet types" are boys who mind their p's and q's, and neither join up with tough guys nor accept a bushboy status. Frequently they are institutionalized boys who have learned to fade into the setting by keeping their emotional distance and cooperating with the boys at the top.

Nate Lane and Stan Kranz experienced inordinate rejection in their lives. Their childhood was spent in foster homes and institutions. Neither of the boys could maintain social relationships. Both were placed on the farm at Hollymeade and because of the odd hours their work-schedule demanded they were excluded from many cottage activities. Their isolation led them to depend heavily upon each other.

Most of the boys found Nate Lane personable but they saw little of him. After a hard day's work he was tired and went to bed upon his return to the cottage. Lane led "just an existence" according to Chet. Stan Kranz, too, was described by his peers as "just another guy, an easy boy to get along with, but who could be antagonizing or obnoxious when he tried to be a part of the group."

d.   The Bushboys

The low-status cliques are characterized by childish regressive behavior. They are a pale imitation of the tough boys farther up in the hierarchy. Preoccupied with their low status, they over-react to anyone's getting something "on them." They ranked each other incessantly. This group manifested the least solidarity; they bickered constantly and displayed blatant hostility among themselves. Petane, Ricky, and Rabin quarreled over the most trivial matters, be it Chinese sauce at the table (spilling it on the other's plate) or possession of a rubber band.

The interactions between members of the lower half of the hierarchy are qualitatively different from those of the "toughs" and "con-artists" in the upper half. Low-status boys' anger was turned inward and was displayed in eccentric behavior, partly because the boys lacked objects in the cottage upon whom to displace it. Note the group's bizarre, self-and-other directed punitiveness:

Lane poured huge amounts of ketchup in his coffee and soup, as well as on his food. . . . For almost an hour Petey banged the wall hard with his strap and fist. . . . At breakfast Rabin ate fifteen pieces of toast, looking to Nate for confirmation. . . . At Table IV Petey and Colorado flipped forks at each other during the meal. . . .

The way in which social position and personality intersect is illustrated in the case of Rabin. After the second year, he became bitterly resentful of his bushboy status in the cottage. He showed paranoid tendencies and overreacted to innocuous situations. As he said, "You just can't trust anybody. If I do anything for someone, I still get bawled out. I get blamed for everything." Once John looked into his room and innocently asked if he was going to clean it up. Rabin walked out muttering to himself, "I'm just a lazy guy, that's all, I'm just lazy."

His mounting anger so unsettled him that he isolated himself from almost everyone in the cottage. During dinner one night Edna asked Rabin why he did not play baseball. Rabin's reply was that he did not like "to get into arguments with the guys around here." While most bushboys manage to ascend from this status, Rabin and Kahn became more firmly bound to it.

e. The Scapegoat

Scapegoating has already been touched upon in the previous chapter. Some of its subtleties may now be elaborated. In the authoritarian social structure there is always one target below to be pecked at, except at the very bottom. In the cottage this rock-bottom target is younger than the other boys, a lone arrival who has difficulty gaining allies.

Colorado was pressured at first by Davis. But not long after Colorado had entered the cottage, he adapted to its bullying ideology and tested his new-found strength on a "green" arrival. How Colorado bullied Strange has been already illustrated. Rick Kahn, a bushboy of long standing, constantly ranked, bullied, and harassed Joe Chase when he first arrived. As a result Joe went AWOL for eight months.

New boys identify first with the lowest status members. They automatically become "punks" unless they have unusual physical strength, courage, or intelligence. A new boy will sleep in the "punk room," eat at Table IV or V, and participate with his low-status clique members in school and recreational activities. The frequent interaction with low-status members consolidates the new boys position as a member of an inferior clique.

A new boy should be prepared physically, socially, and emotionally to be isolated from the others for weeks and even months. What will happen afterward depends in part on his background. If he is of middle-class origin, nonverbal, and effeminate, he may be subjected to prolonged testing and ranking. Depending upon his reactions to this ribbing, he may become further isolated from peers in circular fashion until he is overwhelmed by physical coercion, fear, or anxiety. A case in point was Mavis, a new boy admitted to Hollymeade because of participation in delinquency of a sexual nature. The boys called him "queer" from the outset. He was estranged from the others in the cottage during his whole stay at Hollymeade.

A new boy who gains the reputation of being a "punk" will be ranked out not only by top-status boys but by those lower down as well. Sometimes leaders who see middle-status boys oppressing new boys will step in and stop it. The leaders feel, in these cases, that middle-status boys sometimes ascribe to themselves prerogatives that belong only to the "big men."

As the reader is aware, Werner was an example par excellence of a scapegoat. Petey, a low-status, nonverbal, anti-social, extremely introverted boy, confronted Werner shortly after the latter's arrival. Petey, Rabin, and Meller had succeeded in placing a tack under Werner's seat in the classroom. Werner jumped and angrily yelled, "What the hell's wrong with you comedians?" Petey laughed, Rabin smiled, and Meller bellowed uproariously. Werner looked across the room at Petey, saying, "You try that again and I'll beat your head in." But Werner did not dare move toward Petey, who laughed, while Rabin smiled. Werner was only a "punk."

Scapegoats at the bottom of the pecking order hate their exploiters, their clique "friends," and themselves. They are caught in the most vicious circle at Hollymeade; as catchall targets, it is impossible for them to escape the constant pervasive exploitation of the overbearing toughs and manipulative "con-artists," and they are even prey to bush-boys.

As top leaders move out of the cot-tage, its rigid social structure loosens, and the boys have an opportunity to experiment with new roles. Chuck Small was continually ranked and insulted by Perry Yearwood and Ronny Miles, but when these boys and Davis left Hollymeade, Chuck was able to assume a position of aggressive superiority in the cottage.

Scapegoats, such as Rick Kahn on the other hand, are unable to modify their roles despite the length of time spent in the institution. Here, personality factors are important. Kahn, diagnosed as a borderline schizophrenic, was too obnoxious and unpredictable to become acceptable to the others. He was used (unwittingly, of course) to indoctrinate new boys entering the cottage. Kahn made life so miserable for new boys that they always left his room as soon as a bed was available elsewhere.

THE DELINQUENT SOCIAL SYSTEM

Every social system is stratified in terms of the power and prestige distributed among its members. The recruitment for positions and their consolidation vary with the character of the group and its developmental stages. The criteria that distinguish the superior and inferior strata depend upon the core standards of the group. The durability of Cottage 6's delinquent social structure is supported by sanctions of violence and manipulation that are most efficiently employed by the top-clique boys, but pervade the whole cottage.

It is our fundamental assumption that the deviant interaction described in the foregoing pages is a reflection not only of individual pathology but also of the structure and processes of the group in which the behavior was enacted. The deviant processes are shown in this chapter to become institutionalized into different roles in the social structure.

Just like the individual, the group has a history. Into its evolving network of complementary positions each boy is inducted.

This is where we part company with those who regard psychopathology as dysfunctional to the social system in which it is enacted. The functional approach to deviancy detailed in this chapter views deviant behavior as a crucial component in the equilibrium of cottage social organization.

The big man and the con-artist, on the one hand, the scapegoat and the queer, in the other, constitute the extremes of the cottage role system continuum of peer group behavior in the cottage. Both of these ends of the continuum, as well as those in intermediate positions, are interdependent and define the emotional, intellectual, and social range of cottage life. The social equilibrium built around delinquent or deviant patterns may obtain for long periods until the system in turn gives rise to behavior that is dysfunctional for the group and ends in the breakdown and elimination of boys whose behavior cannot be contained by the deviant cottage system. . . .

It is worth noting in passing that the distribution of power roles in other cottages is somewhat different from the pattern in Cottage 6. In some groups the tough boys, the "power" or the "big men," maintain absolute hegemony and assign the con-artists subsidiary positions. This was the case in Cottage 6. In other cottages, however, the gamblers and con-artists unite with the tough leaders (sometimes individuals combine con-artistry and toughness to rule over the punks or bushboys). Muscles and brains unite to ensure a steady flow of psychic and material services upward.

The power pattern of Cottage 7 seemed to be a clear instance of the foregoing description. Its structure, which is vividly portrayed by Chet Ellins (who lived there for most of his stay in Hollymeade), can be appreciated in light of our growing knowledge of Cottage 6's social organization:

QUESTION. Who ran the cottage when you first came into "7"?

ANSWER. (After naming a few boys) But you see a cottage is never actually run by one guy. One guy has brains, the other guy has muscles, but always four or five, or three guys are the power in the group. They might not be the roughest guys, but they are the power. What they want to do mostly is what the group does, and a lot of smart guys don't actually want to become the leader. They prefer to be the guy in the back; they want to be the power of the group. The cottage guys clique up and hang around together. And these groups, you know, are your power.

QUESTION. When did you become a power in "7"? I know you did, because it was one of the reasons they changed you. Right?

ANSWER. Well, that's true. But I came into power in a different way from a lot of the other kids. I like to gamble, and I'm good at it. And through the fact that you can win, well, then you have money. That automatically makes the group come to you at one point or another.

QUESTION. Is that right?

ANSWER. Guys are going AWOL; they got to come to you to get money. They try to get you to like them. And in order to get you to like them, when you make a suggestion, they follow it because there's no reason to antagonize the hand that's feeding you. So that's how I came into power: guys owed me money, so guys were afraid to get me mad because they'd have to pay. I had my strong arm boys that were willing to collect for me. . . .

QUESTION. Like whom?

ANSWER. Like Foster, and Simon, like myself. You see, I mean I wasn't. . . . The whole point is that I never had to use them. I'd collect my own debts, but yet everybody knew that these guys would help me collect my debts if it ever came to something like that and it never did.

QUESTION. Well, then, were you the three guys who were the top guys up there?

ANSWER. Yes.

Cottage 6 can be visualized as a diamond-shaped social system [Diagram 2] that persists as leaders depart and middle-status and low-status boys rise in the hierarchy. Every stratum combines a cluster of privileges and duties. The translation of each subgroup's and clique's norms into concrete action is seen as the functioning of the diverse roles in the cottage.

SUMMARY

The focalization of power in a few hands at the top of the social hierarchy is the heart of Cottage 6's social system. Toughness summarily gives status, and, together with manipulation, becomes the chief competence for gaining prestige. At their various stations in the social hierarchy the boys are sensitized and preoccupied with their rating because it controls so much of their behavior in the cottage.

Statuses are rigidly fixed and each

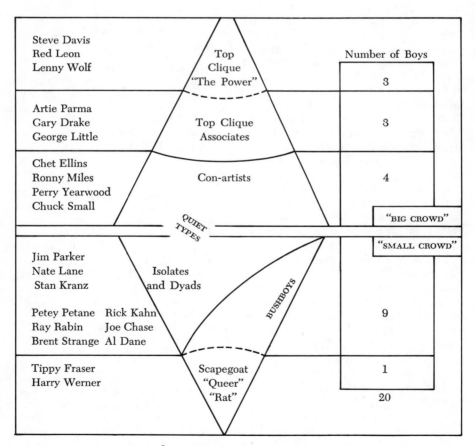

DIAGRAM 2.   A DIAMOND-SHAPED SOCIAL SYSTEM

boy is treated in accordance with the status assigned to him by the social system of the cottage. Social distance is greatest between subgroups and cliques; least among the members of a clique. Within each clique there are pecking orders, miniature reproductions of the cottage social organization. Drake, a high-status "punk," had more in common with Strange and Werner, low-status punks, than with members of his own clique. Dane, on the other hand, as we shall shortly see, had more in common with the big men at the top.

The chief way a boy changes his status is by challenging a higher-status boy to a fight. The outcomes of these encounters are firmly impressed in the boys' memories and drastically change the challenger's status and horizons in the cottage.

The omnipresence of the strong-weak continuum institutionalized in statuses and the lack of alternative identifications exaggerate the toughness norm. Internal aggression in a primary group creates an intense need for aggressors to rationalize their behavior. While exploiting their targets, they cite their queerness, sneakiness, and grubbiness, which justify further aggression until the stereotypes are fixed at both ends.

The drastic restrictions for achieving status within the cottage lead to exaggerated conformity with the peer group standards. These rigid patterns sharply limit the possibilities of personality experimentation and social change. A powerful reference group is thus created and interposed between the child and the staff, and challenges that staff's practices, values, and aspirations.

42.

The Effectiveness of Correctional Programs*

James Robison and Gerald Smith

The introduction of reform measures in correctional programs in the latter part of the nineteenth century was largely the result of a desire for humane treatment of offenders. The offender was no longer regarded as an evil person who "freely chose" to engage in criminal activities; rather, he was viewed as having been "socially determined" to take deviant roles and now in need of "treatment" to "reform" or "rehabilitate" him into a socially adequate individual. His change in status from an "evil" person to one who is "sick" was paralleled by the growth of a "correctional" system to handle the "patients." The retributive slogan, "Let the punishment fit the crime," was displaced by a new principle, "Let the treatment fit the needs of the offended," which called for educational training, psychotherapy (primarily group counseling), and community treatment (usually some variation of probation or parole).

These new correctional programs focused primarily on the offender; however, recent efforts have also been directed toward the community.[1] How effective any of these various reform measures has been in rehabilitating offenders (i.e., in reducing the probability of recidivism) was not studied very rigorously until recently because of numerous problems of evaluation.

Assessment of the relative effectiveness of various correctional programs is difficult because adequate measures of performance have not been authoritatively established. Very often the attempt to measure the behavior of the system's clients is confounded by the reporting procedures of the system. The results of such research yield insights about the personnel of the system but tell us little about its clients.[2]

Research into the correctional system has been concerned with answering these five basic questions about the behavior of convicted persons subjected to alternative procedures:

* Based on a special report by James Robison to the California Legislature Ways and Means Committee, Select Committee on Criminal Justice, 1969.

SOURCE. James Robison and Gerald Smith, "The Effectiveness of Correctional Programs,* from *Crime and Delinquency*, Volume 17, No. 1, January 1971, pp. 67–80. Reprinted with permission.

[1] President's Commission on Law Enforcement and Administration of Justice, *The Challenge of Crime in a Free Society* (Washington, D.C.: U.S. Government Printing Office, 1967).

[2] J. Robison and P. Takagi, "Case Decisions in a State Parole System," California Department of Corrections, Research Division, Administrative Abstract, Research Report No. 31, 1968.

1. Will they act differently if we lock them up rather than place them on probation?

2. Will they recidivate less if we keep them locked up longer?

3. Do educating and "treating" in prison reduce recidivism?

4. Does supervising them more closely in smaller parole caseloads reduce recidivism?

5. What difference does it make whether we discharge prisoners outright or supervise them on parole?

The answers to these questions are not easy to obtain because of all the influences that act on the measuring instruments. Nevertheless, a review of current research will illustrate the problems of evaluation of correctional effectiveness and will yield insights into the probable effects of various penal measures.

1. LOCK THEM UP?

Deciding whether to place an offender on probation or to imprison him is not determined by the relative rehabilitative efficacy of the two approaches. The courts place only their "best risks" on probation; the persons who are imprisoned differ in many ways from those given probation. Hence a simple analysis of the difference in recidivism rates between prison and probation cases will not answer questions about their relative effectiveness. Exploring this difference requires control for case differences.

One possible way to control for case differences is to make random assignment of cases to either probation or prison, as in, for example, the California Youth Authority's Community Treatment Project (CTP), which has been in operation since 1961 and has been widely acclaimed for its promise. After commitment to the Reception Center, wards were randomly assigned either

to (1) a "control" group, confined in an institution and then given regular parole, or to (2) an "experimental" group, released immediately to small special caseloads in the community (9.5 parolees per agent, compared with 55 per agent under regular supervision).[3] A cohort follow-up has demonstrated statistically significant differences favoring community treatment. At the fifteen-months period, 30 per cent of male experimentals had "violated parole or had been unfavorably discharged," compared with 51 per cent of male controls (and 45 per cent of regular statewide Youth Authority releasees). At the 24-months period, these outcomes were 43 per cent and 63 per cent, respectively, again favoring the experimental group. If we take these findings at face value, we are forced to conclude that probation has been proven to be a more effective correctional program than imprisonment for reducing recidivism. But has it?

Within certain boundaries, the recidivism rate can be influenced by the decision-making authorities.[4] The technical violation rate has been shown to vary between parole agents handling similar cases and has markedly influenced the recidivism rates of their wards.[5] In the CTP study, the recidivism rates were managed in such a way as to make the experimentals appear favorable. "The bulk of control failures (68%) was accounted for by the cate-

[3] California Legislature, "Analysis of the Budget Bill of the State of California for the Fiscal Year July 1, 1968, to June 30, 1969," 1969.

[4] Robison and Takagi, *supra* note 2, and J. Robison, M. Gagerstrom, G. Smith, and R. Kingsnorth, "2943 PC Follow-up: Review of the First Year of Adjustment Subsequent to Consideration of Parole Termination," California Department of Corrections, Bay Area Research Unit, 1967.

[5] J. Robison and P. Takagi, "The Parole Violator as an Organization Reject," University of California, School of Criminology, 1968.

gory of Parole Agent Casework Decision (i.e., agent's recommendation to the Youth Authority Board that a given ward's parole be revoked), although this same category accounted for no more than 29% of the Experimental failures."[6] In re-examination of the data, Lerman found that "the chance that an Experimental boy's offense will be handled in a 'revoking' manner is lower if the offense is low or moderate in severity. Experimentals are judged similarly to the Controls only when the offenses are of high severity."[7] The experimentals were no less delinquent in their behavior than the controls; in fact, they committed more "known" delinquent offenses than the controls (2.81 per experimental boy; 1.61 per control boy).[8] This is probably an effect of increased supervision—i.e., if the controls had been watched as carefully, there would have been no differences between the two. The important point, however, is that an ideological belief in the effectiveness of community treatment apparently altered the experimental results.

In the light of these facts CTP gives little support to the thesis that probation is superior to institutionalization for reducing the recidivism rate. There appears to be no difference between the two approaches. One might, however, still argue in favor of "community treatment" on humanitarian and economic grounds.

Another relevant project that attempted to test the relative effectiveness of community treatment was conducted by the Northern California Service League; it involved adult offenders given

professional casework service in lieu of a jail or prison term.

It provided for the treatment of any adult offender referred by the Superior or Municipal Courts of San Francisco who had been found guilty of an offense other than one relating to drunkenness and whose sentence would ordinarily be a county jail or prison term, were the offender not referred to the project for treatment. . . . The second condition, namely that the offender would ordinarily receive a jail or prison term were it not for referral to the project, was to insure that the group treated by the project would be the group that would ordinarily be going to jail or prison and would not include those who would ordinarily be given probation.[9]

Assignment was, thus, not random. Checks upon whether referrals were representative of those being confined revealed that project cases tended to be somewhat younger and included fewer minority ethnic group members, a disproportionately low number of narcotic offenders, and a disproportionately high number of property offenders (e.g., crimes against property, 67 per cent vs. 48 per cent for those jailed and imprisoned in the same year; assaultive crimes, 15 per cent vs. 16 per cent; sexual abuse, 4 per cent vs. 5 per cent; narcotics indulgence or abuse, 12 per cent vs. 25 per cent). The attempt to evaluate outcome matched project cases with jail releasees on age, sex, race, type of offense, and time of release. By the criterion chosen (no arrests or only one or two arrests but no convictions), project cases ($N = 95$) appeared to do better than jail releasees: 80 per cent favorable, compared with 70 per cent; however, the project sponsors consider the findings tentative and comment that

[6] R. Warren, T. Palmer, *et al.*, "An Evaluation of Community Treatment for Delinquents," California Youth Authority, Community Treatment Project Research Report No. 7, 1966.
[7] P. Lerman, "Evaluating the Outcome of Institutions for Delinquents," *Social Work*, July 1968.
[8] *Ibid.*

[9] Conbrose, "Final Report of the San Francisco Rehabilitation Project for Offenders," Northern California Service League, 1966.

the evaluative techniques are faulty.[10] Nevertheless, it would be safe to conclude that project cases did just as well as those confined. The study does not support any claim that institutional confinement is more effective than community supervision.

2. KEEP THEM LOCKED UP LONGER?

The phrase "optimum time for release" suggests that the releasing authority knows when that point in time has been reached and is ready to act on that knowledge. Implicit in it is the notion that there is a relationship between the amount of time served and the probability of recidivism. But is there?

The findings of the California Department of Corrections study of Advanced Release to Parole for the 1954-57 release years are shown in Table 1. The performance difference of 4 per cent in favor of early releases after six months is attributable to their being low risk cases. When base-expectancy controls are introduced for quality of case, early release makes no difference. "All differences appear to be accounted for by base expectancies or length of parole term variability."[11] This was found true when follow-up comparisons were extended to analysis of one-, two-, and three-year exposure periods, and regardless of the size of the parole caseload to which men were released.[12]

On the other hand, there is some evidence that the practice of keeping men in prison longer in itself increases the probability of recidivism. Jaman[13] recently compared parole performances, since 1957, of California first prison releases of persons originally committed for Robbery 1st or 2nd. (On June 30, 1968, 41.6 per cent of the adult felon prison population consisted of men in these offense categories.[14]) They were compared according to whether they had served less or more than the median time in prison for the offense in the particular release year. Cohort follow-up for six-, twelve-, and 24-month periods consistently shows, by almost every criterion (percentage "favorable," percentage returned with new commitment, percentage returned to finish term), a performance advantage favoring those released earlier. To counter the argument that such findings proved merely that the poorer risks were retained longer, Jaman extended the analysis to include control matching on age, ethnic group, base-expectancy level, parole region of release, and type of parole supervision received ("work unit" or "conventional" caseload) and applied it to prisoners released in 1965.

For all offense categories and in all follow-up periods, the percent of favorable outcome among the men who served less than the median time was greater than among those who served more than the median months. Almost half of the testable comparisons showed statistically significant differences. In fact, in the matched samples of men who had been committed for Robbery 1st, those who served less than the median months had a much higher percent of favorable outcome in all three follow-up periods.[15]

It is difficult to escape the conclu-

[10] *Ibid.*

[11] P. Mueller, "Advanced Releases to Parole," California Department of Corrections, Research Division, Research Report No. 20, 1965.

[12] *Ibid.*

[13] D. Jaman, "Parole Outcome and Time Served by First Releases Committed for Robbery and Burglary, 1965 Releases," California Department of Corrections, Measurement Unit, 1968.

[14] California Department of Corrections, "California Prisoners, 1964–66," Research Division, Administrative Statistics Section, 1968.

[15] D. Jaman, "Parole Outcome for First Releases for Selected Commitment Offenses by Time Served before First Release," California Department of Corrections, Research Division, Measurement Unit, 1968.

Table 1

PERCENTAGE OF COMPLETELY CLEAN PAROLE RECORDS WITHIN SIX MONTHS
AFTER RELEASE TO PAROLE IN 1954 TO 1957 BY SIPU ASSIGNMENT
AND TYPES OF PAROLE RELEASE

Type of Parole Release	All Assignments (1954-1957)		Type of Assignment (1954-1957) (Percent)		
	No. Released	Per cent "Clean"	Small or Medium Caseloads	SIPU Large Caseloads	Non-SIPU Large Caseloads
Regular	7,884	68	70	68	69
Advanced	3,116	73	74	72	72
Difference	—	—	4	4	3

sion that the act of incarcerating a person at all will impair whatever potential he has for crime-free future adjustment and that, regardless of which "treatments" are administered while he is in prison, the longer he is kept there the more will he deteriorate and the more likely is it that he will recidivate. In any event, it seems almost certain that releasing men from prison earlier than is now customary in California would not increase recidivism.

The likelihood of recidivism, however, may play relatively little part in the decision to retain many prisoners beyond their legal minimum term.

Sheldon Messinger points to another "hardly surprising" consideration—order within the prisons:

The felt need to maintain control over inmates moves prison officials to seek discretion over sentencing. . . . Prison officials are charged with the management of prisons; whatever the ultimate ends of imprisonment, from the officials' point of view a first requisite is effective influence over inmate conduct. So long as inmates desire freedom, restrictions of freedom—threatened and actual—will provide a possible strategy for control, for effective influence; and the correctional establishment as a whole is premised on the desire of inmates for freedom.[16]

[16] S. Messinger, "Strategies of Control" University of California, Center for the Study of Law and Society, 1968.

Thus, just as prison overcrowding creates a pressure for either shorter average terms or increased capital outlay, the need for inmate control creates a pressure for lengthened confinement to maintain, by example, incentives for cooperative conduct.

3. DO SOMETHING WITH THEM INSIDE?

Group counseling has been one of the most widely applied and recommended prison treatment techniques. Elements of this treatment (e.g., ventilation of feelings and help toward self-understanding) were presumed to advance "rehabilitation" and, secondarily, to support institutional order by helping prisoners "adjust to the frustrations" and "improve the emotional climate of the institution."[17] To assess its effect on the primary goal of rehabilitation (operationally defined as the reduction of recidivism or the probability of recidivism), it is necessary to design an experimental situation utilizing rigorous controls. Only infrequently are treatment programs subject to the types of experimental testing necessary for valid evaluation.[18] Much of the pub-

[17] A. Fenton, "Group Counseling—A Preface to Its Use in Correctional and Welfare Agencies," Sacramento, Calif., Institute for the Study of Crime and Delinquency, 1961.

[18] L. T. Wilkins, *Evaluation of Penal*

lished research on group counseling in a prison setting deals with simple descriptions of the program,[19] theoretical justifications,[20] or shoddy "evaluations" without an adequate control group and random assignment of cases.

A recent study conducted to test the effect of group counseling in prison on postrelease behavior used a randomized assignment procedure and an adequate control group.[21] It is a true cohort follow-up (N=968), with 36-months outcome obtained for each subject regardless of whether he was in custody, still on parole, or discharged from parole. All the subjects were from one prison, "a medium-security institution with its population an almost perfect representation of modal departmental prisoner characteristics"[22]; hence, there was no control group of nonimprisoned felons. While in prison the men were randomly assigned to (1) small counseling groups (Research Group Counseling, $N = 171$), (2) large groups (Community Living, $N = 68$), and (3) a control group (C-Quad, $N = 269$) where no counseling was given; the remainder of the men in the sample chose either to join group counseling (Regular Group Counseling, $N = 274$) or to not participate at all (Voluntary Nonparticipation, $N = 173$). The study sample was limited to those who had at least six months' exposure to programming; the average number of group counseling

sessions was forty. The results of the study are shown in Table 2.

There were no differences in parole outcome by treatment status measured at 6, 12, 24, and 36 months after release, . . . no treatment or control group differences on the number of misdemeanor or felony arrests recorded in the parole record, no differences in total number of weeks spent in jail, and no differences in most serious disposition received within three years after release.[23]

The researchers concluded:

Thousands of inmates and hundreds of staff members were participating in this program at a substantial cost to the Department of Corrections in time, effort, and money. . . . Contrary to the expectations of the treatment theory, there were no significant differences in outcome for those in the various treatment programs or between the treatment groups and the control group.

Furthermore, contrary to sociological expectations, participation in group counseling and community living did not lessen even the limited endorsement of the inmate code, nor did it result in a demonstrable decrease in frequency of prison discipline problems. . . .

It would seem that in order for the Department of Corrections to continue to justify the widespread use of group counseling some new arguments must be advanced, such as "participation in group counseling gives custodial officers a real part in the treatment program and seems to improve their morale" or "group sessions add a little variety to inmate life and take up time."[24]

Nevertheless, the advocates of "treatment" programs can still argue that if

---

Measures (New York: Random House, 1969).

[19] G. Sykes, The Society of Captives (New York: Atheneum, 1966).

[20] R. R. Korn and L. W. McCorkle, Criminology and Penology (New York: Holt, Rinehart, and Winston, 1966), ch. 20.

[21] G. Kassenbaum, D. Ward, and D. Wilner, Prison Treatment and Its Outcome (to be published by John Wiley).

[22] The parole performance of the sample after thirty-six months was nearly identical with that in an earlier study of all men (N = 1,810) released to California parole in 1956.

[23] Kassebaum et al., op. cit. supra note 21.

[24] D. Ward, "Evaluation of Correctional Treatment: Some Implications of Negative Findings," Proceedings of the First National Symposium on Law Enforcement Science and Technology (Washington, D.C.: Thompson Book Co., 1967).

Table 2

POSTRELEASE STATUS AT 36 MONTHS BY TREATMENT STATUS (IN PERCENTAGE)

	Treatment Category				
Returned to Prison	"C" Quad	Voluntary Non-par- ticipation	Com- munity Living	Research Counseling	Regular Counseling
With New Term	16%	18%	27%	20%	15%
To Finish Term	31	37	29	31	34
After Discharge from Parole	1	1	3	—	—
Major Problems					
During Parole	5	3	10	5	6
After Discharge from Parole	4	7	1	1	4
Minor Problems					
During Parole	7	3	7	8	9
After Discharge from Parole	11	8	7	13	10
No Problems					
Still on Parole	4	5	3	4	4
Discharged from Parole	21	18	12	18	18
Total[a]	100%	100%	100%	100%	100%
N=955[b]	(269)	(173)	(68)	(171)	(274)

[a] Percentage totals are rounded.
[b] Not including: Dead = 8, Incomplete Information =5.

group counseling improved in overall quality, it would indeed have an impact on recidivism.

The correctional treatment program just discussed is not atypical; it is unusual only in that it was subjected to a rigorous evaluation. Walter Bailey evaluated one hundred reports on correctional programs and outcome and found no solid indications of treatment efficacy[25]; Robert Martinson completed a similar study for the New York Governor's Special Committee on Criminal Offenders.[26] Despite the continuing popularization of various treatment programs and the increased attention devoted to more rigorous designs for their evaluation, *there are still no treatment techniques which have unequivocally demonstrated themselves capable of reducing recidivism*.

One of the major proposed efforts of the California Department of Corrections in institutional treatment is "medical-psychiatric" programing despite the absence of any evidence that its current model for such operations, the California Medical Facility, is superior in rehabilitative efficacy to routine prison programing.[27] Professionalization and upgrading of treatment services are de-

[25] W. Bailey, "Correctional Outcome: An Evaluation of 100 Reports," University of California, Los Angeles, School of Social Welfare.

[26] R. Martinson, Department of Sociology and Anthropology, City College of New York (personal communication).

[27] Similarly, there has been no evidence that the Department's Outpatient Psychiatric Clinics have any effect on recidivism.

fensible on the grounds of important secondary objectives—special client needs and benefits—but it is doubtful that these services are useful for reducing recidivism.

Processing an offender as ill (and he may, in fact, be ill) is hardly an advance over processing him as evil (and he may also, in fact, be evil). Neither formulation has much relevance in prison, since the inmate's primary status is that of a warehoused object. The California Department of Corrections plans to confer openly the patient status of "medical-psychiatric" bed upon many who are now looked upon as only inmates ("general purpose" beds). The change in nomenclature may enhance the Department's image and will certainly spiral its costs, but any measurable improvement in performance is unlikely.

Just as, historically, the number of witches rose as a consequence of an increase in the number of witch hunters and then declined, not in response to the hunters' rehabilitative efforts but rather as a consequence of corrective excesses that thinned the ranks of the witch hunters,[28] correction may be approaching a turning point. Yet even today, we find passages such as the following, freshly in print:

Society's perception of criminals is changing. Criminals now can be seen as bad or sick. If they are bad, they require custody; if they are sick, they require treatment. The treatment-versus-custody controversy has raged in the Corrections field for several decades, but today the treatment advocates appear to be winning.[29]

[28] With the rise of rationalism, and the disbelief in a personal God, came a corresponding disbelief in his opposite, the Devil. . . . A decline in the acceptance of miracles meant a decline in the acceptance of spells." P. Hughes, *Witchcraft* (Baltimore: Penguin Books, 1965), p. 42.
[29] M. Mathews, "Correctional Rehabilitation: Boom or Bust?" Federal Offenders

Since nothing much is won if either side wins, maybe it's time to call off the game.

The narcotic addict has recently been transferred from the ranks of the bad to those of the sick, through little more than a change in the procedural labels: civil rather than criminal commitment; outpatient rather than parole supervision. Opposition to commitment for a treatment not proven effective has been voiced on the grounds that it is cruel and unusual punishment, that it denies to a person "accused" of illness the stringent legal protections afforded a person accused of crime, and that it is hardly different from imprisonment.[30]

In this movement to civil commitment, California was, as usual, in the forefront, having established in 1961 a model that was recently copied in New York. The program, the California Rehabilitation Center (CRC), has recently been evaluated. Findings from a three-year cohort follow-up on CRC program performance of 1,209 first releasees to outpatient status indicated:

1. Seventeen per cent received a discharge from the program after completing three continuous years on outpatient status.
2. Sixty-seven per cent were returned to the CRC.
3. Thirty-three per cent received a new criminal conviction during their first release (22 per cent misdemeanors and 11 per cent felonies).
4. Seventy-one per cent were detected as having used drugs illegally (63 per cent opiates and 8 per cent other dangerous drugs or marijuana).
5. Characteristics most strongly related to completing the three-year period successfully were: being white;

Rehabilitation Program, Fourth Annual Conference, San Antonio, 1968.
[30] J. Kramer, J. Berecoches, and R. Bass, "Civil Commitment for Addicts," *American Journal of Psychiatry*, December 1968.

staying at CRC a short time; living with one's spouse; living outside of Los Angeles, Orange, San Francisco, or Sacramento counties; and working 75-100 per cent of the time.[31]

The findings, applicable only to first releasees, speak for themselves. Those returned to the center perform even more poorly, of course, upon subsequent release. For example, of all men released in 1966, 50 per cent were returned before a single year in the community had elapsed; the rates were 48 per cent for first releasees, 54 per cent for second releasees, and 61 per cent for third releasees.[32] Note also (see item 3 above) that one out of three shuttled from the ranks of the sick to the ranks of the bad —"new criminal conviction"—though relatively few to the extent of a felony.

When such results are interpreted as "a modest degree of success,"[33] the emphasis certainly belongs on "modest," and one must also ask, "results more successful than what?" That a treatment of this caliber continues to expand and obtain funding makes it obvious that demonstration of effectiveness is a token promise rather than a consequential issue in determining where public investment will be placed. There are now two "habits" to support—the ailment and the costly treatment.

While group counseling has been the most popular special treatment in prison programing, reduced caseload size represents the major approach in parole and probation to the problem of curbing recidivism. Findings on the efficacy of this approach will be reviewed next.

31 J. Berecoches, California Department of Corrections, Research Division, 1968 (personal communication).
32 J. Berecoches, R. Bass, and G. Sing, "Analysis of First-Year Experience of All Released from California Rehabilitation Center to Outpatient Status in 1966," California Rehabilitation Center, Narcotic Addict Outpatient Program Report No. 8, 1968.
33 Kramer *et al.*, *supra* note 30.

4. WATCH THEM MORE CLOSELY AFTERWARD?

The question of caseload size has been more exhaustively studied than any of the others, and hopes attached to caseload reduction have served to justify numerous demonstration projects. These projects typically ask complicated questions about the nature as well as the "intensity" of the supervision technique and explore offender-variable questions as well.

California has led the field in experimentation with caseload size in parole; for the past fifteen years, the Department of Corrections has been involved in manipulation of caseload size. The Special Intensive Parole Unit (SIPU), conducted from 1953 to 1964 in four phases, provides interesting information about the effects of variation in caseload size on recidivism. Following is a summary of the results of each phase of this project:

Phase One (SIPU I)—Provided for random assessment of cases released from the Department of Corrections to special fifteen-man caseloads (experimental) or the regular ninety-man caseloads. Cases remained in an experimental caseload for three months (believed to be the most vulnerable months for failure) and were then transferred to a regular caseload. An evaluation of Phase One revealed that the reduced caseloads had no measurable effect on parole outcome.

Phase Two (SIPU II)—The experimental caseloads were increased to thirty men, and the length of stay was increased to six months before transfer to a regular caseload. Again, no evidence of the superiority of the reduced caseload was demonstrated.

Phase Three (SIPU III)—The experimental caseloads were increased to thirty-five men, and the length of stay was increased to one year before transfer to a regular caseload. A two-year follow-up revealed that reduced caseload parolees did slightly better than those on regular caseloads and that the improvement was attributable to medium-risk parolees.

Phase Four (SIPU IV)—Attempts were made to explore the effects of parolee and officer types on case outcome. Caseload size was reduced to thirty and fifteen, and officers and parolees were matched on characteristics thought to be favorable to parole outcome. The results of the study indicated that these characteristics did not measurably affect parole outcome and that the only variable which mattered was the amount of time an officer had to devote to supervision. The fifteen-man caseload did no better than the thirty-man caseload.[34]

Phase Four of the study has been criticized for lack of precision.[35] There is also evidence that SIPU agents were responding to violations by their parolees in the same fashion as the Youth Authority's Community Treatment Project agents.[36] Thus, it is not known whether significant findings occurred because parolees were behaving differently or because parole agents were reacting differently to violations.

Despite the absence of good evidence supporting reduced caseloads, the California legislature in 1964 gave approval to the Work Unit program in parole. The result was that half the adult male parolees in the state were placed under reduced-caseload supervision, which required the hiring of many parole agents. The assignment of cases to the Work Unit program (average caseloads of about thirty-five based on an elaborate grading system whereby each case is assigned points according to the seriousness of the offense and other factors) was left to the regional classification representative. Thus, Work Unit cases are different from Conventional Unit cases (i.e., regular supervision caseloads averaging about seventy cases), and a comparison of performance for the two has to take this difference into account. In 1965, its first year of operation, there were 2,948 prison releases to Work Unit parole supervision, and 4,353 to Conventional supervision. The performance figures for the two types of supervision, based on a one-year cohort exposure period, are presented in Table 3.[37]

The difference in performance between the two types of supervision appears slight; nevertheless, the 3.2 per cent advantage in favorable outcome of Work Unit over Conventional is statistically significant. In interpreting these data, however, we must remember that the two populations are not directly comparable. For example, all persons classified as having a high potential for violence were assigned to the Work Unit program, which was found to be composed of better-risk parolees as measured by an actuarial prediction device (California Base Expectancy 61A). *When controls for parolee risk level were introduced, the difference in favorable outcome between the Work Unit and the Conventional Unit was erased, and conventional supervision was found to have a significantly lower rate of technical prison return.*[38]

In 1964 the federal probation system inaugurated the San Francisco Project, experimenting with caseloads of four sizes and random assignment. Like the Work Unit program, the project experienced an increase in the technical violation rates accompanying reduction in caseload size:

The minimum supervision caseload has a violation rate of 24.3%; and the "intensive" caseload, a violation rate of 37.5%.

---

[34] See S. Adams, "Some Findings from Correctional Caseload Research," *Federal Probation*, December 1967.

[35] *Ibid.*

[36] See text *supra* at notes 4–8; also, J. Robison, Progress Notes toward the Proposed Study of Parole Operations, California Department of Corrections, Bay Area Research Unit, 1965.

[37] Robison and Takagi, *supra* note 2.

[38] *Ibid.*

Table 3

ACTUAL PAROLE PERFORMANCE BY CASELOAD SIZE

Type of Parole Supervision	No. Released	Outcome (Percent)	
		Favorable	Technical Return
Work Unit Supervision	2948	65.8	15.7
Conventional Supervision	4353	62.6	14.4
Total	7301	63.9	15.0

. . . In the "ideal" caseloads some five or six times as much attention, as measured by direct contact with the offender and with others about him, did not produce a reduction in violations; and in the "intensive" caseloads, despite fourteen times as much attention as provided the minimum supervision cases, the violation rate not only failed to decline significantly, but increased with respect to technical violations. . . .[39]

The researchers concluded that the technical violation rate was a function of the amount of supervision—i.e., the intensified supervision enabled agents to discover a greater number of minor technical violations. Caseload groupings did not differ in regard to nontechnical violations.[40] Thus the small caseload was not demonstrated to be more effective in reducing recidivism.

5. CUT THEM LOOSE OFFICIALLY?

California prides itself on its extensive use of aftercare; about 90 per cent of male felons released from prison in recent years were released to parole supervision. Relatively little attention has been given to comparing men officially discharged from prison with men released on parole.

From 1960 through 1966, 4,854 male felons were discharged from prison at expiration of sentence.[41] Of these, 47 per cent were first releases, and it seems reasonable to assume that many of these men were kept the full time because of problems in their prison adjustment or concerns about releasing them. More than half the prison discharges had been previously returned from parole as violators—10 per cent with a new commitment and 43 per cent to finish their original term. One out of every five men who are returned to prison as technical violators is subsequently discharged from prison and the remainder are reparoled, compared to one out of ten who are returned with new commitment and one out of twelve leaving on first prison release.[42]

In general, then, one would expect men discharged from prison to be poorer risks than those placed on parole. While cohort follow-up is routinely available only for parolees, some return-to-prison data are available from the California Department of Corrections. Examination of these data indicate that discharged men have fewer return-to-prison dispositions than men released to parole supervision. This does not mean that men discharged from prison are better risks. The difference can most likely be accounted for by the circumstance that men in discharged status are not subject to administrative returns as are technical violators of parole.

[39] J. Lohman, A. Wahl, R. Carter, and S. Lewis, "The Intensive Supervision Caseload: A Preliminary Evaluation," University of California, School of Criminology, San Francisco Project No. 11, 1967.
[40] *Ibid.*

[41] California Department of Corrections, *supra* note 14.
[42] These proportions vary slightly from year to year.

In a more detailed study of men discharged or paroled from prison in California (781 discharged vs. 2,858 paroled), Muller found that, during the first two years, discharged cases had a more favorable postinstitutional outcome (i.e., no trouble or no disposition with a sentence over 89 days) than cases released to parole.[43] However, after three years there was no difference between the two groups in postinstitutional dispositions. The parolees' less favorable dispositions during the first two years were probably attributable to their "return to finish term," a disposition not possible for discharged men.[44]

The threshold of criminal or antisocial behavior that may result in return to prison is obviously higher for the exprisoner who is no longer officially under commitment to a correctional system. Does the convenience offered by administrative return to confinement offer sufficient protection to warrant its expense? Are we paying more for protection than it is worth?

CONCLUSION

In the opening section of this essay we noted that reform movements have been generated primarily by humanitarian rather than pragmatic considerations. "Treatment," the presumed antithesis of "punishment," becomes the banner under which such a movement takes shape, and the slogan "Let the treatment fit the offender" replaces "Let the punishment fit the crime." Punishment and treatment, however, are not opposites; the opposite of punishment is reward, and the "law of effect" posits the utility of both in shaping future behavior. Since punishment may be a rehabilitative tool, to talk of punishment *versus* rehabilitation is foolish. But to speak of reward vis-à-vis offenders becomes awkward, since it plays havoc with the concept of deterrence: openly rewarding persons to stop being criminals would seemingly impel others to commit criminal acts in order to secure the benefits offered for retirement from crime. Consequently, it becomes politically more convenient or less embarrassing to introduce the concept of treatment to counterbalance punishment. Punishment is manifestly unpleasant and may or may not "work," whereas treatment, while not intrinsically pleasant, escapes the definitely unpleasant connotations of punishment; furthermore, it is impliedly effective: treatment, almost by definition, is that which results in improvement of a condition. Thus, treatment gains an aura of being both nicer (more humane) and better (more effective).

In correctional practice, treatment and punishment generally coexist and cannot appropriately be viewed as mutually exclusive. Correctional activities (treatments) are undertaken in settings established as places of punishment. Restriction of freedom is a punishment, no matter whether it is imposed by physical confinement (jail or prison) or by surveillance of movement in the community (probation or parole). The punitive conditions are viewed as necessary for the administration of treatment, and the treatments are believed to account for whatever favorable results occur.

The real choice in correction, then, is not between treatment on one hand and punishment on the other but between one treatment-punishment alternative and another.

Analysis of findings in a review of the major California correctional programs that permit relatively rigorous evaluation strongly suggests the following conclusion: *There is no evidence to support any program's claim of superior rehabilitative efficacy.*

[43] Mueller, *supra* note 11.
[44] *Ibid.*

The single answer, then, to each of the five questions originally posed— "Will the clients act differently if we lock them up, or keep them locked up longer, or do something with them inside, or watch them more closely afterward, or cut them loose officially?"—is: *"Probably not."*

Examination of correctional programs in states other than California would probably yield essentially similar results and the conclusion may generally apply. There is considerable evidence that different types of offenders have markedly different likelihoods of recidivating, and there can be little doubt that the different available correctional program options have markedly different degrees of unpleasantness associated with them. Since the more unpleasant or punishing alternatives are more likely to be invoked for those offenders with serious present offenses or multiple past offenses, it is natural that different success

rates and *apparently* different degrees of effectiveness will attach to some alternatives, though these differences of effectiveness are illusory. Since the more unpleasant or punishing alternatives tend also to be the more expensive, the choice of appropriate disposition for offenders should be determined by the amount of punishment we want to impose and the amount of money we are prepared to spend in imposing it; it should not be obscured by illusions of differential rehabilitative efficacy.[45] If the choice is, in fact, merely between greater and lesser punishments, then the rational justification for choosing the greater must, for now, be sought in concepts other than rehabilitation and be tested against criteria other than recidivism.

[45] J. Robison, "It's Time to Stop Counting," Special Report to California Legislature Ways and Means Committee, Select Committee on Criminal Justice, 1969.

43.

Illusions of Treatment in Sentences and Civil Commitments*

Sol Rubin

When I first entered the field of justice and correction, I, like others, accepted the idea of treatment—efforts to rehabilitate criminals—not only as essential but as the motivating spirit of all I wanted to do. The concept of treatment is an article of faith for most people in correction. It is not a bad article of faith. But in recent years I have come to feel that it is not enough as a guide; and standing alone it may be wrong.

Some years ago, in a book on crime and delinquency, I expressed in the introductory chapter what I believe was, and still is, a humanitarian point of view. After going on for a while about rationalism, science, and humanitarianism, I said: "In brief, in the human sciences, to be scientific one must be humanitarian; to be anti-humanitarian is to be unscientific."[1]

It is still not a totally bad statement.

In fact, it isn't a bad statement at all. After all, what is more humanitarian than treatment? But if I were to say it again, I would not say it that way. It seems to me that bad things have been done and are being done under the guise of treatment. Treatment is giving humanitarianism a bad name, especially treatment that stimulates wide use of both criminal commitments and so-called civil commitments.

If I were to rewrite the statement I would be careful to say that it is possible for treatment *not* to be humanitarian, that treatment may be an invasion of civil rights, that there are instances where treatment may be harmful. I would be sure to say that before you decide to treat a person, even a convicted criminal, you must consider whether leaving him alone may not be better, better for him and better for society.

This may sound like a strange utterance from a person who considers himself humanitarian and may possibly be disquieting because only recently has the concept of a right to treatment been recognized.[2] I agree that it is an

* Adapted from a paper given at the University of South Carolina, March 29, 1968.

SOURCE. Sol Rubin, "Illusions of Treatment in Sentences and Civil Commitments" from *Crime and Delinquency*, Volume 16, No. 1, January 1970, pp. 79–92. Reprinted with permission.

[1] Rubin, *Crime and Juvenile Delinquency—A Rational Approach to Penal Problems* 24 (2d ed. 1961).

[2] Note, "The Nascent Right to Treatment," 53 Va. L. Rev. 1134 (1967).

important right and that it must become a protection for individuals. But it must *not* become a cover for depriving them of their liberty.

On reviewing recently what I had written in that book, I see that I was led into the use of the word "treatment" not in isolation, but as contrasted to "punishment." In general, when a criminal was sentenced, we regarded probation as treatment in contrast to imprisonment, which we called punishment, although we acknowledged that therapeutic efforts should be made in prison.

What especially troubles me is that we freely commit people in the name of treatment. But even probation as treatment must be examined. There are many instances when I would say, this defendant should be left alone, not placed on probation.

UNDER THE GUISE OF TREATMENT

My first experience with distortion of the use of treatment in correction, with destructive effect on individuals and correctional systems, came when I encountered the so-called indeterminate sentence.[3] For many years, legislators, judges, and experts of various kinds have talked about the indeterminate sentence as though it were the answer to the main problems in sentencing, including the problem of disparity in sentences, and have proudly rationalized it under the guise of treatment. The indeterminate sentence, they say, is the sentence under which treatment can take place, since release is dependent on the success of the prisoner's readjustment and rehabilitation.

But it does not work out that way at all. In practice, the indeterminate sentence has usually meant the establishment of minimum terms of parole

eligibility and the lengthening of maximum terms of imprisonment. In many jurisdictions the concept of the indeterminate sentence means that every offender committed is committed for the maximum term. The detrimental effect of long sentences, on correctional systems as well as on prisoners, is generally admitted and need not be discussed here.[4]

It must come as a surprise to many, as it did to me when I first encountered it, that the severity of criminal penalties has steadily increased over the years in this country.[5] This is one of the reasons for a steadily increasing ratio of prisoners. Whereas in the middle of the nineteenth century the ratio of state prisoners to the general population was 1 to 2,436, in the middle of the twentieth it was 1 to 1,000. By contrast, the number of prisoners in custody in England in 1930 was less than half what it was a hundred years before, although the population of England had doubled.[6] A number of factors are responsible for the increase in our prison population, but surely one is the introduction of the indeterminate sentence. By this time in most states a defendant who is committed to prison must serve the minimum term before even being considered for parole, and often the minimum term is so high that it completely defeats the theory of parole. A sentence of nineteen to twenty years, nineteen being the minimum term that must be served, is an obviously outrageous instance, but such sentences are handed down and they are upheld by the courts.

Far more common are sentences of five or seven to ten years. But even sentences with lower minimums—sentences, for example, of three to ten

---

[3] Rubin, "The Indeterminate Sentence—Success or Failure?" *Focus*, March 1949 (the article is brought up to date in Rubin, *op. cit. supra* note 1, ch. 8).

[4] See Rubin, Weihofen, Edwards & Rosenzweig, *The Law of Criminal Correction* 137–42.

[5] *Op. cit. supra* note 1, at 132.

[6] *Op. cit. supra* note 4, at 41.

years, also quite common—establish minimum terms of parole eligibility that are so long that a parole board, if it is to fulfill its function, must release the prisoner upon the expiration of the minimum term since, in many instances, earlier release would have been indicated and would have been granted except for the minimum term.

In brief, the principal effect of this treatment idea of indeterminate sentences has been an increase in the length of imprisonment.

Another instance of a treatment concept that boomerangs is the youth authority idea, which was introduced as a solution of the youth crime problem or at least as the way convicted youths should be sentenced. But there is evidence that the result has simply been to increase the percentage of commitments for youthful offenders and to increase the terms of commitment. In part, the attraction of the idea that a youth authority represents treatment induces some liberal judges to commit to youth authorities in cases in which they might otherwise have used probation.[7]

A good example of this development is what has happened under the Youth Corrections Act in the federal system. It is clear that those sentenced under the Act serve longer terms than those sentenced under the ordinary penal statute. In 1959-60 (the latest statistics I have) the average time served before release by all federal offenders—Youth Corrections Act offenders, delinquents, adults—was 16.4 months. Youth Corrections Act offenders served an average of 19.7 months; juvenile delinquents served 18 months; and adults served the smallest amount of time. The actual disparity is even greater than these figures show, since the high figures for juveniles and youths are included in reaching the average for all offenders.[8]

Has treatment for these offenders improved? Is the extra time in the longer term used for application of some treatment purpose that could not have been served under the shorter term? Not that I can discover. The treatment is the same as for prisoners committed under the regular penal laws.

PRISONS

What about commitments to prison under the regular penal law? Are these influenced by the illusion of treatment? Recently I was asked to speak at a conference whose theme was "Reducing Opportunities for Crime." I was instructed to discuss "the need for various levels of *confinement* to reduce opportunity for crime," but my remarks departed from that suggestion. I said that looking for ways to reduce opportunities for crime by treatment in prison was a delusion and that the entire criminal justice system would be wiser to avoid commitments to institutions when that can be done with safety to the community.[9]

The theme suggested to me, however, is a common one; otherwise we would not have the big prison system that we have in this country. With all the attacks on imprisonment, the correctional field is still far from an abolish-prisons movement. What has happened is that the treatment rationale has been superimposed on the ancient system of locking people up. While less brutality occurs in prisons today, it is still far from gone, even in some reputedly modern systems,[10] although some of the harsher forms of discipline—striped uniforms, lockstep, silence—have pretty much vanished. But the essence of im-

[7] *Op. cit. supra* note 1, ch. 7.
[8] *Ibid.*

[9] Proceedings, Indiana Conference on Crime and Prevention, Indiana University, Jan. 18, 1968.
[10] Horrible conditions in a disciplinary cell at Correctional Training Facility at Soledad, Calif., Jordan v. Fitzharris, 257 F. Supp. 674 (1966).

prisonment—the loss of contact with the world of work, family, freedom of movement—is still in operation.

I do not accept the gloss of treatment on modern imprisonment; I do not accept rationalizing imprisonment by the administration of treatment. A good illustration of this rationalization is a large study of imprisonment in the federal system reported in Daniel Glaser's *The Effectiveness of a Prison and Parole System.* The study measures the effectiveness of different forms of treatment in prison by recidivism rates, exactly the same test as was proposed to me in the conference just mentioned.

In exploring success and failure, the study came up with a number of findings. It concluded that some things with prisoners were better or worse than others but that much good was being done. For example, 250 successful releases were asked, "When would you say you changed most permanently from being interested in committing crime?" Four per cent said they had changed before sentencing and 13 percent placed the change at the time of sentencing or between sentencing and imprisonment, but most of the prisoners thought their prison experience was positive. Fifty-two per cent said that they changed their attitudes during imprisonment and 16 per cent said they changed after release. Only 10 per cent denied that they had ever changed, and they were mainly prisoners who said either that they were innocent or that they had been only unwittingly involved in their offense.

Other similar findings seemingly favorable to imprisonment were reported. Why was imprisonment useful? Wouldn't it be nice if it were mainly because of staff work? Glaser writes: "Of the 131 who reported that they changed during imprisonment, 65, or about half, credited a staff member with being influential in their reformation.

Only 11, or 8 per cent, credited the influence of fellow inmates as a factor in their change. The others who reported that their shift from criminal interests occurred in prison credited their own maturation, the deterrent effects of imprisonment, or the influence of persons outside the prison who wrote or visited them."

I do not buy that. The author contends that these data "all suggest that much reformation of criminals does occur with imprisonment, even though prisons certainly have deficiencies and may make some of their inmates more criminal." The data do not necessarily suggest this at all. What if many of these people succeeded *despite* imprisonment? Certainly, comparative statistics with successful releases demonstrate that their success rate would be at least as good if they had been placed on probation. Does inmate interpretation of reasons for change validate the proposition that imprisonment and the forces connected with it effected the change? I doubt it. The impulse to credit imprisonment with a change is especially strong in prisoners who are determined never to commit crime again. At most they would interpret their imprisonment as a reinforcement of a life orientation that they would have even without imprisonment. The possibility also exists of a conscious or subconscious wish to cooperate with the prison authorities or prison researchers.

The study interprets other prison experiences in the same unwarranted fashion, basing inferences on the initial assumption that these persons were in prison because they needed imprisonment to change their attitudes, a proposition not at all examined in the study. The implication of the study is that persons sentenced to prison are (more or less) those who ought to be there. But that is hardly the situation. What if one examined prisoners on the assumption that most of them should not have been committed? If only one of ten convicted felony offenders had been committed, what would the success and failure rates be? I believe that the success rate would be at least as good as when most of such offenders are committed, that the damage to public protection and deterrence would not be greater, and that much money and many people would be saved. Nothing in this study, or any study I know of, negates that assumption.[11]

A number of things support it.

James V. Bennett, while director of the Federal Bureau of Prisons, analyzed the nature of the offenders annually committed to state prisons as follows:

The largest number of these men by far are those who have been convicted of acquisitive crimes—burglary, larceny, forgery, automobile theft, and the like. In this category fall about 65 per cent of the major offenders who are committed to state prisons during a typical year. The next largest number are robberies, 11.7 per cent, and then come the aggravated assault cases and the drug violators, with 10.7 per cent. Homicides, rapes, and kidnapings together account for about 9 per cent. The remainder are for miscellaneous crimes like arson, gun-law violations, and I suppose adultery. These figures are in rather startling contrast with generally held views. The general public has the notion that most criminals and convicts are rapists, robbers, or murderers. This is not the case.[12]

Specific data also point to the potential of a much increased rate of probation. Surveys always show a great disparity in the use of probation from judge to judge, sometimes with a spread as great as from 5 to 80 per cent—

and the success record of the latter group is as great as that of the former.[13] Rhode Island for many years has used probation rather than commitment in 75 per cent of its convictions. A three-year demonstration project in Saginaw, Mich., resulted in cutting state prison commitments in half, to 17 per cent. The reduction was achieved by increasing the use of probation to 68 per cent and by also increasing the use of suspended sentences, fines, and local institutions—all with an improved success rate.[14] It does not take any great improvement over the Rhode Island, Saginaw, and individual judges' rates to reach 90 per cent.

An improvement of only 7 percentage points in the Saginaw rate would achieve our suggested goal of a 10 per cent limit on prison commitments. There is no doubt that this could be achieved. The 17 per cent figure was for all three years of the project, not its lowest rate; also, this project, a demonstration highly visible to the public and regarded with suspicion in some quarters, presumably exercised an excess of caution, a wider safety margin than would be suitable in ordinary situations. In a number of cases of atrocious acts, including rape, where success on probation seemed likely, probation was not granted because of actual or surmised community pressure.

In Hawaii, prison commitments dropped from 28 per cent in 1959 to 9 per cent in 1963.[15]

The author of the federal study concedes that imprisonment has destructive effects and that some of the failures may well be attributed to imprisonment. The likelihood is that imprisonment was harmful to the successes as well as to the failures. It is assumed that, because

---

[11] See letters, Sol Rubin and Daniel Glaser, Fed. Prob., March 1965, pp. 57–58.
[12] Bennett, *A Briefing for Lawyers on Prisoners*, Sterling Lecture Series, Yale University Law School, Feb. 15, 1960.

[13] *Op. cit. supra* note 4, ch. 6 § 28.
[14] Martin, "The Saginaw Project," 6 *Crime & Delin.* 357–64 (1960).
[15] Information from William G. Among, director, Department of Social Services, Hawaii, letter of May 17, 1965.

they succeeded on release, prison helped them; but they may well have been hurt by imprisonment, either in impairments of personality or in adverse effects on their families.

To speak of prisons as training schools for criminals is common. Crime is learned there. One report that substantiates the process is that by William L. Jacks, statistician for the Pennsylvania Board of Parole, who studied convicted parole violators returned to prison over a ten-year period. He compared the crime for which the parolee was returned with the crime that led to the prior conviction. During this period, 3,424 parolees were returned to prison for new crimes. Eighteen of them had been originally committed as drug and narcotic offenders; eleven of the eighteen were returned to prison for new drug crimes—plus 103 other parolees returned for drug offenses. Had prison experience helped them to learn the new crime? Another example: thirteen parolees had been originally convicted for carrying weapons—but 101 of those returned were returned for this crime. "Where did the parolees acquire this habit of carrying weapons, or were they smarter in that they 'beat the rap' for a more serious crime?" asks Jacks.[16] The same sort of question may be asked about the fifty-one parolees returned for receiving stolen goods—the nine parolees who had originally been sentenced for this crime did not repeat it on parole. And the same sort of question may be asked about the recidivists in the Glaser study.

CIVIL COMMITMENTS

Even more than in prison commitments, the concept of treatment is greatly relied on when civil commitments are used in cases in which the criminal law might have been used. Juvenile delinquents are one group dealt with in a so-called civil procedure. Delinquents are people who violate the law[17] but who, because of their youth, are dealt with in what is called a noncriminal proceeding, the principal characteristic of the juvenile court. The statutes say—although it is not so in practice[18]—that the adjudication, which shall not be deemed a conviction of crime, shall not be used against the child.

At long last the Supreme Court of the United States, anticipated by some state courts[19] and legislatures,[20] has said that the juvenile court procedure, which theoretically should provide greater protection for the child, in reality often does not. In one case it said: "There is evidence, in fact, that there may be grounds for concern that the child receives the worst of both worlds: that he gets neither the protections accorded to adults nor the solicitous care and regenerative treatment postulated for children."[21] Accordingly, said the Supreme Court in the next case, many of the protections of criminal procedure must be granted to the juvenile in juvenile court.[22]

---

[16] Jacks, "Why Are Parolees Returned to Prison as Parole Violators?" *Am. J. Corr.*, Nov.-Dec. 1957.

[17] However, children who do not violate the law are also processed as delinquents when they fall within the category of incorrigible, wayward, or beyond the control of their parents. This common type of jurisdiction is condemned in Rubin, "Legal Definitions of Offenses by Children and Youths," U. Ill. L.F. 512 (1960).

[18] Rubin, "The Juvenile in Evolution," 2 *Valparaiso L. Rev.* 1 at 14–18 (1967).

[19] Advisory Council of Judges, Procedure and Evidence in the Juvenile Court (1962).

[20] Standard Juvenile Court Act (1959), drawn upon heavily by numerous legislatures; e.g. Colorado (session laws 1967 ch. 443), Iowa (1965 S.F. 95), Utah (1965 ch. 165), etc.

[21] Kent v. United States, 383 U.S. 541, 86 Sup. Ct. 1045 (1966).

[22] In the Matter of the Application of Gault, 387 U.S. 1, 87 Sup. Ct. 1428 (1967).

In other quasi-criminal commitment procedures the Supreme Court has not been so willing to see through the fiction. A notable instance is the sexual psychopath statutes under which a person who commits a sexual crime (and even, sometimes, a person who does not) may be dealt with through civil procedure and be committed, often for life. The fiction in these cases is well known: the promise of special treatment is not kept; persons under civil commitment for sexual psychopathy receive no more therapy than they would under criminal commitment in prison.[23] The difference between civil commitment and criminal procedure is that, like the juvenile delinquent, the offender receives the worst of both worlds—he is not accorded procedural protections and his loss of liberty is much greater. In most jurisdictions he is committed for a life term, often when the underlying offense is minor and might well have resulted in probation if he had been sentenced under the penal law.

In these cases a little progress is being made. Procedural protections are being required before a man may be committed as a sexual psychopath.[24] But the validity of the statutes themselves is open to question. They have been sustained by a Supreme Court decision that goes back to 1939,[25] upholding a Minnesota statute for civil commitment of so-called sexual psychopaths and accepting the fiction of a treatment procedure. The decision notes that the statute calls the defendant a "patient" four times and clearly implies that a statute referring to a man as a patient will deal with him as such, will treat him, and hence is valid. There is no more in the decision than that.[26]

In my opinion the decision is wrong, and, if reread today, its weakness is not hard to discover. What was done with the defendant is not subjected to examination—the kind of examination of treatment that the Supreme Court made in the recent juvenile court cases; furthermore, sexual misbehavior is not even required. There is not one word in the Supreme Court decision, or in the state Supreme Court decision,[27] telling what the defendant is charged with having done except that it was said to be sexual misconduct.

A recent reminder of the easy acceptance of this point of view is the

[26] On the use of magical words in the correctional field, H. L. Mencken provides an interesting background: "Some time ago, in the *Survey*, the trade journal of the American uplifters, Dr. Thomas Dawes Eliot, associate professor of sociology in Northwestern University, printed a solemn argument [A Limbo for Cruel Words, *Survey*, June 15, 1922] in favor of abandoning all such harsh terms as *reformatory, house of refuge, reform school* and *jail*. "Each time a new phrase is developed," he said, "it seems to bring with it, or at least to be accompanied by, some measure of permanent gain, in standards or in viewpoint, even though much of the old may continue to masquerade as the new. The series, *alms, philanthropy, relief, rehabilitation, case work, family welfare*, shows such a progression from cruder to more refined levels of charity." Among the substitutions proposed by the learned professor were *habit-disease* for *vice*, *psychoneurosis* for *sin*, *failure to compensate* for *disease*, *treatment* for *punishment*, *delinquent* for *criminal*, *unmarried mother* for *illegitimate mother*, *out of wedlock* for *bastard*, *behavior problem* for *prostitute*, *colony* for *penitentiary*, *school* for *reformatory*, *psychopathic hospital* for *insane asylum*, and *house of detention* for *jail*. Many of these terms (or others like them) have been actually adopted. Practically all American insane asylums are now simple *hospitals*, many reformatories and houses of correction have been converted into *homes* or *schools*, all almshouses are now *infirmaries, county-farms*, or *county-homes*, and most of the more advanced American penologists now speak of criminals as *psychopathic personalities*." 1 Mencken, *The American Language* 292–93 (4th ed. 1957).

[27] Minnesota ex rel. Pearson v. Probate Court of Ramsey County, 205 Minn. 545.

---

[23] Gafni, 12 Vill. L. Rev. 183 (1966).
[24] Specht v. Patterson, 386 U.S. 605, 87 Sup. Ct. 1209, 18 L. Ed. 2d 326 (1967).
[25] Minnesota ex rel. Pearson v. Probate Court of Ramsey County, 309 U.S. 270, 60 Sup. Ct. 523 (1939).

Supreme Court case upholding deportation of a homosexual alien under a statute applying to "psychopathic personalities." Is a homosexual a "psychopathic personality"? Yes, said the Supreme Court, if Congress says so, and it inferred from the legislative history of the statute that Congress had said so.[28] Several judges dissented.

The Court is shaky on civil commitment of drug addicts, which it approved in dicta in the much cited Robinson case.[29] I share with others the view that the dicta are not well thought out, that they justify civil commitments by a fiction of treatment that is contradicted by matter-of-fact truth.[30] In California and New York, the principal jurisdictions using civil commitment of drug addicts, the systems for it are in reality no different from prison systems.

The doubts about the Robinson dicta are enhanced by the Supreme Court decision in Powell v. Texas.[31] Again the Court indulged in quite nonlegal dicta, this time on the treatability of chronic alcoholics, concluding that civil commitments for treatment are not really better than short jail terms for chronic alcoholics. So it holds—contrary to much medical opinion—that chronic alcoholism, unlike drug addiction, is not an illness and that a man can be imprisoned for public drunkenness although to some degree he is compelled to drink. Robinson v. California and Powell v. Texas are both unsatisfactory. Proper concepts still have to be worked out.

As is shown by this brief discussion of the cases, the courts are torn by the concept of treatment. Does treatment justify commitment? Recognition of a right to treatment is not enough. Even if treatment is available and even if treatment is needed, those conditions alone do not justify commitment. I have ailments, and whenever possible I avoid medical treatment that others turn to. May I be committed and may treatment be imposed upon me if my ailment is not contagious? Certainly not. If I am dying and refuse a blood transfusion that might save me, a court has no power to order it. There is a right not to be treated.

I have implied that treatment may be punitive. Indeed it often is. I have elaborated this elsewhere, in considering the 1954 Durham decision in the District of Columbia (which replaced the M'Naghten rule of criminal responsibility), pointing out that committing a criminal to a mental hospital does not insure him better treatment than he would receive in a prison; that the environment of a prison is not as abnormal as that of a mental hospital and usually has better activity and training programs; that the term of commitment in a mental hospital, being indefinite and thus potentially for life, is longer than a prison sentence; that the release procedure is demoralizing because of its lack of due process; and, finally, that the defendant committed as mentally ill is automatically committed whereas, if he is convicted in a criminal court, he may well be placed on probation.[32]

The greater punitiveness of the treatment-oriented people is not an accident of law or an unfortunate by-product of the struggle for better treatment services. It is a direct result of their view that institutionalization, if used for treatment, is good.

This view is well represented by Judge David Bazelon not only in his

---

[28] Boutilier v. Immigration and Naturalization Service, 87 Sup. Ct. 1563 (1967).
[29] Robinson v. California, 370 U.S. 660 (1962).
[30] Dissenting opinion of Justice Clark in Robinson v. California, supra note 28. Rubin, Psychiatry and Criminal Law—Illusions, Fictions, and Myths ch. 7 (1965).
[31] Powell v. Texas, 88 Sup. Ct. 2145 (1968).

[32] Rubin, op. cit. supra note 30, ch. 2.

decisions but in his other writings. Recently, on the occasion of the fiftieth anniversary of the Judge Baker Guidance Center in Boston, he gave a paper entitled "The Promise of Treatment."[33] In it he cites the case of a severely disturbed seventeen-year-old who sought a judicial hearing on his claim that he was being illegally held in the receiving home without getting any psychiatric assistance. "He had been at the home for eight months awaiting disposition of a pending charge in the juvenile court. The judge did not hold a hearing to learn what the facts were—because, in his opinion, whether or not the child was receiving psychiatric assistance 'was not germane to the lawfulness of [the juvenile's] confinement.' " Judge Bazelon says that he can "scarcely imagine anything more 'germane' than the fact that the boy was receiving no treatment."

To me it is striking that Judge Bazelon does not maintain that the boy, having been held for eight months without treatment, should have been freed. He does not say that the boy deserved to be freed but complains only that psychiatry should have been involved. Presumably if this boy had been seen once a month by a psychiatrist, the detention would have been justified.

"The central justification," he says, "for assuming jurisdiction over a child in any informal, non-adversary proceeding is the promise to treat him according to his needs." Not exactly. Rather, the essential purpose of the juvenile court proceeding is to avoid a criminal court prosecution and a conviction but without sacrificing due process of law.

Further along Judge Bazelon remarks: "I do not find it objectionable to deprive the child of some procedural safeguards if the individualized treatment he is supposed to get requires the sacrifice and if the new procedures are reasonably fair." No. I know of no individualized treatment that a child is supposed to get in the juvenile court that would be enhanced by depriving him of procedural safeguards.

IF NOT TREATMENT, WHAT?

Where does all this leave me? Do I reject commitments altogether? I would reject commitments made for the purpose of giving treatment—even in the prisons best served by therapeutic services. When one weighs whatever positive ends they achieve against the destructiveness of the prison environment, it is difficult to contend that the balance favors commitment *except when incarceration is called for in the interest of public safety.*[34]

Account must also be taken of damage to the prisoner's family. For example, a man was sentenced to eighteen months in prison. During this period, his seven-year-old son refused to receive first communion; his eight-year-old daughter fell to the bottom of her class; his nine-year-old daughter began suffering from insomnia; his wife became a "disorganized woman"; and three of his six children were seeing a psychiatrist. (In this case, a federal judge released the short-term prisoner because of what was happening to his family.)[35]

I believe commitment is justified only for public safety, and I would not be extravagant in defining public safety. I do not mean that people who are incarcerated should not be treated. Most persons who might justifiably be committed would be those whose offense is violent, with the violence attributable to serious mental illness. Yes, they should

---

[33] Delivered April 14, 1967; published in the New Republic, April 22, 1967, under the title, "Justice for Juveniles."

[34] See analysis of one case in Rubin, "Recognizing and Sentencing the Dangerous Offender," panel discussion, Ninth Annual Meeting of the National Conference of State Trial Judges, 1966.

[35] Chicago Daily News, Dec. 2, 1966; case not reported in law reports.

be treated, but the decision to incarcerate should be based upon security needs.[36] That means that far fewer people would be incarcerated and that many institutions could be closed down.

Earlier I mentioned the demonstration project in Saginaw, Mich. The project was directed by Paul Kalin, a valued colleague of mine, now director of the Midwestern office of the National Council on Crime and Delinquency. I discussed with him the theme of this paper. Among other things he wrote me as follows:

Toward the end of the Saginaw experience I proposed we go beyond the project expectations and used some cases to illustrate the direction. One judge supported the idea, but all the citizens to whom I presented it were cautious because the "public won't accept it."

We worked with an offender who had done time at prison on two or three occasions and had other arrests—virtually all (if not all) for assault with a knife in which the victim was seriously hurt. There was serious consideration given to trying him as a habitual criminal. We recommended probation. He completed it without any violation, and I suspect is still a free citizen in the community. The investigation revealed the victims had "provoked" his reaction by remarks about his promiscuous common-law wife. Basically, the treatment plan suggested divorce, placement of the children with his mother, and acceptance of the fact that his wife was, in fact, a whore.

In another situation, a first offender charged with assault with intent to do serious bodily harm (with a gun), we recommended divorce, remarriage, and getting rid of the gun. Also worked out.

However, we recommended commitment for a young (19–20) first offender charged with purse-snatching. The boy had no court record, but a careful pre-sentence

[36] This is the underlying concept of the Model Sentencing Act (1963).

investigation revealed that his pattern of response to anxiety-provoking situations was assaultive. The judge, who had told me he could not accept our recommendation, interviewed the boy himself and then committed him for a longer term than he might otherwise have done, because the boy responded in the way we had predicted he would.

I would not defend the latter disposition in theory—knowing what could happen to him in prison—but do believe it was a sound disposition in view of the alternatives available. Obviously, there may be some rationalization here—due to my anxiety not to risk a serious violation which might create problems for the project.

By and large what I have said may appear to be an attack on the prison system, which it is. But please note that the test of public security (rather than treatment) may lead to a proper preference for commitment of a nineteen-year-old first offender rather than probation.

Is it simply a matter of finding a new way of attacking prisons and replacing them with probation? No; whether or not probation is equated with treatment, it is also an invasion of one's freedom and should be used only if necessary. Does that mean I advocate less probation? A lot of people on probation should be discharged outright or be fined or be given a suspended sentence, if these are appropriate; probation is for many a burden rather than an aid, and unnecessary probation is also a burden on probation services. Probation has to be used in more effective ways, and for people who are now being committed.

This doctrine is not as far out as it may appear. If a lesson of deterrence is taught by the criminal law process (and it certainly is), much of it comes in the very process of being arrested—or even receiving a ticket—and going through a proceeding that leads to conviction. Conviction of crime is a serious stigma that people want to avoid if possible.

For example, on the question of suspended sentence without probation, Judge Bolitha J. Laws states:

Probation is fairly well developed in many communities and states, but even there the trend to greater use of imprisonment continues. Why? One answer may be that increases in probation grants are made up largely of the obviously safe cases, those for whom fines and suspended sentences were previously used. If that is so, the increased incidence of probation would not reduce the number of prison commitments. In any event, as I see it, we can reduce the prison population only by (a) checking carefully to determine whether we judges should grant probation to many persons now being committed to prison, and (b) increasing the use not only of probation, but of the other forms of community treatment—fines and suspended sentences—as well.

Extensive use of the fine in England has demonstrated its value in a remarkable reduction of institutional commitments. . . .

More frequent use of suspension of sentence without probation, like the fine, is part of the answer to the prison problem. The national average use of probation is probably about one-third of felony convictions. Many of our informed students of crime tell us it can safely be two-thirds, and that public security would not be damaged with that percentage of usage. We achieve success even now with many probationers who receive little or no actual help or guidance from their overworked probation officers. Can we not assume that these offenders would have been equally successful if they had received suspended sentences, without probation? When we speak of trying to achieve greatly increased use of probation, we are really referring to both probation and suspended sentence.[37]

Probation has to be refined if it is to

[37] Laws, "Criminal Courts and Adult Probation," 3 N *NPA J.* 357 (1957).

be used properly. We have to acquire a lot more knowledge about the effective use of probation. I will cite a few instances of such searching.

Intensive supervision is believed to be more therapeutic than occasional contacts between officer and probationer. The following is a summary of a research study on parole, but it would be just as applicable to probation:

In order to evaluate the effects of a special selection and training program of parole officers on recidivism reduction of male delinquents, two control groups of 157 . . . and 152 . . . parolees, all of whom were supervised by regular parole officers, were compared with 95 Experimental Group parolees, who were supervised by 12 specially trained counselors. The three groups were initially matched for background and offense variables. However, when comparison was made for delinquent acts committed during the six-month postparole period of this study, no significant differences were found in the percentage or type of recidivism among the groups. Results should be cautiously interpreted because of the relatively short observation period, factors contributing to the selection of the Experimental Group parolees, and the increased opportunity for the counselors of these parolees to observe maladaptive behavior.[38]

Another study: The San Diego Municipal Court conducted a study of different ways of dealing with chronic alcoholics. It found that probation with supervision by Alcoholics Anonymous, or probation with clinic supervision, produced no better results than no treatment at all.[39]

A similar study of traffic law viola-

[38] Schwitzgebel & Baer, "Intensive Supervision by Parole Officers as a Factor in Recidivism Reduction of Male Delinquents," 67 *Am. J. Psych.* 75 (1967).
[39] Ditman, Crawford, Forgy, Moskowitz & Macandrew, "A Controlled Experiment on the Use of Court Probation for Drunk Arrests," 124 *Am. J. Psychiat.* 2 (1967).

tors was conducted by the Anaheim-Fullerton (Calif.) Municipal Court, whose judge, Claude M. Owens, writes: "Until about four years ago, the judges of this court were satisfied that our drivers' improvement school was effective, because California's Department of Motor Vehicles records showed about 44 per cent of the students had no record of any moving violation convictions in California in the year following completion of school, whereas in the year before attending the school they had at least three such convictions. Then along came an iconoclast who suggested that chance could account for that result—that perhaps the students would have had the same change if they had been placed on probation instead of having to attend the school, or if they had been neither placed on probation nor sent to school."

So they researched it. By now the reader will not be surprised at the results. In the first year following court appearance, about 25 per cent of those who were fined only—no traffic school and no probation—had only one violation, and a smaller percentage had more than one. Defendants sent to drivers' school fared about the same: one-third fewer violations than those who were only fined. Defendants who were placed on probation *and also* sent to drivers' school did not do as well as either of these two groups but did a little better than those only fined.

The experience in the second year, however, was different. Drivers' school alone continued to reduce violations more than just a fine, but probation did not. Instead, after one year of probation, its previously good effect disappeared and the results were not significantly different from those obtained by a fine.[40]

In 1932 the federal probation service consisted of sixty-three officers supervising 23,200 probationers and 2,013 parolees—an average caseload of 400 per officer. Its violation rate was very low, lower than that of probation departments having much smaller caseloads.[41] The thirties, of course, was an archaic, primitive period, and with those high caseloads how much casework could be done? Today the U.S. Probation Office is conducting a project in one of its offices with a caseload of 350 men per officer. During the first six months not one violation was reported.

I do not want to give the impression that probation is a failure. I do not by any means think it is, but I do share the opinion of others, including the federal probation service, that probation is not being used properly. One poor use is in cases where a fine or suspended sentence would be either just as good or better, and we have to find out which cases those are.

• • •

[40] Owens, "Report on a Three Year Controlled Study of the Effectiveness of the Anaheim-Fullerton Municipal Court Drivers Improvement School," *Munic. Ct. Rev.*, Sept. 1967.

[41] Chappell, "The Federal Probation System Today," *Fed. Prob.*, June 1950, p. 30.

44.

The Future of Juvenile Institutions

William E. Amos

In recent years, our society has exhibited more concern about juvenile delinquency and the treatment of youthful offenders than at any time in our history. This concern has been expressed not only in the Congress of the United States, by governors, and other leading citizens in each of our states, but also by individual citizens and private groups throughout the country.

The physical plants and facilities of institutions serving delinquent youth have been updated. Their capacity for housing adjudicated delinquents have increased three or four times. The numbers of staff, both professional and custodial, have increased proportionately. Unfortunately, however, the effectiveness of these institutions has not kept pace with either the demands of the community or the needs of the youngsters. And there is grave concern as to whether the available resources have been utilized efficiently and effectively.

At the present time there are in our country over 400 public and private institutions serving approximately 65,000 boys and girls adjudicated as delin-

quent.[1] The impact made by our institutions is not limited to these young people, but extends to unknown numbers who are influenced by the youths who come from our institutions. Often we hear that only 2 percent of our youngsters are delinquent, so the problem really is not as serious as many believe and that we tend to condemn the majority of our teenagers for the behavior of only a few. This, of course, is only partially true. We overlook the fact that the 2 percent refers only to those of the total youthful population who are adjudicated as delinquents by the court. It does not refer to the significant number that appear before some representative of the court other than the judge. It does not include the large number of youngsters who have contact with the police and are not referred to the court regardless of their guilt or innocence. And it does not include the vast number of youngsters who commit the same acts and exhibit the same attitudes, values, and behaviors as do their adjudicated friends or brothers and, as a result, are as delinquent sociologically as any youngster in our juvenile institutions.

SOURCE. William E. Amos, "The Future of Juvenile Institutions" from *Federal Probation*, Volume 32, No. 1, March 1968, pp. 41–47. Reprinted with permission.

[1] Data supplied by the Children's Bureau, U.S. Department of Health, Education, and Welfare, Washington, D.C.

In some of our heavy delinquency areas, it is estimated that as high as 70 percent of the youngsters between the ages of 9 and 18 could legally be adjudicated as delinquents if their offenses were reported and they appeared before the court. The ineffectiveness of our institutional programs is partially to blame for these numbers because many of the youngsters who return to their neighborhoods, carry with them the added sophistication of a 1-year graduate course in delinquency, manipulation, conning, utilization of the subcultural codes, and assume roles of leadership and influence among other youngsters in their areas.

Seldom do we really know the effectiveness of institutional programs. Most institutions have little knowledge of the recidivism rate of their wards or any systematic way of evaluating changes in their behavior. The general reaction to these failures is that we are aware of them, but do not have the adequate staff to develop evaluative studies. There seems to be very little understanding or desire to use especially equipped agencies to perform these followup studies and to show how to make the most efficient use of their facilities and personnel.

During recent years there has been criticism throughout the country by both professionals and laymen of the present-day efforts of our juvenile institutions. There is a tendency to even reject many of the newer programs and innovations which have been developed in recent years. There is a feeling that little can be done in juvenile correctional institutions and that the emphasis must be placed on prevention since it would be a waste of resources to attempt to modify, change, or alter the current philosophy and programs of the institutional "establishment." Unfortunately there is some validity to these views;

however, the fact is overlooked by many community organization specialists that institutions have a role to play, deal in many instances with the hard-core youngster, and do have the capacity for needed change if the necessary pressure is brought to bear. We have seen the beginnings of change in many programs throughout the country. Within the next decade we will have to think through and accept a variety of new programs, directions, and philosophies in our institutional programs. Some of these include the following:

1. Modification of Treatment Philosophy Within Juvenile Institutions

Even though we give lip service now, very few programs throughout the country are realistically geared to provide a particular type of treatment for a particular type of delinquent. In the future, we will have to see more treatment typologies and prototypes developed, understood, and utilized. This, of course, is basic when we keep in mind the purpose of committing a child to an institution, namely, changing delinquents into nondelinquents.

Until recent years, we have assumed, for the most part, that a youngster who exhibits delinquent behavior could be placed in an institution and receive certain educational and vocational experiences, supplemented by some type of analytically oriented counseling or casework services, and that a favorable change in behavior would result. Unfortunately, this has not been the case. We have voiced the fact that no two human beings are alike and that all persons are unique, but we have not really been able to instill this understanding into institutional programs.

In too many instances we have built large community-style institutions that fail to offer appropriate treatment and rehabilitative experiences for a particu-

The Future of Juvenile Institutions 607

lar type of youngster. We offer, instead, uniform and, in some cases, oppressive experiences that have completely lost the purpose of diagnosis and individual treatment. I should hope to see in the future, then, the development of a classification system that would allow the placement of youngsters in smaller institutions which have individualized programs designed to improve the behavior of a particular type of child. One example of a classification or typology system which will be useful as a guide in the planning of treatment strategy is the interpersonal maturity level classification which is used in the California Youth Authority's community treatment project.[2] In this system, there are provisions for different levels of maturity, from infancy to adulthood. Youngsters are classified, for example, in such terms as an "unsocialized passive youngster," a "cultural conformist," or an "anxious neurotic." The programs aimed at the rehabilitation of these youngsters might, in one case, have a sociological base, in another a psychological base, or a combination of several disciplines. Smaller institutions that can offer specialized facilities and services and specialized programs for a particular type of child have become a necessity in medicine, education, and other disciplines.

I would hypothesize that a majority of the delinquents in major urban areas would be classified as "cultural conformists" and could benefit from programs specifically developed for this type of youngster whose delinquent behavior is a result of a need for social status, peer associates, group identification, and the values and attitude of their culture. There is research that indicates

that treatment which has value for the neurotic child may even make the unsocialized delinquent worse.[3]

2. Minimum Educational Requirements for Professional Staff

This point has caused considerable concern in the last few years. Certain disciplines have been threatened and there has been real resistance to accept the fact that some other discipline, or a person with not professional training at all, might be able to work as successfully and, in some cases, more successfully than the so-called professional.

Research studies have demonstrated that some of these disciplines are not successful with many of our delinquent youngsters and, in fact, may cause harm. There also is evidence that some of our professional people, contrary to their claims, are more inflexible and punitive than nonprofessionals in dealing with the needs of youngsters in institutions. At the same time, there is concern among many of our leading educators that the type of professional person we are turning out in some cases actually knows less about the youngster they are dealing with than many of the people who carry the title of subprofessional. I suspect that in the next few years this will be an area of considerable study, but hopefully one demonstrating progress in our total rehabilitative program.

One of the principal problems involved here is the conflict between the professional and nonprofessional. The term "professional" is not always equated with a person's capability or sensitivity to problems and needs. It is not equated with knowledge of their young charges, their culture, and living

---

[2] Keith S. Griffiths, "The Role of Research," *Delinquent Children in Juvenile Correctional Institutions*, William E. Amos and Raymond L. Manella (editors), Springfield, Illinois: Charles C Thomas, 1966.

[3] R. L. Jenkins and L. Hewitt, "Types of Personality Structures Encountered in Child Guidance Clinics," *American Journal of Orthopsychiatry*, Vol. 14, 1944, pp. 84–94.

conditions. In many instances it has no relationship to the fact that a person has a college degree or even a master's degree. In too many instances it is related simply to the particular discipline or subject area in which a person has a degree. This is particularly true for the field of social work where it is believed that a B.A. or M.A. in psychology, sociology, or education, does not qualify the person for entrance into the professional ranks as a caseworker or a probation officer. This is unfortunate since most authorities recognize that neither probation nor parole is a profession per se. As Barbara Kay states, "Probation is an essentially modern method for the treatment of offenders and, as such, is rooted in the broader social and cultural trends of the modern era."[4]

The point that comes out here is that the type of service which so many of these youth need is not intensive casework as we know it but rather close supervision in the community during weekend and evening hours, help in obtaining community services, and assistance in maintaining a good adjustment in schools and on the job.

I certainly can sympathize with the need to raise standards and improve services to youth. However, I cannot find convincing research that indicates that persons with an M.S.W. degree are necessarily more effective in a correctional setting, when providing the types of services just mentioned, than persons of other disciplines. Judith Benjamin, in her studies of new roles of nonprofessionals in corrections, states that there is some doubt that the social work approach best equips a person to work with delinquent youth. She points out that some experts feel that social work "engenders an attitude of caution or

even of pessimism towards those who manifest serious maladjustments or unstable work or family history."[5]

Miss Benjamin further submits that the social worker, by recommending commitment, limits his clientele to those for whom casework appears to offer success. For this reason it has been suggested that the work of the M.S.W. cannot be reliably compared with that of non-M.S.W. officers.

Some social workers tend to concentrate on good-risk cases. In one agency, for example, it was reported that probation officers who were college graduates but without additional graduate training, performed better with cases adjudged "hopeless" than social workers did.[6]

Since there are indications that institutionalization may be more limited in the future than in the past, and that delinquents will be placed in community-based programs, the social worker model will require a reassessment. It may mean a revision of social work education or acceptance of the other behavioral sciences in a cooperative professional relationship. In the very forseeable future, the apparent need to develop a greater range of services for young people, both within the community and within the institution, may shift the emphasis away from a casework orientation.

In the past there has been some reluctance by psychiatrists, psychologists, and social workers to work in the correctional field, believing it is impossible to work within an authoritarian setting. The error here is the assumption that authority and structure are necessarily hostile and punitive. It is hoped that in

[4] Barbara A. Kay and Clyde B. Vedder, *Probation and Parole.* Springfield, Illinois: Charles C Thomas, 1963.

[5] Judith G. Benjamin, *et al., New Roles for Non-Professionals in Corrections.* New York: National Committee on Employment of Youth, 1965, p. 64.

[6] Milford B. Lytle, "The Unpromising Client," *Crime and Delinquency,* Vol. 10, April 1964, p. 134.

the future, members of the various professions will see treatment in a broader sense than their training has allowed them to do in the past.

3. *Utilization of Noninstitutional Programs*

We are becoming more and more aware that there is little relationship between the time spent in an institution and the degree of positive rehabilitation that results from the institutional experience. In the same vein, we can say that many youngsters might benefit from a very short-term institutional experience or even a weekend institutional experience, and other youngsters might better be returned directly to the community and involved in a variety of treatment and supportive programs based on their particular typologies. This, of course, would require the services of our newest type of juvenile facility—the reception-diagnostic center.

The philosophy behind the reception-diagnostic function is to identify the cause and motivations underlying the delinquent behavior and to provide treatment that will allow the child to re-enter society successfully. At present only about 10 states have such reception-diagnostic facilities. A number of these states do not have the variety of services that would provide individualized treatment plans.

Theoretically, when a child is committed by the court, he would go directly to the reception-diagnostic facility where, during the next 30 to 60 days, the various disciplines would evaluate him and would determine what treatment program would be most appropriate. One example of this type of program is the James Marshall Treatment Program which is conducted by the Calfornia Youth Authority.[7] Geared

[7] Department of the Youth Authority, State of California, *James Marshall Treatment Program*, Sacramento, 1965.

to the 15- to 17-year age group, this program was designed to provide an intensive treatment experience of approximately 90 days in lieu of institutional commitment of adjudicated delinquents. The Marshall program is a residential program, but officials of the California Youth Authority believe the program might be even more successful if the youngsters could return to their own homes each evening.

The Marshall program is geared to the following:[8]

1. Achieving more positive acceptance of authority and limits. Involved in this process is the whole gamut of concern related to the delinquent's concept of authority and authority figures such as parents, teachers, parole agents, and other significant authority figures.

2. Developing a greater degree of adequacy in interpersonal relationships.

3. Being forced to deal with the conflicts which the demands of the conventional versus the delinquent system place upon them.

4. Accepting responsibility for one's own behavior.

5. Developing good work habits.

6. Identifying and recognizing adjustment problem areas.

7. Learning how to handle stress, conflicts, and frustrations.

The program involves 50 boys at any one time. The staff includes parole agents, remedial teachers, social workers, and a school psychologist. The program includes group counseling, remedial education, work experience, physical training, and group discussions. Parents participate in the program and attend group counseling sessions with their sons. There are various review programs where a youngster's progress and his attitudes are discussed

[8] *Ibid.*, p. 1.

with him. It is too early to determine the success of this program, but at the present time staff, parents, and students believe the program has proved itself.

Another such program is the Community Treatment Project in Sacramento, California.[9] Its specific goal is to determine the feasibility of releasing selected youngsters directly from a reception center to a treatment control project in the community. Approximately eight youngsters are assigned to a parole officer who provides close supervision, support, and counseling. The program consists of case conferences with the parole agent, away-from-home placement where it was necessary or appropriate, group or individual counseling from one to four sessions each week, and psychotherapy when needed.

Family counseling is also included as well as special educational tutoring with the following goals:[10]

1. To provide education as a substitute for regular school programs for wards who have been excluded from regular schools;
2. To provide tutoring for wards who will have difficulty in regular schools; and
3. To provide basic remedial education for older wards not returning to a regular school program.

Special recreational and group activities are provided and all wards are required to participate. An interesting aspect of this program is that temporary detention ranging from one day to several days may be utilized by the parole officers to prevent delinquency which may result from an emotional crisis, and to demonstrate the ability and intention

of the parole agent to enforce control. Research has indicated that the program has been successful in preventing recidivism and is less expensive than regular commitments to juvenile institutions.

Another prototype of a noninstitutional program that is gaining support around the country is a school-based program where the child is placed in a special school which provides small classes and remedial education. At the end of each day an individual or group counseling session is available followed by supervised recreation. Probation officers who work from 3 until 11 p.m. provide these services as well as close supervision during the evening hours. The evidence up to this time has indicated that the behavior of the youngsters involved has improved and that the rate of recidivism is relatively low.

These are but a few of the many creative and challenging programs that are being developed in lieu of institutional commitment. Since the results to date indicate that such programs can be effective in changing delinquent behavior and at a lower overall cost, there is every reason to believe that this will be a very active area in juvenile corrections during the next decade.

4. *Use of Community Resources by Institutions and Agencies Not Only During Aftercare but Within the Institutional Program as Well*

We have long contended that our juvenile institutions are desirous of utilizing community resources, but we really did not mean it if it was intended that these agencies should actually come into our institutions and assume certain program responsibilities. Not only from the standpoint of economy and efficiency will this change have to be made, but also there is need to relate the experiences of the institution more directly

[9] Department of the Youth Authority, State of California, *Community Treatment Project*, Sacramento, 1965.
[10] *Ibid.*, p. 8.

to those the child will face in the community.

I am aware of the various administrative problems that may arise when agencies from the community enter an institution for delinquents. Perhaps their lack of understanding of the administrative problems involved in 24-hour-a-day care of hostile, aggressive youngsters and their lack of a sense of responsibility for the total operation of the institution, will undoubtedly create difficult situations. However, in the forseeable future, these problems of administration must be overcome and the resources of the community must be utilized in developing more meaningful and comprehensive programs for the youth committed to institutions. One of the principal agencies involved will be the public school system and its relationship to the educational and vocational programs offered within the institution. A continuous relationship between the school experience in the institution and the school program in the community must be provided if we are to return the youngster to the community better equipped to continue his schooling.

Another agency that institutions should bring into their programs is the state employment service. State employment service counselors should be actively involved in institutional prerelease programs and in the planning of release programs for youngsters. They can provide testing programs, help in job development, lead student discussion groups, and participate in staff training. State departments of vocational rehabilitation can also serve similar functions.

In many of our juvenile institutions there is a lack of adequate mental health service. Public agencies may provide these services if encouraged to do so. In a number of states, representatives of State Bureaus of Mental Hygiene or State Departments of Health

are actively involved in institutional programs and are responsible for providing adequate professional staff. The U. S. Public Health Service has long performed this function for the National Training School as well as other Federal Bureau of Prisons institutions.

In the past decade institutions have increasingly utilized colleges and universities in their programs, but even now their participation is at a very superficial level. Universities should be encouraged to use the training schools as laboratories for research, for internships, for placement of graduates, and as practice teaching sites for students from educational departments. Hopefully this would bring into the institution a steady stream of new blood, new ideas, and new enthusiasm. Under contract, universities can evaluate programs and staff training and conduct research projects.

The increased use of community facilities and programs on a daily basis should be considered. Here the child may leave the institution in the morning, be involved in the community-based program during the day, and return to the institution at night.

During the last few years, various federal programs directed toward improving the educational and vocational qualifications of disadvantaged youth have been developed. An example of this type of program is the Manpower Developed and Training Act. This Act will finance multiskill training programs and provide vocational counseling and placement services. Efforts have been made to encourage juvenile institutions to apply for grants under this Act, but very few have done so.

5. *More Concern with the Role of Prevention by Juvenile Institutions and the Agencies that Administer Them*

Up to this time, juvenile institutions and agencies have assumed little responsibility for preventive services and programs in the community. As a result, there has been a lack of continuity and efficient use of the resources that are available.

The prevention of delinquency should be the responsibility of every citizen, but at the same time one agency should also be held accountable. All delinquency prevention programs could not possibly be placed under one agency, but the responsibility for the operation of selected prevention programs, the determination of prevention needs, the coordination of community efforts, and the evaluation of prevention programs could be the responsibility of a single youth-serving agency.

Authorities who have experience in working with delinquents and with disadvantaged youth recognize that continuity of service is important in any program of rehabilitation and that this continuity often is lacking in programs where differing philosophies prevail, where it is necessary to break through the bureaucratic framework of various agencies, and where the delinquency programs are watered down or diffused because of the pressure of other programs.

6. A Growing Concern for the Legal Rights and Protection of Juveniles

Since the emergence of model juvenile court acts during the past two decades courts and institutions have played the role of an all-powerful father and mother figure who had undeniable rights over the life of the child. There is increasing concern about court decisions that affect the life of the child and the constitutional guarantees that have been ignored, such as adequate notice of the charges, right to counsel, the right to confrontation and cross-examination, and the privilege against self-incrimination. These court decisions will doubtless affect the procedures programs and operations of both our courts and institutions.

For example, let's look at the practice of administrative transfer. In some localities it is now possible to take a child from an institution for dependent children and transfer him to another institution for delinquent children. It is also possible to take a child who has been tried in a juvenile court for involvement in an incident which would not be a crime for an adult and transfer him to an adult penal institution. Both of these types of transfers can be effected without returning the child to court. Both of these types of transfers are receiving increasing attention from the courts and others interested in the constitutional rights of the child.

Another matter concerns the duration of time a child can be kept in a rehabilitation facility. Most authorities agree that the term of a commitment should be as flexible as possible. Those who are in charge of treatment are in a better position to determine when a child is ready to return to the community. However, there are instances where a child may be kept in an institution for years—sometimes because of no fault of the child, as in the case of a poor home situation. Some of the newer juvenile court acts place maximum time limitations so that a child may be committed for an indeterminate sentence not to exceed 3 years. The institution will have to justify to the court why it should not release a child after the 3-year maximum.

In many instances a child released from an institution, but still under the authority of the particular department, may be returned to the institution if his aftercare worker or parole officer believes his behavior and adjustment are not satisfactory. This may occur on the parole officer's recommendation sometimes without a hearing or investigation.

7. *Use of Separate Facilities for Delinquents*

During the past 30 years persons who have been concerned with the rehabilitation of delinquents have fought the battle for separate facilities and individualized services. This has been a necessary battle, one in which considerable progress has been made. However, as any program where chronological age is the principal guideline, some flexibility is desirable.

Many people, however, have regarded flexibility as a threat to traditional juvenile court philosophy and program and also as being punitive. There has been resistance to any procedure that allows sophisticated, older, more aggressive delinquents to be handled in programs outside the juvenile setting. There has been an unwillingness to acknowledge that this type of youth may be a threat to other youngsters and may require an unusual amount of resources to contain him and to protect others. It seems that certain treatment-oriented people have come to the conclusion that a youth of this type may receive better rehabilitative experiences in an institution which has the treatment facilities of the juvenile institution as well as the necessary security features. From this, I would submit, there will be in the years to come greater utilization of youth facilities for the older, sophisticated, more aggressive delinquent. This will not be based on waiver by the juvenile court because of a vicious crime, but rather on the basis of a diagnostic determination that the youth will benefit more from this type of setting both as to rehabilitation and the protection of others. This will not result in a mass transfer and must be done with all legal protection for the youth concerned.

8. *Evaluation of Ongoing Programs*

As mentioned earlier, an evaluation of institutional programs is almost nonexistent today. Our requests for staff, programs, and physical plants are based too much on the operational pressures and on what we believe, and too little on what we actually know. Changes in an institution, as in any administrative structure, are a difficult process. In the future, however, new programs and continuation of old ones must be based on their effectiveness and need as shown by evaluative research. Some believe that outside agencies, such as universities or separate research and evaluation agencies, should perform this task. They believe it is difficult for an ongoing operating agency to evaluate its own programs objectively. Institutions will have to develop this capability or call on someone else to provide this service.